Julie C. Meloni

D1270744

Sams **Teach Yourself**

HTML, CSS and JavaScript

All in One

SECOND EDITION

 800 East 96th Street, Indianapolis, Indiana, 46240 USA

Sams Teach Yourself HTML, CSS and JavaScript All in One, Second Edition

ISBN-13: 978-0-672-33714-7
ISBN-10: 0-672-33714-2

Library of Congress Catalog Card Number: 2014945244

Printed in the United States of America

Second Printing: February 2015

Trademarks

All terms mentioned in this book that are known to be trademarks or service marks have been appropriately capitalized. Sams Publishing cannot attest to the accuracy of this information. Use of a term in this book should not be regarded as affecting the validity of any trademark or service mark.

Warning and Disclaimer

Every effort has been made to make this book as complete and as accurate as possible, but no warranty or fitness is implied. The information provided is on an "as is" basis. The author and the publisher shall have neither liability nor responsibility to any person or entity with respect to any loss or damages arising from the information contained in this book or from the use of the CD or programs accompanying it.

Special Sales

For information about buying this title in bulk quantities, or for special sales opportunities (which may include electronic versions; custom cover designs; and content particular to your business, training goals, marketing focus, or branding interests), please contact our corporate sales department at corpsales@pearsoned.com or (800) 382-3419.

For government sales inquiries, please contact governmentsales@pearsoned.com.

For questions about sales outside the U.S., please contact international@pearsoned.com.

Acquisitions Editor
Mark Taber

Managing Editor
Kristy Hart

Project Editor
Elaine Wiley

Copy Editor
Cheri Clark

Indexer
Ken Johnson

Proofreader
Debbie Williams

Technical Editor
Phil Ballard

Publishing Coordinator
Vanessa Evans

Designer
Gary Adair

Cover Designer
Mark Shirar

Senior Compositor
Gloria Schurick

Contents at a Glance

Mon

Table of Contents

Tue

About the Author

Julie C. Meloni is a software development manager and technical consultant living in Washington, D.C. She has written several books and articles on web-based programming languages and database topics, including the bestselling *Sams Teach Yourself PHP, MySQL and Apache All in One*.

We Want to Hear from You!

As the reader of this book, *you* are our most important critic and commentator. We value your opinion and want to know what we're doing right, what we could do better, what areas you'd like to see us publish in, and any other words of wisdom you're willing to pass our way.

You can email or write to let us know what you did or didn't like about this book—as well as what we can do to make our books stronger.

Please note that we cannot help you with technical problems related to the topic of this book, and that due to the high volume of mail we receive, we might not be able to reply to every message.

When you write, please be sure to include this book's title, edition number, and author, as well as your name and contact information.

Email: feedback@samspublishing.com

Mail: Sams Publishing
         800 East 96th Street
         Indianapolis, IN 46240 USA

Reader Services

Visit our website and register this book at **informit.com/register** for convenient access to any updates, downloads, or errata that might be available for this book.

CHAPTER 1
Understanding How the Web Works

Before you learn the intricacies of HTML (Hypertext Markup Language), CSS (Cascading Style Sheets), and JavaScript, it is important to gain a solid understanding of the technologies that help transform these plain-text files to the rich multimedia displays you see on your computer or handheld device when browsing the World Wide Web.

For example, a file containing markup and client-side code HTML and CSS is useless without a web browser to view it, and no one besides yourself will see your content unless a web server is involved. Web servers make your content available to others who, in turn, use their web browsers to navigate to an address and wait for the server to send information to them. You will be intimately involved in this publishing process because you must create files and then put them on a server to make them available in the first place, and you must ensure that your content will appear to the end user as you intended.

A Brief History of HTML and the World Wide Web

Once upon a time, back when there weren't any footprints on the moon, some farsighted folks decided to see whether they could connect several major computer networks. I'll spare you the names and stories (there are plenty of both), but the eventual result was the "mother of all networks," which we call the Internet.

NOTE

For more information on the history of the World Wide Web, see the Wikipedia article on this topic: http://en.wikipedia.org/wiki/History_of_the_Web.

Until 1990, accessing information through the Internet was a rather technical affair. It was so hard, in fact, that even Ph.D.-holding physicists were often frustrated when trying to swap data. One such physicist, the now-famous (and knighted) Sir Tim Berners-Lee, cooked up a way to easily cross-reference text on the Internet through hypertext links.

This wasn't a new idea, but his simple Hypertext Markup Language (HTML) managed to thrive while more ambitious hypertext projects floundered. Hypertext originally meant text stored in electronic form with cross-reference links between pages. It is now a broader term that refers to just about any object (text, images, files, and so on) that can be linked to other objects. *Hypertext Markup Language* is a language for describing how text, graphics, and files containing other information are organized and linked.

By 1993, only 100 or so computers throughout the world were equipped to serve up HTML pages. Those interlinked pages were dubbed the *World Wide Web (WWW)*, and several web browser programs had been written to enable people to view web pages. Because of the growing popularity of the Web, a few programmers soon wrote web browsers that could view graphical images along with text. From that point forward, the continued development of web browser software and the standardization of the HTML—and XHTML—languages have led us to the world we live in today, one in which more than half a billion websites serve billions of text and multimedia files.

These few paragraphs really are a brief history of what has been a remarkable period. Today's college students have never known a time in which the World Wide Web didn't exist, and the idea of always-on information and ubiquitous computing will shape all aspects of our lives moving forward. Instead of seeing web content creation and management as a set of skills possessed by only a few technically oriented folks (okay, call them geeks, if you will), by the end of this book, you will see that these are skills that anyone can master, regardless of inherent geekiness.

Creating Web Content

You might have noticed the use of the term *web content* rather than *web pages*—that was intentional. Although we talk of "visiting a web page," what we really mean is something like "looking at all the text and the images at one address on our computer." The text that we read and the images that we see are rendered by our web browsers, which are given certain instructions found in individual files.

Those files contain text that is marked up with, or surrounded by, HTML codes that tell the browser how to display the text—as a heading, as a paragraph, in a red font, and so on. Some HTML markup tells the browser to display an image or video file rather than plain text, which brings me back to this point: Different types of content are sent to your web browser, so simply saying web page doesn't begin to cover it. Here we use the term web content instead, to cover the full range of text, image, audio, video, and other media found online.

In later chapters, you'll learn the basics of linking to or creating the various types of multimedia web content found in websites. All you need to remember at this point is that you are in control of the content a user sees when visiting your website. Beginning with the file that contains text to display or codes that tell the server to send a graphic along to the user's web browser, you have to plan, design, and implement all the pieces that will eventually make up your web presence. As you will learn throughout this book, it is not a difficult process as long as you understand all the little steps along the way.

In its most fundamental form, web content begins with a simple text file containing HTML markup. In this book, you'll learn about and compose standards-compliant HTML5 markup. One of the many benefits of writing standards-compliant code is that, in the future, you will not have to worry about having to go back to your code to fundamentally alter it. Instead, your code will (likely) always work for as long as web browsers adhere to standards (hopefully a long time).

Understanding Web Content Delivery

Several processes occur, in many different locations, to eventually produce web content that you can see. These processes occur very quickly—on the order of milliseconds—and occur behind the scenes. In other words, although we might think all we are doing is opening a web browser, typing in a web address, and instantaneously seeing the content we requested, technology in the background is working hard on our behalf. Figure 1.1 shows the basic interaction between a browser and a server.

FIGURE 1.1
A browser request and a server
response.

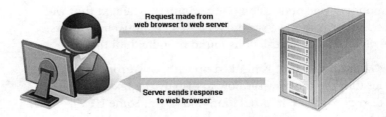

However, the process involves several steps—and potentially several trips between the browser and the server—before you see the entire content of the site you requested.

Suppose you want to do a Google search, so you dutifully type **www.google.com** in the address bar or select the Google bookmark from your bookmarks list. Almost immediately, your browser shows you something like what's shown in Figure 1.2.

FIGURE 1.2
Visiting www.google.com.

Figure 1.2 shows a website that contains text plus one image (the Google logo). A simple version of the processes that occurred to retrieve that text and image from a web server and display it on your screen follows:

1. Your web browser sends a request for the `index.html` file located at the http://www.google.com address. The `index.html` file does not have to be part of the address that you type in the address bar; you'll learn more about the `index.html` file further along in this chapter.

2. After receiving the request for a specific file, the web server process looks in its directory contents for the specific file, opens it, and sends the content of that file back to your web browser.

3. The web browser receives the content of the `index.html` file, which is text marked up with HTML codes, and renders the content based on these HTML codes. While rendering the content, the browser happens upon the HTML code for the Google logo, which you can see in Figure 1.2. The HTML code looks something like this:

    ```
    <img alt="Google" src="/images/srpr/logo4w.png"
        width="275" height="95" />
    ```

    The tag provides attributes that tell the browser the file source location (`src`), width (`width`), and height (`height`) necessary to display the logo. You'll learn more about attributes throughout later chapters.

4. The browser looks at the `src` attribute in the `<img/>` tag to find the source location. In this case, the image `logo3w.png` can be found in the `images` directory at the same web address (www.google.com) from which the browser retrieved the HTML file.

5. The browser requests the file at the http://www.google.com/images/srpr/logo4w.png web address.

6. The web server interprets that request, finds the file, and sends the contents of that file to the web browser that requested it.

7. The web browser displays the image on your monitor.

As you can see in the description of the web content delivery process, web browsers do more than simply act as picture frames through which you can view content. Browsers assemble the web content components and arrange those parts according to the HTML commands in the file.

You can also view web content locally, or on your own hard drive, without the need for a web server. The process of content retrieval and display is the same as the process listed in the previous steps, in that a browser looks for and interprets the codes and content of an HTML file, but the trip is shorter: The browser looks for files on your own computer's hard drive rather than on a remote machine. A web server would be needed to interpret any server-based programming language embedded in the files, but that is outside the scope of this book. In fact, you could work through all the lessons in this book without having a web server to call your own, but then nobody but you could view your masterpieces.

Selecting a Web Hosting Provider

Despite my just telling you that you can work through all the lessons in this book without having a web server, having a web server is the recommended method for continuing. Don't worry—obtaining a hosting provider is usually a quick, painless, and relatively inexpensive process. In fact, you can get your own domain name and a year of web hosting for just slightly more than the cost of the book you are reading now.

If you type **web hosting provider** in your search engine of choice, you will get millions of hits and an endless list of sponsored search results (also known as ads). Not this many web hosting providers exist in the world, although it might seem otherwise. Even if you are looking at a managed list of hosting providers, it can be overwhelming—especially if all you are looking for is a place to host a simple website for yourself or your company or organization.

You'll want to narrow your search when looking for a provider and choose one that best meets your needs. Some selection criteria for a web hosting provider follow:

▶ **Reliability/server "uptime"**—If you have an online presence, you want to make sure people can actually get there consistently.

▶ **Customer service**—Look for multiple methods for contacting customer service (phone, email, chat), as well as online documentation for common issues.

▶ **Server space**—Does the hosting package include enough server space to hold all the multimedia files (images, audio, video) you plan to include in your website (if any)?

▶ **Bandwidth**—Does the hosting package include enough bandwidth that all the people visiting your site and downloading files can do so without your having to pay extra?

▶ **Domain name purchase and management**—Does the package include a custom domain name, or must you purchase and maintain your domain name separately from your hosting account?

▶ **Price**—Do not overpay for hosting. You will see a wide range of prices offered and should immediately wonder, "What's the difference?" Often the difference has little to do with the quality of the service and everything to do with company overhead and what the company thinks it can get away with charging people. A good rule of thumb is that if you are paying more than $75 per year for a basic hosting package and domain name, you are probably paying too much.

Here are three reliable web hosting providers whose basic packages contain plenty of server space and bandwidth (as well as domain names and extra benefits) at a relatively low cost. If you don't go with any of these web hosting providers, you can at least use their basic package descriptions as a guideline as you shop around.

▶ **A Small Orange (www.asmallorange.com)**—The Tiny and Small hosting packages are perfect starting places for the new web content publisher.

▶ **DailyRazor (www.dailyrazor.com)**—Even its Rookie personal hosting package is full-featured and reliable.

▶ **Lunarpages (www.lunarpages.com)**—The Basic hosting package is suitable for many personal and small business websites.

One feature of a good hosting provider is that it provides a "control panel" for you to manage aspects of your account. Figure 1.3 shows the control panel for my own hosting account at DailyRazor. Many web hosting providers offer this particular control panel software, or some control panel that is similar in design—clearly labeled icons leading to tasks you can perform to configure and manage your account.

NOTE

The author has used all these providers (and then some) over the years and has no problem recommending any of them; predominantly, she uses DailyRazor as a web hosting provider, especially for advanced development environments.

FIGURE 1.3
A sample control panel.

You might never need to use your control panel, but having it available to you simplifies the installation of databases and other software, the viewing of web statistics, and the addition of email addresses (among many other features). If you can follow instructions, you can manage your own web server—no special training required.

Testing with Multiple Web Browsers

Now that we've just discussed the process of web content delivery and the acquisition of a web server, it might seem a little strange to step back and talk about testing your websites with multiple web browsers. However, before you go off and learn all about creating websites with HTML and CSS, do so with this very important statement in mind: Every visitor to your website will potentially use hardware and software configurations that are different from your own—their device types (desktop, laptop, netbook, smartphone, iPhone), screen resolutions, browser types, browser window sizes, speed of connections. Remember that you cannot control any aspect of what your visitors use when they view your site. So just as you're setting up your web hosting environment and getting ready to work, think about downloading several web browsers so that you have a local test suite of tools available to you. Let me explain why this is important.

Although all web browsers process and handle information in the same general way, some specific differences among them result in things not always looking the same in different browsers. Even users of the same version of the same web browser can alter how a page appears by choosing different display options and/or changing the size of their viewing windows. All the major web browsers allow users to override the background and fonts the web page author specifies with those of their own choosing. Screen resolution, window size, and optional toolbars can also change how much of a page someone sees when it first appears on their screens. You can ensure only that you write standards-compliant HTML and CSS.

Do not, under any circumstances, spend hours on end designing something that looks perfect only on your own computer—unless you are willing to be disappointed when you look at it on your friend's computer, on the computer in the coffee shop down the street, or on your iPhone.

You should always test your websites with as many of these web browsers as possible:

▶ Apple Safari (http://www.apple.com/safari/) for Mac

▶ Google Chrome (http://www.google.com/chrome) for Mac, Windows, and Linux/UNIX

▶ Mozilla Firefox (http://www.mozilla.com/firefox/) for Mac, Windows, and Linux/UNIX

▶ Microsoft Internet Explorer (http://www.microsoft.com/ie) for Windows

▶ Opera (www.opera.com) for Mac, Windows, and Linux/UNIX

Now that you have a development environment set up, or at least some idea of the type you'd like to set up in the future, let's move on to creating a test file.

NOTE

In Chapter 12, "Creating Fixed or Liquid Layouts," you'll learn a little bit about the concept of responsive web design, in which the design of a site shifts and changes automatically depending on the user's behavior and viewing environment (screen size, device, and so on).

Creating a Sample File

Before we begin, take a look at Listing 1.1. This listing represents a simple piece of web content—a few lines of HTML that print `"Hello World! Welcome to My Web Server."` in large, bold letters on two lines centered within the browser window. You'll learn more about the HTML and CSS used within this file as you move forward in this book.

LISTING 1.1   Our Sample HTML File

```
<!DOCTYPE html>
<html>
<head>
<title>Hello World!</title>
</head>
<body>
<h1 style="text-align: center">Hello World!<br/>
Welcome to My Web Server.</h1>
</body>
</html>
```

To make use of this content, open a text editor of your choice, such as Notepad (on Windows) or TextEdit (on a Mac). Do not use WordPad, Microsoft Word, or other full-featured word processing software because those programs create different sorts of files than the plain-text files we use for web content.

Type the content that you see in Listing 1.1 and then save the file using `sample.html` as the filename. The `.html` extension tells the web server that your file is, indeed, full of HTML. When the file contents are sent to the web browser that requests it, the browser will also know that it is HTML and will render it appropriately.

Now that you have a sample HTML file to use—and hopefully somewhere to put it, such as a web hosting account—let's get to publishing your web content.

Using FTP to Transfer Files

As you've learned so far, you have to put your web content on a web server to make it accessible to others. This process typically occurs by using *File Transfer Protocol (FTP)*. To use FTP, you need an FTP client—a program used to transfer files from your computer to a web server.

FTP clients require three pieces of information to connect to your web server; this information will have been sent to you by your hosting provider after you set up your account:

▶ The hostname, or address, to which you will connect

▶ Your account username

▶ Your account password

When you have this information, you are ready to use an FTP client to transfer content to your web server.

Selecting an FTP Client

Regardless of the FTP client you use, FTP clients generally use the same type of interface. Figure 1.4 shows an example of FireFTP, which is an FTP client used with the Firefox web browser. The directory listing of the local machine (your computer) appears on the left of your screen, and the directory listing of the remote machine (the web server) appears on the right. Typically, you will see right arrow and left arrow buttons, as shown in Figure 1.4. The right arrow sends selected files from your computer to your web server; the left arrow sends files from the web server to your computer. Many FTP clients also enable you to simply select files and then drag and drop those files to the target machines.

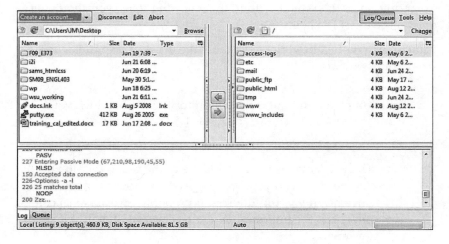

FIGURE 1.4
The FireFTP interface.

Many FTP clients are freely available to you, but you can also transfer files via the web-based File Manager tool that is likely part of your web server's control panel. However, that method of file transfer typically introduces more steps into the process and isn't nearly as streamlined (or simple) as the process of installing an FTP client on your own machine.

Here are some popular free FTP clients:

▶ Classic FTP (http://www.nchsoftware.com/classic/) for Mac and Windows

▶ Cyberduck (cyberduck.ch) for Mac

▶ Fetch (fetchsoftworks.com) for Mac

▶ FileZilla (filezilla-project.org) for all platforms

▶ FireFTP (fireftp.mozdev.org) Firefox extension for all platforms

When you have selected an FTP client and installed it on your computer, you are ready to upload and download files from your web server. In the next section, you'll see how this process works using the sample file in Listing 1.1.

Using an FTP Client

The following steps show how to use Classic FTP to connect to your web server and transfer a file. However, all FTP clients use similar, if not exact, interfaces. If you understand the following steps, you should be able to use any FTP client.

Remember, you first need the hostname, the account username, and the account password.

1. Start the Classic FTP program and click the Connect button. You are prompted to fill out information for the site to which you want to connect, as shown in Figure 1.5.

2. Fill in each of the items shown in Figure 1.5 as described here:

▶ The FTP Server is the FTP address of the web server to which you need to send your web pages. Your hosting provider will have given you this address. It probably is *yourdomain*.com, but check the information you received when you signed up for service.

▶ Complete the User Name field and the Password field using the information your hosting provider gave you.

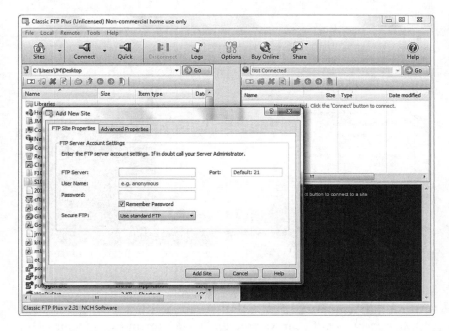

FIGURE 1.5
Connecting to a new site in Classic FTP.

3.   You can switch to the Advanced tab and modify the following optional items, shown in Figure 1.6:

▶ The Site Label is the name you'll use to refer to your own site. Nobody else will see this name, so enter whatever you want.

▶ You can change the values for Initial Remote Directory on First Connection and Initial Local Directory on First Connection, but you might want to wait until you have become accustomed to using the client and have established a workflow.

4.   When you're finished with the settings, click Add Site to save the settings. You can then click Connect to establish a connection with the web server.

You will see a dialog box indicating that Classic FTP is attempting to connect to the web server. Upon successful connection, you will see an interface like the one in Figure 1.7, showing the contents of the local directory on the left and the contents of your web server on the right.

FIGURE 1.6
The Advanced connection options
in Classic FTP.

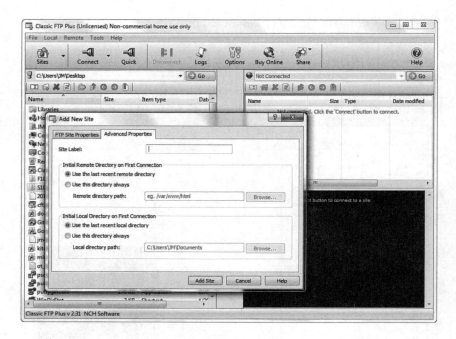

5. You are now *almost* ready to transfer files to your web server. All that remains is to change directories to what is called the *document root* of your web server. The document root of your web server is the directory that is designated as the top-level directory for your web content—the starting point of the directory structure, which you'll learn more about later in this chapter. Often, this directory is named `public_html`, www (because www has been created as an alias for `public_html`), or htdocs. You do not have to create this directory; your hosting provider will have created it for you.

   Double-click the document root directory name to open it. The display shown on the right of the FTP client interface changes to show the contents of this directory (it will probably be empty at this point, unless your web hosting provider has put placeholder files in that directory on your behalf).

6. The goal is to transfer the `sample.html` file you created earlier from your computer to the web server. Find the file in the directory listing on the left of the FTP client interface (navigate if you have to), and click it once to highlight the filename.

7. Click the right-arrow button in the middle of the client interface to send the file to the web server. When the file transfer

completes, the right side of the client interface refreshes to show you that the file has made it to its destination.

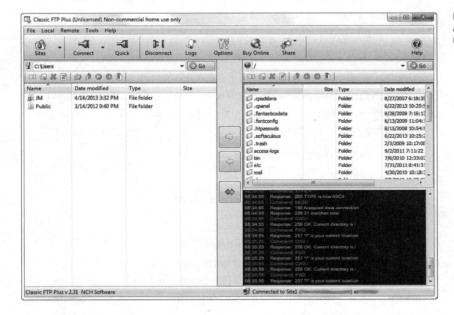

8. Click the Disconnect button to close the connection, and then exit the Classic FTP program.

These steps are conceptually similar to the steps you take anytime you want to send files to your web server via FTP. You can also use your FTP client to create subdirectories on the remote web server. To create a subdirectory using Classic FTP, click the Remote menu and then click New Folder. Different FTP clients have different interface options to achieve the same goal.

Understanding Where to Place Files on the Web Server

An important aspect of maintaining web content is determining how you will organize that content—not only for the user to find, but also for you to maintain on your server. Putting files in directories helps you manage those files.

Naming and organizing directories on your web server, and developing rules for file maintenance, is completely up to you. However, maintaining a well-organized server makes your management of its content more efficient in the long run.

Basic File Management

As you browse the Web, you might have noticed that URLs change as you navigate through websites. For instance, if you're looking at a company's website and you click on graphical navigation leading to the company's products or services, the URL probably changes from

http://www.*companyname*.com/

to

http://www.*companyname*.com/products/

or

http://www.*companyname*.com/services/

In the preceding section, I used the term *document root* without really explaining what that is all about. The document root of a web server is essentially the trailing slash in the full URL. For instance, if your domain is *yourdomain*.com and your URL is http://*www.yourdomain*. com/, the document root is the directory represented by the trailing slash (/). The document root is the starting point of the directory structure you create on your web server; it is the place where the web server begins looking for files requested by the web browser.

If you put the `sample.html` file in your document root as previously directed, you will be able to access it via a web browser at the following URL:

http://www.*yourdomain*.com/sample.html

If you entered this URL into your web browser, you would see the rendered `sample.html` file, as shown in Figure 1.8.

However, if you created a new directory within the document root and put the `sample.html` file in that directory, the file would be accessed at this URL:

http://www.*yourdomain*.com/newdirectory/sample.html

FIGURE 1.8
The sample.html file accessed via a web browser.

If you put the sample.html file in the directory you originally saw upon connecting to your server—that is, you did *not* change directories and place the file in the document root—the sample.html file would not be accessible from your web server at any URL. The file will still be on the machine that you know as your web server, but because the file is not in the document root—where the server software knows to start looking for files—it will never be accessible to anyone via a web browser.

The bottom line? Always navigate to the document root of your web server before you start transferring files.

This is especially true with graphics and other multimedia files. A common directory on web servers is called images, where, as you can imagine, all the image assets are placed for retrieval. Other popular directories include css for style sheet files (if you are using more than one) and js for external JavaScript files. Alternatively, if you know that you will have an area on your website where visitors can download many types of files, you might simply call that directory downloads.

Whether it's a ZIP file containing your art portfolio or an Excel spreadsheet with sales numbers, it's often useful to publish files on the Internet that aren't simply web pages. To make available on the Web a file that isn't an HTML file, just upload the file to your website as if it were an HTML file, following the instructions earlier in this chapter for uploading. After the file is uploaded to the web server, you can create a link to it (as you'll learn in Chapter 7, "Using External and Internal Links"). In other words, your web server can serve much more than HTML.

Here's a sample of the HTML code that you will learn more about later in this book. The following code would be used for a file named `artfolio.zip`, located in the `downloads` directory of your website, and with link text that reads `Download my art portfolio!`:

```
<a href="/downloads/artfolio.zip">Download my art portfolio!</a>
```

Using an Index Page

When you think of an index, you probably think of the section in the back of a book that tells you where to look for various keywords and topics. The index file in a web server directory can serve that purpose—if you design it that way. In fact, that's where the name originates.

The `index.html` file (or just *index file*, as it's usually referred to) is the name you give to the page you want people to see as the default file when they navigate to a specific directory in your website.

Another function of the index page is that users who visit a directory on your site that has an index page but who do not specify that page will still land on the main page for that section of your site—or for the site itself.

For instance, you can type either of the following URLs and land on Apple's iPhone informational page:

> http://www.apple.com/iphone/
>
> http://www.apple.com/iphone/index.html

Had there been no `index.html` page in the `iphone` directory, the results would depend on the configuration of the web server. If the server is configured to disallow directory browsing, the user would have seen a "Directory Listing Denied" message when attempting to access the URL without a specified page name. However, if the server is configured to allow directory browsing, the user would have seen a list of the files in that directory.

Your hosting provider will already have determined these server configuration options. If your hosting provider enables you to modify server settings via a control panel, you can change these settings so that your server responds to requests based on your own requirements.

Not only is the index file used in subdirectories, but it's used in the top-level directory (or document root) of your website as well. The first page of your website—or *home page* or *main page*, or however you like to refer to the web content you want users to see when they first visit your domain—should be named `index.html` and placed in the document root of your web server. This ensures that when users type `http://www.yourdomain.com/` into their web browsers, the server responds with the content you intended them to see (instead of "Directory Listing Denied" or some other unintended consequence).

Distributing Content Without a Web Server

Publishing HTML and multimedia files online is obviously the primary reason to learn HTML and create web content. However, there are also situations in which other forms of publishing simply aren't viable. For example, you might want to distribute CD-ROMs, DVD-ROMs, or USB drives at a trade show with marketing materials designed as web content—that is, hyperlinked text viewable through a web browser, but without a web server involved. You might also want to include HTML-based instructional manuals on removable media for students at a training seminar. These are just two examples of how HTML pages can be used in publishing scenarios that don't involve the Internet.

This process is also called creating *local* sites; even though no web server is involved, these bundles of hypertext content are still called sites. The *local* term comes into play because your files are accessed locally and not remotely (via a web server).

Publishing Content Locally

Let's assume that you need to create a local site that you want to distribute on a USB drive. Even the cheapest USB drives hold so much data these days—and basic hypertext files are quite small—that you can distribute an entire site and a fully functioning web browser all on one little drive.

Simply think of the directory structure of your USB drive just as you would the directory structure of your web server. The top level of the USB drive directory structure can be your document root. Or if you are distributing a web browser along with the content, you might have two directories—for example, one named `browser` and one named `content`. In that case, the `content` directory would be your document root. Within the document root, you could have additional subfolders in which you place content and other multimedia assets.

NOTE

Distributing a web browser isn't required when you are creating and distributing a local site, although it's a nice touch. You can reasonably assume that users have their own web browsers and will open the `index.html` file in a directory to start browsing the hyperlinked content. However, if you want to distribute a web browser on the USB drive, go to www.portableapps.com and look for Portable Firefox or Portable Chrome.

It's as important to maintain good organization with a local site as it is with a remote website so that you avoid broken links in your HTML files. You'll learn more about the specifics of linking files in Chapter 7.

Publishing Content on a Blog

You might have a blog hosted by a third party, such as WordPress, Tumblr, or Blogger, and thus have already published content without having a dedicated web server or even knowing any HTML. These services offer *visual editors* in addition to *source editors*, meaning that you can type your words and add presentational formatting such as bold, italics, or font colors without knowing the HTML for these actions. Still, the content becomes actual HTML when you click the Publish button in these editors.

However, with the knowledge you will acquire throughout this book, your blogging will be enhanced because you will be able to use the source editor for your blog post content and blog templates, thus affording you more control over the look and feel of that content. These actions occur differently from the process you learned for creating an HTML file and uploading it via FTP to your own dedicated web server, but I would be remiss if I did not note that blogging is, in fact, a form of web publishing.

Tips for Testing Web Content

Whenever you transfer files to your web server or place them on removable media for local browsing, you should immediately test every page thoroughly. The following checklist helps ensure that your web content behaves the way you expected. Note that some of the terms might be unfamiliar to you at this point, but come back to this checklist as you progress through this book and create larger projects:

▶ Before you transfer your files, test them locally on your machine to ensure that the links work and the content reflects the visual design you intended. After you transfer the pages to a web server or removable device, test them all again.

▶ Perform these tests with as many browsers as you can—Chrome, Firefox, Internet Explorer, Opera, and Safari is a good list—and on both Mac and Windows platforms. If possible, check at low resolution (800×600) and high resolution (1920×1080).

▶ Turn off auto image loading in your web browser before you start testing so that you can see what each page looks like without the graphics. Check your alt tag messages, and then turn image loading back on to load the graphics and review the page carefully again.

▶ Use your browser's font size settings to look at each page in various font sizes to ensure that your layout doesn't fall to pieces if users override your font specifications with their own.

▶ Wait for each page to completely finish loading, and then scroll all the way down to make sure that all images appear where they should.

▶ Time how long it takes each page to load. Does it take more than a few seconds to load? If so, is the information on that page valuable enough to keep users from going elsewhere before the page finishes loading? Granted, broadband connections are common, but that doesn't mean you should load up your pages with 1MB images.

If your pages pass all those tests, you can rest easy; your site is ready for public viewing.

Summary

This chapter introduced you to the concept of using HTML to mark up text files to produce web content. You also learned that there is more to web content than just the "page"—web content also includes image, audio, and video files. All this content lives on a web server—a remote machine often far from your own computer. On your computer or other device, you use a web browser to request, retrieve, and eventually display web content on your screen.

You learned the criteria to consider when determining whether a web hosting provider fits your needs. After you have selected a web hosting provider, you can begin to transfer files to your web server, which you also learned how to do, using an FTP client. You also learned a bit about web server directory structures and file management, as well as the very important purpose of the `index.html` file in a given web server directory. In addition, you learned that you can distribute web content on removable media, and you learned how to go about structuring the files and directories to achieve the goal of viewing content without using a remote web server.

Finally, you learned the importance of testing your work in multiple browsers after you've placed it on a web server. Writing valid, standards-compliant HTML and CSS helps ensure that your site looks reasonably similar for all visitors, but you still shouldn't design without receiving input from potential users outside your development team—it is even more important to get input from others when you are a design team of one!

Q&A

Q. I've looked at the HTML source of some web pages on the Internet, and it looks frighteningly difficult to learn. Do I have to think like a computer programmer to learn this stuff?

A. Although complex HTML pages can indeed look daunting, learning HTML is much easier than learning actual software programming languages (such as C++ or Java). HTML is a markup language rather than a programming language; you mark up text so that the browser can render the text a certain way. That's a completely different set of thought processes than developing a computer program. You really don't need any experience or skill as a computer programmer to be a successful web content author.

One of the reasons the HTML behind many commercial websites looks complicated is that it was likely created by a visual web design tool—a "what you see is what you get" (WYSIWYG) editor that uses whatever markup its software developer told it to use in certain circumstances (as opposed to being hand-coded, in which you are completely in control of the resulting markup). In this book, you are taught fundamental coding from the ground up, which typically results in clean, easy-to-read source code. Visual web design tools have a knack for making code difficult to read and for producing code that is convoluted and not standards compliant.

Q. Running all the tests you recommend would take longer than creating my pages! Can't I get away with less testing?

A. If your pages aren't intended to make money or provide an important service, it's probably not a big deal if they look funny to some users or produce errors once in a while. In that case, just test each page with a couple different browsers and call it a day. However, if you need to project a professional image, there is no substitute for rigorous testing.

Q. Seriously, who cares how I organize my web content?

A. Believe it or not, the organization of your web content does matter to search engines and potential visitors to your site. But overall, having an organized web server directory structure helps you keep track of content that you are likely to update frequently. For instance, if you have a dedicated directory for images or multimedia, you know exactly where to look for a file you want to update—no need to hunt through directories containing other content.

Workshop

The Workshop contains quiz questions and exercises to help you solidify your understanding of the material covered. Try to answer all questions before looking at the "Answers" section that follows.

Quiz

1. How many files would you need to store on a web server to produce a single web page with some text and two images on it?

2. What are some of the features to look for in a web hosting provider?

3. What three pieces of information do you need in order to connect to your web server via FTP?

4. What is the purpose of the `index.html` file?

5. Does your website have to include a directory structure?

Answers

1. You would need three: one for the web page itself, which includes the text and the HTML markup, and one for each of the two images.

2. Look for reliability, customer service, web space and bandwidth, domain name service, site-management extras, and price.

3. You need the hostname, your account username, and your account password.

4. The `index.html` file is typically the default file for a directory within a web server. It enables users to access http://www.*yourdomain*.com/*somedirectory*/ without using a trailing filename and still end up in the appropriate place.

5. No. Using a directory structure for file organization is completely up to you, although using one is highly recommended because it simplifies content maintenance.

Exercises

▶ Get your web hosting in order—are you going to move through the lessons in this book by viewing files locally on your own computer, or are you going to use a web hosting provider? Note that most web hosting providers will have you up and running the same day you purchase your hosting plan.

▶ If you are using an external hosting provider, then using your FTP client, create a subdirectory within the document root of your website. Paste the contents of the `sample.html` file into another file named `index.html`, change the text between the `<title>` and `</title>` tags to something new, and change the text between the `<h1>` and `</h1>` tags to something new. Save the file and upload it to the new subdirectory. Use your web browser to navigate to the new directory on your web server, and see that the content in the `index.html` file appears. Then, using your FTP client, delete the `index.html` file from the remote subdirectory. Return to that URL with your web browser, reload the page, and see how the server responds without the `index.html` file in place.

▶ Using the same set of files created in the preceding exercise, place these files on a removable media device—a CD-ROM or a USB drive, for example. Use your browser to navigate this local version of your sample website, and think about the instructions you would have to distribute with this removable media so that others could use it.

CHAPTER 2
Structuring an HTML Document

In the first chapter, you got a basic idea of the process behind creating web content and viewing it online (or locally, if you do not yet have a web hosting provider). In this chapter, we get down to the business of explaining the various elements that must appear in an HTML file so that it is displayed appropriately in your web browser.

In general, this chapter provides a summary of HTML basics and gives some practical tips to help you make the most of your time as a web page developer. You'll begin to dive a bit deeper into the theory behind it all as you learn about the HTML5 elements that enable you to enhance the semantics—the meaning—of the information that you provide in your marked-up text. You'll take a closer look at six elements that are fundamental to solid semantic structuring of your documents: `<header>`, `<section>`, `<article>`, `<nav>`, `<aside>`, and `<footer>`.

Throughout the remainder of this book, you will see these tags used appropriately in the code samples, so this lesson makes sure that you have a good grasp of their meaning before we continue.

Getting Prepared

Here's a review of what you need to do before you're ready to use the rest of this book:

1. Get a computer. I used a Windows laptop to test the sample web content and capture the figures in this book, but you can use any Windows, Macintosh, or Linux/UNIX machine to create and view your web content.

WHAT YOU'LL LEARN IN THIS CHAPTER:

▶ How to create a simple web page in HTML

▶ How to include all the HTML tags that every web page must have

▶ How to organize a page with paragraphs and line breaks

▶ How to organize your content with headings

▶ How to use the semantic elements of HTML5

▶ How to use semantic tags to indicate header and footer content

▶ How to use semantic tags to indicate navigational and secondary content

▶ How to use semantic tags to better structure body content

2. Get a connection to the Internet. Whether you have a dial-up, wireless, or broadband connection doesn't matter for the creation and viewing of your web content, but the faster the connection, the better for the overall experience. The Internet service provider (ISP), school, or business that provides your Internet connection can help you with the details of setting it up properly. Additionally, many public spaces such as coffee shops, bookstores, and libraries offer free wireless Internet service that you can use if you have a laptop computer with Wi-Fi network support.

3. Get web browser software. This is the software your computer needs in order to retrieve and display web content. As you learned in the first chapter, the most popular browsers (in alphabetical order) are Apple Safari, Google Chrome, Microsoft Internet Explorer, Mozilla Firefox, and Opera. It's a good idea to install several of these browsers so that you can experiment and make sure that your content looks consistent across them all; you can't make assumptions about the browsers other people are using.

4. Explore! Use a web browser to look around the Internet for websites that are similar in content or appearance to those you'd like to create. Note what frustrates you about some pages, what attracts you and keeps you reading others, and what makes you come back to some pages over and over again. If a particular topic interests you, consider searching for it using a popular search engine such as Google (www.google.com) or Bing (www.bing.com).

Getting Started with a Simple Web Page

In the first chapter, you learned that a web page is just a text file that is marked up by (or surrounded by) HTML codes that tell the browser how to display the text. To create these text files, use a text editor such as Notepad (on Windows) or TextEdit (on a Mac)—do not use WordPad, Microsoft Word, or other full-featured word-processing software because those create different sorts of files than the plain-text files we use for web content.

Before you begin working, you should start with some text that you want to put on a web page:

1. Find (or write) a few paragraphs of text about yourself, your family, your company, your softball team, or some other subject in which you're interested.

2. Save this text as plain, standard ASCII text. Notepad (on Windows) and most simple text editors always save files as plain text, but if you're using another program, you might need to choose this file type as an option (after selecting File, Save As).

As you go through this chapter, you will add HTML markup (called *tags*) to the text file, thus making it into web content.

When you save files containing HTML tags, always give them a name ending in `.html`. This is important—if you forget to type the `.html` at the end of the filename when you save the file, most text editors will give it some other extension (such as `.txt`). If that happens, you might not be able to find the file when you try to look at it with a web browser; if you find it, it certainly won't display properly. In other words, web browsers expect a web page file to have a file extension of `.html` and to be in plain-text format.

When visiting websites, you might also encounter pages with a file extension of `.htm`, which is another acceptable file extension to use. You might find other file extensions used on the Web, such as `.jsp` (Java Server Pages), `.asp` (Microsoft Active Server Pages), or `.php` (PHP: Hypertext Preprocessor), but these file types use server-side technologies that are beyond the scope of HTML and the lessons throughout this book. However, these files also contain HTML in addition to the programming language; although the programming code in those files is compiled on the server side and all you would see on the client side is the HTML output, if you looked at the source files, you would likely see some intricate weaving of programming and markup codes.

Listing 2.1 shows an example of text you can type and save to create a simple HTML page. If you opened this file with Chrome, you would see the page shown in Figure 2.1. Every web page you create must include a `<!DOCTYPE>` declaration, as well as `<html></html>`, `<head></head>`, `<title></title>`, and `<body></body>` tag pairs.

CAUTION

We reiterate this point because it is very important to both the outcome and the learning process itself: Do not create your first HTML file with Microsoft Word or any other HTML-compatible word processor; most of these programs attempt to rewrite your HTML for you in strange ways, potentially leaving you totally confused. The same holds true when you use Microsoft Word and "Save As" HTML—you are likely to get a verbose and noncompliant file full of HTML that will not validate and will cause you headaches to edit.

Additionally, I recommend that you *not* use a graphical, what-you-see-is-what-you-get (WYSIWYG) editor, such as Adobe Dreamweaver. You'll likely find it easier and more educational to start with a simple text editor while you're just learning HTML.

LISTING 2.1   The `<html>`, `<head>`, `<title>`, and `<body>` Tags

```
<!DOCTYPE html>
<html lang="en">
  <head>
    <title>The First Web Page</title>
  </head>

  <body>
   <p>
      In the beginning, Tim created the HyperText Markup Language.
      The Internet was without form and void, and text was upon
      the face of the monitor and the Hands of Tim were moving
      over the face of the keyboard. And Tim said, Let there be
      links; and there were links. And Tim saw that the links were
      good; and Tim separated the links from the text. Tim called
      the links Anchors, and the text He  called Other Stuff. And
      the whole thing together was the first Web Page.
   </p>
  </body>
</html>
```

FIGURE 2.1
When you save the text in Listing 2.1 as an HTML file and view it with a web browser, only the actual title and body text are displayed.

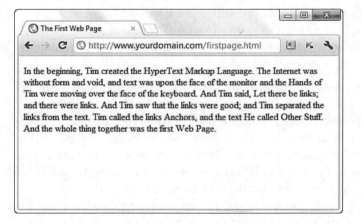

In Listing 2.1, as in every HTML page, the words starting with < and ending with > are actually coded commands. These coded commands are called *HTML tags* because they "tag" pieces of text and tell the web browser what kind of text it is. This allows the web browser to display the text appropriately.

The first line in the document is the document type declaration; you are *declaring* that it is `html` (specifically, HTML5) because `html` is the value used to declare a document as HTML5 in the `<!DOCTYPE>` tag.

Before you learn the meaning of the HTML tags used in Listing 2.1, you might want to see exactly how I went about creating and viewing the document itself. Follow these steps:

1. Type all the text in Listing 2.1, including the HTML tags, in Windows Notepad (or use Macintosh TextEdit or another text editor of your choice).

2. Select File, Save As. Be sure to select plain text (or ASCII text) as the file type.

3. Name the file `firstpage.html`.

4. Choose the folder on your hard drive where you want to keep your web pages—and remember which folder you choose! Click the Save or OK button to save the file.

5. Now start your favorite web browser. (Leave Notepad running, too, so you can easily switch between viewing and editing your page.)

In Internet Explorer, select File, Open and click Browse. If you're using Firefox, select File, Open File. Navigate to the appropriate folder and select the `firstpage.html` file. Some browsers and operating systems also enable you to drag and drop the `firstpage.html` file onto the browser window to view it.

Voilà! You should see the page shown in Figure 2.1.

TRY IT YOURSELF ▼

Creating and Viewing a Basic Web Page

NOTE

You don't need to be connected to the Internet to view a web page stored on your own computer. By default, your web browser tries to connect to the Internet every time you start it, which makes sense most of the time. However, this can be a hassle if you're developing pages locally on your hard drive (offline) and you keep getting errors about a page not being found. If you have a full-time web connection via a LAN, a cable modem, Wi-Fi, or DSL, this is a moot point because the browser will never complain about being offline. Otherwise, the appropriate action depends on your breed of browser; check the options under your browser's Tools menu.

If you have obtained a web hosting account, you could use FTP at this point to transfer the `firstpage.html` file to the web server. In fact, from this chapter forward, the instructions assume that you have a hosting provider and are comfortable sending files back and forth via FTP; if that is not the case, you should review the first chapter before moving on. Alternatively, if you are consciously choosing to work with files locally (without a web host), be prepared to adjust the instructions to suit your particular needs (such as ignoring the commands "transfer the files" and "type in the URL").

HTML Tags Every Web Page Must Have

The time has come for the secret language of HTML tags to be revealed to you. When you understand this language, you will have creative powers far beyond those of other humans. Don't tell the other humans, but it's really pretty easy.

The first line of code is the document type declaration; in HTML5, this is simply

```
<!DOCTYPE html>
```

This declaration identifies the document as being HTML5, which then ensures that web browsers know what to expect and prepare to render content in HTML5.

Many HTML tags have two parts: an *opening tag*, which indicates where a piece of text begins, and a *closing tag*, which indicates where the piece of text ends. Closing tags start with a / (forward slash) just after the < symbol.

Another type of tag is the *empty tag*, which is different, in that it doesn't include a pair of matching opening and closing tags. Instead, an empty tag consists of a single tag that starts with < and ends with / just before the > symbol. Although the ending slash is no longer explicitly required in HTML5, it does aid in compatibility with XHTML—if you have a pile of old XHTML in your website, it will not break while you're in the process of upgrading it.

Following is a quick summary of these three tags, just to make sure you understand the role each plays:

▶ An *opening tag* is an HTML tag that indicates the start of an HTML command; the text affected by the command appears after the opening tag. Opening tags always begin with < and end with >, as in `<html>`.

▶ A *closing tag* is an HTML tag that indicates the end of an HTML command; the text affected by the command appears before the closing tag. Closing tags always begin with </ and end with >, as in `</html>`.

▶ An *empty tag* is an HTML tag that issues an HTML command without enclosing any text in the page. Empty tags always begin with < and end with />, as in `<br />` and `<img />`.

For example, the `<body>` tag in Listing 2.1 tells the web browser where the actual body text of the page begins, and `</body>` indicates where it ends. Everything between the `<body>` and `</body>` tags appears in the main display area of the web browser window, as shown in Figure 2.1.

The very top of the browser window (refer to Figure 2.1) shows title text, which is any text that is located between `<title>` and `</title>`. The title text also identifies the page on the browser's Bookmarks or Favorites menu, depending on which browser you use. It's important to provide titles for your pages so that visitors to the page can properly bookmark them for future reference; search engines also use titles to provide a link to search results.

You will use the `<body>` and `<title>` tag pairs in every HTML page you create because every web page needs a title and body text. You will also use the `<html>` and `<head>` tag pairs, which are the other two tags shown in Listing 2.1. Putting `<html>` at the very beginning of a document simply indicates that the document is a web page. The `</html>` at the end indicates that the web page is over.

Within a page, there is a head section and a body section. Each section is identified by `<head>` and `<body>` tags. The idea is that information in the head of the page somehow describes the page but isn't actually displayed by a web browser. Information placed in the body, however, is displayed by a web browser. The `<head>` tag always appears near the beginning of the HTML code for a page, just after the opening `<html>` tag.

The `<title>` tag pair used to identify the title of a page appears within the head of the page, which means it is placed after the opening `<head>` tag and before the closing `</head>` tag. In the upcoming chapters, you'll learn about some other advanced header information that can go between `<head>` and `</head>`, such as style sheet rules for formatting the page.

The `<p>` tag in Listing 2.1 encloses a paragraph of text. You should enclose your chunks of text in the appropriate container elements whenever possible; you'll learn more about container elements as the book moves forward.

NOTE

You no doubt noticed in Listing 2.1 that there is some extra code associated with the `<html>` tag. This code consists of the language attribute (`lang`), which is used to specify additional information related to the tag. In this case, it specifies that the language of the text within the HTML is English. If you are writing in a different language, replace the `en` (for English) with the language identifier relevant to you.

TIP

You might find it convenient to create and save a bare-bones page (also known as a *skeleton* page, or *template*) with just the DOCTYPE and opening and closing `<html>`, `<head>`, `<title>`, and `<body>` tags, similar to the document in Listing 2.1. You can then open that document as a starting point whenever you want to make a new web page and save yourself the trouble of typing all those obligatory tags every time.

Organizing a Page with Paragraphs and Line Breaks

When a web browser displays HTML pages, it pays no attention to line endings or the number of spaces between words. For example, the top version of the poem in Figure 2.2 appears with a single space between all words, even though that's not how it's entered in Listing 2.2. This is because extra whitespace in HTML code is automatically reduced to a single space. Additionally, when the text reaches the edge of the browser window, it automatically wraps to the next line, no matter where the line breaks were in the original HTML file.

FIGURE 2.2
When the HTML in Listing 2.2 is viewed as a web page, line and paragraph breaks appear only where there are <br /> and <p> tags.

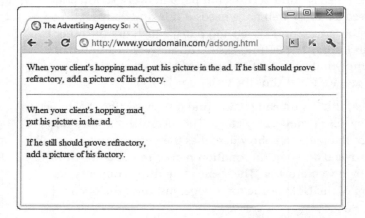

LISTING 2.2   HTML Containing Paragraph and Line Breaks

```
<!DOCTYPE html>

<html lang="en">
  <head>
    <title>The Advertising Agency Song</title>
  </head>

  <body>
    <p>
      When your client's    hopping mad,
      put his picture in the ad.

      If he still should    prove refractory,
      add a picture of his factory.
    </p>
    <hr />
    <p>
```

```
      When your client's hopping mad,<br />
      put his picture in the ad.
   </p>
   <p>
      If he still should prove refractory,<br />
      add a picture of his factory.
   </p>
 </body>
</html>
```

You must use HTML tags if you want to control where line and paragraph breaks actually appear. When text is enclosed within the `<p></p>` container tags, a line break is assumed after the closing tag. In later chapters, you'll learn to control the height of the line break using CSS. The `<br />` tag forces a line break within a paragraph. Unlike the other tags you've seen so far, `<br />` doesn't require a closing `</br>` tag—this is one of those empty tags discussed earlier.

The poem in Listing 2.2 and Figure 2.2 shows the `<br />` and `<p>` tags used to separate the lines and verses of an advertising agency song. You might have also noticed the `<hr />` tag in the listing, which causes a horizontal rule line to appear on the page (see Figure 2.2). Inserting a horizontal rule with the `<hr />` tag also causes a line break, even if you don't include a `<br />` tag along with it. Like `<br />`, the `<hr />` horizontal rule tag is an empty tag and, therefore, never gets a closing `</hr>` tag.

NOTE

If a closing slash isn't required for empty elements, you might ask why it's used throughout this book. One reason is that over the years, closing tags went from not being required, to required, to not being required (again), and your author is simply stuck in her ways using the perfectly valid but no longer required closing slash. Another reason is that because that middle period was relatively long, a *lot* of code editors, code generators, and templates use the closing slash, so you will see it used more often than not. It doesn't matter which way you choose to write because both ways are valid; just be sure that whatever coding style you follow, you are consistent in its use.

TRY IT YOURSELF ▼

Formatting Text in HTML

Try your hand at formatting a passage of text as proper HTML:

1. Add `<html><head><title>My Title</title></head><body>` to the beginning of the text (using your own title for your page instead of *My Title*). Also include the boilerplate code at the top of the page that takes care of meeting the requirements of standard HTML.

2. Add `</body></html>` to the very end of the text.

3. Add a `<p>` tag at the beginning of each paragraph and a `</p>` tag at the end of each paragraph.

4. Use `<br />` tags anywhere you want single-spaced line breaks.

5. Use `<hr />` to draw horizontal rules separating major sections of text, or wherever you'd like to see a line across the page.

▼ TRY IT YOURSELF

Formatting Text in HTML
continued

6. Save the file as `mypage.html` (using your own filename instead of `mypage`).

7. Open the file in a web browser to see your web content. (Send the file via FTP to your web hosting account, if you have one.)

8. If something doesn't look right, go back to the text editor to make corrections and save the file again (and send it to your web hosting account, if applicable). You then need to click Reload/Refresh in the browser to see the changes you made.

CAUTION

If you are using a word processor to create the web page, be sure to save the HTML file in plain-text or ASCII format.

NOTE

By now, you've probably caught on to the fact that HTML code is often indented by its author to reveal the relationship between different parts of the HTML document, as well as for simple ease of reading. This indentation is entirely voluntary—you could just as easily run all the tags together with no spaces or line breaks, and they would still look fine when viewed in a browser. The indentations are for you so that you can quickly look at a page full of code and understand how it fits together. Indenting your code is another good web design habit and ultimately makes your pages easier to maintain, both for yourself and for anyone else who might pick up where you leave off.

Organizing Your Content with Headings

When you browse web pages on the Internet, you'll notice that many of them have a heading at the top that appears larger and bolder than the rest of the text. Listing 2.3 is sample code and text for a simple web page containing an example of a heading as compared to normal paragraph text. Any text between the `<h1>` and `</h1>` tags will appear as a large heading. Additionally, `<h2>` and `<h3>` make progressively smaller headings, and so on, as far down as `<h6>`.

LISTING 2.3　Heading Tags

```
<!DOCTYPE html>

<html lang="en">
  <head>
    <title>My Widgets</title>
  </head>

  <body>
    <h1>My Widgets</h1>
    <p>My widgets are the best in the land. Continue reading to
    learn more about my widgets.</p>

    <h2>Widget Features</h2>
    <p>If I had any features to discuss,  you can bet I'd do
    it here.</p>

    <h3>Pricing</h3>
    <p>Here, I would talk about my widget pricing.</p>

    <h3>Comparisons</h3>
    <p>Here, I would talk about how my widgets compare to my
```

```
    competitor's widgets.</p>
  </body>
</html>
```

As you can see in Figure 2.3, the HTML that creates headings couldn't be simpler. In this example, the phrase "My Widgets" is prominently displayed using the `<h1>` tag. To create the biggest (level 1) heading, just put an `<h1>` tag at the beginning and an `</h1>` tag at the end of the text you want to use as a heading. For a slightly smaller (level 2) heading—for information that is of lesser importance than the title—use the `<h2>` and `</h2>` tags around your text. For content that should appear even less prominently than a level 2 heading, use the `<h3>` and `</h3>` tags around your text.

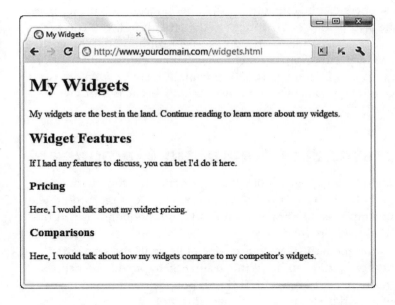

FIGURE 2.3
Using three levels of headings shows the hierarchy of content on this sample product page.

However, bear in mind that your headings should follow a content hierarchy; use only one level 1 heading, have one (or more) level 2 headings after the level 1 heading, use level 3 headings directly after level 2 headings, and so on. Do not fall into the trap of assigning headings to content just to make that content display a certain way. Instead, ensure that you are categorizing your content appropriately (as a main heading, a secondary heading, and so on), while using display styles to make that text render a particular way in a web browser.

Theoretically, you can also use `<h4>`, `<h5>`, and `<h6>` tags to make progressively less important headings, but these aren't used very often. Web browsers seldom show a noticeable difference between these headings and the `<h3>` headings anyway—although you can control that with your own CSS—and content usually isn't displayed in such a manner that you'd need six levels of headings to show the content hierarchy.

It's important to remember the difference between a *title* and a *heading*. These two words are often interchangeable in day-to-day English, but when you're talking HTML, `<title>` gives the entire page an identifying name that isn't displayed on the page itself; it's displayed only on the browser window's title bar. The heading tags, on the other hand, cause some text on the page to be displayed with visual emphasis. There can be only one `<title>` per page, and it must appear within the `<head>` and `</head>` tags; on the other hand, you can have as many `<h1>`, `<h2>`, and `<h3>` headings as you want, in any order that suits your fancy. However, as I mentioned before, you should use the heading tags to keep tight control over content hierarchy; do not use headings as a way to achieve a particular look, because that's what CSS is for.

Understanding Semantic Elements

HTML5 includes tags that enable you to enhance the semantics—the meaning—of the information that you provide in your marked-up text. Instead of simply using HTML as a presentation language, as was the practice in the very early days when `<b>` for bold and `<i>` for italics was the norm, modern HTML has as one of its goals the separation of presentation and meaning. While using CSS to provide guidelines for presentation, composers of HTML can provide meaningful names within their markup for individual elements, not only through the use of IDs and class names (which you'll learn about later in this book), but also through the use of semantic elements.

Some of the semantic elements available in HTML5 follow:

> ▶ `<header></header>`—This might seem counterintuitive, but you can use multiple `<header>` tags within a single page. The `<header>` tag should be used as a container for introductory information, so it might be used only once in your page (likely at the top)—but you also might use it several times if your page

---

Don't forget that anything placed in the head of a web page is not intended to be viewed on the page, whereas everything in the body of the page *is* intended for viewing.

Peeking at Other Designers' Pages

Given the visual and sometimes audio pizzazz present in many popular web pages, you probably realize that the simple pages described in this lesson are only the tip of the HTML iceberg. Now that you know the basics, you might surprise yourself with how much of the rest you can pick up just by looking at other people's pages on the Internet. You can see the HTML for any page by right-clicking and selecting View Source in any web browser.

Don't worry if you aren't yet able to decipher what some HTML tags do or exactly how to use them yourself. You'll find out about all those things as the book moves forward. However, sneaking a preview now will show you the tags that you do know in action and give you a taste of what you'll soon be able to do with your web pages.

content is broken into sections. Any container element can have a `<header>` element; just make sure that you're using it to include introductory information about the element it is contained within.

▶ `<footer></footer>`—The `<footer>` tag is used to contain additional information about its containing element (page or section), such as copyright and author information or links to related resources.

▶ `<nav></nav>`—If your site has navigational elements, such as links to other sections within a site or even within the page itself, these links go in a `<nav>` tag. A `<nav>` tag typically is found in the first instance of a `<header>` tag, just because people tend to put navigation at the top and consider it introductory information, but that is not a requirement. You can put your `<nav>` element anywhere (as long as it includes navigation), and you can have as many on a page as you need (often no more than two, but you might feel otherwise).

▶ `<section></section>`—The `<section>` tag contains anything that relates thematically; it can also contain a `<header>` tag for introductory information and possibly a `<footer>` tag for other related information. You can think of a `<section>` as carrying more meaning than a standard `<p>` (paragraph) or `<div>` (division) tag, which typically conveys no meaning at all; the use of `<section>` conveys a relationship between the content elements it contains.

▶ `<article></article>`—An `<article>` tag is like a `<section>` tag, in that it can contain a `<header>`, a `<footer>`, and other container elements such as paragraphs and divisions. But the additional meaning carried with the `<article>` tag is that it is, well, like an article in a newspaper or some other publication. Use this tag around blog posts, news articles, reviews, and other items that fit this description. One key difference between an `<article>` and a `<section>` is that an `<article>` is a standalone body of work, whereas a `<section>` is a thematic grouping of information.

▶ `<aside></aside>`—Use the `<aside>` tag to indicate secondary information; if the `<aside>` tag is within a `<section>` or an `<article>`, the relationship will be to those containers; otherwise, the secondary relationship will be to the overall page or site itself. It might make sense to think of the `<aside>` as a sidebar—either for all the content on the page or for an article or other thematic container of information.

These semantic elements will become clearer as you practice using them. In general, using semantic elements is a good idea because they provide additional meaning not only for you and other designers and programmers reading and working with your markup, but also for machines. Web browsers and screen readers will respond to your semantic elements by using these elements to determine the structure of your document; screen readers will report a deeper meaning to users, thus increasing the accessibility of your material.

One of the best ways to understand the HTML5 semantic elements is to see them in action, but that can be a little difficult when the primary purpose of these elements is to provide *meaning* rather than design. That's not to say that you can't add design to these elements—you most certainly can, and you will in later lessons. But the "action" of the semantic elements is to hold content and provide meaning through doing so, as in Figure 2.4, which shows a common use of semantic elements for a basic web page.

FIGURE 2.4
Showing basic semantic elements in a web page.

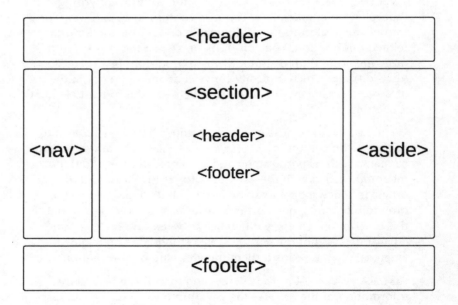

Initially, you might think, "Of *course*, that makes total sense, with the header at the top and the footer at the bottom," and feel quite good about yourself for understanding semantic elements at first glance—and you should! A second glance should then raise some questions:

What if you want your navigation to be horizontal under your header? Does an aside have to be (literally) on the side? What if you don't want any asides? What's with the use of `<header>` and `<footer>` again within the main body section? And that's just to name a few! Another question you might ask is where the `<article>` element fits in; it isn't shown in this example but is part of this chapter.

This is the time when conceptualizing the page—and specifically the page *you* want to create—comes into play. If you understand the content you want to mark up and you understand that you can use any, all, or none of the semantic elements and still create a valid HTML document, then you can begin to organize the content of your page in the way that makes the most sense for it and for you (and, hopefully, for your readers).

Let's take a look at the elements used in Figure 2.4 before moving on to a second example and then a deeper exploration of the individual elements themselves. In Figure 2.4, you see a `<header>` at the top of the page and a `<footer>` at the bottom—straightforward, as already mentioned. The use of a `<nav>` element on the left side of the page matches a common display area for navigation, and the `<aside>` element on the right side of the page matches a common display area for secondary notes, pull quotes, helper text, and "for more information" links about the content. In Figure 2.5, you'll see some of these elements shifted around, so don't worry—Figure 2.4 is not some immutable example of semantic markup.

Something you might be surprised to see in Figure 2.5 is the `<header>` and `<footer>` inside the `<section>` element. As you'll learn shortly, the role of the `<header>` element is to introduce a second example and then a deeper exploration of the individual elements themselves. In Figure 2.4, you see a `<header>` at the top of the page and a `<footer>` at the bottom—straightforward, as already mentioned. The use of a `<nav>` element on the left side of the page matches the content that comes after it, and the `<header>` element itself does not convey any level in a document outline. Therefore, you can use as many as you need to mark up your content appropriately; a `<header>` at the beginning of the page might contain introductory information about the page as a whole, and the `<header>` element within the `<section>` element might just as easily and appropriately contain introductory information about the content within it. The same is true for the multiple appearances of the `<footer>` element in this example.

> **NOTE**
>
> Although you do not need to use semantic elements to create a valid HTML document, even a minimal set is recommended so that web browsers and screen readers can determine the structure of your document. Screen readers are capable of reporting a deeper meaning to users, thus increasing the accessibility of your material.
>
> (If this note were marked up in an HTML document, it would use the `<aside>` element.)

FIGURE 2.5
Using nested semantic elements to add more meaning to the content.

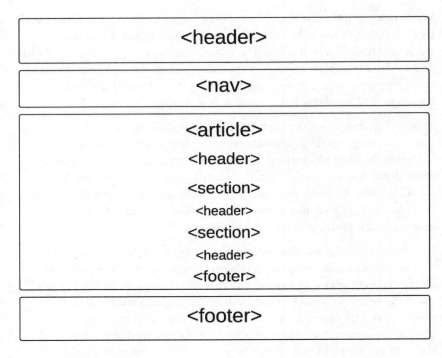

Let's move on to Figure 2.5, which shifts around the <nav> element and also introduces use of the <article> element.

In Figure 2.5, the <header> and <nav> elements at the beginning of the page, and the <footer> element at the bottom of the page, should make perfect sense to you. And, although we haven't talked about the <article> element yet, if you think about it as a container element that has sections (<section>s, even!), with each of those sections having its own heading, then the chunk of semantic elements in the middle of the figure should make sense, too. As you can see, there's no single way to conceptualize page content—there's the conceptualization that you should do of each individual page's content.

If you marked up some content in the structure shown in Figure 2.5, it might look like Listing 2.4.

LISTING 2.4   Semantic Markup of Basic Content

```html
<!DOCTYPE html>

<html lang="en">
  <head>
    <title>Semantic Example</title>
  </head>
  <body>
    <header>
        <h1>SITE OR PAGE LOGO GOES HERE</h1>
    </header>
    <nav>
        SITE OR PAGE NAV GOES HERE.
    </nav>
    <article>
        <header>
            <h2>Article Heading</h2>
        </header>
        <section>
            <header>
                <h3>Section 1 Heading</h3>
            </header>
            <p>Section 2 content here.</p>
        </section>
        <section>
            <header>
                <h3>Section 2 Heading</h3>
            </header>
            <p>Section 2 content here.</p>
        </section>
        <footer>
            <p>Article footer goes here.</p>
        </footer>
    </article>
    <footer>
        SITE OR PAGE FOOTER HERE
    </footer>
  </body>
</html>
```

If you opened this HTML document in your web browser, you would
see something like what's shown in Figure 2.6—a completely unstyled
document, but one that has semantic meaning (even if no one can
"see" it).

FIGURE 2.6
The output of Listing 2.4.

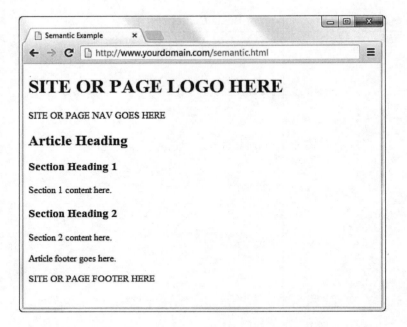

Just because there is no visible styling doesn't mean the meaning is lost; as noted earlier in this section, machines can interpret the structure of the document as provided for through the semantic elements. You can see the outline of this basic document in Figure 2.7, which shows the output of this file after examination by the HTML5 Outline tool at http://gsnedders.html5.org/outliner/.

FIGURE 2.7
The outline of this document follows the semantic markup.

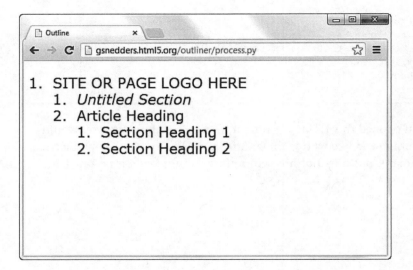

Now that you've seen some examples of conceptualizing the information represented in your documents, you're better prepared to start marking up those documents. The sections that follow take a look at the semantic elements individually.

Using `<header>` in Multiple Ways

At the most basic level, the `<header>` element contains introductory information. That information might take the form of an actual `<h1>` (or other level) element, or it might simply be a logo image or text contained within a `<p>` or `<div>` element. The *meaning* of the content should be introductory in nature, to warrant its inclusion within a `<header></header>` tag pair.

As you've seen in the examples so far in this lesson, a common placement of a `<header>` element is at the beginning of a page. When it's used in this way, containing a logo or an `<h1>`-level title makes sense, such as here:

```
<header>
    <img src="acmewidgets.jpg" alt="ACME Widgets LLC"/>
</header>
```

Or even this:

```
<header>
    <img src="acmewidgets.jpg" alt="ACME Widgets LLC"/>
    <h1>The finest widgets are made here!</h1>
</header>
```

Both snippets are valid uses of `<header>` because the information contained within them is introductory to the page overall.

As you've also seen in this chapter, you are not limited to only one `<header>`. You can go crazy with your `<header>` elements, as long as they are acting as containers for introductory information—Listing 2.4 showed the use of `<header>` elements for several `<section>` elements within an `<article>`, and this is a perfectly valid use of the element:

```
<section>
   <header>
     <h3>Section 1 Heading</h3>
   </header>
   <p>Section 2 content here.</p>
</section>
<section>
```

TIP

Using the HTML5 Outline tool is a good way to check that you've created your headers, footers, and sections; if you examine your document and see "untitled section" anywhere, and those untitled sections do not match up with a `<nav>` or `<aside>` element (which have more relaxed guidelines about containing headers), then you have some additional work to do.

NOTE

In general, *flow content* elements are elements that contain text, images, or other multimedia embedded content; HTML elements fall into multiple categories.

If you want to learn more about the categorization of elements into content models, see http://www.w3.org/TR/2011/WD-html5-20110525/content-models.html.

```
<header>
    <h3>Section 2 Heading</h3>
</header>
<p>Section 2 content here.</p>
</section>
```

The `<header>` element can contain any other element in the flow content category, of which it is also a member. This means that a `<header>` *could* contain a `<section>` element, if you wanted, and be perfectly valid markup. However, when you are conceptualizing your content, think about whether that sort of nesting makes sense before you go off and do it.

The only exceptions to the permitted content within `<header>` are that the `<header>` element cannot contain *other* `<header>` elements and it cannot contain a `<footer>` element. Similarly, the `<header>` element cannot be contained within an `<address>` or `<footer>` element.

Understanding the `<section>` Element

The `<section>` element has a simple definition: It is "a generic section of a document" that is also "a thematic grouping of content, typically with a heading." That sounds pretty simple to me, and probably does to you as well. So you might be surprised to find that if you type "difference between section and article in HTML5" in your search engine of choice, you'll find tens of thousands of entries talking about the differences because the definitions trip people up all the time. We first discuss the `<section>` element and then cover the `<article>` element—and hopefully avoid any of the misunderstandings that seem to plague new web developers.

In Listing 2.4, you saw a straightforward example of using `<section>` within an `<article>` (repeated here); in this example, you can easily imagine that the `<section>`s contain a "thematic grouping of content," which is supported by the fact that they each have a heading.

```
<article>
    <header>
        <h2>Article Heading</h2>
    </header>
    <section>
        <header>
            <h3>Section 1 Heading</h3>
```

```
      </header>
      <p>Section 2 content here.</p>
   </section>
   <section>
      <header>
         <h3>Section 2 Heading</h3>
      </header>
      <p>Section 2 content here.</p>
   </section>
   <footer>
      <p>Article footer goes here.</p>
   </footer>
</article>
```

But here's an example of a perfectly valid use of `<section>` with no `<article>` element in sight:

```
<section>
   <header>
      <h1>Super Heading</h1>
   </header>
   <p>Super content!</p>
</section>
```

So what's a developer to do? Let's say you have some generic content that you know you want to divide into sections with their own headings. In that case, use `<section>`. If you need to only *visually* delineate chunks of content (such as with paragraph breaks) that do not require additional headings, then `<section>` isn't for you—use `<p>` or `<div>` instead.

Because the `<section>` element can contain any other flow content element, and can be contained within any other flow content element (except the `<address>` element), it's easy to see why, without other limitations and with generic guidelines for use, the `<section>` element is sometimes misunderstood.

Using `<article>`

Personally, I believe that a lot of the misunderstanding regarding the use of `<section>` versus `<article>` has to do with the name of the `<article>` element. When I think of an article, I think specifically about an article in a newspaper or a magazine. I don't naturally think "any standalone body of work," which is how the `<article>` element is commonly defined. The HTML5 recommended specification defines it as "a complete, or self-contained, composition in a document, page, application, or site and that is, in principle, independently distributable or reusable," such as "a forum post, a magazine or newspaper article, a blog entry, a user-submitted comment, an interactive widget or gadget, or any other independent item of content."

In other words, an `<article>` element could be used to contain the entire page of a website (whether or not it is an article in a publication), an actual article in a publication, a blog post anywhere and everywhere, part of a threaded discussion in a forum, a comment on a blog post, and as a container that displays the current weather in your city. It's no wonder there are tens of thousands of results for a search on "difference between section and article in HTML5."

A good rule of thumb when you're trying to figure out when to use `<article>` and when to use `<section>` is simply to answer the following question: Does this content make sense on its own? If so, then no matter what the content seems to be to you (for example, a static web page, not an article in *The New York Times*), start by using the `<article>` element. If you find yourself breaking it up, do so in `<section>`s. And if you find yourself thinking that your "article" is, in fact, part of a greater whole, then change the `<article>` tags to `<section>` tags, find the beginning of the document, and surround it from there with the more appropriately placed `<article>` tag at a higher level.

Implementing the `<nav>` Element

The `<nav>` element seems so simple (`<nav>` implies *navigation*), and it ultimately is—but it can also be used incorrectly. In this section, you'll learn some basic uses and also some incorrect uses to avoid. If your site has any navigational elements at all, either sitewide or within a long page of content, you have a valid use for the `<nav>` element.

For that sitewide navigation, you typically find a `<nav>` element within the primary `<header>` element; you are not required to do so, but if you want your navigational content to be introductory (and omnipresent in your template), you can easily make a case for your primary `<nav>` element to appear within the primary `<header>`. More important, that is valid HTML (as is `<nav>` outside a `<header>`)—a `<nav>` element can appear within any flow content, as well as contain any flow content.

The following code snippet shows the main navigational links of a website, placed within a <header> element:

```
<header>
    <img src="acmewidgets.jpg" alt="ACME Widgets LLC"/>
    <h1>The finest widgets are made here!</h1>
    <nav>
      <ul>
          <li><a href="#">About Us</a></li>
          <li><a href="#">Products</a></li>
          <li><a href="#">Support</a></li>
          <li><a href="#">Press</a></li>
      </ul>
    </nav>
</header>
```

You are not limited to a single <nav> element in your documents, which is good for site developers who create templates that include both primary *and* secondary navigation. For example, you might see horizontal primary navigation at the top of a page (often contained within a <header> element), and then vertical navigation in the left column of a page, representing the secondary pages within the main section. In that case, you simply use a second <nav> element, not contained within the <header>, placed and styled differently to delineate the two types visually in addition to semantically.

Remember, the <nav> element is used for *major* navigational content—primary and secondary navigation both count, as does the inclusion of tables of content within a page. For good and useful semantic use of the <nav> element, do not simply apply it to every link that allows a user to navigate anywhere. Note that I said "good and useful" semantic use, not necessarily "valid" use—it's true that you could apply <nav> to any list of links, and it would be valid according to the HTML specification because links are flow content. But it wouldn't be particularly *useful*—it wouldn't add meaning—to surround a list of links to social media sharing tools with the <nav> element.

When to Use <aside>

As you'll see by the number of tips and notes from me throughout this book, I'm a big fan of the type of content that is most appropriately marked up within the <aside> element. The <aside> element is meant to contain any content that is tangentially related to the content around it—additional explanation, links to related resources, pull quotes, helper text, and so on. You might think of the `<aside>` element as a sidebar, but be careful not to think of it only as a *visual* sidebar, or a column on the side of a page where you can stick anything and everything you want, whether or not it's related to the content or site at hand.

In Figure 2.8, you can see how content in an `<aside>` is used to create a *pull quote*, or a content excerpt that is specifically set aside to call attention to it. The `<aside>`, in this case, is used to highlight an important section of the text, but it could also have been used to define a term or link to related documents.

FIGURE 2.8
Using *<aside>* to create meaningful pull quotes.

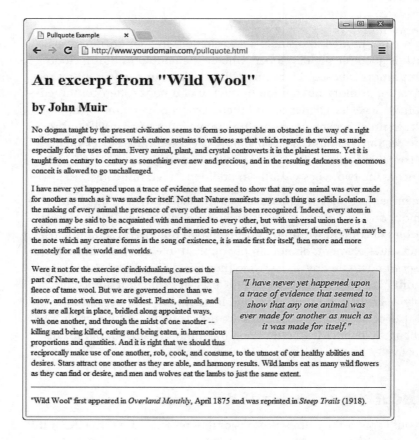

When determining whether to use the `<aside>` element, think about the content you want to add. Is it related directly to the content in which the `<aside>` would be contained, such as a definition of terms used in an article or a list of related links for the article? If your answer is an easy yes, that's great! Use `<aside>` to your heart's content. If you're thinking of including an `<aside>` outside a containing element that is itself full of content, just make sure that the content of the `<aside>` is reasonably related to your site overall and that you're not just using the `<aside>` element for visual effect.

Using `<footer>` Effectively

The counterpart to the `<header>` element, the `<footer>` element, contains additional information about its containing element. The most common use of the `<footer>` element is to contain copyright information at the bottom of a page, such as here:

```
<footer>
    <p>&copy; 2014 Acme Widgets, LLC. All Rights Reserved.</p>
</footer>
```

Similar to the `<header>` element, the `<footer>` element can contain any other element in the flow content category, of which it is also a member, with the exception of *other* `<footer>` or `<header>` elements. Additionally, a `<footer>` element cannot be contained within an `<address>` element, but a `<footer>` element can contain an `<address>` element—in fact, a `<footer>` element is a common location for an `<address>` element to reside in.

Placing useful `<address>` content within a `<footer>` element is one of the most effective uses of the `<footer>` element (not to mention the `<address>` element) because it provides specific contextual information about the page or section of the page to which it refers. The following snippet shows a use of `<address>` within `<footer>`:

```
<footer>
    <p>&copy; 2014 Acme Widgets, LLC. All Rights Reserved.</p>
    <p>Copyright Issues? Contact:</p>
        <address>
        Our Lawyer<br/>
        123 Main Street<br/>
        Somewhere, CA 95128<br/>
        <a href="mailto:lawyer@richperson.com">lawyer@richperson.
        com</a>
        </address>
</footer>
```

As with the `<header>` element, you are not limited to only one `<footer>`. You can use as many `<footer>` elements as you need, as long as they are containers for additional information about the containing element—Listing 2.4 showed the use of `<footer>` elements for both the page and an `<article>`, both of which are valid.

Summary

This chapter introduced the basics of what web pages are and how they work. You learned that coded HTML commands are included in a text file, and you saw that typing HTML text yourself is better than using a graphical editor to create HTML commands for you—especially when you're learning HTML.

You were introduced to the most basic and important HTML tags. By adding these coded commands to any plain-text document, you can quickly transform it into a bona fide web page. You learned that the first step in creating a web page is to put a few obligatory HTML tags at the beginning and end, including adding a title for the page. You can then mark where paragraphs and lines end and add horizontal rules and headings, if you want them. You also got a taste of some of the semantic tags in HTML5, which are used to provide additional meaning by delineating the types of content your pages contain (not just the content itself). Table 2.1 summarizes all the tags introduced in this chapter.

TABLE 2.1   HTML Tags Covered in Chapter 2

Tag	Function
`<html>...</html>`	Encloses the entire HTML document.
`<head>...</head>`	Encloses the head of the HTML document. Used within the `<html>` tag pair.
`<title>...</title>`	Indicates the title of the document. Used within the `<head>` tag pair.
`<body>...</body>`	Encloses the body of the HTML document. Used within the `<html>` tag pair.
`<p>...</p>`	Encloses a paragraph; skips a line between paragraphs.
` `	Indicates a line break.

`<hr />`	Displays a horizontal rule line.
`<h1>...</h1>`	Encloses a first-level heading.
`<h2>...</h2>`	Encloses a second-level heading.
`<h3>...</h3>`	Encloses a third-level heading.
`<h4>...</h4>`	Encloses a fourth-level heading (seldom used).
`<h5>...</h5>`	Encloses a fifth-level heading (seldom used).
`<h6>...</h6>`	Encloses a sixth-level heading (seldom used).
`<header>...</header>`	Contains introductory information.
`<footer>...</footer>`	Contains supplementary material for its containing element (commonly a copyright notice or author information).
`<nav>...</nav>`	Contains navigational elements.
`<section>...</section>`	Contains thematically similar content, such as a chapter of a book or a section of a page.
`<article>...</article>`	Contains content that is a standalone body of work, such as a news article.
`<aside>...</aside>`	Contains secondary information for its containing element.
`<address>...</address>`	Contains address information related to its nearest `<article>` or `<body>` element, often contained within a `<footer>` element.

Q&A

Q. I've created a web page, but when I open the file in my web browser, I see all the text, including the HTML tags. Sometimes I even see weird gobbledygook characters at the top of the page. What did I do wrong?

A. You didn't save the file as plain text. Try saving the file again, being careful to save it as Text Only or ASCII Text. If you can't quite figure out how to get your word processor to do that, don't stress. Just type your HTML files in Notepad or TextEdit instead, and everything should work just fine. (Also, always make sure that the filename of your web page ends in `.html` or `.htm`.)

Q. I've seen web pages on the Internet that don't have `<!DOCTYPE>` or `<html>` tags at the beginning. You said pages always have to start with these tags. What's the deal?

A. Many web browsers will forgive you if you forget to include the `<!DOCTYPE>` or `<html>` tag and will display the page correctly anyway. However, it's a very good idea to include it because some software does need it to identify the page as valid HTML. Besides, you want your pages to be bona fide HTML pages so that they conform to the latest web standards.

Q. Do I have to use semantic markup at all? Didn't you say throughout this lesson that pages are valid with or without it?

A. True, none of these elements is required for a valid HTML document. You don't have to use any of them, but I urge you to think beyond the use of markup for visual display only and think about it for semantic meaning as well. Visual display is meaningless to screen readers, but semantic elements convey a ton of information through these machines.

Q. I'm still completely befuddled about when to use `<section>` and when to use `<aside>`. Can you make it more clear?

A. I don't blame you. There's a resource available at the HTML5 Doctor website that is one of the best I've seen to help eliminate the confusion. It's a flowchart for HTML5 sectioning, found at http://html5doctor.com/downloads/h5d-sectioning-flowchart.png. This flowchart asks the right questions about your content and helps you determine the correct container element to use.

Workshop

The Workshop contains quiz questions and exercises to help you solidify your understanding of the material covered. Try to answer all questions before looking at the "Answers" section that follows.

Quiz

1. What five tags does every HTML page require?

2. What HTML tags and text do you use to produce the following body content:

▶ A heading with the words `We are Proud to Present...`

▶ A secondary heading with the one word `Orbit`

▶ A heading of lesser importance with the words `The Geometric Juggler`

3. What code would you use to create a complete HTML web page with the title Foo Bar, a heading at the top that reads Happy Hour at the Foo Bar, and then the words Come on down! in regular type? Try to use some of the semantic elements you just learned.

4. Which of the semantic elements discussed in this chapter is appropriate for containing the definition of a word used in an article?

5. Do you have to use an `<h1>`, `<h2>`, `<h3>`, `<h4>`, `<h5>`, or `<h6>` element within a `<header>` element?

6. How many different `<nav>` elements can you have in a single page?

Answers

1. Every HTML page requires `<html>`, `<head>`, `<title>`, and `<body>` (along with their closing tags, `</html>`, `</head>`, `</title>`, and `</body>`), plus `<!DOCTYPE html>` on the very first line.

2. The code within the body would look like this:

```
<h1>We are Proud to Present...</h1>
<h2>Orbit</h2>
<h3>The Geometric Juggler</h3>
```

3. Your code could look like this:

```
<!DOCTYPE html>

<html lang="en">
  <head>
    <title>Foo Bar</title>
  </head>

  <body>
    <header>
        <h1>Happy Hour at the Foo Bar</h1>
    </header>
    <section>
        <p>Come on Down!</p>
    </section>
  </body>
</html>
```

4. The `<aside>` element is appropriate for this.

5. No. The `<header>` element can contain any other flow content besides another `<header>` element or a `<footer>` element. However, a heading element (`<h1>` through `<h6>`) is not required in a `<header>` element.

6. You can have as many `<nav>` elements as you need. The trick is to "need" only a few (perhaps for primary and secondary navigation only); otherwise, the meaning is lost.

Exercises

▶ Even if your main goal in reading this book is to create web content for your business, you might want to make a personal web page just for practice. Type a few paragraphs to introduce yourself to the world, and use the HTML tags you learned in this chapter to make them into a web page.

▶ Throughout the book, you'll be following along with the code examples and making pages of your own. Take a moment now to set up a basic document template containing the document type declaration and tags for the core HTML document structure. That way, you can be ready to copy and paste that information whenever you need it.

▶ Building off a single page template, create a few more related pieces of content. Remember that some of your pages might contain `<article>` elements with no sections, but others might contain `<section>` elements with `<header>` and `<footer>` elements as well.

CHAPTER 3
Understanding Cascading Style Sheets

In the preceding chapter, you learned the basics of HTML, including how to set up a skeletal HTML template for all your web content. In this chapter, you'll learn how to fine-tune the display of your web content using *Cascading Style Sheets (CSS)*.

The concept behind style sheets is simple: You create a style sheet document that specifies the fonts, colors, spacing, and other characteristics that establish a unique look for a website. You then link every page that should have that look to the style sheet instead of specifying all those styles repeatedly in each separate document. Therefore, when you decide to change your official corporate typeface or color scheme, you can modify all your web pages at once just by changing one or two entries in your style sheet—you don't have to change them in all your static web files. So a *style sheet* is a grouping of formatting instructions that control the appearance of several HTML pages at once.

Style sheets enable you to set a great number of formatting characteristics, including exact typeface controls, letter and line spacing, and margins and page borders, just to name a few. Style sheets also enable you to specify sizes and other measurements in familiar units, such as inches, millimeters, points, and picas. In addition, you can use style sheets to precisely position graphics and text anywhere on a web page, either at specific coordinates or relative to other items on the page.

In short, style sheets bring a sophisticated level of display to the Web. And they do so, if you'll pardon the expression, with style.

WHAT YOU'LL LEARN IN THIS CHAPTER:

▶ How to create a basic style sheet
▶ How to use style classes
▶ How to use style IDs
▶ How to construct internal style sheets and inline styles

⇒ How Inlay for Connect CSS.

⇒ How many kind Selectors

NOTE

If you have three or more web pages that share (or should share) similar formatting and fonts, you might want to create a style sheet for them as you read this chapter. Even if you choose not to create a complete style sheet, you'll find it helpful to apply styles to individual HTML elements directly within a web page.

NOTE

You might notice that I use the term *element* a fair amount in this chapter (and I do in the rest of the book, for that matter). An *element* is simply a piece of information (content) in a web page, such as an image, a paragraph, or a link. Tags are used to mark up elements, and you can think of an element as a tag, complete with descriptive information (attributes, text, images, and so on) within the tag.

How CSS Works

The technology behind style sheets is called CSS, or Cascading Style Sheets. CSS is a language that defines style constructs such as fonts, colors, and positioning, which describe how information on a web page is formatted and displayed. CSS styles can be stored directly in an HTML web page or in a separate style sheet file. Either way, style sheets contain style rules that apply styles to elements of a given type. When used externally, style sheet rules are placed in an external style sheet document with the file extension .css.

A *style rule* is a formatting instruction that can be applied to an element on a web page, such as a paragraph of text or a link. Style rules consist of one or more style properties and their associated values. An *internal style sheet* is placed directly within a web page, whereas an *external style sheet* exists in a separate document and is simply linked to a web page via a special tag—more on this tag in a moment.

The *cascading* part of the name CSS refers to the manner in which style sheet rules are applied to elements in an HTML document. More specifically, styles in a CSS style sheet form a hierarchy in which more specific styles override more general styles. It is the responsibility of CSS to determine the precedence of style rules according to this hierarchy, which establishes a cascading effect. If that sounds a bit confusing, just think of the cascading mechanism in CSS as being similar to genetic inheritance, in which general traits are passed from parents to a child, but more specific traits are entirely unique to the child. Base-style rules are applied throughout a style sheet but can be overridden by more specific style rules.

A quick example should clear things up. Take a look at the following code to see whether you can tell what's going on with the color of the text:

```
<div style="color:green">
  This text is green.
  <p style="color:blue">This text is blue.</p>
  <p>This text is still green.</p>
</div>
```

In the preceding example, the color green is applied to the `<div>` tag via the `color` style property. Therefore, the text in the `<div>` tag is colored green. Because both `<p>` tags are children of the `<div>` tag, the green text style cascades down to them. However, the first `<p>` tag overrides the color style and changes it to blue. The end result is that the first line (not surrounded by a paragraph tag) is green, the first official paragraph is blue, and the second official paragraph retains the cascaded green color.

If you made it through that description on your own and came out on the other end unscathed, congratulations—that's half the battle. Understanding CSS isn't like understanding rocket science, and the more you practice, the more it will become clear. The real trick is developing the aesthetic design sense that you can then apply to your online presence through CSS.

Like many web technologies, CSS has evolved over the years. The original version of CSS, known as *Cascading Style Sheets Level 1* (*CSS1*), was created in 1996. The later CSS2 standard was created in 1998, and CSS2 is still in use today; all modern web browsers support CSS2. The latest version of CSS is CSS3, which builds on the strong foundation laid by its predecessors but adds advanced functionality to enhance the online experience. Throughout this book, you'll learn core CSS, including new elements of CSS3 that are applicable to the basic design and functionality that this text covers. So when I talk about CSS throughout the book, I'm referring to CSS3.

You'll find a complete reference guide to CSS at http://www.w3.org/Style/CSS/. The rest of this chapter explains the basics of putting CSS to good use.

A Basic Style Sheet

Despite their intimidating power, style sheets can be simple to create. Consider the web pages shown in Figures 3.1 and 3.2. These pages share several visual properties that can be put into a common style sheet:

- ▶ They use a large, bold Verdana font for the headings and a normal-size and -weight Verdana font for the body text.
- ▶ They use an image named `logo.gif` floating within the content and on the right side of the page.
- ▶ All text is black except for subheadings, which are purple.
- ▶ They have margins on the left side and at the top.
- ▶ They include vertical space between lines of text.
- ▶ They include a footer that is centered and in small print.

FIGURE 3.1
This page uses a style sheet to fine-tune the appearance and spacing of the text and images.

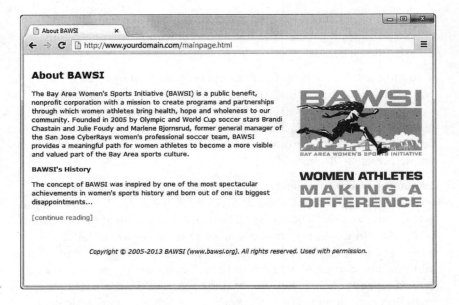

FIGURE 3.2
This page uses the same style sheet as the one in Figure 3.1, thus maintaining a consistent look and feel.

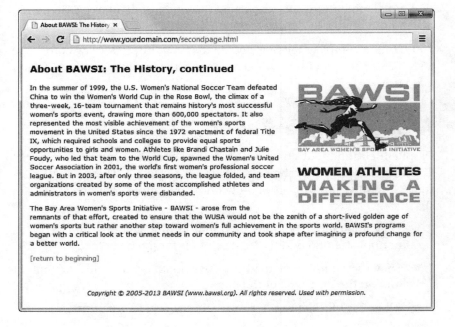

Listing 3.1 shows the CSS used in a style sheet to specify these properties.

LISTING 3.1   A Single External Style Sheet

```
body {
  font-size: 10pt;
  font-family: Verdana, Geneva, Arial, Helvetica, sans-serif;
  color: black;
  line-height: 14pt;
  padding-left: 5pt;
  padding-right: 5pt;
  padding-top: 5pt;
}

h1 {
  font: 14pt Verdana, Geneva, Arial, Helvetica, sans-serif;
  font-weight: bold;
  line-height: 20pt;
}

p.subheader {
  font-weight: bold;
  color: #593d87;
}

img {
  padding: 3pt;
  float: right;
}

a {
  text-decoration: none;
}

a:link, a:visited {
  color: #8094d6;
}

a:hover, a:active {
  color: #FF9933;
}

footer {
  font-size: 9pt;
  font-style: italic;
  line-height: 12pt;
  text-align: center;
  padding-top: 30pt;
}
```

This might initially appear to be a lot of code, but if you look closely, you'll see that there isn't a lot of information on each line of code. It's fairly standard to place individual style rules on their own line, to help make style sheets more readable, but that is a personal preference; you could put all the rules on one line as long as you kept using the semicolon to separate each rule (more on that in a bit). Speaking of code readability, perhaps the first thing you noticed about this style sheet code is that it doesn't look anything like normal HTML code. CSS uses a syntax all its own to specify style sheets.

Of course, the listing includes some familiar HTML tags (although not all tags require an entry in the style sheet). As you might guess, `body`, `h1`, `p`, `img`, `a`, and `footer` in the style sheet refer to the corresponding tags in the HTML documents to which the style sheet will be applied. The curly braces after each tag name describe how all content within that tag should appear.

In this case, the style sheet says that all `body` text should be rendered at a size of 10 points, in the Verdana font (if possible), and with the color black, with 14 points between lines. If the user does not have the Verdana font installed, the list of fonts in the style sheet represents the order in which the browser should search for fonts to use: Geneva, then Arial, and then Helvetica. If the user has none of those fonts, the browser uses whatever default sans-serif font is available. Additionally, the page should have left, right, and top padding of 5 points each.

Any text within an `<h1>` tag should be rendered in boldface Verdana at a size of 14 points. Moving on, any paragraph that uses only the `<p>` tag inherits all the styles indicated by the body element. However, if the `<p>` tag uses a special class named `subheader`, the text appears bold and in the color `#593d87` (a purple color).

The `pt` after each measurement in Listing 3.1 means *points* (there are 72 points in an inch). If you prefer, you can specify any style sheet measurement in inches (`in`), centimeters (`cm`), pixels (`px`), or "widths of a letter *m*," which are called ems (`em`).

NOTE

You can specify font sizes as large as you like with style sheets, although some display devices and printers do not correctly handle fonts larger than 200 points.

You might have noticed that each style rule in the listing ends with a semicolon (`;`). Semicolons are used to separate style rules from each other. It is therefore customary to end each style rule with a semicolon so that you can easily add another style rule after it. Review the remainder of the style sheet in Listing 3.1 to see the presentation formatting applied to additional tags. Don't worry—you'll learn more about each of these types of entries throughout the lessons in this book.

To link this style sheet to HTML documents, include a `<link />` tag in the `<head>` section of each document. Listing 3.2 shows the HTML code for the page shown in Figure 3.1. It contains the following `<link />` tag:

```
<link rel="stylesheet" type="text/css" href="styles.css" />
```

This assumes that the style sheet is stored under the name `styles.css` in the same folder as the HTML document. As long as the web browser supports style sheets—and all modern browsers do—the properties specified in the style sheet will apply to the content in the page without the need for any special HTML formatting code. This meets one of the goals of HTML, which is to provide a separation between the content in a web page and the specific formatting required to display that content.

LISTING 3.2   HTML Code for the Page Shown in Figure 3.1

```
<!DOCTYPE html>

<html lang="en">
  <head>
    <title>About BAWSI</title>
    <link rel="stylesheet" type="text/css" href="styles.css" />
  </head>
  <body>
    <section>

    <header>
    <h1>About BAWSI</h1>
    </header>

    <p><img src="logo.gif" alt="BAWSI logo"/>The Bay Area Women's
    Sports Initiative (BAWSI) is a public benefit, nonprofit
    corporation with a mission to create programs and partnerships
    through which women athletes bring health, hope and wholeness to
    our community. Founded in 2005 by Olympic and World Cup soccer
    stars Brandi Chastain and Julie Foudy and Marlene Bjornsrud,
    former general manager of the San Jose CyberRays women's
    professional soccer team, BAWSI provides a meaningful path for
    women athletes to become a more visible and valued part of the
    Bay Area sports culture.</p>

    <p class="subheader">BAWSI's History</p>

    <p>The concept of BAWSI was inspired by one of the most
    spectacular achievements in women's sports history and born out
    of one its biggest disappointments... </p>
```

TIP

In most web browsers, you can view the style rules in a style sheet by opening the `.css` file and choosing Notepad or another text editor as the helper application to view the file. (To determine the name of the `.css` file, look at the HTML source of any web page that links to it.) To edit your own style sheets, just use a text editor.

NOTE

Not every browser's support of CSS is flawless. To find out how major browsers compare to each other in terms of CSS support, take a look at this website: http://www. quirksmode.org/css/contents. html.

```
<p><a href="secondpage.html">[continue reading]</a></p>
  </section>


  <footer>
  Copyright &copy; 2005-2013 BAWSI (www.bawsi.org).
  All rights reserved.  Used with permission.
  </footer>
  </body>
</html>
```

The code in Listing 3.2 is interesting because it contains no formatting of any kind. In other words, nothing in the HTML code dictates how the text and images are to be displayed—no colors, no fonts, nothing. Yet the page is carefully formatted and rendered to the screen, thanks to the link to the external style sheet, `styles.css`. The real benefit to this approach is that you can easily create a site with multiple pages that maintains a consistent look and feel. And you have the benefit of isolating the visual style of the page to a single document (the style sheet) so that one change impacts all pages.

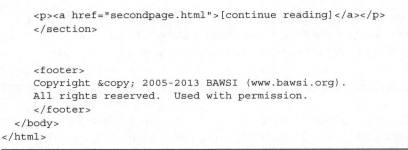

▼ TRY IT YOURSELF

Create a Style Sheet of Your Own

Starting from scratch, create a new text document called `mystyles.css` and add some style rules for the following basic HTML tags: `<body>`, `<p>`, `<h1>`, and `<h2>`. After creating your style sheet, make a new HTML file that contains these basic tags. Play around with different style rules, and see for yourself how simple it is to change entire blocks of text in paragraphs with one simple change in a style sheet file.

A CSS Style Primer

You now have a basic knowledge of CSS style sheets and how they are based on style rules that describe the appearance of information in web pages. The next few sections of this chapter provide a quick overview of some of the most important style properties and enable you to get started using CSS in your own style sheets.

CSS includes various style properties that are used to control fonts, colors, alignment, and margins, to name just a few. The style properties in CSS can be generally grouped into two major categories:

▶ Layout properties, which consist of properties that affect the positioning of elements on a web page, such as margins, padding, and alignment

▶ Formatting properties, which consist of properties that affect the visual display of elements within a website, such as the font type, size, and color

Basic Layout Properties

CSS layout properties determine how content is placed on a web page. One of the most important layout properties is the `display` property, which describes how an element is displayed with respect to other elements. The `display` property has four basic values:

▶ `block`—The element is displayed on a new line, as in a new paragraph.

▶ `list-item`—The element is displayed on a new line with a list-item mark (bullet) next to it.

▶ `inline`—The element is displayed inline with the current paragraph.

▶ `none`—The element is not displayed; it is hidden.

Understanding the `display` property is easier if you visualize each element on a web page occupying a rectangular area when displayed—the `display` property controls the manner in which this rectangular area is displayed. For example, the `block` value results in the element being placed on a new line by itself, whereas the `inline` value places the element next to the content just before it. The `display` property is one of the few style properties that can be applied in most style rules. Following is an example of how to set the `display` property:

```
display: block;
```

You control the size of the rectangular area for an element with the `width` and `height` properties. As with many size-related CSS properties, `width` and `height` property values can be specified in several different units of measurement:

▶ `in`—Inches

▶ `cm`—Centimeters

▶ `mm`—Millimeters

NOTE

The `display` property relies on a concept known as *relative positioning*, which means that elements are positioned relative to the location of other elements on a page. CSS also supports *absolute positioning*, which enables you to place an element at an exact location on a page, independent of other elements. You'll learn more about both of these types of positioning in Chapter 10, "Understanding the CSS Box Model and Positioning."

▶ %—Percentage

▶ px—Pixels

▶ pt—Points

You can mix and match units however you choose within a style sheet, but it's generally a good idea to be consistent across a set of similar style properties. For example, you might want to stick with points for font properties and pixels for dimensions. Following is an example of setting the width of an element using pixel units:

```
width: 200px;
```

Basic Formatting Properties

CSS formatting properties are used to control the appearance of content on a web page, as opposed to controlling the physical positioning of the content. One of the most popular formatting properties is the border property, which establishes a visible boundary around an element with a box or partial box. Note that a border is always present in that space is always left for it, but the border does not appear in a way that you can see unless you give it properties that make it visible (like a color). The following border properties provide a means of describing the borders of an element:

▶ border-width—The width of the border edge

▶ border-color—The color of the border edge

▶ border-style—The style of the border edge

▶ border-left—The left side of the border

▶ border-right—The right side of the border

▶ border-top—The top of the border

▶ border-bottom—The bottom of the border

▶ border—All the border sides

The border-width property establishes the width of the border edge. It is often expressed in pixels, as the following code demonstrates:

```
border-width: 5px;
```

Not surprisingly, the `border-color` and `border-style` properties set the border color and style. Following is an example of how these two properties are set:

```
border-color: blue;
border-style: dotted;
```

The `border-style` property can be set to any of the following basic values (you'll learn about some more advanced border tricks later in this book):

- ▶ `solid`—A single-line border
- ▶ `double`—A double-line border
- ▶ `dashed`—A dashed border
- ▶ `dotted`—A dotted border
- ▶ `groove`—A border with a groove appearance
- ▶ `ridge`—A border with a ridge appearance
- ▶ `inset`—A border with an inset appearance
- ▶ `outset`—A border with an outset appearance
- ▶ `none`—No border
- ▶ `hidden`—Effectively the same as `none`

The default value of the `border-style` property is `none`, which is why elements don't have a border *unless* you set the border property to a different style. Although `solid` is the most common border style, you will also see the other styles in use.

The `border-left`, `border-right`, `border-top`, and `border-bottom` properties enable you to set the border for each side of an element individually. If you want a border to appear the same on all four sides, you can use the single `border` property by itself, which expects the following styles separated by a space: `border-width`, `border-style`, and `border-color`. Following is an example of using the `border` property to set a border that consists of two (double) red lines that are a total of 10 pixels in width:

```
border: 10px double red;
```

Whereas the color of an element's border is set with the `border-color` property, the color of the inner region of an element is set using the `color` and `background-color` properties. The `color` property sets the color of text in an element (foreground), and the `background-color` property sets the color of the background behind the text. Following is an example of setting both color properties to predefined colors:

```
color: black;
background-color: orange;
```

You can also assign custom colors to these properties by specifying the colors in hexadecimal (covered in more detail in Chapter 8, "Working with Colors, Images, and Multimedia") or as RGB (Red, Green, Blue) decimal values:

```
background-color: #999999;
color: rgb(0,0,255);
```

You can also control the alignment and indentation of web page content without too much trouble. This is accomplished with the `text-align` and `text-indent` properties, as the following code demonstrates:

```
text-align: center;
text-indent: 12px;
```

When you have an element properly aligned and indented, you might be interested in setting its font. The following basic font properties set the various parameters associated with fonts (you'll learn about some more advanced font usage in Chapter 6, "Working with Fonts, Text Blocks, Lists, and Tables"):

- ▶ `font-family`—The family of the font
- ▶ `font-size`—The size of the font
- ▶ `font-style`—The style of the font (`normal` or `italic`)
- ▶ `font-weight`—The weight of the font (`normal`, `lighter`, `bold`, `bolder`, and so on)

The `font-family` property specifies a prioritized list of font family names. A prioritized list is used instead of a single value to provide alternatives in case a font isn't available on a given system. The `font-size` property specifies the size of the font using a unit of measurement, usually points. Finally, the `font-style` property sets the style of the font, and the `font-weight` property sets the weight of the font. Following is an example of setting these font properties:

```
font-family: Arial, sans-serif;
font-size: 36pt;
font-style: italic;
font-weight: normal;
```

Now that you know a whole lot more about style properties and how they work, refer to Listing 3.1 and see whether it makes a bit more sense. Here's a recap of the style properties used in that style sheet, which you can use as a guide for understanding how it works:

▶ font—Lets you set many font properties at once. You can specify a list of font names separated by commas; if the first is not available, the next is tried, and so on. You can also include the words bold and/or italic and a font size. Alternatively, you can set each of these font properties separately with font-family, font-size, font-weight, and font-style.

▶ line-height—Is also known in the publishing world as *leading*. This sets the height of each line of text, usually in points.

▶ color—Sets the text color using the standard color names or hexadecimal color codes (see Chapter 8 for more details).

▶ text-decoration—Is useful for turning off link underlining; simply set it to none. The values of underline, italic, and line-through are also supported. Chapter 7, "Using External and Internal Links," covers applying styles to links in more detail.

▶ text-align—Aligns text to the left, right, or center, along with justifying the text with a value of justify.

▶ padding—Adds padding to the left, right, top, and bottom of an element; this padding can be in measurement units or a percentage of the page width. Use padding-left and padding-right if you want to add padding to the left and right of the element independently. Use padding-top or padding-bottom to add padding to the top or bottom of the element, as appropriate. You'll learn more about these style properties in Chapter 9, "Working with Margins, Padding, Alignment, and Floating," and Chapter 10, "Understanding the CSS Box Model and Positioning."

Using Style Classes

This is a "teach yourself" book, so you don't have to go to a single class to learn how to give your pages great style—although you *do* need to learn what a style class is. Whenever you want some of the text on your pages to look different from the other text, you can create what amounts to a custom-built HTML tag. Each type of specially formatted text you define is called a *style class*. A *style class* is a custom set of formatting specifications that can be applied to any element in a web page.

Before showing you a style class, I need to take a quick step back and clarify some CSS terminology. First off, a CSS *style property* is a specific style that you can assign a value, such as `color` or `font-size`. You associate a style property and its respective value with elements on a web page by using a selector. A *selector* is used to identify tags on a page to which you apply styles. Following is an example of a selector, a property, and a value all included in a basic style rule:

```
h1 { font: 36pt Courier; }
```

In this code, `h1` is the selector, `font` is the style property, and `36pt Courier` is the value. The selector is important because it means that the font setting will be applied to all `h1` elements in the web page. But maybe you want to differentiate between some of the `h1` elements— what then? The answer lies in style classes.

Suppose you want two different kinds of `<h1>` headings for use in your documents. You create a style class for each one by putting the following CSS code in a style sheet:

```
h1.silly { font: 36pt Comic Sans; }
h1.serious { font: 36pt Arial; }
```

Notice that these selectors include a period (.) after `h1`, followed by a descriptive class name. To choose between the two style classes, use the `class` attribute, like this:

```
<h1 class="silly">Marvin's Munchies Inc. </h1>
<p>Text about Marvin's Munchies goes here. </p>
```

Or you could use this:

```
<h1 class="serious">MMI Investor Information</h1>
<p>Text for business investors goes here.</p>
```

When referencing a style class in HTML code, simply specify the class name in the `class` attribute of an element. In the preceding example, the words `Marvin's Munchies Inc.` would appear in a 36-point Comic Sans font, assuming that you included a `<link />` to the style sheet at the top of the web page and that the user has the Comic Sans font installed. The words MMI Investor Information would appear in the 36-point Arial font instead. You can see another example of classes in action in Listing 3.2; look for the subheader <p> class.

What if you want to create a style class that can be applied to any element instead of just headings or some other particular tag? In your CSS, simply use a period (.) followed by any style class name you make up and any style specifications you choose. That class can specify any number of font, spacing, and margin settings all at once. Wherever you want to apply your custom tag in a page, just use an HTML tag plus the class attribute, followed by the class name you created.

For example, the style sheet in Listing 3.1 includes the following style class specification:

```
p.subheader {
  font-weight: bold;
  color:#593d87;
}
```

This style class is applied in Listing 3.2 with the following tag:

```
<p class="subheader">
```

Everything between that tag and the closing </p> tag in Listing 3.2 appears in bold purple text.

What makes style classes so valuable is how they isolate style code from web pages, effectively enabling you to focus your HTML code on the actual content in a page, not on how it is going to appear on the screen. Then you can focus on how the content is rendered to the screen by fine-tuning the style sheet. You might be surprised by how a relatively small amount of code in a style sheet can have significant effects across an entire website. This makes your pages much easier to maintain and manipulate.

Using Style IDs

When you create custom style classes, you can use those classes as many times as you like—they are not unique. However, in some instances, you want precise control over unique elements for layout or formatting purposes (or both). In such instances, look to IDs instead of classes.

TIP

You might have noticed a change in the coding style when a style rule includes multiple properties. For style rules with a single style, you'll commonly see the property placed on the same line as the rule, like this:

```
p.subheader { font-weight:
bold; }
```

However, when a style rule contains multiple style properties, it's much easier to read and understand the code if you list the properties one per line, like this:

```
p.subheader {
  font-weight: bold;
  color:#593d87;
}
```

A *style ID* is a custom set of formatting specifications that can be applied to only one element in a web page. You can use IDs across a set of pages, but only once per time within each page.

For example, suppose you have a title within the body of all your pages. Each page has only one title, but all the pages themselves include one instance of that title. Following is an example of a selector with an ID indicated, plus a property and a value:

```
p#title {font: 24pt Verdana, Geneva, Arial, sans-serif}
```

Notice that this selector includes a hash mark, or pound sign (#), after p, followed by a descriptive ID name. When referencing a style ID in HTML code, simply specify the ID name in the id attribute of an element, like so:

```
<p id="title">Some Title Goes Here</p>
```

Everything between the opening and closing `<p>` tags will appear in 24-point Verdana text—but only once on any given page. You often see style IDs used to define specific parts of a page for layout purposes, such as a header area, footer area, main body area, and so on. These types of areas in a page appear only once per page, so using an ID rather than a class is the appropriate choice.

Internal Style Sheets and Inline Styles

In some situations, you want to specify styles that will be used in only one web page. You can enclose a style sheet between `<style>` and `</style>` tags and include it directly in an HTML document. Style sheets used in this manner must appear in the `<head>` of an HTML document. No `<link />` tag is needed, and you cannot refer to that style sheet from any other page (unless you copy it into the beginning of that document too). This kind of style sheet is known as an internal style sheet, as you learned earlier in the chapter.

Listing 3.3 shows an example of how you might specify an internal style sheet.

NOTE

The `<span>` and `</span>` tags are dummy tags that do nothing in and of themselves except specify a range of content to apply any `style` attributes that you add. The only difference between `<div>` and `<span>` is that `<div>` is a block element and, therefore, forces a line break, whereas `<span>` doesn't. Therefore, you should use `<span>` to modify the style of any portion of text that is to appear in the middle of a sentence or paragraph without any line break.

LISTING 3.3   A Web Page with an Internal Style Sheet

```
<!DOCTYPE html>

<html lang="en">
  <head>
    <title>Some Page</title>

    <style type="text/css">
      footer {
        font-size: 9pt;
        line-height: 12pt;
        text-align: center;
      }
    </style>
  </head>
  <body>
  ...
  <footer>
  Copyright 2013 Acme Products, Inc.
  </footer>
  </body>
</html>
```

In the listing code, the `footer` style class is specified in an internal style sheet that appears in the head of the page. The style class is now available for use within the body of this page. In fact, it is used in the body of the page to style the copyright notice.

Internal style sheets are handy if you want to create a style rule that is used multiple times within a single page. However, in some instances, you might need to apply a unique style to one particular element. This calls for an inline style rule, which enables you to specify a style for only a small part of a page, such as an individual element. For example, you can create and apply a style rule within a `<p>`, `<div>`, or `<span>` tag via the `style` attribute. This type of style is known as an *inline style* because it is specified right there in the middle of the HTML code.

Here's how a sample `style` attribute might look:

```
<p style="color: green">
  This text is green, but <span style="color: red">this text is
  red.</span>
  Back to green again, but...
</p>
<p>
  ...now the green is over, and we're back to the default color
  for this page.
</p>
```

> **CAUTION**
>
> Using inline styles isn't considered a best practice when used beyond page-level debugging or the process of trying out new things in a controlled setting. The best practice of all is having your pages link to a centrally maintained style sheet so that changes are immediately reflected in all pages that use it.

This code makes use of the `<span>` tag to show how to apply the `color` style property in an inline style rule. In fact, both the `<p>` tag and the `<span>` tag in this example use the `color` property as an inline style. What's important to understand is that the `color: red` style property overrides the `color: green` style property for the text between the `<span>` and `</span>` tags. Then in the second paragraph, neither of the `color` styles applies because it is a completely new paragraph that adheres to the default color of the entire page.

Validate Your Style Sheets

Just as it is important to validate your HTML or XHTML markup, it is important to validate your style sheet. You can find a specific validation tool for CSS at http://jigsaw.w3.org/css-validator/. You can point the tool to a web address, upload a file, or paste content into the form field provided. The ultimate goal is a result like the one in Figure 3.3: `valid!`

FIGURE 3.3
The W3C CSS Validator shows there are no errors in the style sheet contents of Listing 3.1.

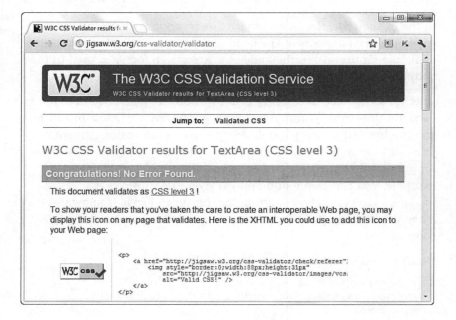

Summary

In this chapter, you learned that a style sheet can control the appearance of many HTML pages at once. It can also give you extremely precise control over the typography, spacing, and positioning of HTML elements. You also learned that, by adding a `style` attribute to almost any HTML tag, you can control the style of any part of an HTML page without referring to a separate style sheet document.

You learned about three main approaches to including style sheets in your website: a separate style sheet file with the extension `.css` that is linked to in the `<head>` of your documents, a collection of style rules placed in the head of the document within the `<style>` tag, and rules placed directly in an HTML tag via the `style` attribute (although the latter is not a best practice for long-term use).

Table 3.1 summarizes the tags discussed in this chapter. Refer to the CSS style sheet standards at www.w3c.org for details on what options can be included after the `<style>` tag or the `style` attribute.

TABLE 3.1   HTML Tags and Attributes Covered in Chapter 3

Tag/Attributes	Function
Tag	
`<style>...</style>`	Allows an internal style sheet to be included within a document. Used between `<head>` and `</head>`.
Attribute	
`type="contenttype"`	The Internet content type. (Always `"text/css"` for a CSS style sheet.)
Tag	
`<link />`	Links to an external style sheet (or other document type). Used in the `<head>` section of the document.
Attributes	
`href="url"`	The address of the style sheet.
`type="contenttype"`	The Internet content type. (Always `"text/css"` for a CSS style sheet.)
`rel="stylesheet"`	The link type. (Always `"stylesheet"` for style sheets.)

Tag

`<span>...</span>`   Does nothing but provide a place to put `style` or other attributes. (Similar to `<div>...</div>`, but does not cause a line break.)

Attribute

`style="style"`   Includes inline style specifications. (Can be used in `<span>`, `<div>`, `<body>`, and most other HTML tags.)

Q&A

Q. Say I link a style sheet to my page that says all text should be blue, but there's a `<span style="font-color: red">` **tag in the page somewhere. Will that text display as blue or red?**

A. Red. Local inline styles always take precedence over external style sheets. Any style specifications you put between `<style>` and `</style>` tags at the top of a page also take precedence over external style sheets (but not over inline styles later in the same page). This is the cascading effect of style sheets that I mentioned earlier in the chapter. You can think of cascading style effects as starting with an external style sheet, which is overridden by an internal style sheet, which is overridden by inline styles.

Q. Can I link more than one style sheet to a single page?

A. Sure. For example, you might have a sheet for formatting (text, fonts, colors, and so on) and another one for layout (margins, padding, alignment, and so on)—just include a `<link />` for both. Technically, the CSS standard requires web browsers to give the user the option to choose between style sheets when multiple sheets are presented via multiple `<link />` tags. However, in practice, all major web browsers simply include every style sheet unless it has a `rel="alternate"` attribute. The preferred technique for linking in multiple style sheets involves using the special `@import` command. The following is an example of importing multiple style sheets with `@import`:

```
@import url(styles1.css);
@import url(styles2.css);
```

Similar to the `<link />` tag, the `@import` command must be placed in the head of a web page.

Workshop

The Workshop contains quiz questions and exercises to help you solidify your understanding of the material covered. Try to answer all questions before looking at the "Answers" section that follows.

Quiz

1. What code would you use to create a style sheet to specify 30-point blue Arial headings and all other text in 10-point blue Times Roman (or the default browser font)?

2. If you saved the style sheet you made for Question 1 as `corporate.css`, how do you apply it to a web page named `intro.html`?

3. How many different ways are there to ensure that style rules can be applied to your content?

Answers

1. Your style sheet would include the following:

```
h1 { font: 30pt blue Arial; }
body { font: 10pt blue "Times New Roman"; }
```

2. Put the following tag between the `<head>` and `</head>` tags of the `intro.html` document:

```
<link rel="stylesheet" type="text/css" href="corporate.css" />
```

3. Three: externally, internally, and inline.

Exercises

▶ Using the style sheet you created earlier in this chapter, add some style classes to your style sheet. To see the fruits of your labor, apply those classes to the HTML page you created as well. Use classes with your `<h1>` and `<p>` tags to get the feel for things.

▶ Develop a standard style sheet for your website, and link it into all your pages. (Use internal style sheets and/or inline styles for pages that need to deviate from it.) If you work for a corporation, chances are, it has already developed font and style specifications for printed materials. Get a copy of those specifications, and follow them for company web pages too.

▶ Be sure to explore the official style sheet specs at http://www.w3.org/Style/CSS/, and try some of the more esoteric style properties not covered in this chapter.

CHAPTER 4
Understanding JavaScript

The World Wide Web (WWW) began as a text-only medium—the first browsers didn't even support images within web pages. The Web has come a long way since those early days. Today's websites include a wealth of visual and interactive features in addition to useful content: graphics, sounds, animation, and video. Web scripting languages, such as JavaScript, are one of the easiest ways to spice up a web page and to interact with users in new ways.

The first part of this chapter introduces the concept of web scripting and the JavaScript language. As the chapter moves ahead, you'll learn how to include JavaScript commands directly in your HTML documents, and how your scripts will be executed when the page is viewed in a browser. You will work with a simple script, edit it, and test it in your browser, all the while learning the basic tasks involved in creating and using JavaScript scripts.

Learning Web Scripting Basics

You already know how to use one type of computer language: HTML. You use HTML tags to describe how you want your document formatted, and the browser obeys your commands and shows the formatted document to the user. But because HTML is a simple text markup language, it can't respond to the user, make decisions, or automate repetitive tasks. Interactive tasks such as these require a more sophisticated language: a programming language or a *scripting* language.

Although many programming languages are complex, scripting languages are generally simple. They have a simple syntax, can

NOTE

Interpreted languages have their disadvantages—they can't execute really quickly, so they're not ideally suited for complicated work, such as graphics. Also, they require the interpreter (in JavaScript's case, usually a browser) in order to work.

perform tasks with a minimum of commands, and are easy to learn. JavaScript is a web scripting language that enables you to combine scripting with HTML to create interactive web pages.

Scripts and Programs

A movie or a play follows a script—a list of actions (or lines) for the actors to perform. A web script provides the same type of instructions for the web browser. A script in JavaScript can range from a single line to a full-scale application. (In either case, JavaScript scripts usually run within a browser.)

Some programming languages must be *compiled*, or translated, into machine code before they can be executed. JavaScript, on the other hand, is an *interpreted* language: The browser executes each line of script as it comes to it.

There is one main advantage to interpreted languages: Writing or changing a script is very simple. Changing a JavaScript script is as easy as changing a typical HTML document, and the change is enacted as soon as you reload the document in the browser.

Introducing JavaScript

JavaScript was developed nearly 20 years ago by Netscape Communications Corporation, the maker of the long-defunct Netscape web browser. JavaScript was the first web scripting language to be supported by browsers, and it is still by far the most popular.

NOTE

A bit of history: JavaScript was originally called LiveScript and was first introduced in Netscape Navigator 2.0 in 1995. It was soon renamed JavaScript to indicate a marketing relationship with Sun's Java language, although there is no other relationship, structurally or otherwise, between Java and JavaScript.

JavaScript is almost as easy to learn as HTML, and it can be included directly in HTML documents. Here are a few of the things you can do with JavaScript:

▶ Display messages to the user as part of a web page, in the browser's status line, or in alert boxes

▶ Validate the contents of a form and make calculations (for example, an order form can automatically display a running total as you enter item quantities)

▶ Animate images or create images that change when you move the mouse over them

▶ Create ad banners that interact with the user, rather than simply displaying a graphic

▶ Detect the browser in use or its features and perform advanced functions only on browsers that support them

▶ Detect installed plug-ins and notify the user if a plug-in is required

▶ Modify all or part of a web page without requiring the user to reload it

▶ Display or interact with data retrieved from a remote server

You can do all this and more with JavaScript, including creating entire applications. We'll explore the uses of JavaScript throughout this book.

How JavaScript Fits into a Web Page

Using the `<script>` tag, you can add a short script (in this case, just one line) to a web document, as shown in Listing 4.1. The `<script>` tag tells the browser to start treating the text as a script, and the closing `</script>` tag tells the browser to return to HTML mode. In most cases, you can't use JavaScript statements in an HTML document except within `<script>` tags. The exception is event handlers, described later in this chapter.

LISTING 4.1   A Simple HTML Document with a Simple Script

```
<!DOCTYPE html>

<html lang="en">
  <head>
    <title>The American Eggplant Society</title>
  </head>

  <body>
    <h1>The American Eggplant Society</h1>
    <p>Welcome to our site. Unfortunately, it is still
    under construction.</p>
    <p>We last worked on it on this date:
    <script type="text/javascript">
    <!-- Hide the script from old browsers
    document.write(document.lastModified);
    // Stop hiding the script -->
    </script>
    </p>
  </body>
</html>
```

JavaScript's `document.write` statement, which you'll learn more about later, sends output as part of the web document. In this case, it displays the modification date of the document, as shown in Figure 4.1.

FIGURE 4.1
Using `document.write` to display a last-modified date.

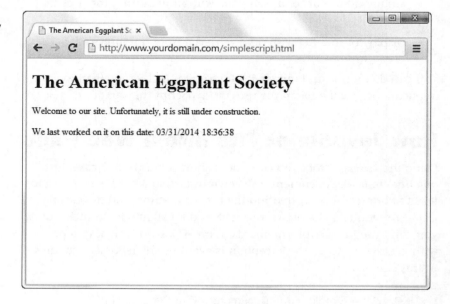

In this example, we placed the script within the body of the HTML document. There are actually four places where you might use scripts:

▶ **In the body of the page**—In this case, the script's output is displayed as part of the HTML document when the browser loads the page.

▶ **In the header of the page between the** `<head>` **tags**—Scripts in the header should not be used to create output within the `<head>` section of an HTML document, since that would likely result in poorly-formed and invalid HTML documents, but these scripts can be referred to by other scripts here and elsewhere. The `<head>` section is often used for functions—groups of JavaScript statements that can be used as a single unit. You will learn more about functions in Chapter 14, "Getting Started with JavaScript Programming."

▶ **Within an HTML tag, such as** `<body>` **or** `<form>`—This is called an *event handler* and it enables the script to work with HTML elements. When using JavaScript in event handlers, you don't need to use the `<script>` tag. You'll learn more about event handlers in Chapter 14.

▶ **In a separate file entirely**—JavaScript supports the use of files with the `.js` extension containing scripts; these can be included by specifying a file in the `<script>` tag. While the `.js` extension is a convention, scripts can actually have any file extension, or none.

Using Separate JavaScript Files

When you create more complicated scripts, you'll quickly find that your HTML documents become large and confusing. To avoid this problem, you can use one or more external JavaScript files. These are files with the `.js` extension that contain JavaScript statements.

External scripts are supported by all modern browsers. To use an external script, you specify its filename in the `<script>` tag:

```
<script type="text/javascript" src="filename.js"></script>
```

Because you'll be placing the JavaScript statements in a separate file, you don't need anything between the opening and closing `<script>` tags—in fact, anything between them will be ignored by the browser.

You can create the `.js` file using a text editor. It should contain one or more JavaScript commands, and only JavaScript—don't include `<script>` tags, other HTML tags, or HTML comments. Save the `.js` file in the same directory as the HTML documents that refer to it.

Understanding JavaScript Events

Many of the useful things you can do with JavaScript involve interacting with the user, and that means responding to *events*—for example, a link or a button being clicked. You can define event handlers within HTML tags to tell the browser how to respond to an event. For example, Listing 4.2 defines a button that displays a message when clicked.

TIP
External JavaScript files have a distinct advantage: You can link to the same `.js` file from two or more HTML documents. Because the browser stores this file in its cache, this can reduce the time it takes your web pages to display.

LISTING 4.2   A Simple Event Handler

```
<!DOCTYPE html>

<html lang="en">
  <head>
    <title>Event Test</title>
  </head>

  <body>
    <h1>Event Test</h1>
    <button type="button"
            onclick="alert('You clicked the button.')">
            Click Me!</button>
  </body>
</html>
```

In various places throughout this book, you'll learn more about JavaScript's event model and how to create simple and complex event handlers.

Exploring JavaScript's Capabilities

If you've spent any time browsing the Web, you've undoubtedly seen lots of examples of JavaScript in action. Here are some brief descriptions of typical applications for JavaScript, all of which you'll explore further, later in this book.

Improving Navigation

Some of the most common uses of JavaScript are in navigation systems for websites. You can use JavaScript to create a navigation tool—for example, a drop-down menu to select the next page to read, or a submenu that pops up when you hover over a navigation link.

When it's done right, this kind of JavaScript interactivity can make a site easier to use, while still remaining usable for browsers that don't support JavaScript (or HTML5/CSS3, which can also be used to create great navigation).

Validating Forms

Form validation is another common use of JavaScript, although the form validation features of HTML5 have stolen a lot of JavaScript's thunder here as well. A simple script can read values the user types into a form and make sure they're in the right format, such as with ZIP Codes, phone numbers, and e-mail addresses. This type of client-side validation enables users to fix common errors without waiting for a response from the web server telling them that their form submission was invalid. You'll learn how to work with form data in Chapter 26, "Working with Web-Based Forms."

Special Effects

One of the earliest and most annoying uses of JavaScript was to create attention-getting special effects—for example, scrolling a message in the browser's status line or flashing the background color of a page.

These techniques have fortunately fallen out of style, but thanks to the W3C DOM and the latest browsers, some more impressive effects are possible with JavaScript—for example, creating objects that can be dragged and dropped on a page, or creating fading transitions between images in a slideshow. Some developers have HTML5, CSS3, and JavaScript working in tandem to create fully functioning interactive games.

Remote Scripting (AJAX)

For a long time, the biggest limitation of JavaScript was that there was no way for it to communicate with a web server. For example, you could use JavaScript to verify that a phone number had the right number of digits, but not to look up the user's location in a database based on the number.

Now that some of JavaScript's advanced features are supported by most browsers, this is no longer the case. Your scripts can get data from a server without loading a page, or send data back to be saved. These features are collectively known as AJAX (Asynchronous JavaScript and XML), or *remote scripting*. You'll learn how to develop AJAX scripts in Chapter 25, "AJAX: Remote Scripting."

You've seen AJAX in action if you've used Google's Gmail mail application, Facebook, or any online news site that allows you to comment on stories, vote for favorites, or participate in a poll. All of these use remote scripting to present you with a responsive user interface that works with a server in the background.

NOTE

UTC stands for Universal Time (Coordinated), and is the atomic time standard based on the old GMT (Greenwich Mean Time) standard. This is the time at the prime meridian, which runs through Greenwich, London, England.

CAUTION

Remember to include only valid JavaScript statements between the starting and ending `<script>` tags. If the browser finds anything but valid JavaScript statements within the `<script>` tags, it will display a JavaScript error message.

Displaying Time with JavaScript

One common use of JavaScript is to display dates and times in the browser, and that's where we'll start putting some scripting pieces together. Because JavaScript runs on the browser, the times it displays will be in the user's current time zone. However, you can also use JavaScript to calculate "universal" (UTC) time.

Your script, like most JavaScript programs, begins with the HTML `<script>` tag. As you learned earlier in this chapter, you use the `<script>` and `</script>` tags to enclose a script within the HTML document.

To begin creating the script, open your favorite text editor and type the beginning and ending `<script>` tags as shown:

```
<script type="text/javascript"></script>
```

In this script, you'll use JavaScript to determine the local and UTC times and then display them in the browser. Fortunately, all the hard parts, such as converting between date formats, are built in to the JavaScript interpreter—this is one of the reasons that displaying dates and times is a good starting place for beginners.

Storing Data in Variables

To begin the script, you will use a *variable* to store the current date. You will learn more about variables in Chapter 16, "Using JavaScript Variables, Strings, and Arrays," but for now just understand that a *variable* is a container that can hold a value—a number, some text, or, in this case, a date.

NOTE

Notice the semicolon at the end of the code snippet creating a variable called `now`. This semicolon tells the browser that it has reached the end of a statement. Semicolons are optional, but using them helps you avoid some common errors. We'll use them throughout this book for clarity.

To start writing the script, add the following line after the first `<script>` tag. Be sure to use the same combination of capital and lowercase letters in your version because JavaScript commands and variable names are case sensitive.

```
now = new Date();
```

This statement creates a variable called `now` and stores the current date and time in it. This statement and the others you will use in this script use JavaScript's built-in `Date` object, which enables you to conveniently handle dates and times. You'll learn more about working with dates in Chapter 17, "Using JavaScript Functions and Objects."

Calculating the Results

Internally, JavaScript stores dates as the number of milliseconds since January 1, 1970. Fortunately, JavaScript includes a number of functions to convert dates and times in various ways, so you don't have to figure out how to convert milliseconds to day, date, and time.

To continue your script, add the following two statements before the final `</script>` tag:

```
localtime = now.toString();
utctime = now.toGMTString();
```

These statements create two new variables: `localtime`, containing the current time and date in a nice readable format, and `utctime`, containing the UTC equivalent.

NOTE

The `localtime` and `utctime` variables store a piece of text, such as January 1, 2001 12:00 PM. In programming parlance, a piece of text is called a *string*.

Creating Output

You now have two variables—`localtime` and `utctime`—which contain the results we want from our script. Of course, these variables don't do us much good unless we can see them. JavaScript includes several ways to display information, and one of the simplest is the `document.write` statement.

The `document.write` statement displays a text string, a number, or anything else you throw at it. Because your JavaScript program will be used within a web page, the output will be displayed as part of the page. To display the result, add these statements before the final `</script>` tag:

```
document.write("<p><strong>Local time:</strong> " + localtime +
"</p>");
document.write("<p><strong>UTC time:</strong> " + utctime +
"</p>");
```

These statements tell the browser to add some text to the web page containing your script. The output will include some brief strings introducing the results, and the contents of the `localtime` and `utctime` variables.

Notice the HTML elements, such as `<p>` and `<strong>`, within the quotation marks—because JavaScript's output appears within a web page, it needs to be formatted using HTML.

NOTE

Notice the plus signs (+) used between the text and variables in the `document.write()` code snippets. In this case, it tells the browser to combine the values into one string of text. If you use the plus sign between two numbers, they are added together.

Adding the Script to a Web Page

You should now have a complete script that calculates a result and displays it. Your listing should match Listing 4.3.

LISTING 4.3   The Complete Date and Time Script

```
<script type="text/javascript">
now = new Date();
localtime = now.toString();
utctime = now.toGMTString();
document.write("<p><strong>Local time:</strong> " + localtime +
"</p>");
document.write("<p><strong>UTC time:</strong> " + utctime +
"</p>");
</script>
```

To use your script, you'll need to add it to an HTML document. If you use the general template you've seen in the chapters so far, you should end up with something like Listing 4.4.

LISTING 4.4   The Date and Time Script in an HTML Document

```
<!DOCTYPE html>

<html lang="en">
  <head>
    <title>Displaying Times and Dates</title>
  </head>

  <body>
    <h1>Current Date and Time</h1>
    <script type="text/javascript">
     now = new Date();
     localtime = now.toString();
     utctime = now.toGMTString();
     document.write("<p><strong>Local time:</strong> "
         + localtime + "</p>");
     document.write("<p><strong>UTC time:</strong> " + utctime
         + "</p>");
    </script>
  </body>
</html>
```

Now that you have a complete HTML document, save it with an .html extension.

Testing the Script

To test your script, you simply need to load the HTML document you created in a web browser. If you typed the script correctly, your browser should display the result of the script, as shown in Figure 4.2. (Of course, your result won't be the same as mine, but it should be the same as the setting of your computer's clock.)

NOTE

Notepad and other Windows text editors might try to be helpful and add the `.txt` extension to your script. Be sure your saved file has the correct extension.

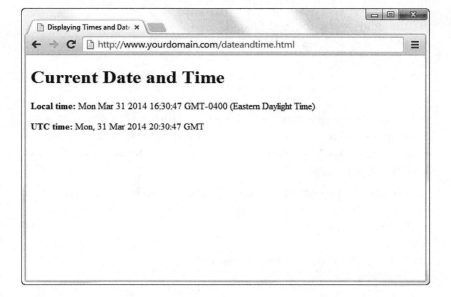

Current Date and Time

Local time: Mon Mar 31 2014 16:30:47 GMT-0400 (Eastern Daylight Time)

UTC time: Mon, 31 Mar 2014 20:30:47 GMT

FIGURE 4.2
Using JavaScript to display the date and time.

A note about Internet Explorer: Depending on your security settings, the script might not execute, and your browser might display a security warning. In this case, follow your browser's instructions to allow your script to run. (This happens because the default security settings allow JavaScript in online documents, but not in local files.)

Modifying the Script

Although the current script does indeed display the current date and time, its display isn't nearly as attractive as the clock on your wall or desk. To remedy that situation, you can use some additional JavaScript features and a bit of HTML to display a large clock.

To display a large clock, we need the hours, minutes, and seconds in separate variables. Once again, JavaScript has built-in functions to do most of the work:

```
hours = now.getHours();
mins = now.getMinutes();
secs = now.getSeconds();
```

These statements load the `hours`, `mins`, and `secs` variables with the components of the time using JavaScript's built-in date functions.

After the hours, minutes, and seconds are in separate variables, you can create `document.write` statements to display them:

```
document.write("<p><strong>");
document.write(hours + ":" + mins + ":" + secs);
document.write("</p></strong>");
```

The first statement displays an HTML `<h2>` header tag to display the clock as a second-level header element. The second statement displays the `hours`, `mins`, and `secs` variables, separated by colons, and the third adds the closing `</h2>` tag.

You can add the preceding statements to the original date and time script to add the large clock display. Listing 4.5 shows the complete modified version of the script.

LISTING 4.5   The Date and Time Script with Large Clock Display

```
<!DOCTYPE html>

<html lang="en">
  <head>
    <title>Displaying Times and Dates</title>
  </head>

  <body>
    <h1>Current Date and Time</h1>
    <script type="text/javascript">
      now = new Date();
      localtime = now.toString();
      utctime = now.toGMTString();
      document.write("<p><strong>Local time:</strong> "
          + localtime + "</p>");
      document.write("<p><strong>UTC time:</strong> " + utctime
          + "</p>");
      hours = now.getHours();
      mins = now.getMinutes();
      secs = now.getSeconds();
      document.write("<h2>");
      document.write(hours + ":" + mins + ":" + secs);
```

```
      document.write("</h2>");
    </script>
  </body>
</html>
```

Now that you have modified the script, save the HTML file and open the modified file in your browser. If you left the browser running, you can simply use the Reload button to load the new version of the script. Try it and verify that the same time is displayed in both the upper portion of the window and the new large clock. Figure 4.3 shows the results.

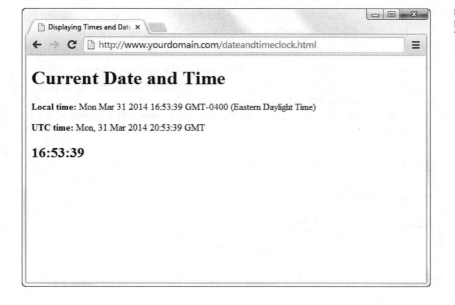

FIGURE 4.3
Displaying the modified Date and Time script.

Dealing with JavaScript Errors

As you develop more complex JavaScript applications, you're going to run into errors from time to time. JavaScript errors are usually caused by mistyped JavaScript statements.

To see an example of a JavaScript error message, modify the statement you added in the preceding section. We'll use a common error: omitting one of the parentheses. Change the last `document.write` statement in Listing 4.5 to read

```
document.write("</h2>";
```

NOTE

The time formatting produced by this script isn't perfect: Hours after noon are in 24-hour time; and there are no leading zeroes, so 12:04 is displayed as 12:4. See Chapter 17 for solutions to these issues.

Save your HTML document again and load the document into the browser. Depending on the browser version you're using, one of two things will happen: Either an error message will be displayed, or the script will simply fail to execute.

If an error message is displayed, you're halfway to fixing the problem by adding the missing parenthesis. If no error was displayed, you should configure your browser to display error messages so that you can diagnose future problems:

▶ In Firefox, you can also select Tools, JavaScript Console from the menu.

▶ In Chrome, select Tools, JavaScript Console from the Options menu. A console displays in the bottom of the browser window. The console is shown in Figure 4.4, displaying the error message you created in this example.

▶ In Internet Explorer, select Tools, Internet Options. On the Advanced page, uncheck the Disable Script Debugging box and check the Display a Notification About Every Script Error box. (If this is disabled, a yellow icon in the status bar still notifies you of errors.)

FIGURE 4.4
Showing an error in the JavaScript console in Chrome.

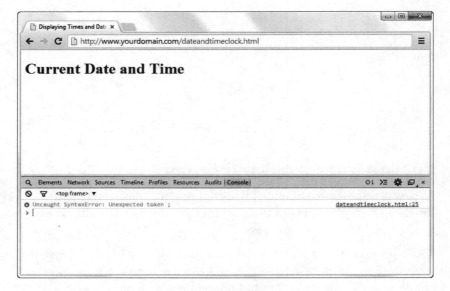

The error we get in this case is Uncaught SyntaxError and it points to line 25. In this case, clicking on the name of the script takes you directly to the highlighted line containing the error, as shown in Figure 4.5.

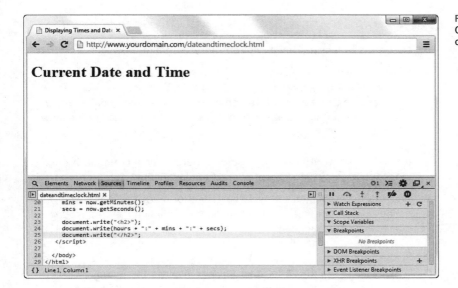

Most modern browsers contain JavaScript debugging tools such as the one you just witnessed. You'll learn more about this in the next chapter.

Summary

During this chapter, you've learned what web scripting is and what JavaScript is. You've also learned how to insert a script into an HTML document or refer to an external JavaScript file, what sorts of things JavaScript can do, and how JavaScript differs from other web languages. You also wrote a simple JavaScript program and tested it using a web browser. You also learned how to modify and test scripts, and what happens when a JavaScript program runs into an error.

In the process of writing this script, you have used some of JavaScript's basic features: variables, the document.write statement, and functions for working with dates and times.

Now that you've learned a bit of JavaScript syntax, you're ready to continue on to learn all manner and sorts of things about web development before settling in to write interactive websites using client-side scripting.

Q&A

Q. **Do I need to test my JavaScript on more than one browser?**

A. In an ideal world, any script you write that follows the standards for JavaScript will work in all browsers, and 98% of the time (give or take) that's true in the real world. But browsers do have their quirks, and you should test your scripts in Chrome, Internet Explorer, and Firefox at a minimum.

Q. **If I plan to learn PHP, Ruby, or some other server-side programming language anyway, will I have any use for JavaScript?**

A. Certainly. JavaScript is the ideal language for many parts of a web-based application, such as form validation. Although PHP, Ruby, and other server-side languages have their uses, they can't interact directly with the user on the client side.

Q. **When I try to run my script, the browser displays the actual script in the browser window instead of executing it. What did I do wrong?**

A. This is most likely caused by one of three errors. First, you might be missing the beginning or ending `<script>` tags. Check them, and verify that the first reads `<script type="text/javascript">`. Second, your file might have been saved with a `.txt` extension, causing the browser to treat it as a text file. Rename it to `.htm` or `.html` to fix the problem. Third, make sure your browser supports JavaScript, and that it is not disabled in the Preferences dialog.

Q. **Why are the `<strong>` and `<br />` tags allowed in the statements to print the time? I thought HTML tags weren't allowed within the `<script>` tags.**

A. Because this particular tag is inside quotation marks, it's considered a valid part of the script. The script's output, including any HTML tags, is interpreted and displayed by the browser. You can use other HTML tags within quotation marks to add formatting, such as the `<h2>` tags we added for the large clock display.

Workshop

The workshop contains quiz questions and exercises to help you solidify your understanding of the material covered. Try to answer all questions before looking at the "Answers" section that follows.

Quiz

1. When a user views a page containing a JavaScript program, which machine actually executes the script?

    a. The user's machine running a web browser

    b. The web server

    c. A central machine deep within Netscape's corporate offices

2. What tool do you use to create and edit JavaScript programs?

    a. A browser

    b. A text editor

    c. A pencil and a piece of paper

3. What are variables used for in JavaScript programs?

    a. Storing numbers, dates, or other values

    b. Varying randomly

    c. Causing high-school algebra flashbacks

4. What should appear at the very end of a JavaScript script embedded in an HTML file?

    a. The `<script type="text/javascript">` tag

    b. The `</script>` tag

    c. The `END` statement

Answers

1. a. JavaScript programs execute on the web browser. (There is actually a server-side version of JavaScript, but that's another story.)

2. b. Any text editor can be used to create scripts. You can also use a word processor if you're careful to save the document as a text file with the `.html` or `.htm` extension.

3. **a.** Variables are used to store numbers, dates, or other values.

4. **b.** Your script should end with the `</script>` tag.

Exercises

▶ Add a millisecond field to the large clock. You can use the `getMilliseconds` function, which works just like `getSeconds` but returns milliseconds.

▶ Modify the script to display the time, including milliseconds, twice. Notice whether any time passes between the two time displays when you load the page.

CHAPTER 5
Validating and Debugging Your Code

It doesn't matter if you're a beginner or a seasoned expert—bugs happen. It's a fact of life for developers of all skill levels, and I would even venture to say that if your code doesn't contain errors at some point during its creation, then you're just not trying hard enough. So don't worry about the bugs, just worry about identifying and fixing them before clients or customers experience the side effects.

In this chapter, you'll learn about how to validate and debug your HTML and CSS as you develop it, as well as how to use some handy tools built directly into your web browser to identify and debug issues with your JavaScript.

Validating Your Web Content

In the first chapter of this book, I discussed ways to test the web pages you create; one very important way to test your pages is to *validate* them. Think of it this way: It's one thing to design and draw a beautiful set of house plans, but it's quite another for an architect to stamp it as a safe structure suitable for construction. Validating your web pages is a similar process; in this case, however, the architect is a web-based application, not a person.

In brief, validation is the process of testing your pages with a special application that searches for errors and makes sure your pages adhere to the current HTML and CSS standards. Validation is simple. In fact, the standards body responsible for developing web standards, the World Wide Web Consortium (W3C), offers an online validation tool you can use. To validate the HTML of a web page, follow this URL: http://validator.w3.org/. Figure 5.1 shows the options for using the W3C Markup Validation Service.

WHAT YOU'LL LEARN IN THIS CHAPTER:

▶ How to validate your HTML and CSS

▶ How to use Developer Tools to debug HTML and CSS

▶ How to use the JavaScript console to debug JavaScript

FIGURE 5.1
The W3C Markup Validation
Service enables you to validate an
HTML document to ensure that it
has been coded accurately.

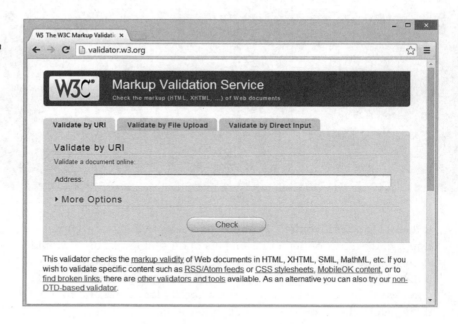

If you've already published a page online, you can use the Validate by URI tab. Use the Validate by File Upload tab to validate files stored on your local computer file system. The Validate by Direct Input tab enables you to paste the contents of a file from your text editor. If all goes well, your page will get a passing report, such as that shown in Figure 5.2, which validates a code listing from Chapter 2, "Structuring an HTML Document."

The W3C also provides a tool to validate CSS; visit http://jigsaw. w3.org/css-validator/ and enter a URL or upload a file using the options provided. If the W3C Markup or CSS Validation Service encounters an error, it provides specific details (including the line numbers of the offending code). Figure 5.3 shows an example of an error report; in this instance I have purposely used the CSS property `padding-up`—a property that does not exist—instead of `padding-top`.

Using basic validation services is a great way to hunt down problems and rid your HTML and CSS of invalid code, such as incorrectly named CSS properties and mismatched HTML tags. Validation not only informs you when your pages are constructed properly, but also assists you in finding and fixing problems in the code before you publish pages for the world to see.

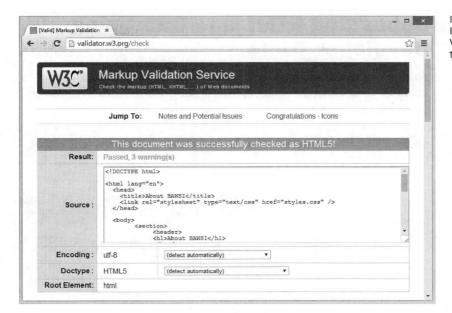

FIGURE 5.2
If a page passes the W3C Markup Validation Service, you know that the code is ready for prime time.

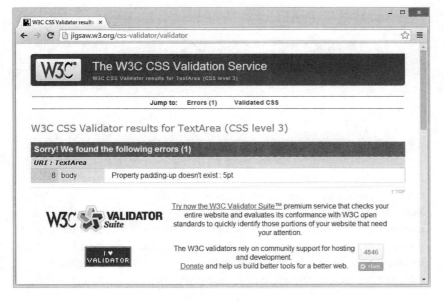

FIGURE 5.3
The W3C CSS Validation Service, like the W3C Markup Validation Service, provides useful error reports.

Debugging HTML and CSS Using Developer Tools

You can extend your debugging efforts beyond basic validation by using more advanced Developer Tools that are built into most major browsers. Figures 5.4, 5.5, and 5.6 show what some of the major browsers look like with Developer Tools turned on; in each figure you'll notice some consistencies in the names and functionalities of certain tools.

FIGURE 5.4
Inspecting an element containing the Google logo using Developer Tools in Firefox.

Although the examples we'll go through in this section use the Chrome Developer Tools, you can see similarities in all the Developer Tools shown previously. In this specific case, the ability to inspect an element is present in all three sets of tools. When you are selecting an element on the screen with your mouse, the additional window panels in the Developer Tools show the exact HTML used to render that element, as well as the style rules currently applied to that element.

This functionality of the inspector is quite useful because it provides a visual way to see the relationship between the node in the DOM tree and the rendered web page; additionally, note the use of breadcrumbs in each set of tools, which shows the hierarchy of nodes from the root `html` node down to the `img` node (with the ID value of `#hplogo`).

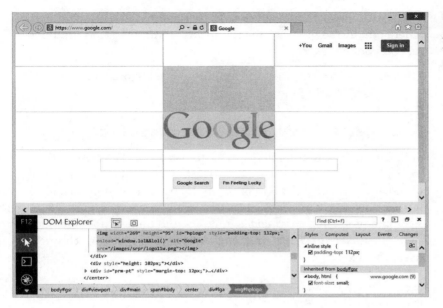

FIGURE 5.5
Inspecting an element containing the Google logo using Developer Tools in Microsoft Internet Explorer.

FIGURE 5.6
Inspecting an element containing the Google logo using Developer Tools in Chrome.

This use of breadcrumbs serves to further assist your understanding of where a rendered visual element appears within the DOM (and not just on your screen).

The next few sections will take you through some practical applications of using these tools.

Debugging HTML Using the Inspector

To illustrate how to use the inspector to debug HTML, consider the code in Listing 5.1, which is just a basic HTML document containing a list of movies, and the word "Favorite" in the heading is supposed to be in italics. However, if you look at the rendered version in Figure 5.7, you'll see some problems: *Everything* is in italics and there is no bullet in front of the first list item. These problems are caused by just two characters in all the text.

LISTING 5.1   A Simple HTML Document with Some HTML Syntax Errors Illustrated in Figure 5.7

```
<!DOCTYPE html>
<html lang="en">
  <head>
    <title>Favorite Movies</title>
  </head>
  <body>
    <h1><i>Favorite<i> Movies</h1>
    <ul>
      <ll>Lord of the Rings</li>
      <li>Harry Potter</li>
      <li>Narnia</li>
      <li>Hot Lead and Cold Feet</li>
    </ul>
  </body>
</html>
```

Follow along with these steps to find and fix the HTML syntax problems using the inspector in Chrome Developer Tools:

1. Add the code in Listing 5.1 to a new file and save the document, and then open it in Chrome. You can keep the document on your local machine or put it on your web server—it doesn't matter for this example, as long as you can open the file in your web browser.

FIGURE 5.7
This web page has two problems:
only the word "Favorite" should be
in italics, and there is no bullet in
front of the first list item.

2. Open Chrome and navigate to Tools, Developer Tools from
the menu (you can also use F12 or Ctrl+Shift+i on Windows, or
Cmd+Opt+i on a Mac). You should see something like what's
shown in Figure 5.8, with the Elements tab preselected and the
`<body>` element highlighted.

FIGURE 5.8
The Elements tab is selected by
default.

3. Click on the arrows in the Elements panel to expand the `<h1>`
    tag, as shown in Figure 5.9. Notice there's an `<i>` element under
    the `<h1>` element, but now also another `<i></i>` tag pair. That
    isn't right, because you remember (and can see in your source
    file) that you didn't put `<i>` elements all over your code, so why
    do they appear? Well, if you look closely at the Elements panel,
    and then the source code, you will notice there is a missing / that
    would make the second instance of the `<i>` tag the closing `</i>`
    tag that you want. That means the browser is rendering (and the
    inspector is showing) what appear to be `<i></i>` elements around
    every single element in your code, because the first `<i>` element
    was never closed—the rendering engine is interpreting that all of
    these phantom `<i>` elements are present.

FIGURE 5.9
This HTML Inspector shows more
`<i>` elements in the DOM than are
in your source code.

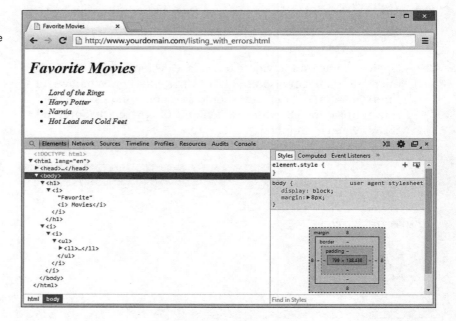

4. In your source file, change the second `<i>` tag to a closing `</i>`
    tag and save the document. Put it on your web server if that's
    where you originally placed it.

5. Refresh the document in the browser. Notice, as in Figure 5.10, that the word "Favorite" is now in italics, as it should be, and all the phantom `<i>` elements are gone from the inspector; however, the bullet point is still missing in the browser's display.

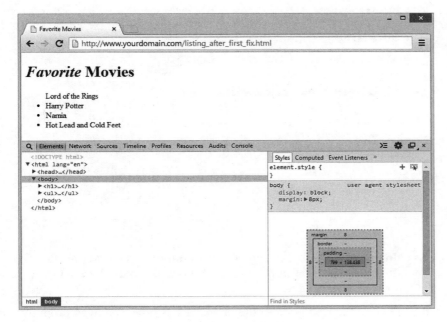

FIGURE 5.10
This web page now has only one problem: no bullet point on the first list item.

6. Go back to the Elements panel and expand the `<ul>` element, and then the `<ll>`, as shown in Figure 5.11. Notice that instead of a set of four appropriately opened and closed `<li>` elements under the `<ul>` element, there is an open `<ll>` tag followed by three `<li>` elements within it, and then a closing `</li>` tag. Although we haven't covered the HTML list item tags yet in this book (it's in the next chapter), you can probably deduce that since the three lines with opening and closing `<li>` tags show bullets, and in the source code the `<ll>` element is closed by an `</li>` tag, the opening tag should indeed be an `<li>` tag.

FIGURE 5.11
Viewing the DOM reveals that the
browser sees an `<ll>` tag under
the `<ul>` tag, not a set of `<li>`
tags.

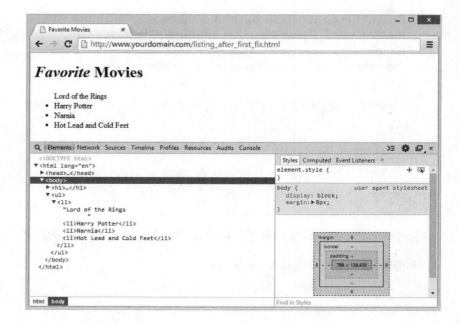

7.   In your source file, change the `<ll>` tag to a `<li>` tag and save
      the document. Put it on your web server if that's where you
      originally placed it.

8.   Reload the web page in the browser. It is now displayed properly,
      as shown in Figure 5.12.

FIGURE 5.12
Chrome now displays the web page
formatted as intended.

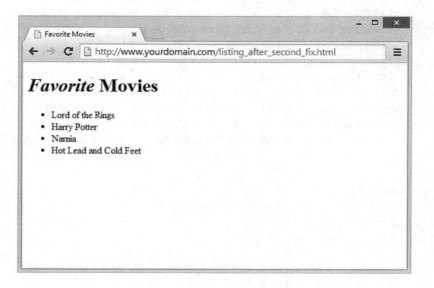

Although going through all the steps as you just did shows you some ways in which the inspector can be used to help spot issues, you might wonder just how much more efficient and helpful that process actually is versus just using a validator. After all, the issues seen earlier were purely validation errors and would have easily been caught by using the W3C Validator you learned about previously. Figure 5.13 shows some of the validation errors present in the original listing.

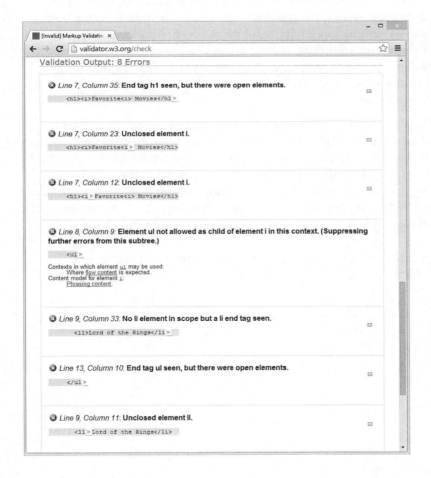

FIGURE 5.13
The W3C Validator clearly shows errors.

It's true that a validator will more quickly identify pure syntax issues, and that using the inspector assumes that you have the knowledge and experience to see the issue straightaway if it's presented in a different context rather than the raw source code. In other words, I still recommend that beginners run their code through a validator first, but seeing alternative views of the DOM rendering is quite useful for an ongoing learning process.

Debugging CSS Using the Inspector

Everything you just learned about debugging HTML with the inspector is also true when it comes to CSS; you can use the Developer Tools to uncover issues with style definitions and inheritance. These built-in tools become especially useful when you are working with more advanced development, such as when you are using JavaScript to modify the CSS of particular elements beyond their original state in the source code, but can still be useful in the beginning stages of your development.

The steps below go through a brief example of using the inspector when working with CSS—specifically, some ill-formed yet valid CSS as shown in Listing 5.2. Although you're encountering this chapter (and therefore these examples) very early in your development process, I am quite certain that within a few chapters you'll remember the steps you've learned here and will be using Developer Tools to enhance your debugging and development throughout the rest of the book.

LISTING 5.2   Valid HTML and CSS That Doesn't Display Nicely

```
<!DOCTYPE html>
<html lang="en">
  <head>
    <style type="text/css">
    #container {
      margin: 30px;
      padding: 5px;
    }

    #tabs {
      padding: 0px;
      width: 50px;
    }

    #content {
      border: 1px solid #000000;
      height: 100px;
      width: 300px;
      clear: both;
    }
    span {
```

```
      margin: 5px;
      width: 100px;
      background-color: #C0C0C0;
      font-weight: bold;
      border-color: #C0C0C0;
      border: 1px solid #000000;
      border-radius: 5px 5px 0px 0px;
      padding: 3px;
      float: left;
      text-align: center;
    }

    span:hover {
      background-color: #3030FF;
      color: #FFFFFF;
      cursor: pointer;
    }

    p {
      font-weight: bold;
      text-align: center;
    }
  </style>
  <title>Sample Page</title>
</head>
<body>
  <div id="container">
    <div id="tabs">
      <span>Name/Title</span>
      <span>Contact Info</span>
      <span>Biography</span>
    </div>

    <div id="content">
      <p>Jimbo Jones</p>
      <p>Rabble-Rouser</p>
    </div>
  </div>
</body>
</html>
```

If you run this HTML and CSS through a validator, it will produce
no errors since it is valid HTML and CSS. However, as you can see in
Figure 5.14, it's just not right. The tabs are supposed to align across
the top of the box that contains text. The idea, if we could get past
this initial layout issue, is that a user could click on the tabs and the
contents in the box would change. But we can't move forward and

make that happen until this initial display works as we intend it to work. This is a classic example of a debugging problem in HTML and CSS—it's not wrong (invalid), but it just isn't right (displaying the way we want it to).

FIGURE 5.14
The result of valid HTML and CSS that needs some additional debugging to look better.

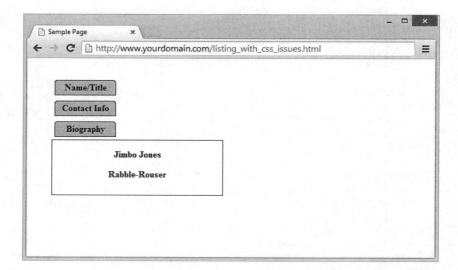

FIGURE 5.14
The result of valid HTML and CSS that needs some additional debugging to look better.

Follow along with these steps to uncover and fix some of the issues using the inspector:

1. Add the code in Listing 5.2 to a new file and save the document, and then open it in Chrome. You can keep the document on your local machine or put it on your web server—it doesn't matter for this example, as long as you can open the file in your web browser.

2. Open Chrome and navigate to Tools, Developer Tools from the menu (you can also use F12 or Ctrl+Shift+i on Windows, or Cmd+Opt+i on a Mac).

3. Click on the arrows in the Elements panel to expand the `<div>` element with the ID of `"container"`, and then the `<div>` element with the ID of `"tabs"`. Click on the `<div>` element with the ID of `"tabs"` so that it is highlighted on your screen, as shown in Figure 5.15. The width of this particular `<div>` will be shown; in this case it is 50 pixels wide. This should lead you to wonder if the width of this particular `<div>`, which is less than the width of any of the `<span>` elements within it, let alone all three of them, is causing an issue with your layout.

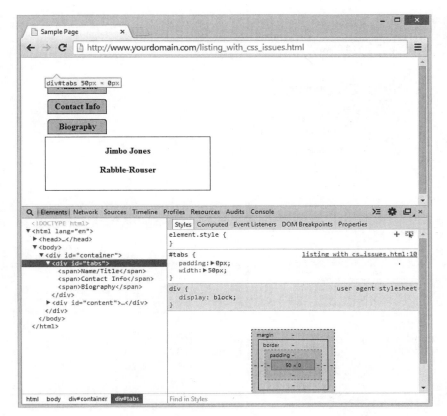

FIGURE 5.15
The selected <div> element is only 50 pixels wide.

4. Following your instincts from the preceding step, click on the <div> element with the ID of "container" so that it is highlighted on your screen and so that the style is given focus in the style panel. Note that the width of this particular <div> element is 300 pixels.

5. In the Elements pane, again click on the <div> element with the ID of "tabs" so that its styles are in focus in the style panel. Within the style panel, double-click on the width value so that the field becomes editable, and change that value to be 300px, as shown in Figure 5.16.

FIGURE 5.16
The layout changes immediately,
although it still isn't correct.

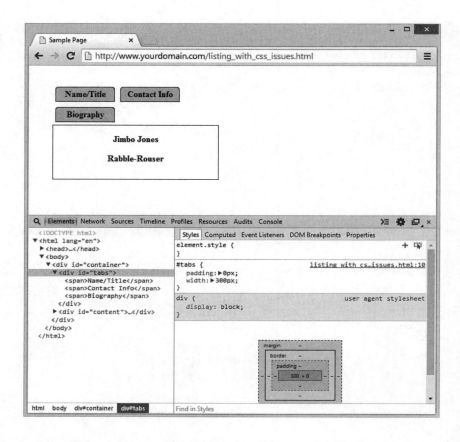

FIGURE 5.16
The layout changes immediately, although it still isn't correct.

TIP

Using the inspector within
Developer Tools isn't just for
your own code. You can turn on
Developer Tools and look at the
source code of any page and
get a sense for how the page
is constructed—and you can
change HTML and CSS values
to see how these changes
affect the display, as well, just
as you did here.

Without making any changes to the underlying source code, either
locally or on your web server, you can use the inspector as a sort of
editor to review possible changes to HTML and CSS. Although the code
in this example still is far from looking "good," you can continue to
make changes on your own and see how the display reacts. You might
have better results after working through later chapters, but even
without detailed knowledge of alignment, margins, and padding, you
can experience a sort of trial-and-error debugging without having to
commit changes in your code.

Debugging JavaScript Using Developer Tools

The Developer Tools within Chrome (and other major browsers) can also help you debug your JavaScript, from catching basic syntax errors in the Console to working through advanced debugging steps using the Sources panel and all that it contains. As we go through the tools in this section, we'll use the code in Listing 5.3.

LISTING 5.3   A Simple HTML Document with a Few Different JavaScript Errors

```html
<!DOCTYPE html>
<html lang="en">
  <head>
    <title>Sample Page</title>

    <script src="http://code.jquery.com/jquery-latest.min.js">
    </script>

    <script type="text/javascript">
    function incCount(){
      var count = 0;
      count += 1;
      return count;
    }

    function countIt(){
      $("#counter").html(incCount);
    }
    </script>

    <style type="text/css">
    button {
      background-color: #0066AA;
      color: #FFFFFF;
      font-weight: bold;
      border: 2px solid #C0C0C0;
      width: 100px;
    }
    </style>
  </head>

  <body>
      <button onclick="countit()">Click Me</button>
      <div id="counter"></div>
  </body>
</html>
```

If you add the code in Listing 5.3 to a new file and save the document, and then open it in Chrome from either your local machine or your server, you'll see this completely unassuming little button as in Figure 5.17.

FIGURE 5.17
Showing the initial output of Listing 5.3.

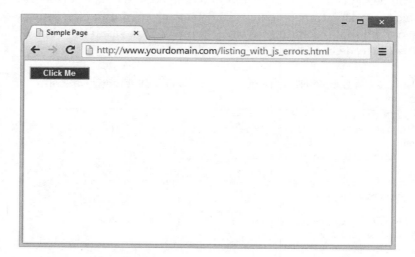

However, if you follow along with these steps, you'll soon uncover issues with this code by using the Console:

1. Open Chrome and navigate to Tools, Developer Tools from the menu (you can also use F12 or Ctrl+Shift+i on Windows, or Cmd+Opt+i on a Mac).

2. Switch to the Console pane by clicking the Console tab in Developer Tools.

3. Click the Click Me button that has been rendered by the browser. You should see an error like that shown in Figure 5.18, which indicates there is an error in the code.

4. Click on the link that will take you to the precise line in the file that contains the error (in this instance, the link is `listing_with_js_errors.html:32`), and you will see that the JavaScript function being called is `countit()`, whereas the function was originally defined in line 15 as `countIt()`. As you learned in the preceding chapter, case matters in JavaScript.

FIGURE 5.18
The Console shows where there is
a syntax error in the code.

If you correct the underlying source file by using `countIt()` in line 32 instead of `countit()`, and then reload the document and click the Click Me button, you will no longer see an error in the Console. However, as you'll soon see, there are more issues with this document.

In the `<head>` section of the document, we find a link to a JavaScript library (jQuery, actually) that is stored externally, as well as some JavaScript code that defines two functions. The `<body>` section includes a `<button>` tag with an `onclick` event to invoke the `countIt()` JavaScript function, as well as a `<div>` element that is used to display the string containing the current count of the number of times the button has been clicked. That's all fine and dandy, except if you actually click the Click Me button more than once, the number will not increase past 1 and no error is present in the Console. This situation calls for more advanced debugging.

Taking a Closer Look at the Sources Panel

The Sources panel contains a set of tools that enable you to pause, resume, and step through code that is loaded in the web browser. By setting breakpoints, you can watch individual sections of your code execute, which is especially helpful when you are trying to track down issues that are unrelated to basic syntax (which the Console will helpfully display without intervention on your part).

With the code in Listing 5.3 loaded into your browser and Developer Tools enabled, click on the Sources tab to show the Sources panel and its related tools. It should look something like what's shown in Figure 5.19.

FIGURE 5.19
Showing the Sources panel in Developer Tools, along with some important tools for this example.

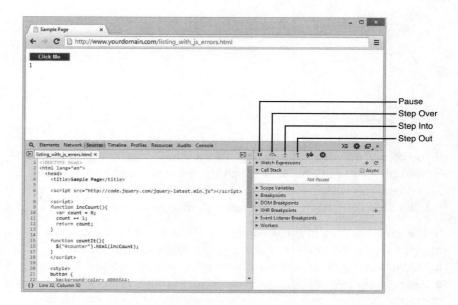

NOTE

For a thorough understanding of all the icons in the Sources panel, see https://developer. chrome.com/devtools/docs/ javascript-debugging.

To debug our script, we'll focus on setting breakpoints and stepping through the code using the tools highlighted in Figure 5.19. But first, some explanations of terms:

▶ **Breakpoints**—Breakpoints enable you to specify where you would like to stop the JavaScript from executing. When you set a breakpoint, the browser stops executing and breaks into the debugger before it executes that line of code—this enables you to see the state of the code at that specific point. You set breakpoints by clicking on a line number in the code listing, and you remove a breakpoint by clicking the line number again; breakpoints are then indicated by a highlighted blue arrow icon. The Breakpoints tab shows you a list of breakpoints that have been set. You can disable the breakpoint by unchecking the checkbox next to it.

▶ **Step Over**—When you click the Step Over icon, the code advances one line. If the line of code is to execute another function, that function is executed and you are taken to the next line of code in the current function. If a breakpoint is encountered when stepping over a function, the browser stops executing at that location in the script.

▶ **Step Into**—When you click the Step Into icon, the code advances one line. If the line of code is to execute another function, you are taken to the first line of code in that function.

▶ **Step Out**—When you click the Step Out icon, the current function finishes executing and you are taken to the next line of code in the calling function.

Now, let's start debugging the script in Listing 5.3 and see why it won't advance the count past 1.

1. Set a breakpoint on line 10 by clicking to the left of the line number. A blue arrow should appear, as shown in Figure 5.20. Also note that the Scope Variables section of the right-most pane is open. I've done this because I want to watch how the value of `count` changes as the script moves forward. After all, it's this value that is the problem, since it's not changing after the first click.

FIGURE 5.20
A breakpoint is set on line 10 of the script.

2. Now click the button on the web page. You should see a yellow arrow appear in the body of the web page indicating that the script is paused in the debugger, and line 10 in the code listing will be highlighted. In the script, line 10 is the first line of the `incCount()` function; the `incCount()` function is supposed to determine the value of the counter string, represented by the variable `count`. In the Scope Variables area, you should see that the value of `count` is currently undefined.

3. Click the Step Over icon. In the Scope Variables area, you should see the value of `count` go to `0`—the value has been defined with a starting number of `0`.

4. Click the Step Over icon again. Now the value of `count` is 1, as expected, changed by the `count += 1;` line, which says "take the current value of `count` and increment it by one."

5. Click the Step Out icon three times to step out of this function and the jQuery functions in between. Notice that the value on the web page has gone to `1`.

6. Click the Continue icon (the Pause icon will change to a Continue icon as soon as the script is started) to allow the script to complete. So far, so good.

7. Click the button again in the web page. The debugger should activate again and be stopped in the same location as step 2. Notice that the value of `count` is undefined again, when common sense (but not our code) tells us it should be 1.

8. Click the Step Over icon; `count` changes to `0`. Click Step Over again and `count` changes to `1`. As the button is clicked, `count` is reset to undefined, set to `0`, and then incremented to `1`. This is not the desired behavior.

9. To fix the problem, return to the source code and switch lines 9 and 10 so that the definition of `count` happens before the definition of the function that uses it (`incCount()`). This change defines the variable `count` and sets the value only once when the script is loaded, and before the function is defined.

If you load the newly debugged file, you'll find that the counter increments as expected.

The preceding example was a basic example, but it was made simple so that it would be easy to follow the steps and get used to how the debugger works, early on in your education. Keep in mind these basic steps, and set a breakpoint and watch the variables as you step through the code.

Summary

In this chapter you learned various ways to validate and debug issues in your HTML, CSS, and JavaScript. You learned how to use the inspector within Chrome's Developer Tools to see the HTML elements and CSS styles and properties that the browser has rendered while loading a web page. Additionally, you learned the basics of reviewing JavaScript syntax errors in the console, and setting breakpoints and systematically stepping through the code to debug more complex problems.

The methods you learned in this chapter will be very helpful to you as you finish this book, not to mention in future projects, because they will save a lot of time and frustration with simple validation and syntax errors that always seem to creep into code (no matter how experienced you are).

Q&A

Q. I've seen web pages that don't have a `<!DOCTYPE>` tag at the beginning, yet it looks just fine. How is that possible?

A. Many web browsers forgive you if you forget to include the `<!DOCTYPE>` tag and display the page anyway by using their best guess as to which standard to follow. However, it's a good idea to include a proper `<!DOCTYPE>` tag not only because you want your pages to be bona fide valid HTML pages that conform to the latest web standards, but also because if you don't, and the browser applies a default standard that doesn't include the tags you've used in the code, the display will look incorrect.

Q. The Developer Tools seem really rich—what else can I debug with them?

A. You're right—there are a lot of elements of the Developer Tools in Chrome that aren't covered here, not to mention the idiosyncrasies of the other major browsers' implementations of Developer Tools. But in general you can use the Developer Tools to debug values stored in cookies, the status of external resources used by your script (are they found/not found, are they slow to load, and so on), and the amount of memory used by the page and its scripts, among other things.

Workshop

The Workshop contains quiz questions and exercises to help you solidify your understanding of the material covered. Try to answer all questions before looking at the "Answers" section that follows.

Quiz

1. Using Chrome's Developer Tools, how would you find the current value of the `background-color` CSS property for a specific `<div>` tag in a document?

2. Using a debugger, how do you stop code execution on a specific line of code?

3. Which section of Chrome Developer Tools enabled you to see the value of a variable as a script was stepped through?

Answers

1. Click on the Elements tab to open the Elements panel, and then select the specific `<div>` you're interested in—the current style values will appear in the right-most panel.

2. You can stop script execution on a particular line by setting a breakpoint. This is true of most debugging tools and is not specific to the Chrome Developer Tools.

3. The Scope Variables section of the Sources panel enables you to see the value of variables used in a script.

Exercises

▶ Continue debugging Listing 5.2 until the elements line up in ways that look appealing to you. As a hint, since you haven't explicitly learned these skills yet, try modifying values for widths and values for padding in the CSS.

▶ Use console logging to output specific strings at different points throughout your script. You can log to the console by inserting code like the following in your JavaScript, and then review these strings in the Console panel as the script executes:

```
console.log("Some string.");
```

CHAPTER 6
Working with Fonts, Text Blocks, Lists, and Tables

In the early days of the Web, text was displayed in only one font and one size. However, a combination of HTML and CSS now makes it possible to control the appearance of text (font type, size, color) and how it is aligned and displayed on a web page. In this chapter you'll learn how to change the visual display of the font—its font family, size, and weight—and how to incorporate boldface, italics, superscripts, subscripts, and strikethrough text into your pages. You will also learn how to change typefaces and font sizes. Then, after becoming conversant in these textual aspects, you'll learn the basics of text alignment and some advanced text tips and tricks, such as the use of lists. Because lists are so common, HTML provides tags that automatically indent text and add numbers, bullets, or other symbols in front of each listed item. You'll learn how to format different types of lists, which are part of the many ways to display content in your website. Finally, you'll learn how to build HTML tables that you can use to control the spacing, layout, and appearance of tabular data in your web content. Although you can achieve similar results using CSS, there are definitely times when a table is the best way to present information in rows and columns. You also see in this chapter how designers had to use tables for page layout in the past—and how to avoid ever doing that in the future.

WHAT YOU'LL LEARN IN THIS CHAPTER:

► How to use boldface, italics, and special text formatting

► How to tweak the font

► How to use special characters

► How to align text on a page

► How to use the three types of HTML lists

► How to place lists within lists

► How to create simple tables

► How to control the size of tables

► How to align content and span rows and columns within tables

► How to use CSS columns

▼ TRY IT YOURSELF

Preparing Sample Text

You can make the most of learning how to style text throughout this chapter if you have some sample text that you can use to display different fonts and colors, and that you can indent, center, or otherwise manipulate. It doesn't really matter what type of text you use because there are so many stylistic possibilities to try that they would never appear all on the same web page anyway (unless you wanted to drive your visitors batty). Take this opportunity just to get a feel for how text-level changes can affect the appearance of your content.

▶ If the text you'll be using is from a word processing or database program, be sure to save it to a new file in plain-text or ASCII format. You can then add the appropriate HTML tags and style attributes to format it as you go through this lesson.

▶ Any text will do, but try to find (or type) some text you want to put onto a web page. The text from a company brochure or from your résumé might be a good choice.

▶ Any type of outline, bullet points from a presentation, numbered steps, glossary, or list of textual information from a database will serve as good material to work with.

▶ Before you use the code introduced in this chapter to format the body text, add the set of skeleton HTML tags you've used in previous hours (at least the `<!DOCTYPE>`, `<html>`, `<head>`, `<title>`, and `<body>` tags).

NOTE

When viewing other designers' web content, you might notice methods of marking up text that are different from those this book teaches. Some telltale signs of the old way of formatting text include the use of the `<b></b>` tag pair to indicate when a word should be bolded, the `<i></i>` tag pair to indicate when a word should be in italics, and the `<font></font>` tag pair to specify font family, size, and other attributes. However, this method is being phased out of HTML, and CSS is considerably more powerful.

Working with Special Characters

Before we rush headlong into font changes, let's talk for a minute about special characters within fonts. Most fonts include special characters for European languages, such as the accented *é* in *café*. You'll also find a few mathematical symbols and special punctuation marks, such as the circular • bullet.

You can insert these special characters at any point in an HTML document using the appropriate codes in Table 6.1. You'll find an even more extensive list of codes for multiple character sets at the following URL:

    http://www.webstandards.org/learn/reference/named_entities.html

For example, you can produce the word *café* using either of the following methods:

```
caf&eacute;
caf&#233;
```

Table 6.1 Commonly Used English-Language Special Characters

Character	Numeric Code	Code Name	Description
" "	&#34;	&quot;	Quotation mark
&	&#38;	&amp;	Ampersand
<	&#60;	&lt;	Less than
>	&#62;	&gt;	Greater than
¢	&#162;	&cent;	Cents sign
£	&#163;	&pound;	Pound sterling
&#124;	&#166;	¦ or &brkbar;	Broken vertical bar
§	&#167;	&sect;	Section sign
©	&#169;	&copy;	Copyright
®	&#174;	&reg;	Registered trademark
°	&#176;	&deg;	Degree sign
±	&#177;	&plusmn;	Plus over minus
2	&#178;	&sup2;	Superscript two
3	&#179;	&sup3;	Superscript three
·	&#183;	&middot;	Middle dot
1	&#185;	&sup1;	Superscript one
¼	&#188;	&frac14;	Fraction one-fourth
½	&#189;	&frac12;	Fraction one-half
¾	&#190;	&frac34;	Fraction three-fourths
Æ	&#198;	&AElig;	Capital AE ligature
æ	&#230;	&aelig;	Small ae ligature
É	&#201;	&Eacute;	Accented capital E
é	&#233;	&eacute;	Accented lowercase e
×	&#215;	&times;	Multiplication sign
÷	&#247;	&divide;	Division sign

TIP

Looking for the copyright (©) and registered trademark (®) symbols? Those codes are © and ®, respectively.

To create an unregistered trademark (™) symbol, use ™.

Although you can specify character entities by number, each symbol also has a mnemonic name that is often easier to remember.

HTML uses a special code known as a *character entity* to represent special characters such as © and ®. Character entities are always specified starting with & and ending with ;. Table 6.1 lists the most commonly used character entities, although HTML supports many more.

Table 6.1 includes codes for the angle brackets, quotation, and ampersand. You must use those codes if you want these symbols to appear on your pages; otherwise, the web browser interprets them as HTML commands.

Listing 6.1 and Figure 6.1 show several of the symbols from Table 6.1 in use.

LISTING 6.1   Special Character Codes

```
<!DOCTYPE html>

<html lang="en">
  <head>
    <title>Punctuation Lines</title>

    <style type="text/css">
    section {
      margin-bottom: 20px;
    }
    </style>

  </head>

  <body>
    <section>
      Q: What should you do when a British banker picks a fight
      with you?<br />
      A: &pound; some &cent;&cent; into him.
    </section>
    <section>
      Q: What do you call it when a judge takes part of a law
      off the books?<br />
      A: &sect; violence.
    </section>
    <section>
      Q: What did the football coach get from the locker room
      vending machine in the middle of the game?<br />
      A: A &frac14; back at &frac12; time.
    </section>
    <section>
      Q: How hot did it get when the police detective interrogated
      the mathematician?<br />
      A: x&sup3;&deg;
    </section>
    <section>
      Q: What does a punctilious plagiarist do?<br />
      A: &copy;
    </section>
  </body>
</html>
```

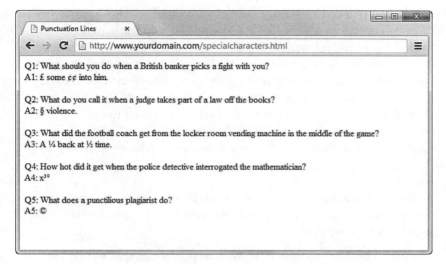

FIGURE 6.1
This is how the HTML page in Listing 6.1 looks in most web browsers.

Boldface, Italics, and Special Text Formatting

Way back in the age of the typewriter, we were content with a plain-text display and with using an occasional underline to show emphasis. Today, **boldface** and *italic* text have become de rigueur in all paper communication. Naturally, you can add bold and italic text to your web content as well. Several tags and style rules make text formatting possible.

The old-school approach—discussed briefly here because invariably you will see it in the source code of many websites, if you choose to look—to adding bold and italic formatting to text involves the `<b></b>` and `<i></i>` tag pairs. For boldface text, you wrap the `<b>` and `</b>` tags around your text. Similarly, to make any text appear in italics, you enclose it in `<i>` and `</i>` tags. Although this approach still works fine in browsers, it isn't as flexible or powerful as the CSS style rules for text formatting and should be avoided.

NOTE

Although you want to use styles wherever possible to affect presentation, an alternative to style rules when it comes to bold and italic text involves the `<strong></strong>` and `<em></em>` tag pairs. The `<strong>` tag does the same thing as the `<b>` tag in most browsers, whereas the `<em>` tag acts just like the tag `<i>` by formatting text as italics. Of course, you can style these tags however you'd like, but those are the defaults.

The `<strong>` and `<em>` tags are considered an improvement over `<b>` and `<i>` because they imply only that the text should receive special emphasis; they don't dictate exactly how that effect should be achieved. In other words, a browser doesn't necessarily have to interpret `<strong>` as meaning bold or `<em>` as meaning italic. This makes `<strong>` and `<em>` more fitting in HTML5 because they add meaning to text, along with affecting how the text should be displayed.

Part III, "Advanced Web Page Design with CSS," covers CSS style rules in more depth, but a little foreshadowing is appropriate here just so that you understand some basic text formatting options. The `font-weight` style rule enables you to set the weight, or boldness, of a font using a style rule. Standard settings for `font-weight` include `normal`, `bold`, `bolder`, and `lighter` (with `normal` being the default). Italic text is controlled via the `font-style` rule, which you can set to `normal`, `italic`, or `oblique`. You can specify style rules together as well if you want to apply more than one rule, as the following example demonstrates:

```
<p style="font-weight:bold; font-style:italic">This paragraph is
bold and italic!</p>
```

In this example, both style rules are specified in the `style` attribute of the `<p>` tag. The key to using multiple style rules is that they must be separated by a semicolon (`;`).

You aren't limited to using font styles in paragraphs, however. The following code shows how to italicize text in a bulleted list:

```
<ul>
  <li style="font-style:italic">Important Stuff</li>
  <li style="font-style:italic">Critical Information</li>
  <li style="font-style:italic">Highly Sensitive Material</li>
  <li>Nothing All That Useful</li>
</ul>
```

CAUTION

In the past, a `<u>` tag was useful in creating underlined text, but you don't want to use it now, for a couple of reasons. First, users expect underlined text to be a link, so they might get confused if you underline text that isn't a link. Second, the `<u>` tag is *obsolete*, which means that it has been phased out of the HTML language (as has the `<strike>` tag). Both tags are still supported in web browsers and likely will be for quite a while, but using CSS is the preferred approach to creating underlined and strikethrough text.

You can also use the `font-weight` style rule within headings, but a heavier font usually doesn't have an effect on headings because they are already bold by default.

Although using CSS enables you to apply richer formatting, there are a few other HTML5 tags that are good for adding special formatting to text when you don't necessarily need to be as specific as CSS enables you to be. Following are some of these tags. Listing 6.2 and Figure 6.2 demonstrate each tag in action.

▶ `<sup></sup>`—Superscript text

▶ `<sub></sub>`—Subscript text

▶ `<em></em>`—Emphasized (typically italic) text

▶ `<strong></strong>`—Strong (typically boldface) text

▶ `<pre></pre>`—Monospaced text, preserving spaces and line breaks

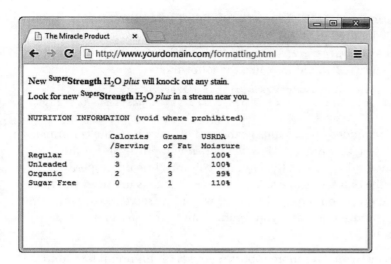

FIGURE 6.2
Here's what the character formatting from Listing 6.2 looks like.

LISTING 6.2 Special Formatting Tags

```
<!DOCTYPE html>

<html lang="en">
  <head>
    <title>The Miracle Product</title>
  </head>

  <body>
    <p>
      New <sup>Super</sup><strong>Strength</strong> H<sub>2</sub>O
      <em>plus</em> will knock out any stain.<br/>Look for new
       <sup>Super</sup><strong>Strength</strong>
      H<sub>2</sub>O <em>plus</em> in a stream near you.
    </p>
    <pre>
NUTRITION INFORMATION (void where prohibited)

              Calories   Grams   USRDA
              /Serving   of Fat  Moisture
Regular          3          4      100%
Unleaded         3          2      100%
Organic          2          3       99%
Sugar Free       0          1      110%
    </pre>
  </body>
</html>
```

The `<pre>` tag causes text to appear in the monospaced font—and does something else unique and useful. As you learned in Chapter 2,

"Structuring an HTML Document," multiple spaces and line breaks are normally ignored in HTML files, but `<pre>` causes exact spacing and line breaks to be preserved. For example, without `<pre>`, the text at the end of Figure 6.2 would look like the following:

```
calories grams usrda /serving of fat moisture regular
3 4 100% unleaded 3 2 100% organic 2 3 99% sugar free 0 1 110%
```

Even if you added `<br />` tags at the end of every line, the columns wouldn't line up properly. However, when you put `<pre>` at the beginning and `</pre>` at the end, the columns line up properly because the exact spaces are kept—no `<br />` tags are needed. The `<pre>` tag gives you a quick and easy way to preserve the alignment of any monospaced text files you might want to transfer to a web page with minimum effort.

CSS provides you with more robust methods for lining up text (and doing anything with text, actually), and you'll learn more about them throughout Part III.

Tweaking the Font

Sometimes you want a bit more control over the size and appearance of your text than just some boldface or italics. Before I get into the appropriate way to tinker with the font using CSS, let's briefly look at how things were done *before* CSS—you might still find examples of this method when you look at the source code for other websites. Remember, just because these older methods are in use doesn't mean you should follow suit.

Before style sheets entered the picture, the now-phased-out `<font>` tag was used to control the fonts in web page text.

For example, the following HTML was once used to change the size and color of some text on a page:

```
<font size="5" color="purple">This text will be big and purple.
</font>
```

As you can see, the size and color attributes of the `<font>` tag made it possible to alter the font of the text without too much effort. Although this approach worked fine, it was replaced with a far superior approach to font formatting, thanks to CSS style rules. Following are a few of the main style rules used to control fonts:

▶ `font-family`—Sets the family (typeface) of the font

▶ `font-size`—Sets the size of the font

▶ `color`—Sets the color of the font

The `font-family` style rule enables you to set the typeface used to display text. You can and usually should specify more than one value for this style (separated by commas) so that if the first font isn't available on a user's system, the browser can try an alternative.

Providing alternative font families is important because each user potentially has a different set of fonts installed, at least beyond a core set of common basic fonts (Arial, Times New Roman, and so forth). By providing a list of alternative fonts, you have a better chance of your pages gracefully falling back on a known font when your ideal font isn't found.

Following is an example of the `font-family` style used to set the typeface for a paragraph of text:

```
<p style="font-family:arial, sans-serif, 'times roman'">
```

This example has several interesting parts. First, `arial` is specified as the primary font. Capitalization does not affect the font family, so `arial` is no different from `Arial` or `ARIAL`. Another interesting point about this code is how single quotes are used around the times roman font name because it has a space in it. However, because `'times roman'` appears after the generic specification of `sans-serif`, it is unlikely that `'times roman'` would be used. Because `sans-serif` is in the second position, it says to the browser "if Arial is not on this machine, use the default sans-serif font."

The `font-size` and `color` style rules are also commonly used to control the size and color of fonts. The `font-size` style can be set to a predefined size (such as `small`, `medium`, or `large`), or you can set it to a specific point size (such as `12pt` or `14pt`). The `color` style can be set to a predefined color (such as `white`, `black`, `blue`, `red`, or `green`), or you can set it to a specific hexadecimal color (such as `#ffb499`). Following is a better version of the previous paragraph example, and with the font size and color specified:

```
<p style="font-family:arial, 'times roman', sans-serif;
        font-size:14pt; color:green">
```

NOTE

You'll learn more about controlling the color of the text on your pages in Chapter 8, "Working with Colors, Images, and Multimedia." That chapter also shows you how to create your own custom colors and how to control the color of text links.

NOTE

You'll learn about hexadecimal colors in Chapter 8. For now, just understand that the `color` style rule enables you to specify exact colors beyond just using `green`, `blue`, `orange`, and so forth.

The sample web content in Listing 6.3 and shown in Figure 6.3 uses some font style rules to create the beginning of a basic online résumé.

LISTING 6.3   Using Font Style Rules to Create a Basic Résumé

```
<!DOCTYPE html>

<html lang="en">
  <head>
    <title>R&eacute;sum&eacute; for Jane Doe</title>

    <style type="text/css">
      body {
        font-family: Verdana, sans-serif;
        font-size: 12px;
      }

      header {
        text-align: center;
      }

      h1 {
        font-family:Georgia, serif;
        font-size: 28px;
        text-align: center;
      }

      p.contactinfo {
        font-size: 14px;
      }

      p.categorylabel {
        font-size: 12px;
        font-weight: bold;
        text-transform: uppercase;
      }

      div.indented {
        margin-left: 25px;
      }
    </style>
  </head>
  <body>
      <header>
      <h1>Jane Doe</h1>
      <p class="contactinfo">1234 Main Street, Sometown,
      CA 93829<br/>
      tel: 555-555-1212, e-mail: jane@doe.com</p>
      </header>
      <section>
      <p class="categorylabel">Summary of Qualifications</p>
```

```
<ul>
<li>Highly skilled and dedicated professional offering a
solid background in whatever it is you need.</li>
<li>Provide comprehensive direction for whatever it is
that will get me a job.</li>
<li>Computer proficient in a wide range of industry-related
computer programs and equipment. Any industry.</li>
</ul>

</section>
<section>
<p class="categorylabel">Professional Experience</p>
<div class="indented">
        <p><strong>Operations Manager,
        Super Awesome Company, Some City, CA [Sept 2002 -
        present]</strong></p>
        <ul>
        <li>Direct all departmental operations</li>
        <li>Coordinate work with internal and external
        resources</li>
        <li>Generally in charge of everything</li>
        </ul>
        <p><strong>Project Manager,
        Less Awesome Company, Some City, CA [May 2000 - Sept
        2002]</strong></p>
        <ul>
        <li>Direct all departmental operations</li>
        <li>Coordinate work with internal and external
        resources</li>
        <li>Generally in charge of everything</li>
        </ul>
</div>
</section>
<section>
<p class="categorylabel">Education</p>
<ul>
<li>MBA, MyState University, May 2002</li>
<li>B.A, Business Administration, MyState University,
May 2000</li>
</ul>
</section>
<section>
<p class="categorylabel">References</p>
<ul>
<li>Available upon request.</li>
</ul>
</section>
</body>
</html>
```

FIGURE 6.3
Here's what the code used in Listing 6.3 looks like.

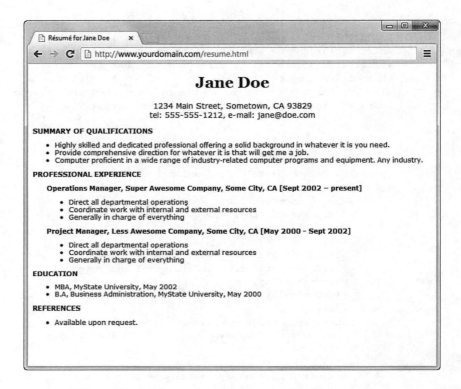

Using CSS, which organizes sets of styles into classes—as you learned in Chapter 3, "Understanding Cascading Style Sheets"—you can see how text formatting is applied to different areas of this content. If you look closely at the definition of the `div.indented` class, you will see the use of the `margin-left` style. This style, which you will learn more about in Part III, applies a certain amount of space (25 pixels, in this example) to the left of the element. That space accounts for the indentation shown in Figure 6.3.

Using Web Fonts

In the preceding section, you saw uses of font families that we're pretty sure reside on everyone's computers. That is, you can be assured that most computers would render Arial or Times New Roman, or have a go-to default font for serif and sans-serif, if that's what your stylesheet calls for. But with the inclusion of the `@font-face` feature in CSS3, you can wield even greater design power over the content you place online.

In brief, the `@font-face` feature enables you to define fonts for use in your HTML5 markup so that they are displayed to users regardless of whether they have those fonts installed on their computer (and chances are incredibly great that users do not have your selected fancy font on their own computer). The definition of the font can be local (to your web server, if you care to include font files there) or remote (you can link to locations where many fonts are stored).

In your stylesheet, to define a new font for use throughout your page(s), you can simply use the following structure:

```
@font-face {
    font-family: 'some_name_goes_here';
    src: url('some_location_of_the_font_file');
}
```

After it's defined, you can refer to the `font-family` as you would anywhere else in your stylesheet, such as here:

```
h1 {
  font-family: 'some_name_goes_here';
  font-size: 28px;
  text-align: center;
}
```

But where do you get fonts, you might ask? You can obtain fonts from many locations—some free, others not. A widely popular location is Google Web Fonts (http://www.google.com/fonts), not only because the fonts are free but also because Google is widely recognized as providing a stable platform, which is important if your web typography relies on a font that's sitting on someone else's web server. Some other reliable pay sites for obtaining fonts are TypeKit (typekit.com/) and Fontspring (www.fontspring.com). Pay sites aren't necessarily bad—artists have to make money, too; I have a personal TypeKit subscription and am very happy with their service, but I also use Google Web Fonts for many projects.

Let's take a look at modifying the code in Listing 6.3 to include a Google Web Font for the `h1` element. If you go to www.google.com/fonts and select a font you like, Google gives you code to include in your HTML and CSS. I've selected a font called Cherry Swash, and Google has advised me to include the following in my HTML template, in the `<head>` section:

```
<link href='http://fonts.googleapis.com/css?family=Cherry+
Swash:400,700'
    rel='stylesheet' type='text/css' />
```

NOTE

If you look at the Google link location, you can see that it is Google's `@font-face` definition already done for us. Specifically, it says:

```
@font-face {
  font-family: 'Cherry
Swash';
  font-style: normal;
  font-weight: 400;
  src: local('Cherry
Swash'),
local('CherrySwash-
Regular'), url(http://
themes.googleusercontent.
com/static/fonts/
cherryswash/v1/
HqOk7C7J1TZ5i3L-
ejF0vnhCUOGz7vYGh680lGh-
uXM.woff) format('woff');
}
@font-face {
  font-family: 'Cherry
Swash';
  font-style: normal;
  font-weight: 700;
  src: local('Cherry
Swash Bold'),
local('CherrySwash-
Bold'), url(http://themes.
googleusercontent.com/
static/fonts/cherryswash/
v1/-CfyMyQqfucZPQNB0nvYy
Hl4twXkwp3_
u9ZoePkT564.woff)
format('woff');
}
```

Now that my code knows where to look for the font, we just refer to it:

```
h1 {
  font-family:'Cherry Swash';
  font-size:28px;
  text-align:center;
}
```

Figure 6.4 shows the new résumé with the web font in use.

FIGURE 6.4
The résumé, using Cherry Swash
as the font in the heading.

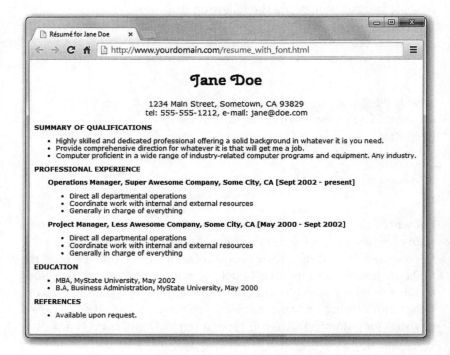

Aligning Text on a Page

It's easy to take for granted the fact that most paragraphs are automatically aligned to the left when you're reading information on the Web. However, there certainly are situations in which you might choose to align content to the right or even the center of a page. HTML gives you the option to align a single HTML block-level element, such as text contained within a `<p></p>` or `<div></div>` tag pair. Before we get into the details of aligning block elements, however, let's briefly note how attributes work.

Using Attributes

Attributes provide additional information related to an HTML tag. *Attributes* are special code words used inside an HTML tag to control exactly what the tag does. They are very important in even the simplest bit of web content, so it's important that you are comfortable using them.

Attributes invoke the use of styles, classes, or IDs that are applied to particular tags. If you define a particular class or ID in a style sheet—as you learned in Chapter 3—then you can invoke that class or ID using `class="someclass"` or `id="someid"` within the tag itself. When the browser renders the content for display, it will look to the style sheet to determine exactly how the content will appear according to the associated style definitions. Similarly, you can use the `style` attribute to include style information for a particular element without connecting the element to an actual style sheet—this is the inline style format you learned about in Chapter 3.

In the following example, each paragraph could be left-aligned:

```
<p style="text-align: left;">Text goes here.</p>
<p class="leftAlignStyle">Text goes here.</p>
<p id="firstLeftAlign">Text goes here.</p>
```

In the first paragraph, the style appears directly in the `style` attribute—this is useful for debugging or for short-term formatting tests, but not so much for ongoing maintenance of your web content. In the second paragraph, the paragraph will be left-aligned if the style sheet entry for the `leftAlignStyle` class includes the `text-align` statement; remember, using a class means that other tags can reuse the class. Similarly, the third paragraph will be left-aligned if the style sheet entry for the `firstLeftAlign` id includes the `text-align` statement; remember, using an `id` means that these styles can be applied to only the one identified tag.

Aligning Block-Level Elements

To align text in a block-level element such as `<p>` to the right margin without creating a separate class or ID in a style sheet, simply place `style="text-align:right"` inside the `<p>` tag at the beginning of the paragraph (or define it in a class or an `id`). Similarly, to center the text in the element, use `<p style="text-align:center">`. To align text in a paragraph to the left, use `<p style="text-align:left">`.

NOTE

Every attribute and style rule in HTML has a default value that is assumed when you don't set the attribute yourself. In the case of the `text-align` style rule of the `<p>` tag, the default value is `left`, so using the bare-bones `<p>` tag has the same effect as using `<p style="text-align:left">`. Learning the default values for common style rules is an important part of becoming a good web page developer.

The `text-align` part of the `style` attribute is referred to as a *style rule*, which means that it is setting a particular style aspect of an HTML element. You can use many style rules to carefully control the formatting of web content.

The `text-align` style rule is not reserved for just the `<p>` tag. In fact, you can use the `text-align` style rule with any block-level element, which includes semantic elements such as `<section>` and `<header>`, as well as `<h1>`, `<h2>`, the other heading-level tags, and the `<div>` tag, among others. The `<div>` tag is especially handy because it can encompass other block-level elements and thus allow you to control the alignment of large portions of your web content all at once. The *div* in the `<div>` tag is for *division*.

Listing 6.4 demonstrates the `style` attribute and `text-align` style rule with different block-level elements. Figure 6.5 displays the results.

LISTING 6.4   The `text-align` Style Rule Used with the `style` Attribute

```
<!DOCTYPE html>

<html lang="en">
  <head>
    <title>Bohemia</title>
  </head>

  <body>
    <section style="text-align:center">

    <header>
      <h1>Bohemia</h1>
      <h2>by Dorothy Parker</h2>
    </header>
    </section>
    <section>
      <p style="text-align:left">
      Authors and actors and artists and such<br />
      Never know nothing, and never know much.<br />
      Sculptors and singers and those of their kidney<br />
      Tell their affairs from Seattle to Sydney.
      </p>
      <p style="text-align:center">
      Playwrights and poets and such horses' necks<br />
      Start off from anywhere, end up at sex.<br />
      Diarists, critics, and similar roe<br />
      Never say nothing, and never say no.
      </p>
      <p style="text-align:right">
```

```
      People Who Do Things exceed my endurance;<br />
      God, for a man that solicits insurance!
      </p>
      </section>
   </body>
</html>
```

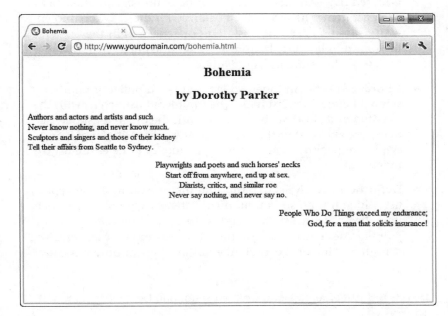

FIGURE 6.5
The results of using the text alignment in Listing 6.4.

The use of `<section style="text-align:center">` ensures that the content area, including the two headings, is centered. However, the inline styles applied to the individual paragraphs within the `<section>` override the setting and ensure that the text of the first paragraph is left-aligned, the second paragraph is centered, and the third paragraph is right-aligned.

The Three Types of HTML Lists

For clarity, it's often useful to present information on a web page as a list of items. There are three basic types of HTML lists. All three are shown in Figure 6.6, and Listing 6.5 reveals the HTML used to construct them.

► **Ordered list**—An indented list that has numbers or letters before each list item. The ordered list begins with the `<ol>` tag and ends with a closing `</ol>` tag. List items are enclosed in the `<li></li>` tag pair and line breaks appear automatically at each opening `<li>` tag. The entire list is indented.

► **Unordered list**—An indented list that has a bullet or another symbol before each list item. The unordered list begins with the `<ul>` tag and closes with `</ul>`. As with the ordered list, its list items are enclosed in the `<li></li>` tag pair. A line break and symbol appear at each opening `<li>` tag, and the entire list is indented.

► **Definition list**—A list of terms and their meanings. This type of list, which has no special number, letter, or symbol before each item, begins with `<dl>` and ends with `</dl>`. The `<dt></dt>` tag pair encloses each term and the `<dd></dd>` tag pair encloses each definition. Line breaks and indentations appear automatically.

LISTING 6.5   Unordered Lists, Ordered Lists, and Definition Lists

```
<!DOCTYPE html>

<html lang="en">
  <head>
    <title>How to Be Proper</title>
  </head>

  <body>
    <article>

    <header>
      <h1>How to Be Proper</h1>
    </header>
    <section>
      <header>
        <h1>Basic Etiquette for a Gentleman Greeting a
        Lady Acquaintance</h1>
```

```
    </header>
    <ul>
    <li>Wait for her acknowledging bow before tipping your
    hat.</li>
    <li>Use the hand farthest from her to raise the hat.</li>
    <li>Walk with her if she expresses a wish to converse;
    never make a lady stand talking in the street.</li>
    <li>When walking, the lady must always have the wall.</li>
    </ul>
</section>

<section>
    <header>
        <h1>Recourse for a Lady Toward Unpleasant Men Who
        Persist in Bowing</h1>
    </header>
    <ol>
    <li>A simple stare of iciness should suffice in most
    instances.</li>
    <li>A cold bow discourages familiarity without offering
    insult.</li>
    <li>As a last resort: "Sir, I have not the honour of your
    acquaintance."</li>
    </ol>
</section>

<section>
    <header>
        <h1>Proper Address of Royalty</h1>
    </header>

    <dl>
    <dt>Your Majesty</dt>
    <dd>To the king or queen.</dd>
    <dt>Your Royal Highness</dt>
    <dd>To the monarch's spouse, children, and siblings.</dd>
    <dt>Your Highness</dt>
    <dd>To nephews, nieces, and cousins of the sovereign.</dd>
    </dl>
</section>
</article>
</body>
</html>
```

FIGURE 6.6
The three basic types of HTML lists.

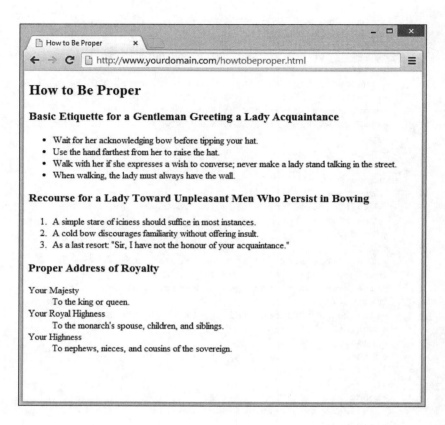

Note the use of semantic elements (`<article>`, `<section>`, and `<header>`) in Listing 6.5 to provide a better sense of the content outline, including how the chunks of text relate to one another. Each of these elements could have their own styles applied to them, which would provide further visual separation of the elements.

Placing Lists Within Lists

Although definition lists are officially supposed to be used for defining terms, many web page authors use them anywhere they'd like to see some indentation. In practice, you can indent any text simply by putting `<dl><dd>` at the beginning of it and `</dd></dl>` at the end and skipping over the `<dt></dt>` tag pair.

Because of the level of control over the display of your items that you have when using CSS, there is no need to use *nested* lists to achieve the visual appearance of indentation. Reserve your use of nested lists for when the content warrants it. In other words, use nested lists to show a hierarchy of information, such as in Listing 6.6.

Ordered and unordered lists can be nested inside one another, down to as many levels as you want. In Listing 6.6, a complex indented outline is constructed from several unordered lists. Notice in Figure 6.7 that the web browser automatically uses a different type of bullet for each of the first three levels of indentation, making the list very easy to read. This is common in modern browsers.

NOTE

Nesting refers to a tag that appears entirely within another tag. Nested tags are also referred to as *child tags* of the (parent) tag that contains them. It is a common (but not required) coding practice to indent nested tags so that you can easily see their relationship to the parent tag.

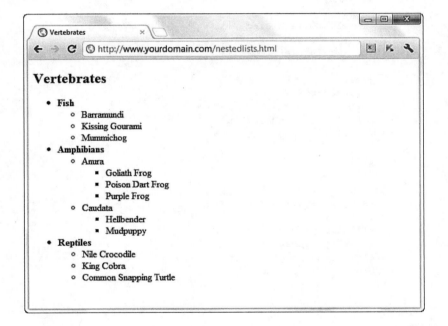

FIGURE 6.7
Multilevel unordered lists are neatly indented and bulleted for improved readability.

LISTING 6.6   Using Lists to Build Outlines

```
<!DOCTYPE html>

<html lang="en">
  <head>
    <title>Vertebrates</title>
  </head>

  <body>
    <section>

      <header>
      <h1>Vertebrates</h1>
```

```
    </header>

    <ul>
      <li><strong>Fish</strong>
        <ul>
          <li>Barramundi</li>
          <li>Kissing Gourami</li>
          <li>Mummichog</li>
        </ul>
      </li>
      <li><strong>Amphibians</strong>
        <ul>
          <li>Anura
            <ul>
              <li>Goliath Frog</li>
              <li>Poison Dart Frog</li>
              <li>Purple Frog</li>
            </ul>
          </li>
          <li>Caudata
            <ul>
              <li>Hellbender</li>
              <li>Mudpuppy</li>
            </ul>
          </li>
        </ul>
      </li>
      <li><strong>Reptiles</strong>
        <ul>
          <li>Nile Crocodile</li>
          <li>King Cobra</li>
          <li>Common Snapping Turtle</li>
        </ul>
      </li>
    </ul>
  </body>
</html>
```

As Figure 6.7 shows, a web browser normally uses a solid disc for the first-level bullet, a hollow circle for the second-level bullet, and a solid square for all deeper levels. However, you can explicitly choose which type of bullet to use for any level by using `<ul style="list-style-type:disc">`, `<ul style="list-style-type:circle">`, or `<ul style="list-style-type:square">` instead of `<ul>`, either inline or in a specific style sheet.

You can even change the bullet for any single point within an unordered list by using the `list-style-type` style rule in the `<li>` tag.

For example, the following code displays a hollow circle in front of the words `extra` and `super`, and a solid square in front of the word `special`:

```
<ul style="list-style-type:circle">
  <li>extra</li>
  <li>super</li>
  <li style="list-style-type:square">special</li>
</ul>
```

The `list-style-type` style rule also works with ordered lists, but instead of choosing a type of bullet, you choose the type of numbers or letters to place in front of each item. Listing 6.7 shows how to use Roman numerals (`list-style-type:upper-roman`), capital letters (`list-style-type:upper-alpha`), lowercase letters (`list-style-type:lower-alpha`), and ordinary numbers in a multilevel list. Figure 6.8 shows the resulting outline, which is nicely formatted.

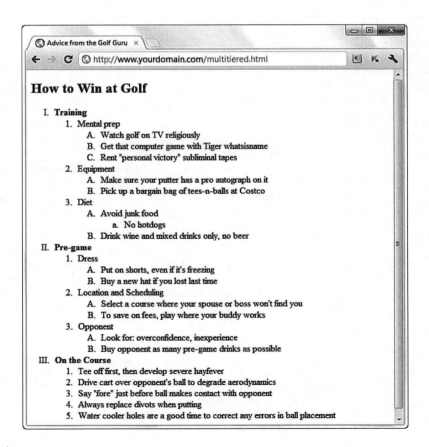

FIGURE 6.8
A well-formatted outline can make almost any plan look more plausible.

Although Listing 6.7 uses the `list-style-type` style rule only with the `<ol>` tag, you can also use it for specific `<li>` tags within a list (though it's hard to imagine a situation when you would want to do this). You can also explicitly specify ordinary numbering with `list-style-type:decimal`, and you can make lowercase Roman numerals with `list-style-type:lower-roman`.

LISTING 6.7   Using the `list-style-type` Style Rule with the `style` Attribute in Multitiered Lists

```
<!DOCTYPE html>

<html lang="en">
  <head>
    <title>Advice from the Golf Guru</title>
  </head>

  <body>
    <article>

    <header>
    <h1>How to Win at Golf</h1>
    </header>

    <ol style="list-style-type:upper-roman">
      <li><strong>Training</strong>
        <ol>
          <li>Mental prep
            <ol style="list-style-type:upper-alpha">
              <li>Watch golf on TV religiously</li>
              <li>Get that computer game with Tiger whatsisname
              </li>
              <li>Rent "personal victory" subliminal tapes</li>
            </ol>
          </li>
          <li>Equipment
            <ol style="list-style-type:upper-alpha">
              <li>Make sure your putter has a pro autograph on it
              </li>
              <li>Pick up a bargain bag of tees-n-balls at Costco
              </li>
            </ol>
          </li>
          <li>Diet
            <ol style="list-style-type:upper-alpha">
              <li>Avoid junk food
                <ol style="list-style-type:lower-alpha">
                  <li>No hotdogs</li>
                </ol>
              </li>
```

```
        <li>Drink wine and mixed drinks only, no beer</li>
      </ol>
    </li>
  </ol>
</li>
<li><strong>Pre-game</strong>
  <ol>
    <li>Dress
      <ol style="list-style-type:upper-alpha">
        <li>Put on shorts, even if it's freezing</li>
        <li>Buy a new hat if you lost last time</li>
      </ol>
    </li>
    <li>Location and Scheduling
      <ol style="list-style-type:upper-alpha">
        <li>Select a course where your spouse or boss won't
        find you</li>
        <li>To save on fees, play where your buddy works</li>
      </ol>
    </li>
    <li>Opponent
      <ol style="list-style-type:upper-alpha">
        <li>Look for: overconfidence, inexperience</li>
        <li>Buy opponent as many pre-game drinks as
        possible</li>
      </ol>
    </li>
  </ol>
</li>
<li><strong>On the Course</strong>
  <ol>
    <li>Tee off first, then develop severe hayfever</li>
    <li>Drive cart over opponent's ball to degrade
    aerodynamics</li>
    <li>Say "fore" just before ball makes contact with
    opponent</li>
    <li>Always replace divots when putting</li>
    <li>Water cooler holes are a good time to correct any
    errors in Ball placement</li>
  </ol>
</li>
  </ol>
  </article>
  </body>
</html>
```

Creating a Simple Table

Another method for controlling the layout of information within your web pages is to display that information within a table. A table consists of rows of information with individual cells inside. To make tables, you have to start with a `<table>` tag. Of course, you end your tables with the `</table>` tag. CSS contains numerous properties that enable you to modify the table itself, such as the various border properties you learned about in previous chapters.

With the `<table>` tag in place, you next need the `<tr>` tag. The `<tr>` tag creates a table row, which contains one or more cells of information before the closing `</tr>`. To create these individual cells, use the `<td>` tag (`<td>` stands for *table data*). Place the table information between the `<td>` and `</td>` tags. A *cell* is a rectangular region that can contain any text, images, and HTML tags. Each row in a table consists of at least one cell. Multiple cells within a row form columns in a table.

One more basic tag is involved in building tables. The `<th>` tag works exactly like a `<td>` tag, except that `<th>` indicates that the cell is part of the heading of the table. Most web browsers automatically render the text in `<th>` cells as centered and boldface, as you can see with Chrome in Figure 6.9. However, if your browser does not automatically render this element with a built-in style, you have an element that you can style using CSS without using a class to differentiate among types of table data elements.

FIGURE 6.9
The code in Listing 6.8 creates a table with six rows and four columns.

You can create as many cells as you want, but each row in a table should have the same number of columns as the other rows. The HTML code in Listing 6.8 creates a simple table using only the four table tags I've mentioned thus far.

LISTING 6.8   Creating Tables with the `<table>`, `<tr>`, `<td>`, and `<th>` Tags

```
<!DOCTYPE html>

<html lang="en">
  <head>
    <title>Baseball Standings</title>
  </head>

  <body>
  <h1>Baseball Standings</h1>
    <table>
      <tr>
        <th>Team</th>
        <th>W</th>
        <th>L</th>
        <th>GB</th>
      </tr>
      <tr>
        <td>San Francisco Giants</td>
        <td>54</td>
        <td>46</td>
        <td>8.0</td>
      </tr>
      <tr>
        <td>Los Angeles Dodgers</td>
        <td>62</td>
        <td>38</td>
        <td>—</td>
      </tr>
      <tr>
      <tr>
        <td>Colorado Rockies</td>
        <td>54</td>
        <td>46</td>
        <td>8.0</td>
      </tr>
      <tr>
        <td>Arizona Diamondbacks</td>
        <td>43</td>
        <td>58</td>
        <td>19.5</td>
      </tr>
```

TIP

You might find your HTML tables easier to read (and less prone to time-wasting errors) if you use spaces to indent `<tr>` and `<td>` tags, as I did in Listing 6.8. Remember, browsers ignore spaces when rendering HTML, so the layout of your code has no effect on the layout of the table that people will see.

```
    <tr>
       <td>San Diego Padres</td>
       <td>39</td>
       <td>62</td>
       <td>23.5</td>
    </tr>
  </table>
 </body>
</html>
```

The table in the example contains baseball standings, which are perfect for arranging in rows and columns—but they're a little plain. For instance, this example doesn't even have any borders! You'll learn to jazz things up a bit in just a moment. The headings in the table show the Team, Wins (W), Losses (L), and Games Behind (GB) in the standings.

Adding the following stylesheet entries takes care of adding a basic border around the table and its cells:

```
table, tr, th, td {
   border: 1px solid black;
   border-collapse: collapse;
   padding: 3px;
}
```

You might wonder why you have to specify these styles for all four elements used to create the table instead of just the overall table element itself. Basically, this is because a table is made up of its elements, and each element can have these styles applied. The following figures demonstrate how the table would look with various elements styles or unstyled, to emphasize this point.

Figure 6.10 shows the output of the styles just listed. The `border-collapse` property, with a value of `collapse`, makes all the borders of the `<table>`, `<tr>`, and `<th>` or `<td>` elements collapse into one shared border. The padding adds a little breathing room to the content of the cells.

In Figure 6.11, you can see what the table would look like without the `border-collapse` property specified (the default value then takes effect, which is `separate`, for separate borders).

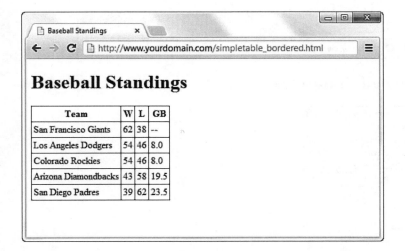

FIGURE 6.10
Adding some CSS styles to the table, including the use of `border-collapse`.

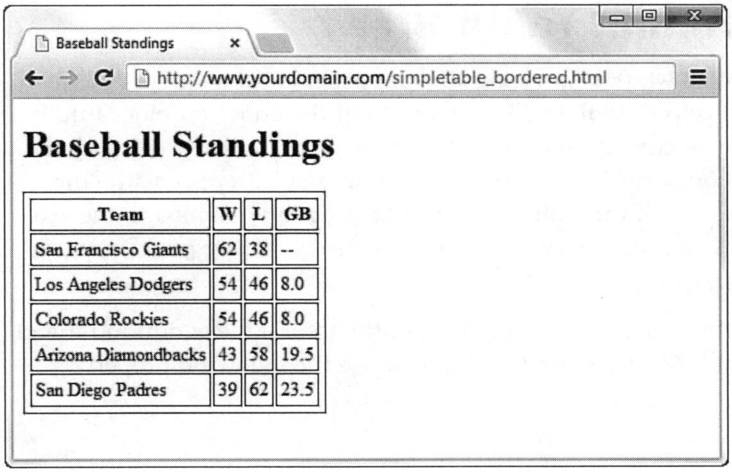

FIGURE 6.11
Removing the `border-collapse` property shows borders for all the elements.

In Figure 6.12, you can see what the table would look like without specifying any of the previous styles for the `<th>` and `<td>` elements—note the lack of border denoting the columns.

FIGURE 6.12
Removing the styles for the <th> and <td> elements.

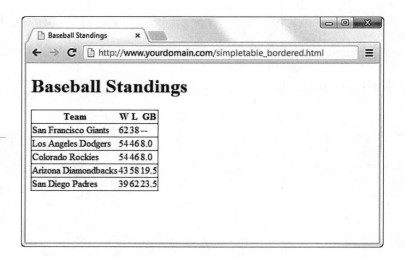

Baseball Standings ×

http://www.yourdomain.com/simpletable_bordered.html

Baseball Standings

Team	W	L	GB
San Francisco Giants	62	38	--
Los Angeles Dodgers	54	46	8.0
Colorado Rockies	54	46	8.0
Arizona Diamondbacks	43	58	19.5
San Diego Padres	39	62	23.5

TIP

You can employ three other useful but not required table-related tags when creating simple tables:

▶ <thead></thead>— Wrap your header rows in this element to add more meaning to the grouping and also allow these header rows to be printed across all pages (if your table is that long). You can then style the <thead> element instead of individual <th> cells.

▶ <tbody></tbody>—Wrap the rows that make up the "body" of this table (everything besides the header and the footer rows) in this element, to add more meaning to the grouping; you can then also style the <tbody> element as a whole instead of styling individual <td> cells.

▶ <tfoot></tfoot>—Much like the <thead> element, use this to wrap your footer rows (if you have any) in this element, to add more meaning to the grouping and style it as a whole. An example of a footer row might be a summation of the data presented in the columns, such as financial totals.

Controlling Table Sizes

When a table width is not specified, the size of a table and its individual cells automatically expand to fit the data you place into it. However, you can control the width of the entire table by defining the width CSS property for the <table> element; you can also define the width of each cell through the width CSS property assigned to the <td> elements. The width property can be specified as either pixels, ems, or percentages.

To make the first cell of a table 20% of the total table width and the second cell 80% of the table width, you use the following property definitions:

```
<table style="width:100%">
  <tr>
   <td style="width:20%">skinny cell</td>
   <td style="width:80%">fat cell</td>
  </tr>
</table>
```

Notice that the table is sized to 100%, which ensures that it fills the entire width of the browser window. When you use percentages instead of fixed pixel sizes, the table resizes automatically to fit any size browser window while maintaining the aesthetic balance you're seeking. In this case, the two cells within the table are automatically resized to 20% and 80% of the total table width, respectively.

In Listing 6.9, the simple table from Listing 6.8 (plus the border-related styles) is expanded to show very precise control over table cell widths (plus, the border-related styles have been added).

LISTING 6.9   Specifying Table Cell Widths

```
<!DOCTYPE html>

<html lang="en">
  <head>
    <title>Baseball Standings</title>

    <style type="text/css">
    table, tr, th, td {
       border: 1px solid black;
       border-collapse: collapse;
       padding: 3px;
    }
    </style>
  </head>

 <body>
  <h1>Baseball Standings</h1>
    <table>
      <tr>
        <th style="width: 200px;">Team</th>
        <th style="width: 25px;">W</th>
        <th style="width: 25px;">L</th>
        <th style="width: 25px;">GB</th>
      </tr>
      <tr>
        <td>San Francisco Giants</td>
        <td>62</td>
        <td>38</td>
        <td>--</td>
      </tr>
      <tr>
        <td>Los Angeles Dodgers</td>
        <td>54</td>
        <td>46</td>
        <td>8.0</td>
      </tr>
      <tr>
        <td>Colorado Rockies</td>
        <td>54</td>
        <td>46</td>
        <td>8.0</td>
      </tr>
      <tr>
        <td>Arizona Diamondbacks</td>
```

```
          <td>43</td>
          <td>58</td>
          <td>19.5</td>
        </tr>
        <tr>
          <td>San Diego Padres</td>
          <td>39</td>
          <td>62</td>
          <td>23.5</td>
        </tr>
      </table>
    </body>
</html>
```

You can see the consistent column widths in Figure 6.13.

The addition of a specific width style for each `<th>` element in the first row defines the widths of the columns. The first column is defined as 200px wide, and the second, third, and fourth columns are each 25px wide. In Figure 6.13, you can see whitespace after the text in the first column, indicating that the specified width is indeed greater than the column width would have been had the table been allowed to render without explicit width indicators.

FIGURE 6.13
The code in Listing 6.9 creates a table with six rows and four columns, with specific widths used for each column.

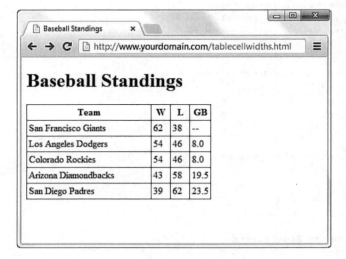

Also note that these widths are not repeated in the `<td>` elements in subsequent rows. Technically, you need to define the widths in only the first row; the remaining rows will follow suit because they are all part of the same table. However, if you had used another formatting style (such as a style to change font size or color), you would've had to repeat that style for each element that should have those display properties.

Alignment and Spanning Within Tables

By default, anything you place inside a table cell is aligned to the left and vertically centered. All the figures so far in this lesson have shown this default alignment. However, you can align the contents of table cells both horizontally and vertically with the `text-align` and `vertical-align` style properties.

You can apply these alignment attributes to any `<tr>`, `<td>`, or `<th>` tag. Alignment attributes assigned to a `<tr>` tag apply to all cells in that row. Depending on the size of your table, you can save yourself some time and effort by applying these attributes at the `<tr>` level and not in each `<td>` or `<th>` tag.

The HTML code in Listing 6.10 uses a combination of text alignment styles to apply a default alignment to a row, but it is overridden in a few individual cells. Figure 6.14 shows the result of the code in Listing 6.10.

Following are some of the more commonly used `vertical-align` style property values: `top`, `middle`, `bottom`, `text-top`, `text-bottom`, and `baseline` (for text). These property values give you plenty of flexibility in aligning table data vertically.

LISTING 6.10   Alignment, Cell Spacing, Borders, and Background Colors in Tables

```
<!DOCTYPE html>

<html lang="en">
  <head>
    <title>Things to Fear</title>
    <style type="text/css">
    table {
       border: 2px solid black;
```

TIP

Keeping the structure of rows and columns organized in your mind can be the most difficult part of creating tables with cells that span multiple columns or rows. The tiniest error can often throw the whole thing into disarray. You can save yourself time and frustration by sketching complicated tables on paper before you start writing the HTML to implement them.

```css
          border-collapse: collapse;
          padding: 3px;
          width: 100%;
      }

      tr, th, td {
          border: 2px solid black;
          border-collapse: collapse;
          padding: 3px;
      }

      thead {
          background-color: #ff0000;
          color: #ffffff;
      }

      .aligntop {
          vertical-align:top;
      }

      .description {
          font-size: 14px;
          font-weight: bold;
          vertical-align: middle;
          text-align: center;
      }

       .weight {
          text-align: center;
      }
      </style>

</head>

<body>
  <h1>Things to Fear</h1>
  <table>
    <thead>
       <tr>
       <th colspan="2">Description</th>
       <th>Size</th>
       <th>Weight</th>
       <th>Speed</th>
       </tr>
    </thead>
    <tr class="aligntop">
       <td><img src="handgun.gif" alt=".38 Special"/></td>
       <td class="description">.38 Special</td>
       <td>Five-inch barrel.</td>
       <td class="weight">20 oz.</td>
```

```
            <td>Six rounds in four seconds.</td>
        </tr>
        <tr class="aligntop">
            <td><img src="rhino.gif" alt="Rhinoceros" /></td>
            <td class="description">Rhinoceros</td>
            <td>Twelve feet, horn to tail.</td>
            <td class="weight">2 tons</td>
            <td>Thirty-five miles per hour in bursts.</td>
        </tr>
        <tr class="aligntop">
            <td><img src="axeman.gif" alt="Broad Axe" /></td>
            <td class="description">Broad Axe</td>
            <td>Thirty-inch blade.</td>
            <td class="weight">12 lbs.</td>
            <td>Sixty miles per hour on impact.</td>
        </tr>
    </table>
  </body>
</html>
```

NOTE

You often see alternating row colors in a table. For instance, one row might have a gray background, and the next row might have a white background. Alternating the row colors helps users read the content of your table more clearly, especially if the table is large.

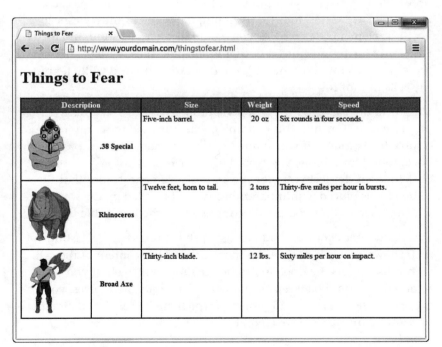

FIGURE 6.14
The code in Listing 6.10 shows the use of the colspan attribute and some alignment styles.

At the top of Figure 6.14, a single cell (`Description`) spans two columns. This is accomplished with the `colspan` attribute in the `<th>` tag for that cell. As you might guess, you can also use the `rowspan` attribute to create a cell that spans more than one row.

Spanning is the process of forcing a cell to stretch across more than one row or column of a table. The `colspan` attribute causes a cell to span multiple columns; `rowspan` has the same effect on rows.

Additionally, text styles are defined in the stylesheet and applied to the cells in the Description column to create bold text that is both vertically aligned to the middle and horizontally aligned to the center of the cell.

A few tricks in Listing 6.10 haven't been explained yet. You can give an entire table—and each individual row or cell in a table—its own background, distinct from any background you might use on the web page itself. You can do this by placing the `background-color` or `background-image` style in the `<table>`, `<tr>`, `<td>`, `<th>`, `<thead>`, `<tbody>`, or `<tfooter>` tags (or assigning the value in the stylesheet for these elements), exactly as you would in the `<body>` tag. In Listing 6.10, only the top row has a background color; the stylesheet defines the `<thead>` element as one with a red background and white text in the cells in that row.

Similar to the `background-color` style property is the `background-image` property (not shown in this example), which is used to set an image for a table background. If you wanted to set the image `leaves.gif` as the background for a table, you would use `background-image:url(leaves.gif)` in the stylesheet entry for the `<table>` element. Notice that the image file is placed within parentheses and preceded by the word `url`, which indicates that you are describing where the image file is located.

Tweaking tables goes beyond just using style properties. As Listing 6.10 shows, you can control the space around the content of the cell, within its borders, by applying some padding to the cell. If you want to add some space between the borders of the cells themselves, you can use the `border-spacing` CSS property, which enables you to define the horizontal and vertical spacing like so:

```
border-spacing: 2px 4px;
```

In the example, spacing is defined as 2 pixels of space between the horizontal borders, and 4 pixels of space between the vertical borders. If you use only one value, the value is applied to all four borders.

Page Layout with Tables

At the beginning of this chapter, I indicated that designers have used tables for page layout, as well as to display tabular information. You will still find many examples of table-based layouts if you peek at another designer's source code. This method of design grew out of inconsistencies in browser support for CSS in the mid-1990s to early 2000s. Because all browsers supported tables, and in generally the same way, web designers latched on to the table-based method of content layout to achieve the same visual page display across all browsers. However, now that support for CSS is relatively similar across all major browsers, designers can follow the long-standing standards-based recommendation *not* to use tables for page layout.

The World Wide Web Consortium (W3C), the standards body that oversees the future of the web, has long promoted style sheets as the proper way to lay out pages (instead of using tables). Style sheets are ultimately much more powerful than tables, which is why the bulk of this book teaches you how to use style sheets for page layout.

The main reasons for avoiding using tables for layout include these:

▶ **Mixing presentation with content**—One goal of CSS and standards-compliant web design is to separate the presentation layer from the content layer.

▶ **Creating unnecessarily difficult redesigns**—To change a table-based layout, you have to change the table-based layout on every single page of your site (unless it is part of a complicated, dynamically driven site, in which case you have to undo all the dynamic pieces and remake them).

▶ **Addressing accessibility issues**—Screen reading software looks to tables for content and often tries to read layout tables as content tables.

▶ **Rendering on mobile devices**—Table layouts are often not flexible enough to scale downward to small screens (see Chapter 12, "Creating Fixed or Liquid Layouts").

These are but a few of the issues in table-based web design. For a closer look at some of these issues, see the popular presentation "Why Tables for Layout Is Stupid," at http://www.hotdesign.com/seybold/everything.html.

Using CSS Columns

If you have a large amount of text-only information, you might want to present it much like a physical newspaper does: in columns. Over a hundred years of research have shown a correlation between the length of a line and reading speed, and indicated a "sweet spot," or optimum length of a line that allows for a quick and enjoyable reading experience. The continued presence of this sweet spot—lines that are around 4 inches long—is why physical newspapers still present information in columns.

If you have a lot of information to present to readers, or if you simply want to mimic the aesthetic of a newspaper layout, you can use CSS columns. True, you could also use a table, because tables are made of rows and columns, but the preceding section explained some of the reasons to avoid a table-based layout. Also, columns aren't just for text; you can put anything you want into defined columns, such as advertisements or related text in a sidebar.

In Figure 6.15, you can see a basic use of CSS columns, to define a traditional newspaper-type layout. The code in Listing 6.11 shows this layout.

FIGURE 6.15
The code in Listing 6.11 shows a three-column layout.

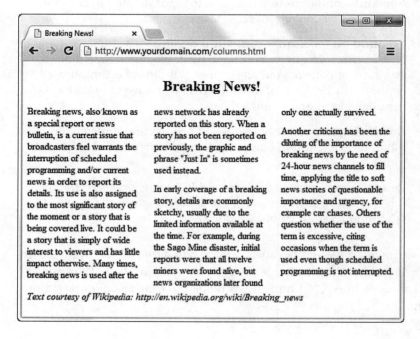

LISTING 6.11 Alignment, Cell Spacing, Borders, and Background Colors in
Tables

```
<!DOCTYPE html>

<html lang="en">
  <head>
    <title>Breaking News!</title>
    <style type="text/css">
    article {
        -webkit-column-count: 3;
        -webkit-column-gap: 21px;

        -moz-column-count: 3;
        -moz-column-gap: 21px;

        column-count: 3;
        column-gap: 21px;
    }

    h1 {
        text-align: center;
        -webkit-column-span: all;
        -moz-column-span: all;
        column-span: all;
    }

    p {
        margin-top: 0px;
        margin-bottom: 12px;
    }

    footer {
        -webkit-column-span: all;
        -moz-column-span: all;
        column-span: all;
    }
    </style>
  </head>

  <body>
    <article>

      <header>
        <h1>Breaking News!</h1>
      </header>

        <p>Breaking news, also known as a special report or news
        bulletin, is a current issue that broadcasters feel warrants
        the interruption of scheduled programming and/or current news
```

```
in order to report its details. Its use is also assigned to
the most significant story of the moment or a story that is
being covered live. It could be a story that is simply of
wide interest to viewers and has little impact otherwise.
Many times, breaking news is used after the news network has
already reported on this story. When a story has not been
reported on previously, the graphic and phrase "Just In" is
sometimes used instead.</p>

<p>In early coverage of a breaking story, details are
commonly sketchy, usually due to the limited information
available at the time. For example, during the Sago Mine
disaster, initial reports were that all twelve miners were
found alive, but news organizations later found only one
actually survived.</p>

<p>Another criticism has been the diluting of the importance
of breaking news by the need of 24-hour news channels to
fill time, applying the title to soft news stories of
questionable importance and urgency, for example car chases.
Others question whether the use of the term is excessive,
citing occasions when the term is used even though scheduled
programming is not interrupted.</p>

   <footer>
     <em>Text courtesy of Wikipedia:
   http://en.wikipedia.org/wiki/Breaking_news</em>
   </footer>

  </article>
 </body>
</html>
```

NOTE

In the stylesheet, note that, for each column-related property in the stylesheet, I've added two additional entries with `-webkit` and `-moz` prefixes. Because browser support for column-related CSS is still a bit inconsistent, using the properties with these prefixes ensures that the properties will work in all browsers.

The code in Listing 6.11 is from a fake news article, so I've used the `<article>` element to hold all the content. Inside the `<article>` element is a `<header>` element that contains the "Breaking News!" heading (at the `<h1>` level), followed by three paragraphs of text and a `<footer>` element. All the styling is handled in the stylesheet at the beginning of the listing; styles are provided for four of the elements just named: `<article>`, `<h1>`, `<p>`, and `<footer>`.

In the stylesheet, I'm applying the primary definition of the columns within the `<article>` element. I've used `column-count` to define three columns, and I've used `column-gap` to define the space between the columns as 21 pixels wide. Next, I've added a definition for the `<h1>` element, first to make the text align in the center of the page, and second to ensure that the text spans all the columns. I applied the same `column-span` property to the entry for the `<footer>` element, for the same reason.

After the entry for the `<h1>` element, I added some specific margins to the `<p>` element, namely, a top margin of 0 pixels and a bottom margin of 12 pixels. I could have left well enough alone and just allowed the `<p>` elements to display as the default style, but that would have created a margin at the top of each paragraph. "What's the big deal?" you might ask, because it looks as though I've manually added space between the paragraphs anyway—and that's true. However, I added the space *after* each paragraph and took away the space *before* each paragraph so that the first column doesn't begin with a space and thus misalign the tops of each of the three columns.

You can even add vertical lines between columns, as shown in Figure 6.16. The stylesheet entries I added to achieve this appearance are shown here; note that they look remarkably similar to how you define borders (which you will learn about in the next chapter).

```
-webkit-column-rule-width: 1px;
-moz-column-rule-width: 1px;
column-rule-width: 1px;
-webkit-column-rule-style: solid;
-moz-column-rule-style: solid;
column-rule-style: solid;
-webkit-column-rule-color: #000;
-moz-column-rule-color: #000;
column-rule-color: #000;
```

FIGURE 6.16
The code in Listing 6.11, with the addition of vertical lines between the columns.

Summary

In this chapter, you learned how to make text appear as boldface or italic and how to code superscripts, subscripts, special symbols, and accented letters. You saw how to make the text line up properly in preformatted passages of monospaced text and how to control the size, color, and typeface of any section of text on a web page. You also learned that attributes are used to specify options and special behavior of many HTML tags, and you learned to use the `style` attribute with CSS style rules to affect the appearance of text. You also learned how to create and combine three basic types of HTML lists: ordered lists, unordered lists, and definition lists. Lists can be placed within other lists to create outlines and other complex arrangements of text.

Finally, you learned to arrange text and images into organized rows and columns called tables. You learned the basic tags for creating tables and several CSS properties for controlling the alignment, spacing, and appearance of tables. You also learned that tables are *never* to be used for layout purposes, but that you can achieve a multicolumn layout using CSS columns.

Table 6.2 summarizes the tags and attributes discussed in this chapter. Don't feel as though you have to memorize all these tags, by the way!

TABLE 6.2   HTML Tags and Attributes Covered in Chapter 6

Tag/Attribute	Function
`<em>...</em>`	Emphasis (usually italic).
`<strong>...</strong>`	Stronger emphasis (usually bold).
`<pre>...</pre>`	Preformatted text (exact line endings and spacing will be preserved—usually rendered in a monospaced font).
`<sub>...</sub>`	Subscript.
`<sup>...</sup>`	Superscript.
`<div>...</div>`	A region of text to be formatted.
`<dl>...</dl>`	A definition list.
`<dt>...</dt>`	A definition term, as part of a definition list.
`<dd>...</dd>`	The corresponding definition to a definition term, as part of a definition list.
`<ol>...</ol>`	An ordered (numbered) list.
`<ul>...</ul>`	An unordered (bulleted) list.
`<li>...</li>`	A list item for use with `<ol>` or `<ul>`.
`<table>...</table>`	Creates a table that can contain any number of rows and columns.
`<thead>...</thead>`	Defines the heading row of a table.
`<tbody>...</tbody>`	Defines the body rows of a table.
`<tfoot>...</tfoot>`	Defines the footer row of a table.
`<tr>...</tr>`	Defines a table row containing one or more cells (`<td>` tags).
`<th>...</th>`	Defines a table heading cell. (Accepts all the same styles as `<td>`.)
`<td>...</td>`	Defines a table data cell.

Attribute	Function
`style="font-family:typeface"`	The typeface (family) of the font, which is the name of a font, such as `Arial`. (Can also be used with `<p>`, `<h1>`, `<h2>`, `<h3>`, and so on.)

`style="font-size:size"`	The size of the font, which can be set to `small`, `medium`, or `large`, as well as `x-small`, `x-large`, and so on. Can also be set to a specific point size (such as `12pt`).
`style="color:color"`	Changes the color of the text.
`style="text-align:alignment"`	Aligns text to `center`, `left`, or `right`. (Can also be used with `<p>`, `<h1>`, `<h2>`, `<h3>`, and so on.)
`style="list-style-type:numtype"`	The type of numerals used to label the list. Possible values are `decimal`, `lower-roman`, `upper-roman`, `lower-alpha`, `upper-alpha`, and `none`.
`style="list-style-type:bullettype"`	The bullet dingbat used to mark list items. Possible values are `disc`, `circle`, `square`, and `none`.
`style="list-style-type:type"`	The type of bullet or number used to label this item. Possible values are `disc`, `circle`, `square`, `decimal`, `lower-roman`, `upper-roman`, `lower-alpha`, `upper-alpha`, and `none`.

Q&A

Q. How do I find out the exact name for a font I have on my computer?

A. On a Windows computer, open the Control Panel and click the `Fonts` folder—the fonts on your system are listed (Vista users might have to switch to Classic View in the Control Panel). On a Mac, open `Font Book` in the `Applications` folder. When specifying fonts in the `font-family` style rule, use the exact spelling of font names. Font names are not case sensitive, however.

Q. How do I put Kanji, Arabic, Chinese, and other non-European characters on my pages?

A. First of all, users who need to read these characters on your pages must have the appropriate language fonts installed. They must also have selected that language character set and its associated font for their web browsers. You can use the Character Map program in Windows (or a similar program in other operating systems) to get the numerical codes for each character in any language font. To find Character Map, click Start, All Programs, Accessories, and then System

Tools. (On a Mac, open `Font Book` in the `Applications` folder.) If the character you want has a code of `214`, use `&#214;` to place it on a web page. If you cannot find the Character Map program, use your operating system's built-in Help function to find the specific location.

The best way to include a short message in an Asian language (such as `We Speak Tamil-Call Us!`) is to include it as a graphics image. That way every user will see it, even if they use English as their primary language for web browsing. But even to use a language font in a graphic, you will likely have to download a specific language pack for your operating system. Again, check your system's Help function for specific instructions.

Q. **I've seen web pages that use three-dimensional little balls or other special graphics for bullets. How do they do that?**

A. That trick is a little bit beyond what this chapter covers. You'll learn how to do it yourself in Chapter 8.

Q. **I made a big table, and when I load the page, nothing appears on the page for a long time. Why the wait?**

A. Complex tables can take a while to appear on the screen. The web browser has to figure out the size of everything in the table before it can display any part of it. You can speed things up a bit by always including `width` and `height` attributes for every graphics image within a table. Defining specific widths for the `<table>` and `<td>` elements also helps.

Workshop

The workshop contains quiz questions and activities to help you solidify your understanding of the material covered. Try to answer all questions before looking at the "Answers" section that follows.

Quiz

1. How would you create a paragraph in which the first three words are bold, using styles rather than the `<b>` or `<strong>` tags?

2. How would you represent the chemical formula for water?

3. How do you display "© 2014, Webwonks Inc." on a web page?

4. How would you center everything on an entire page?

5. How can you create a simple two-row, two-column table with a single-pixel black border to outline the table?

Answers

1. You can use this code:

```
<p><span style="font-weight: bold">First three words</span>
are bold.</p>
```

2. You can use H₂O.

3. You can use either of the following:

```
&copy; 2014, Webwonks Inc.
&#169; 2014, Webwonks Inc.
```

4. If you thought about putting a `<div style="text-align:center">` immediately after the `<body>` tag at the top of the page, and `</div>` just before the `</body>` tag at the end of the page, then you're correct. However, the `text-align` style is also supported directly in the `<body>` tag, which means you can forgo the `<div>` tag and place the `style="text-align:center"` style directly in the `<body>` tag. Presto, the entire page is centered!

5. Use the following HTML:

```
<table style="border: 1px solid #000000; border-collapse:
collapse;">
  <tr>
    <td>Top left...</td>
    <td>Top right...</td>
  </tr>
  <tr>
    <td>Bottom left...</td>
    <td>Bottom right...</td>
  </tr>
</table>
```

Exercises

▶ Apply the font-level style attributes you learned about in this chapter to various block-level elements such as `<p>`, `<div>`, `<ul>`, and `<li>` items. Try nesting your elements to get a feel for how styles do or do not cascade through the content hierarchy.

▶ Use the text alignment style attributes to place blocks of text in various places on your web page. Try nesting your paragraphs and divisions (`<p>` and `<div>`) to get a feel for how styles do or do not cascade through the content hierarchy.

▶ Try producing an ordered list outlining the information you'd like to put on your web pages. This will give you practice formatting HTML lists and also give you a head start on thinking about the issues covered in later chapters of this book.

▶ You often see alternating row colors in a table, with one row having a gray background and the next a white background. The goal of alternating colors in table rows is so that the individual rows are easier to discern when the viewer is looking quickly at the table full of data. Create a table with alternating row colors and text colors (if necessary).

CHAPTER 7

Using External and Internal Links

So far, you have learned how to use HTML tags to create some basic web pages. However, at this point, those pieces of content are islands unto themselves, with no connection to anything else (although it is true that, in Chapter 3, "Understanding Cascading Style Sheets," I sneaked a few page links into the examples). To turn your work into real web content, you need to connect it to the rest of the Web—or at least to your other pages within your own personal or corporate sites.

This chapter shows you how to create hypertext links to content within your own document and how to link to other external documents. Additionally, you will learn how to style hypertext links so that they display in the color and decoration you desire—not necessarily the default blue underlined display.

Using Web Addresses

The simplest way to store web content for an individual website is to place all the files in the same folder. When files are stored together like this, you can link to them by simply providing the name of the file in the `href` attribute of the `<a>` tag.

An *attribute* is an extra piece of information associated with a tag that provides further details about the tag. For example, the `href` attribute of the `<a>` tag identifies the address of the page to which you are linking.

When you have more than a few pages, or when you start to have an organization structure to the content in your site, you should put your files into directories (or *folders*, if you will) whose names reflect the content within them. For example, all your images could be in an

WHAT YOU'LL LEARN IN THIS CHAPTER:

▶ How to use anchor links

▶ How to link between pages on your own site

▶ How to link to external content

▶ How to link to an email address

▶ How to use window targeting with your links

▶ How to style your links with CSS

NOTE

Before we begin, you might want a refresher on the basics of where to put files on your server and how to manage files within a set of directories. This information is important to know when creating links in web content. Refer to Chapter 1, "Understanding How the Web Works," specifically the section titled "Understanding Where to Place Files on the Web Server."

images directory, corporate information could be in an about directory, and so on. Regardless of how you organize your documents within your own web server, you can use relative addresses, which include only enough information to find one page from another.

A *relative address* describes the path from one web page to another, instead of a full (or *absolute*) Internet address.

As you recall from Chapter 1, the document root of your web server is the directory designated as the top-level directory for your web content. In web addresses, that document root is represented by the forward slash (/). All subsequent levels of directories are separated by the same type of forward slash. For example:

```
/directory/subdirectory/subsubdirectory/
```

Suppose you are creating a page named zoo.html in your document root, and you want to include a link to pages named african.html and asian.html in the elephants subdirectory. The links would look like the following:

```
<a href="/elephants/african.html">Learn about African elephants.</a>
<a href="/elephants/asian.html">Learn about Asian elephants.</a>
```

These specific addresses are actually called *relative-root addresses*, in that they are relative addresses that lack the entire domain name, but they are specifically relative to the document root specified by the forward slash.

Using a regular relative address, you can skip the initial forward slash. This type of address allows the links to become relative to whatever directory they are in—it could be the document root, or it could be another directory one or more levels down from the document root:

```
<a href="elephants/african.html">Learn about African elephants.</a>
<a href="elephants/asian.html">Learn about Asian elephants.</a>
```

Your african.html and asian.html documents in the elephants subdirectory could link back to the main zoo.html page in either of these ways:

```
<a href="http://www.yourdomain.com/zoo.html">Return to the zoo.</a>
<a href="/zoo.html">Return to the zoo.</a>
<a href="../zoo.html">Return to the zoo.</a>
```

The first link is an absolute link. With an absolute link, there is *absolutely* no doubt where the link should go because the full URL is provided—domain name included.

The second link is a relative-root link. It is relative to the domain you are currently browsing and, therefore, does not require the protocol type (for example, `http://`) or domain name (for example, `www.yourdomain.com`); the initial forward slash is provided to show that the address begins at the document root.

In the third link, the *double dot* (`..`) is a special command that indicates the folder that contains the current folder—in other words, the *parent folder*. Anytime you see the double dot, just think to yourself, "Go up a level in the directory structure."

If you use relative addressing consistently throughout your web pages, you can move directories of pages to another folder, disk drive, or web server without changing the links.

Relative addresses can span quite complex directory structures, if necessary. Chapter 27, "Organizing and Managing a Website," offers more detailed advice for organizing and linking large numbers of web pages.

TIP

The general rule surrounding relative addressing (`elephants/african.html`) versus absolute addressing (`http://www.takeme2thezoo.com/elephants/african.html`) is that you should use relative addressing when linking to files that are stored together, such as files that are all part of the same website. Use absolute addressing when you're linking to files somewhere else—another computer, another disk drive, or, more commonly, another website on the Internet.

TRY IT YOURSELF ▼

Creating a Simple Site Architecture

Hopefully by now you've created a page or two of your own while working through the lessons. Follow these steps to add a few more pages and link them:

1. Use a home page as a main entrance and as a central hub to which all your other pages are connected. If you created a page about yourself or your business, use that page as your home page. You also might like to create a new page now for this purpose.

2. On the home page, put a list of links to the other HTML files you've created (or placeholders for the HTML files you plan to create soon). Be sure that the exact spelling of the filename, including any capitalization, is correct in every link.

3. On every other page besides the home page, include a link at the bottom (or top) leading back to your home page. That makes navigating around your site simple and easy.

4. You might also want to include a list of links to related or interesting sites, either on your home page or on a separate links page. People often include a list of their friends' personal pages on their own home page. However, businesses should be careful not to lead potential customers away to other sites too quickly—there's no guarantee they'll remember to use relative addressing for links between your own pages and absolute addressing for links to other sites.

Linking Within a Page Using Anchors

The `<a>` tag—the tag responsible for hyperlinks on the Web—got its name from the word *anchor*, because a link serves as a designation for a spot in a web page. In examples throughout this book so far, you've learned how to use the `<a>` tag to link to somewhere else, but that's only half its usefulness. Let's get started working with anchor links that link to content within the same page.

Identifying Locations in a Page with Anchors

The `<a>` tag can be used to mark a spot on a page as an anchor, enabling you to create a link that points to that exact spot. Listing 7.1, presented a bit later in this chapter, demonstrates a link to an anchor within a page. To see how such links are made, let's take a quick peek ahead at the first `<a>` tag in the listing:

```
<a id="top"></a>
```

TIP

You can actually use an `id` attribute on many container elements in HTML5, and use the `</a>` tag to point to those elements as anchor links as well.

The `<a>` tag normally uses the `href` attribute to specify a hyperlinked target. The `<a href>` is what you click, and `<a id>` is where you go when you click there. In this example, the `<a>` tag is still specifying a target, but no actual link is created. Instead, the `<a>` tag gives a name to the specific point on the page where the tag occurs. The `</a>` tag must be included and a unique name must be assigned to the `id` attribute, but no text between `<a>` and `</a>` is necessary.

Linking to Anchor Locations

Figure 7.1 shows a site with various anchor points placed throughout a single page. Take a look at the last `<a>` tag in Listing 7.1 to see an example:

```
<a href="#top">Return to Index.</a>
```

The # symbol means that the word `top` refers to a named anchor point within the current document rather than to a separate page. When a user clicks `Return to Index`, the web browser displays the part of the page starting with the `<a id="top">` tag.

LISTING 7.1   Setting Anchor Points by Using the `<a>` Tag with an `id` Attribute

```
<!DOCTYPE html>

<html lang="en">
```

```
<head>
 <title>Alphabetical Shakespeare</title>
</head>

<body>
  <article>

  <header>
    <h1><a id="top"></a>First Lines of Shakespearean Sonnets</h1>
  </header>

  <p>Don't you just hate when you go a-courting, and you're down
  on one knee about to rattle off a totally romantic
  Shakespearean sonnet, and zap! You space it. <em>"Um... It was,
  uh... I think it started with a B..."</em></p>
  <p>Well, appearest thou no longer the dork. Simply refer to
  this page, click on the first letter of the sonnet you want,
  and get an instant reminder of the first line to get you
  started. <em>"Beshrew that heart that makes my heart to
  groan..."</em></p>

  <p style="text-align:center"><strong>Alphabetical Index
  </strong></p>
  <div style="text-align:center">
  <a href="#A">A</a> <a href="#B">B</a> <a href="#C">C</a>
  <a href="#D">D</a> <a href="#E">E</a> <a href="#F">F</a>
  <a href="#G">G</a> <a href="#H">H</a> <a href="#I">I</a>
  <a href="#J">J</a> <a href="#K">K</a> <a href="#L">L</a>
  <a href="#M">M</a> <a href="#N">N</a> <a href="#O">O</a>
  <a href="#P">P</a> <a href="#Q">Q</a> <a href="#R">R</a>
  <a href="#S">S</a> <a href="#T">T</a> <a href="#U">U</a>
  <a href="#V">V</a> <a href="#W">W</a> <a href="#X">X</a>
  <a href="#Y">Y</a> <a href="#Z">Z</a>
  </div>
  <hr />

  <section>

  <header>
  <h1><a id="A"></a>A</h1>
  </header>
  <ul>
  <li>A woman's face with nature's own hand painted,</li>
  <li>Accuse me thus, that I have scanted all, </li>
  <li>Against my love shall be as I am now</li>
  <li>Against that time (if ever that time come) </li>
  <li>Ah wherefore with infection should he live, </li>
  <li>Alack what poverty my muse brings forth, </li>
  <li>Alas 'tis true, I have gone here and there, </li>
  <li>As a decrepit father takes delight, </li>
```

NOTE

Near the end of Listing 7.1 you see a line that reads:

```
<!-- continue with the
alphabet -->
```

This text (an HTML comment) will appear in your source code but will not be displayed by the browser. You can learn more about commenting your code in Chapter 27.

CAUTION

Anchor names specified via the id attribute in the <a> tag must start with a letter. So if you want to simply number the IDs of anchors, be sure to start them with text (as in photo1, photo2, and so on) instead of just 1, 2, and so on.

```
<li>As an unperfect actor on the stage, </li>
<li>As fast as thou shalt wane so fast thou grow'st, </li>
</ul>
<p><a href="#top">Return to Index.</a></p>
</section>
<hr />
<!-- continue with the alphabet -->
<section>

<header>
  <h1><a id="Z"></a>Z</h1>
</header>

<p>(No sonnets start with Z.)</p>
<p><a href="#top"><em>Return to Index.</em></a></p>
</section>

</article>
</body>
</html>
```

FIGURE 7.1
The `<a id>` tags in Listing 7.1 don't appear at all on the web page. The `<a href>` tags appear as underlined links.

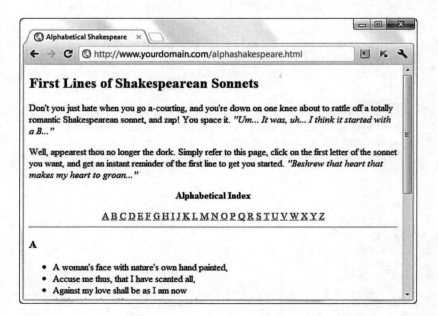

Each of the `<a href>` links in Listing 7.1 makes an underlined link leading to a corresponding `<a id>` anchor—or it would if I had filled in all the text. Only A and Z will work in this example because only the A and Z links have corresponding text to link to, but feel free to fill in the rest on your own! Clicking the letter Z under Alphabetical Index in Figure 7.1, for example, takes you to the part of the page shown in Figure 7.2.

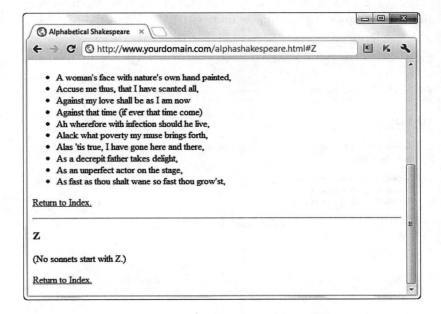

FIGURE 7.2
Clicking the letter Z on the page shown in Figure 7.1 takes you to the appropriate section of the same page.

Having mastered the concept of linking to sections of text within a single page, you can now learn to link other pieces of web content.

Linking Between Your Own Web Content

As you learned earlier in this chapter, you do not need to include `http://` before each address specified in the `href` attribute when linking to content within your domain (or on the same computer, if you are viewing your site locally). When you create a link from one file to another file within the same domain or on the same computer, you don't need to specify a complete Internet address. In fact, if the two files are stored in the same folder, you can simply use the name of the HTML file by itself:

```
<a href="pagetwo.html">Go to Page 2.</a>
```

As an example, Listing 7.2 and Figure 7.3 show a quiz page with a link to the answers page shown in Listing 7.3 and Figure 7.4. The answers page contains a link back to the quiz page. Because the page in Listing 7.2 links to another page in the same directory, the filename can be used in place of a complete address.

FIGURE 7.3
This is the `historyquiz.html` file listed in Listing 7.2 and referred to by the link in Listing 7.3.

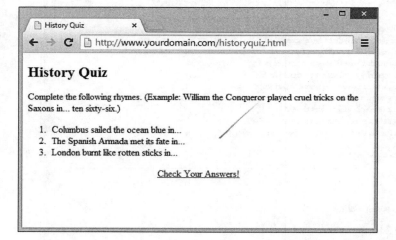

FIGURE 7.4
The `Check Your Answers!` link in Figure 7.3 takes you to this answers page. The `Return to the Questions` link takes you back to what's shown in Figure 7.3.

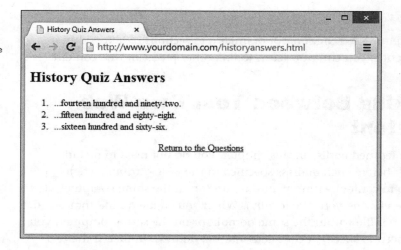

LISTING 7.2 **The** `historyanswers.html` **File**

```
<!DOCTYPE html>

<html lang="en">
 <head>
  <title>History Quiz</title>
 </head>

 <body>
  <section>

  <header>
  <h1>History Quiz</h1>
  </header>

  <p>Complete the following rhymes. (Example: William the
  Conqueror played cruel tricks on the Saxons in... ten
  sixty-six.)</p>
  <ol>
  <li>Columbus sailed the ocean blue in...</li>
  <li>The Spanish Armada met its fate in...</li>
  <li>London burnt like rotten sticks in...</li>
  </ol>
  <p style="text-align: center;">
  <a href="historyanswers.html">Check Your Answers!</a>
  </p>

  </section>
 </body>
</html>
```

LISTING 7.3 **The** `historyanswers.html` **File That** `historyquiz.html`
Links To

```
<!DOCTYPE html>

<html lang="en">
 <head>
  <title>History Quiz Answers</title>
 </head>

 <body>
  <section>

  <header>
  <h1>History Quiz Answers</h1>
  </header>

  <ol>
   <li>...fourteen hundred and ninety-two.</li>
```

NOTE

In both Listing 7.2 and Listing 7.3, you'll see the use of the `<section></section>` tag pair around the bulk of the content. You might wonder whether that is entirely necessary—after all, it is the only content on the page. The answer is, no, it isn't entirely necessary. The HTML would validate just fine, and no one looking at this code would be confused by its organization if the `<section></section>` tags were not present. They are used here just to make sure you get used to seeing them throughout these code examples, and to enable me to write this note about how you *might* use the `<section> </section>` tags at some point in the future. For example, if you were to put both the questions section and the answers section on one page, and apply the use of styles and a little bit of JavaScript-based interactivity, you could hide one section (the questions) until the reader clicked a link that would then show the other section (the answers). This action is beyond the scope of the book, but it is an example of how the simplest bit of markup can set you up for bigger things later.

```
    <li>...fifteen hundred and eighty-eight.</li>
    <li>...sixteen hundred and sixty-six.</li>
    </ol>
    <p style="text-align: center;">
    <a href="historyquiz.html">Return to the Questions</a>
    </p>
    </section>
  </body>
</html>
```

Using filenames instead of complete Internet addresses saves you a lot of typing. More important, the links between your pages will work properly no matter where the group of pages is stored. You can test the links while the files are still on your computer's hard drive. You can then move them to a web server, a CD-ROM, a DVD, or a memory card, and all the links will still work correctly. There is nothing magic about this simplified approach to identifying web pages—it all has to do with web page addressing, as you've already learned.

Linking to External Web Content

The only difference between linking to pages within your own site and linking to external web content is that when linking outside your site, you need to include the full address to that bit of content. The full address includes the http:// before the domain name and then the full pathname to the file (for example, an HTML file, an image file, a multimedia file, and so on).

For example, to include a link to Google from within one of your own web pages, you would use this type of absolute addressing in your `<a>` link:

```
<a href="http://www.google.com/">Go to Google</a>
```

You can apply what you learned in previous sections to creating links to named anchors on other pages. Linked anchors are not limited to the same page. You can link to a named anchor on another page by including the address or filename followed by # and the anchor name. For example, the following link would take you to an anchor named `photos` within the african.html page inside the `elephants` directory on the (fictional) domain www.takeme2thezoo.com.

```
<a href="http://www.takeme2thezoo.com/elephants/african.
html#photos">
Check out the African Elephant Photos!</a>
```

CAUTION

As you might know, you can leave out the `http://` at the front of any address when typing it into most web browsers. However, you *cannot* leave that part out when you type an Internet address into an `<a href>` link on a web page.

CAUTION

Be sure to include the # symbol only in `<a href>` link tags. Don't put the # symbol in the `<a id>` tag; links to that name won't work in that case.

If you are linking from another page already on the www.
takeme2thezoo.com domain (because you are, in fact, the site
maintainer), your link might simply be as follows:

```
<a href="/elephants/african.html#photos">Check out the
African Elephant Photos!</a>
```

The `http://` and the domain name would not be necessary in that
instance, as you have already learned.

Linking to an Email Address

In addition to linking between pages and between parts of a single
page, the `<a>` tag enables you to link to email addresses. This is the
simplest way to enable your web page visitors to talk back to you. Of
course, you could just provide visitors with your email address and
trust them to type it into whatever email programs they use, but that
increases the likelihood for errors. By providing a clickable link to your
email address, you make it almost completely effortless for them to
send you messages and eliminate the chance for typos.

An HTML link to an email address looks like the following:

```
<a href="mailto:yourusername@yourdomain.com">Send me an
email message.</a>
```

The words `Send me an email message` will appear just like any other
`<a>` link.

If you want people to see your actual email address (so that they can
make note of it or send a message using a different email program),
include it both in the `href` attribute and as part of the message
between the `<a>` and `</a>` tags, like this:

```
<a href="mailto:you@yourdomain.com">you@yourdomain.com</a>
```

In most web browsers, when a user clicks the link, that person gets a
window into which he or she can type a message that is immediately
sent to you—the email program the person uses to send and receive
email will automatically be used. You can provide some additional
information in the link so that the subject and body of the message
also have default values. You do this by adding `subject` and `body`
variables to the `mailto` link. You separate the variables from the email
address with a question mark (?), separate the value from the variable

TIP

If you want to specify only an
email message subject and not
the body, you can just leave off
the ampersand and the `body`
variable, equal sign, and value
text string, as follows:

```
<a href="mailto:author@
somedomain.com?subject=
Book Question">author@
somedomain.com</a>
```

TIP

If you put an email contact link in the footer of all your web pages, you make it easy for others to contact you; you give them a way to tell you about any problems with the page that your testing might have missed. Just don't forget to use the email address character entity trick so that your address flies under the radar of spammers.

with an equal sign (=), and then separate each of the variable and value pairs with an ampersand (&). You don't have to understand the variable/value terminology at this point. Here is an example of specifying a subject and body for the preceding email example:

```
<a href="mailto:author@somedomain.com?subject=Book Question&body=
When is the next edition coming out?">author@somedomain.com</a>
```

When a user clicks this link, an email message is created with `author@somedomain.com` as the recipient, `Book Question` as the subject of the message, and `When is the next edition coming out?` as the message body.

Before you run off and start plastering your email address all over your web pages, I have to give you a little warning and then let you in on a handy trick. You're no doubt familiar with spammers that build up databases of email addresses and then bombard them with junk mail advertisements. One way spammers harvest email addresses is using programs that automatically search web pages for `mailto` links.

Fortunately, a little trick will thwart many (but not all) spammers. This trick involves using character entities to encode your email address, which confuses scraper programs that attempt to harvest your email address from your web pages. As an example, consider the email address `jcmeloni@gmail.com`. If you replace the letters in the address with their character entity equivalents, some email harvesting programs will be thrown off. Lowercase ASCII character entities begin at `&#97;` for the letter *a* and increase through the alphabet in order. For example, the letter *j* is `&#106`, *c* is `&#99`, and so on. Replacing all the characters with their ASCII attributes produces the following:

```
<a href="mailto:&#106;&#099;&#109;&#101;&#108;&#111;&#110;&#105;
&#064;&#103;&#109;&#097;&#105;&#108;&#046;&#099;&#111;&#109;">
Send me an email message.</a>
```

Because the browser interprets the character encoding as, well, characters, the end result is the same from the browser's perspective. However, automated email harvesting programs search the raw HTML code for pages, which, in this case, is showing a fairly jumbled-looking email address. If you don't want to figure out the character encoding for your own address, just type "email address encoder" into your search engine, and you will find some services online that will produce an encoded string for you.

Opening a Link in a New Browser Window

Now that you have a handle on how to create addresses for links—both internal (within your site) and external (to other sites)—there is one additional method of linking: forcing the user to open links in new windows.

You've no doubt heard of *pop-up windows*, which are browser windows—typically advertising products or services—that are intended to be opened and displayed automatically without the user's approval (many modern browsers disallow this behavior). However, the concept of opening another window or targeting another location serves a valid purpose in some instances. For example, you might want to present information in a smaller secondary browser window but still allow the user to see the information in the main window. This is often the case when the user is clicking on a link to an animated demo, a movie clip, or some other multimedia element. You might also want to target a new browser window when you are linking to content off-site.

The word *target* is important because that is the name of the attribute used with the `<a>` tag. The `target` attribute points to a valid browsing context, or "new window to open."

A valid HTML link that opens in a new window is constructed like so:

```
<a href="/some/file.html" target="_blank">Open a Window!</a>
```

Remember, opening a new browser window on behalf of your user—especially when it's a full-size new window—goes against some principles of usability and accessibility, so be considerate if and when you do it.

Using CSS to Style Hyperlinks

The default display of a text-based hyperlink on a web page is underlined blue text. You might also have noticed that links you have previously visited appear as underlined purple text—that color is also a default. If you've spent any time at all on the Web, you will also have noticed that not all links are blue or purple—and for that, I think, we are all thankful. Using a little CSS and knowledge of the various pseudoclasses for the `<a>` link, you can make your links look however you want.

> **NOTE**
>
> You can use graphics as links (instead of using text as links) by putting an `<img />` tag between the opening `<a>` and closing `</a>` tags.

A *pseudoclass* is a class that describes styles for elements that apply to certain circumstances, such as various states of user interaction with that element.

For example, the common pseudoclasses for the `<a>` tag are `link`, `visited`, `hover`, and `active`. You can remember them with the mnemonic "Love–Hate" (LV for *love* and HA for *hate*) if you choose.

▶ `a:link` describes the style of a hyperlink that has not been visited previously.

▶ `a:visited` describes the style of a hyperlink that has been visited previously and is present in the browser's memory.

▶ `a:hover` describes the style of a hyperlink as a user's mouse hovers over it (and before it has been clicked).

▶ `a:active` describes the style of a hyperlink that is in the act of being clicked but has not yet been released.

NOTE

The colors in this example are indicated by their hexadecimal values.

For example, let's say you want to produce a link with the following styles:

▶ A font that is bold and Verdana (and not underlined, meaning it has no text decoration)

▶ A base color that is light blue

▶ A color of red when users hover over it or when they are clicking it

▶ A color of *gray* after users have visited it

Your style sheet entries might look like the following:

```
a {
    font-family: Verdana, sans-serif;
    font-weight: bold;
    text-decoration: none;
}
a:link {
    color: #6479A0;
}
a:visited {
    color: #cccccc;
}
a:hover {
    color: #e03a3e;
}
```

```
a:active {
    color: #e03a3e;
}
```

Because the sample link will be Verdana bold (and not underlined)
regardless of the state it is in, those three property and value pairs
can reside in the rule for the a selector. However, because each
pseudoclass must have a specific color associated with it, we use a rule
for each pseudoclass, as shown in the code example. The pseudoclass
inherits the style of the parent rule, unless the rule for the pseudoclass
specifically overrides that rule. In other words, all the pseudoclasses
in the preceding example will be Verdana bold (and not underlined).
However, if we had used the following rule for the hover pseudoclass,
the text would display in Comic Sans when users hovered over it (if, in
fact, the user has the Comic Sans font installed):

```
a:hover {
    font-family: "Comic Sans MS";
    color: #e03a3e;
}
```

Additionally, because the active and hover pseudoclasses use the same
font color, you can combine style rules for them:

```
a:hover, a:active {
    color: #e03a3e;
}
```

Listing 7.4 puts these code snippets together to produce a page using
styled pseudoclasses; Figure 7.5 shows the results of this code.

FIGURE 7.5
A link can use particular styles to
control the visual display.

LISTING 7.4   Using Styles to Display Link Pseudoclasses

```html
<!DOCTYPE html>

<html lang="en">
 <head>
  <title>Sample Link Style</title>

  <style type="text/css">
  a {
    font-family: Verdana, sans-serif;
    font-weight: bold;
    text-decoration: none;
  }
  a:link {
    color: #6479a0;
  }
  a:visited {
    color: #cccccc;
  }
  a:hover, a:active {
    color: #ff0000;
  }
  </style>
 </head>
 <body>
        <h1>Sample Link Style</h1>
        <p><a href="simplelinkstyle.html">The first time you see
        me, I should be a light blue, bold, non-underlined link
        in the Verdana font</a>.</p>
 </body>
</html>
```

If you view the example in your web browser, indeed the link should be a light blue, bold, nonunderlined Verdana font. If you hover over the link, or click the link without releasing it, it should turn red. If you click and release the link, the page simply reloads because the link points to the file with the same name. However, at that point, the link is in your browser's memory and thus is displayed as a visited link—and it appears gray instead of blue.

You can use CSS to apply a wide range of text-related changes to your links. You can change fonts, sizes, weights, decoration, and so on. Sometimes you might want several sets of link styles in your style sheet. In that case, you can create classes; you aren't limited to working with only one set of styles for the `<a>` tag. The following example is a set of style sheet rules for a `footerlink` class for links I might want to place in the footer area of my website:

```
a.footerlink {
    font-family: Verdana, sans-serif;
    font-weight: bold;
    font-size: 75%;
    text-decoration: none;
}
a.footerlink:link, a.footerlink:visited {
    color: #6479a0;
}
a.footerlink:hover, a.footerlink:active {
    color: #e03a3e;
}
```

As you can see in the example that follows, the class name (`footerlink`) appears after the selector name (`a`), separated by a dot, and before the pseudoclass name (`hover`), separated by a colon:

```
selector.class:pseudoclass
a.footerlink:hover
```

Summary

The `<a>` tag is what makes hypertext "hyper." With it, you can create links between pages, as well as links to specific anchor points on any page. This chapter focused on creating and styling simple links to other pages using either relative or absolute addressing to identify the pages.

You learned that when you're creating links to other people's pages, it's important to include the full Internet address of each page in an `<a href>` tag. For links between your own pages, include just the filenames and enough directory information to get from one page to another.

You also learned how to create named anchor points within a page and how to create links to a specific anchor. You learned how to link to your email address so that users can easily send you messages. You even learned how to protect your email address from spammers. Finally, you learned methods for controlling the display of your links using CSS.

Table 7.1 summarizes the `<a>` tag discussed in this chapter.

TABLE 7.1   HTML Tags and Attributes Covered in Chapter 7

Tag/Attribute	Function
`<a>...</a>`	With the `href` attribute, creates a link to another document or anchor. With the `id` attribute, creates an anchor that can be linked to.
Attributes	*Function*
`href="address"`	The address of the document or anchor point to link to.
`id="name"`	The name for this anchor point in the document.

Q&A

Q. **What happens if I link to a page on the Internet, and then the person who owns that page deletes or moves it?**

A. That depends on how the maintainer of that external page has set up his web server. Usually, you will see a `page not found` message or something to that effect when you click a link that has been moved or deleted. You can still click the Back button to return to your page. As a site maintainer, you can periodically run link-checking programs to ensure that your internal and external links are valid. An example of this is the Link Checker service, at http://validator.w3.org/checklink.

Q. **One of the internal links on my website works fine on my computer, but when I put the pages on the Internet, the link doesn't work anymore. What's up?**

A. These are the most likely culprits:

▶ **Capitalization problems**—On Windows computers, linking to a file named `MyFile.html` with `<a href="myfile.html">` works. On most web servers, the link must be `<a href="MyFile.html">` (or you must change the name of the file to `MyFile.html`). To make matters worse, some text editors and file transfer programs actually change the capitalization without telling you. The best solution is to stick with all-lowercase filenames for web pages.

▶ **Spaces in filenames**—Most web servers don't allow filenames with spaces. For example, you should never name a web page `my page.html`. Instead, name it `mypage.html` or even `my_page.html` or `my-page.html` (using an underscore or dash instead of a space).

▶ **Local absolute addresses**—If you link to a file using a local absolute address, such as `C:\mywebsite\news.html`, the link won't work when you place the file on the Internet. You should never use local absolute addresses; when this occurs, it is usually an accident caused by a temporary link that was created to test part of a page. So be careful to remove any test links before publishing a page on the Web.

Q. Can I put both `href` and `id` in the same `<a>` tag? Would I want to for any reason?

A. You can, and it might save you some typing if you have a named anchor point and a link right next to each other. It's generally better, however, to use `<a href>` and `<a id>` separately to avoid confusion because they play very different roles in an HTML document.

Q. What happens if I accidentally misspell the name of an anchor or forget to put the `#` in front of it?

A. If you link to an anchor name that doesn't exist within a page or you misspell the anchor name, the link goes to the top of that page.

Workshop

The Workshop contains quiz questions and exercises to help you solidify your understanding of the material covered. Try to answer all questions before looking at the "Answers" section that follows.

Quiz

1. Your best friend from elementary school finds you on the Internet and says he wants to trade home page links. How do you put a link to his site at http://www.supercheapsuits.com/~billybob/ on one of your pages?

2. What HTML would you use to make it possible for someone clicking the words "About the Authors" at the top of a page to skip down to a list of credits somewhere else on the page?

3. If your email address is bon@soir.com, how would you make the text "goodnight greeting" into a link that people can click to compose and send you an email message?

Answers

1. Put the following on your page:

```
<a href="http://www.supercheapsuits.com/~billybob/">Billy
Bob's site</a>
```

2. Type this at the top of the page:

```
<a href"#credits"></a>
```

Type this at the beginning of the credits section:

```
<a id="credits">About the Authors</a>
```

3. Type the following on your web page:

```
Send me a <a href="mailto:bon@soir.com">goodnight greeting
</a>!
```

Exercises

▶ Create an HTML file consisting of a formatted list of your favorite websites. You might already have these sites bookmarked in your web browser, in which case you can visit them to find the exact URL in the browser's address bar.

▶ If you have created any pages for a website, look through them and consider whether there are any places in the text where you'd like to make it easy for people to contact you. Include a link to your email address there. You can never provide too many opportunities for people to contact you and tell you what they need or what they think about your products—especially if you're running a business.

CHAPTER 8
Working with Colors, Images, and Multimedia

You're right, there are a lot of topics covered in this chapter—but have no fear, for each of these tasks is short and sweet, and will help you move your web development experience from the white background/ black text examples so far in this book to more interesting (or at least colorful) examples. But that's not to say that dark text on a light background is bad—in fact, it's the most common color combination you'll find online.

Paying attention to color schemes and producing a visually appealing website is important, but you don't have to be an artist by trade to implement high-impact color schemes in your website, or to put a few appealing flourishes on what otherwise would be a drab, square world. You don't need to spend hundreds or thousands of dollars on software packages, either, just to manipulate digital photographs or other source graphics you might want to use. The topics in this chapter should help you understand the very basics of color theory and how to modify colors using CSS, as well as how to create images you can use in your website.

After you learn to create the graphics themselves, you'll be ready to include them in your website. Beyond just the basics of using the HTML `<img/>` tag to include images for display in a web browser, you'll learn how to provide descriptions of these images (and why). You'll also learn about image placement, including how to use images as backgrounds for different elements. You'll also learn how to use imagemaps, which enable you to use a single image as a link to multiple locations.

Finally, you'll learn a little bit about working with multimedia. The term *multimedia* encompasses everything we see and hear on a web

NOTE

Although the sample figures in this chapter use a popular and free graphics program for Windows, Mac, and Linux users (GNU Image Manipulation Program, or GIMP), you can apply the knowledge you learn in this chapter to any major Windows or Macintosh graphics application—although the menus and options will look different, of course.

page: audio, video, and animation, as well as static images and text. Although you won't learn how to create any particular audio or video, you will learn how to include such files in your site, through either linking or embedding the content.

Best Practices for Choosing Colors

I can't tell you exactly which colors to use in your website, but I can help you understand certain considerations when selecting those colors on your own. The colors you use can greatly influence your visitors; for example, if you are running an e-commerce site, you want to use colors that entice your users to view your catalog and eventually purchase something. If you are creating a text-heavy site, you want to make sure the color scheme leads to easy-to-read text. Overall, you want to make sure you use colors judiciously and with respect.

You might wonder how respect enters into the mix when talking about colors, but remember that the World Wide Web is an international community and that people's interpretations differ. For instance, pink is very popular in Japan but very unpopular in Eastern European countries. Similarly, green is the color of money in the United States, but the vast majority of other countries have multicolored paper bills—"the color of money" thus isn't a single color at all, so the metaphor would be of no value to international visitors.

Besides using culturally sensitive colors, other best practices include the following:

▶ Use a natural palette of colors. This doesn't mean you should use earth tones, but use colors that you would naturally see on a casual stroll around town—avoid ultrabright colors that can cause eye strain.

▶ Use a small color palette. You don't need to use 15 colors to achieve your goals. In fact, if your page includes text and images in 15 colors, you might reevaluate the message you're attempting to send. Focus on three or four main colors, with a few complementary colors at most.

▶ Consider your demographics. You likely can't control your demographics, so you have to find a middle ground that accommodates everyone. The colors younger people enjoy are not necessarily the same ones older people appreciate, just as there are color biases between men and women and people from different geographic regions and cultures.

You now might be thinking that your color options are limited. Not so—you simply need to think about the decisions you're making before you make them. A search for "color theory" in the search engine of your choice should give you more food for thought, as will the use of the color wheel.

The *color wheel* is a chart that shows the organization of colors in a circular manner. Its method of display is an attempt to help you visualize the relationships among primary, secondary, and complementary colors. Color schemes are developed from working with the color wheel; understanding color schemes can help you determine the color palette to use consistently throughout your website. For example, knowing something about color relationships will hopefully enable you to avoid using orange text on a light blue background, or bright blue text on a brown background.

Some common color schemes in web design are given here:

- **Analogous**—Using colors that are adjacent to each other on the color wheel, such as yellow and green. One color is the dominant color, and its analogous friend enriches the display.

- **Complementary**—Using colors that are opposite each other on the color wheel, such as a warm color (red) and a cool color (green).

- **Triadic**—Using three colors that are equally spaced around the color wheel. The triadic scheme provides balance while still allowing rich color use.

Entire books and courses are devoted to understanding color theory, so continuing the discussion in this book would indeed be a tangent. However, if you intend to work in web design and development, you will be served well with a solid understanding of the basics of color theory. Spend some time reading about it—an online search will provide a wealth of information.

Additionally, spend some hands-on time with the color wheel. The Color Scheme Designer at http://colorschemedesigner.com/ enables you to start with a base color and produce monochromatic, complementary, triadic, tetradic, analogic, and accented analogic color schemes.

NOTE

For a complete list of the 140 descriptive color names, as well as their hexadecimal codes and an example of the color as displayed by your browser, visit http://www.w3.org/TR/SVG/types.html#ColorKeywords.

TIP

It's worth pointing out that color names are not case sensitive. So Black, black, and BLACK are all black, although most web designers stick with lowercase or mixed case (if they use color names at all—most designers use the hexadecimal notation, for a more nuanced approach to color use).

Understanding Web Colors

Specifying a background color other than white for a web page is easier than you probably realize. For example, to specify blue as the background color for a page, put `style="background-color:blue"` inside the `<body>` tag or in the style sheet rule for the body element. Of course, you can use many colors other than blue. In fact, the W3C standards list 17 colors: aqua, black, blue, fuchsia, gray, green, lime, maroon, navy, olive, orange, purple, red, silver, teal, white, and yellow.

Obviously, many more than just those 17 colors are displayed on the Web—in fact, you can use 140 color names with the assurance that all browsers will display these colors similarly. Here's a partial list of the 140 descriptive color names: azure, bisque, cornflowerblue, darksalmon, firebrick, honeydew, lemonchiffon, papayawhip, peachpuff, saddlebrown, thistle, tomato, wheat, and whitesmoke.

But names are subjective—for instance, if you look at the color chart of 140 cross-browser color names, you'll see that you can't distinguish between fuchsia and magenta. The associated hexadecimal color values for those two terms, fuchsia and magenta, are also exactly the same: `#ff00ff`. You'll learn about hexadecimal color values in the next section, but for now, know that if you want to be standards compliant and use more than the 16 color names the W3C standards dictate, you need to use the hexadecimal color codes whenever possible.

Hexadecimal color codes make possible 16 million colors, and most modern computer displays can display all of them. However, be aware that not all computer monitors display colors in the same hues. What might appear as a beautiful light blue background color on your monitor might be more of a purple hue on another user's monitor. Neutral, earth-tone colors (such as medium gray, tan, and ivory) can produce even more unpredictable results on many computer monitors. These colors might even seem to change color on a single monitor, depending on lighting conditions in the room or the time of day.

In addition to changing the background of your pages to a color other than white, you can change the color of text links, including various properties of links (such as the color for when a user hovers over a link versus when the user clicks a link—as you learned in previous chapters). You can also set the background color of container elements (such as paragraphs, divs, blockquotes, and table cells), and you can use colors to specify the borders around those elements. You'll see some examples of colors and container elements later in this chapter.

There are plenty of very bad websites, some created by earnest people with no trace of irony whatsoever. However, the World's Worst Website, in Figure 8.1, was purposefully created to show some of the more egregious sins of website design, especially with its use of colors. A screenshot does not do it justice—visit and experience the site for yourself, at http://www.angelfire.com/super/badwebs/main.htm.

FIGURE 8.1
A partial screenshot of the World's Worst Website.

If you search for "bad website examples" in your search engine, you will find many sites that collect examples of bad design and explain just why such a site should be in a Hall of Shame rather than a Hall of Fame. Many sites are considered bad because of their visual displays, and that display begins with color selection. Therefore, understanding colors, as well as the nuances of their specification and use, is a crucial step to creating a good website.

Using Hexadecimal Values for Colors

To remain standards compliant, as well as to retain precise control over the colors in your website, you can reference colors by their hexadecimal value. The hexadecimal value of a color is an indication of how much red, green, and blue light should be mixed into each color. It works a little bit like Play-Doh—just mix in the amounts of red, blue, and green you want in order to get the appropriate color.

The hexadecimal color format is #rrggbb, in which rr, gg, and bb are two-digit hexadecimal values for the red (rr), green (gg), and blue (bb) components of the color. If you're not familiar with hexadecimal numbers, don't sweat it. Just remember that ff is the maximum and 00 is the minimum. Use one of the following codes for each component:

- ff means full brightness.
- cc means 80% brightness.
- 99 means 60% brightness.
- 66 means 40% brightness.
- 33 means 20% brightness.
- 00 means none of this color component.

For example, bright red is #ff0000, dark green is #003300, bluish-purple is #660099, and medium gray is #999999. To make a page with a red background and dark green text, you could use the following HTML code within inline styles:

```
<body style="background-color:#ff0000; color:#003300">
```

Although only six examples of two-digit hexadecimal values are shown here, there are actually 256 combinations of two-digit hexadecimal values: 0–9 and a–f, paired up. For example, f0 is a possible hex value (decimal value 240), 62 is a possible hex value (decimal value 98), and so on.

As previously discussed, the rr, gg, and bb in the #rrggbb hexadecimal color code format stand for the red, green, and blue components of the color. Each of those components has a decimal value ranging from 0 (no color) to 255 (full color).

So white (or #ffffff) translates to a red value of 255, a green value of 255, and a blue value of 255. Similarly, black (#000000) translates to a red value of 0, a green value of 0, and a blue value of 0. True red is #ff0000 (all red, no green, and no blue), true green is #00ff00 (no red, all green, no blue), and true blue is #0000ff (no red, no green, and all blue). All other hexadecimal notations translate to some variation of the 255 possible values for each of the three colors. The cross-browser-compatible color name CornflowerBlue is associated with the hexadecimal notation #6495ed—a red value of 100, a green value of 149, and a blue value of 237 (almost all of the available blue values).

When picking colors, either through a graphics program or by finding something online that you like, you might see the color notation in hexadecimal or decimal. If you type "hexadecimal color converter" into your search engine, you will find numerous options to help you convert color values into something you can use in your style sheets.

Using CSS to Set Background, Text, and Border Colors

When using CSS, you can use color values in three instances: when specifying the background color, the text color, or the border color of elements. In Chapter 7, "Using External and Internal Links," you learned about using colors for various link states, so in this chapter, we focus on basic element display.

Figure 8.2 shows an example of color usage that could very easily go into a web design Hall of Shame. I can't imagine ever using these combinations of colors and styles in a serious website, but it serves here as an example of how color style *could* be applied to various elements. The image printed in this book will likely not do justice to the horrific colors used, so be sure to open the sample file or type up the code in Listing 8.1 and load it in your browser.

FIGURE 8.2
You can set background, text, and
border colors using CSS.

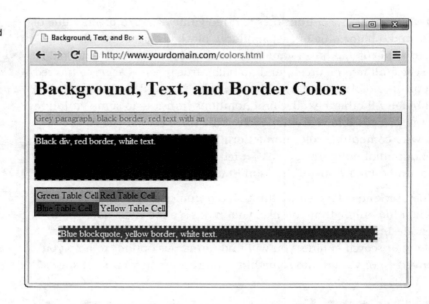

Listing 8.1 shows the HTML and CSS styles used to produce Figure 8.2.

LISTING 8.1   Using Styles to Produce Background, Text, and Border
Colors

```
<!DOCTYPE html>

<html lang="en">
  <head>
    <title>Background, Text, and Border Colors</title>

    <style type="text/css">
    #uglyparagraph {
       background-color: #cccccc;
       color: #ff0000;
       border:1px solid #000000;
    }
    .orange {
       color: #ffa500
    }
    #uglydiv {
       width: 300px;
       height: 75px;
       margin-bottom: 12px;
       background-color: #000000;
       border: 2px dashed #ff0000;
       color: #ffffff;
    }
```

```
    table {
         border-width: 1px solid #000;
         border-spacing: 2px;
         border-style: outset;
         border-collapse: collapse;
    }
    .greencell {
       background-color: #00ff00;
    }
    .redcell {
       background-color: #ff0000;
    }
    .bluecell {
       background-color: #0000ff;
    }
    .yellowcell {
       background-color: #ffff00;
    }
    #uglybq {
       background-color: #0000ff;
       border:4px dotted #ffff00;
       color:#ffffff;
    }
    </style>
</head>

<body>
     <h1>Background, Text, and Border Colors</h1>

     <p id="uglyparagraph">Grey paragraph, black border, red text
     with an <span class="orange">orange span</span>.</p>

     <div id="uglydiv ">Black div, red border, white text. </div>

     <table>
     <tr>
     <td class="greencell">Green Table Cell</td>
     <td class="redcell">Red Table Cell</td>
     </tr>
     <tr>
     <td class="bluecell">Blue Table Cell</td>
     <td class="yellowcell">Yellow Table Cell</td>
     </tr>
     </table>

     <blockquote id="uglybq">
     Blue blockquote,  yellow border, white text.
     </blockquote>
  </body>
</html>
```

Looking at the styles in Listing 8.1, you should be able to figure out almost everything except some of the border styles. In CSS you can't designate borders as a color without also having a width and type. In the first example in Listing 8.1, for `uglyparagraph`, the border width is `1px` and the border type is `solid`. In the example for `uglydiv`, the border width is `2px` and the border type is `dashed`. In the `uglybq` example, the border width is `4px` and the border type is `dotted`.

When picking colors for your website, remember that a little bit goes a long way—if you really like a bright and spectacular color, use it as an accent color, not throughout the primary design elements. For readability, remember that light backgrounds with dark text are much easier to read than dark backgrounds with light text.

Finally, consider the not-insignificant portion of your audience that might be colorblind. For accessibility, you might consider using the Colorblind Web Page Filter tool at http://colorfilter.wickline.org/ to see how your site looks to a person with colorblindness.

Choosing Graphics Software

NOTE

Without a doubt, Adobe Photoshop is the cream of the crop when it comes to image-editing programs. However, it is expensive and quite complex if you don't have experience working with computer graphics. For more information on Adobe's products, visit the Adobe website at www.adobe.com. If you are in the market for one of the company's products, you can download a free evaluation version from the site.

You can use almost any graphics program to create and edit images for your website, from the simple painting or drawing program that typically comes free with your computer's operating system, to an expensive professional program such as Adobe Photoshop. Similarly, if you have a digital camera or scanner attached to your computer, it probably came with some graphics software capable of creating images suitable for online use. Several free image editors also are available for download—or even online as a web application—and deal just with the manipulation of photographic elements.

If you already have software you think might be good for creating web graphics, try using it to do everything described in these next sections. If your software can't handle some of the tasks covered here, it probably isn't a good tool for web graphics. In that case, download and install GIMP from www.gimp.org. This fully functional graphics program is completely free and can definitely perform the actions shown in this chapter.

If GIMP doesn't suit you, consider downloading the evaluation version of Adobe Photoshop or Corel DRAW. For photo manipulation only, you have many free options, all with helpful features. Google's Picasa, available free at http://picasa.google.com/, is one such option. Pixlr (pixlr.com) is another good option. Both of these programs are suited for editing images rather than creating them from scratch, and Picasa is also oriented toward organizing your digital photograph collection. These types of programs won't necessarily help you design a banner or button image for your site; however, they can help you work with some supplementary images, and they are powerful enough that they're worth checking out.

The Least You Need to Know About Graphics

Two forces are always at odds when you post graphics and multimedia on the Internet. The users' eyes and ears want all your content to be as detailed and accurate as possible, and they also want that information displayed immediately. Intricate, colorful graphics mean big file sizes, which increase the transfer time even over a fast connection. How do you maximize the quality of your presentation while minimizing file size? To make these choices, you need to understand how color and resolution work together to create a subjective sense of quality.

The resolution of an image is the number of individual dots, or pixels, that make up an image (typically 72 dots per inch, or 72dpi). Large, high-resolution images generally take longer to transfer and display than small, low-resolution images. Image dimensions are usually specified as the width times the height of the image, expressed in pixels; a 300×200 image, for example, is 300 pixels wide and 200 pixels high.

You might be surprised to find that resolution isn't the most significant factor in determining an image file's storage size (and transfer time). This is because images used on web pages are always stored and transferred in compressed form. Image compression is the mathematical manipulation that images are put through to squeeze out repetitive patterns. The mathematics of image compression is complex, but the basic idea is that repeating patterns or large areas of the same color can be squeezed out when the image is stored on a disk. This makes the image file much smaller and allows it to be transferred faster over the Internet. The web browser then restores the original appearance of the image when the image is displayed.

Using Images Found Elsewhere

One of the best ways to save time creating the graphics and media files for web pages is, of course, to avoid creating them altogether. Grabbing a graphic from any web page is as simple as right-clicking it (or Option + Click an Apple mouse) and selecting Save Image As or Save Picture As (depending on your browser). Extracting a background image from a page is just as easy: Right-click it and select Save Background As.

However, you should *never* use images without the explicit permission of the owner, either by asking or by looking for a Creative Commons license. To take images without explicit permission is a copyright violation (and is also distasteful). To learn more about copyrights, I recommend the "Copyright Crash Course" online tutorial from the University of Texas, at http://copyright.lib.utexas.edu/.

You might also want to consider royalty-free clip art, which doesn't require you to get copyright permission. Or, Clipart.com is another popular clip art destination; for a small fee you have access to thousands of stock images.

Several types of image resolution are used, including pixel, spatial, spectral, temporal, and radiometric. You could spend hours just learning about each type—and if you were taking a graphics design class, you might do just that. For now, however, all you need to remember is that large images take longer to download and also use a lot of space in your display. Display size and storage or transfer size are factors to take into consideration when you are designing your website.

In the sections that follow, you'll learn how to create graphics with big visual impact but small file sizes. The techniques you use to accomplish this depend on the contents and purpose of each image. There are as many uses for web graphics as there are web pages, but four types of graphics are by far the most common:

- ▶ Photos of people, products, and places
- ▶ Graphical banners and logos
- ▶ Buttons or icons to indicate actions and provide links
- ▶ Background textures for container elements

Preparing Photographic Images

To put photos on your web pages, you need to convert your print-based photos to digital images or create photos digitally by using a digital camera, which includes the ubiquitous camera in your smartphone. In the case of some older models of hardware, you might need to use the custom software that came with your device to transfer images to your hard drive, but in most cases, you should be able to connect your device and then drag and drop files to your hard drive. If you are using a scanner to create digital versions of your print photos, you can control just about any scanner directly from the graphics program of your choice—see your software documentation for details.

After you transfer the digital image files to your computer, you can use your graphics program to crop, resize, color-correct, and compress to get them ready for use in your website.

Cropping an Image

Because you want web page graphics to be as compact as possible, you usually need to crop your digital photos. When you *crop* a photo, you select the area you want to display and crop away the rest.

If you don't have a scanner or digital camera, note that almost all film developers offer a service that transfers photos from 35mm film to a CD-ROM or DVD-ROM for a modest fee. You can then copy the files to your hard drive and use your graphics program to open and modify the image files.

The GIMP toolbox offers quick access to the crop tool and its possible attributes. Find an image file—either a digital image you have taken with your camera and stored on your hard drive, or an image you found online. After opening the image in GIMP, perform the following steps to crop it in GIMP:

Cropping in GIMP

1. In the GIMP toolbox, click the Crop tool (see Figure 8.3). Depending on the tool you select, you might have additional attributes you can select. For example, Figure 8.3 shows the attributes for the cropping tool (such as the aspect ratio, position, size, and so on).

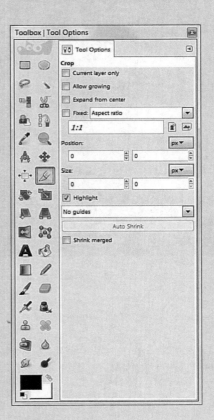

FIGURE 8.3
Select the Crop tool from the toolbox.

Cropping in GIMP
continued

FIGURE 8.4
Select the area of the image that you want to display.

2. In the image you want to crop, draw a box around the selection by clicking the upper-left corner of the portion of the image you want to keep and holding the left mouse button while you drag down to the lower-right corner. See Figure 8.4.

3. Click one of the corners of the selection to apply the cropping.

Your graphics program will likely have a different method than the one shown, but the concept is the same: Select the area to keep and then crop out the rest.

Even after your image has been cropped, it might be larger than it needs to be for a web page. Depending on the design of a specific web page, you might want to limit large images to no more than 800×600 pixels (if it is shown on a page by itself, such as an item catalog) or even 640×480 pixels or smaller. When shown alongside text, images tend to be in the range of 250 to 350 pixels for width, so there's just enough room for the text as well. In some cases, you might want to also provide a thumbnail version of the image that links to a larger version; then you'll probably stick closer to 100 pixels in the larger dimension for the thumbnail.

TIP
Your graphics software will likely have an omnipresent size display somewhere in the image window itself. In GIMP, you can see the current image size in the window title bar. Other programs might show it in the lower-right or lower-left corners. You might also see the magnification ratio in the window, and you might be able to change it by zooming in or out.

Resizing an Image

The exact tool necessary to change an image's size depends on the program you are using. In GIMP, go to the Image menu and click Scale Image to open the Scale Image dialog box (see Figure 8.5).

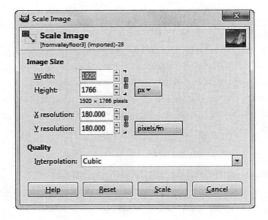

FIGURE 8.5
Use the Scale Image dialog box to change the size of an image.

You'll almost always want to resize using the existing aspect ratio, meaning that when you enter the width you'd like the image to be, the height is calculated automatically (and vice versa), to keep the image from squishing out of shape. In GIMP, the aspect ratio is locked by default, as indicated by the chain link displayed next to the Width and Height options shown in Figure 8.5. Clicking once on the chain unlocks it, enabling you to specify pixel widths and heights of your own choosing—squished or not.

NOTE
As with many of the features in GIMP, the Scale Image dialog box appears in front of the window containing the image being resized. This placement enables you to make changes in the dialog box, apply them, and see the results immediately.

In most, if not all, graphics programs, you can also resize the image based on percentages instead of providing specific pixel dimensions. For example, if my image started out as 1815×1721 and I didn't want to do the math to determine the values necessary to show it as half that width, I could simply select Percent (in this instance, from the drop-down next to the pixel display in Figure 8.5) and change the default setting (100) to 50. The image width would then become 908 pixels wide by 861 high—and no math was necessary on my part.

Tweaking Image Colors

If you are editing photographic images instead of creating your own graphics, you might need to use some color-correction tools to get the photo just right. As in many image-editing programs, GIMP offers several options for adjusting an image's brightness, contrast, and color balance, as well as a filter to reduce the dreaded red-eye. To remove red-eye using GIMP, go to Filters, click Enhance, and then click Red Eye Removal.

Most of these options are pretty intuitive. If you want the image to be brighter, adjust the brightness. If you want more red in your image, adjust the color balance. In GIMP, the Colors menu gives you access to numerous tools. As with the Scale Image dialog box described in the preceding section, each tool displays a dialog box in the foreground of your workspace. As you adjust the colors, the image reflects those changes. This preview function is a feature included in most image-editing software.

Figure 8.6 shows the Adjust Hue/Lightness/Saturation tool, one of the many tools provided on the Colors menu. As shown in the figure, you can achieve many color-related changes by using various sliders in dialog boxes to adjust the values you are working with. The Preview feature enables you to see what you are doing as you are doing it. The Reset Color button returns the image to its original state without any changes applied.

Because of the numerous tools available to you, and the preview function available with each tool, a little playful experimentation is the best way to find out what each tool does.

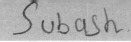

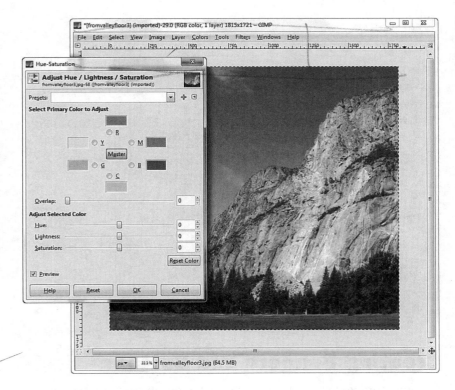

FIGURE 8.6
The Adjust Hue/Lightness/
Saturation tool is one of many
slider-based color-modification
tools available in GIMP.

Controlling JPEG Compression

Photographic images on the Web work best when saved in the JPEG file format rather than GIF; JPEG enables you to retain the number of colors in the file while still keeping the overall file size to a manageable level. When you're finished adjusting the size and appearance of your photo, select File, Export and choose JPEG as the file type. Your graphics program will likely provide you with another dialog box for controlling various JPEG options, such as compression.

Figure 8.7 shows the Export Image as JPEG dialog box you'll see when you export a JPEG in GIMP. You can see here that you can control the compression ratio for saving JPEG files by adjusting the Quality slider between 1 (low quality, small file size) and 100 (high quality, large file size).

You might want to experiment a bit to see how various JPEG compression levels affect the quality of your images, but 85% quality (or 15% compression) is generally a good compromise between file size (and, therefore, download speed) and quality for most photographic images.

FIGURE 8.7
GIMP enables you to reduce file size while still retaining image quality by saving in the JPEG format.

Creating Banners and Buttons

Graphics that you create from scratch, such as banners and buttons, require you to make considerations uniquely different from those that apply to photographs.

The first decision you need to make when you produce a banner or button is how big it should be. Most people accessing the web now have a computer with a screen that is at least 1024×768 pixels in resolution, if not considerably larger. For example, my screen is currently set at 1440×900 pixels; 1366×768 is another popular resolution. It's a nice touch to plan your graphics so that they always fit within smaller screens (1024×768), with room to spare for scrollbars and margins. These days, though, you won't run into much trouble if you're designing for the desktop and nudge that minimal width up by a few pixels.

Assuming that you target a minimum resolution of 1024×768 pixels, full-size banners and title graphics should be no more than 900 pixels wide, which is the generally available viewable width of the page after you've accounted for scrollbars, toolbars, and other parts of the browser window. Within a page, normal photos and other images should be from 100 to 300 pixels in each dimension, and smaller buttons and icons should be 20 to 100 pixels tall and wide. Over the years, some generally acceptable sizes have been used for banner graphics and other advertisement-size images; you can see these sizes in use if you look at the banner ads available for affiliate and partner programs, such as the Amazon Affiliate program (see https://affiliate-program.amazon.com/). Common sizes include 120×600, 234×60, and 300×250, to name a new.

To create a new image in GIMP, go to File and choose New. The Create a New Image dialog box displays (see Figure 8.8). If you aren't sure how big the image needs to be, just accept the default size of 640×480. Or you can choose one of the other predetermined sizes in the Template drop-down, such as Web Banner Common 468×60 or Web Banner Huge 728×90. Those two settings are conservative, yet perfectly acceptable, interpretations of "common" and "huge" for banners. From this dialog box, you can also enter your own width and height for the new image.

TIP

For many years, designing for 800×600 screen resolution was the norm. Still keep that low number in mind because many people do not open applications in full-screen mode. However, designing for a baseline 1024×768 screen resolution is not a bad idea.

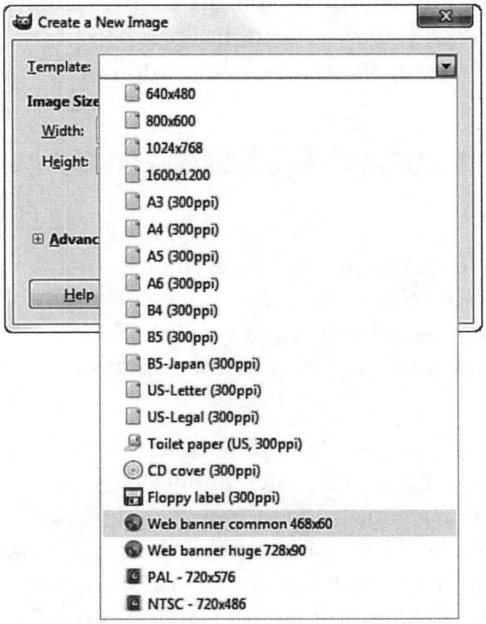

FIGURE 8.8
You must decide on the size of an image before you start working on it.

Create a New Image

Template:

- 640x480
- 800x600
- 1024x768
- 1600x1200
- A3 (300ppi)
- A4 (300ppi)
- A5 (300ppi)
- A6 (300ppi)
- B4 (300ppi)
- B5 (300ppi)
- B5-Japan (300ppi)
- US-Letter (300ppi)
- US-Legal (300ppi)
- Toilet paper (US, 300ppi)
- CD cover (300ppi)
- Floppy label (300ppi)
- Web banner common 468x60
- Web banner huge 728x90
- PAL - 720x576
- NTSC - 720x486

For the image's background color, you should usually choose white to match the background that most web browsers use for web pages (although as you learned previously, that color can be changed). When you know that you'll be creating a page with a background other than white, you can choose a different background color for your image. Or you might want to create an image with no background at all, in which case you select Transparency as the background color. When the final, web-ready image includes a transparent background, the web page (and its background color) behind the image is allowed to show through. In GIMP, select the background color for your new image by opening the Advanced Options in the Create a New Image dialog box.

After you enter the width and height of the image in pixels and click OK, you are faced with a blank canvas—an intimidating sight if you're as art-phobic as most of us! However, so many image-creation tutorials (not to mention entire books) are available to lead you through the process that I'm comfortable leaving you to your own creative devices. This section is all about introducing you to the things you want to keep in mind when creating graphics for use in your sites. This section does not necessarily teach you exactly how to do it, because being comfortable with the tool *you* choose is the first step to mastering it.

Reducing or Removing Colors in an Image

One of the most effective ways to reduce the size of an image—and, therefore, its download time—is to reduce the number of colors used in the image. This can drastically reduce the visual quality of some photographic images, but it works great for most banners, buttons, and other icons.

You'll be glad to know that there is a special file format for images with a limited number of colors, the Graphics Interchange Format (GIF). When you save or export an image as a GIF, you might be prompted to flatten layers or reduce the number of colors by converting to an indexed image because those are requirements for GIFs; check your software's help file regarding layers and indexed colors for a full understanding of what you might need to do.

Remember, the GIF image format is designed for images that contain areas of solid colors, such as web page titles and other illustrated graphics; the GIF format is not ideal for photographs (use JPG or PNG files instead).

PNG (pronounced "ping") is a useful file format that is supported in all major web browsers. Whereas the GIF image format enables you to specify a single transparent color, which means that the background of the web page will show through those areas of an image, the PNG format takes things a step further by enabling you to specify varying degrees of transparency.

You might have seen websites that use background colors or images in their container elements but also have images present in the foreground that allow the background to show through parts of the foreground graphics. In these cases, the images in the foreground have portions that are transparent so that the images themselves—which are always on a rectangular canvas—do not show the areas of the canvas where the design does not occur. You often want to use these types of partially transparent images to make graphics look good over any background color or background image you have in place.

To make part of an image transparent, the image must be saved in the GIF or PNG file format. As mentioned previously in this chapter, most graphics programs that support the GIF format enable you to specify one color to be transparent, whereas PNG images allow for a range of transparency. Largely because of this transparency range, the PNG format is superior to GIF. All the latest web browsers already support PNG images.

The process of creating a transparent image depends on the type of image you are creating (GIF or PNG) and the graphics software you are using to create it. For instructions, look in your graphics program's help files or type "transparent images with [*your program here*]" into your search engine.

Creating Tiled Background Images

You can use any GIF, JPG, or PNG image as a background tile within a container element, but before you go off and create a tiled background, especially a highly patterned tiled background, ask yourself what that tiled background adds to the overall look and feel of your website.

More important, ask yourself whether the text of the site can be read easily when placed over that pattern.

Think about the websites you frequent every day, and consider the fact that few use tiled, heavily patterned backgrounds on their entire pages. If you restrict your browsing to websites for companies, products, sports teams, or other sites in which information (primarily text) is privileged, the number of sites with tiled, heavily patterned backgrounds decreases even further. The web affords everyone the right of individuality in design, but if you are creating a site for your business, you might want to avoid using a highly patterned background with contrasting colored text.

If you do use a tiled background image for your entire site, remember that tiled images look best when you can't tell they're tiled images. In other words, you know you have a good image when the top edge of a background tile matches seamlessly with the bottom edge, and the left edge matches with the right.

Figures 8.9 and 8.10 show background tiles in use, both with seamless background, but with varying degrees of effectiveness.

FIGURE 8.9
This is an example of a seamless background image in which you can tell the background is tiled because you can see six identical shapes.

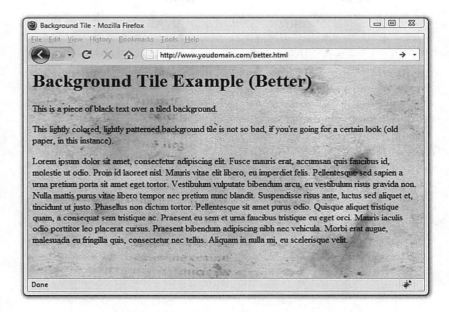

Later in this chapter, you'll learn how to place background images within your container elements. Despite my warnings so far in this section, background images can be powerful weapons in your design arsenal—just not when heavily patterned. You can find some great (and freely available) examples of background images—often referred to as *textures*—at the Subtle Patterns website (subtlepatterns.com). I haven't shown an example of a good subtle tiled background because for it to be an element of good design, it would likely be so subtle that it wouldn't be visible in a printed book.

Creating Animated Web Graphics

The GIF image format enables you to create animated images that add some motion to spice up any web page. Animated GIF images also transfer much faster than most of the video or multimedia files that are often used for similar effect. With the GIMP software package, you can create animated GIFs by creating multiple layers within an image and then modifying the Animated GIF options when saving the file. Additionally, if you have a series of images you want to animate, you can use the free, web-based GIF animation service at Gickr (www.gickr.com).

The first step in creating a GIF animation is to create a series of images to be displayed one after the other—or a series of layers, depending on your particular software program. Each of these images is called a *frame.* In the same way as movies or cartoons are put together, the images that you see on the movie or television screen and the images in animated graphics are made up of many individual frames that have slight differences in their appearance. When you have your graphical frames in mind, the process of tying them together is relatively simple—the planning stage is the most difficult. Take some time to sketch out the frames in storyboard fashion, especially if you plan to have more than just a few frames. When you know how your frames are going to fit together, use the Gickr service mentioned earlier in this section, or read the documentation for your graphics software to learn its particular process for pulling it all together.

▼ TRY IT YOURSELF

Preparing Images for Use in Your Website

You should get two or three images ready now so that you can try putting them on your own pages as you follow along with the rest of this chapter. If you have some image files already saved in the GIF, PNG, or JPEG formats (the filenames end in .gif, .png, or .jpg), use those. It's also fine to use any graphics you created while reading the preceding section.

Search engines such as Google can become a gold mine of images by leading you to sites related to your own theme. Search engines can also help you discover the oodles of sites specifically dedicated to providing free and cheap access to reusable media collections. Other valuable sources include Google Images (images.google.com/) and Flickr (www.flickr.com)—look for images using Creative Commons licenses that allow free use with attribution.

Placing Images on a Web Page

To get started with image placement on your website, first move the image file into the same folder as the HTML file or into a directory named images—often used for easy organization.

In this first example, let's assume you have placed an image called myimage.gif in the same directory as the HTML file you want to use to display it. To display it, insert the following HTML tag at the point in the text where you want the image to appear, using the name of your image file instead of myimage.gif:

```
<img src="myimage.gif" alt="My Image" />
```

If your image file were in the `images` directory below the document root, you would use the following code, which you can see now contains the full path to `myimage.gif` in the `images` directory:

```
<img src="/images/myimage.gif" alt="My Image" />
```

Both the `src` and the `alt` attributes of the `<img />` tag are required for valid HTML web pages. The `src` attribute identifies the image file, and the `alt` attribute enables you to specify descriptive text about the image. The `alt` attribute is intended to serve as an alternative to the image if a user is unable to view the image either because it is unavailable or because the user is using a text-only browser or screen reader. You'll read more on the `alt` attribute later, in the section "Describing Images with Text."

As an example of how to use the `<img />` tag, Listing 8.2 inserts an image at the top of the page, before a paragraph of text. Whenever a web browser displays the HTML file in Listing 8.2, it automatically retrieves and displays the image file as shown in Figure 8.11.

NOTE

It doesn't matter to the web server, web browser, or end user just where you put your images, as long as you know where they are and you use the correct paths in your HTML code.

Personally, I prefer to put all my images in a separate `images` directory, or in a subdirectory of a generic `assets` directory (such as `assets/images`), so that all my images or other assets, such as multimedia and JavaScript files, are neatly organized.

FIGURE 8.11
When a web browser displays the HTML code shown in Listing 8.2, it renders the `hd.jpg` image.

NOTE

The `<img />` tag is one of the HTML tags that also supports a `title` attribute; you can also use this attribute to describe an image, much like the `alt` attribute. However, the `title` attribute is problematic, in that it is displayed inconsistently across different user agents and thus cannot be relied on. You might see the `title` attribute being used, and your HTML will be valid if you use it, but please do not use it in place of an `alt` attribute; doing so will limit your site's usefulness on many types of devices.

NOTE

You can include an image from any website within your own pages. In those cases, the image is retrieved from the other page's web server whenever your page is displayed. You could do this, but you shouldn't! Not only is it bad manners (and probably a copyright violation) because you are using the other person's bandwidth for your own personal gain, but it also can make your pages display more slowly. Additionally, you have no way of controlling when the image might be changed or deleted.

If you are granted permission to republish an image from another web page, always transfer a copy of that image to your computer and use a local file reference, such as `<img src="myimage.jpg" />` instead of `<img src="http://www.otherserver.com/theirimage.jpg" />`. This advice is not applicable, however, when you host your images—such as photographs—at a service specifically meant as an image repository, such as Flickr (www.flickr.com). Services such as Flickr provide you with a URL for each image, and each URL includes Flickr's domain in the address. The same is true if you want to link to images you have taken with mobile applications such as Instagram—these types of services also provide you with a full URL to an image that you can then link to in your own website.

LISTING 8.2   Using the `<img />` Tag to Place Images on a Web Page

```html
<!DOCTYPE html>
<html lang="en">
 <head>
  <title>A Spectacular Yosemite View</title>
 </head>

 <body>
  <section>
    <header>
      <h1>A Spectacular Yosemite View</h1>
    </header>
     <img src="hd.jpg" alt="Half Dome" />
    <p><strong>Half Dome</strong> is a granite dome in Yosemite
    National Park,located in northeastern Mariposa County,
    California, at the eastern end of Yosemite Valley. The
    granite crest rises more than 4,737 ft (1,444 m) above
    the valley floor.</p>
    <p>This particular view is of Half Dome as seen from Washburn
    Point.</p>
  </section>
 </body>
</html>
```

If you guessed that `img` refers to "image," you're right. Likewise, `src` refers to "source," or a reference to the location of the image file. As discussed at the beginning of this book, an image is always stored in a file separate from the text of your web page (your HTML file), even though it appears to be part of the same page when viewed in a browser.

As with the `<a>` tag used for hyperlinks, you can specify any complete Internet address as the location of an image file in the `src` attribute of the `<img />` tag. You can also use relative addresses, such as `/images/birdy.jpg` or `../smiley.gif`.

Describing Images with Text

The `<img />` tag in Listing 8.2 includes a short text message—in this case, `alt="Half Dome"`. The `alt` stands for *alternate text*, which is the message that appears in place of the image itself if it does not load. An image might not load if its address is incorrect, if the Internet connection is very slow and the data has not yet transferred, or if the user is using a text-only browser or screen reader. Figure 8.12 shows one example of `alt` text used in place of an image. Each web browser renders `alt` text differently, but the information is still provided when it is part of your HTML document.

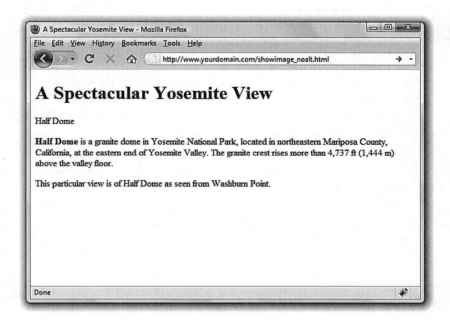

FIGURE 8.12
Users will see `alt` messages when images do not appear.

Even when graphics have fully loaded and are visible in the web browser, the `alt` message might appear in a little box (known as a *tooltip*) whenever the mouse pointer passes over an image. The `alt` message also helps any user who is visually impaired (or is using a voice-based interface to read the web page).

You must include a suitable `alt` attribute in every `<img />` tag on your web pages, keeping in mind the variety of situations in which people might see that message. A very brief description of the image is usually best, but web page authors sometimes put short advertising messages or subtle humor in their `alt` messages; too much humor and not enough information is frowned upon, because it is not all that useful. For small or unimportant images, it's tempting to omit the `alt` message altogether, but the `alt` attribute is a required attribute of the `<img />` tag. If you omit it, this doesn't mean your page won't display properly, but it does mean you'll be in violation of HTML standards. I recommend assigning an empty text message to `alt` if you absolutely don't need it (`alt=""`), which is sometimes the case with small or decorative images.

TIP

The height and width specified for an image don't have to match the image's actual height and width. A web browser tries to squish or stretch the image to display whatever size you specify. However, this is generally a bad idea because browsers aren't particularly good at resizing images. If you know you want an image to display smaller, you're definitely better off just resizing it in an image editor.

NOTE

At the time of this writing, web developers and designers are discussing the creation and implementation of what are known as responsive images, or images that are displayed at different sizes and resolutions depending on the browser and media type. A new HTML5 element called `<picture>` has been introduced but is not yet part of the standard, nor is it implemented by many web browsers. If you plan to do any work with images on the Web in the future, file away this information and check up on the status of this new element from time to time at http://picture. responsiveimages.org/.

Specifying Image Height and Width

Because text moves over the Internet much faster than graphics, most web browsers end up displaying the text on a page before they display images. This gives users something to read while they're waiting to see the pictures, which makes the whole page seem to load faster.

You can make sure that everything on your page appears as quickly as possible and in the right places by explicitly stating each image's height and width. That way, a web browser can immediately and accurately make room for each image as it lays out the page and while it waits for the images to finish transferring.

For each image you want to include in your site, you can use your graphics program to determine its exact height and width in pixels. You might also be able to find these image properties by using system tools. For example, in Windows, you can see an image's height and width by right-clicking the image, selecting Properties, and then selecting Details. When you know the height and width of an image, you can include its dimensions in the `<img />` tag, like this:

```
<img src="myimage.gif" alt="Fancy Picture" width="200"
height="100" />
```

Aligning Images

Just as you can align text on a page, you can align images on the page using special attributes. You can align images both horizontally and vertically with respect to text and other images that surround them.

Horizontal Image Alignment

As discussed in Chapter 6, "Working with Fonts, Text Blocks, Lists and Tables," you can use the `text-align` CSS property to align content within an element as centered, aligned with the right margin, or aligned with the left margin. These style settings affect both text and images, and they can be used within any block element, such as `<p>`.

Like text, images are normally lined up with the left margin unless another alignment setting indicates that they should be centered or right-justified. In other words, `left` is the default value of the `text-align` CSS property.

You can also wrap text around images by using the `float` CSS property directly within the `<img />` tag.

In Listing 8.3, `<img style="float:left" />` aligns the first image to the left and wraps text around the right side of it, as you might expect. Similarly, `<img style="float:right" />` aligns the second image to the right and wraps text around the left side of it. Figure 8.13 shows how these images align on a web page. There is no concept of floating an image to the center because there would be no way to determine how to wrap text on each side of it.

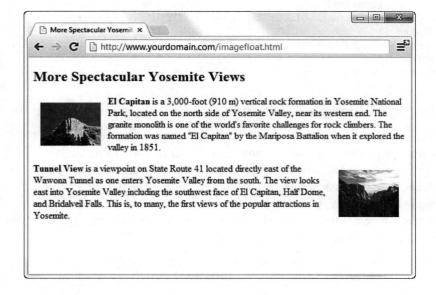

FIGURE 8.13
Showing the image alignment from Listing 8.3.

LISTING 8.3   Using `float` Style Properties to Align Images on a Web Page

```
<!DOCTYPE html>

<html lang="en">
 <head>
  <title>More Spectacular Yosemite Views</title>
 </head>

 <body>
  <section>
    <header>
    <h1>More Spectacular Yosemite Views</h1>
    </header>
    <p><img src="elcap_sm.jpg" alt="El Capitan" width="100"
```

NOTE

Notice the addition of padding in the style attribute for both `<img/>` tags used in Listing 8.3. This padding provides some breathing room between the image and the text—12 pixels on all four sides of the image. You'll learn more about padding in Chapter 9, "Working with Margins, Padding, Alignment, and Floating."

```
height="75" style="float:left; padding: 12px;"/><strong>El
Capitan</strong> is a 3,000-foot (910 m) vertical rock
formation in Yosemite National Park, located on the north
side of Yosemite Valley, near its western end. The granite
monolith is one of the world's favorite challenges for rock
climbers. The formation was named "El Capitan" by the
Mariposa Battalion when it explored the valley in 1851.</p>
<p><img src="tunnelview_sm.jpg" alt="Tunnel View" width="100"
height="80" style="float:right; padding: 12px;"/><strong>
Tunnel View</strong> is a viewpoint on State Route 41 located
directly east of the Wawona Tunnel as one enters Yosemite
Valley from the south. The view looks east into Yosemite
Valley including the southwest face of El Capitan, Half Dome,
and Bridalveil Falls. This is, to many, the first views of
the popular attractions in Yosemite.</p>
    </section>
  </body>
</html>
```

Vertical Image Alignment

Sometimes you want to insert a small image in the middle of a line of text, or you want to put a single line of text next to an image as a caption. In either case, having some control over how the text and images line up vertically would be handy. Should the bottom of the image line up with the bottom of the letters, or should the text and images all be arranged so that their middles line up? You can choose between these and several other options:

▶ To line up the top of an image with the top of the tallest image or letter on the same line, use this:

```
<img style="vertical-align:text-top" />
```

▶ To line up the bottom of an image with the bottom of the text, use this:

```
<img style="vertical-align:text-bottom" />
```

▶ To line up the middle of an image with the overall vertical center of everything on the line, use this:

```
<img style="vertical-align:middle" />
```

NOTE

The `vertical-align` CSS property also supports values of `top` and `bottom`, which can align images with the overall top or bottom of a line of elements, regardless of any text on the line.

▶ To line up the bottom of an image with the baseline of the text, use this:

```
<img style="vertical-align:baseline" />
```

All four of these options are used in Listing 8.4 and displayed in Figure 8.14. Four thumbnail images are now listed vertically down the page, along with descriptive text next to each image. Various settings for the `vertical-align` CSS property are used to align each image and its relevant text. This is certainly not the most beautiful page, but the various alignments should be clear to you.

LISTING 8.4   Using `vertical-align` Styles to Align Text with Images

```
<!DOCTYPE html>

<html lang="en">
 <head>
  <title>Small But Mighty Spectacular Yosemite Views</title>
 </head>

 <body>
  <section>
    <header>
      <h1>Small But Mighty Yosemite Views</h1>
    </header>
    <p><img src="elcap_sm.jpg" alt="El Capitan" width="100"
    height="75" style="vertical-align:text-top;"/><strong>El
    Capitan</strong> is a 3,000-foot (910 m) vertical rock
    formation in Yosemite National Park.</p>
    <p><img src="tunnelview_sm.jpg" alt="Tunnel View" width="100"
    height="80" style="vertical-align:text-bottom;"/><strong>
    Tunnel View</strong> looks east into Yosemite Valley.</p>
    <p><img src="upperyosefalls_sm.jpg" alt="Upper Yosemite
    Falls" width="87" height="100" style="vertical-
    align:middle;"/>
    <strong>Upper Yosemite Falls</strong> are 1,430 ft and are
    among the twenty highest waterfalls in the world. </p>
    <p><img src="hangingrock_sm.jpg" alt="Hanging Rock"
    width="100" height="75" style="vertical-align:baseline;"/>
    <strong>Hanging Rock</strong>, off Glacier Point, used to be
    a popular spot for people to, well, hang from. Crazy
    people.</p>
  </section>
 </body>
</html>
```

TIP

If you don't assign any `vertical-align` CSS property in an `<img />` tag or class used with an `<img />` tag, the bottom of the image will line up with the baseline of any text next to it. That means you never actually have to use `vertical-align:baseline` because it is assumed by default. However, if you specify a margin for an image and intend for the alignment to be a bit more exact in relation to the text, you might want to explicitly set the `vertical-align` attribute to `text-bottom`.

Turning Images into Links

You probably noticed in Figure 8.11 that the image on the page is quite large. This is fine in this particular example, but it isn't ideal when you're trying to present multiple images. It makes more sense to create smaller image thumbnails that link to larger versions of each image. Then you can arrange the thumbnails on the page so that visitors can easily see all the written content, even if they see only a smaller version of the actual (larger) image. Thumbnails are one of the many ways you can use image links to spice up your pages.

To turn any image into a clickable link to another page or image, you can use the <a> tag that you learned about in Chapter 7 to make text links. Listing 8.5 contains the code to display thumbnails of images within text, with those thumbnails linking to larger versions of the images. To ensure that the user knows to click the thumbnails, the image and some helper text are enclosed in a <div>, as shown in Figure 8.15.

LISTING 8.5   Using Thumbnails for Effective Image Links

```
<!DOCTYPE html>

<html lang="en">
 <head>
  <title>More Spectacular Yosemite Views</title>
   <style type="text/css">
   div.imageleft {
    float: left;
    clear: all;
    text-align: center;
    font-size: 10px;
    font-style: italic;
   }
   div.imageright {
    float: right;
    clear: all;
    text-align: center;
    font-size: 10px;
    font-style: italic;
   }
   img {
    padding: 6px;
    border: none;
   }
   </style>
 </head>
 <body>
  <section>
    <header>
    <h1>More Spectacular Yosemite Views</h1>
    </header>
    <div class="imageleft">
    <a href="http://www.flickr.com/photos/nofancyname/614253439/"><img
    src="elcap_sm.jpg" alt="El Capitan" width="100" height="75"/></a>
    <br/>click image to enlarge</div>
    <p><strong>El Capitan</strong> is a 3,000-foot (910 m) vertical
    rock formation in Yosemite National Park, located on the north
    side of Yosemite Valley, near its western end. The granite
    monolith is one of the world's favorite challenges for rock
    climbers. The formation was named "El Capitan" by the Mariposa
    Battalion when it explored the valley in 1851.</p>
    <div class="imageright">
    <a href="http://www.flickr.com/photos/nofancyname/614287355/"><img
    src="tunnelview_sm.jpg" alt="Tunnel View" width="100" height="80"
    /></a> <br/>click image to enlarge</div>
    <p><strong>Tunnel View</strong> is a viewpoint on State Route 41
    located directly east of the Wawona Tunnel as one enters Yosemite
    Valley from the south. The view looks east into Yosemite Valley
    including the southwest face of El Capitan, Half Dome, and
```

```
     Bridalveil Falls. This is, to many, the first views of the
     popular attractions in Yosemite.</p>
     </section>
   </body>
</html>
```

FIGURE 8.15
Using thumbnails as links improves
the layout of a page that uses
large images.

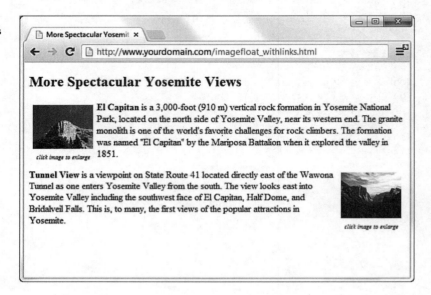

The code in Listing 8.5 uses additional styles that are explained in more detail in later chapters, but you should be able to figure out the basics:

▶ The <a> tags link these particular images to larger versions, which, in this case, are stored on an external server (at Flickr).

▶ The <div> tags, and their styles, are used to align those sets of graphics and caption text (and also include some padding).

Unless instructed otherwise, web browsers display a colored rectangle around the edge of each image link. As with text links, the rectangle usually appears blue for links that haven't been visited recently and purple for links that have been visited recently—unless you specify different-colored links in your style sheet. Because you seldom, if ever, want this unsightly line around your linked images, you should usually include style="border:none" in any <img /> tag within a link.

In this instance, the `border:none` style is made part of the style sheet entry for the `img` element because we use the same styles twice.

When you click one of the thumbnail images on the sample page shown, the link opens in the browser, as shown in Figure 8.16.

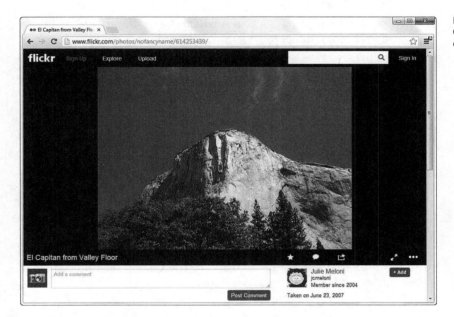

FIGURE 8.16
Clicking a linked thumbnail image opens the target of the link.

Using Background Images

As you learned earlier in this chapter, you can use background images to act as a sort of wallpaper in a container element so that the text or other images appear on top of this underlying design.

The basic CSS properties that work together to create a background are listed here:

▶ `background-color`—Specifies the background color of the element. Although it is not image related, it is part of the set of background-related properties. If an image is transparent or does not load, the user will see the background color instead.

▶ `background-image`—Specifies the image to use as the background of the element using the following syntax: `url('imagename.gif')`.

▶ `background-repeat`—Specifies how the image should repeat, both horizontally and vertically. By default (without specifying anything), background images repeat both horizontally and vertically. Other options are `repeat` (same as default), `repeat-x` (horizontal), `repeat-y` (vertical), and `no-repeat` (only one appearance of the graphic).

▶ `background-position`—Specifies where the image should be initially placed, relative to its container. Options include `top-left`, `top-center`, `top-right`, `center-left`, `center-center`, `center-right`, `bottom-left`, `bottom-center`, `bottom-right`, and specific pixel and percentage placements.

When specifying a background image, you can put all these specifications together into one property, like so:

```
body {
    background: #ffffff url('imagename.gif') no-repeat top right;
}
```

In the preceding style sheet entry, the body element of the web page will be white and will include a graphic named `imagename.gif` at the top right. Another use for the `background` property is the creation of custom bullets for your unordered lists. To use images as bullets, first define the style for the `<ul>` tag as shown here:

```
ul {
  list-style-type: none;
  padding-left: 0;
  margin-left: 0;
}
```

Next, change the declaration for the `<li>` tag to this:

```
li {
  background: url(mybullet.gif) left center no-repeat
}
```

Make sure that `mybullet.gif` (or whatever you name your graphic) is on the web server and accessible; in this case, all unordered list items will show your custom image instead of the standard filled-disc bullet.

We return to the specific use of background properties in Part III, "Advanced Web Page Design with CSS," when using CSS for overall page layouts.

Using Imagemaps

Sometimes you want to use an image as navigation, but beyond the simple button-based or link-based navigation that you often see in websites. For example, perhaps you have a website with medical information, and you want to show an image of the human body that links to pages that provide information about various body parts. Or you have a website that provides a world map that users can click to access information about countries. You can divide an image into regions that link to different documents, depending on where users click within that image. This is called an *imagemap*, and any image can be made into an imagemap.

Why Imagemaps Aren't Always Necessary

The first point to know about imagemaps is that you probably won't need to use them except in very special cases. It's almost always easier and more efficient to use several ordinary images that are placed directly next to one another and provide a separate link for each image.

For example, see Figure 8.17. This is a web page that shows 12 different corporate logos; this example is a common type of web page in the business world, in which you give a little free advertisement to your partners. You *could* present these logos as one large image and create an imagemap that provides links to each of the 12 companies. Users could click each logo in the image to visit each company's site. But every time you wanted to add a new logo to the imagemap, you would have to modify the entire image and remap the hotspots—not a good use of anyone's time. Instead, in this case when an imagemap is not warranted, you simply display the images on the page as in this example, by using 12 separate images (one for each company) and having each image include a link to that particular company.

An imagemap is the best choice for an image that has numerous parts, is oddly arranged, or has a design that is itself too complicated to divide into separate images. Figure 8.18 shows an image that is best suited as an imagemap—a public domain image provided by the United States CIA of the standard time zones of the world.

```
<a href ="http: // www.google.com"> <img src ="image.jpg />
</a>
```

FIGURE 8.17
A web page with 12 different logos;
this could be presented as a
single imagemap or divided into 12
separate pieces.

FIGURE 8.18
This image wouldn't respond well
to being sliced up into perfectly
equal parts—better make it an
imagemap.

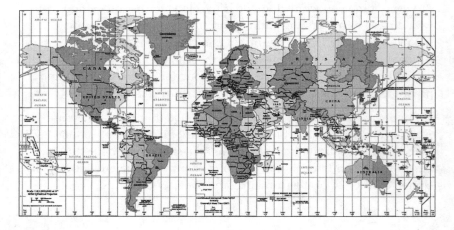

Mapping Regions Within an Image

To create any type of imagemap, you need to figure out the numerical pixel coordinates of each region within the image that you want to turn into a clickable link. These clickable links are also known as *areas*. Your graphics program might provide you with an easy way to find these coordinates. Or you might want to use a standalone imagemapping tool such as Mapedit (http://www.boutell.com/mapedit/) or an online imagemap maker such as the one at www.image-maps.com/. In addition to helping you map the coordinates, these tools provide the HTML code necessary to make the maps work.

Using an imagemapping tool is often as simple as using your mouse to draw a rectangle (or a custom shape) around the area you want to be a link. Figure 8.19 shows the result of one of these rectangular selections, as well as the interface for adding the URL and the title or alternate text for this link. Several pieces of information are necessary to creating the HTML for your imagemap: coordinates, target URL, and alternate text for the link.

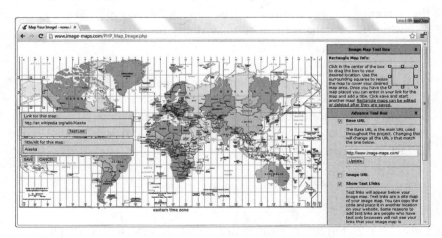

FIGURE 8.19
Using an imagemapping tool to create linked areas of a single graphic.

You're more likely to remember how to make imagemaps if you get an image of your own and turn it into an imagemap as you continue with this chapter:

▶ For starters, it's easiest to choose a fairly large image that is visually divided into roughly rectangular regions.

▶ If you don't have a suitable image handy, use your favorite graphics program to make one. Perhaps use a single photograph showing several people, and use each person as an area of the imagemap.

▶ Try a few different imagemapping tools to determine which you like best. Start with standalone software such as Mapedit (http://www.boutell.com/mapedit/), and move to the online imagemap maker at www.image-maps.com/. There are others; use the search engine of your choice to find variations on the imagemap software theme.

Creating the HTML for an Imagemap

If you use an imagemap generator, it will provide the necessary HTML for creating the imagemap. However, it is a good idea to understand the parts of the code so that you can check it for accuracy. The following HTML code is required to start any imagemap:

```
<map name="mapname">
```

Keep in mind that you can use whatever name you want for the name of the `<map>` tag, although it helps to make it as descriptive as possible. Next, you need an `<area />` tag for each region of the image. Following is an example of a single `<area />` tag that was produced by the actions shown in Figure 8.19:

```
<area shape="rect" coords="1,73,74,163"
   href="http://en.wikipedia.org/wiki/Alaska"
   alt="Alaska"    title="Alaska" />
```

This `<area />` tag has five attributes, which you use with every area you describe in an imagemap:

▶ shape indicates whether the region is a rectangle (shape="rect"), a circle (shape="circle"), or an irregular polygon (shape="poly").

▶ coords gives the exact pixel coordinates for the region. For rectangles, give the x,y coordinates of the upper-left corner followed by the x,y coordinates of the lower-right corner. For circles, give the x,y center point followed by the radius in pixels. For polygons, list the x,y coordinates of all the corners in a connect-the-dots order.

Here is an example of a mapped polygon—they can get a little crazy looking:

```
<area shape="poly"
coords="233,0,233,20,225,22,225,101,216,121,212,154,212,167,
212,181,222,195,220,209,226,214,226,234,232,252,224,253,223,
261,231,264,232,495,254,497,274,495,275,482,258,463,275,381,
270,348,257,338,266,329,272,313,271,301,258,292,264,284,262,
262,272,263,272,178,290,172,289,162,274,156,274,149,285,151,
281,134,272,137,274,3"
href="http://en.wikipedia.org/wiki/Eastern_Time_Zone"
alt="Eastern Time Zone" title="Eastern Time Zone"/>
```

▶ `href` specifies the location to which the region links. You can use any address or filename that you would use in an ordinary `<a>` link tag.

▶ `alt` enables you to provide a piece of text that is associated with the shape; as you learned previously, providing this text is important to users browsing with text-only browsers or screen readers.

▶ The use of `title` ensures that tooltips containing the information are also visible when the user accesses the designated area.

Each distinct clickable region in an imagemap must be described as a single area, which means that a typical imagemap consists of a list of areas. After you've coded the `<area />` tags, you are done defining the imagemap, so wrap things up with a closing `</map>` tag.

The last step in creating an imagemap is wiring it up to the actual map image. The map image is placed on the page using an ordinary `<img />` tag. However, an extra `usemap` attribute is coded like this:

```
<img src="timezonemap.png" usemap="#timezonemap"
  style="border:none; width:977px;height:498px "
  alt=" World Timezone Map " />
```

When specifying the value of the `usemap` attribute, use the name you put in the `id` of the `<map>` tag (and don't forget the # symbol). Also include the `style` attribute to specify the height and width of the image and to turn off the border around the imagemap, which you might or might not elect to keep in imagemaps of your own.

NOTE

One method of producing mapped images relies solely on CSS, not the HTML `<map>` tag. You will learn more about this in Chapter 11, "Using CSS to Do More with Lists, Text, and Navigation."

Listing 8.6 shows the complete code for a sample web page containing the map graphic, its imagemap, and a few mapped areas.

LISTING 8.6   Defining the Regions of an Imagemap with `<map>` and `<area />` Tags

```
<!DOCTYPE html>

<html lang="en">
 <head>
  <title>Testing an Imagemap</title>
 </head>

 <body>
  <section>
    <header>
      <h1>Testing an Imagemap</h1>
    </header>
    <div style="text-align:center"> Click on an area to learn
    more about that location or time zone.<br/>
    <img src="timezonemap.png" usemap="#timezonemap"
    style="border:none; width:977px;height:498px "
    alt="World Timezone Map" /></div>

    <map name="timezonemap" id="timezonemap">
    <area shape="poly" coords=" 233,0,233,20,225,22,225,101,216,
    121,212,154,212,167,212,181,222,195,220,209,226,214,226,234,
    232,252,224,253,223,261,231,264,232,495,254, 497,274,495,275,
    482,258,463,275,381,270,348,257, 338,266,329,272,313,271,301,
    258,292,264,284,262, 262,272,263,272,178,290,172,289,162,
    274,156,274,149,285,151,281,134,272,137,274,3 "
    href="http://en.wikipedia.org/wiki/eastern_time_zone"
    alt="Eastern Time Zone" title="Eastern Time Zone" />
    <area shape="rect" coords="1,73,74,163 "
    href="http://en.wikipedia.org/wiki/Alaska"
    alt="Alaska" title="Alaska" />
    </map>
  </section>
  </body>
</html>
```

Figure 8.20 shows the imagemap in action. When you hover the mouse over an area, the `alt` or `title` text for that area—in this example, `Eastern Time Zone`—is displayed on the imagemap.

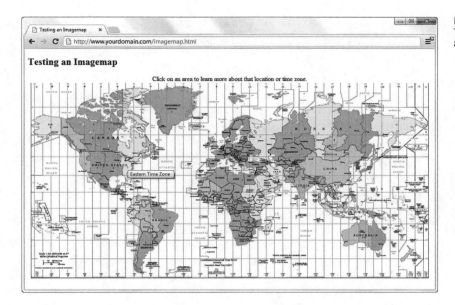

FIGURE 8.20
The imagemap defined in Listing 8.6 as it displays on the web page.

Linking to Multimedia Files

Let's move away from static images for a moment and move into more exciting multimedia such as audio and video. The simplest and most reliable option for incorporating a video or audio file into your website is to simply link it in with an `<a>` tag, exactly as you would link to another HTML file.

For example, you could use the following line to offer an MOV video of an adorable kitten:

```
<a href="cute_kitten.mov">View an adorable kitten!</a>
```

When the user clicks the words `View an adorable kitten!`, the `cute_kitten.mov` QuickTime video file is transferred to his or her computer from your web server. Whichever helper application or plug-in the user has installed automatically starts as soon as the file has finished downloading. If no compatible helper or plug-in can be found, the web browser offers the user a chance to download the appropriate plug-in or save the video on the hard drive for later viewing.

NOTE

In case you're unfamiliar with *helper applications* (*helper apps* for short), they are the external programs that a web browser calls on to display any type of file it can't handle on its own. Generally, the helper application associated with a file type is called on whenever a web browser can't display that type of file on its own.

Plug-ins are a special sort of helper application installed directly into a web browser. They enable you to view multimedia content directly in the browser window.

▼ TRY IT YOURSELF

Create or Find Some Multimedia to Use in Your Website

Before you learn how to place multimedia on your web pages, you need to have some multimedia content.

Creating multimedia of any kind can be a challenging and complicated task. If you're planning to create your own content from scratch, you need far more than this book to become the next crackerjack multimedia developer. When you have some content, however, you can use the tips in this chapter to show you how to place your new creations into your web pages.

If you're artistically challenged, you can obtain useful multimedia assets in several alternative ways. Aside from the obvious (such as hiring an artist), here are a few suggestions:

▶ Much of the material on the Internet is free. Of course, it's still a good idea to double-check with the author or current owner of the content; you don't want to be sued for copyright infringement. In addition, various offices of the U.S. government generate content that, by law, belongs to all Americans. (For example, any NASA footage found online is free for your use.)

▶ Many search engines have specific search capabilities for finding multimedia files. As long as you are careful about copyright issues, this can be an easy way to find multimedia related to a specific topic. A simple search for "sample Flash animations," "sample QuickTime movie," or "sample audio files" will produce more results than you can handle.

▶ If you are creatively inclined, determine the medium you like most—video production, audio production, or animation, for example. When you have a starting point, look into the various types of software that will enable you to create such artistic masterpieces. Many companies, including Adobe (www.adobe.com) and Apple (www.apple.com), provide multimedia software.

Listing 8.7 contains the code for a web page that uses a simple image link to play a video in Windows Media file format. In addition to the image link, a link is placed within the text to provide context for the user.

LISTING 8.7   Linking an Image to a Windows Media Video

```
<!DOCTYPE html>

<html lang="en">
  <head>
    <title>This Kitten Loves to Play!</title>
  </head>

  <body>
    <h1>This Kitten Loves to Play!</h1>
    <div style="border-style:none; float:left; padding:12px">
    <a href="kitten.wmv"><img src="projector.gif"
      alt="Kitten Video" /></a>
    </div>
    <p>All kittens love to play, but this one is particularly
    fond of her yellow stuffed banana toy!</p>
    <p>Click <a href="kitten.wmv">here</a> or on the projector
    graphic to see a movie clip of this kitten in action.</p>
  </body>
</html>
```

This code simply uses the `projector.gif` GIF image as a link to the `kitten.wmv` video clip. Figure 8.21 shows the kitten sample page with the projector image in view. When the image is clicked, the Windows Media Player is invoked and begins to play the movie.

To view the video, you need only click the animated projector (or the text link in the paragraph). This action results in the browser either playing the video with the help of a plug-in (if one is found that can play the clip) or deferring to a suitable helper application.

If you change the link from `kitten.wmv` (Windows Media) to `kitten.mov` (QuickTime), your browser handles the link differently. Instead of launching another program, the QuickTime plug-in enables you to view the movie clip directly in the browser window (see Figure 8.22).

As you might have guessed, this approach of using a simple link to play multimedia files offers the best backward compatibility because the browser bears all the responsibility of figuring out how to play a multimedia clip. The downside to this is that you don't have much control over how a clip is played, and you definitely can't play a clip directly in the context of a page.

NOTE

If your browser has no support for QuickTime, you can download the QuickTime player free from Apple at http://www.apple.com/quicktime/. Even if you do have QuickTime installed, some browsers play QuickTime movies differently based on whether a plug-in is installed. For example, on my Windows computer, Internet Explorer and Firefox both play QuickTime movies directly in the browser window via a plug-in, whereas Opera launches QuickTime as a helper application.

FIGURE 8.21
The `projector.gif` GIF image is used as an image link to a Windows Media file that launches an external helper application.

FIGURE 8.22
When you follow the image link, the `kitten.mov` QuickTime movie is played using the QuickTime browser plug-in.

Embedding Multimedia Files

HTML has long contained a standard `<object>` element for embedding multimedia files in a web page. This element is widely supported in both desktop and mobile browsers and is used to represent a type of resource to be viewed or played in the browser but using an external plug-in.

Embedding a multimedia file into a web page produces a set of software controls that enable the file to be played directly—no secondary window is necessary, and there's no need to navigate away from the page you are on. Following is code to embed the kitten video, which you saw earlier, using the `<object>` tag:

```
<object
  width="320"
  height="240"
  type="video/x-ms-wmv"
  data="kitten.wmv"
</object>
```

You can see the result of this code in Figure 8.23. This code isn't much more complicated than adding an image to your web page; the only real difference is that here you specify the file type (in this case, `video/x-ms-wmv`).

NOTE

It's important to note that Windows Media Player is a sophisticated enough media player that it automatically *streams* multimedia files, which means that it begins playing them after loading only the first few seconds of content. The idea is that the rest of the content is loaded in the background while you're watching or listening to earlier portions. Visitors thus don't have to wait through long download times when viewing or listening to your multimedia clips.

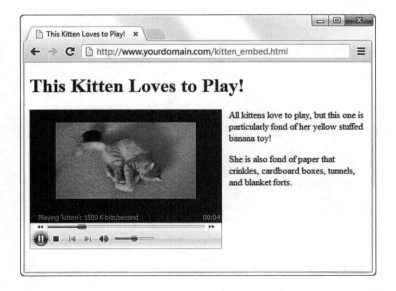

FIGURE 8.23
The `<object>` tag enables you to embed a video clip on a web page.

The `width` and `height` attributes of the `<object>` element determine the size of the embedded player (Windows Media Player, in this example). Some browsers automatically size the embedded player to fit the content if you leave these attributes off, whereas others don't show anything. Play it safe by setting them to a size that suits the multimedia content being played.

Only two other attributes are necessary to display the appropriate video file: the `data` attribute, which has a value of the filename (or URL to the file) you want to play, and the `type` attribute, which identifies the type of media being displayed. In this case, the file is a Windows Media Video (WMV) file, specified by the MIME types. A *MIME type* is an identifier for uniquely identifying different types of media objects on the Internet. MIME stands for Multipurpose Internet Mail Extensions, and this name comes from the fact that MIME types were originally used to identify email attachments. These MIME types should be used in the `type` attribute of the `<object>` element to identify what kind of multimedia object the `data` attribute is referencing.

Following are the MIME types for several popular sound and video formats you might want to use in your web pages:

▶ WAV Audio—`audio/vnd.wave`

▶ MP3 Audio—`audio/mpeg`

▶ MP4 Audio—`audio/mp4`

▶ WMV—`video/x-ms-wmv`

▶ MPEG Video—`video/mpeg`

▶ MPEG4 Video—`video/mp4`

▶ QuickTime—`video/quicktime`

Listing 8.8 shows the relevant code for the kitten web page, where you can see the `<object>` element as it appears in context.

LISTING 8.8   Using an `<object>` Element to Directly Embed a WMV Video Clip

```
<!DOCTYPE html>

<html lang="en">
  <head>
    <title>This Kitten Loves to Play!</title>
  </head>
```

```
<body>
  <h1>This Kitten Loves to Play!</h1>
  <div style="float:left; padding:12px">
  <object
     width="320"
     height="240"
     data="kitten.wmv"
     type="video/x-ms-wmv">
  </object>
  </div>
  <p>All kittens love to play, but this one is particularly
  fond of her yellow stuffed banana toy!</p>
  <p>She is also fond of paper that crinkles, cardboard boxes,
  tunnels, and blanket forts.</p>
  </body>
</html>
```

Although this section has discussed "embedding" a multimedia object using the `<object>` element, you can use another element to achieve the same goal: the appropriately named `<embed />` element. There's a good reason I didn't talk about the `<embed />` element first: It has a negative and confusing history. In the days before HTML5, multimedia objects could be embedded in web pages in two ways: using `<object>` (part of the official specification) or using `<embed />` (not part of the official specification, but implemented by the old Netscape browser). During this time, if you wanted to ensure that your embedded multimedia object was visible in all browsers, you used a little trickery and wrapped your `<embed />` element inside an `<object>` element, like so:

```
<object
      width="320"
      height="240"
      data="kitten.wmv"
      type="video/x-ms-wmv">

      <embed
            width="320"
            height="240"
            type="video/x-ms-wmv"
            src="kitten.wmv" />
</object>
```

Browsers that knew what to do with `<object>` elements did so and ignored the `<embed />` element. But browsers that ignored the `<object>` element and knew what to do with the `<embed />` element did just that. This was as annoying to web developers then as it is confusing to explain now.

Now, in the era of HTML5, both the `<object>` and the `<embed />` elements are valid, and you can use either one without having to use both. The only difference between the general usage of the two is that the `<object>` element uses the `data` attribute to refer to the multimedia resource, whereas the `<embed />` element uses the `src` attribute (much like the `<img />` tag).

Using Pure HTML5 for Audio and Video Playback

In the preceding section, you learned more about the confusing history of the `<object>` and `<embed />` elements than you probably imagined existed. The end result of this confusing history is that although you most certainly can continue to use `<object>` or `<embed />` elements to embed audio or video in your web pages, and rely on external plug-ins to play those files, HTML5 contains native elements for playing audio and video. In this instance, *native* refers to the browser's capability to play multimedia files without external plug-ins, and all major browsers on all platforms (including mobile) support these elements. This will be the preferred method of playing back audio and video moving forward.

Listing 8.9 shows how to use the `<audio>` element to embed an audio file that will be played natively by the browser. The `<audio>` element is quite simple and requires only one attribute: `src`, or the location of the resource you want to play. However, as you see in Listing 8.9, you'll probably want to use a few other handy attributes.

LISTING 8.9   Using the `<audio>` Element to Embed and Play an Audio File

```
<!DOCTYPE html>

<html lang="en">
  <head>
    <title>Let's Hear Some Music</title>
  </head>
```

```
<body>
   <h1>Let's Hear Some Music</h1>
   <p>Better yet, let's use the HTML5 &lt;audio&gt; element
   to do so!</p>
   <audio
         src="manhattan_beach.mp3"
         preload="auto"
         controls
         autoplay
         loop>

         <!-- Message to display in case the audio element isn't
         supported. -->
         <p>Your browser does not support the audio element.</p>
   </audio>
   </body>
</html>
```

TIP

Notice the inclusion of a message to users inside the `<audio>` element. Although current versions of all major browsers support the `<audio>` element, if a user's browser does not, that user will instead see the message within the `<p></p>` tags.

In addition to the `src` attribute, which, in this case, has a value of `manhattan_beach.mp3` because that is the name of the audio file I want to play, I'm using four other attributes in this `<audio>` element:

▶ `preload`—Has three possible values: `none`, `auto`, and `metadata`. Use `none` if you do not want to buffer the file, use `auto` to buffer the file, and use `metadata` if you want to buffer only the metadata for the file.

▶ `controls`—If present, shows the controls for the audio player.

▶ `autoplay`—If present, plays the file as soon as it loads.

▶ `loop`—If present, continues to play the file repeatedly until it is manually stopped.

Figure 8.24 shows the page in Listing 8.9 as rendered by the Chrome web browser.

In practice, you probably wouldn't want to automatically play and loop a sound file in your website—doing so is typically considered a particularly negative user experience. However, if you *do* automatically play a sound file (please don't!), be sure to include the player controls so that users can immediately turn off the sound.

FIGURE 8.24
Using the `<audio>` element to
play a sound file.

Using the HTML5 `<video>` element is quite similar to using the `<audio>` element. Listing 8.10 shows an example of this, in which the only real changes besides some text changes are the use of `height` and `width` attributes to define the space taken up by the video player and the video clip.

LISTING 8.10   Using the `<video>` Element to Embed and Play a Video File

```
<!DOCTYPE html>

<html lang="en">
  <head>
    <title>Let's Watch a Video</title>
  </head>

  <body>
    <h1>Let's Watch a Video</h1>
    <p>Better yet, let's use the HTML5 &lt;video&gt; element
    to do so!</p>
    <video
          src="kitten.mov"
          preload="auto"
          width="320"
          height="240"
          controls
          autoplay
          loop>
```

```
        <!-- Message to display in case the video element
        isn't supported. -->
        <p>Your browser does not support the video element.</p>
    </video>
    </body>
</html>
```

The `preload`, `controls`, `autoplay`, and `loop` attributes do exactly the same for the `<video>` element as they do for the `<audio>` element. Figure 8.25 shows the page in Listing 8.10 as rendered by the Chrome web browser.

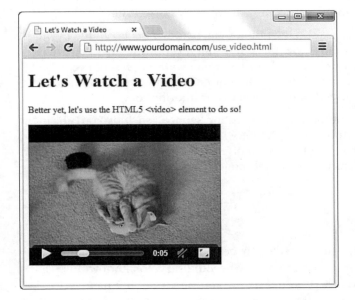

FIGURE 8.25
Using the `<video>` element to play a video file.

Additional Tips for Using Multimedia

Before you add video, audio, or animations to your website, ask yourself whether you really should do so. When you use these types of multimedia, be sure to do so for a reason. Gratuitous sound and video, just like gratuitous images, can detract from your overall message. Then again, if your message is "Look at the videos I've made" or "Listen to my music and download some songs," then multimedia absolutely must play a role in your website.

Keep a few additional tips in mind:

▶ Don't include multimedia in a page and set it to automatically play when the page loads. Always give users the option to start (and stop) your sound or video.

▶ When providing files for direct download, give users a choice of file type. Don't limit yourself to providing multimedia content playable by only one type of player on only one operating system.

▶ Multimedia files are larger than the typical graphics and text files, which means you need to have the space on your web server to store them, as well as the bandwidth allotment to transfer them to whomever requests them via your website.

▶ If your site is entirely audio or video and offers very little by way of text or graphics, understand that a certain segment of your audience won't see or hear what you want to present because of the limitations of their system or bandwidth. Provide these users with additional options to get your information.

▶ Leverage free online video hosting services, such as YouTube (www.youtube.com). Not only does YouTube provide storage for your video clips, but it also gives you the code necessary to embed the video in your own web page.

Summary

In this chapter, you learned a few best practices for color use, and you learned how to use the color wheel to find colors that will complement your text. Additionally, you learned about hexadecimal notation for colors—all colors are expressed in notations related to the amount of red, green, and blue in them—and saw how hexadecimal notation enables you to apply nuanced colors to your elements. More important, you learned about the three color-related style properties that you can use to apply color to container backgrounds, borders, and text using CSS. Additionally, you learned the basics of preparing graphics for use on web pages. If nothing else, you learned that this is a complex topic, and you learned just enough in this chapter to whet your appetite. The examples in this chapter used the popular (and free!) GIMP software package, but feel free to use the graphics software that best suits your needs. Among the actions you learned were how to crop, resize, and tweak image colors, and you also learned about the different file formats. You must keep in mind many considerations when including graphics in your site, including graphic size and resolution, and how to use transparency, animated GIFs, and tiled backgrounds.

After creating images, you also learned how to use images in your web pages. You learned how to place them in your pages using the `<img />` tag, and how to include a short text message that appears in place of the image as it loads and that also appears whenever users move the mouse pointer over the image. You also learned how to control the horizontal and vertical alignment of each image, and how to wrap text around the left or right of an image. To make your pages more interactive, you learned how to use images as links—either by using the `<a>` tag around the images or by creating imagemaps. Finally, you learned how to embed video and sound in a web page. You learned how to use a simple link to a multimedia file, which is the most broadly supported but least flexible option for playing media content. You then learned how to use the `<object>` or `<embed />` elements to embed a media player directly in a web page, which can be used to include a vast array of media types, including WAV, MP3, AVI, WMV, and QuickTime videos, to name just a few. You also learned about the `<audio>` and `<video>` elements in HTML5, which enable the browser to render audio or video files natively, or without external plug-in support.

Table 8.1 summarizes the tags and attributes covered in this chapter.

TABLE 8.1   Tags and Attributes Covered in Chapter 8

Tag	Function
`<img />`	Places an image file within the page.
Attribute/Style	*Function*
`style="background-color:color"`	Sets the background color of an element (such as `<body>`, `<p>`, `<div>`, `<blockquote>`, and other containers).
`style="color:color"`	Sets the color of text within an element.
`style="border:size type color"`	Sets the color of the four borders around an element. Border colors cannot be used without also specifying the width and type of the border.

`src="address"`	Gives the address or filename of the image.
`alt="altdescription"`	Gives an alternative description of the image that is displayed in place of the image, primarily for users who can't view the image itself.
`title="title"`	A text message that is displayed as an image title, typically in a small pop-up box (tooltip) over the image.
`width="width"`	Specifies the width of the image (in pixels).
`height="height"`	Specifies the height of the image (in pixels).

Attribute/Style	*Function*
`style="border:attributes"`	Gets rid of the border around the image if the image is serving as a link.
`style="vertical-align: alignment"`	Aligns the image vertically to `text-top`, `top`, `text-bottom`, `bottom`, `middle`, or `baseline`.
`style="float:float"`	Floats the image to one side so that text can wrap around it. Possible values are `left`, `right`, and `none` (default).

Tag	**Function**
`<map>...</map>`	A client-side imagemap referenced by `<img usemap="..." />`. Includes one or more `<area />` tags.
`<area />`	Defines a clickable link within a client-side imagemap.

Attribute/Style	*Function*
`usemap="name"`	The name of an imagemap specification for client-side imagemapping. Used with `<map>` and `<area />`.
`shape="value"`	Within the `<area />` tag, specifies the shape of the clickable area. Valid options for this attribute are `rect`, `poly`, and `circle`.
`coords="values"`	Within the `<area />` tag, specifies the coordinates of the clickable region within an image. Its meaning and setting vary according to the type of area.
`href="linkurl"`	Within the `<area />` tag, specifies the URL that should be loaded when the area is clicked.

Tag	Function
`<object>...</object>`	Embeds images, videos, Java applets, ActiveX controls, or other objects into a document.

Attribute/Style	Function
`width="width"`	Specifies the width of the embedded object in pixels.
`height="height"`	Specifies the height of the embedded object in pixels.
`data="mediaurl"`	Gives the URL of the resource you want to embed.
`type="mimetype"`	Specifies the MIME type of the multimedia content.

Tag	Function
`<embed />`	Embeds a multimedia file to be read or displayed by a plug-in application.

Attribute/Style	Function
`width="width"`	Specifies the width of the embedded object in pixels.
`height="height"`	Specifies the height of the embedded object in pixels.
`src="mediaurl"`	Gives the URL of the file to embed.
`type="mimetype"`	Specifies the MIME type of the multimedia content.

Tag	Function
`<audio>...</ audio >`	Plays an audio file natively in the browser.

Attribute/Style	Function
`src="mediaurl"`	Gives the URL of the file to embed.
`preload="preloadtype"`	Tells whether to preload the media file. Options are `none`, `auto`, and `metadata`.
`controls`	Instructs the browser to show the audio player controls.
`autoplay`	Instructs the browser to play the file when it has finished loading.
`loop`	Instructs the browser to play the file until it is explicitly stopped.

Tag	Function
`<video>...</ video >`	Plays a video file natively in the browser.

Attribute/Style	Function
`src="mediaurl"`	Gives the URL of the file to embed.
`preload="preloadtype"`	Tells whether to preload the media file. Options are `none`, `auto`, and `metadata`.

`width="width"`	Specifies the width of the embedded object in pixels.
`height="height"`	Specifies the height of the embedded object in pixels.
`controls`	Instructs the browser to show the video player controls.
`autoplay`	Instructs the browser to play the file when it has finished loading.
`loop`	Instructs the browser to play the file until it is explicitly stopped.

Q&A

Q. I've produced graphics for printing on paper. Are web page graphics any different?

A. Yes. In fact, many of the rules for print graphics are reversed on the Web. Web page graphics have to be low resolution, whereas print graphics should be as high resolution as possible. White washes out black on computer screens, whereas black bleeds into white on paper. Also, someone might stop a web page from loading when only half the graphics have been downloaded, which isn't a consideration when one is looking at images in print. Try to avoid falling into old habits if you've done a lot of print graphics design.

Q. I used the `<img />` tag just as you advised, but when I view the page, all I see is a little box with some shapes in it. What's wrong?

A. The broken image icon you're seeing can mean one of two things: Either the web browser couldn't find the image file or the image isn't saved in a format the browser recognizes. To solve these problems, first check to make sure that the image is where it is supposed to be. If it is, then open the image in your graphics editor and save it again as a GIF, JPG, or PNG.

Q. I hear a lot about streaming video and audio. What does that mean?

A. In the past, video and audio files took minutes and sometimes hours to retrieve through most modems, which severely limited the inclusion of video and audio on web pages. The goal everyone is moving toward is streaming video or audio, which plays while the data is being received. In other words, you don't have to completely download the clip before you can start to watch it or listen to it.

Streaming playback is now widely supported through most media players, in both standalone versions and plug-ins. When you embed a media object using the `<object>` or `<embed />` elements, the underlying media player automatically streams the media clip if the player supports streaming. When using the `<video>` element, you have more fine-grained control over the buffering and playback of your multimedia resource.

Q. What happens if I overlap areas on an imagemap?

A. You are allowed to overlap areas on an imagemap. Just keep in mind that, in the determination of which link to follow, one area has precedence over the other area. Precedence is assigned according to which areas are listed first in the imagemap. For example, the first area in the map has precedence over the second area, which means that a click in the overlapping portion of the areas will link to the first area. If you have an area within an imagemap that doesn't link to anything (known as a *dead area*), you can use this overlap trick to deliberately prevent this area from linking to anything. To do this, just place the dead area before other areas so that the dead area overlaps them, and then set its `href` attribute to `""`.

Workshop

The Workshop contains quiz questions and exercises to help you solidify your understanding of the material covered. Try to answer all questions before looking at the "Answers" section that follows.

Quiz

1. How would you give a web page a black background and make all text bright green? Based on what you've learned in this chapter, would you even want to use that color combination?

2. What CSS properties and values would you use to ensure that a paragraph had a white background, orange text, and a 3-pixel-wide dashed green border?

3. If you have a square image of a blue flower on a transparent background, and the background color of the containing element is gray, will your flower image appear on the page as a square or some other shape?

4. If you had an image called `myimage.png` and you wanted to align it so that a line of text lined up at the middle of the image, what style property would you use?

5. What's the simplest method to provide access to a video on your website for the widest possible audience?

Answers

1. Although it is highly recommended that you don't do it, you would put the following at the beginning of the web page or use a style rule for the `body` element:

```
<body style="background-color:#000000; color:#00FF00">
```

2. The following properties and values would work:

```
background-color: #ffffff;
color: #ffa500;
border: 3px dashed #00ff00;
```

3. It will appear as the shape of the flower because the image has a transparent background. The gray background of the containing element will show through.

4. You would use `vertical-align:middle` to ensure that the text lined up at the middle of the image.

5. Just link to it:

```
<a href="myvideo.mov">my video</a>
```

Exercises

▶ Select a base color that you like—perhaps a lovely blue or an earthy tone—and use the Color Scheme Designer at http://colorschemedesigner.com/ to come up with a set of colors that you can use in a website. I recommend the tetrad or accented analogic scheme types.

▶ When you have a set of colors—or a few options for sets of colors—create a basic HTML page with an `<h1>` element, a paragraph of text, and perhaps some list items. Use the color-related styles you learned about in this chapter to change the background color of the page and the text of the various block-level elements, to see how these sets of colors might work together. See how they interact, and determine which colors are best used for containers and which are best used for plain text, header text, and link text.

▶ Practicing any of the image placement methods in this chapter will go a long way toward helping you determine the role that images can, and will, play in the websites you design. Using a few sample images, practice using the `float` style to place images and text in relation to one another. Remember, the possible values for `float` are `left`, `right`, and `none` (default).

▶ Find some freely available audio and video clips on the web, and practice placement within your text using the HTML5 `<audio>` and `<video>` elements.

CHAPTER 9
Working with Margins, Padding, Alignment, and Floating

Now that you've learned some of the basics of creating web content, in this chapter you'll learn the nitty-gritty of using CSS to enhance that content. In the chapters that follow, you dive in to using CSS to control aspects of your entire web page, not just individual pieces of text or graphics.

Before you tackle page layout, however, it is important to understand four particular CSS properties individually before putting them all together:

- ▶ **The** margin **and** padding **properties**—For adding space around elements

- ▶ **The** align **and** float **properties**—To place your elements in relation to others

The examples provided in this chapter are not the most stylish examples of web content ever created, but they are not intended to be. Instead, the examples clearly show just how HTML5 and CSS are working together. Although this chapter is short in terms of page count, the concepts deserve careful reading and hands-on practice. When you master CSS through this and other sections of the book, and through ongoing practice of what you've learned, you'll be able to use your own design skills to enhance what can be (and often is) the relatively basic underlying scaffolding.

WHAT YOU'LL LEARN IN THIS CHAPTER:

- ▶ How to add margins around elements

- ▶ How to add padding within elements

- ▶ How to keep everything aligned

- ▶ How to use the float property

Using Margins

Style sheet *margins* enable you to add empty space around the *outside* of the rectangular area for an element on a web page. It is important to remember that the `margin` property works with space outside the element.

Following are the style properties for setting margins:

▶ `margin-top`—Sets the top margin

▶ `margin-right`—Sets the right margin

▶ `margin-bottom`—Sets the bottom margin

▶ `margin-left`—Sets the left margin

▶ `margin`—Sets the top, right, bottom, and left margins as a single property

You can specify margins using any of the individual margin properties or using the single `margin` property. Margins can be specified as auto, meaning that the browser itself sets the margin in specific lengths (pixels, points, or ems) or in percentages. If you decide to set a margin as a percentage, keep in mind that the percentage is calculated based on the size of the containing element. So if you set the `margin-left` property of an element within the body to 25%, the left margin of the element will end up being 25% of the width of the entire page. However, if you set the `margin-left` property of an element within *that* element to 25%, it will be 25% of whatever that original 25% was calculated to be.

The code in Listing 9.1 produces four rectangles on the page, each 250 pixels wide and 100 pixels high, with a 5-pixel solid black border (see Figure 9.1). Each rectangle—or `<div>`, in this case—has a different background color. We want the margin around each `<div>` to be 15 pixels on all sides, so we can use the following:

```
margin-top: 15px;
margin-right: 15px;
margin-bottom: 15px;
margin-left: 15px;
```

You can also write that in shorthand, using the `margin` property:

```
margin: 15px 15px 15px 15px;
```

When you use the `margin` property (or `padding` or `border`) and you want all four values to be the same, you can simplify this even further and use this:

```
margin: 15px;
```

When using shorthand for setting margins, padding, or borders, four approaches apply, which vary based on how many values you use when setting the property:

- ▶ **One value**—The size of all the margins

- ▶ **Two values**—The size of the top/bottom margins and the left/right margins (in that order)

- ▶ **Three values**—The size of the top margin, the left and right margins (they are given the same value), and the bottom margin (in that order)

- ▶ **Four values**—The size of the top, right, bottom, and left margins (in that order)

You might find it easier to stick to either using one value or using all four values, but that's certainly not a requirement.

LISTING 9.1 Simple Code to Produce Four Colored `<div>`s with Borders and Margins

```
<!DOCTYPE html>

<html lang="en">
  <head>
  <title>Color Blocks</title>
    <style type="text/css">
        div {
            width: 250px;
            height: 100px;
            border: 5px solid #000000;
            color: black;
            font-weight: bold;
            text-align: center;
        }

        div#d1 {
            background-color: red;
            margin: 15px;
        }

        div#d2 {
            background-color: green;
```

NOTE

You can remember the shorthand order in at least two different ways. First, if you think of an element as a rectangle, start at the top and work your way clockwise around the sides: top side, right side, bottom side, left side. Or you can use a first-letter mnemonic device and remember *TRBL* (pronounced "trouble" or "tribble," if you're a *Star Trek* fan), which also represents a possible state of being in case you forget the order of the margin properties.

Also note that the TRBL order is valid for padding properties and border properties as well.

```
            margin: 15px;
        }

        div#d3 {
            background-color: blue;
            margin: 15px;
        }

        div#d4 {
            background-color: yellow;
            margin: 15px;
        }
    </style>
</head>

<body>
    <div id="d1">DIV #1</div>
    <div id="d2">DIV #2</div>
    <div id="d3">DIV #3</div>
    <div id="d4">DIV #4</div>
</body>
</html>
```

You can see the output of Listing 9.1 in Figure 9.1.

FIGURE 9.1
The basic color blocks sample
page shows four color blocks, each
with equal margins.

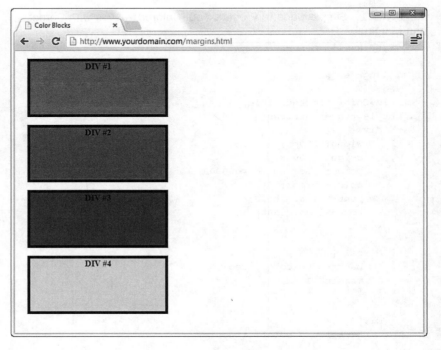

Next, working with just the `margin` property in the style sheet entries in Listing 9.1, let's shift the margins. In this example, you can't really see the right-side margin on any of these `<div>` elements because there's nothing to the right of them and they're not aligned to the right. With that in mind, let's set `margin-right` to `0px` in all of these. Beyond that, the next set of goals is to produce the following:

▶ No margin around the first color block

▶ A left-side margin of 15 pixels, a top margin of 5 pixels, and no bottom margin around the second color block

▶ A left-side margin of 75 pixels and no top margin or bottom margin around the third color block

▶ A left-side margin of 250 pixels and a top margin of 25 pixels around the fourth color block

This seems as though it would be straightforward—no margin is being set around the first block. But we want a margin at the top of the second block, so really there *will* be a visible margin between the first and second blocks, even if we are not specifying a margin for the first block.

The new style sheet entries for the four named `<div>`s now look like this:

```
div#d1 {
  background-color: red;
  margin: 0px;
}

div#d2 {
  background-color: green;
  margin: 5px 0px 0px 15px;
}

div#d3 {
  background-color: blue;
  margin: 0px 0px 0px 75px;
}

div#d4 {
  background-color: yellow;
  margin: 25px 0px 0px 250px;
}
```

The result of the code changes (see Figure 9.2) seems random but is actually quite useful for pointing out a few other important points. For example, when you recall that one of the goals was to produce no margin around the first color block, you might expect the border of the color block to be flush with the browser window. But as Figure 9.2 shows, there is a clear space between the content of the page and the frame of the browser window.

FIGURE 9.2
Modifications to the color blocks sample page display some different margins.

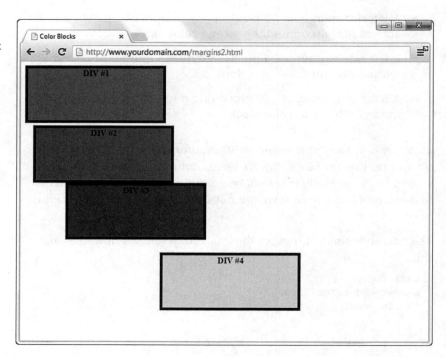

If we were working on element placement—which we get to in the next chapter—this would cause a problem in the layout. To ensure that your placements and margins are counted from a position flush with the browser, you need to address the margin of the <body> element itself. In this case, you add the following to your style sheet:

```
body {
  margin: 0px;
}
```

Another "gotcha" to remember is that if you have two bordered elements stacked on top of each other, but with no margin between them, the point at which they touch appears to have a double border. You might then consider making the top element's `border-bottom` half the width and then also make the bottom element's `border-top` half the width. If you do this, the borders appear to be the same width as the other sides when stacked on top of each other.

In addition, you might have thought that using a left-side margin of 250 pixels—the width of the `<div>`s—would begin the fourth color block where the third color block ended. That is not the case, however, because the third color block has a `margin-left` of 75 pixels. For them to even be close to lining up, the `margin-left` value for the fourth `<div>` would have to be 325 pixels.

Changing the styles to those shown in the following code produces the spacing shown in Figure 9.3.

```
body {
  margin: 0px;
}
div {
  width: 250px;
  height: 100px;
  color: black;
  font-weight: bold;
  text-align: center;
}
div#d1 {
  border: 5px solid #000000;
  background-color: red;
  margin: 0px;
}
div#d2 {
  border-width: 6px 6px 3px 6px;
  border-style: solid;
  border-color: #000000;
  background-color: green;
  margin: 10px 0px 0px 15px;
}
div#d3 {
  border-width: 3px 6px 6px 6px;
  border-style: solid;
  border-color: #000000;
  background-color: blue;
  margin: 0px 0px 0px 15px;
}
div#d4 {
  border: 5px solid #000000;
  background-color: yellow;
  margin: 0px 0px 0px 265px;
}
```

FIGURE 9.3
A third modification to the color blocks pulls items into closer relation with each other.

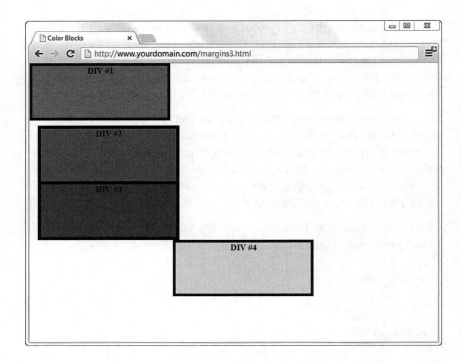

These changes give the `<body>` element a zero margin, thus ensuring that a `margin-left` value of 25 pixels truly is 25 pixels from the edge of the browser frame. It also shows the second and third color blocks stacked on top of each other, but with modifications to the `border` element so that a double border does not appear. Additionally, the fourth color block begins where the third color block ends.

As you can see in Figure 9.3, some overlap occurs between the right edge of the third color block and the left edge of the fourth color block. Why is that the case, if the color blocks are 250 pixels wide, the third color block has a `margin-left` value of 15 pixels, and the fourth color block is supposed to have a 265-pixel margin to its left? Well, it does have that 265-pixel margin, but that margin size is not enough because you also have to factor in the 6 pixels of border. Changing the `margin` property for the fourth color block to reflect the following code makes the third and fourth blocks line up according to plan (see Figure 9.4):

```
margin: 0px 0px 0px 276px;
```

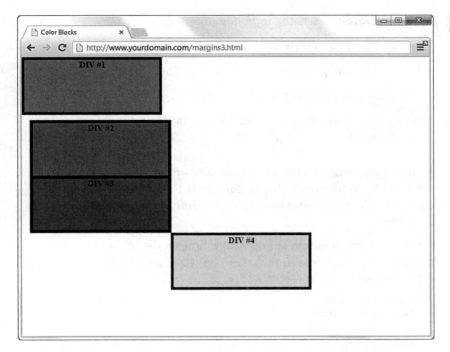

FIGURE 9.4
Changing the margin to allow for
11 pixels of border width.

As shown in these examples, margin specifications are incredibly useful for element placement, but you must use caution when setting these specifications.

Padding Elements

Padding is similar to margins, in that it adds extra space to elements. The big difference is where that space is located. Recall that margins are added to the outside of elements. On the other hand, padding adds space *inside* the rectangular area of an element. As an example, if you create a style rule for an element that establishes a width of 50 pixels and a height of 30 pixels, and then sets the padding of the rule to 5 pixels, the remaining content area will be 40 pixels by 20 pixels. Also, because the padding of an element appears within the element's content area, it assumes the same style as the content of the element, including the background color.

You specify the padding of a style rule using one of the `padding` properties, which work much like the `margin` properties. The following padding properties are available for use in setting the padding of style rules:

▶ `padding-top`—Sets the top padding

▶ `padding-right`—Sets the right padding

▶ `padding-bottom`—Sets the bottom padding

▶ `padding-left`—Sets the left padding

▶ `padding`—Sets the top, right, bottom, and left padding as a single property

As with margins, you can set the padding of style rules using individual padding properties or the single `padding` property. You can also express padding using either a unit of measurement or a percentage.

Following is an example of how you might set the left and right padding for a style rule so that there are 10 pixels of padding on each side of an element's content:

```
padding-left: 10px;
padding-right: 10px;
```

As with margins, you can set all the padding for an element with a single property (the `padding` property). To set the `padding` property, you can use the same four approaches available for the `margin` property. Following is an example of how you would set the vertical padding (top/bottom) to 12 pixels and the horizontal padding (left/right) to 8 pixels for a style rule:

```
padding: 12px 8px;
```

Following is more explicit code that performs the same task by specifying all the padding values:

```
padding: 12px 8px 12px 8px;
```

In all the previous figures, note that the text DIV #1, DIV #2, and so on appears at the top of the colored block, with just a little space between the border and the text. That amount of space hasn't been specified by any padding value, but it appears as a sort of default within the element. If you want specific control over your element padding, Listing 9.2 shows some examples. All the color blocks are 250 pixels wide and 100 pixels high, have a 5-pixel solid black border, and have 25 pixels of margin (see Figure 9.5). The fun stuff happens within the padding values for each individual `<div>`.

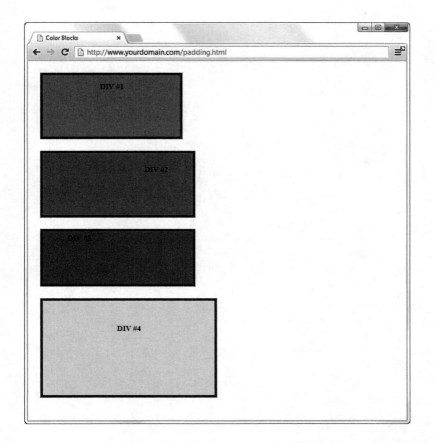

FIGURE 9.5
The basic color blocks sample
page shows four color blocks with
variable padding.

LISTING 9.2 Simple Code to Produce Four Colored `<div>`s with Borders,
Margins, and Padding

```
<!DOCTYPE html>

<html lang="en">
  <head>
    <title>Color Blocks</title>
    <style type="text/css">
      body {
         margin: 0px;
      }
      div {
         width: 250px;
         height: 100px;
         border: 5px solid #000000;
         color: black;
         font-weight: bold;
         margin: 25px;
```

```
      }

      div#d1 {
         background-color: red;
         text-align: center;
         padding: 15px;
      }

      div#d2 {
         background-color: green;
         text-align: right;
         padding: 25px 50px 6px 6px;
      }

      div#d3 {
         background-color: blue;
         text-align: left;
         padding: 6px 6px 6px 50px;
      }

      div#d4 {
         background-color: yellow;
         text-align: center;
         padding: 50px;
      }
   </style>
  </head>

  <body>
    <div id="d1">DIV #1</div>
    <div id="d2">DIV #2</div>
    <div id="d3">DIV #3</div>
    <div id="d4">DIV #4</div>
  </body>
</html>
```

You should immediately recognize that something is amiss in this example. The color blocks are all supposed to be 250 pixels wide and 100 pixels high. The color blocks in Figure 9.5 are not uniform because, despite our efforts to control the size of the <div>, the padding applied later overrides that initial size declaration.

If you place the text in a <p> element and give that element a white background (see Figure 9.6), you can see where the padding is in relation to the text. When there just isn't room to use all the padding that is defined, the surrounding element has to make adjustments. You will learn about this effect in detail in Chapter 10, "Understanding the CSS Box Model and Positioning."

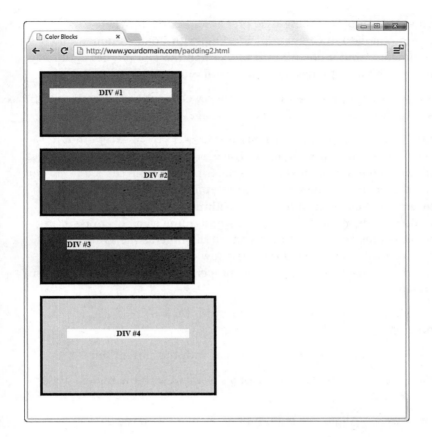

FIGURE 9.6
Showing the padding in relation to the text.

The greatest number of tweaks or nudges you make in your web design with CSS will have to do with margins and padding. Just remember: Margins are outside the element; padding is inside it.

Keeping Everything Aligned

Because content on a web page doesn't always fill the entire width of the rectangular area in which it is displayed, it is often helpful to control the alignment of the content. Even if text within a rectangular area extends to multiple lines, alignment enters the picture because you might want the text left-justified, right-justified, or centered. Two style properties enable you to control the alignment of elements: `text-align` and `vertical-align`.

You saw examples of these style properties in action (when aligning images) in Chapter 8, "Working with Colors, Images, and Multimedia," but it doesn't hurt to mention these properties again here because alignment plays a role in overall page design as well.

As a refresher, using `text-align` aligns an element horizontally within its bounding area, and it can be set to `left`, `right`, `center`, or `justify`.

The `vertical-align` property is similar to `text-align` except that it is used to align elements vertically. The `vertical-align` property specifies how an element is aligned with its parent or, in some cases, the current line of elements on the page. "Current line" refers to the vertical placement of elements that appear within the same parent element—in other words, inline elements. If several inline elements appear on the same line, you can set their vertical alignments the same to align them vertically. A good example is a row of images that appear one after the next—the `vertical-align` property enables you to align them vertically.

Following are common values for use with the `vertical-align` property:

▶ `top`—Aligns the top of an element with the current line

▶ `middle`—Aligns the middle of an element with the middle of its parent

▶ `bottom`—Aligns the bottom of an element with the current line

▶ `text-top`—Aligns the top of an element with the top of its parent

▶ `baseline`—Aligns the baseline of an element with the baseline of its parent

▶ `text-bottom`—Aligns the bottom of an element with the bottom of its parent

Alignment works in conjunction with margins, padding, and (as you'll learn in the next section) the `float` property to enable you to maintain control over your design.

Understanding the `Float` **Property**

Understanding the `float` property is fundamental to understanding CSS-based layout and design; it is one of the last pieces in the puzzle of how all these elements fit together. Briefly stated, the float property allows elements to be moved around in the design so that other elements can wrap around them. You often find float used in conjunction with images (as you saw in Chapter 8), but you can—and many designers do—float all sorts of elements in the layout.

Elements float horizontally, not vertically, so all you have to concern yourself with are two possible values: right and left. When used, an element that floats will float as far right or as far left (depending on the value of float) as the containing element will allow it. For example, if you have three <div>s with float values of left, they will all line up to the left of the containing body element. If you have your <div>s within another <div>, they will line up to the left of *that* element, even if that element itself is floated to the right.

You can best understand floating by seeing a few examples, so let's move on to Listing 9.3. This listing simply defines three rectangular <div>s and floats them next to each other (floating to the left).

LISTING 9.3   Using float to Place <div>s

```
<!DOCTYPE html>

<html lang="en">
  <head>
    <title>Color Blocks</title>
    <style type="text/css">
      body {
          margin:0px;
      }
      div {
          width: 250px;
          height: 100px;
          border: 5px solid #000000;
          color: black;
          font-weight: bold;
          margin: 25px;
      }

      div#d1 {
          background-color: red;
          float: left;
      }

      div#d2 {
          background-color: green;
          float: left;
```

```
        }

        div#d3 {
            background-color: blue;
            float: left;
        }
    </style>
</head>

<body>
    <div id="d1">DIV #1</div>
    <div id="d2">DIV #2</div>
    <div id="d3">DIV #3</div>
</body>
</html>
```

Figure 9.7 shows the resulting page. Already you can see a problem—these three color blocks were supposed to be floated next to each other.

FIGURE 9.7
Using float to place the color blocks.

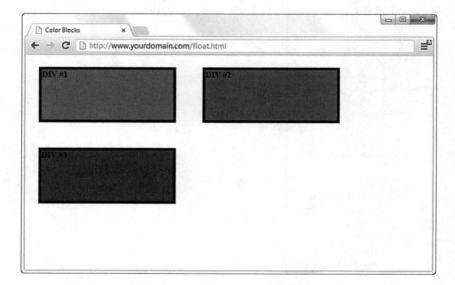

Well, actually they *are* floated next to each other, but the browser window is not wide enough to display these three 250-pixel-wide blocks with 25 pixels of margin between them. Because they are floating, the third one simply floats to the next line.

You can imagine that this could be a problem in a specifically designed visual layout, so pay attention to your margins, padding, alignment, and floating while also testing within a target browser window size. Granted, the browser window in Figure 9.7 is a small one to make this point about floating elements moving to the next line when there is no room for them to fit where they should. In other words, if you open the same HTML file with a larger browser window, you might not see the issue—this is why you should also check your sites at different resolutions to see whether a fix is needed. The fix here is to adjust the margins and other size-related properties of your `<div>`s.

Figure 9.8 shows another interesting possibility when the `float` property is used. The only changes made to the code from Listing 9.3 involved making the color blocks only 100 pixels wide, reducing the margins to 10px, and changing the `float` alignment of the second color block to `right` (instead of `left`).

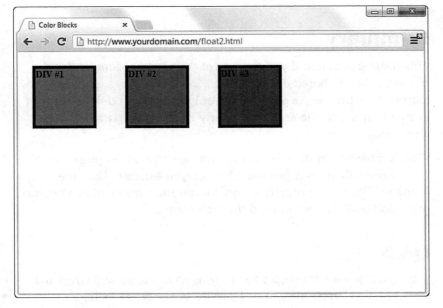

FIGURE 9.8
Using float to place the color blocks.

However, something interesting happened. The second color block now appears visually as the third color block because it is flush right. The second color block has a `float` value of `right`, so it has floated all the way to the right. The first and third color blocks are floating as left as possible, regardless of the way in which the `<div>` code appears in the HTML, which is as follows:

```
<div id="d1">DIV #1</div>
<div id="d2">DIV #2</div>
<div id="d3">DIV #3</div>
```

Floating takes a lot of practice to get used to, especially when your page has additional elements in your page, not just a few colored blocks. For example, what happens when you add a basic paragraph to the mix? All elements placed after the floating element then float around that element. To avoid that problem, use the `clear` property.

The `clear` property has five possible values: `left`, `right`, `both`, `none`, and `inherit`. The most common values are `left`, `right`, and `both`. Specifying `clear:left` ensures that no other floating elements are allowed to the left, `clear:right` ensures that no other floating elements are allowed to the right, and so on. Floating and clearing is a learn-by-doing process, so look for more situations in the Workshop at the end of this chapter.

Summary

This chapter introduced you to some of the most fundamental style properties in CSS-based design: `margin`, `padding`, and `float`. You learned how the `margin` property controls space around the outside of elements and how the `padding` property works with space within the elements.

After a refresher on the `text-align` and `vertical-align` properties you learned about in a previous chapter, you learned about the `float` property. The `float` property allows for specific placement of elements and additional content around those elements.

Q&A

Q. The examples of margins and padding all had to do with boxes and text. Can I apply margins and padding to images as well?

A. Yes, you can apply margins and padding to any block-level element, such as a `<p>`, a `<div>`, an `<img/>`, and lists such as `<ul>` and `<ol>`, as well as list items (`<li>`)—just to name a few.

Workshop

The Workshop contains quiz questions and exercises to help you solidify your understanding of the material covered. Try to answer all questions before looking at the "Answers" section that follows.

Quiz

1. To place two `<div>` elements next to each other, but with a 30-pixel margin between them, what entry or entries can you use in the style sheet?

2. Which CSS style property and value are used to ensure that content does not appear to the left of a floating element?

3. What style sheet entry is used to place text within a `<div>` to appear 12 pixels from the top of the element?

Answers

1. You can use several entries. The first `<div>` uses a style property of `margin-right:15px`. The second `<div>` uses a style property of `margin-left:15px`. Or you can assign the full 30 pixels to either `<div>` using `margin-right` or `margin-left`, as appropriate. Additionally, at least the first `<div>` needs to have `float:left` assigned to it.

2. In this instance, use `clear:left`.

3. You would use `padding-top:12px`.

Exercises

▶ Fully understanding margins, padding, alignment, and floating takes practice. Using the color blocks code or `<div>`s of your own, practice all manner and sorts of spacing and floating before moving on to the next chapter. The next chapter discusses the CSS box model as a whole, which encompasses the individual items discussed in this chapter.

▶ While you're at it, practice applying margins and padding to every block-level element you've learned so far. Get used to putting images within blocks of text and putting margins around the images so that the text does not run right up to the edge of the graphic.

CHAPTER 10
Understanding the CSS Box Model and Positioning

In the preceding chapter, I mentioned the CSS box model a few times. This chapter begins with a discussion of the box model and explains how the information you learned in the preceding chapter helps you understand this model. It's important to spend some time focusing on and practicing working with the box model, because if you have a good handle on how the box model works, you won't tear your hair out when you create a design and then realize that the elements don't line up or that they seem a little "off." You'll know that, in almost all cases, something—the margin, the padding, the border—just needs a little tweaking.

You'll also learn more about CSS positioning, including stacking elements on top of each other in a three-dimensional way (instead of a vertical way). Finally, you'll learn about controlling the flow of text around elements using the `float` property.

The CSS Box Model

Every element in HTML is considered a "box," whether it is a paragraph, a `<div>`, an image, and so on. Boxes have consistent properties, whether we see them or not, and whether the style sheet specifies them or not. They're always present, and as designers, we have to keep their presence in mind when creating a layout.

Figure 10.1 is a diagram of the box model. The box model describes the way in which every HTML block-level element has the potential for a border, padding, and margin and, specifically, how the border, padding, and margin are applied. In other words, all elements have some padding between the content and the border of the element.

WHAT YOU'LL LEARN IN
THIS CHAPTER:

▶ How to conceptualize the CSS box model

▶ How to position your elements

▶ How to control the way elements stack up

▶ How to manage the flow of text

Additionally, the border might or might not be visible, but space for it is here, just as there is a margin between the border of the element and any other content outside the element.

FIGURE 10.1
Every element in HTML is represented by the CSS box model.

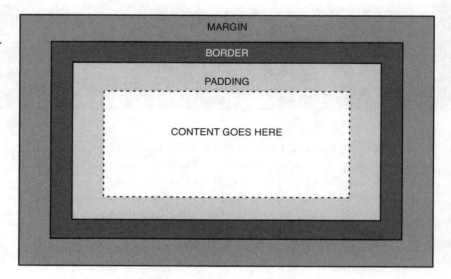

Here's yet another explanation of the box model, going from the outside inward:

- The *margin* is the area outside the element. It never has color; it is always transparent.
- The *border* extends around the element, on the outer edge of any padding. The border can be of several types, widths, and colors.
- The *padding* exists around the content and inherits the background color of the content area.
- The *content* is surrounded by padding.

Here's where the tricky part comes in: To know the true height and width of an element, you have to take all the elements of the box model into account. Think back to the example from the preceding chapter: Despite the specific indication that a <div> should be 250 pixels wide and 100 pixels high, that <div> had to grow larger to accommodate the padding in use.

You already know how to set the width and height of an element using the width and height properties. The following example shows how to define a `<div>` that is 250 pixels wide and 100 pixels high, with a red background and a black single-pixel border:

```css
div {
    width: 250px;
    height: 100px;
    background-color: #ff0000;
    border: 1px solid #000000;
}
```

Figure 10.2 shows this simple `<div>`.

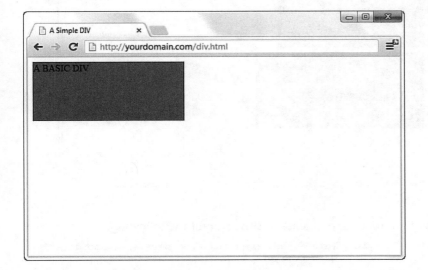

FIGURE 10.2
This is a simple `<div>`.

If we define a second element with these same properties, but also add `margin` and `padding` properties of a certain size, we begin to see how the size of the element changes. This is because of the box model.

The second `<div>` is defined as follows, just adding 10 pixels of margin and 10 pixels of padding to the element:

```css
div#d2 {
    width: 250px;
    height: 100px;
    background-color: #ff0000;
    border: 5px solid #000000;
    margin: 10px;
    padding: 10px;
}
```

The second `<div>`, shown in Figure 10.3, is defined as the same height and width as the first one, but the overall height and width of the entire box surrounding the element itself is much larger when margins and padding are put in play.

FIGURE 10.3
This is supposed to be another simple `<div>`, but the box model affects the size of the second `<div>`.

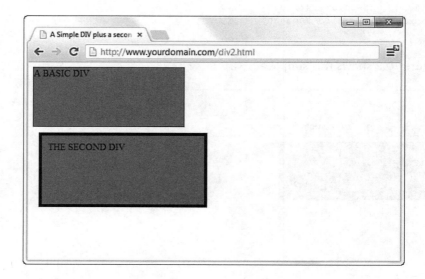

NOTE

Throughout this book, you've been drilled in the use of the DOCTYPE declaration—all sample code includes a DOCTYPE. Continue this practice not only so that your code validates, but because a very specific issue arises with some versions of Internet Explorer and the CSS box model: If a DOCTYPE is not defined, some versions of Internet Explorer manipulate the height and width of your elements in a way you did not intend. This causes browser incompatibility issues with your layout. So remember to include a DOCTYPE.

The total *width* of an element is the sum of the following:

```
width + padding-left + padding-right + border-left + border-right
+ margin-left + margin-right
```

The total *height* of an element is the sum of the following:

```
height + padding-top + padding-bottom + border-top + border-
bottom + margin-top + margin-bottom
```

Therefore, the second `<div>` has an actual width of 300 (250 + 10 + 10 + 5 + 5 + 10 + 10) and an actual height of 150 (100 + 10 + 10 + 5 + 5 + 10 + 10).

By now, you can begin to see how the box model affects your design. Let's say that you have only 250 pixels of horizontal space, but you like 10 pixels of margin, 10 pixels of padding, and 5 pixels of border on all sides. To accommodate what you like with what you have room to display, you must specify the width of your `<div>` as only 200 pixels so that 200 + 10 + 10 + 5 + 5 + 10 + 10 adds up to that 250 pixels of available horizontal space.

The mathematics of the model are important as well. In dynamically driven sites or sites in which user interactions drive the client-side display (such as through JavaScript events), your server-side or client-side code could draw and redraw container elements on the fly. In other words, your code will produce the numbers, but you have to provide the boundaries.

Now that you've been schooled in the way of the box model, keep it in mind throughout the rest of the work you do in this book and in your web design. Among other things, it will affect element positioning and content flow, which are the two topics we tackle next.

The Whole Scoop on Positioning

Relative positioning is the default type of positioning HTML uses. You can think of relative positioning as being akin to laying out checkers on a checkerboard: The checkers are arranged from left to right, and when you get to the edge of the board, you move on to the next row. Elements that are styled with the `block` value for the `display` style property are automatically placed on a new row, whereas `inline` elements are placed on the same row immediately next to the element preceding them. As an example, `<p>` and `<div>` tags are considered block elements, whereas the `<span>` tag is considered an inline element.

The other type of positioning CSS supports is known as *absolute positioning* because it enables you to set the exact position of HTML content on a page. Although absolute positioning gives you the freedom to spell out exactly where an element is to appear, the position is still relative to any parent elements that appear on the page. In other words, absolute positioning enables you to specify the exact location of an element's rectangular area with respect to its parent's area, which is very different from relative positioning.

With the freedom of placing elements anywhere you want on a page, you can run into the problem of overlap, when an element takes up space another element is using. Nothing is stopping you from specifying the absolute locations of elements so that they overlap. In this case, CSS relies on the z-index of each element to determine which element is on the top and which is on the bottom. You'll learn more about the z-index of elements later in this chapter. For now, let's look at exactly how you control whether a style rule uses relative or absolute positioning.

The type of positioning (relative or absolute) a particular style rule uses is determined by the `position` property, which is capable of having one of the following two values: `relative` or `absolute`. After specifying the type of positioning, you provide the specific position using the following properties:

▶ `left`—The left position offset

▶ `right`—The right position offset

▶ `top`—The top position offset

▶ `bottom`—The bottom position offset

You might think that these position properties make sense only for absolute positioning, but they actually apply to both types of positioning. Under relative positioning, the position of an element is specified as an offset relative to the original position of the element. So if you set the `left` property of an element to `25px`, the left side of the element shifts over 25 pixels from its original (relative) position. An absolute position, on the other hand, is specified relative to the parent of the element to which the style is applied. So if you set the `left` property of an element to `25px` under absolute positioning, the left side of the element appears 25 pixels to the right of the parent element's left edge. On the other hand, using the `right` property with the same value positions the element so that its *right* side is 25 pixels to the right of the parent's *right* edge.

Let's return to the color-blocks example to show how positioning works. In Listing 10.1, the four color blocks have relative positioning specified. As you can see in Figure 10.4, the blocks are positioned vertically.

LISTING 10.1   Showing Relative Positioning with Four Color Blocks

```
<!DOCTYPE html>

<html lang="en">
 <head>
  <title>Positioning the Color Blocks</title>
   <style type="text/css">
   div {
     position: relative;
     width: 250px;
     height: 100px;
     border: 5px solid #000;
```

```
   color: black;
   font-weight: bold;
   text-align: center;
   }
   div#d1 {
   background-color: red;
   }

   div#d2 {
   background-color: green;
   }

   div#d3 {
   background-color: blue;
   }

   div#d4 {
   background-color: yellow;
   }
  </style>

 </head>
 <body>
  <div id="d1">DIV #1</div>
  <div id="d2">DIV #2</div>
  <div id="d3">DIV #3</div>
  <div id="d4">DIV #4</div>
 </body>
</html>
```

The style sheet entry for the `<div>` element itself sets the `position` style property for the `<div>` element to `relative`. Because the remaining style rules are inherited from the `<div>` style rule, they inherit its relative positioning. In fact, the only difference between the other style rules is that they have different background colors.

Notice in Figure 10.4 that the `<div>` elements are displayed one after the next, which is what you would expect with relative positioning. But to make things more interesting, which is what we're here to do, you can change the positioning to absolute and explicitly specify the placement of the colors. In Listing 10.2, the style sheet entries are changed to use absolute positioning to arrange the color blocks.

FIGURE 10.4
The color blocks are positioned
vertically, with one on top of the
other.

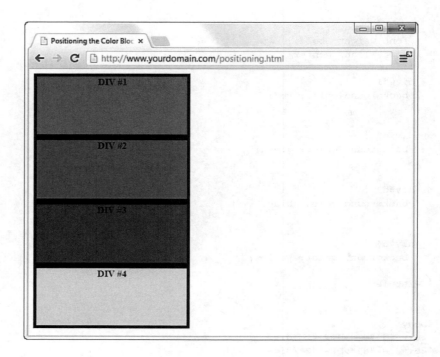

FIGURE 10.4
The color blocks are positioned vertically, with one on top of the other.

LISTING 10.2   Using Absolute Positioning of the Color Blocks

```html
<!DOCTYPE html>

<html lang="en">
 <head>
  <title>Positioning the Color Blocks</title>
    <style type="text/css">
    div {
     position: absolute;
     width: 250px;
     height: 100px;
     border: 5px solid #000;
     color: black;
     font-weight: bold;
     text-align: center;
    }
    div#d1 {
     background-color: red;
     left: 0px;
     top: 0px;
    }
```

```
    div#d2 {
     background-color: green;
     left: 75px;
     top: 25px;
    }
    div#d3 {
     background-color: blue;
     left: 150px;
     top: 50px;
    }
    div#d4 {
     background-color: yellow;
     left: 225px;
     top: 75px;
    }
    </style>
 </head>
 <body>
    <div id="d1">DIV #1</div>
    <div id="d2">DIV #2</div>
    <div id="d3">DIV #3</div>
    <div id="d4">DIV #4</div>
 </body>
</html>
```

This style sheet sets the `position` property to `absolute`, which is necessary for the style sheet to use absolute positioning. Additionally, the `left` and `top` properties are set for each of the inherited `<div>` style rules. However, the position of each of these rules is set so that the elements are displayed overlapping each other, as Figure 10.5 shows.

Now we're talking layout! Figure 10.5 shows how absolute positioning enables you to place elements exactly where you want them. It also reveals how easy it is to arrange elements so that they overlap. You might be curious about how a web browser knows which elements to draw on top when they overlap. The next section covers how you can control stacking order.

FIGURE 10.5
The color blocks are displayed
using absolute positioning.

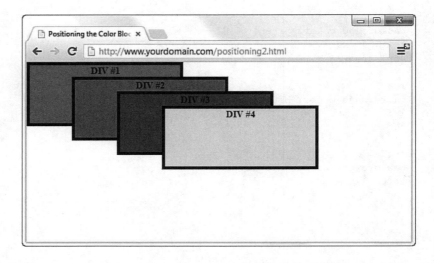

NOTE

Regardless of the z-index
value you set for a style rule, an
element displayed with the rule
will always appear on top of its
parent.

Controlling the Way Things Stack Up

In certain situations, you want to carefully control the manner in which elements overlap each other on a web page. The z-index style property enables you to set the order of elements with respect to how they stack on top of each other. The name *z-index* might sound a little strange, but it refers to the notion of a third dimension (Z) that points into the computer screen, in addition to the two dimensions that go across (X) and down (Y) the screen. Another way to think of the z-index is to consider the relative position of a single magazine within a stack of magazines. A magazine nearer the top of the stack has a higher z-index than a magazine lower in the stack. Similarly, an overlapped element with a higher z-index is displayed on top of an element with a lower z-index.

The z-index property is used to set a numeric value that indicates the relative z-index of a style rule. The number assigned to z-index has meaning only with respect to other style rules in a style sheet, which means that setting the z-index property for a single rule doesn't mean much. On the other hand, if you set z-index for several style rules that apply to overlapped elements, the elements with higher z-index values appear on top of elements with lower z-index values.

Listing 10.3 contains another version of the color-blocks style sheet and HTML that uses z-index settings to alter the natural overlap of elements.

LISTING 10.3 Using `z-index` to Alter the Display of Elements in the Color-Blocks Sample

```html
<!DOCTYPE html>

<html lang="en">
 <head>
  <title>Positioning the Color Blocks</title>
   <style type="text/css">
   div {
     position: absolute;
     width: 250px;
     height: 100px;
     border: 5px solid #000;
     color: black;
     font-weight: bold;
     text-align: center;
    }
    div#d1 {
     background-color: red;
     left: 0px;
     top: 0px;
     z-index: 0;
    }
    div#d2 {
     background-color: green;
     left: 75px;
     top: 25px;
     z-index: 3;
    }
    div#d3 {
     background-color: blue;
     left: 150px;
     top: 50px;
     z-index: 2;
    }
    div#d4 {
     background-color: yellow;
     left: 225px;
     top: 75px;
     z-index: 1;
    }
   </style>
 </head>
 <body>
  <div id="d1">DIV #1</div>
  <div id="d2">DIV #2</div>
  <div id="d3">DIV #3</div>
  <div id="d4">DIV #4</div>
 </body>
</html>
```

The only change in this code from what you saw in Listing 10.2 is the addition of the `z-index` property in each of the numbered `div` style classes. Notice that the first numbered `div` has a `z-index` setting of 0, which should make it the lowest element in terms of the z-index, whereas the second `div` has the highest z-index. Figure 10.6 shows the color-blocks page as displayed with this style sheet, which clearly shows how the z-index affects the displayed content and makes it possible to carefully control the overlap of elements.

Although the examples show color blocks that are simple `<div>` elements, the `z-index` style property can affect any HTML content, including images.

FIGURE 10.6
Using `z-index` to alter the display of the color blocks.

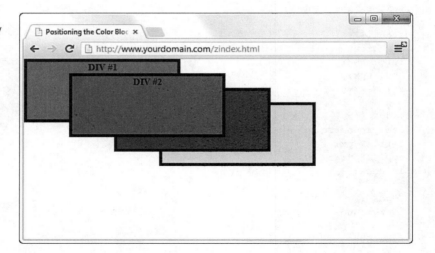

Managing the Flow of Text

Now that you've seen some examples of placing elements relative to other elements or placing them absolutely, it's time to revisit the flow of content around elements. The conceptual *current line* is an invisible line used to place elements on a page. This line has to do with the flow of elements on a page; it comes into play as elements are arranged next to each other across and down the page. Part of the flow of elements is the flow of text on a page. When you mix text with other elements (such as images), it's important to control how the text flows around those other elements.

You've already seen two of these style properties in Chapter 9, "Working with Margins, Padding, Alignment, and Floating." Following are some style properties that give you control over text flow:

▶ `float`—Determines how text flows around an element

▶ `clear`—Stops the flow of text around an element

▶ `overflow`—Controls the overflow of text when an element is too small to contain all the text

The `float` property controls how text flows around an element. It can be set to either `left` or `right`. These values determine where to position an element with respect to flowing text. So setting an image's `float` property to `left` positions the image to the left of flowing text.

As you learned in the preceding chapter, you can prevent text from flowing next to an element by using the `clear` property, which you can set to `none`, `left`, `right`, or `both`. The default value for the clear property is `none`, indicating that text is to flow with no special considerations for the element. The `left` value causes text to stop flowing around an element until the left side of the page is free of the element. Likewise, the `right` value means that text is not to flow around the right side of the element. The `both` value indicates that text isn't to flow around either side of the element.

The `overflow` property handles overflow text, which is text that doesn't fit within its rectangular area; this can happen if you set the `width` and `height` of an element too small. The `overflow` property can be set to `visible`, `hidden`, or `scroll`. The `visible` setting automatically enlarges the element so that the overflow text fits within it; this is the default setting for the property. The `hidden` value leaves the element the same size, allowing the overflow text to remain hidden from view. Perhaps the most interesting value is `scroll`, which adds scrollbars to the element so that you can move around and see the text.

Summary

This chapter began with an important discussion about the CSS box model and how to calculate the width and height of elements when taking margins, padding, and borders into consideration. The chapter continued by tackling absolute positioning of elements, and you learned about positioning using `z-index`. You then learned about a few nifty style properties that enable you to control the flow of text on a page.

This lesson was brief but chock-full of fundamental information about controlling the design of your site. It is worth rereading and working through the examples so that you have a good foundation for your work.

Q&A

Q. How would I determine when to use relative positioning and when to use absolute positioning?

A. Although there are no set guidelines regarding the usage of relative versus absolute positioning, the general idea is that absolute positioning is required only when you want to exert a finer degree of control over how content is positioned. This has to do with the fact that absolute positioning enables you to position content down to the exact pixel, whereas relative positioning is much less predictable in terms of how it positions content. This isn't to say that relative positioning can't do a good job of positioning elements on a page; it just means that absolute positioning is more exact. Of course, this also makes absolute positioning potentially more susceptible to changes in screen size, which you can't really control.

Q. If I don't specify the z-index of two elements that overlap each other, how do I know which element will appear on top?

A. If the `z-index` property isn't set for overlapping elements, the element that appears later in the web page will appear on top. The easy way to remember this is to think of a web browser drawing each element on a page as it reads it from the HTML document; elements read later in the document are drawn on top of those that were read earlier.

Workshop

The Workshop contains quiz questions and exercises to help you solidify your understanding of the material covered. Try to answer all questions before looking at the "Answers" section that follows.

Quiz

1. What's the difference between relative positioning and absolute positioning?

2. Which CSS style property controls the manner in which elements overlap each other?

3. What HTML code could you use to display the words `Where would you like to` starting exactly at the upper-left corner of the browser window, and display the words `GO TODAY?` in large type exactly 80 pixels down and 20 pixels to the right of the corner?

Answers

1. In relative positioning, content is displayed according to the flow of a page, with each element physically appearing after the element preceding it in the HTML code. Absolute positioning, on the other hand, enables you to set the exact position of content on a page.

2. The `z-index` style property controls the manner in which elements overlap each other.

3. You can use this code:

```
<span style="position:absolute;left:0px;top:0px">
Where would you like to</span>
<h1 style="position:absolute;right:20px;top:80px">GO TODAY?</h1>
```

Exercises

▶ Practice working with the intricacies of the CSS box model by creating a series of elements with different margins, padding, and borders, and see how these properties affect their height and width.

▶ Find a group of images that you like, and use absolute positioning and maybe even some `z-index` values to arrange them in a sort of gallery. Try to place your images so that they form a design (such as a square, triangle, or circle).

CHAPTER 11
Using CSS to Do More with Lists, Text, and Navigation

In Chapter 6, "Working with Fonts, Text Blocks, Lists, and Tables," you were introduced to three types of HTML lists, and in Chapter 9, "Working with Margins, Padding, Alignment, and Floating," you learned about margins, padding, and alignment of elements. In this chapter, you will learn how margins, padding, and alignment styles can be applied to different types of HTML lists, helping you produce some powerful design elements purely in HTML and CSS.

Specifically, you will learn how to modify the appearance of list elements—beyond the use of the list-style-type property that you learned in Chapter 6—and how to use a CSS-styled list to replace the client-side imagemaps you learned about in Chapter 8, "Working with Colors, Images, and Multimedia." You will put into practice many of the CSS styles you've learned thus far, and the knowledge you will gain in this chapter will lead directly into using lists for more than just simply presenting a bulleted or numbered set of items. You will learn a few of the many ways to use lists as vertical or horizontal navigation, including how to use lists to create drop-down menus.

The methods explained in this chapter represent a very small subset of the numerous and varied navigation methods you can create using lists. However, the concepts are all similar; different results come from your own creativity and application of these basic concepts. To help you get your creative juices flowing, I will provide pointers to other examples of CSS-based navigation at the end of this chapter.

WHAT YOU'LL LEARN IN THIS CHAPTER:

▶ How the CSS box model affects lists
▶ How to customize the list item indicator
▶ How to use list items and CSS to create an imagemap
▶ How navigation lists differ from regular lists
▶ How to create vertical navigation with CSS
▶ How to create horizontal navigation with CSS

HTML List Refresher

As you learned in Chapter 6, there are three basic types of HTML lists. Each presents content in a slightly different way based on its type and the context:

▶ The *ordered list* is an indented list that displays numbers or letters before each list item. The ordered list is surrounded by `<ol>` and `</ol>` tags and list items are enclosed in the `<li></li>` tag pair. This list type is often used to display numbered steps or levels of content.

▶ The *unordered list* is an indented list that displays a bullet or another symbol before each list item. The unordered list is surrounded by `<ul>` and `</ul>` tags, and list items are enclosed in the `<li></li>` tag pair. This list type is often used to provide a visual cue that brief, yet specific, bits of information will follow.

▶ A *definition list* is often used to display terms and their meanings, thereby providing information hierarchy within the context of the list itself—much like the ordered list but without the numbering. The definition list is surrounded by `<dl>` and `</dl>` tags with `<dt>` and `</dt>` tags enclosing the term and `<dd>` and `</dd>` tags enclosing the definitions.

When the content warrants it, you can nest your ordered and unordered lists—or place lists within other lists. Nested lists produce a content hierarchy, so reserve their use for when your content actually has a hierarchy you want to display (such as content outlines or tables of content). Or, as you will learn later in this chapter, you can use nested lists when your site navigation contains subnavigational elements.

How the CSS Box Model Affects Lists

Specific list-related styles include `list-style-image` (for placement of an image as a list-item marker), `list-style-position` (indicating where to place the list-item marker), and `list-style-type` (the type of list-item marker itself). But although these styles control the structure of the list and list items, you can use `margin`, `padding`, `color`, and `background-color` styles to achieve even more specific displays with your lists.

In Chapter 9, you learned that every element has some padding between the content and the border of the element; you also learned there is a margin between the border of the element and any other content. This is true for lists, and when you are styling lists, you must remember that a "list" is actually made up of two elements: the parent list element type (`<ul>` or `<ol>`) and the individual list items themselves. Each of these elements has margins and padding that can be affected by a style sheet.

The examples in this chapter show you how different CSS styles affect the visual display of HTML lists and list items. Keep these basic differences in mind as you practice working with lists in this chapter, and you will be able to use lists to achieve advanced visual effects within site navigation.

Listing 11.1 creates a basic list containing three items. In this listing, the unordered list itself (the `<ul>`) is given a blue background, a black border, and a specific width of 100 pixels, as shown in Figure 11.1. The list items (the individual `<li>`) have a gray background and a yellow border. The list item text and indicators (the bullet) are black.

NOTE

Some older browsers handle margins and padding differently, especially around lists and list items. However, at the time of writing, the HTML and CSS in this and other chapters in this book are displayed identically in current versions of the major web browsers (Apple Safari, Google Chrome, Microsoft Internet Explorer, Mozilla Firefox, and Opera). Of course, you should still review your web content in all browsers before you publish it online, but the need for "hacking" style sheets to accommodate the rendering idiosyncrasies of browsers is fading away.

LISTING 11.1 Creating a Basic List with Color and Border Styles

```
<!DOCTYPE html>

<html lang="en">
  <head>
    <title>List Test</title>
    <style type="text/css">
      ul {
         background-color: #6666ff;
         border: 1px solid #000000;
         width: 100px;
      }
      li {
         background-color: #cccccc;
         border: 1px solid #ffff00;
      }
    </style>
  </head>

  <body>
    <h1>List Test</h1>
    <ul>
      <li>Item #1</li>
      <li>Item #2</li>
      <li>Item #3</li>
```

```
        </ul>
      </body>
</html>
```

FIGURE 11.1
Styling the list and list items with colors and borders.

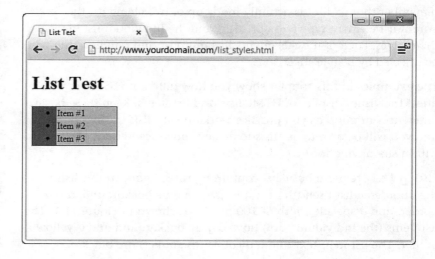

NOTE

You can test the default
`padding-left` value as
displayed by different browsers
by creating a simple test
file such as that shown in
Listing 11.1, and then adding
`padding-left: 40px;` to the
declaration for the `ul` selector
in the style sheet. If you reload
the page and the display does
not change, you know that your
test browser uses 40 pixels as
a default value for `padding-
left`.

As Figure 11.1 shows, the `<ul>` creates a box in which the individual
list items are placed. In this example, the entirety of the box has a
blue background. But also note that the individual list items—in this
example, they use a gray background and a yellow border—do not
extend to the left edge of the box created by the `<ul>`.

This is because browsers automatically add a certain amount of
padding to the left side of the `<ul>`. Browsers don't add padding to
the margin, because that would appear around the outside of the
box. They add padding inside the box and only on the left side. That
padding value is approximately 40 pixels.

The default left-side padding value remains the same regardless of the
type of list. If you add the following line to the style sheet, creating a
list with no item indicators, you will find that the padding remains the
same (see Figure 11.2):

```
list-style-type: none;
```

When you are creating a page layout that includes lists of any type,
play around with padding to place the items "just so" on the page.
Similarly, just because no default margin is associated with lists doesn't

mean you can't assign some to the display; adding `margin` values to the declaration for the `ul` selector provides additional layout control.

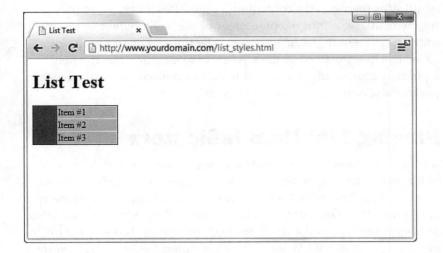

FIGURE 11.2
The default left-side padding remains the same with or without list item indicators.

But remember, so far we've worked with only the list definition itself; we haven't worked with the application of styles to the individual list items. In Figures 11.1 and 11.2, the gray background and yellow border of the list item show no default padding or margin. Figure 11.3 shows the different effects created by applying padding or margin values to list items rather than the overall list "box" itself.

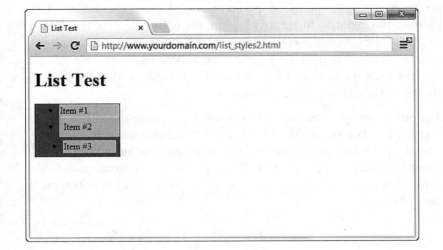

FIGURE 11.3
Different values affect the padding and margins on list items.

The first list item is the base item, with no padding or margin applied to it. However, the second list item uses a class called `padded`, defined in the style sheet as `padding: 6px`; you can see the 6 pixels of padding on all sides (between the content and the yellow border surrounding the element). Note that the placement of the bullet remains the same as the placement of the first list item. The third list item uses a class called `margined`, defined in the style sheet as `margin: 6px`, to apply 6 pixels of margin around the list item; this margin allows the blue background of the `<ul>` to show through.

Placing List Item Indicators

All this talk of margins and padding raises another issue: the control of list item indicators (when used) and how text should wrap around them (or not). The default value of the `list-style-position` property is `outside`—this placement means that the bullets, numbers, and other indicators are kept to the left of the text, outside the box created by the `<li></li>` tag pair. When text wraps within the list item, it wraps within that box and remains flush left with the left border of the element.

But when the value of `list-style-position` is `inside`, the indicators are inside the box created by the `<li></li>` tag pair. Not only are the list item indicators then indented further (they essentially become part of the text), but the text wraps beneath each item indicator.

Figure 11.4 shows an example of both outside and inside list style positions. The only changes between Listing 11.1 and the code used to produce the example in Figure 11.4 (not including the filler text added to Item #2 and Item #3) is that the second list item uses a class called `outside`, defined in the style sheet as `list-style-position: outside`, and the third list item uses a class called `inside`, defined in the style sheet as `list-style-position: inside`.

The additional filler text used for the second list item shows how the text wraps when the width of the list is defined as a value that is too narrow to display all on one line. You could have achieved the same result without using `list-style-position: outside` because that is the default value of `list-style-position` without any explicit statement in the code.

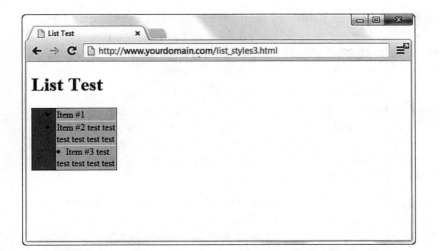

FIGURE 11.4
The difference between outside and inside values for list-style-position.

However, you can clearly see the difference when the `inside` position is used. In the third list item, the bullet and the text are both within the gray area bordered by yellow—the list item itself. Margins and padding affect list items differently when the value of `list-style-position` is `inside` (see Figure 11.5).

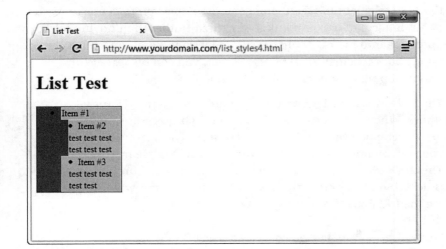

FIGURE 11.5
Margin and padding change the display of items using the inside list-style-position.

In Figure 11.5, the second and third list items both have a `list-style-position` value of `inside`. However, the second list item has a `margin-left` value of 12 pixels and the third list item has a `padding-left` value of 12 pixels. Although both content blocks (list indicator plus the text) show text wrapped around the bullet, and the placement of these blocks within the gray area defining the list item is the same, the affected area is the list item within the list itself.

As you would expect, the list item with the `margin-left` value of 12 pixels displays 12 pixels of red showing through the transparent margin surrounding the list item. Similarly, the list item with the `padding-left` value of 12 pixels displays 12 pixels of gray background (of the list item) before the content begins. Padding is within the element; margin is outside the element.

By understanding the way margins and padding affect both list items and the list in which they appear, you can create navigation elements in your website that are pure CSS and do not rely on external images. Later in this hour, you'll learn how to create both vertical and horizontal navigation menus, as well as menu drop-downs.

Creating Imagemaps with List Items and CSS

In Chapter 8 you learned how to create client-side imagemaps using the `<map>` element in HTML. Imagemaps enable you to define an area of an image and assign a link to that area (rather than having to slice an image into pieces, apply links to individual pieces, and stitch the image back together in HTML). However, you can also create an imagemap purely out of valid HTML and CSS.

The code in Listing 11.2 produces the imagemap that Figure 11.6 shows. When the code is rendered in a web browser, it simply looks like a web page with an image placed in it. The actions happen when your mouse hovers over a "hot" area, as you can see in Figure 11.6: The thick white border and image `alt` text show the area the mouse is hovering over, and in the lower left of the browser window, you can see the URL assigned to that hotspot.

LISTING 11.2   Creating an Imagemap Using CSS

```
<!DOCTYPE html>

<html lang="en">
  <head>
    <title>CSS Imagemap Example</title>
    <style type="text/css">
```

```
#theImg {
    width: 500px;
    height: 375px;
    background: url(tea_shipment.jpg) no-repeat;
    position: relative;
    border: 1px solid #000000;
}
#theImg ul {
    margin: 0px;
    padding: 0px;
    list-style: none;
}
#theImg a {
    position: absolute;
    text-indent: -1000em;
}
#theImg a:hover {
    border: 4px solid #ffffff;
}
#ss a {
    top: 0px;
    left: 5px;
    width: 80px;
    height: 225px;
}
#gn a {
    top: 226px;
    left: 15px;
    width: 70px;
    height: 110px;
}
#ib a {
    top: 225px;
    left: 85px;
    width: 60px;
    height: 90px;
}
#iTEA1 a {
    top: 100px;
    left: 320px;
    width: 178px;
    height: 125px;
}
#iTEA2 a {
    top: 225px;
    left: 375px;
    width: 123px;
    height: 115px;
}
    </style>
</head>
```

```
<body>
  <div id="theImg">
  <ul>
  <li id="ss"><a href="[some URL]"
      title="Sugarshots">Sugarshots</a></li>
  <li id="gn"><a href="[some URL]"
      title="Golden Needle">Golden Needle</a></li>
  <li id="ib"><a href="[some URL]"
      title="Irish Breakfast">Irish Breakfast</a></li>
  <li id="iTEA1"><a href="[some URL]"
      title="IngenuiTEA">IngenuiTEA</a></li>
  <li id="iTEA2"><a href="[some URL]"
      title="IngenuiTEA">IngenuiTEA</a></li>
  </ul>
  </div>
  </body>
</html>
```

FIGURE 11.6
CSS enables you to define
hotspots in an imagemap.

As Listing 11.2 shows, the style sheet has quite a few entries, but the actual HTML is quite short. List items are used to create five distinct clickable areas; those "areas" are list items that are assigned a specific height and width and then placed over an image that sits in the background. If the image is removed from the background of the `<div>` that surrounds the list, the list items still exist and are still clickable.

Let's walk through the style sheet so that you understand the pieces that make up this HTML and CSS imagemap, which is—at its most basic level—just a list of links.

The list of links is enclosed in a `<div>` named `theImg`. In the style sheet, this `<div>` is defined as a block element that is 500 pixels wide and 375 pixels high, with a 1-pixel solid black border. The background of this element is an image named `tea_shipment.jpg` that is placed in one position and does not repeat. The next bit of HTML that you see is the beginning of the unordered list (`<ul>`). In the style sheet, this unordered list is given margin and padding values of 0 pixels all around and a `list-style` of `none`—list items will not be preceded by any icon.

The list item text itself never appears to the user because of this trick in the style sheet entry for all `<a>` tags within the `<div>`:

```
text-indent: -1000em;
```

By indenting the text *negative* 1,000 ems, you can be assured that the text will never appear. It does exist, but it exists in a nonviewable area 1,000 ems to the left of the browser window. In other words, if you raise your left hand and place it to the side of your computer monitor, `text-indent: -1000em` places the text somewhere to the left of your pinky finger. But that's what we want because we don't need to see the text link. We just need an area to be defined as a link so that the user's cursor changes as it does when rolling over any link in a website.

When the user's cursor hovers over a list item containing a link, that list item shows a 4-pixel border that is solid white, thanks to this entry in the style sheet:

```
#theImg a:hover {
    border: 4px solid #ffffff;
}
```

The list items themselves are then defined and placed in specific positions based on the areas of the image that are supposed to be the clickable areas. For example, the list item with the `ss` ID, for Sugarshots—the name of the item shown in the figure—has its top-left corner placed 0 pixels from the top of the `<div>` and 5 pixels in from the left edge of the `<div>`. This list item is 80 pixels wide and 225 pixels high. Similar style declarations are made for the `#gn`, `#ib`, `#iTEA1`, and

#iTEA2 list items so that the linked areas associated with those IDs appear in certain positions relative to the image.

How Navigation Lists Differ from Regular Lists

When we talk about using lists to create navigation elements, we really mean using CSS to display content in the way website visitors expect navigation to look—in short, *different* from simple bulleted or numbered lists. Although it is true that a set of navigation elements is essentially a list of links, those links are typically displayed in a way that makes it clear that users should interact with the content:

▶ The user's mouse cursor will change to indicate that the element is clickable.

▶ The area around the element changes appearance when the mouse hovers over it.

▶ The content area is visually set apart from regular text.

Older methods of creating navigation tended to rely on images—such as graphics with beveled edges and the use of contrasting colors for backgrounds and text—plus client-side programming with JavaScript to handle image swapping based on mouse actions. But using pure CSS to create navigation from list elements produces a more usable, flexible, and search-engine-friendly display that is accessible by users using all manner and sorts of devices.

Regardless of the layout of your navigational elements—horizontal or vertical—this chapter discusses two levels of navigation: primary and secondary. *Primary navigation* takes users to the introductory pages of main sections of your site; *secondary navigation* reflects those pages within a certain section.

Creating Vertical Navigation with CSS

Depending on your site architecture—both the display template you have created and the manner in which you have categorized the information in the site—you might find yourself using vertical navigation for either primary navigation or secondary navigation.

For example, suppose you have created a website for your company and the primary sections are About Us, Products, Support, and Press. Within the primary About Us section, you might have several other pages, such as Mission, History, Executive Team, and Contact Us— these other pages are the secondary navigation within the primary About Us section.

Listing 11.3 sets up a basic secondary page with vertical navigation in the side of the page and content in the middle of the page. The links in the side and the links in the content area of the page are basic HTML list elements.

This listing and the example shown in Figure 11.7 provide a starting point for showing you how CSS enables you to transform two similar HTML structures into two different visual displays (and thus two different contexts).

LISTING 11.3   Basic Page with Vertical Navigation in a List

```
<!DOCTYPE html>

<html lang="en">
  <head>
    <title>About Us</title>
    <style type="text/css">
      body {
          font: 12pt Verdana, Arial, Georgia, sans-serif;
      }
      nav {
          width: 150px;
          float: left;
          margin-top: 12px;
          margin-right: 18px;
      }
      section {
          width: 550px;
          float: left;
      }
    </style>
  </head>

  <body>
    <nav>
    <ul>
      <li><a href="#">Mission</a></li>
      <li><a href="#">History</a></li>
      <li><a href="#">Executive Team</a></li>
      <li><a href="#">Contact Us</a></li>
    </ul>
```

```
      </nav>
      <section>
        <header>
        <h1>About Us</h1>
        </header>
        <p>On the introductory pages of main sections, it can be
        useful to repeat the secondary navigation and provide more
        context, such as:</p>
        <ul>
        <li><a href="#">Mission</a>: Learn more about our corporate
        mission and philanthropic efforts.</li>
        <li><a href="#">History</a>: Read about our corporate
        history and learn how we grew to become the largest widget
        maker in the country.</li>
        <li><a href="#">Executive Team</a>: Our team of executives
        makes the company run like a well-oiled machine (also
        useful for making widgets).</li>
        <li><a href="#">Contact Us</a>: Here you can find multiple
        methods for contacting us (and we really do care what you
        have to say).</li>
        </ul>
      </section>
    </body>
</html>
```

FIGURE 11.7
The starting point: unstyled list navigation.

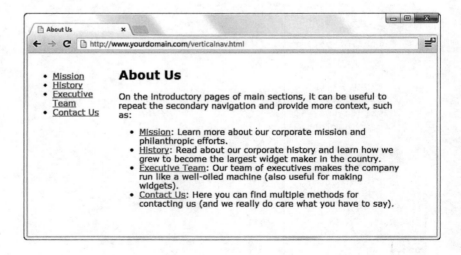

The contents of this page are set up in two sections: a `<nav>` element containing navigation, and a single `<section>` element containing the primary text of the page. The only styles assigned to anything in this basic page are the width, margin, and float values associated with each element. No styles have been applied to the list elements.

To differentiate between the links present in the list in the content area and the links present in the list in the side navigation, add the following styles to the style sheet:

```
nav a {
   text-decoration: none;
}
section a {
   text-decoration: none;
   font-weight: bold;
 }
```

These styles simply say that all `<a>` links in the `<nav>` have no underline, and all `<a>` links in the `<section>` have no underline and are bold. Figure 11.8 shows the difference.

But to really make the side navigation list look like something special, you have to dig deeper into the style sheet.

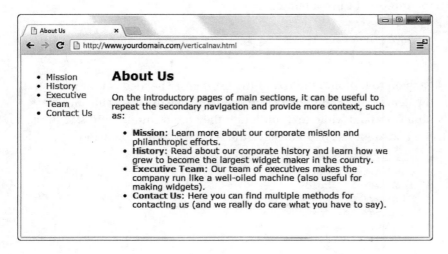

FIGURE 11.8
Differentiating the list elements using CSS.

Styling the Single-Level Vertical Navigation

The goal with this particular set of navigation elements is simply to present them as a block of links without bullets and with background and text colors that change depending on their link state (regular link, visited link, hovering over the link, or activated link). The first step in the process is already complete: separating the navigation from the content. We've done that by putting the navigation in a `<nav>` element.

Next, you need to modify the `<ul>` that defines the link within the `<nav>` element. Let's take away the list indicator and ensure that there is no extra margin or padding hanging around besides the top margin. That top margin is used to line up the top of the navigation with the top of the "About Us" header text in the content area of the page:

```
nav ul {
    list-style: none;
    margin: 12px 0px 0px 0px;;
    padding: 0px;
}
```

Because the navigation list items themselves will appear as colored areas, give each list item a bottom border so that some visual separation of the content can occur:

```
nav li {
    border-bottom: 1px solid #ffffff;
}
```

Now on to building the rest of the list items. The idea is that when the list items simply sit there acting as links, they are a special shade of blue with bold white text (although they are a smaller font size than the body text itself). To achieve that effect, add the following:

```
nav li a:link, nav li a:visited {
    font-size: 10pt;
    font-weight: bold;
    display: block;
    padding: 3px 0px 3px 3px;
    background-color: #628794;
    color: #ffffff;
}
```

All the styles used previously should be familiar to you, except perhaps the use of `display: block;` in the style sheet entry. Setting the `display` property to `block` ensures that the entire `<li>` element is in play when a user hovers his mouse over it. Figure 11.9 shows the vertical list menu with these new styles applied to it.

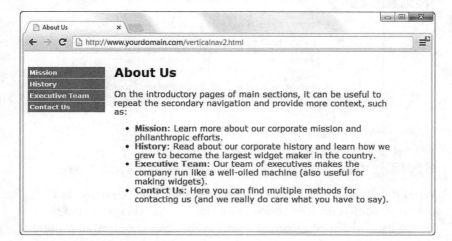

FIGURE 11.9
The vertical list is starting to look like a navigation menu.

When the user's mouse hovers over a navigational list element, the idea is for some visual change to take place so that the user knows that the element is clickable. This is akin to how most software menus change color when a user's cursor hovers over the menu items. In this case, we'll change the background color of the list item and change the text color of the list item; they'll be different from the blue and white shown previously.

```css
nav li a:hover, nav li a:active {
    font-size: 10pt;
    font-weight: bold;
    display: block;
    padding: 3px 0px 3px 3px;
    background-color: #6cac46;
    color: #000000;
}
```

Figure 11.10 shows the results of all the stylistic work so far. A few entries in a style sheet have transformed the simple list into a visually differentiated menu.

FIGURE 11.10
The list items now change color
when the mouse hovers over them.

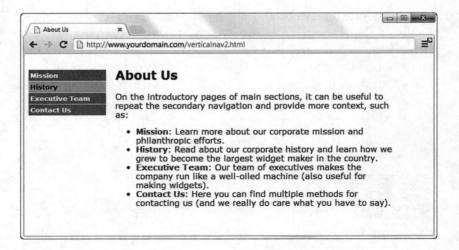

Styling the Multilevel Vertical Navigation

What if your site architecture calls for another level of navigation
that you want your users to see at all times? That is represented by
nested lists (which you learned about in previous chapters) and more
style sheet entries. In this case, assume that there are four navigation
elements under the Executive Team link. In the HTML, modify the list
as shown here:

```
<ul>
  <li><a href="#">Mission</a></li>
  <li><a href="#">History</a></li>
  <li><a href="#">Executive Team</a>
    <ul>
    <li><a href="#">&raquo; CEO</a>
    <li><a href="#">&raquo; CFO</a>
    <li><a href="#">&raquo; COO</a>
    <li><a href="#">&raquo; Other Minions</a>
    </ul>
  </li>
  <li><a href="#">Contact Us</a></li>
</ul>
```

This code produces a nested list under the Executive Team link (see
Figure 11.11). The » HTML entity produces the right-pointing
arrows that are displayed before the text in the new links.

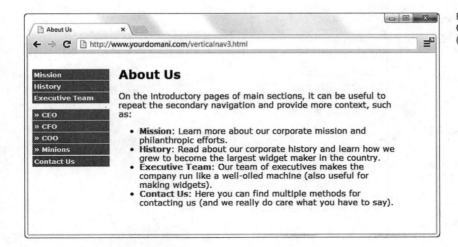

FIGURE 11.11
Creating a nested navigation list
(but one that is not yet styled well).

The new items appear as block elements within the list, but the hierarchy of information is not visually represented. To add some sort of visual element that identifies these items as subnavigational elements attached to the Executive Team link, modify the style sheet again to add some indentation.

But before doing that, you want to modify some of the other style sheet entries as well. In the preceding section, we added selectors such as `nav ul` and `nav li`, which indicate "all `<ul>` in the `<nav>` element" and "all `<li>` in the `<nav>` element," respectively. However, we now have two instances of `<ul>` and another set of `<li>` elements with the `<nav>` element, all of which we want to appear different from the original set.

To ensure that both sets of list items are styled appropriately, make sure that the style sheet selectors clearly indicate the hierarchy of the lists. To do that, use entries such as `nav ul` and `nav ul li` for the first level of lists, and use `nav ul ul` and `nav ul ul li` for the second level of lists. Listing 11.4 shows the new version of style sheet entries and the HTML that produces the menu shown in Figure 11.12.

LISTING 11.4   Multilevel Vertical Navigation in a List

```
<!DOCTYPE html>

<html lang="en">
  <head>
    <title>About Us</title>
    <style type="text/css">
```

```
body {
    font: 12pt Verdana, Arial, Georgia, sans-serif;
}
nav {
    width: 150px;
    float: left;
    margin-top: 12px;
    margin-right: 18px;
}
section {
    width: 550px;
    float: left;
}
nav a {
    text-decoration: none;
}
section a {
    text-decoration: none;
    font-weight: bold;
}
nav ul {
    list-style: none;
    margin: 12px 0px 0px 0px;
    padding: 0px;
}
nav ul li {
    border-bottom: 1px solid #ffffff;
}
nav ul li a:link, nav ul li a:visited {
    font-size: 10pt;
    font-weight: bold;
    display: block;
    padding: 3px 0px 3px 3px;
    background-color: #628794;
    color: #ffffff;
}
nav ul li a:hover, nav ul li a:active {
    font-size: 10pt;
    font-weight: bold;
    display: block;
    padding: 3px 0px 3px 3px;
    background-color: #c6a648;
    color: #000000;
}
nav ul ul {
    margin: 0px;
    padding: 0px;
}
nav ul ul li {
    border-bottom: none;
```

```
        }
    nav ul ul li a:link, nav ul ul li a:visited {
        font-size: 8pt;
        font-weight: bold;
        display: block;
        padding: 3px 0px 3px 18px;
        background-color: #628794;
        color: #ffffff;
    }
    nav ul ul li a:hover, nav ul ul li a:active {
        font-size: 8pt;
        font-weight: bold;
        display: block;
        padding: 3px 0px 3px 18px;
        background-color: #c6a648;
        color: #000000;
    }
    </style>
</head>

<body>
  <nav>
  <ul>
    <li><a href="#">Mission</a></li>
    <li><a href="#">History</a></li>
    <li><a href="#">Executive Team</a>
        <ul>
        <li><a href="#">&raquo; CEO</a></li>
        <li><a href="#">&raquo; CFO</a></li>
        <li><a href="#">&raquo; COO</a></li>
        <li><a href="#">&raquo; Other Minions</a></li>
        </ul>
    </li>
    <li><a href="#">Contact Us</a></li>
  </ul>
  </nav>
  <section>
    <header>
    <h1>About Us</h1>
    </header>
    <p>On the introductory pages of main sections, it can be
    useful to repeat the secondary navigation and provide more
    context, such as:</p>
    <ul>
    <li><a href="#">Mission</a>: Learn more about our corporate
    mission and philanthropic efforts.</li>
    <li><a href="#">History</a>: Read about our corporate
    history and learn how we grew to become the largest widget
    maker in the country.</li>
```

```
      <li><a href="#">Executive Team</a>: Our team of executives
      makes the company run like a well-oiled machine (also
      useful for making widgets).</li>
      <li><a href="#">Contact Us</a>: Here you can find multiple
      methods for contacting us (and we really do care what you
      have to say).</li>
      </ul>
    </section>
  </body>
</html>
```

FIGURE 11.12
Creating two levels of vertical
navigation using CSS.

The different ways of styling vertical navigation are limited only by
your own creativity. You can use colors, margins, padding, background
images, and any other valid CSS to produce vertical navigation that is
quite flexible and easily modified. If you type **CSS vertical navigation**
in your search engine, you will find thousands of examples—and they
are all based on the simple principles you've learned in this chapter.

Creating Horizontal Navigation with CSS

The lessons on navigation began with vertical navigation because the concept of converting a list into navigation is easier to grasp when the navigation still looks like a list of items that you might write vertically on a piece of paper, like a grocery list. When creating horizontal navigation, you still use HTML list elements but instead of a vertical display achieved by using the inline value of the display property for both the `<ul>` and the `<li>`, use the block value of the display property. It really is as simple as that.

Listing 11.5 shows a starting point for a page featuring horizontal navigation. The page contains a `<header>` element for a logo and navigation and a `<section>` element for content. Within the `<header>` element, a `<div>` containing a logo is floated next to a `<nav>` element containing the navigational links. The list that appears in the `<nav>` element has a display property value of inline for both the list and the list items. You can see these elements and their placement in Figure 11.13.

LISTING 11.5   Basic Horizontal Navigation from a List

```
<!DOCTYPE html>

<htmllang="en">
  <head>
    <title>ACME Widgets LLC</title>
    <style type="text/css">
      body {
         font: 12pt Verdana, Arial, Georgia, sans-serif;
      }
      header {
         width: auto;
      }
      #logo {
         float: left;
      }
      nav {
         float: left;
      }
      nav ul {
         list-style: none;
         display: inline;
      }
      nav li {
```

Positions
Fixed : —③
Relavantive : —②
absolute —④
Static : —①

Relative
follow static

Outside Margin
inside Padding

All tags are boxs

<uli>

```
            display: inline;
        }
        section {
            width: auto;
            float: left;
            clear: left;
        }
        section a {
            text-decoration: none;
            font-weight: bold;
        }
    </style>
</head>
<body>
    <header>
        <div id="logo">
            <img src="acmewidgets.jpg" alt="ACME Widgets LLC" />
        </div>
        <nav>
            <ul>
            <li><a href="#">About Us</a></li>
            <li><a href="#">Products</a></li>
            <li><a href="#">Support</a></li>
            <li><a href="#">Press</a></li>
            </ul>
        </nav>
    </header>
    <section>
        <p><strong>ACME Widgets LLC</strong> is the greatest
        widget-maker in all the land.</p>
        <p>Don't believe us? Read on...</p>
        <ul>
        <li><a href="#">About Us</a>: We are pretty great.</li>
        <li><a href="#">Products</a>: Our products are the best.</li>
        <li><a href="#">Support</a>: It is unlikely you will need
        support, but we provide it anyway.</li>
        <li><a href="#">Press</a>: Read what others are saying
        (about how great we are).</li>
        </ul>
    </section>
</body>
</html>
```

FIGURE 11.13
Creating functional—but not
necessarily beautiful—horizontal
navigation using inline list
elements.

Modifying the display of this list occurs purely through CSS; the
structure of the content within the HTML itself is already set. To
achieve the desired display, use the following CSS. First, the `<nav>`
element is modified to be a particular width, display a background
color and border, and use a top margin of 85 pixels (so that it displays
near the bottom of the logo).

```
nav {
    float:left;
    margin: 85px 0px 0px 0px;
    width: 400px;
    background-color: #628794;
    border: 1px solid black;
}
```

The definition for the `<ul>` remains the same as in Listing 11.5 except
for the changes in margin and padding:

```
nav ul {
    margin: 0px;
    padding: 0px;
    list-style: none;
    display: inline;
}
```

The definition for the `<li>` remains the same as in Listing 11.5 except
it has been given a `line-height` value of `1.8em`:

```
nav li {
    display: inline;
    line-height: 1.8em;
}
```

The link styles are similar to those used in the vertical navigation; these entries have different padding values, but the colors and font sizes remain the same:

```
nav ul li a:link, nav ul li a:visited {
    font-size: 10pt;
    font-weight: bold;
    text-decoration: none;
    padding: 7px 10px 7px 10px;
    background-color: #628794;
    color: #ffffff;
}
nav ul li a:hover, nav ul li a:active {
    font-size: 10pt;
    font-weight: bold;
    text-decoration: none;
    padding: 7px 10px 7px 10px;
    background-color: #c6a648;
    color: #000000;
}
```

Putting these styles together, you produce the display shown in Figure 11.14.

FIGURE 11.14
Creating horizontal navigation with some style.

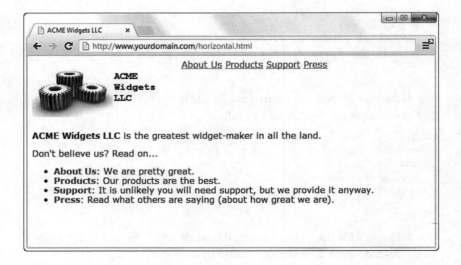

When the user rolls over the navigation elements, the background and text colors change in the same way they did when the user hovered her mouse over the vertical navigation menu. Also, just as you did with the vertical navigation menu, you can use nested lists to produce drop-down functionality in your horizontal menu. Try it yourself!

Summary

This chapter began with examples of how lists and list elements are affected by padding and margin styles. You first learned about the default padding associated with lists and how to control that padding. Next you learned how to modify padding and margin values and how to place the list item indicator either inside the list item or outside it, so you could begin to think about how styles and lists can affect your overall site design. Finally, you learned how to leverage lists and list elements to create a pure HTML and CSS imagemap, thus reducing the need for slicing up linked images or using the <map> element.

After learning to "think outside the (list) box," if you will, you learned how to use unordered lists to produce horizontal or vertical navigation within your website. By using CSS instead of graphics, you will have more flexibility in both the display and the maintenance of your site. Throughout this chapter, you learned that with a few entries in your style sheet, you can turn plain underlined text links into areas with borders and background colors and other text styles. Additionally, you learned how to present nested lists within menus.

Q&A

Q. An awful lot of web pages talk about the "box model hack" regarding margins and padding, especially for lists and list elements. Are you sure I don't have to use a hack?

A. At the beginning of this chapter, you learned that the HTML and CSS in this chapter (and others) all look the same in the current versions of the major web browsers. This is the product of several years of web developers having to do code hacks and other tricks before modern browsers began handling things according to CSS specifications, not their own idiosyncrasies. Additionally, there is a growing movement to rid Internet users of the *very* old web browsers that necessitated most of these hacks in the first place. So although I wouldn't necessarily advise you to design *only* for the current versions of the major web browsers, I also wouldn't recommend that you spend a ton of time implementing hacks for the older versions of browsers—which less than 5% of the Internet population uses, by the way. You should continue to write solid code that validates and adheres to design principles, test your pages in a suite of browsers that best reflects your audience, and release your site to the world.

Q. The CSS imagemap seems like a lot of work. Is the `<map>` element so bad?

A. The `<map>` element isn't at all bad, and is valid HTML5. The determination of coordinates used in client-side imagemaps can be difficult, however, especially without graphics software or software intended for the creation of client-side imagemaps. The CSS version gives you more options for defining and displaying clickable areas, only one of which you've seen here.

Q. Can I use graphics in the navigation menus as a custom list indicator?

A. Yes. You can use graphics within the HTML text of the list item or as background images within the `<li>` element. You can style your navigation elements just as you style any other list element. The only differences between an HTML unordered list and a CSS-based horizontal or vertical navigation list is that you are calling it that and you are using the unordered list for a specific purpose outside of the body of the text. Along with that, you then style the list to show the user that it is indeed something different—and you can do that with small graphics to accentuate your lists.

Q. Where can I find more examples of what I can do with lists?

A. The last time I checked, typing CSS navigation in a search engine returned approximately 44 million results. Here are a few starting places:

▶ A List Apart's CSS articles at http://www.alistapart.com/topics/code/

▶ Maxdesign's CSS Listamatic at http://css.maxdesign.com.au/listamatic/

▶ Vitaly Friedman's CSS Showcase at http://www.alvit.de/css-showcase/

Workshop

The workshop contains quiz questions and activities to help you solidify your understanding of the material covered. Try to answer all questions before looking at the "Answers" section that follows.

Quiz

1. What is the difference between the `inside` and `outside` `list-style-position` values? Which is the default value?

2. Does a `list-style` with a value of `none` still produce a structured list, either ordered or unordered?

3. When creating list-based navigation, how many levels of nested lists can you use?

4. When creating a navigation list of any type, can the four pseudoclasses for the `a` selector have the same values?

Answers

1. The `list-style-position` value of `inside` places the list item indicator inside the block created by the list item. A value of `outside` places the list item indicator outside the block. When `inside`, content wraps beneath the list item indicator. The default value is `outside`.

2. Yes. The only difference is that no list item indicator is present before the content within the list item.

3. Technically, you can nest your lists as deeply as you want to. But from a usability standpoint, there is a limit to the number of levels that you would *want* to use to nest your lists. Three levels is typically the limit—more than that and you run the risk of creating a poorly organized site or simply giving users more options than they need to see at all times.

4. Sure, but then you run the risk of users not realizing that your beautiful menus are indeed menus (because no visual display would occur for a mouse action).

Exercises

▶ Find an image and try your hand at mapping areas using the technique shown in this chapter. Select an image that has areas in which you could use hot spots or clickable areas leading to other web pages on your site or to someone else's site. Then create the HTML and CSS to define the clickable areas and the URLs to which they should lead.

▶ Using the techniques shown for a multilevel vertical list, add subnavigation items to the vertical list created at the end of the chapter.

▶ Look at the numerous examples of CSS-based navigation used in websites and find some tricky-looking actions. Using the View Source function of your web browser, look at the CSS used by these sites and try to implement something similar for yourself.

CHAPTER 12
Creating Fixed or Liquid Layouts

So far, you've learned a lot about styling web content, from font sizes and colors to images, block elements, lists, and more. But what we haven't yet discussed is a high-level overview of page layout. In general, there are two types of layouts: fixed and liquid. But it's also possible to use a combination of the two, with some elements fixed and others liquid.

In this chapter, you'll first learn about the characteristics of these two types of layouts and see a few examples of websites that use them. At the end of the chapter, you'll see a basic template that combines elements of both types of layouts. Ultimately, the type of layout you choose is up to you—it's hard to go wrong as long as your sites follow HTML and CSS standards.

WHAT YOU'LL LEARN IN THIS CHAPTER:

► How fixed layouts work
► How liquid layouts work
► How to create a fixed/ liquid hybrid layout
► How to think about and begin to implement a responsive design

TRY IT YOURSELF ▼
Finding Examples of Layouts You Like

A good place for examples of liquid layouts is the WordPress Themes Directory, at http://wordpress.org/themes/. WordPress began as a blogging platform but in recent years has seen an increase in use as a nonblog content or site-management tool. The WordPress Themes Directory shows hundreds of examples of both fixed-width and liquid layouts that give you an idea, if not all the code, for what you can create. Even though you are not working with a WordPress blog or site as part of the exercises in this book, the Themes Directory is a place where you can see and interact with many variations on designs.

Spend some time looking at the WordPress examples and perhaps the CSS Zen Garden as well, at www.csszengarden.com. This will help you get a feel for the types of layouts you like without being swayed by the content within the layout.

Understanding Fixed Layouts

A fixed layout, or fixed-width layout, is just that: a layout in which the body of the page is set to a specific width. That width is typically controlled by a master "wrapper" element that contains all the content. The `width` property of a wrapper element, such as a `<div>`, is set in the style sheet entry if the `<div>` was given an ID value such as `main` or `wrapper` (although the name is up to you).

When creating a fixed-width layout, the most important decision is determining the minimum screen resolution you want to accommodate. For many years, 800×600 was the "lowest common denominator" for web designers, resulting in a typical fixed width of approximately 760 pixels. However, the number of people using 800×600 screen resolution for nonmobile browsers is now less than 4%. Given that, many web designers consider 1,024×768 the current minimum screen resolution, so if they create fixed-width layouts, the fixed width typically is somewhere between 800 and 1,000 pixels wide.

A main reason for creating a fixed-width layout is so that you can have precise control over the appearance of the content area. However, if users visit your fixed-width site with smaller or much larger screen resolutions than the resolution you had in mind while you designed it, they will encounter scrollbars (if their resolution is smaller) or a large amount of empty space (if their resolution is greater). Finding fixed-width layouts is difficult among the most popular websites these days because site designers know they need to cater to the largest possible audience (and therefore make no assumptions about browser size). However, fixed-width layouts still have wide adoption, especially by site administrators using a content management system with a strict template.

The following figures show one such site, for San Jose State University (university websites commonly use a strict template and content management system, so this was an easy example to find); it has a wrapper element fixed at 960 pixels wide. In Figure 12.1, the browser window is a shade under 900 pixels wide. On the right side of the image, important content is cut off (and at the bottom of the figure, a horizontal scrollbar displays in the browser).

CAUTION

Remember, the web browser window contains nonviewable areas, including the scrollbar. So if you are targeting a 1,024-pixel-wide screen resolution, you really can't use all 1,024 of those pixels.

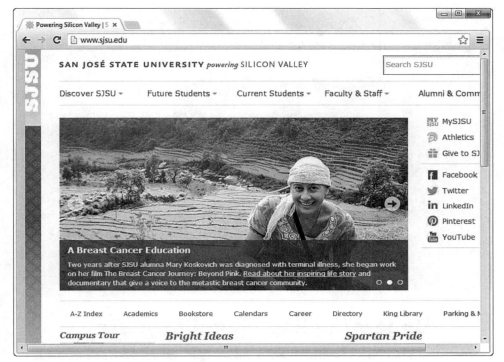

FIGURE 12.1
A fixed-width example
with a smaller screen
size.

However, Figure 12.2 shows how this site looks when the browser window is more than 1,400 pixels wide: You see a lot of empty space (or "real estate") on both sides of the main body content, which some consider aesthetically displeasing.

Besides the decision to create a fixed-width layout in the first place is the task of determining whether to place the fixed-width content flush left or center it. Placing the content flush left produces extra space on the right side only; centering the content area creates extra space on both sides. However, centering at least provides balance, whereas a flush-left design could end up looking like a small rectangle shoved in the corner of the browser, depending on the size and resolution of a user's monitor.

FIGURE 12.2
A fixed-width example
with a larger screen
size.

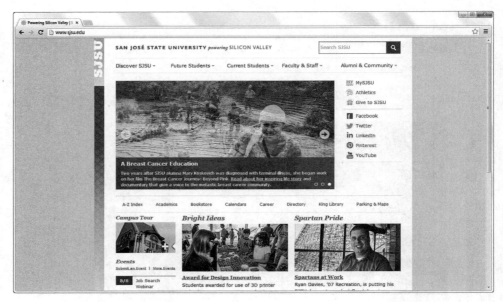

Understanding Liquid Layouts

A liquid layout—also called a *fluid* layout—is one in which the body of the page does not use a specified width in pixels, although it might be enclosed in a master "wrapper" element that uses a percentage width. The idea behind the liquid layout is that it can be perfectly usable and still retain the overall design aesthetic even if the user has a very small or very wide screen.

Figures 12.3, 12.4, and 12.5 show three examples of a liquid layout in action.

In Figure 12.3, the browser window is approximately 770 pixels wide. This example shows a reasonable minimum screen width before a horizontal scrollbar appears. In fact, the scrollbar does not appear until the browser is 735 pixels wide. On the other hand, Figure 12.4 shows a very small browser window (less than 600 pixels wide).

FIGURE 12.3
A liquid layout as viewed in a relatively small screen.

In Figure 12.4, you can see a horizontal scrollbar; in the header area of the page content, the logo graphic is beginning to take over the text and appear on top of it. But the bulk of the page is still quite usable. The informational content on the left side of the page is still legible and is sharing the available space with the input form on the right side.

Figure 12.5 shows how this same page looks in a very wide screen. In Figure 12.5, the browser window is approximately 1,330 pixels wide. There is plenty of room for all the content on the page to spread out. This liquid layout is achieved because all the design elements have a percentage width specified (instead of a fixed width). In doing so, the layout makes use of all the available browser real estate.

FIGURE 12.4
A liquid layout as viewed in a very small screen.

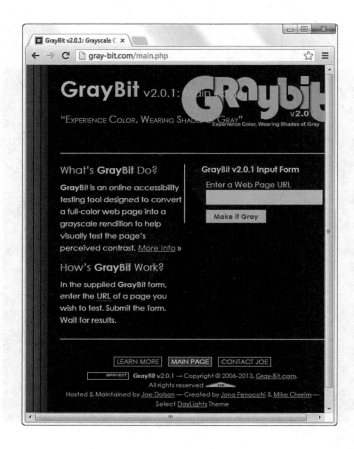

FIGURE 12.5
A liquid layout as viewed in a wide screen.

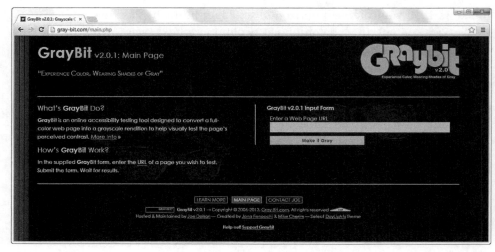

The liquid layout approach might seem like the best approach at first glance—after all, who wouldn't want to take advantage of all the screen real estate available? But there's a fine line between taking advantage of space and not allowing the content to breathe. Too much content is overwhelming; not enough content in an open space is underwhelming.

The pure liquid layout can be quite impressive, but it requires a significant amount of testing to ensure that it is usable in a wide range of browsers at varying screen resolutions. You might not have the time and effort to produce such a design; in that case, a reasonable compromise is the fixed/liquid hybrid layout, or a fully responsive design, as you'll learn about later in this chapter.

Creating a Fixed/Liquid Hybrid Layout

A fixed/liquid hybrid layout is one that contains elements of both types of layouts. For example, you could have a fluid layout that includes fixed-width content areas either within the body area or as anchor elements (such as a left-side column or as a top navigation strip). You can even create a fixed content area that acts like a frame, in which a content area remains fixed even as users scroll through the content.

Starting with a Basic Layout Structure

In this example, you'll learn to create a template that is liquid but with two fixed-width columns on either side of the main body area (which is a third column, if you think about it, only much wider than the others). The template also has a delineated header and footer area. Listing 12.1 shows the basic HTML structure for this layout.

LISTING 12.1   Basic Fixed/Liquid Hybrid Layout Structure

```
<!DOCTYPE html>

<html lang="en">
  <head>
    <title>Sample Layout</title>
    <link href="layout.css" rel="stylesheet" type="text/css" />
  </head>
```

```
<body>
  <header>HEADER</header>
  <div id="wrapper">
      <div id="content_area">CONTENT</div>
      <div id="left_side">LEFT SIDE</div>
      <div id="right_side">RIGHT SIDE</div>
  </div>
  <footer>FOOTER</footer>
</body>
</html>
```

First, note that the style sheet for this layout is linked to with the `<link>` tag instead of included in the template. Because a template is used for more than one page, you want to be able to control the display elements of the template in the most organized way possible. This means you need to change the definitions of those elements in only one place—the style sheet.

Next, notice that the basic HTML is just that: extremely basic. Truth be told, this basic HTML structure can be used for a fixed layout, a liquid layout, or the fixed/liquid hybrid you see here because all the actual styling that makes a layout fixed, liquid, or hybrid happens in the style sheet.

With the HTML structure in Listing 12.1, you actually have an identification of the content areas you want to include in your site. This planning is crucial to any development; you have to know what you want to include before you even think about the type of layout you are going to use, let alone the specific styles that will be applied to that layout.

At this stage, the `layout.css` file includes only this entry:

```
body {
    margin:0;
    padding:0;
}
```

If you look at the HTML in Listing 12.1 and say to yourself, "But those `<div>` elements will just stack on top of each other without any styles," you are correct. As shown in Figure 12.6, there is no layout to speak of.

NOTE

I am using elements with named identifiers in this example instead of the semantic elements such as `<section>` or `<nav>` because I'm illustrating the point in the simplest way possible without being prescriptive to the content itself. However, if you know that the `<div>` on the left side is going to hold navigation, you should use the `<nav>` tag instead of a `<div>` element with an id of `left_side`.

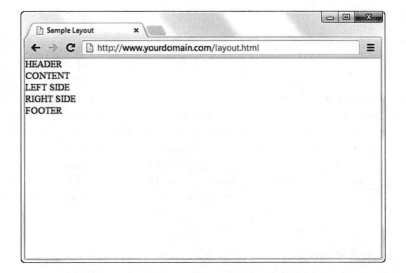

Defining Two Columns in a Fixed/Liquid Hybrid Layout

We can start with the easy things. Because this layout is supposed to be liquid, we know that whatever we put in the header and footer areas will extend the width of the browser window, regardless of how narrow or wide the window might be.

Adding the following code to the style sheet gives the header and footer area each a width of 100% as well as the same background color and text color.

```
header, footer {
  float: left;
  width: 100%;
  background-color: #7152f4;
  color: #ffffff;
}
```

Now things get a little trickier. We have to define the two fixed columns on either side of the page, plus the column in the middle. In the HTML we're using here, note that a <div> element, called wrapper, surrounds both. This element is defined in the style sheet as follows:

```
#wrapper {
  float: left;
  padding-left: 200px;
  padding-right: 125px;
}
```

The two padding definitions essentially reserve space for the two fixed-width columns on the left and right of the page. The column on the left will be 200 pixels wide, the column on the right will be 125 pixels wide, and each will have a different background color. But we also have to position the items relative to where they would be placed if the HTML remained unstyled (see Figure 12.6). This means adding `position: relative` to the style sheet entries for each of these columns. Additionally, we indicate that the `<div>` elements should float to the left.

But in the case of the `left_side` `<div>`, we also indicate that we want the rightmost margin edge to be 200 pixels in from the edge (this is in addition to the column being defined as 200 pixels wide). We also want the margin on the left side to be a full negative margin; this will pull it into place (as you will soon see). The `right_side` `<div>` does not include a value for `right`, but it does include a negative margin on the right side:

```
#left_side {
  position: relative;
  float: left;
  width: 200px;
  background-color: #52f471;
  right: 200px;
  margin-left: -100%;
}

#right_side {
  position: relative;
  float: left;
  width: 125px;
  background-color: #f452d5;
  margin-right: -125px;
}
```

At this point, let's also define the content area so that it has a white background, takes up 100% of the available area, and floats to the left relative to its position:

```
#content_area {
  position: relative;
  float: left;
```

```
    background-color: #ffffff;
    width: 100%;
}
```

At this point, the basic layout should look something like Figure 12.7, with the areas clearly delineated.

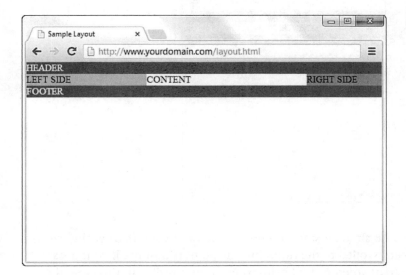

FIGURE 12.7
A basic HTML template after some styles have been put in place.

However, there's a problem with this template if the window is resized below a certain width. Because the left column is 200 pixels wide and the right column is 125 pixels wide, and you want at least *some* text in the content area, you can imagine that this page will break if the window is only 350 to 400 pixels wide. We address this issue in the next section.

Setting the Minimum Width of a Layout

Although users won't likely visit your site with a desktop browser that displays less than 400 pixels wide, the example serves its purpose within the confines of this chapter. You can extrapolate and apply this information broadly: Even in fixed/liquid hybrid sites, at some point, your layout will break down unless you do something about it.

One of those "somethings" is to use the `min-width` CSS property. The `min-width` property sets the minimum width of an element, not including padding, borders, or margins. Figure 12.8 shows what happens when `min-width` is applied to the `<body>` element.

Figure 12.8 shows a small portion of the right column after the screen has been scrolled to the right, but the point is that the layout does not break apart when resized below a minimum width. In this case, the minimum width is 525 pixels:

```
body {
  margin: 0;
  padding: 0;
  min-width: 525px;
}
```

The horizontal scrollbar appears in this example because the browser window itself is less than 500 pixels wide. The scrollbar disappears when the window is slightly larger than 525 pixels wide.

Handling Column Height in a Fixed/Liquid Hybrid Layout

This example is all well and good except for one problem: It has no content. When content is added to the various elements, more problems arise. As Figure 12.9 shows, the columns become as tall as necessary for the content they contain.

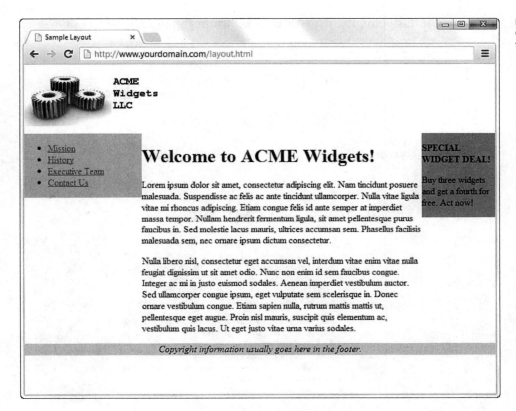

FIGURE 12.9
Columns are only as
tall as their contents.

Because you cannot count on a user's browser being a specific height, or the content always being the same length, you might think this poses a problem with the fixed/liquid hybrid layout. Not so. If you think a little outside the box, you can apply a few more styles to bring all the pieces together.

First, add the following declarations in the style sheet entries for the `left_side`, `right_side`, and `content_area` ids:

```
margin-bottom: -2000px;
padding-bottom: 2000px;
```

These declarations add a ridiculous amount of padding and assign a too-large margin to the bottom of all three elements. You must also add `position: relative` to the footer element definitions in the style sheet so that the footer is visible despite this padding.

NOTE

Because we have moved beyond the basic layout example, I also took the liberty to remove the background and text color properties for the header and footer, which is why the example no longer shows white text on a very dark background. Additionally, I've centered the text in the `<footer>` element, which now has a light gray background.

At this point, the page looks as shown in Figure 12.10—still not what we want, but closer.

FIGURE 12.10
Color fields are now
visible, despite the
amount of content in
the columns.

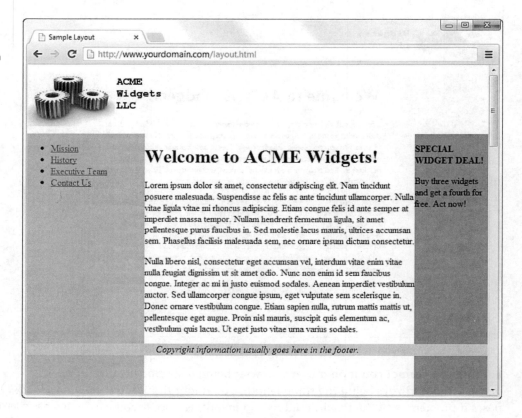

To clip off all that extra color, add the following to the style sheet for the wrapper ID:

```
overflow: hidden;
```

Figure 12.11 shows the final result: a fixed-width/liquid hybrid layout with the necessary column spacing. I also took the liberty of styling the navigational links and adjusting the margin around the welcome message; you can see the complete style sheet in Listing 12.3.

The full HTML code appears in Listing 12.2, and Listing 12.3 shows the final style sheet.

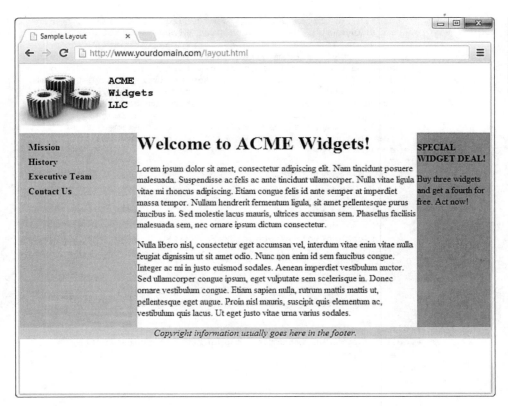

FIGURE 12.11
Congratulations!
It's a fixed-width/
liquid hybrid layout
(although you'll want
to do something about
those colors!).

LISTING 12.2   Basic Fixed/Liquid Hybrid Layout Structure (with Content)

```
<!DOCTYPE html>

<html lang="en">
  <head>
    <title>Sample Layout</title>
    <link href="layout.css" rel="stylesheet" type="text/css" />
  </head>

  <body>
    <header><img src="acmewidgets.jpg" alt="ACME Widgets
      LLC"/></header>
    <div id="wrapper">
      <div id="content_area">
        <h1>Welcome to ACME Widgets!</h1>
        <p>Lorem ipsum dolor sit amet, consectetur adipiscing elit.
        Nam tincidunt posuere malesuada. Suspendisse ac felis ac
        ante tincidunt ullamcorper. Nulla vitae ligula vitae mi
        rhoncus adipiscing. Etiam congue felis id ante semper at
        imperdiet massa tempor. Nullam hendrerit fermentum ligula,
        sit amet pellentesque purus faucibus in. Sed molestie lacus
```

```
      mauris, ultrices accumsan sem. Phasellus facilisis
      malesuada sem, nec ornare ipsum dictum consectetur.</p>
      <p>Nulla libero nisl, consectetur eget accumsan vel,
      interdum vitae enim vitae nulla feugiat dignissim ut sit
      amet odio. Nunc non enim id sem faucibus congue. Integer ac
      mi in justo euismod sodales. Aenean imperdiet vestibulum
      auctor. Sed ullamcorper congue ipsum, eget vulputate sem
      scelerisque in. Donec ornare vestibulum congue. Etiam
      sapien nulla, rutrum mattis mattis ut, pellentesque eget
      augue. Proin nisl mauris, suscipit quis elementum ac,
      vestibulum quis lacus. Ut eget justo vitae urna varius
      sodales. </p>
    </div>
    <div id="left_side">
      <ul>
      <li><a href="#">Mission</a></li>
      <li><a href="#">History</a></li>
      <li><a href="#">Executive Team</a></li>
      <li><a href="#">Contact Us</a></li>
      </ul>
    </div>
    <div id="right_side">
      <p><strong>SPECIAL WIDGET DEAL!</strong></p>
      <p>Buy three widgets and get a fourth for free. Act now!</p>
    </div>
  </div>
  <footer>Copyright information usually goes here in the
  footer.</footer>
 </body>
</html>
```

LISTING 12.3   Full Style Sheet for Fixed/Liquid Hybrid Layout

```
body {
  margin:0;
  padding:0;
  min-width: 525px;
}

header {
  float: left;
  width: 100%;
}

footer {
  position:relative;
  float: left;
  width: 100%;
  background-color: #cccccc;
  text-align:center;
  font-style: italic;
}
```

```
#wrapper {
  float: left;
  padding-left: 200px;
  padding-right: 125px;
  overflow: hidden;
}

#left_side {
  position: relative;
  float: left;
  width: 200px;
  background-color: #52f471;
  right: 200px;
  margin-left: -100%;
  margin-bottom: -2000px;
  padding-bottom: 2000px;

}

#right_side {
  position: relative;
  float: left;
  width: 125px;
  background-color: #f452d5;
  margin-right: -125px;
  margin-bottom: -2000px;
  padding-bottom: 2000px;

}

#content_area {
  position: relative;
  float: left;
  background-color: #ffffff;
  width: 100%;
  margin-bottom: -2000px;
  padding-bottom: 2000px;

}

h1 {
  margin: 0;
}

#left_side ul {
  list-style: none;
  margin: 12px 0px 0px 12px;
  padding: 0px;
}

#left_side li a:link, #nav li a:visited {
  font-size: 12pt;
  font-weight: bold;
```

```
    padding: 3px 0px 3px 3px;
    color: #000000;
    text-decoration: none;
    display: block;
}

#left_side li a:hover, #nav li a:active {
    font-size: 12pt;
    font-weight: bold;
    padding: 3px 0px 3px 3px;
    color: #ffffff;
    text-decoration: none;
    display: block;
}
```

Considering a Responsive Web Design

In 2010, web designer Ethan Marcotte coined the term *responsive web design* to refer to a web design approach that builds on the basics of fluid design you just learned a bit about. The goal of a responsive web design is that content is easy to view, read, and navigate, regardless of the device type and size on which you are viewing it. In other words, a designer who sets out to create a responsive website is doing so to ensure that the site is similarly enjoyable to and usable by audience members viewing on a large desktop display, a small smartphone, or a medium-size tablet.

Responsive design is based on fluid (liquid) grid layouts, much as you learned about earlier in this chapter, but with a few modifications and additions. First, those grid layouts should always be in relative units rather than absolute ones. In other words, designers should use percentages rather than pixels to define container elements.

Second—and this is something we have not discussed in previous chapters—all images should be flexible. By this, I mean that instead of using a specific height and width for each image, relative percentages are used so that the images always display within the (relatively sized) element that contains them.

Finally, spend some time developing specific style sheets for each media type, and use media queries to employ these different rules based on the type. You can specify a link to a style sheet like the following:

```
<link rel="stylesheet" type="text/css"
    media="screen and (max-device-width: 480px)"
    href="wee.css" />
```

In this example, the `media` attribute contains a type and a query: The type is `screen` and the query portion is `(max-device-width: 480px)`. This means that if the device attempting to render the display is one with a screen and the horizontal resolution (device width) is less than 480 pixels wide—as with a smartphone—then load the style sheet called `wee.css` and render the display using the rules found within it.

Of course, a few short paragraphs in this book cannot do justice to the entirety of responsive web design. I highly recommend reading Marcotte's book *Responsive Web Design* (http://www.abookapart.com/products/responsive-web-design) after you have firmly grounded yourself in the basics of HTML5 and CSS3 that this book is teaching you. Additionally, several of the HTML and CSS frameworks discussed in Chapter 27, "Organizing and Managing a Website," take advantage of principles of responsive design, and that makes a great starting point for building up a responsive site and tinkering with the fluid grid, image resizing, and media queries that make it so.

Summary

In this chapter, you saw some practical examples of the three main types of layouts: fixed, liquid, and a fixed/liquid hybrid. In the third section of the lesson, you saw an extended example that walked you through the process of creating a fixed/liquid hybrid layout in which the HTML and CSS all validate properly. Remember, the most important part of creating a layout is figuring out the sections of content you think you might need to account for in the design.

Finally, you were introduced to the concept of responsive web design, which itself is a book-length topic. Given the brief information you learned here, such as using a fluid grid layout, responsive images, and media queries, you have some basic concepts to begin testing on your own.

Q&A

Q. I've heard about something called an elastic layout. How does that differ from the liquid layout?

A. An *elastic layout* is a layout whose content areas resize when the user resizes the text. Elastic layouts use ems, which are inherently proportional to text and font size. An em is a typographical unit of measurement equal to the point size of the current font. When ems are used in an elastic layout, if a user forces the text size to increase or decrease in size using Ctrl and the mouse scroll wheel, the areas containing the text increase or decrease proportionally. Elastic layouts are often quite difficult to achieve.

Q. You've spent a lot of time talking about liquid layouts and hybrid layouts—are they better than a purely fixed layout?

A. *Better* is a subjective term; in this book, the concern is with standards-compliant code. Most designers will tell you that liquid layouts take longer to create (and perfect), but the usability enhancements are worth it, especially when it leads to a responsive design. When might the time not be worth it? If your client does not have an opinion and is paying you a flat rate instead of an hourly rate. In that case, you are working only to showcase your own skills (that might be worth it to you, however).

Workshop

The Workshop contains quiz questions and activities to help you solidify your understanding of the material covered. Try to answer all questions before looking at the "Answers" section that follows.

Quiz

1. Which is the best layout to use, in general: fixed, liquid, or a hybrid?

2. Can you position a fixed layout anywhere on the page?

3. What does `min-width` do?

Answers

1. This was a trick question; there is no "best" layout. It depends on your content and the needs of your audience. (Note that the author ultimately leans toward liquid and then responsive layouts as the "best," however, if you have the time and resources to implement them.)

2. Sure. Although most fixed layouts are flush left or centered, you can assign a fixed position on an x-y axis where you could place a `<div>` that contains all the other layout `<div>`s.

3. The `min-width` property sets the minimum width of an element, not including padding, borders, or margins.

Exercises

▶ Figure 12.11 shows the finished fixed/liquid hybrid layout, but notice a few areas for improvement: There isn't any space around the text in the right-side column, there aren't any margins between the body text and either column, the footer strip is a little sparse, and so on. Take some time to fix these design elements.

▶ Using the code you fixed in the preceding exercise, try to make it responsive, using only the brief information you learned in this chapter. Just converting container elements to relative sizes should go a long way toward making the template viewable on your smartphone or other small device, but a media query and alternative style sheet certainly wouldn't hurt, either.

CHAPTER 13

Understanding Dynamic Websites and HTML5 Applications

The term *dynamic* means something active or something that motivates another person to become active. A dynamic website is one that incorporates interactivity into its functionality and design, but also motivates a user to take an action—read more, purchase a product, and so on. In this chapter, you'll learn about the types of interactivity that can make a site dynamic, including information about both server-side and client-side scripting (as well as some practical examples of the latter).

You've had a brief introduction to client-side scripting in Chapter 4, "Understanding JavaScript," and you used a little of it in Chapter 11, "Using CSS to Do More with Lists, Text, and Navigation," when you used event attributes and JavaScript to change the styles of particular elements—that is called manipulating the Document Object Model (DOM). You'll do a bit more of that type of manipulation in this chapter. Specifically, after learning about the different technologies, you'll use JavaScript to display a random quote upon page-load and swap images based on user interaction. Finally, having learned at least the keywords and the basic concept of putting the HTML, CSS, and JavaScript pieces together, you'll be introduced to the possibilities that exist when you're creating HTML5 applications.

Understanding the Different Types of Scripting

In web development, two types of scripting exist: server side and client side. Both types of scripting—which is, in fact, a form of computer programming—are beyond the scope of this book. However, they are

WHAT YOU'LL LEARN IN THIS CHAPTER:

▶ How to conceptualize different types of dynamic content

▶ How to include JavaScript in your HTML

▶ How to display randomized text with JavaScript

▶ How to change images using JavaScript and user events

▶ How to begin thinking ahead to putting all the pieces together to create HTML5 applications not *too* far beyond this book. Two very useful and popular books in the *Sams Teach Yourself* series are natural extensions of this one: *Sams Teach Yourself PHP, MySQL, and Apache All in One* (for server-side scripting) and *Sams Teach Yourself JavaScript in 24 Hours* (for client-side scripting).

Server-side scripting refers to scripts that run on the web server, which then sends results to your web browser. If you have ever submitted a form at a website (which includes using a search engine), you have experienced the results of a server-side script. Some popular (and relatively easy-to-learn) server-side scripting languages include the following (to learn more, visit the websites listed):

- ▶ PHP (PHP: Hypertext Preprocessor)—http://www.php.net
- ▶ Ruby—http://www.ruby-lang.org
- ▶ Python—http://www.python.org
- ▶ Perl—http://www.perl.org

TIP

Despite its name, JavaScript is not a derivation of or any other close relative to the object-oriented programming language called Java. Released by Sun Microsystems in 1995, Java is closely related to the server-side scripting language JSP. JavaScript was created by Netscape Communications, also in 1995, and given the name to indicate a similarity in appearance to Java but not a direct connection with it.

On the other hand, *client-side scripting* refers to scripts that run within your web browser—no interaction with a web server is required for the scripts to run. By far the most popular client-side scripting language is *JavaScript*. For several years, research has shown that more than 98% of all web browsers have JavaScript enabled.

Another client-side scripting language is Microsoft's *VBScript (Visual Basic Scripting Edition)*. This language is available only with the Microsoft Internet Explorer web browser and, therefore, should not be used unless you are very sure that users will access your site with that web browser (such as in a closed corporate environment). This chapter (and of course the rest of the book) assumes the use of JavaScript for client-side scripting; the coding examples in these chapters are all JavaScript.

Including JavaScript in HTML

JavaScript code can live in one of two places within your files:

- ▶ In its own file with a `.js` extension
- ▶ Directly in your HTML files

External files are often used for script libraries (code you can reuse throughout many pages), whereas code that appears directly in the

HTML files tends to achieve functionality specific to those individual pages. Regardless of where your JavaScript lives, your browser learns of its existence through the use of the `<script></script>` tag pair.

When you store your JavaScript in external files, it is referenced in this manner:

```
<script type="text/javascript" src="/path/to/script.js"></script>
```

These `<script></script>` tags are typically placed between the `<head></head>` tags because, strictly speaking, they are not content that belongs in the `<body>` of the page. Instead, the `<script>` tag makes available a set of JavaScript functions or other information that the rest of the page can then use. However, you can also just encapsulate your JavaScript functions or code snippets with the `<script>` tag and place them anywhere in the page, as needed. Listing 13.1 shows an example of a JavaScript snippet placed in the `<body>` of an HTML document.

> NOTE
>
> It is also quite common to find scripts loaded at the bottom of your page, just before the close of the `<body>` element. This ensures that your pages render without waiting to load the script. However, you cannot use this method of loading scripts if you also use your scripts to write content out to the page—it would just write it at the end, which is likely not your intention.

LISTING 13.1 Using JavaScript to Print Some Text

```
<!DOCTYPE html>

<html lang="en">
  <head>
    <title>JavaScript Example</title>
  </head>

  <body>
    <h1>JavaScript Example</h1>
    <p>This text is HTML.</p>
    <script type="text/javascript">
    <!-- Hide the script from old browsers
    document.write('<p>This text comes from JavaScript.</p>');
    // Stop hiding the script -->
    </script>
  </body>
</html>
```

Between the `<script></script>` tags is a single JavaScript command that outputs the following HTML:

```
<p>This text comes from JavaScript.</p>
```

When the browser renders this HTML page, it sees the JavaScript between the `<script></script>` tags, stops for a millisecond to execute the command, and then returns to rendering the output that now includes the HTML output from the JavaScript command. Figure 13.1 shows that this page appears as any other HTML page appears. It's an HTML page, but only a small part of the HTML comes from a JavaScript command.

FIGURE 13.1
The output of a JavaScript snippet looks like any other output.

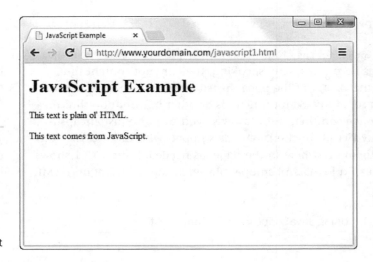

TIP

You might have noticed these two lines in Listing 13.1:

```
<!-- Hide the script from
old browsers
// Stop hiding the script
-->
```

This is an HTML comment. Anything between the `<!--` start and `-->` end will be visible in the source code but will not be rendered by the browser. In this case, JavaScript code is surrounded by HTML comments, on the off chance that your visitor is running a very old web browser or has JavaScript turned off. These days, nearly all browsers use or ignore JavaScript appropriately, but there's no harm in commenting it out for very old browsers or screenreaders that do not handle JavaScript at all.

Displaying Random Content

You can use JavaScript to display something different each time a page loads. Maybe you have a collection of text or images that you find interesting enough to include in your pages.

I'm a sucker for a good quote. If you're like me, or plenty of other people creating personal websites, you might find it fun to incorporate an ever-changing quote into your web pages. To create a page with a quote that changes each time the page loads, you must first gather all your quotes, along with their respective sources. You then place these quotes into a JavaScript *array*, which is a special type of storage unit in programming languages that is handy for holding lists of items.

After the quotes are loaded into an array, the JavaScript used to pluck out a quote at random is fairly simple (we explain it momentarily). You've already seen the snippet that will print the output to your HTML page.

Listing 13.2 contains the complete HTML and JavaScript code for a web page that displays a random quote each time it loads.

Listing 13.2   A Random-Quote Web Page

```
<!DOCTYPE html>

<html lang="en">
  <head>
    <title>Quotable Quotes</title>

    <script type="text/javascript">
      <!-- Hide the script from old browsers
      function getQuote() {
        // Create the arrays
        quotes = new Array(4);
        sources = new Array(4);

        // Initialize the arrays with quotes
        quotes[0] = "When I was a boy of 14, my father was so " +
        "ignorant...but when I got to be 21, I was astonished " +
        "at how much he had learned in 7 years.";
        sources[0] = "Mark Twain";

        quotes[1] = "Everybody is ignorant. Only on different " +
        "subjects.";
        sources[1] = "Will Rogers";

        quotes[2] = "They say such nice things about people at " +
        "their funerals that it makes me sad that I'm going to " +
        "miss mine by just a few days.";
        sources[2] = "Garrison Keillor";

        quotes[3] = "What's another word for thesaurus?";
        sources[3] = "Steven Wright";

        // Get a random index into the arrays
        i = Math.floor(Math.random() * quotes.length);

        // Write out the quote as HTML
        document.write("<p style='background-color: #ffb6c1' >\"");
        document.write(quotes[i] + "\"");
        document.write("<em>- " + sources[i] + "</em>");
        document.write("</p>");
      }
      // Stop hiding the script -->
    </script>
  </head>

  <body>
    <h1>Quotable Quotes</h1>
    <p>Following is a random quotable quote. To see a new quote just
    reload this page.</p>
    <script type="text/javascript">
      <!-- Hide the script from old browsers
      getQuote();
```

```
      // Stop hiding the script -->
    </script>
  </body>
</html>
```

Although this code looks kind of long, a lot of it consists of just the four quotes available for display on the page.

The large number of lines between the first set of `<script></script>` tags is creating a function called `getQuote()`. After a function is defined, it can be called in other places in the same page, which you see later in the code. Note that if the function existed in an external file, the function could be called from all your pages.

If you look closely at the code, you will see some lines like this:

```
// Create the arrays
```

and

```
// Initialize the arrays with quotes
```

These are code comments. A developer uses these types of comments to leave notes in the code so that anyone reading it has an idea of what the code is doing in that particular place. After the first comment about creating the arrays, you can see that two arrays are created—one called `quotes` and one called `sources`, each containing four elements:

```
quotes = new Array(4);
sources = new Array(4);
```

After the second comment (about initializing the arrays with quotes), four items are added to the arrays. Let's look closely at one of them, the first quote by Mark Twain:

```
quotes[0] = "When I was a boy of 14, my father was so " +
"ignorant...but when I got to be 21, I was astonished at " +
"how much he had learned in 7 years.";
sources[0] = "Mark Twain";
```

You already know that the arrays are named quotes and sources. But the variables to which values are assigned (in this instance) are called `quotes[0]` and `sources[0]`. Because quotes and sources are arrays, each item in the array has its own position. When you're using arrays, the first item in the array is not in slot #1—it is in slot #0. In other words, you begin counting at 0 instead of 1, which is typical in programming—just file that away as an interesting and useful note for the future (or a good trivia answer). Therefore, the text of the first quote (a value) is assigned to `quotes[0]` (a variable). Similarly, the text of the first source is assigned to `source[0]`.

Text strings are enclosed in quotation marks. However, in JavaScript, a line break indicates an end of a command, so the following would cause problems in the code:

```
quotes[0] = "When I was a boy of 14, my father was so
ignorant...but when I got to be 21, I was astonished at
how much he had learned in 7 years.";
```

Therefore, you see that the string is built as a series of strings enclosed in quotation marks, with a plus sign (+) connecting the strings (this plus sign is called a *concatenation operator*).

The next chunk of code definitely looks the most like programming; this line is generating a random number and assigning that value to a variable called `i`:

```
i = Math.floor(Math.random() * quotes.length);
```

But you can't just pick any random number—the purpose of the random number is to determine which of the quotes and sources should be printed, and there are only four quotes. So this line of JavaScript does the following:

▶ Uses `Math.random()` to get a random number between 0 and 1. For example, 0.5482749 might be a result of `Math.random()`.

▶ Multiplies the random number by the length of the quotes array, which is currently 4; the length of the array is the number of elements in the array. If the random number is 0.5482749 (as shown previously), multiplying that by 4 results in 2.1930996.

▶ Uses `Math.floor()` to round the result down to the nearest whole number. In other words, 2.1930996 turns into 2.

▶ Assigns the variable i a value of 2 (for example).

The rest of the function should look familiar, with a few exceptions. First, as you learned earlier this chapter, `document.write()` is used to write HTML that the browser then renders. Next, the strings are separated to clearly indicate when something needs to be handled differently, such as escaping the quotation marks with a backslash when they should be printed literally (\) or when the value of a variable is substituted. The actual quote and source that are printed are the ones that match `quotes[i]` and `sources[i]`, where `i` is the number determined by the mathematical functions noted previously.

But the act of simply writing the function doesn't mean that any output will be created. Further on in the HTML, you can see `getQuote();` between two `<script></script>` tags—that is how the function is called. Wherever that function call is made, that is where the output of the function will be placed. In this example, the output displays below a paragraph that introduces the quotation.

Figure 13.2 shows the Quotable Quotes page as it appears when loaded in a web browser. When the page reloads, there is a one-in-four chance that a different quote displays—it is random, after all!

FIGURE 13.2
The Quotable Quotes page displays a random quote each time it is loaded.

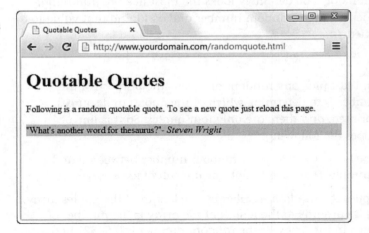

Keep in mind that you can easily modify this page to include your own quotes or other text that you want to display randomly. You can also increase the number of quotes available for display by adding more entries in the `quotes` and `sources` arrays in the code. And of course, you can modify the HTML output and style it however you'd like.

If you use the Quotable Quotes page as a starting point, you can easily alter the script and create your own interesting variation on the idea. And if you make mistakes along the way, so be it. The trick to getting past mistakes in script code is to be patient and carefully analyze the code you've entered. You can always remove code to simplify a script until you get it working, and then add new code one piece at a time to make sure each piece works.

Understanding the Document Object Model *DOM*

This section could also be called "The Least You Need to Know About the Document Object Model to Begin Working with It and Learning More in the Future," but that would make for a terrible section title even if it is true. As you've read, client-side interactivity using JavaScript typically takes the form of manipulating the Document Object Model in some way. The DOM is the invisible structure of all documents—not the HTML structure or the way in which you apply semantic formatting, but a sort of overall framework or container. If this description seems vague, that's because it is; it's not a tangible object.

JavaScript follows hirarchy.

Where HTML follows codes.

The overall container object is called the document. Any container that you create within the document, that you've given an ID, can be referenced by that ID. For example, if you have a <div> with an ID called wrapper, then in the DOM that element is referenced as follows:

```
document.wrapper
```

For example, you can change the visibility of a specific element by changing the style object associated with it. Similarly, if you wanted to access the background-color style of the <div> with an ID called wrapper (to then do something with it), it would be referred to as follows:

```
document.wrapper.style.background-color
```

To change the value of that style to something else, perhaps based on an interactive user event, use the following to change the color to white:

```
document.wrapper.style.background-color="#ffffff"
```

The DOM is the framework behind your ability to refer to elements and their associated objects in this way. Obviously, this is a brief overview of something quite complicated, but at least you can now begin to grasp what this document-dot-something business is all about. To learn a lot more about the DOM, visit the World Wide Web Consortium information about the DOM at http://www.w3.org/DOM/.

Changing Images Based on User Interaction

Chapter 4 introduced you to the concept of user interaction events, such as `onclick`. In that chapter, you invoked changes in window display based on user interaction; in this section, you'll see an example of a visible type of interaction that is both practical and dynamic.

Figure 13.3 shows a page that contains one large image with some text next to it, and three small images farther down the page. If you look closely at the list of small images, you might notice that the first small image is, in fact, a smaller version of the large image that is displayed. This is a common display for a type of small gallery, such as one that you might see in an online catalog, in which an item has a description and a few alternate views of the product. Although close-up images of the details of products are important to the potential buyer, using several large images on a page becomes unwieldy from both a display and bandwidth point of view, so this type of gallery view is a popular way to display alternative images. I don't personally have products to sell, but I do have pictures of big trees that I can use as an example (see Figure 13.3).

The large image on the page is called using this `<img/>` tag:

```
<img
    id="large_photo"
    style="border: 1px solid black; margin-right: 13px;"
    src="mariposa_large_1.jpg"
    alt="large photo" />
```

The `style`, `src`, and `alt` attributes should all make sense to you at this stage of the game. Additionally, as you can see, this image is given an ID of `large_photo`. Therefore, this image exists in the DOM as `document.images['large_photo']`—images are referred to by their ID. This is important because a bit of JavaScript functionality enables us to dynamically change the value of `document.images['large_image']`. `src`, which is the source (`src`) of the image.

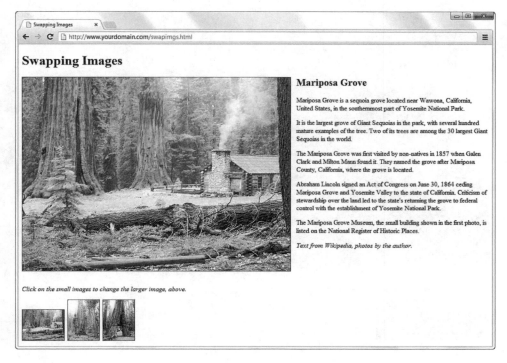

FIGURE 13.3
An informational
page with a main
image and alternative
images ready to click
and view.

The following code snippet creates the third small image in the group
of three images shown at the bottom of Figure 13.3. The `onclick` event
indicates that when the user clicks on this small image, the value of
`document.images['large_image'].src`—the large image slot—is filled
with the path to a matching large image.

```
<a href="#"
  onclick="javascript:document.images['large_photo'].src =
 'mariposa_large_1.jpg'">
<img
  style="border: 1px solid black; margin-right: 3px;"
  src="mariposa_small_1.jpg"
  alt="photo #1" /></a>
```

Figure 13.4 shows the same page, but not reloaded by the user. The slot
for the large image is filled by a different image when the user clicks
on one of the other smaller images at the bottom of the page.

FIGURE 13.4
The large image is
replaced when the
user clicks on a
smaller one.

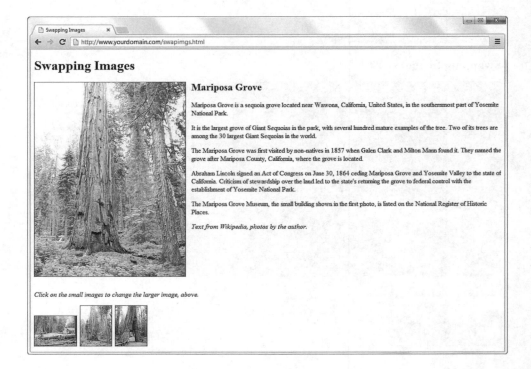

Figure 13.4 (continued): The large image is replaced when the user clicks on a smaller one.

Thinking Ahead to Developing HTML5 Applications

I'm not going to lie—there's a pretty big difference between a basic website built with HTML, CSS, and a little JavaScript, and comprehensive applications that use some of the advanced features of HTML5 and the latest JavaScript frameworks. But it's important to your understanding of HTML, the language of the Web, to have some idea of just how far you can extend it (it's pretty far, as it turns out). Beyond basic markup, HTML5 extends to include APIs (application programming interfaces) for complex applications, beginning with the native integration of audio and video elements, as you learned in previous lessons, and going all the way to built-in offline storage mechanisms that allow full-blown applications to be accessed and run (and data stored on the client side) even without a network connection.

Although HTML5 is incredibly rich, the creation of highly interactive HTML5 websites and applications—including mobile applications—doesn't happen in isolation. Interactivity comes when HTML5 is paired with a client-side language such as JavaScript, which then reaches back into the server and talks to a server-side language (PHP, Ruby, Python, and so on) through a persistent connection called a *web socket*. With this connection open and talking to some server-side code that is (for example) talking to a database or performing some calculation, the browser can relay a bundle of information that is additionally processed by JavaScript and finally rendered in HTML5. Be it a video game, a word processing program, or an email or Twitter client, just to name a few popular types of HTML5 applications, the combination of the advanced features of HTML5 plus JavaScript—and, specifically, the feature-rich JavaScript libraries such as jQuery (http://jquery.com/)—really makes the opportunities limitless when it comes to application creation.

The depth of the technologies involved in HTML5 application creation is beyond the scope of this basic book, but the foundation you should have in standards-compliant HTML5, CSS3, and JavaScript will serve you well if you begin to think outside the box of a basic website. To learn more about HTML5 application creation, take a look at *Sams Teach Yourself HTML5 Mobile Application Development in 24 Hours* for an introduction to some of the core features. Throughout *this* book, you get a solid foundation in the basics of HTML5. I am confident that, with additional instruction, you can take the next step and begin to learn and build basic interactions in an HTML5 application.

Summary

In this chapter, you learned about the differences between server-side scripting and client-side scripting, and you learned how to include JavaScript in your HTML files to add a little interactivity to your websites. You also learned how to use the JavaScript `document.write()` method to display random quotes upon page load. Finally, you learned a bit about the Document Object Model.

By applying the knowledge you've gained from the preceding chapter, you've learned how to use client-side scripting to make images on a web page respond to mouse movements. Although they are simple in their construction, these types of interactions are some of the basic JavaScript-based interactions that form the foundation of web applications. Hopefully this will spur your desire to learn more about server-side programming so that you can give your websites even more complex interactive features, including taking a step into the world of creating HTML5 applications.

Q&A

Q. If I want to use the random-quote script from this lesson, but I want to have a library of a lot of quotes, do I have to put all the quotes in each page?

A. Yes. Each item in the array must be there. This is where you can begin to see a bit of a tipping point between something that can be client side and something that is better dealt with on the server side. If you have a true library of random quotations and only one is presented at any given time, it's probably best to store those items in a database table and use a little piece of server-side scripting to connect to that database, retrieve the text, and print it on the page. Alternatively, you can always continue to carry all the quotes with you in JavaScript, but you should at least put that JavaScript function into a different file that can be maintained separately from the text.

Q. I've seen some online catalogs that display a large image in what looks to be a layer on top of the website content—I can see the regular website content underneath it, but the focus is on the large image. How is that done?

A. The description sounds like an effect created by a JavaScript library called Lightbox. The Lightbox library enables you to display an image, or a gallery of images, in a layer that is placed over your site content. This is a very popular library used to show the details of large images or just a set of images deemed important enough to showcase "above" the content. The library is freely available from its creator at http://lokeshdhakar.com/projects/lightbox/. To install and use it, follow the instructions included with the software; you will be able to integrate it into your site using the knowledge you've gained in this book so far.

Workshop

The Workshop contains quiz questions and activities to help you solidify your understanding of the material covered. Try to answer all questions before looking at the "Answers" section that follows.

Quiz

1. You've made a picture of a button and named it `button.gif`. You've also made a simple GIF animation of the button so that it flashes green and white. You've named that GIF `flashing.gif`. What HTML and JavaScript code can you use to make the button flash whenever a user moves the mouse pointer over it and also link to a page named `gohere.html` when a user clicks the button?

2. How can you modify the code you wrote for Question 1 so that the button flashes when a user moves the mouse over it and continues flashing even if the user then moves the mouse away from it?

3. What does the plus sign mean in the following context?

```
document.write('This is a text string ' + 'that I have
created.');
```

Answers

1. Your code might look something like this:

```
<a href="gohere.html"
onmouseover="javascript:document.images['flasher'].
src='flashing.gif'"
onmouseout="javascript:document.images['flasher'].
src='button.gif'">
<img src="button.gif" id="flasher" style="border-style:
none" /></a>
```

2. Your code might look something like this:

```
<a href="gohere.html"
onmouseover="javascript:document.images['flasher'].
src='flashing.gif'">
<img src="button.gif" id="flasher" style="border-style:
none" /></a>
```

3. The plus sign (+) joins two strings together.

Exercises

▶ Do you have any pages that would look flashier or be easier to understand if the navigation icons or other images changed when the mouse passed over them? If so, try creating some highlighted versions of the images, and try modifying your own page using the information presented in this chapter.

▶ You can display random images—such as graphical banners or advertisements—in the same way you learned to display random content using JavaScript earlier in this chapter. Instead of printing text, just print the `<img/>` tag for the images you want to display.

CHAPTER 14
Getting Started with JavaScript Programming

The preceding chapter reminded you of some of the basic uses of JavaScript and how to include JavaScript in your HTML documents. In this chapter, you'll learn a few more basic JavaScript concepts and script components that you'll use in just about every bit of JavaScript script you will write. Additionally, you'll learn about JSON (JavaScript Object Notation), which is a simple structured way to store information that can be used on the client side. Understanding these components will prepare you for the remaining chapters of this book, in which you'll explore specific JavaScript functions and features in greater depth.

Basic Concepts

There are a few basic concepts and terms you'll run into throughout this book. In the following sections, you'll learn about the basic building blocks of JavaScript.

Statements

Statements are the basic units of a JavaScript program. A statement is a section of code that performs a single action. For example, the following four statements are from the date and time example in Chapter 4, "Understanding JavaScript." These statements create a new Date object and then assign the values for the current hour, minutes, and seconds into variables called hours, mins, and secs, respectively. You can then use these variables in your JavaScript code.

WHAT YOU'LL LEARN IN THIS CHAPTER:

▶ How and why to organize scripts using functions
▶ What objects are and how JavaScript uses them
▶ How JavaScript can respond to events
▶ How and when to use conditional statements and loops
▶ How browsers execute scripts in the proper order
▶ Basic syntax rules for avoiding JavaScript errors
▶ What JSON is and how it can be used

object ← *variables.*

```
now = new Date();
hours = now.getHours();
mins = now.getMinutes();
secs = now.getSeconds();
```

Although a statement is typically a single line of JavaScript, this is not a rule—it's possible (and fairly common) to break a statement across multiple lines, or to include more than one statement in a single line.

A semicolon marks the end of a statement, but you can also omit the semicolon if you start a new line after the statement—if that is your coding style. In other words, these are three valid JavaScript statements:

```
hours = now.getHours()
mins = now.getMinutes()
secs = now.getSeconds()
```

However, if you combine statements into a single line, you must use semicolons to separate them. For example, the following line is valid:

```
hours = now.getHours(); mins = now.getMinutes(); secs =
now.getSeconds();
```

This line is invalid:

```
hours = now.getHours() mins = now.getMinutes() secs =
now.getSeconds();
```

Combining Tasks with Functions

Functions are groups of JavaScript statements that are treated as a single unit. A statement that uses a function is referred to as a *function call*. For example, you might create a function called alertMe, which produces an alert when called, like so:

```
function alertMe() {
    alert("I am alerting you!");
}
```

→ *built in function.*

When this function is called, a JavaScript alert pops up and the text I am alerting you! is displayed.

Functions can take parameters—the expression inside the parentheses—to tell them what to do. Additionally, a function can return a value to a waiting variable. For example, the following function call prompts the user for a response and stores it in the text variable:

```
text = prompt("Enter some text.")
```

Creating your own functions is useful for two main reasons: First, you can separate logical portions of your script to make it easier to understand. Second, and more important, you can use the function several times or with different data to avoid repeating script statements.

Variables

If you recall the basic introduction to JavaScript in Chapter 4, you'll remember that variables are containers that can store a number, a string of text, or another value. For example, the following statement creates a variable called `fred` and assigns it the value `27`:

```
var fred = 27;
```

JavaScript variables can contain numbers, text strings, and other values. You'll learn more about variables in much greater detail in Chapter 16, "Using JavaScript Variables, Strings, and Arrays."

Understanding Objects

JavaScript also supports *objects*. Like variables, objects can store data— but they can store two or more pieces of data at once. As you'll learn throughout the JavaScript-specific chapters of this book, using built-in objects and their methods is fundamental to JavaScript—it's one of the ways the language works, by providing a predetermined set of actions you can perform. For example, the `document.write` functionality you saw earlier in this chapter is actually a situation in which you use the `write` method of the `document` object to output text to the browser for eventual rendering.

The data stored in an object are called the *properties* of the object. For example, you could use objects to store information about people in an address book. The properties of each person object might include a name, an address, and a telephone number.

You'll want to become intimately familiar with object-related syntax, because you will see objects quite a lot even if you don't build your own. You'll definitely find yourself using built-in objects, and objects will very likely form a large part of any JavaScript libraries you import for use. JavaScript uses periods to separate object names and property names. For example, for a person object called Bob, the properties might include `Bob.address` and `Bob.phone`.

NOTE

An entire chapter of this book is devoted to learning how to create and use functions. You will learn how to define, call, and return values from your own functions in Chapter 17, "Using JavaScript Functions and Objects."

Objects can also include *methods*. These are functions that work with the object's data. For example, our person object for the address book might include a `display()` method to display the person's information. In JavaScript terminology, the statement `Bob.display()` would display Bob's details.

Don't worry if this sounds confusing—you'll be exploring objects in much more detail later in this book. For now, you just need to know the basics. JavaScript supports three kinds of objects:

- ▶ *Built-in objects* are built in to the JavaScript language. You've already encountered one of these, `Date`, in Chapter 4. Other built-in objects include `Array` and `String`, which you'll explore in Chapter 16; `Math`, which is explained in Chapter 17; `Boolean`; `Number`; and `RegExp`.

- ▶ *DOM (Document Object Model) objects* represent various components of the browser and the current HTML document. For example, the `alert()` function you used earlier in this chapter is actually a method of the `window` object. You'll explore these in more detail in Chapter 15, "Working with the Document Object Model (DOM)."

- ▶ *Custom objects* are objects you create yourself. For example, you could create a `person` object, as mentioned earlier in this section.

Conditionals

Although you can use event handlers to notify your script (and potentially the user) when something happens, you might need to check certain conditions yourself as your script runs. For example, you might want to validate on your own that a user entered a valid email address in a web form.

JavaScript supports conditional statements, which enable you to answer questions like this. A typical conditional uses the `if` statement, as in this example:

```
if (count == 1) {
   alert("The countdown has reached 1.");
}
```

This compares the variable count with the constant 1, and displays an alert message to the user if they are the same. It is quite likely you will use one or more conditional statements like this in most of your scripts, and as such an entire chapter is devoted to this concept, Chapter 18, "Controlling Flow with Conditions and Loops."

Loops

Another useful feature of JavaScript—and most other programming languages—is the capability to create *loops*, or groups of statements that repeat a certain number of times. For example, these statements display the same alert 10 times, greatly annoying the user:

```
for (i=1; i<=10; i++) {
    alert("Yes, it's yet another alert!");
}
```

The `for` statement is one of several statements JavaScript uses for loops. This is the sort of thing computers are supposed to be good at—performing repetitive tasks. You will use loops in many of your scripts, in much more useful ways than this example, as you'll see in Chapter 18.

Event Handlers

As mentioned in Chapter 4, not all scripts are located within `<script>` tags. You can also use scripts as event handlers. Although this might sound like a complex programming term, it actually means exactly what it says: Event handlers are scripts that handle events. You learned a little bit about events in Chapter 13, "Understanding Dynamic Websites and HTML5 Applications," but not to the extent you'll read about now or learn in Chapter 19, "Responding to Events."

In real life, an event is something that happens to you. For example, the things you write on your calendar are events, such as "Dentist appointment" or "Fred's birthday." You also encounter unscheduled events in your life, for example, a traffic ticket, an IRS audit, or an unexpected visit from relatives.

Whether events are scheduled or unscheduled, you probably have normal ways of handling them. Your event handlers might include things such as *When Fred's birthday arrives, send him a present* or *When relatives visit unexpectedly, turn out the lights and pretend nobody is home*.

Event handlers in JavaScript are similar: They tell the browser what to do when a certain event occurs. The events JavaScript deals with aren't as exciting as the ones you deal with—they include such events as

When the mouse button is pressed and *When this page is finished loading*. Nevertheless, they're a very useful part of JavaScript.

Many JavaScript events (such as mouse clicks, which you've seen previously) are caused by the user. Rather than doing things in a set order, your script can respond to the user's actions. Other events don't involve the user directly—for example, an event can be triggered when an HTML document finishes loading.

Each event handler is associated with a particular browser object, and you can specify the event handler in the tag that defines the object. For example, images and text links have an event, onmouseover, that happens when the mouse pointer moves over the object. Here is a typical HTML image tag with an event handler:

```
<img src="button.gif" onmouseover="highlight();" />
```

You specify the event handler as an attribute within the HTML tag and include the JavaScript statement to handle the event within the quotation marks. This is an ideal use for functions because function names are short and to the point and can refer to a whole series of statements.

▼ TRY IT YOURSELF

Using an Event Handler

Here's a simple example of an event handler, which will give you some practice setting up an event and working with JavaScript without using `<script>` tags. Listing 14.1 shows an HTML document that includes a simple event handler.

LISTING 14.1 An HTML Document with a Simple Event Handler

```
<!DOCTYPE html>

<html lang="en">
  <head>
    <title>Event Handler Example</title>
  </head>

  <body>
    <h1>Event Handler Example</h1>
    <div>
    <a href="http://www.google.com/"
    onclick="alert('A-ha! An Event!');">Go to Google</a>
    </div>
  </body>
</html>
```

The event handler is defined with the following `onclick` attribute within the `<a>` tag that defines a link:

```
onclick="alert('Aha! An Event!');"
```

This event handler uses the DOM's built-in `alert` method of the `window` object to display a message when you click on the link; after you click OK to dismiss the alert, your browser will continue on to the URL. In more complex scripts, you will usually define your own functions to act as event handlers. Figure 14.1 shows this example in action.

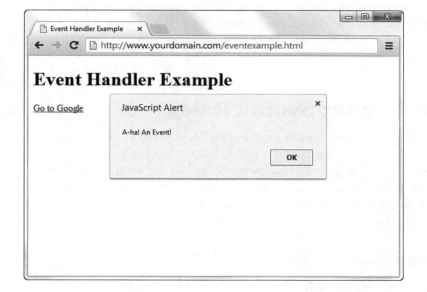

FIGURE 14.1
The browser displays an alert when you click the link.

You'll use other event handlers throughout this book, leading up to a more comprehensive lesson in Chapter 19.

Which Script Runs First?

You are not limited to a single script within a web document: one or more sets of `<script>` tags, external JavaScript files, and any number of event handlers can be used within a single document. With all of these scripts, you might wonder how the browser knows which to execute first. Fortunately, this is done in a logical fashion:

TIP

After you click the OK button to dismiss the alert, the browser follows the link defined in the `<a>` tag. Your event handler could also stop the browser from following the link, as you will learn in Chapter 19.

► Sets of `<script>` tags within the `<head>` element of an HTML document are handled first, whether they include embedded code or refer to a JavaScript file. Because scripts in the `<head>` element will not create output in the web page, it's a good place to define functions for use later.

► Sets of `<script>` tags within the `<body>` section of the HTML document are executed after those in the `<head>` section, while the web page loads and displays. If there are two or more scripts in the body, they are executed in order.

► Event handlers are executed when their events happen. For example, the `onload` event handler is executed when the body of a web page loads. Because the `<head>` section is loaded before any events, you can define functions there and use them in event handlers.

JavaScript Syntax Rules

JavaScript is a simple language, but you do need to be careful to use its *syntax*—the rules that define how you use the language—correctly. The rest of this book covers many aspects of JavaScript syntax, but there are a few basic rules you can begin to keep in mind now, throughout the chapters in this book, and then when you are working on your own.

Case Sensitivity

Almost everything in JavaScript is *case sensitive*: You cannot use lowercase and capital letters interchangeably. Here are a few general rules:

► JavaScript keywords, such as `for` and `if`, are always lowercase.

► Built-in objects such as `Math` and `Date` are capitalized.

► DOM object names are usually lowercase, but their methods are often a combination of capitals and lowercase. Usually capitals are used for all but the first word, as in `setAttribute` and `getElementById`.

When in doubt, follow the exact case used in this book or another JavaScript reference. If you use the wrong case, the browser will usually display an error message.

Variable, Object, and Function Names

When you define your own variables, objects, or functions, you can choose their names. Names can include uppercase letters, lowercase letters, numbers, and the underscore (_) character. Names must begin with a letter or an underscore.

You can choose whether to use capitals or lowercase in your variable names, but remember that JavaScript is case sensitive: score, Score, and SCORE would be considered three different variables. Be sure to use the same name each time you refer to a variable.

Reserved Words

One more rule for variable names: They must not be reserved words. These include the words that make up the JavaScript language, such as if and for, DOM object names such as window and document, and built-in object names such as Math and Date.

A list of JavaScript reserved words can be found at https://developer.mozilla.org/en-US/docs/Web/JavaScript/Reference/Reserved_Words.

Spacing

Blank space (known as *whitespace* by programmers) is ignored by JavaScript. You can include spaces and tabs within a line, or blank lines, without causing an error. Blank space often makes the script more readable, so do not hesitate to use it.

Using Comments

JavaScript *comments* enable you to include documentation within your script. Brief documentation is useful if someone else needs to understand the script, or even if you try to understand it after returning to your code after a long break. To include comments in a JavaScript program, begin a line with two slashes, as in this example:

```
//this is a comment.
```

You can also begin a comment with two slashes in the middle of a line, which is useful for documenting a script. In this case, everything on the line after the slashes is treated as a comment and ignored by the browser. For example, the following line is a valid JavaScript statement followed by a comment explaining what is going on in the code:

```
a = a + 1; // add 1 to the value of the variable a
```

JavaScript also supports C-style comments (also used in PHP), which begin with /* and end with */. These comments can extend across more than one line, as the following example demonstrates:

```
/* This script includes a variety
of features, including this comment. */
```

Because JavaScript statements within a comment are ignored, this type of comment is often used for commenting out sections of code. If you have some lines of JavaScript that you want to temporarily take out of the picture while you debug a script, you can add /* at the beginning of the section and */ at the end.

Best Practices for JavaScript

Now that you've learned some of the very basic rules for writing valid JavaScript, it's also a good idea to follow a few *best practices*. The following practices are not required, but you'll save yourself and others some headaches if you begin to integrate them into your development process.

▶ **Use comments liberally**—These make your code easier for others to understand, and also easier for you to understand when you edit them later. They are also useful for marking the major divisions of a script.

▶ **Use a semicolon at the end of each statement, and use only one statement per line**—Although you learned in this chapter that semicolons are not necessary to end a statement (if you use a new line), using semicolons and only one statement per line will make your scripts easier to read and also easier to debug.

▶ **Use separate JavaScript files whenever possible**—Separating large chunks of JavaScript makes debugging easier, and also encourages you to write modular scripts that can be reused.

▶ **Avoid being browser-specific**—As you learn more about JavaScript, you'll learn some features that work in only one browser. Avoid them unless absolutely necessary, and always test your code in more than one browser.

► **Keep JavaScript optional**—Don't use JavaScript to perform an essential function on your site—for example, the primary navigation links. Whenever possible, users without JavaScript should be able to use your site, although it might not be quite as attractive or convenient. This strategy is known as *progressive enhancement*.

There are many more best practices involving more advanced aspects of JavaScript. You'll learn about them not only as you progress through the chapters, but also over time and as you collaborate with others on web development projects.

Understanding JSON

Although JSON, or *JavaScript Object Notation*, is not a part of the core JavaScript language, it is in fact a common way to structure and store information either used by or created by JavaScript-based functionality on the client side. Now is a good time to familiarize yourself with JSON (pronounced "Jason") and some of its uses.

JSON-encoded data is expressed as a sequence of parameter and value pairs, with each pair using a colon to separate parameter from value. These "parameter":"value" pairs are themselves separated by commas:

```
"param1":"value1", "param2":"value2", "param3":"value3"
```

Finally, the whole sequence is enclosed between curly braces to form a JSON object; the following example creates a variable called yourJSONObject:

```
var yourJSONObject = {
    "param1":"value1",
    "param2":"value2",
    "param3":"value3"
}
```

JSON objects can have properties and methods accessed directly using the usual dot notation, such as this:

```
alert(yourJSONObject.param1); // alerts 'value1'
```

More generally, though, JSON is a general-purpose syntax for exchanging data in a string format. It is then easy to convert the JSON object into a string by a process known as serialization; serialized data is convenient for storage or transmission around networks. You'll see some uses of serialized JSON objects as this book progresses.

One of the most common uses of JSON these days is as a data interchange format used by APIs, or application programming interfaces, and other data feeds that are consumed by a front-end application that uses JavaScript to parse this data. This increased use of JSON in place of other data formats such as XML has come about because JSON is

- ▶ Easy to read for both people and computers
- ▶ Simple in concept, a JSON object being nothing more than a series of "parameter": "value" pairs enclosed by curly braces
- ▶ Largely self-documenting
- ▶ Fast to create and parse
- ▶ A subset of JavaScript, meaning that no special interpreters or other additional packages are necessary

You will gain practical experience working with JSON in Chapter 25, "AJAX: Remote Scripting."

Summary

Throughout this chapter you were introduced to several components of JavaScript programming and syntax, such as functions, objects, event handlers, conditions, and loops. You also learned how to use JavaScript comments to make your script easier to read, and looked at a simple example of an event handler. Finally, you were introduced to JSON, a data interchange format that is commonly used by JavaScript-based applications.

Q&A

Q. I've heard the term object-oriented applied to languages such as C++ and Java. If JavaScript supports objects, is it an object-oriented language?

A. Yes, although it might not fit some people's strict definitions. JavaScript objects do not support all the features that languages such as C++ and Java support, although the latest versions of JavaScript have added more object-oriented features.

Q. Having several scripts that execute at different times seems confusing. Why would I want to use event handlers?

A. Event handlers are the ideal way (and in JavaScript, the only way) to handle advanced interactions within a web page, such as using buttons, checkboxes, and text fields in ways beyond simply completing a form and sending it to a recipient. Rather than writing a script that sits and waits for a button to be pushed, you can simply create an event handler and let the browser do the waiting for you, while allowing the user to continue viewing elements and text on the page.

Workshop

The workshop contains quiz questions and exercises to help you solidify your understanding of the material covered. Try to answer all questions before looking at the "Answers" section that follows.

Quiz

1. A script that executes when the user clicks the mouse button is an example of what?

    a. An object

    b. An event handler

    c. An impossibility

2. Which of the following are capabilities of functions in JavaScript?

    a. Accept parameters

    b. Return a value

    c. Both of the above

3. Which of the following is executed first by a browser?

    a. A script in the `<head>` section

    b. A script in the `<body>` section

    c. An event handler for a button

Answers

1. **b.** A script that executes when the user clicks the mouse button is an event handler.

2. **c.** Functions can both accept parameters and return values.

3. **a.** Scripts defined in the `<head>` section of an HTML document are executed first by the browser.

Exercises

To further explore the JavaScript features you learned about in this chapter, you can perform the following exercises:

▶ Examine the Date and Time script you created in Chapter 4 and find any examples of methods and objects being used.

▶ Add JavaScript comments to the Date and Time script to make it more clear what each line does. Verify that the script still runs properly.

CHAPTER 15

Working with the Document Object Model (DOM)

The preceding chapter introduced you to the basic concepts of programming in JavaScript; this chapter will help you better understand the Document Object Model (or DOM), which is the structured framework of a document within a web browser. Using JavaScript objects, methods, and other functionality (in addition to basic HTML), controlling the DOM enables you to develop rich user experiences.

Understanding the Document Object Model

One advantage that JavaScript has over plain HTML is that these client-side scripts can manipulate the web browser and documents (including their contents) right there in the browser after the content has been loaded. Your script can load a new page into the browser, work with parts of the browser window and the loaded document, open new windows, and even modify text within the page—all dynamically, without requiring additional page loads from a server.

To work with the browser and documents, JavaScript uses the hierarchy of parent and child objects found within the DOM. These objects are organized into a treelike structure, and represent all the content and components of a web document and the browser that renders it.

WHAT YOU'LL LEARN IN THIS CHAPTER:

▶ How the W3C DOM standard makes dynamic pages easier to control

▶ The basics of the standard DOM objects: `window`, `document`, `history`, and `location`

▶ How to work with DOM nodes, parents, children, and siblings

▶ How to access and use the properties of DOM nodes

▶ How to access and use DOM node methods

▶ How to control element positioning with JavaScript

▶ How to hide and show elements with JavaScript

▶ How to add and modify text within a page with JavaScript

NOTE

The DOM is not part of JavaScript or any other programming language—rather, it's an API (application programming interface) built into the browser.

The objects in the DOM have *properties* that describe the web browser or document, and *methods*, or built-in code that enables you to work with parts of the web browser or document. You'll learn more about these properties and methods, and will practice referencing or using them, as this chapter moves forward.

You've seen DOM object notation already in this book, even if it wasn't called out as such. When you refer to a DOM object, you use the parent object name followed by the child object name or names, separated by periods. For example, if you need to refer to a specific image loaded in your web browser, these are child objects of the document object. But that document object, in turn, is a child of the DOM's window object. So to reference an image called logo_image, the DOM object notation would look like this:

```
window.document.logo_image
```

Using window Objects

At the top of the browser object hierarchy is the window object, which represents a browser window. You've already used at least one method of the window object: alert(), which displays a message in an alert box.

A user might have several windows open at a time, each with its own distinct window object, since different documents will presumably be loaded in each window. Even if the same document is loaded into two or more windows, they are considered distinct window objects because they are in fact distinct instances of the browser. However, when referencing window.document (or just document) in your JavaScript, the reference is interpreted to be the window currently in focus—the one actively being used. You'll learn more about windows, including how to reference those out-of-focus windows, in Chapter 20, "Using Windows."

The window object is the parent object for all the objects we will be looking at in this chapter. Figure 15.1 shows the window section of the DOM object hierarchy and a variety of its objects.

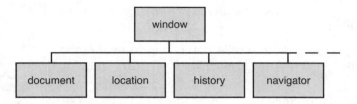

FIGURE 15.1
The `window` section of the DOM object hierarchy, and some of its children.

Working with the `document` **Object**

Just like it sounds, the `document` object represents a web document. Web documents are displayed within browser windows, so it shouldn't surprise you to learn that the `document` object is a child of the `window` object. Because the `window` object always represents the current window, as you learned in the preceding section, you can use `window.document` to refer to the current document. You can also simply refer to `document`, which automatically refers to the current window.

In the following sections, you will look at some of the properties and methods of the `document` object that will be useful in your scripting.

Getting Information About the Document

Several properties of the `document` object include information about the current document in general:

> ▶ `document.URL` specifies the document's URL, and you (or your code) cannot change the value of this property.

> ▶ `document.title` refers to the title of the current page, defined by the HTML `<title>` tag; you can change the value of this property.

> ▶ `document.referrer` returns the URL of the page the user was viewing before the current page—usually, the page with a link to the current page. As with `document.URL`, you cannot change the value of `document.referrer`. Note that `document.referrer` will be blank if a user has directly accessed a given URL directly.

> ▶ `document.lastModified` is the date the document was last modified. This date is sent from the server along with the page.

NOTE

In previous chapters, you've already used the `document.write` method to display text within a web document. The examples in earlier chapters used only a single window and document, so it was unnecessary to use `window.document.write`—but this longer syntax would have worked equally well.

▶ `document.cookie` enables you to read or set a cookie used within the document.

▶ `document.images` returns a collection of images used in the document.

As an example of a document property, Listing 15.1 shows a short HTML document that displays its last modified date using JavaScript.

LISTING 15.1   Displaying the Last Modified Date

```html
<!DOCTYPE html>

<html lang="en">
  <head>
    <title>Displaying the Last Modified Date</title>
  </head>
  <body>
    <h1>Displaying the Last Modified Date</h1>
    <p>This page was last modified on:
    <script type="text/javascript">
        document.write(document.lastModified);
    </script>
    </p>
</body>
</html>
```

Figure 15.2 shows the output of Listing 15.1.

FIGURE 15.2
Viewing the last modified date of a document.

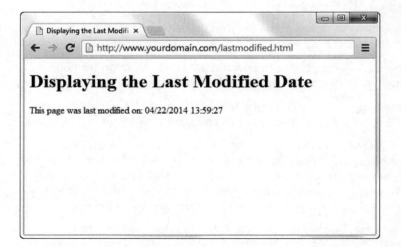

If you use JavaScript to display the value of this document property, you don't have to remember to update the date each time you modify the page, should you choose to expose this information to the user. (You could also use the script to always print the current date instead of the last modified date, but that would be cheating.)

Writing Text in a Document

The simplest document object methods are also the ones you will use most often. In fact, you've used one of them already, even in the most basic examples in this book so far. The document.write method prints text as part of the HTML in a document window. An alternative statement, document.writeln, also prints text, but it also includes a newline (\n) character at the end. This is handy when you want your text to be the last thing on the line in your source code.

You can use these methods only within the body of the web page; you can't use these methods to add to a page that has already loaded without reloading it. You *can* write new content for a document, however, as the next section explains.

The document.write method can be used within a <script> tag in the body of an HTML document. You can also use it in a function, provided you include a call to the function within the body of the document, as shown in Listing 15.1.

Using Links and Anchors

Another child of the document object is the link object. There can be, and very likely are, multiple link objects in a document. Each link object includes information about a link to another location or to an anchor.

You can access link objects through the links array. Each member of the array is one of the link objects in the current page. A property of the links array, document.links.length, indicates the number of links in the page. You might use the document.links.length property in a script to first determine how many links there are, before performing additional tasks such as dynamically changing the display or a certain number of links, and so on.

Each `link` object (or member of the `links` array) has a list of properties defining the URL that is ultimately stored in the object. The `href` property contains the entire URL, and other properties define other, smaller, portions of it. The link object uses the same property names as the `location` object, defined later in this chapter, so after you commit one set to memory, you will also know the other set.

You can refer to a property by indicating the link number, or position within the array, and property name. For example, the following statement assigns the entire URL of the first link stored in the array to the variable `link1`:

```
var link1 = links[0].href;
```

The `anchor` objects are also children of the `document` object. Each `anchor` object represents an anchor in the current document—a particular location that can be jumped to directly.

As with links, you can access anchors using an array; this one is called `anchors`. Each element of this array is an `anchor` object. The `document.anchors.length` property gives you the number of elements in the `anchors` array. An example of using the `anchors` array to your advantage would be to use JavaScript to loop through all the anchors on a given page, to dynamically generate a table of contents at the top of the page.

Accessing Browser History

The `history` object is another child (property) of the `window` object. This object holds information about the locations (URLs) that have been visited before and after the current one, and it includes methods to go to previous or next locations.

The `history` object has one property you can access:

▶ `history.length` keeps track of the length of the history list—in other words, the number of different locations that the user has visited.

The `history` object has three methods you can use to move through the history list:

▶ `history.go()` opens a URL from the history list. To use this method, specify a positive or negative number in parentheses.

For example, `history.go(-2)` is equivalent to pressing the Back button twice.

▶ `history.back()` loads the preceding URL in the history list—equivalent to pressing the Back button or to `history.go(-1)`.

▶ `history.forward()` loads the next URL in the history list, if available. This is equivalent to pressing the Forward button or to `history.go(1)`.

You can use the `back` and `forward` methods of the `history` object to add your own Back and Forward buttons to a web document. The browser already has Back and Forward buttons, of course, but sometimes it is useful (or provides a better user experience) to include your own links that serve the same purpose.

Suppose you wanted to create a script that displays Back and Forward buttons and use these methods to navigate the browser. Here's the code that will create the Back button:

```
<button type="button" onclick="history.back();">Go Back</button>
```

In the preceding snippet, the `<button>` element defines a button labeled Go Back. The `onclick` event handler uses the `history.back()` method to go to the preceding page in the browser's history. The code for a Go Forward button is similar:

```
<button type="button" onclick="history.forward();">Go Forward
</button>
```

Let's take a look at these in the context of a complete web page. Listing 15.2 shows a complete HTML document, and Figure 15.3 shows a browser's display of the document. After you load this document into a browser, visit other URLs and make sure the Go Back and Go Forward buttons work as expected.

LISTING 15.2 A Web Page That Uses JavaScript to Include Back and Forward Buttons

```
<!DOCTYPE html>

<html lang="en">
  <head>
    <title>Using Custom Go Back and Go Forward Buttons</title>
  </head>
  <body>
    <h1>Using Custom Go Back and Go Forward Buttons</h1>
```

```
    <p>Buttons on this page allow you to go back or forward in
    your history list.</p>
    <p>These buttons should be the equivalent of the back
    and forward arrow buttons in your browser's toolbar.</p>
    <div>
    <button type="button"
            onclick="history.back();">Go Back</button>
    <button type="button"
            onclick="history.forward();">Go Forward</button>
    </div>
  </body>
</html>
```

FIGURE 15.3
Showing custom Go Back and Go
Forward buttons.

Working with the `location` **Object**

Another child of the `window` object is the `location` object. This object
stores information about the current URL loaded in the browser
window. For example, the following JavaScript statement loads a URL
into the current window by assigning a value to the `href` property of
this object:

```
window.location.href="http://www.google.com";
```
not advised.

The `href` property contains the entire URL of the window's current
location. Using JavaScript, you can access portions of the URL through

various properties of the `location` object. To understand these properties a bit better, consider the following URL:

http://www.google.com:80/search?q=javascript

The following properties represent parts of the URL:

▶ `location.protocol` is the protocol part of the URL (`http` in the example).

▶ `location.hostname` is the hostname of the URL (`www.google.com` in the example).

▶ `location.port` is the port number of the URL (`80` in the example).

▶ `location.pathname` is the filename part of the URL (`search` in the example).

▶ `location.search` is the query portion of the URL, if any (`q=javascript` in the example).

Unused in this example but also accessible are the following:

▶ `location.host` is the hostname of the URL plus the port number (`www.google.com:80` in the example).

▶ `location.hash` is the anchor name used in the URL, if any.

The `link` object, introduced earlier in this chapter, also uses this list of properties for accessing portions of the URL found in the `link` object.

The `location` object has three methods:

▶ `location.assign()` loads a new document when used as follows:

```
location.assign("http://www.google.com")
```

▶ `location.reload()` reloads the current document. This is the same as using the Reload button on the browser's toolbar. If you optionally include the `true` parameter when calling this method, it will ignore the browser's cache and force a reload whether the document has changed or not.

▶ `location.replace()` replaces the current location with a new one. This is similar to setting the `location` object's properties yourself. The difference is that the `replace` method does not affect the browser's history. In other words, the Back button can't be used to go to the preceding location. This is useful for splash screens or temporary pages that it would be useless to return to.

CAUTION

Although the `location.href` property usually contains the same URL as the `document.URL` property described earlier in this chapter, you can't change the `document.URL` property. Always use `location.href` to load a new page in a given window.

More About the DOM Structure

Previously in this chapter, you learned how some of the most important DOM objects are organized: The `window` object is a parent to the `document` object, and so on. Although these objects were the only ones available in the original conception of the DOM years ago, the modern DOM adds objects under the `document` object for every element of a page.

To better understand the concept of a `document` object for every element, let's look at the simple HTML document in Listing 15.3. This document has the usual `<head>` and `<body>` sections, plus a heading and a single paragraph of text.

LISTING 15.3   A Simple HTML Document

```
<!DOCTYPE html>

<html lang="en">
  <head>
    <title>A Simple HTML Document</title>
  </head>
  <body>
    <h1>This is a Level-1 Heading.</h1>
    <p>This is a simple paragraph.</p>
</body>
</html>
```

Like all HTML documents, this one is composed of various *containers* and their contents. The `<html>` tags form a container that includes the entire document, the `<body>` tags contain the body of the page, and so on.

In the DOM, each container within the page and its contents are represented by an object. The objects are organized into a treelike structure, with the `document` object itself at the root of the tree, and with individual elements such as the heading and paragraph of text at the leaves of the tree. Figure 15.4 shows a diagram of these relationships.

In the following sections, you will examine the structure of the DOM more closely.

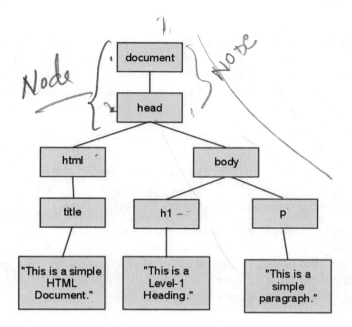

FIGURE 15.4
How the DOM represents an HTML document.

NOTE

Don't worry if this tree structure confuses you right now; just understand you can assign IDs to elements and refer to them in your JavaScript. Further on, you will look at more complicated examples that will use this newfound information about how objects are organized in the DOM.

Nodes

Each container or element in a document is called a *node* in the DOM. In the example in Figure 15.4, each of the objects in boxes is a node, and the lines represent the relationships between the nodes.

You will often need to refer to individual nodes in scripts. You can do this by assigning an ID, or by navigating the tree using the relationships between the nodes. You will get plenty of practice with nodes as you move forward in this book; it's a good word to know.

Parents and Children

As you have already learned, an object can have a *parent*—an object that contains it—and can also have *children*—objects that it contains. The DOM uses the same terminology as JavaScript in this regard.

In Figure 15.4, the document object is the parent object for the other objects shown, and does not have a parent itself explicitly listed, although as you've learned previously the document object is a child of the window object. The html object is the parent of the head and body objects, and the h1 and p objects are children of the body object.

Text nodes work a bit differently. The actual text in the paragraph is a node in itself, and is a child of the p object, rather than being a grandchild of the body object. Similarly, the text within the <h1> tags is a child of the h1 object. Don't worry, we'll return to this concept throughout the rest of this book.

Siblings

The DOM also uses another term for organization of objects: *siblings*. As you might expect, this refers to objects that have the same parent—in other words, objects at the same level in the DOM object tree.

In Figure 15.4, the h1 and p objects are siblings, because both are children of the body object. Similarly, the head and body objects are siblings under the html object. There's not a lot of practical use in knowing which objects are siblings, but it is offered here as some knowledge that completes the family tree.

NOTE

The following sections describe only the most important properties and methods of nodes, and those that are supported by current browsers. For a complete list of available properties, see the W3C's DOM specification at http://www.w3.org/TR/DOM-Level-3-Core/.

Working with DOM Nodes

As you've seen, the DOM organizes objects within a web page into a treelike structure. Each node (object) in this tree can be accessed in JavaScript. In the next sections you will learn how you can use the properties and methods of nodes to manage them.

Basic Node Properties

Previously in this book, you used the style property of nodes to change their style sheet values. Each node also has a number of basic properties that you can examine or set. These include the following:

▶ nodeName is the name of the node (not the ID). For nodes based on HTML tags, such as <p> or <body>, the name is the tag name: p or body. For the document node, the name is a special code: #document. Similarly, text nodes have the name #text. This is a read-only value.

▶ nodeType is an integer describing the node's type, such as 1 for normal HTML tags, 3 for text nodes, and 9 for the document node. This is a read-only value.

▶ nodeValue is the actual text contained within a text node. This property returns null for other types of nodes.

▶ innerHTML is the HTML content of any node. You can assign a value including HTML tags to this property and change the DOM child objects for a node dynamically.

Node Relationship Properties

In addition to the basic properties described previously, each node has various properties that describe its relation to other nodes. These include the following read-only properties:

▶ firstChild is the first child object for a node. For nodes that contain text, such as h1 or p, the text node containing the actual text is the first child.

▶ lastChild is the node's last child object.

▶ childNodes is an array that includes all of a node's child nodes. You can use a loop with this array to work with all the nodes under a given node.

▶ previousSibling is the sibling (node at the same level) previous to the current node.

▶ nextSibling is the sibling after the current node.

Document Methods

The document node itself has several methods you might find useful. You have already used one of these in exercises in this book (getElementById) to refer to DOM objects by their ID properties. The document node's methods include the following:

▶ getElementById(id) returns the element with the specified id attribute.

▶ getElementsByTagName(tag) returns an array of all the elements with a specified tag name. You can use the wildcard * to return an array containing all the nodes in the document.

▶ createTextNode(text) creates a new text node containing the specified text, which you can then add to the document.

▶ createElement(tag) creates a new HTML element for the specified tag. As with createTextNode, you need to add the element to the document after creating it. You can assign content within the element by changing its child objects or the innerHTML property.

Node Methods

Each node within a page has a number of methods available. Which of these are valid depends on the node's position in the page, and whether it has parent or child nodes. These include the following:

▶ `appendChild(new)` appends the specified new node after all the object's existing nodes.

▶ `insertBefore(new, old)` inserts the specified new child node before the specified old child node, which must already exist.

▶ `replaceChild(new, old)` replaces the specified old child node with a new node.

▶ `removeChild(node)` removes a child node from the object's set of children.

▶ `hasChildNodes()` returns a Boolean value of `true` if the object has one or more child nodes, or `false` if it has none.

▶ `cloneNode()` creates a copy of an existing node. If a parameter of `true` is supplied, the copy will also include any child nodes of the original node.

Creating Positionable Elements (Layers)

Now that you understand a little more about how the DOM is structured, you should be able to start thinking about how you can control any element in a web page, such as a paragraph or an image. For example, you can use the DOM to change the position, visibility, and other attributes of an element.

Before the W3C DOM and CSS2 standards (remember, we're now on CSS3), you could only reposition *layers*, or special groups of elements defined with a proprietary tag. Although you can now position any element individually, it's still useful to work with groups of elements in many cases.

You can effectively create a layer, or a group of HTML objects that can be controlled as a group, using the `<div>` container element, which you learned about early in this book.

To create a layer with `<div>`, enclose the content of the layer between the two division tags and specify the layer's properties in the `style` attribute of the `<div>` tag. Here's a simple example:

```
<div id="layer1" style="position:absolute; left:100px;
top:100px">
This is the content of the layer.
</div>
```

This code defines a layer with the name `layer1`. This is a movable layer positioned 100 pixels down and 100 pixels to the right of the upper-left corner of the browser window.

You've already learned about the positioning properties and seen them in action in Parts II and III of this book. This includes setting object size (such as `height` and `width`) and position (such as `absolute` or `relative`), object visibility, and object background and borders. The remaining examples in this chapter use HTML and CSS much like that you've already seen in this book, but show you JavaScript-based interactions with the DOM in action.

Controlling Positioning with JavaScript

Using the code snippet from the preceding section, in this section you'll see an example of how you can control the positioning attributes of an object, using JavaScript.

Here is our sample layer (a `<div>`):

```
<div id="layer1" style="position:absolute; left:100px;
top:100px">
This is the content of the layer.
</div>
```

To move this layer up or down within the page using JavaScript, you can change its `style.top` attribute. For example, the following statements move the layer 100 pixels down from its original position:

```
var obj = document.getElementById("layer1");
obj.style.top=200;
```

The `document.getElementById()` method returns the object corresponding to the layer's `<div>` tag, and the second statement sets the object's `top` positioning property to 200px; you can also combine these two statements:

```
document.getElementById("layer1").style.top = 200;
```

NOTE

As you've learned in earlier chapters, you can specify CSS properties such as the `position` property and other layer properties in a `<style>` block, in an external style sheet, or in the `style` attribute of an HTML tag, and then control these properties using JavaScript. The code snippets shown here use properties in the `style` attribute rather than in a `<style>` block just because it is a snippet of an example and not a full code listing.

NOTE

Some CSS properties, such
as text-indent and
border-color, have hyphens
in their names. When you use
these properties in JavaScript,
you combine the hyphenated
sections and use a capital
letter: textIndent and
borderColor.

This simply sets the style.top property for the layer without assigning a variable to the layer's object.

Now let's create an HTML document that defines a layer, and combine it with a script to allow the layer to be moved, hidden, or shown using buttons. Listing 15.4 shows the HTML document that defines the buttons and the layer. The script itself (position.js) follows in Listing 15.5.

LISTING 15.4   The HTML Document for the Movable Layer Example

```html
<!DOCTYPE html>

<html lang="en">
  <head>
   <title>Positioning Elements with JavaScript</title>
   <script type="text/javascript" src="position.js"></script>
   <style type="text/css">
   #buttons {
       text-align:center;
   }
   #square {
       position: absolute;
       top: 150px;
       left: 100px;
       width: 200px;
       height: 200px;
       border: 2px solid black;
       padding: 10px;
       background-color: #e0e0e0;
   }
   div {
       padding: 10px;
   }
   </style>
  </head>
<body>
   <h1>Positioning Elements</h1>
   <div id="buttons">
   <button type="button" name="left"
     onclick="pos(-1,0);">Left</button>
   <button type="button" name="right"
     onclick="pos(1,0);">Right</button>
   <button type="button" name="up"
     onclick="pos(0,-1);">Up</button>
   <button type="button" name="down"
     onclick="pos(0,1);">Down</button>
   <button type="button" name="hide"
     onclick="hideSquare();">Hide</button>
   <button type="button" name="show"
     onclick="showSquare();">Show</button>
```

```
   </div>
   <hr />
   <div id="square">
   This square is an absolutely positioned layer
   that you can move using the buttons above.
   </div>
   </body>
</html>
```

In addition to some basic HTML, Listing 15.4 contains the following:

▶ The `<script>` tag in the header reads a script called `position.js`, which is shown in Listing 15.5.

▶ The `<style>` section is a brief style sheet that defines the properties for the movable layer. It sets the `position` property to `absolute` to indicate that it can be positioned at an exact location, sets the initial position in the `top` and `left` properties, and sets `border` and `background-color` properties to make the layer clearly visible.

▶ The `<button>` tags define six buttons: four to move the layer left, right, up, or down, and two to control whether it is visible or hidden.

▶ The `<div>` section defines the layer itself. The `id` attribute is set to the value `"square"`. This `id` is used in the style sheet to refer to the layer, and will also be used in your script.

If you load the HTML into a browser, you should see the buttons and the `"square"` layer, but the buttons won't do anything yet. The script in Listing 15.5 adds the capability to use the actions. When you load the code in Listing 15.4 into your browser, it should look as shown in Figure 15.5.

Listing 15.5 shows the JavaScript variables and functions that are called in the HTML in Listing 15.4. This code is expected (by the `<script>` tag) to be in a file called `position.js`.

LISTING 15.5 The Script for the Movable Layer Example

```
var x=100,y=150;
function pos(dx,dy) {
    if (!document.getElementById) return;
    x += 30*dx;
    y += 30*dy;
    obj = document.getElementById("square");
    obj.style.top=y + "px";
```

```
        obj.style.left=x + "px";
}
function hideSquare() {
    if (!document.getElementById) return;
    obj = document.getElementById("square");
    obj.style.display="none";
}
function showSquare() {
    if (!document.getElementById) return;
    obj = document.getElementById("square");
    obj.style.display="block";
}
```

FIGURE 15.5
The movable layer, ready to
be moved.

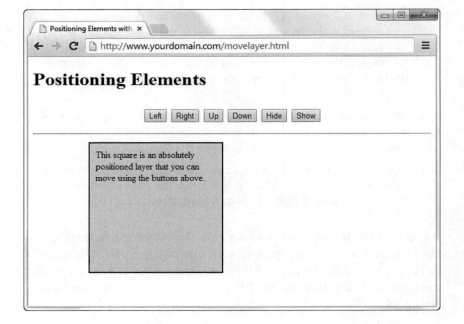

The var statement at the beginning of the script defines two variables,
x and y, that will store the current position of the layer. The pos
function is called by the event handlers for all four of the movement
buttons.

The parameters of the pos() function, dx and dy, tell the script how
the layer should move: If dx is negative, a number is subtracted from
x, moving the layer to the left. If dx is positive, a number is added to x,
moving the layer to the right. Similarly, dy indicates whether to move
up or down.

The `pos()` function begins by making sure the `getElementById()` function is supported, so it won't attempt to run in older browsers. It then multiplies `dx` and `dy` by 30 (to make the movement more obvious) and applies them to `x` and `y`. Finally, it sets the `top` and `left` properties to the new position (including the "px" to indicate the unit of measurement), thus moving the layer.

Two more functions, `hideSquare()` and `showsquare()`, hide or show the layer by setting its `display` property to `"none"` (hidden) or `"block"` (shown).

To use this script, save it as `position.js` and then load the HTML document in Listing 15.4 into your browser. Figure 15.6 shows this script in action—well, after an action, at least. Figure 15.6 shows the script after the Right button has been pressed four times, and the Down button five times.

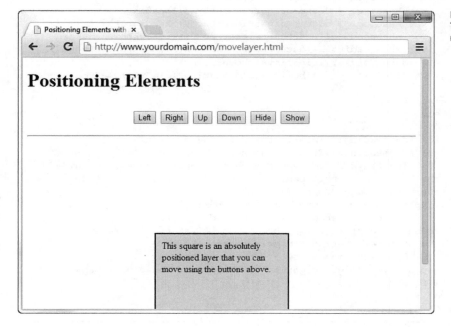

FIGURE 15.6
The movable layer has been moved.

Hiding and Showing Objects

In the preceding example, you saw some functions that could be used to hide or show the "square." In this section, we'll take a closer look at hiding and showing objects within a page.

As a refresher, objects have a `visibility` style property that specifies whether they are currently visible within the page:

```
Object.style.visibility="hidden"; // hides an object
Object.style.visibility="visible"; // shows an object
```

Using this property, you can create a script that hides or shows objects in either browser. Listing 15.6 shows the HTML document for a script that allows two headings to be shown or hidden.

LISTING 15.6   Hiding and Showing Objects

```
<!DOCTYPE html>

<html lang="en">
  <head>
    <title>Hiding or Showing Objects</title>
    <script type="text/javascript">
    function showHide() {
        if (!document.getElementById) return;
        var heading1 = document.getElementById("heading1");
        var heading2 = document.getElementById("heading2");
        var showheading1 = document.checkboxform.checkbox1.checked;
        var showheading2 = document.checkboxform.checkbox2.checked;
        heading1.style.visibility=(showheading1) ? "visible" : "hidden";
        heading2.style.visibility=(showheading2) ? "visible" : "hidden";
    }
    </script>
  </head>
  <body>
    <h1 id="heading1">This is the first heading</h1>
    <h1 id="heading2">This is the second heading</h1>
    <p>Using the W3C DOM, you can choose whether to show or hide
    the headings on this page using the checkboxes below.</p>
    <form name="checkboxform">
    <input type="checkbox" name="checkbox1"
           onclick="showHide();" checked="checked" />
    <span style="font-weight:bold">Show first heading</span><br/>
    <input type="checkbox" name="checkbox2"
           onclick="showHide();" checked="checked" />
    <span style="font-weight:bold">Show second heading</span><br/>
    </form>
  </body>
</html>
```

The `<h1>` tags in this document define headings with IDs of `head1` and `head2`. Inside the `<form>` element are two checkboxes, one for each of these headings. When a checkbox is modified (checked or unchecked), the `onclick` method calls the JavaScript `showHide()` function to perform an action.

The `showHide()` function is defined within the `<script>` tag in the header. This function assigns the objects for the two headings to two variables named `heading1` and `heading2`, using the `getElementById()` method. Next, it assigns the value of the checkboxes within the form to the `showheading1` and `showheading2` variables. Finally, the function uses the `style.visibility` attributes to set the visibility of the headings.

Figure 15.7 shows this example in action. In the figure, the second heading's checkbox has been unchecked, so only the first heading is visible.

FIGURE 15.7

TIP

The lines that set the `visibility` property might look a bit strange. The `?` and `:` characters create *conditional expressions*, a shorthand way of handling `if` statements. You'll learn more about these conditional expressions in Chapter 18, "Controlling Flow with Conditions and Loops."

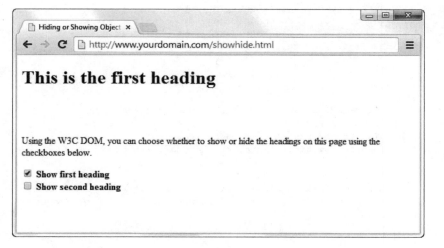

The text hiding/showing example in action.

Modifying Text Within a Page

You can also create a simple script to modify the contents of a heading within a web page (or any element, for that matter). As you learned earlier in this chapter, the `nodeValue` property of a text node contains its actual text, and the text node for a heading is a child of that heading. Thus, the syntax to change the text of a heading with the identifier `head1` would be

```
var heading1 = document.getElementById("heading1");
heading1.firstChild.nodeValue = "New Text Here";
```

This assigns the heading's object to the variable called `heading1`. The `firstChild` property returns the text node that is the only child of the heading, and its `nodeValue` property contains the heading text.

Using this technique, it's easy to create a page that allows the heading to be changed dynamically. Listing 15.7 shows the complete HTML document for a script that does just that.

LISTING 15.7   The Complete Text-Modifying Example

```
<!DOCTYPE html>

<html lang="en">
  <head>
    <title>Dynamic Text in JavaScript</title>
    <script type="text/javascript">
    function changeTitle() {
       if (!document.getElementById) return;
       var newtitle = document.changeform.newtitle.value;
       var heading1 = document.getElementById("heading1");
       heading1.firstChild.nodeValue=newtitle;
    }
    </script>
  </head>
  <body>
    <h1 id="heading1">Dynamic Text in JavaScript</h1>
    <p>Using the W3C DOM, you can dynamically change the
    heading at the top of this page.</p>
    <p>Enter a new title and click the Change! button. </p>

    <form name="changeform">
    <input type="text" name="newtitle" size="40" />
    <button type="button" onclick="changeTitle();">Change!</button>
    </form>
  </body>
</html>
```

This example defines a form that enables the user to enter a new heading for the page. Pressing the button calls the `changeTitle()` function, defined in the `<script>` tag in the `<head>` element. This JavaScript function gets the value the user entered in the form, and changes the heading's value to the new text by assigning the value of the input to the `heading1.firstChild.nodeValue` property.

Figure 15.8 shows this page in action after a new title has been entered and the Change! button has been clicked.

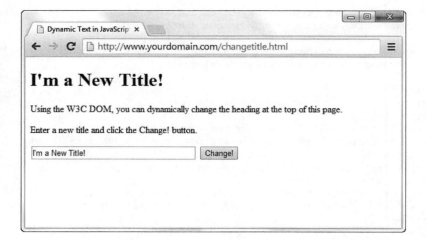

FIGURE 15.8
The heading-modification example
in action.

Adding Text to a Page

Next, you can create a script that actually adds text to a page rather
than just changing existing text. To do this, you must first create a
new text node. This statement creates a new text node with the text
"this is a test":

```
var node=document.createTextNode("this is a test");
```

Next, you can add this node into the document. To do this, you use
the `appendChild` method. The text can be added to any element that
can contain text, but in this example we will just use a paragraph.
The following statement adds the text node defined previously to the
paragraph with the identifier `paragraph1`:

```
document.getElementById("paragraph1").appendChild(node);
```

Listing 15.8 shows the HTML document for a complete example that
uses this technique, using a form to allow the user to specify text to
add to the page.

LISTING 15.8   Adding Text to a Page

```
<!DOCTYPE html>

<html lang="en">
  <head>
    <title>Adding Text to a Page</title>
    <script type="text/javascript">
    function addText() {
```

```
        if (!document.getElementById) return;
        var sentence=document.changeform.sentence.value;
        var node=document.createTextNode(" " + sentence);
        document.getElementById("paragraph1").appendChild(node);
        document.changeform.sentence.value="";
      }
    </script>
  </head>
  <body>
    <h1 id="heading1">Create Your Own Content</h1>
    <p id="paragraph1"> Using the W3C DOM, you can dynamically add
    sentences to this paragraph.</p>
    <p>Type a sentence and click the Add! button.</p>
    <form name="changeform">
    <input type="text" name="sentence" size="65" />
    <button type="button" onclick="addText();">Add!</button>
    </form>
  </body>
</html>
```

In this example, the `<p>` element with the ID of `paragraph1` is the paragraph that will hold the added text. The `<form>` element creates a form with a text field called `sentence`, and an Add! button, which calls the `addText()` function when pressed. This JavaScript function is defined in the `<script>` tag in the `<head>` element. The `addText()` function first assigns text typed in the text field to the `sentence` variable. Next, the script creates a new text node containing the value of the `sentence` variable, and appends the new text node to the paragraph.

Load this document into a browser to test it, and try adding several sentences by typing them and clicking the Add! button. Figure 15.9 shows this document after several sentences have been added to the paragraph.

FIGURE 15.9
The text-addition example in action.

Summary

In this chapter, you learned a lot about the Document Object Model (DOM), which creates a hierarchy of web browser and document objects that you can access via JavaScript. You learned how you can use the `document` object to work with documents, and used the `history` and `location` objects to control the current URL displayed in the browser.

Additionally, you learned the methods and properties you can use to manage DOM objects, and created sample scripts to hide and show elements within a page, modify existing text, and add to existing text. You also learned how to use HTML and CSS to define a positionable layer, and how you can use positioning properties dynamically with JavaScript.

This foundational knowledge of the DOM puts you in position (no pun intended) to more effectively work with JavaScript in advanced ways, as you'll learn in the chapters that follow.

Q&A

Q. Can I avoid assigning an `id` attribute to every DOM object I want to handle with a script?

A. Yes. Although the scripts in this chapter typically use the `id` attribute for convenience, you can actually locate any object in the page by using combinations of node properties such as `firstChild` and `nextSibling`. However, keep in mind that any change you make to the HTML can change an element's place in the DOM hierarchy, so the `id` attribute is a reliable recommended way to handle this.

Q. I can use `history` and `document` instead of `window.history` and `window.document`. Can I leave out the `window` object in other cases?

A. Yes. For example, you can use `alert` instead of `window.alert` to display a message. The `window` object contains the current script, so it's treated as a default object. However, be warned that you shouldn't omit the `window` object's name when you're using multiple windows or in an event handler.

Q. Can I change history entries, or prevent the user from using the Back and Forward buttons?

A. You can't change the history entries. Additionally, you can't prevent the use of the Back and Forward buttons, but you can use the `location.replace()` method to load a series of pages that don't appear in the history. There are a few tricks for preventing the Back button from working properly, but I don't recommend them—that's the sort of thing that gives JavaScript a bad reputation.

Workshop

The workshop contains quiz questions and exercises to help you solidify your understanding of the material covered. Test your knowledge of JavaScript and the DOM by answering the following questions. Try to answer all questions before looking at the "Answers" section that follows.

Quiz

1. Which of the following DOM objects never has a parent node?

    a. `body`

    b. `div`

    c. `document`

2. Which of the following is the correct syntax to get the DOM object for a heading with the identifier `heading1`?

    a. `document.getElementById("heading1")`

    b. `document.GetElementByID("heading1")`

    c. `document.getElementsById("heading1")`

3. Which of the following tags can be used to create a layer?

    a. `<layer>`

    b. `<div>`

    c. `<style>`

4. Which property controls an element's left-to-right position?

    a. `left`

    b. `width`

    c. `lrpos`

5. Which of the following CSS rules would create a heading that is not currently visible in the page?

    a. `h1 {visibility: invisible;}`

    b. `h1 {display: none;}`

    c. `h1 {style: invisible;}`

Answers

1. c. The `document` object is the root of the DOM object tree, and has no parent object.

2. a. `getElementById` has a lowercase *g* at the beginning, and a lowercase *d* at the end, contrary to what you might know about normal English grammar.

3. b. The `<div>` tag is one of several container elements that can be used to create positionable layers (but the only one valid in this list).

4. a. The `left` property controls an element's left-to-right position.

5. b. The `none` value for the `display` property makes it invisible. The `visibility` property could also be used, but its possible values are `visible` or `hidden`.

Exercises

▶ Modify the Back and Forward example in Listing 15.2 to include a Reload button along with the Back and Forward buttons. (This button would trigger the `location.reload()` method.)

▶ Modify the positioning example in Listings 15.4 and 15.5 to move the square 1 pixel at a time rather than 30 at a time.

▶ Add a third checkbox to Listing 15.6 to allow the paragraph of text to be shown or hidden. You will need to add an `id` attribute to the `<p>` tag, add a checkbox to the form, and add the appropriate lines to the script.

CHAPTER 16
Using JavaScript Variables, Strings, and Arrays

Now that you have learned some of the fundamentals of JavaScript and the DOM, it's time to dig into more details of the JavaScript language.

In this chapter, you'll learn three tools for storing data in JavaScript: *variables*, which store numbers or text; *strings*, which are special variables for working with text; and *arrays*, which are multiple variables you can refer to by number. Variables, strings, and arrays are not the most exciting elements of any programming language when described individually, but as you will see throughout the rest of this book, variables, strings, and arrays are fundamental to just about every bit of complex JavaScript that you'll develop.

Using Variables

Unless you skipped over all the JavaScript-related chapters so far in this book, you've already used a few variables. You probably can also figure out how to use a few more without any help from me. Nevertheless, there are some aspects of variables you haven't learned yet, which are covered in the next few sections.

Choosing Variable Names

As a reminder, *variables* are named containers that can store data (for example, a number, a text string, or an object). As you learned earlier in this book, every variable has a unique name, of your choosing. However, there are rules you must follow when choosing a variable name:

[Handwritten margin note: strings are Word (alphabetic) always mention within quotes " "]

▶ Variable names can include letters of the alphabet, both upper-
and lowercase. They can also include the digits 0–9 and the
underscore (_) character.

▶ Variable names cannot include spaces or any other punctuation
characters.

▶ The first character of the variable name must be either a letter or
an underscore.

▶ Variable names are case sensitive—totalnum, Totalnum, and
TotalNum are interpreted as separate variable names.

▶ There is no official limit on the length of variable names, but
they must fit on one line. Frankly, if your variable names are
longer than that—or even longer than 25 or so characters, you
might consider a different naming convention.

NOTE

You can choose to use either
friendly, easy-to-read names
or completely cryptic ones. Do
yourself a favor: Use longer (but
not too long), friendly names
whenever possible. Although you
might remember the difference
between a, b, x, and x1 right
now, you might not after a few
days away from the code, and
someone who isn't you most
certainly won't understand
your cryptic naming convention
without some documentation.

Using these rules, the following are examples of valid variable names:

```
total_number_of_fish
LastInvoiceNumber
temp1
a
_var39
```

Using Local and Global Variables

Some computer languages require you to declare a variable before
you use it. JavaScript includes the var keyword, which can be used to
declare a variable. You can omit var in many cases; the variable is still
declared the first time you assign a value to it.

To understand where to declare a variable, you will need to understand
the concept of *scope*. A variable's scope is the area of the script in
which that variable can be used. There are two types of variables:

▶ *Global variables* have the entire script (and other scripts in
the same HTML document) as their scope. They can be used
anywhere, even within functions.

▶ Local variables have a single function as their scope. They can be
used only within the function they are created in.

[Handwritten margin note: Within function variable called Local — outside the function variable called Global — Same variable name can be use in different function and they are not related]

To create a global variable, you declare it in the main script, outside any functions. You can use the var keyword to declare the variable, as in this example:

```
var students = 25;
```

This statement declares a variable called students and assigns it a value of 25. If this statement is used outside functions, it creates a global variable. The var keyword is optional in this case, so this statement is equivalent to the preceding one:

```
students = 25;
```

Arrays carries multiple variable's values

Before you get in the habit of omitting the var keyword, be sure you understand exactly when it's required. It's actually a good idea to always use the var keyword—you'll avoid errors and make your script easier to read, and it won't usually cause any trouble.

A local variable belongs to a particular function. Any variable you declare with the var keyword in a function is a local variable. Additionally, the variables in the function's parameter list are always local variables.

To create a local variable within a function, you *must* use the var keyword. This forces JavaScript to create a local variable, even if there is a global variable with the same name. However, try to keep your variable names distinct, even if you are using them in different scopes.

You should now understand the difference between local and global variables. If you're still a bit confused, don't worry—if you use the var keyword every time, you'll usually end up with the right type of variable.

Assigning Values to Variables

As you learned in Chapter 4, "Understanding JavaScript," you use the equal sign to assign a value to a variable. For example, this statement assigns the value 40 to the variable lines:

```
var lines = 40;
```

You can use any expression to the right of the equal sign, including other variables. You have used this syntax earlier to add one to a variable:

```
lines = lines + 1;
```

Because incrementing or decrementing variables is quite common, JavaScript includes two types of shorthand for this syntax. The first is the += operator, which enables you to create the following shorter version of the preceding example:

```
lines += 1;
```

Similarly, you can subtract a number from a variable using the -= operator:

```
lines -= 1;
```

If you still think that's too much to type, JavaScript also includes the increment and decrement operators, ++ and --. This statement adds one to the value of lines:

```
lines++;
```

Similarly, this statement subtracts one from the value of lines:

```
lines--;
```

You can alternatively use the ++ or -- operators before a variable name, as in ++lines. However, these are not identical. The difference is in when the increment or decrement happens:

▶ If the operator is after the variable name, the increment or decrement happens *after* the current expression is evaluated.

▶ If the operator is before the variable name, the increment or decrement happens *before* the current expression is evaluated.

This difference is an issue only when you use the variable in an expression and increment or decrement it in the same statement. As an example, suppose you have assigned the lines variable the value 40. The following two statements have different effects:

```
alert(lines++);
alert(++lines);
```

NOTE

The increment and decrement operators are strictly for your convenience. If it makes more sense to you to stick to lines = lines + 1, do it—your script won't suffer.

The first statement displays an alert with the value 40, and then increments lines to 41. The second statement first increments lines to 41, then displays an alert with the value 41.

Understanding Expressions and Operators

An *expression* is a combination of variables and values that the JavaScript interpreter can evaluate to a single value, like 2+2 = 4. The characters that are used to combine these values, such as + and /, are called *operators*.

TIP
Along with variables and constant values, expressions can also include function calls that return results.

Using JavaScript Operators

In the basic JavaScript examples so far in this book, you've already used some operators, such as the + sign (addition) and the increment and decrement operators. Table 16.1 lists some of the most important (and common) operators used in JavaScript expressions.

TABLE 16.1   Common JavaScript Operators

Operator	Description	Example
+	Concatenate (combine) strings	message="this is"+ " a test";
+	Add	result = 5 + 7;
-	Subtract	score = score - 1;
*	Multiply	total = quantity * price;
/	Divide	average = sum / 4;
%	Modulo (remainder)	remainder = sum % 4;
++	Increment	tries++;
--	Decrement	total--;

Along with these, there are also many other operators used in conditional statements—you'll learn about these in Chapter 18, "Controlling Flow with Conditions and Loops."

Operator Precedence

When you use more than one operator in an expression, JavaScript uses rules of *operator precedence* to decide how to calculate the value. Table 16.1 lists the operators from lowest to highest precedence, and operators with highest precedence are evaluated first. For example, consider this statement:

```
result = 4 + 5 * 3;
```

If you try to calculate this result, there are two ways to do it. You could multiply 5 * 3 first and then add 4 (result: 19) or add 4 + 5 first and then multiply by 3 (result: 27). JavaScript solves this dilemma by following the precedence rules: Because multiplication has a higher precedence than addition, it first multiplies 5 * 3 and then adds 4, producing a result of 19.

Sometimes operator precedence doesn't produce the result you want. For example, consider this statement:

```
result = a + b + c + d / 4;
```

This is an attempt to average four numbers by adding them all together and then dividing by four. However, because JavaScript gives division a higher precedence than addition, it will divide the d variable by 4 before adding the other numbers, producing an incorrect result.

You can control precedence by using parentheses. Here's the working statement to calculate an average:

```
result = (a + b + c + d) / 4;
```

The parentheses ensure that the four variables are added first, and then the sum is divided by four.

Data Types in JavaScript

In some computer languages, you have to specify the type of data a variable will store, for example, a number or a string. In JavaScript, you don't need to specify a data type in most cases. However, you should know the types of data JavaScript can deal with.

These are the basic JavaScript data types:

▶ *Numbers*, such as 3, 25, or 1.4142138. JavaScript supports both integers and floating-point numbers.

▶ *Boolean*, or logical values. These can have one of two values: true or false. These are useful for indicating whether a certain condition is true.

NOTE

If you're familiar with any other programming languages, you'll find that the operators and precedence in JavaScript work, for the most part, the same way as those in C, C++, and Java, as well as web scripting languages such as PHP.

TIP

If you're unsure about operator precedence, you can use parentheses to make sure things work the way you expect and to make your script more readable.

NOTE

You'll learn more about Boolean values, and about using conditions in JavaScript, in Chapter 18.

- *Strings*, such as `"I am a jelly doughnut"`. These consist of one or more characters of text. (Strictly speaking, these are `string` objects, which you'll learn about later in this chapter.)

- The *null value*, represented by the keyword `null`. This is the value of an undefined variable. For example, the statement `document.write(fig)` will result in this value (and an error message) if the variable `fig` has not been previously used or defined.

Although JavaScript keeps track of the data type currently stored in each variable, it doesn't restrict you from changing types midstream. For example, suppose you declared a variable by assigning it a value:

```
var total = 31;
```

This statement declares a variable called `total` and assigns it the value of `31`. This is a numeric variable. Now suppose you changed the value of `total`:

```
total = "albatross";
```

This assigns a string value to `total`, replacing the numeric value. JavaScript will not display an error when this statement executes; it's perfectly valid, although it's probably not a very useful "total."

Converting Between Data Types

JavaScript handles conversions between data types for you whenever it can. For example, you've already used statements like this:

```
document.write("The total is " + total);
```

This statement prints out a message such as `"The total is 40"`. Because the `document.write` function works with strings, the JavaScript interpreter automatically converts any nonstrings in the expression (in this case, the value of `total`) to strings before performing the function.

This works equally well with floating-point and Boolean values. However, there are some situations in which it won't work. For example, the following statement will work fine if the value of `total` is `40`:

```
average = total / 3;
```

NOTE

Although this feature of JavaScript is convenient and powerful, it can also make it easy to make a mistake. For example, if the `total` variable was later used in a mathematical calculation, the result would be invalid—but JavaScript does not warn you that you've made this mistake.

However, the `total` variable could also contain a string; in this case, the preceding statement would result in an error.

In some situations, you might end up with a string containing a number, and need to convert it to a regular numeric variable. JavaScript includes two functions for this purpose:

- `parseInt()`—Converts a string to an integer number.
- `parseFloat()`—Converts a string to a floating-point number.

NOTE

These functions look for a number of the appropriate type at the beginning of the string. If a valid number is not found, the function returns the special value `NaN`, meaning *not a number*.

Both of these functions will read a number from the beginning of the string and return a numeric version. For example, these statements convert the string `"30 angry polar bears"` to a number:

```
var stringvar = "30 angry polar bears";
var numvar = parseInt(stringvar);
```

After these statements execute, the `numvar` variable contains the number `30`; the nonnumeric portion of the string is ignored.

Using `String` Objects

You've already used several strings in the brief JavaScript examples found in previous chapters. Strings store a group of text characters, and are named similarly to other variables. As a simple example, this statement assigns the string `This is a test` to a string variable called `stringtest`:

```
var stringtest = "This is a test";
```

In the following sections, you'll learn a little more about the `String` object and see it in action in a full script.

Creating a `String` Object

JavaScript stores strings as `String` objects. You usually don't need to worry about this piece of information—that your strings are in fact objects—but it will explain some of the common techniques you'll see for working with strings, which use methods (built-in functions) of the `String` object.

There are two ways to create a new String object. The first is the one you've already used, whereas the second uses object-oriented syntax. The following two statements create the same string:

```
var stringtest = "This is a test";
stringtest = new String("This is a test");
```

The second statement uses the new keyword, which you use to create objects. This tells the browser to create a new String object containing the text This is a test, and assigns it to the variable stringtest.

NOTE

Although you can create a string using object-oriented syntax, the standard JavaScript syntax is simpler, and there is no difference in the strings created by these two methods.

Assigning a Value

You can assign a value to a string in the same way as any other variable. Both of the examples in the preceding section assigned an initial value to the string. You can also assign a value after the string has already been created. For example, the following statement replaces the contents of the stringtest variable with a new string:

```
var stringtest = "This is only a test.";
```

You can also use the concatenation operator (+) to combine the values of two strings. Listing 16.1 shows a simple example of assigning and combining the values of strings.

LISTING 16.1 Assigning Values to Strings and Combining Them

```
<!DOCTYPE html>

<html lang="en">
  <head>
    <title>String Text</title>
  </head>

  <body>
    <h1>String Test</h1>
    <script type="text/javascript">
      var stringtest1 = "This is a test. ";
      var stringtest2 = "This is only a test.";
      var bothstrings = stringtest1 + stringtest2;
      alert(bothstrings);
    </script>
</body>
</html>
```

This script assigns values to two string variables, `stringtest1` and `stringtest2`, and then displays an alert with their combined value (the variable `bothstrings`). If you load this HTML document in a browser, your output should resemble what's shown in Figure 16.1.

In addition to using the + operator to concatenate two strings, you can use the += operator to add text to a string. For example, this statement adds a period to the current contents of a string variable named `sentence`:

```
sentence += ".";
```

Calculating the String's Length

From time to time, you might find it useful to know how many characters a string variable contains. You can do this with the `length` property of `string` objects, which you can use with any string. To use this property, type the string's name followed by `.length`.

For example, `stringtest.length` refers to the length of the `stringtest` string. Here is an example of this property:

```
var stringtest = "This is a test.";
document.write(stringtest.length);
```

The first statement assigns the string `This is a test.` to the `stringtest` variable. The second statement displays the length of the string—in this case, 15 characters. The `length` property is a read-only property, so you cannot assign a value to it to change a string's length.

NOTE

Remember that although `stringtest` refers to a string variable, the value of `stringtest.length` is a number and can be used in any numeric expression.

Converting the String's Case

Two methods of the `String` object enable you to convert the contents of a string to all uppercase or all lowercase:

▶ `toUpperCase()`—Converts all characters in the string to uppercase

▶ `toLowerCase()`—Converts all characters in the string to lowercase

For example, the following statement displays the value of the `stringtest` string variable in lowercase:

```
document.write(stringtest.toLowerCase());
```

Assuming that this variable contained the text `This Is A Test`, the result would be the following string:

```
this is a test
```

Note that the statement doesn't change the value of the `stringtest` variable. These methods return the upper- or lowercase version of the string, but they don't change the string itself. If you want to change the string's value, you can use a statement like this:

```
stringtest = stringtest.toLowerCase();
```

NOTE

Note that the syntax for these methods is similar to the `length` property introduced earlier. The difference is that methods always use parentheses, whereas properties don't. The `toUpperCase` and `toLowerCase` methods do not take any parameters, but you still need to use the parentheses.

Working with Substrings

In the short examples so far, you've worked only with entire strings. Like most programming languages, JavaScript also enables you to work with *substrings*, or portions of a string. You can use the `substring` method to retrieve a portion of a string, or the `charAt` method to get a single character. These are explained in the following sections.

Using Part of a String

The `substring` method returns a string consisting of a portion of the original string between two index values, which you must specify in parentheses. For example, the following statement displays the fourth through sixth characters of the `stringtest` string:

```
document.write(stringtest.substring(3,6));
```

At this point, you're probably wondering where the 3 and the 6 come from. There are three things you need to understand about using index parameters, regardless of when you're using them:

▶ Indexing starts with 0 for the first character of the string, so the fourth character is actually index 3.

▶ The second index is noninclusive. A second index of 6 includes up to index 5 (the sixth character).

▶ You can specify the two indexes in either order. The smaller one will be assumed to be the first index. In the previous example, `(6,3)` would have produced the same result. Of course, there is rarely a reason to use the reverse order.

As another example, suppose you defined a string called `alpha` to hold an upper-case version of the alphabet:

```
var alpha = "ABCDEFGHIJKLMNOPQRSTUVWXYZ";
```

The following are examples of the `substring()` method using the `alpha` string:

▶ `alpha.substring(0,4)` returns ABCD.

▶ `alpha.substring(10,12)` returns KL.

▶ `alpha.substring(12,10)` also returns KL. Because 10 is the smaller of the two values, it's is used as the first index.

▶ `alpha.substring(6,7)` returns G.

▶ `alpha.substring(24,26)` returns YZ.

▶ `alpha.substring(0,26)` returns the entire alphabet.

▶ `alpha.substring(6,6)` returns the `null` value, an empty string. This is true whenever the two index values are the same.

Getting a Single Character

The `charAt` method is a simple way to grab a single character from a specified position within a string. To use this method, specify the character's index, or position, in parentheses. As you've learned, the index begins at 0 for the first character. Here are a few examples of using the `charAt` method on the `alpha` string:

▶ `alpha.charAt(0)` returns A.

▶ `alpha.charAt(12)` returns M.

▶ `alpha.charAt(25)` returns Z.

▶ `alpha.charAt(27)` returns an empty string because there is no character at that position.

Finding a Substring

Another use for substrings is to find a string within another string. One way to do this is with the `indexOf` method. To use this method, add `indexOf` to the string you want to search, and specify the string to search for in the parentheses. This example searches for "this" in the `string` string and assigns the result to a variable called `location`:

```
var location = stringtest.indexOf("this");
```

The value returned in the `location` variable is an index into the string, similar to the first index in the `substring` method. The first character of the string is index 0.

You can specify an optional second parameter in this method, to indicate the index value to begin the search. For example, this statement searches for the word `fish` in the moretext string, starting with the 20th character:

```
var newlocation = moretext.indexOf("fish",19);
```

A second method, `lastIndexOf()`, works the same way but finds the *last* occurrence of the string. It searches the string backward, starting with the last character. For example, this statement finds the last occurrence of `Fred` in the `names` string:

```
var namelocation = names.lastIndexOf("Fred");
```

As with `indexOf()`, you can specify a location to search from as the second parameter. In this case, the string will be searched backward starting at that location.

CAUTION

As with most JavaScript methods and property names, `indexOf` is case sensitive. Make sure you type it exactly as shown here when you use it in scripts.

NOTE

One use for the second parameter of this method is to search for multiple occurrences of a string. After finding the first occurrence, you search starting with that location for the second one, and so on.

Using Numeric Arrays

An *array* is a numbered group of data items that you can treat as a single unit. For example, you might use an array called `scores` to store several scores for a game. Arrays can contain strings, numbers, objects, or other types of data. Each item in an array is called an *element* of the array.

Creating a Numeric Array

Unlike most other types of JavaScript variables, you typically need to declare an array before you use it. The following example creates an array with four elements:

```
scores = new Array(4);
```

To assign a value to the array, you use an index in brackets. As you've seen earlier in this chapter, indexes begin with 0, so the elements of the array in this example would be numbered 0 to 3. These statements assign values to the four elements of the array:

```
scores[0] = 39;
scores[1] = 40;
scores[2] = 100;
scores[3] = 49;
```

You can also declare an array and specify values for elements at the same time. This statement creates the same `scores` array in a single line:

```
scores = new Array(39,40,100,49);
```

You can also use a shorthand syntax to declare an array and specify its contents. The following statement is an alternative way to create the `scores` array:

```
scores = [39,40,100,49];
```

Understanding Array Length

Like strings, arrays have a `length` property. This tells you the number of elements in the array. If you specified the length when creating the

TIP

Remember to use parentheses when declaring an array with the `new` keyword, as in `a = new Array(3,4,5)`, and use brackets when declaring an array without `new`, as in `a = [3,4,5]`. Otherwise, you'll run into JavaScript errors.

array, this value becomes the `length` property's value. For example, these statements would print the number 30:

```
scores = new Array(30);
document.write(scores.length);
```

You can declare an array without a specific length, and change the length later by assigning values to elements or changing the `length` property. For example, these statements create a new array and assign values to two of its elements:

```
test = new Array();
test[0]=21;
test[5]=22;
```

In this example, because the largest index number assigned so far is 5, the array has a `length` property of 6—remember, elements are numbered starting at 0.

Accessing Array Elements

You can read the contents of an array using the same notation you used when assigning values. For example, the following statements would display the values of the first three elements of the `scores` array:

```
scoredisplay = "Scores: " + scores[0] + "," + scores[1] +
    "," + scores[2];

document.write(scoredisplay);
```

TIP

Looking at this example, you might imagine it would be inconvenient to display all the elements of a large array. This is an ideal job for loops, which enable you to perform the same statements several times with different values. You'll learn all about loops in Chapter 18.

Using String Arrays

So far, you've used arrays of numbers. JavaScript also enables you to use *string arrays*, or arrays of strings. This is a powerful feature that enables you to work with a large number of strings at the same time.

Creating a String Array

You declare a string array in the same way as a numeric array—in fact, JavaScript does not make a distinction between them:

```
names = new Array(30);
```

You can then assign string values to the array elements:

```
names[0] = "John H. Watson";
names[1] = "Sherlock Holmes";
```

As with numeric arrays, you can also specify a string array's contents when you create it. Either of the following statements would create the same string array as the preceding example:

```
names = new Array("John H. Watson", "Sherlock Holmes");
names = ["John H. Watson", "Sherlock Holmes"];
```

You can use string array elements anywhere you would use a string. You can even use the string methods introduced earlier. For example, the following statement prints the first four characters of the first element of the names array, resulting in John:

```
document.write(names[0].substring(0,4));
```

Splitting a String

JavaScript includes a string method called split, which splits a string into its component parts. To use this method, specify the string to split and a character to divide the parts:

```
name = "John Q. Public";
parts = name.split(" ");
```

In this example, the name string contains the name John Q. Public. The split method in the second statement splits the name string at each space, resulting in three strings. These are stored in a string array called parts. After the sample statements execute, the elements of parts contain the following:

▶ parts[0] = "John"

▶ parts[1] = "Q."

▶ parts[2] = "Public"

JavaScript also includes an array method, join, that performs the opposite function. This statement reassembles the parts array into a string:

```
fullname = parts.join(" ");
```

The value in the parentheses specifies a character to separate the parts of the array. In this case, a space is used, resulting in the final string `John Q. Public`. If you do not specify a character, commas are used.

Sorting a String Array

JavaScript also includes a `sort` method for arrays, which returns an alphabetically sorted version of the array. For example, the following statements initialize an array of four names and sort it:

```
names[0] = "Public, John Q.";
names[1] = "Doe, Jane";
names[2] = "Duck, Daisy";
names[3] = "Mouse, Mickey";
sortednames = names.sort();
```

The last statement sorts the `names` array and stores the result in a new array, `sortednames`.

Sorting a Numeric Array

Because the `sort` method sorts alphabetically, it won't work with a numeric array—at least not the way you'd expect. If an array contains the numbers 4, 10, 30, and 200, for example, it would sort them as 10, 200, 30, 4—not even close. Fortunately, there's a solution: You can specify a function in the `sort` method's parameters, and that function is used to compare the numbers. The following code sorts a numeric array correctly:

```
function numbercompare(a,b) {
    return a-b;
}
numbers = new Array(30, 10, 200, 4);
sortednumbers = numbers.sort(numbercompare);
```

This example defines a simple function, `numbercompare`, that subtracts the two numbers. After you specify this function in the `sort` method, the array is sorted in the correct numeric order: 4, 10, 30, 200.

NOTE

JavaScript expects the comparison function to return a negative number if `a` belongs before `b`, 0 if they are the same, or a positive number if `a` belongs after `b`. This is why `a-b` is all you need for the function to sort numerically.

To gain more experience working with JavaScript's string and array features,
you can create a script that enables the user to enter a list of names, and
displays the list in sorted form.

Because this will be a larger script, you will create separate HTML and
JavaScript files, as described in Chapter 14, "Getting Started with JavaScript
Programming." First, the sort.html file will contain the HTML structure
and form fields for the script to work with. Listing 16.2 shows the HTML
document.

LISTING 16.2   The HTML Document for the Sorting Example

```
<!DOCTYPE html>

<html lang="en">
  <head>
    <title>Array Sorting Example</title>
    <script type="text/javascript" src="sort.js"></script>
  </head>

  <body>
    <h1>Sorting String Arrays</h1>
    <p>Enter two or more names in the field below,
    and the sorted list of names will appear in the
    textarea.</p>
    <form name="theform">
    Name:
    <input type="text" name="newname" size="20" />
    <input type="button" name="addname" value="Add"
    onclick="SortNames();">
    <br/>
    <h2>Sorted Names</h2>
    <textarea cols="60" rows="10" name="sorted">
    The sorted names will appear here.
    </textarea>
    </form>
</body>
</html>
```

Because the script will be in a separate document, the <script> tag in the
header of this document uses the src attribute to include a JavaScript file
called sort.js. You will create this file next.

This document defines a form named theform, a text field named newname,
an addname button, and a textarea named sorted. Your script will use these
form fields as its user interface.

Listing 16.3 provides the JavaScript necessary for the sorting process.

LISTING 16.3   The JavaScript File for the Sorting Example

```javascript
// initialize the counter and the array
var numbernames=0;
var names = new Array();
function SortNames() {
    // Get the name from the text field
    thename=document.theform.newname.value;
    // Add the name to the array
    names[numbernames]=thename;
    // Increment the counter
    numbernames++;
    // Sort the array
    names.sort();
    document.theform.sorted.value=names.join("\n");
}
```

TRY IT YOURSELF ▼

Sorting and Displaying Names
continued

The script begins by defining two variables with the `var` keyword: `numbernames` is a counter that increments as each name is added, and the `names` array stores the names.

When you type a name into the text field and click the button, the `onclick` event handler calls the `SortNames` function. This function stores the text field value in a variable, `thename`, and then adds the name to the `names` array using `numbernames` as the index. It then increments `numbernames` to prepare for the next name.

The final section of the script sorts the names and displays them. First, the `sort()` method is used to sort the `names` array. Next, the `join()` method is used to combine the names, separating them with line breaks, and display them in the textarea.

To test the script, save it as `sort.js`, and then load the `sort.html` file you created previously into a browser. You can then add some names and test the script. Figure 16.2 shows the result after several names have been sorted.

▼ TRY IT YOURSELF

Sorting and Displaying Names

continued

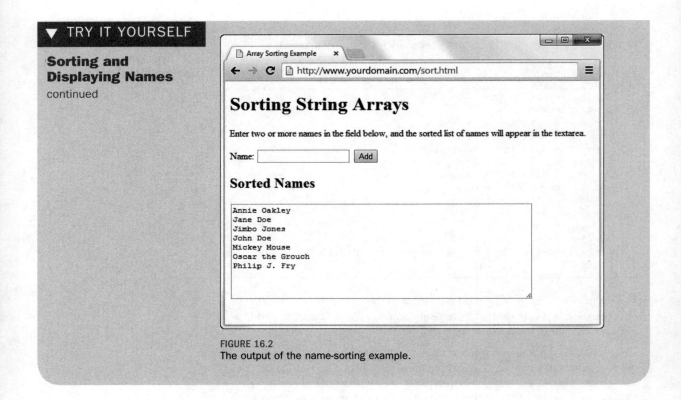

FIGURE 16.2
The output of the name-sorting example.

Summary

In this chapter, the lessons focused on variables and how JavaScript handles them. You've learned how to name variables, how to declare them, and the differences between local and global variables. You also explored the data types supported by JavaScript and how to convert between them.

You also learned about JavaScript's more complex variable types—strings and arrays—and looked at the features that enable you to perform operations on them, such as converting strings to uppercase or sorting arrays.

In the next chapter, you'll continue your foundational JavaScript education by learning more about two additional key features: functions and objects.

Q&A

Q. **What is the importance of the** `var` **keyword? Should I always use it to declare variables?**

A. You only need to use `var` to define a local variable in a function. However, if you're unsure at all, it's always safe to use `var`. Using it consistently will help you keep your scripts organized and error free.

Q. **Is there any reason I would want to use the** `var` **keyword to create a local variable with the same name as a global one?**

A. Not on purpose. The main reason to use `var` is to avoid conflicts with global variables you might not know about. For example, you might add a global variable in the future, or you might add another script to the page that uses a similar variable name. This is more of an issue with large, complex scripts.

Q. **What good are Boolean variables?**

A. Often in scripts you'll need a variable to indicate whether something has happened—for example, whether a phone number the user has entered is in the right format. Boolean variables are ideal for this; they're also useful in working with conditions, as you'll see in Chapter 18.

Q. **Can I store other types of data in an array? For example, can I have an array of dates?**

A. Absolutely. JavaScript enables you to store any data type in an array.

Q. **What about two-dimensional arrays?**

A. These are arrays with two indexes (such as columns and rows). JavaScript does not directly support this type of array, but you can use objects to achieve the same effect. You will learn more about objects in the next chapter.

Workshop

The workshop contains quiz questions and exercises to help you solidify your understanding of the material covered. Try to answer all questions before looking at the "Answers" section that follows.

Quiz

1. Which of the following is *not* a valid JavaScript variable name?

    a. `2names`

    b. `first_and_last_names`

    c. `FirstAndLast`

2. If the statement `var fig=2` appears in a function, which type of variable does it declare?

    a. A global variable

    b. A local variable

    c. A constant variable

3. If the string `test` contains the value `The eagle has landed.`, what would be the value of `test.length`?

    a. `4`

    b. `21`

    c. `The`

4. Using the same sample string, which of these statements would return the word `eagle`?

    a. `test.substring(4,9)`

    b. `test.substring(5,9)`

    c. `test.substring("eagle")`

5. What will be the result of the JavaScript expression `31 + "  angry polar bears"`?

    a. An error message

    b. 32

    c. "31 angry polar bears"

Answers

1. **a.** `2names` is an invalid JavaScript variable name because it begins with a number. The others are valid, although they're probably not ideal choices for names.

2. **b.** Because the variable is declared in a function, it is a local variable. The `var` keyword ensures that a local variable is created.

3. **b.** The length of the string is 21 characters.

4. a. The correct statement is `test.substring(4,9)`. Remember that the indexes start with `0`, and that the second index is noninclusive.

5. c. JavaScript converts the whole expression to the string `"31 angry polar bears"`. (No offense to polar bears, who are seldom angry and rarely seen in groups this large.)

Exercises

▶ Modify the sorting example in Listing 16.3 to convert the names to all uppercase before sorting and displaying them.

▶ Modify Listing 16.3 to display a numbered list of names in the textarea.

CHAPTER 17
Using JavaScript Functions and Objects

In this chapter, you'll learn about two more key JavaScript concepts that you'll use throughout the rest of this book (and in your future JavaScript endeavors). First, you'll learn the details of creating and using functions, which enable you to group any number of statements into a single block. Functions are useful for creating reusable sections of code, and you can create functions that accept parameters and return values for later use.

Whereas functions enable you to group sections of code, objects enable you to group data—you can use objects to combine related data items and functions for working with the data. You'll learn how to define and use objects and their methods, and will work specifically with two more useful objects built in to JavaScript: Math and Date.

Using Functions

The scripts you've seen so far in this book have been simple lists of instructions. The browser begins with the first statement after the <script> tag and follows each instruction in order until it reaches the closing </script> tag (or encounters an error).

Although this is a straightforward approach for short scripts, it can be confusing to read a longer script written in this fashion. To make it easier for you to organize your scripts, JavaScript supports functions, which you learned about briefly in Chapter 14, "Getting Started with JavaScript Programming." In this section, you will learn how to define and use functions.

Defining a Function

Functions are groups of JavaScript statements that can be treated as a single unit. To use a function, you must first define it. Here is a simple example of a function definition:

```
function Greet() {
    alert("Greetings!");
}
```

This snippet defines a function that displays an alert message to the user. This begins with the `function` keyword followed by the name you're giving to the function—in this case, the function's name is `Greet`. Notice the parentheses after the function's name. As you'll learn in short order, the space between them is not always empty as it is here.

The first and last lines of the function definition include curly braces ({ and }). You use these curly braces to enclose all the statements within the function. The browser uses the curly braces to determine where the function begins and ends.

Between the braces is the core JavaScript code of the function. This particular function contains a single line that invokes the `alert` method, which displays an alert message to the user. The message contains the text "Greetings!"

Now, about those parentheses. The current version of the `Greet` function always does the same thing: Each time you use it, it displays the same message in the alert pop-up window.

To make this function more flexible, you can add *parameters*, also known as *arguments*. These are variables that are received by the function each time it is called. For example, you can add a parameter called `who` that tells the function the name of the person to greet, based on the value of that parameter when the function is called. Here is the modified `Greet` function:

```
function Greet(who) {
    alert("Greetings, " + who + "!");
}
```

Of course, to actually call this function and see its behavior in action, you need to include it in an HTML document. Traditionally, the best place for a function definition is within the `<head>` section of the document. Because the statements in the `<head>` section are executed first, this ensures that the function is defined before it is used.

Listing 17.1 shows the `Greet` function embedded in the header section of an HTML document, but not yet called into action.

LISTING 17.1   The `Greet` Function in an HTML Document

```
<!DOCTYPE html>

<html lang="en">
  <head>
    <title>Functions</title>
    <script type="text/javascript">
    function Greet(who) {
        alert("Greetings, " + who + "!");
    }
    </script>
  </head>
  <body>
    <p>This is the body of the page.</p>
  </body>
</html>
```

Calling the Function

You have now defined a function and placed it in an HTML document. However, if you load Listing 17.1 into a browser, you'll notice that it does absolutely nothing besides display the text "This is the body of the page." This lack of action is because the function is defined—ready to be used—but we haven't used it yet.

Making use of a function is referred to as *calling* the function. To call a function, use the function's name as a statement in a script or as an action associated with an event. To call a function, you need to include the parentheses and the values for the function's parameters, if any. For example, here's a statement that calls the `Greet` function:

```
Greet("Fred");
```

TIP

Functions can have more than one parameter. To define a function with multiple parameters, list a variable name for each parameter, separated by commas. To call the function, specify values for each parameter separated by commas.

This tells the JavaScript interpreter to go ahead and start processing the first statement in the Greet function. Calling the function in this manner, with a parameter within the parentheses, passes the parameter "Fred" to the function. This value of "Fred" is then assigned to the who variable inside the function.

Listing 17.2 shows a complete HTML document that includes the function definition and a few buttons within the page that call the function as an action associated with an event. To demonstrate the usefulness of functions, we'll call it twice to greet two different people—using two different parameters.

LISTING 17.2   The Complete Function Example

```html
<!DOCTYPE html>

<html lang="en">
  <head>
    <title>Functions</title>
    <script type="text/javascript">
    function Greet(who) {
        alert("Greetings, " + who + "!");
    }
    </script>
  </head>
  <body>
    <h1>Function Example</h1>
    <p>Who are you?</p>
    <button type="button" onclick="Greet('Fred');">I am Fred
    </button>
    <button type="button" onclick="Greet('Ethel');">I am Ethel
    </button>
  </body>
</html>
```

This listing includes two buttons, each of which calls the Greet function a bit differently—with a different parameter associated with the call from each button.

Now that you have a script that actually does something, try loading it into a browser. If you press one of the buttons, you should see something like the screen in Figure 17.1, which shows the alert that appears when one of the buttons is pressed (I Am Ethel, in this case).

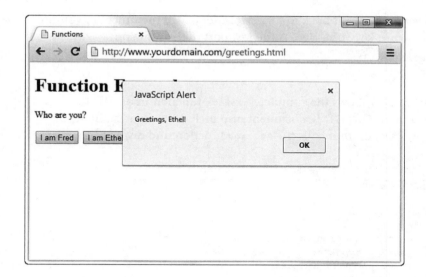

FIGURE 17.1
The output of the `Greet` function example, with one button pressed.

Returning a Value

The function you created in the preceding example displays a message to the user in an alert pop-up, but functions can also return a value to the script that called them. This enables you to use functions to calculate values. As an example, let's create a function that averages four numbers.

As usual, your function should begin with the `function` keyword, the function's name, and the parameters it accepts. We will use the variable names a, b, c, and d for the four numbers to average. Here is the first line of the function:

```
function Average(a,b,c,d) {
```

Next, the function needs to calculate the average of the four parameters. You can calculate this by adding them, and then dividing by the number of parameters (in this case, 4). Thus, here is the next line of the function:

```
var result = (a + b + c + d) / 4;
```

This statement creates a variable called `result` and calculates the value assigned to `result` by adding the four numbers, and then dividing by 4. (The parentheses are necessary to tell JavaScript to be absolutely sure to perform the addition before the division.)

NOTE

I've also included the opening brace ({) on the first line of the function. This is a common style, but you can also place the brace on the next line or on a line by itself.

To send this result back to the script that called the function, you use the `return` keyword. Here is the last part of the function:

```
return result;
}
```

Listing 17.3 shows the complete `Average` function in an HTML document. This HTML document also includes a small script in the `<body>` section that calls the `Average` function and displays the result.

LISTING 17.3　The `Average` Function in an HTML Document

```
<!DOCTYPE html>

<html lang="en">
  <head>
    <title>Function Example: Average</title>
    <script type="text/javascript">
    function Average(a,b,c,d)  {
        var result = (a + b + c + d) / 4;
        return result;
    }
    </script>
  </head>
  <body>
    <h1>Function Example: Average</h1>
    <p>The following is the result of the function call.</p>
    <script type="text/javascript">
    var score = Average(3,4,5,6);
    document.write("The average is: " + score);
    </script>
  </body>
</html>
```

If you open the script in Listing 17.3 in your web browser, you will see something like the result shown in Figure 17.2, which shows the average printed on the screen, courtesy of the `document.write` method.

You can use a variable with the function call, as shown in this listing. This statement averages the numbers 3, 4, 5, and 6 and stores the result in a variable called `score`:

```
var score = Average(3,4,5,6);
```

TIP

You can also use the function call directly in an expression. For example, you could use the `alert` statement to display the result of the function `alert(Average(1,2,3,4))`.

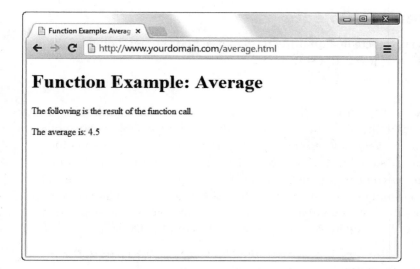

FIGURE 17.2
The output of the Average function example.

Introducing Objects

In the preceding chapter, you learned how to use variables to represent different kinds of data in JavaScript. JavaScript also supports *objects*, a more complex kind of variable that can store multiple data items and functions. Although a variable can have only one value at a time, an object can contain multiple values, which enables you to group related data items into a single object.

In this chapter, you'll learn how to define and use your own objects. You've already worked with some of them, including the following:

- ▶ **DOM objects**—These objects enable your scripts to interact with elements of the web browser and web documents. You learned about these in Chapter 15, "Working with the Document Object Model (DOM)."

- ▶ **Built-in objects**—These include strings and arrays, which you learned about in Chapter 16, "Using JavaScript Variables, Strings, and Arrays."

The syntax for working with all three types of objects—DOM objects, built-in objects, and custom objects—is the same, so even if you don't end up creating your own objects, you should have a good understanding of JavaScript's object terminology and syntax.

Creating Objects

When you created an array in the preceding chapter, you used the following JavaScript statement:

```
scores = new Array(4);
```

The `new` keyword tells the JavaScript interpreter to use built-in functionality to create an object of the `Array` type. Objects have one or more *properties*—essentially, properties are variables, with values, that are stored within the object. For example, in Chapter 15, you learned you can use the `location.href` property to give you the URL of the current document, because the value (the URL) is assigned to that property, just as a value is assigned to a variable. The `href` property is one of the properties of the `location` object in the DOM.

You've also used the `length` property of `string` objects, as in the following example from the preceding chapter:

```
var stringtest = "This is a test.";
document.write(stringtest.length);
```

NOTE

An object can also be a property of another object. This is referred to as a *child object*.

To reiterate, as with variables, each object property has a *value*. To read a property's value, you simply reference the object name and property name, separated by a period, in any expression—the example you just saw uses `stringtest.length`. You can change a property's value using the `=` operator, just as you can change the assignment of a value to a variable. The following example sends the browser to a new URL by assigning a new variable to the `location.href` property:

```
location.href="http://www.google.com/";
```

Understanding Methods

Along with properties, each object can have one or more *methods*. These are functions that work with the object's data. For example, the following JavaScript statement reloads the current document, as you learned in Chapter 15:

```
location.reload();
```

When you use the `reload()` method, you're using a method of the `location` object. Like other functions, methods can accept arguments in parentheses, and can return values. Each object type in JavaScript has its own list of built-in methods. For example, a list of built-in

methods for the `Array` object can be found at https://developer.mozilla.
org/en-US/docs/Web/JavaScript/Reference/Global_Objects/Array/
prototype#Methods.

Using Objects to Simplify Scripting

Although JavaScript's variables and arrays are versatile ways to store
data, sometimes you need a more complicated structure, which is
when objects are useful. For example, suppose you are creating a script
to work with a business card database that contains names, addresses,
and phone numbers for various people.

If you were using regular variables, you would need several separate
variables for each person in the database: a name variable, an address
variable, and so on. This would be very confusing, not to mention
quite lengthy to define.

Arrays would improve things, but only slightly. You could have a
names array, an addresses array, and a phone number array. Each
person in the database would have an entry in each array. This would
be more convenient than many, many individually named variables,
but still not perfect.

With objects, you can make the variables that store the database as
logical as the physical business cards they are supposed to represent.
Each person could be represented by a new `Card` object, which
would contain properties for name, address, and phone number.
You can even add methods to the object to display or work with the
information, which is where the real power of using objects comes
into play.

In the following sections, you'll use JavaScript to create a `Card` object
and some properties and methods. Later in this chapter, you'll use
the `Card` object in a script that will be used to display information for
several members of this datastore you've created through the use of
objects.

Defining an Object

The first step in creating an object is to name it and its properties.
We've already decided to call the object a `Card` object. Each object will
have the following properties:

- ▶ name
- ▶ email
- ▶ address
- ▶ phone

The first step in using this object in a JavaScript program is to create a function to make new `Card` objects. This function is called the *constructor* for an object. Here is the constructor function for the `Card` object:

```
function Card(name,email,address,phone) {
    this.name = name;
    this.email = email;
    this.address = address;
    this.phone = phone;
}
```

The constructor is a simple function that accepts parameters to initialize a new object and assigns them to the corresponding properties. You can think of it like setting up a template for the object. The `Card` function in particular accepts several parameters from any statement that calls the function, and then assigns these parameters as properties of an object. Because the function is called `Card`, the object created is a `Card` object.

Notice the `this` keyword. You'll use it anytime you create an object definition. Use `this` to refer to the current object—the one that is being created by the function.

Defining an Object Method

Next, you will create a method to work with the `Card` object. Because all `Card` objects will have the same properties, it might be handy to have a function that prints the properties in a neat format. Let's call this function `printCard`.

Your `printCard` function will be used as a method for `Card` objects, so you don't need to ask for parameters. Instead, you can use the `this` keyword again to refer to the current object's properties. Here is a function definition for the `printCard()` function:

```
function printCard() {
    var name_line = "Name: " + this.name + "<br/>\n";
    var email_line = "Email: " + this.email + "<br/>\n";
```

```
    var address_line = "Address: " + this.address + "<br/>\n";
    var phone_line = "Phone: " + this.phone + "<hr/>\n";
    document.write(name_line, email_line, address_line,
    phone_line);
}
```

This function simply reads the properties from the current object (`this`), prints each one with a label string before it, and then creates a new line.

You now have a function that prints a card, but it isn't officially a method of the `Card` object. The last thing you need to do is make `printCard` part of the function definition for `Card` objects. Here is the modified function definition:

```
function Card(name,email,address,phone) {
    this.name = name;
    this.email = email;
    this.address = address;
    this.phone = phone;
    this.printCard = printCard;
}
```

The added statement looks just like another property definition, but it refers to the `printCard` function. This new method will now work so long as `printCard` has its own function definition elsewhere in your script. Methods are essentially properties that define a function rather than a simple value.

Creating an Object Instance

Now let's use the object definition and method you just created. To use an object definition, you create a new object using the `new` keyword. This is the same keyword you've already used to create `Date` and `Array` objects.

The following statement creates a new `Card` object called `tom`:

```
tom = new Card("Tom Jones", "tom@jones.com",
               "123 Elm Street, Sometown ST 77777",
               "555-555-9876");
```

As you can see, creating an object is easy. All you do is call the `Card()` function (the object definition) and enter the required attributes in the same order as you defined originally (in this case, the parameters: name, email, address, phone).

> **TIP**
>
> The previous example uses lowercase names such as `address` for properties, and a mixed-case name (`printCard`) for the method. You can use any case for property and method names, but this is one way to make it clear that `printCard` is a method rather than an ordinary property.

After this statement executes, you will have a new object to hold Tom's information. This new object, now named `tom`, is called an *instance* of the `Card` object. Just as there can be several string variables in a program, there can be several instances of an object you define.

Rather than specifying all the information for a card with the `new` keyword, you can assign them after the fact. For example, the following script creates an empty `Card` object called `holmes`, and then assigns its properties:

```
holmes = new Card();
holmes.name = "Sherlock Holmes";
holmes.email = "sherlock@holmes.com";
holmes.address = "221B Baker Street";
holmes.phone = "555-555-3456";
```

After you've created an instance of the `Card` object using either of these methods, you can use the `printCard()` method to display its information. For example, this statement displays the properties of the `tom` card:

```
tom.printCard();
```

Now you've created a new object to store business cards and a method to print them. As a final demonstration of objects, properties, functions, and methods, you will now use this object in a web page to display data for several cards.

Your script will need to include the function definition for `printCard`, along with the function definition for the `Card` object. You will then create three cards and print them in the body of the document. We will use separate HTML and JavaScript files for this example. Listing 17.4 shows the complete script.

LISTING 17.4   A Sample Script That Uses the `Card` Object

```
// define the functions
function printCard() {
    var name_line = "<strong>Name: </strong>" + this.name +
    "<br/>\n";
    var email_line = "<strong>Email: </strong>" + this.email +
    "<br/>\n";
    var address_line = "<strong>Address: </strong>" + this.address
    + "<br/>\n";
    var phone_line = "<strong>Phone: </strong>" + this.phone +
    "<hr/>\n";
    document.write(name_line, email_line, address_line, phone_
    line);
}
```

```
function Card(name,email,address,phone) {
   this.name = name;
   this.email = email;
   this.address = address;
   this.phone = phone;
   this.printCard = printCard;
}

// Create the objects
var sue = new Card("Sue Suthers", "sue@suthers.com", "123 Elm
        Street, Yourtown ST 99999", "555-555-9876");
var fred = new Card("Fred Fanboy", "fred@fanboy.com", "233 Oak
        Lane, Sometown ST 99399", "555-555-4444");
var jimbo = new Card("Jimbo Jones", "jimbo@jones.com", "233
        Walnut Circle, Anotherville ST 88999", "555-555-1344");

// Now print them
sue.printCard();
fred.printCard();
jimbo.printCard();
```

TRY IT YOURSELF ▼

Storing Data in Objects

continued

Notice that the `printCard()` function has been modified slightly to make things look good with the labels in boldface. To prepare to use this script, save it as `cards.js`. Next, you'll need to include the `cards.js` script in a simple HTML document. Listing 17.5 shows the HTML document for this example.

LISTING 17.5 The HTML File for the `Card` Object Example

```
<!DOCTYPE html>

<html lang="en">
  <head>
    <title>JavaScript Business Cards</title>
  </head>
  <body>
    <h1>JavaScript Business Cards</h1>
    <p>External script output coming up...</p>
    <script type="text/javascript" src="cards.js"></script>
    <p>External script output has ended.</p>
  </body>
</html>
```

To test the complete script, save this HTML document in the same directory as the `cards.js` file you created earlier, and then load the HTML document into a browser. The browser's display of this example is shown in Figure 17.3.

▼ TRY IT YOURSELF

Storing Data in Objects

continued

FIGURE 17.3
Displaying the output of the business card example.

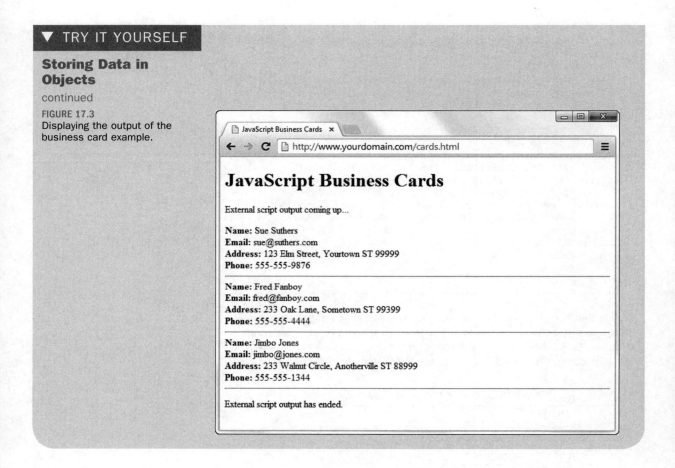

Extending Built-in Objects

JavaScript includes a feature that enables you to extend the definitions of built-in objects. For example, if you think the `String` object doesn't quite fit your needs, you can extend it by adding a new property or method. This might be very useful if you were creating a large script that used many strings and manipulated those strings in unique ways.

You can add both properties and methods to an existing object by using the `prototype` keyword. (A *prototype* is another name for an object's definition, or constructor function.) The `prototype` keyword enables you to change the definition of an object outside its constructor function.

As an example, let's add a method to the `string` object definition.
You will create a method called `heading`, which converts a string into
an HTML heading. The following statement defines a string called
`myTitle`:

```
var myTitle = "Fred's Home Page";
```

This statement would output the contents of the `myTitle` string as an
HTML level 1 heading:

```
document.write(myTitle.heading(1));
```

Listing 17.6 adds a `heading` method to the `string` object definition that
will display the string as a heading, and then displays three headings
using the new method.

LISTING 17.6   Adding a Method to the `string` Object

```
<!DOCTYPE html>

<html lang="en">
  <head>
    <title>Test of Heading Method</title>
  </head>
  <body>
    <script type="text/javascript">
    function addHeading(level) {
       var html = "h" + level;
       var text = this.toString();
       var opentag = "<" + html + ">";
       var closetag = "</" + html + ">";
       return opentag + text + closetag;
    }
    String.prototype.heading = addHeading;
    document.write("This is a heading 1".heading(1));
    document.write("This is a heading 2".heading(2));
    document.write("This is a heading 3".heading(3));
    </script>
  </body>
</html>
```

First, you define the `addHeading()` function, which will serve as the
new string method. It accepts a number to specify the heading level.
The `opentag` and `closetag` variables are used to store the HTML "begin
heading tag" and "end heading tag" tags, such as `<h1>` and `</h1>`.

After the function is defined, use the `prototype` keyword to add it as
a method of the `string` object. You can then use this method on any

String object or, in fact, any JavaScript string. This is demonstrated by the last three statements, which display quoted text strings as level 1, 2, and 3 headings.

If you load this document into a browser, it should look something like what's shown in Figure 17.4.

FIGURE 17.4
Displaying the dynamic heading example.

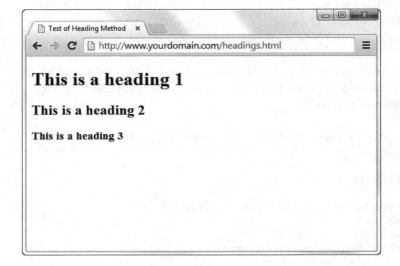

Using the Math **Object**

The Math object is a built-in JavaScript object that includes math constants and functions. You'll never need to create a Math object, because it exists automatically in any JavaScript program. The Math object's properties represent mathematical constants, and its methods are mathematical functions. If you're working with numbers in any way in your JavaScript, the Math object will be your new best friend.

Rounding and Truncating

Three of the most useful methods of the Math object enable you to round decimal values up and down:

▶ Math.ceil() rounds a number up to the next integer.

▶ Math.floor() rounds a number down to the next integer.

▶ Math.round() rounds a number to the nearest integer.

All of these methods take the number to be rounded as their only parameter. You might notice one thing missing: the capability to round to a decimal place, such as for dollar amounts. Fortunately, you can easily simulate this, as is shown in this simple function that rounds numbers to two decimal places:

```
function round(num) {
    return Math.round(num * 100) / 100;
}
```

The function shown here multiplies the value by 100 to move the decimal, and then rounds the number to the nearest integer. Finally, the value is divided by 100 to restore the decimal to its original position.

Generating Random Numbers

One of the most commonly used methods of the Math object is the Math.random() method, which generates a random number. This method doesn't require any parameters. The number it returns is a random decimal number between zero and one.

You'll usually want a random number between one and some predetermined value. You can do this with a general-purpose random number function. The following function generates random numbers between one and the parameter you send it:

```
function rand(num) {
    return Math.floor(Math.random() * num) + 1;
}
```

This function multiplies a random number by the value specified in the num parameter, and then converts it to an integer between one and the number by using the Math.floor() method.

Other Math Methods

The Math object includes many methods beyond those you've looked at here. For example, Math.sin() and Math.cos() calculate sines and cosines. The Math object also includes properties for various mathematical constants, such as Math.PI. You can see a list of all the built-in methods you can use with the Math object at https://developer. mozilla.org/en-US/docs/Web/JavaScript/Reference/Global_Objects/ Math#Methods.

Working with Math **Methods**

The `Math.random` method generates a random number between 0 and 1. However, it's very difficult for a computer to generate a truly random number. (It's also hard for a human being to do so—that's why dice were invented.) Today's computers do reasonably well at generating random numbers, but just how good is JavaScript's `Math.random` function? One way to test it is to generate many random numbers and calculate the average of all of them.

In theory, the average of all generated numbers should be somewhere near .5, or halfway between 0 and 1. The more random values you generate, the closer the average should get to this middle ground. To really do this test, let's create a script that tests JavaScript's random number function by generating 5,000 random numbers and calculates their average.

This example will use a `for` loop, which you'll learn more about in the next chapter, but this is a simple enough example that you should be able to follow along. In this case, the `for` loop will generate the random numbers. You'll be surprised how fast JavaScript can do this.

To begin your script, initialize a variable called `total`. This variable will store a running total of all the random values, so it's important that it starts at 0:

```
var total = 0;
```

Next, begin a loop that will execute 5,000 times. Use a `for` loop because you want it to execute for a fixed number of times (in this case 5,000):

```
for (i=1; i<=5000; i++) {
```

Within the `for` loop, you will need to create a random number and add its value to the `total` variable. Here are the statements that do this and continue with the next iteration of the loop:

```
    var num = Math.random();
    total += num;
}
```

Depending on the speed of your computer, it might take a few seconds to generate those 5,000 random numbers. Just to be sure something is happening, let's have the script display a status message after each 1,000 numbers:

```
if (i % 1000 == 0) {
   document.write("Generated " + i + " numbers...<br/>");
}
```

The final part of your script will calculate the average by dividing the value of the total variable by 5,000. Let's also round the average to three decimal places, for fun:

```
var average = total / 5000;
average = Math.round(average * 1000) / 1000;
document.write("<h2>Average of 5000 numbers is: " + average +
"</h2>");
```

To test this script and see just how random those numbers are, combine the complete script with an HTML document and <script> tags. Listing 17.7 shows the complete random number testing script.

LISTING 17.7   A Script to Test JavaScript's Random Number Function

```
<!DOCTYPE html>

<html lang="en">
  <head>
    <title>Math Example</title>
  </head>
  <body>
    <h1>Math Example</h1>
    <p>How random are JavaScript's random numbers?<br/>
    Let's generate 5000 of them and find out.</p>

    <script type="text/javascript">
    var total = 0;
    for (i=1; i<=5000; i++) {
      var num = Math.random();
      total += num;
      if (i % 1000 == 0) {
         document.write("Generated " + i + " numbers...<br/>");
      }
    }
    var average = total / 5000;
    average = Math.round(average * 1000) / 1000;
    document.write("<h2>Average of 5000 numbers is: " + average +
    "</h2>");
    </script>

  </body>
</html>
```

To test the script, load the HTML document into a browser. After a short delay, you should see a result. If it's close to `.5`, the numbers are reasonably random. My result was `.505`, as shown in Figure 17.5. If you reload the page, you'll likely get different results, but they should all be around `.5`.

FIGURE 17.5
The random number testing script in action.

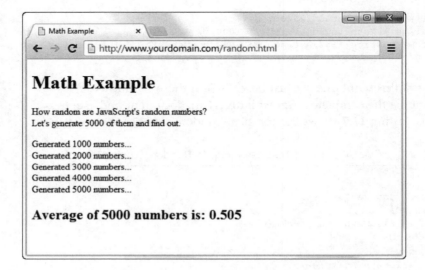

Working with Dates

The `Date` object is a built-in JavaScript object that enables you to work more easily with dates and times. You can create a `Date` object anytime you need to store a date, and use the `Date` object's methods to work with the date.

You encountered one example of a `Date` object in Chapter 4, "Understanding JavaScript," with the time/date script. The `Date` object has no properties of its own. To set or obtain values from a `Date` object, use the methods described in the next section.

Creating a `Date` Object

You can create a `Date` object using the `new` keyword. You can also optionally specify the date to store in the object when you create it. You can use any of the following formats:

```
birthday = new Date();
birthday = new Date("November 1, 2014 08:00:00");
birthday = new Date(11,1, 2014);
birthday = new Date(11,1,2014, 8, 0, 0);
```

You can choose any of these formats, depending on which values you want to set. If you use no parameters, as in the first example, the current date is stored in the object. You can then set the values using the set methods, described in the next section.

Setting Date Values

Various set methods enable you to set components of a Date object to values:

▶ setDate() sets the day of the month.

▶ setMonth() sets the month. JavaScript numbers the months from 0 to 11, starting with January (0).

▶ setFullYear() sets the year.

▶ setTime() sets the time (and the date) by specifying the number of milliseconds since January 1, 1970.

▶ setHours(), setMinutes(), and setSeconds() set the time.

As an example, the following statement sets the year of a Date object called holiday to 2014:

```
holiday.setFullYear(2014);
```

Reading Date Values

You can use the get methods to get values from a Date object. This is the only way to obtain these values, because they are not available as properties. Here are the available get methods for dates:

▶ getDate() gets the day of the month.

▶ getMonth() gets the month.

▶ getFullYear() gets the year.

▶ getTime() gets the time (and the date) as the number of milliseconds since January 1, 1970.

▶ getHours(), getMinutes(), getSeconds(), and getMilliseconds() get the components of the time.

NOTE

Along with setFullYear and getFullYear, which require four-digit years, JavaScript includes setYear and getYear methods, which use two-digit year values.

Working with Time Zones

Finally, a few functions are available to help your `Date` objects work with local time values and time zones:

▶ The `getTimeZoneOffset()` function gives you the local time zone's offset from UTC (Coordinated Universal Time, based on the old Greenwich Mean Time standard). In this case, *local* refers to the location of the browser. (Of course, this works only if the user has set his or her system clock accurately.)

▶ The `toUTCString()` function converts the `date` object's time value to text, using UTC.

▶ The `toLocalString()` function converts the `date` object's time value to text, using local time.

Along with these basic functions, JavaScript includes UTC versions of several of the functions described previously. These are identical to the regular commands, but work with UTC instead of local time:

▶ The `getUTCDate()` function gets the day of the month in UTC time.

▶ The `getUTCDay()` function gets the day of the week in UTC time.

▶ The `getUTCFullYear()` function gets the four-digit year in UTC time.

▶ The `getUTCMonth()` function returns the month of the year in UTC time.

▶ The `getUTCHours()`, `getUTCMinutes()`, `getUTCSeconds()`, and `getUTCMilliseconds()` functions return the components of the time in UTC.

▶ The `setUTCDate()`, `setUTCFullYear()`, `setUTCMonth()`, `setUTCHours()`, `setUTCMinutes()`, `setUTCSeconds()`, and `setUTCMilliseconds()` functions set the time in UTC.

Converting Between Date Formats

Two special methods of the `Date` object enable you to convert between date formats. Instead of using these methods with a `Date` object you created, you use them with the built-in object `Date` itself. These include the following:

▶ The `Date.parse()` method converts a date string, such as November 1, 2014, to a `Date` object (number of milliseconds since 1/1/1970).

▶ The `Date.UTC()` method does the opposite. It converts a `Date` object value (number of milliseconds) to a UTC (GMT) time.

Summary

In this chapter, you learned several important features of JavaScript. First, you learned how to use functions to group JavaScript statements, and how to call functions and use the values they return. Next, you learned about JavaScript's object-oriented features—defining objects with constructors, creating object instances, and working with properties, property values, and methods.

As an example of these object-oriented features, you looked closer at the `Math` and `Date` objects built into JavaScript, and learned more than you ever wanted to know about random numbers.

Q&A

Q. Many objects in JavaScript, such as DOM objects, include parent and child objects. Can I include child objects in my custom object definitions?

A. Yes. Just create a constructor function for the child object, and then add a property to the parent object that corresponds to it. For example, if you created a `Nicknames` object to store several nicknames for a person in the card file example, you could add it as a child object in the `Card` object's constructor: `this.nick = new Nicknames();`.

Q. Can I create an array of custom objects?

A. Yes. First, create the object definition as usual and define an array with the required number of elements. Then assign a new object to each array element (for example, `cardarray[1] = new Card();`). You can use a loop, described in the next chapter, to assign objects to an entire array at once.

Q. Can I modify all properties of objects?

A. With custom objects, yes—but this varies with built-in objects and DOM objects. For example, you can use the `length` property to find the length of a string, but it is a *read-only property* and cannot be modified.

Workshop

The workshop contains quiz questions and activities to help you solidify your understanding of the material covered. Try to answer all questions before looking at the "Answers" section that follows.

Quiz

1. What JavaScript keyword is used to create an instance of an object?

    a. `object`

    b. `new`

    c. `instance`

2. What is the meaning of the `this` keyword in JavaScript?

    a. The current object.

    b. The current script.

    c. It has no meaning.

3. Which of the following objects *cannot* be used with the `new` keyword?

    a. `Date`

    b. `Math`

    c. `String`

4. How does JavaScript store dates in a `Date` object?

    a. The number of milliseconds since January 1, 1970

    b. The number of days since January 1, 1900

    c. The number of seconds since Netscape's public stock offering

5. What is the range of random numbers generated by the `Math.random` function?

    a. Between `1` and `100`

    b. Between `1` and the number of milliseconds since January 1, 1970

    c. Between `0` and `1`

Answers

1. **b.** The `new` keyword creates an object instance.

2. **a.** The `this` keyword refers to the current object.

3. **b.** The `Math` object is static; you can't create a `Math` object.

4. **a.** Dates are stored as the number of milliseconds since January 1, 1970.

5. **c.** JavaScript's random numbers are between `0` and `1`.

Exercises

▶ Modify the definition of the `Card` object to include a property called `personal_notes` to store your own notes about the person. Modify the object definition and `printCard` function in Listings 17.4 and 17.5 to include this property.

▶ Modify the random number script in Listing 17.7 to run three times, calculating a total of 15,000 random numbers, and display separate totals for each set of 5,000. (As a hint, you'll need to use another `for` loop that encloses most of the script.)

CHAPTER 18
Controlling Flow with Conditions and Loops

Statements in a JavaScript program generally execute in the order in which they appear, one after the other. Because this order isn't always practical, most programming languages provide *flow control* statements that let you control the order in which code is executed. Functions, which you learned about in the preceding chapter, are one type of flow control—although a function might be defined first thing in your code, its statements can be executed anywhere in the script.

In this chapter, you'll look at two other types of flow control in JavaScript: conditions, which allow a choice of different options depending on values that are tested, and loops, which allow statements to repeat based on certain conditions.

The `if` Statement

One of the most important features of a computer language is the capability to test and compare values, and to perform different actions based on the results of the test or the values that are present. This allows your scripts to behave differently based on the values of variables, or based on input from the user.

The `if` statement is the main conditional statement in JavaScript. This statement means much the same in JavaScript as it does in English—for example, here is a typical conditional statement in English:

If the phone rings, answer it.

This statement consists of two parts: a condition (*If the phone rings*) and an action (*answer it*). The `if` statement in JavaScript works much the same way. Here is an example of a basic `if` statement:

```
if (a == 1)alert("I found a 1!");
```

This statement includes a condition (if a equals 1) and an action (display a message). This statement checks the variable a and, if it has a value of 1, displays an alert message. Otherwise, it does nothing.

If you use an if statement like the preceding example, that is, all on one line, you can use only a single statement as the action. However, you can also use multiple statements for the action by enclosing the entire if statement in curly braces ({}), as shown here:

```
if (a == 1) {
    alert("I found a 1!");
    a = 0;
}
```

This block of statements checks the variable a once again. If the value of the variable matches 1, it displays a message and sets a back to 0.

It's up to you, as a matter of personal style, whether you use the curly braces for single statements within flow control structures. Some people (such as me) find it easier to read if all the flow control structures are clearly delineated through the use of curly braces no matter their length, and other developers are perfectly happy using a mix of single-line conditional statements and statements within braces. It doesn't really matter which you use; just try to use them consistently for easier ongoing maintenance.

Conditional Operators

NOTE

Either side of the conditional expression can be a variable, a constant, or an expression. You can compare a variable and a value, or compare two variables. (You can also compare two constants, but there's usually no reason to.)

The action part of an if statement can include any of the JavaScript statements you've already learned (and those you haven't, for that matter), but the condition part of the statement uses its own syntax. This is called a *conditional expression*.

A conditional expression usually includes two values to be compared (in the preceding example, the values were a and 1). These values can be variables, constants, or even expressions in themselves.

Between the two values to be compared is a *conditional operator*. This operator tells JavaScript how to compare the two values. For instance, the == operator that you saw in the preceding section is used to test whether the two values are equal.

Various conditional operators are available:

- `==` —Is equal to
- `!=` —Is not equal to
- `<` —Is less than
- `>` —Is greater than
- `>=` —Is greater than or equal to
- `<=` —Is less than or equal to

Combining Conditions with Logical Operators

Often, you'll want to check a variable for more than one possible value, or check more than one variable at once. JavaScript includes *logical operators*, also known as Boolean operators, for this purpose. For example, the following two statements check different conditions and use the same action:

```
if (phone == "") alert("error!");
if (email == "") alert("error!");
```

Using a logical operator, you can combine them into a single statement:

```
if ((phone == "") || (email == "")) alert("Something Is
Missing!");
```

This statement uses the logical `or` operator (`||`) to combine the conditions. Translated to English, this would be, "If the phone number is blank or the email address is blank, display an error message."

An additional logical operator is the `And` operator, `&&`. Consider this statement:

```
if ((phone == "") && (email == "")) alert("Both Values Are
Missing!");
```

In this case, the error message will be displayed only if *both* the email address and phone number variables are blank.

A third logical operator is the exclamation mark (`!`), which means `Not`. It can be used to invert an expression—in other words, a true

CAUTION

Be sure not to confuse the equality operator (`==`) with the assignment operator (`=`), even though they both might be read or referred to as "equals." Remember to use `=` when *assigning* a value to a variable, and `==` when *comparing* values. Confusing these two is one of the most common mistakes in programming (JavaScript or otherwise).

TIP

If the JavaScript interpreter discovers the answer to a conditional expression before reaching the end, it does not evaluate the rest of the condition. For example, if the first of two conditions separated by the `||` operator is true, the second is not evaluated because the condition (one or the other) has already been met. You can take advantage of operators to improve the speed of your scripts.

TIP

Logical operators are powerful, but it's easy to accidentally create an impossible condition with them. For example, the condition ((a < 10) && (a > 20)) might look correct at first glance. However, if you read it out loud, you get "If a is less than 10 and a is greater than 20"—an impossibility in our universe. In this case, Or (||) should have been used to make a meaningful condition.

expression would become false, and a false one would become true. For example, here's a statement that uses the Not operator:

```
if (!phone == "") alert("phone is OK");
```

In this statement, the ! (Not) operator inverts the condition, so the action of the if statement is executed only if the phone number variable is *not* blank. You could also use the != (Not equal) operator to simplify this statement:

```
if (phone != "") alert("phone is OK");
```

Both of the preceding statements will alert you if the phone variable has a value assigned to it (it is not blank, or null).

The else Keyword

An additional feature of the if statement is the else keyword. Much like its English-language counterpart, else tells the JavaScript interpreter what to do if the condition in the if statement isn't met. The following is a simple example of the else keyword in action:

```
if (a == 1) {
    alert("Found a 1!");
    a = 0;
} else {
    alert("Incorrect value: " + a);
}
```

NOTE

Like the if statement, else can be followed either by a single action statement or by a number of statements enclosed in braces.

This snippet displays a message and resets the variable a if the condition is met. If the condition is *not* met (if a is not 1), a different message is displayed courtesy of the else statement.

Using Shorthand Conditional Expressions

In addition to the if statement, JavaScript provides a shorthand type of conditional expression that you can use to make quick decisions. This uses a peculiar syntax that is also found in other languages, such as C. A conditional expression looks like this:

```
variable = (condition) ? (value if true) : (value if false);
```

This construction ends up assigning one of two values to the variable: one value if the condition is true, and another value if it is false. Here is an example of a conditional expression:

```
value = (a == 1) ? 1 : 0;
```

This statement might look confusing, but it is equivalent to the following `if` statement:

```
if (a == 1) {
   value = 1;
} else {
   value = 0;
}
```

In other words, the value directly after the question mark (?) will be used if the condition is true, and the value directly after the colon (:) will be used if the condition is false. The colon and what follows represents the `else` portion of the statement, were it written as an `if...else` statement and, like the `else` portion of the `if` statement, is optional.

These shorthand expressions can be used anywhere JavaScript expects a value. They provide a quick way to make simple decisions about values. As an example, here's a quick way to display a grammatically correct message about a variable:

```
document.write("Found " + counter +
    ((counter == 1) ? " word." : " words."));
```

This prints the message `Found 1 word` if the `counter` variable has a value of `1`, and `Found 2 words` if its value is `2` or greater. You might, in fact, find that conditional expressions are not quicker or easier for you to use, and that is perfectly fine. You should, however, know what they look like and how to read them, should you encounter them in someone else's code in the future.

Testing Multiple Conditions with `if` **and** `else`

You now have all the pieces necessary to create a script using `if` and `else` statements to control flow. In Chapter 4, "Understanding JavaScript," you created a simple script that displays the current date and time. We'll use that knowledge here as you create a script that uses conditions to display a greeting that depends on the time: "Good morning," "Good afternoon," "Good evening," or "Good day." To accomplish this task, you can use a combination of several `if` statements:

```
if (hour_of_day < 10)  {
    document.write("Good morning.");
}  else if ((hour_of_day >= 14) && (hour_of_day <= 17))  {
    document.write("Good afternoon.");
}  else if (hour_of_day >= 17)  {
    document.write("Good evening.");
}  else {
    document.write("Good day.");
}
```

The first statement checks the `hour_of_day` variable for a value less than 10—in other words, it checks whether the current time is before 10:00 a.m. If so, it displays the greeting "Good morning."

The second statement checks whether the time is between 2:00 p.m. and 5:00 p.m. and, if so, displays "Good afternoon." This statement uses `else if` to indicate that this condition will be tested only if the preceding one failed—if it's morning, there's no need to check whether it's afternoon. Similarly, the third statement checks for times after 5:00 p.m. and displays "Good evening."

The final statement uses a simple `else`, meaning it will be executed if none of the previous conditions matched. This covers the times between 10:00 a.m. and 2:00 p.m. (neglected by the other statements) and displays "Good day."

The HTML File

To try this example in a browser, you'll need an HTML file. We will keep the JavaScript code separate, so Listing 18.1 is the complete HTML file. Save it as `timegreet.html` but don't load it into the browser until you've prepared the JavaScript file in the next section.

LISTING 18.1 The HTML File for the Time and Greeting Example

```
<!DOCTYPE html>

<html lang="en">
  <head>
    <title>Time Greet Example</title>
  </head>
  <body>
```

```
      <h1>Current Date and Time</h1>
      <script type="text/javascript" src="timegreet.js" > </script>
   </body>
</html>
```

The JavaScript File

Listing 18.2 shows the complete JavaScript file for the time-greeting example. This uses the built-in `Date` object functions to find the current date and store it in `hour_of_day`, `minute_of_hour`, and `seconds_of_minute` variables. Next, `document.write` statements display the current time, and the `if` and `else` statements introduced earlier display an appropriate greeting.

LISTING 18.2   A Script to Display the Current Time and a Greeting

```
// Get the current date
now = new Date();

// Split into hours, minutes, seconds
hour_of_day = now.getHours();
minute_of_hour = now.getMinutes();
seconds_of_minute = now.getSeconds();

// Display the time
document.write("<h2>");
document.write(hour_of_day + ":" + minute_of_hour +
               ":" + seconds_of_minute);
document.write("</h2>");

// Display a greeting
document.write("<p>");
if  (hour_of_day < 10)   {
     document.write("Good morning.");
}  else if ((hour_of_day >= 14) && (hour_of_day <= 17)) {
     document.write("Good afternoon.");
}  else if (hour_of_day >= 17)  {
     document.write("Good evening.");
}  else  {
     document.write("Good day.");
}
document.write("</p>");
```

To try this example, save this file as `timegreet.js` and then load the `timegreet.html` file into your browser. Figure 18.1 shows the results of this script.

FIGURE 18.1
The output of the time-greeting example.

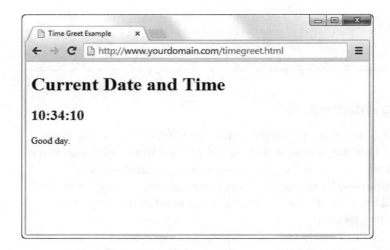

Using Multiple Conditions with switch

In Listing 18.2, you used several if...else statements in a row to test for different conditions. Here is another example of this technique:

```
if (button=="next") {
    window.location="next.html";
} else if (button=="previous") {
    window.location="previous.html";
} else if (button=="home") {
    window.location="home.html";
} else if (button=="back") {
    window.location="menu.html";
}
```

Although this construction is a logical way of doing things, this method can get messy if each if statement has its own block of code with several statements in it. As an alternative, JavaScript includes the switch statement, which enables you to combine several tests of the same variable or expression into a single block of statements. The following shows the same example converted to use switch:

```
switch(button) {
    case "next":
        window.location="next.html";
        break;
    case "previous":
        window.location="previous.html";
        break;
```

```
case "home":
    window.location="home.html";
    break;
case "back":
    window.location="menu.html";
    break;
default:
    window.alert("Wrong button.");
}
```

The switch statement has several components:

▶ The initial switch statement. This statement includes the value to test (in this case, button) in parentheses.

▶ Braces ({ and }) enclose the contents of the switch statement, similar to a function or an if statement.

▶ One or more case statements. Each of these statements specifies a value to compare with the value specified in the switch statement. If the values match, the statements after the case statement are executed. Otherwise, the next case is tried.

▶ The break statement is used to end each case. This skips to the end of the switch. If break is not included, statements in multiple cases might be executed whether or not they match.

▶ Optionally, the default case can be included and followed by one or more statements that are executed if none of the other cases was matched.

NOTE

You can use multiple statements after each case statement within the switch structure, and not just the single line statements shown here. You don't need to enclose them in braces. If the case matches, the JavaScript interpreter executes statements until it encounters a break or the next case.

One of the main benefits of using a switch statement instead of an if...else statement is readability—in one glance you know that all the conditional tests are for the same expression, and therefore you can focus on understanding the desired outcome of the conditional tests. But using a switch statement is purely optional—you might find you prefer if...else statements, and there's nothing wrong with that. Any efficiency gains in using a switch statement instead of an if...else statement will not be noticeable to human eyes, if any is even present at all. The bottom line is this: Use what you like.

Using for Loops

The for keyword is the first tool to consider for creating loops, much as you saw in the preceding chapter during the random number example. A for loop typically uses a variable (called a *counter* or an *index*) to keep track of how many times the loop has executed, and it stops when the counter reaches a certain number. A basic `for` statement looks like this:

```
for (var = 1; var < 10; var++) {
   // more code
}
```

There are three parameters to the `for` loop, each separated by semicolons:

▶ The first parameter (`var = 1` in the example) specifies a variable and assigns an initial value to it. This is called the *initial expression* because it sets up the initial state for the loop.

▶ The second parameter (`var < 10` in the example) is a condition that must remain true to keep the loop running. This is called the *condition* of the loop.

▶ The third parameter (`var++` in the example) is a statement that executes with each iteration of the loop. This is called the *increment expression* because it is typically used to increment the counter. The increment expression executes at the end of each loop iteration.

After the three parameters are specified, a left brace (`{`) is used to signal the beginning of a block. A right brace (`}`) is used at the end of the block. All the statements between the braces will be executed with each iteration of the loop.

The parameters for a `for` loop might sound a bit confusing, but after you're used to it, you'll use `for` loops frequently. Here is a simple example of this type of loop:

```
for (i=0; i<10; i++) {
   document.write("This is line " + i + "<br />");
}
```

These statements define a loop that uses the variable `i`, initializes it with the value of `0`, and loops as long as the value of `i` is less than `10`. The increment expression, `i++`, adds one to the value of `i` with each iteration of the loop. Because this happens at the end of the loop, the output will be nine lines of text.

When a loop includes only a single statement between the braces, as in this example, you can omit the braces if you want. The following statement defines the same loop without braces:

```
for (i=0; i<10; i++)
    document.write("This is line " + i + "<br />");
```

The loop in this example contains a document.write statement that will be repeatedly executed. To see just what this loop does, you can add it to a <script> section of an HTML document as shown in Listing 18.3.

LISTING 18.3 A Loop Using the for Keyword

```
<!DOCTYPE html>

<html lang="en">
  <head>
    <title>Using a for Loop</title>
  </head>
  <body>
    <h1>Using a for Loop</h1>
    <p>The following is the output of the <strong>for</strong>
    loop:</p>
    <script type="text/javascript">
    for (i=1;i<10;i++) {
       document.write("This is line " + i + "<br />");
    }
    </script>
  </body>
</html>
```

This example displays a message containing the current value of the loop's counter during each iteration. The output of Listing 18.3 is shown in Figure 18.2.

Notice that the loop was executed only nine times. This is because the conditional is i<10—i is less than 10. When the counter (i) is incremented to 10, the expression is no longer true. If you want the loop to count to 10, you will have to change the conditional; either i<=10 or i<11 will work fine.

The for loop is traditionally used to count from one number to another, but you can use just about any statement for the initialization, condition, and increment. However, there's usually a better way to do other types of loops with the while keyword, described in the next section.

TIP

It's a good style convention to use braces with all loops whether they contain one statement or many statements. This makes it easy to add statements to the loop later without causing syntax errors.

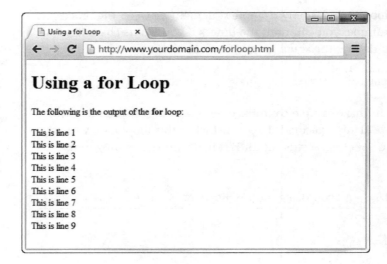

Using while **Loops**

Another keyword for loops in JavaScript is while. Unlike for loops, while loops don't necessarily use a variable to count. Instead, they continue to execute as long as a condition is true. In fact, if the condition starts out as false, the statements won't execute at all.

The while statement includes the condition in parentheses, and it is followed by a block of statements within braces, just like a for loop. Here is a simple while loop:

```
while (total < 10) {
    n++;
    total += values[n];
}
```

This loop uses a counter, n, to iterate through the values array. Rather than stopping at a certain count, however, it stops when the total of the values reaches 10.

You might have thought that you could have done the same thing with a for loop, and you'd be correct:

```
for (n=0;total < 10; n++) {
    total += values[n];
}
```

As a matter of fact, the `for` loop is nothing more than a special kind of `while` loop that handles an initialization and an increment for you all in one line. You can generally use `while` for any loop. However, it's best to choose whichever type of loop makes the most sense for the job, or takes the least amount of typing.

Using `do...while` Loops

JavaScript, like many other programming languages, includes a third type of loop: the `do...while` loop. This type of loop is similar to an ordinary `while` loop, with one difference: The condition is tested at +the *end* of the loop rather than the beginning. Here is a typical `do...while` loop:

```
do {
    n++;
    total += values[n];
}
while (total < 10);
```

As you've probably noticed, this is basically an upside-down version of the previous `while` example. There is one difference: With the `do` loop, the condition is tested at the *end* of the loop. This means that the statements in the loop will always be executed at least once, even if the condition is never true.

NOTE

As with the `for` and `while` loops, the `do` loop can include a single statement without braces, or a number of statements enclosed in braces.

Working with Loops

Although you can use simple `for` and `while` loops for straightforward tasks, there are some considerations you should make when using more complicated loops. In the next sections, we'll look at infinite loops (to be avoided!) and the `break` and `continue` statements, which give you more control over the execution of your loops.

Creating an Infinite Loop

The `for` and `while` loops give you quite a bit of control over the loop. In some cases, this can cause problems if you're not careful. For example, look at the following loop code:

```
while (i < 10) {
    n++;
    values[n] = 0;
}
```

There's a mistake in this example. The condition of the `while` loop refers to the `i` variable, but that variable doesn't actually change during the loop—the `n` variable does. This creates an *infinite loop*. The loop will continue executing until the user stops it, or until it generates an error of some kind.

Infinite loops can't always be stopped by the user, except by quitting the browser—and some loops can even prevent the browser from quitting, or cause a crash.

Obviously, infinite loops are something to avoid. They can also be difficult to spot because JavaScript won't give you an error that actually tells you there is an infinite loop. Thus, each time you create a loop in a script, you should be careful to make sure there's a way out.

Occasionally, you might want to create a long-running and seemingly infinite loop deliberately. For example, you might want your program to execute until the user explicitly stops it, or until you provide an escape route with the `break` statement, which is introduced in the next section. Here's an easy way to create an infinite loop:

```
while (true) {
    //more code
}
```

Because the value `true` is the conditional, this loop will always find its condition to be true.

Escaping from a Loop

There is a way out of a long-running and seemingly infinite loop. You can use the `break` statement at some point during the loop to exit immediately and continue with the first statement after the loop. Here is a simple example of the use of `break`:

```
while (true) {
    n++;
    if (values[n] == 1) break;
}
```

Although the `while` statement is set up as an infinite loop, the `if` statement checks the corresponding value of an array, and if it finds a value of `1`, it exits the loop.

When the JavaScript interpreter encounters a `break` statement, it skips the rest of the loop and continues the script with the first statement after the right brace at the loop's end. You can use the `break` statement in any type of loop, whether infinite or not. This provides an easy way to exit if an error occurs, or if another condition is met.

Continuing a Loop

One more JavaScript statement is available to help you control the execution of a loop. The `continue` statement skips the rest of the loop but, unlike `break`, it continues with the next iteration of the loop. Here is a simple example:

```
for (i=1; i<21; i++) {
   if (score[i]==0) continue;
   document.write("Student number "+ i + ", Score: "
   + score[i] + "<br/>");
}
```

This script uses a `for` loop to print scores for 20 students, stored in the `score` array (not shown here). The `if` statement is used to check for scores with a value of `0`. The script assumes that a score of `0` means that the student didn't take the test, so it continues the loop without printing that score.

Looping Through Object Properties

Yet another type of loop is available in JavaScript. The `for...in` loop is not as flexible as an ordinary `for` or `while` loop, but it is specifically designed to perform an operation on each property of an object.

For example, the built-in `navigator` object contains properties that describe the user's browser. You can use `for...in` to display this object's properties:

```
for (i in navigator) {
    document.write("<p>Property: " + i + "<br/>");
    document.write("Value: " + navigator[i] + "</p>");
}
```

Like an ordinary `for` loop, this type of loop uses an index variable (`i` in the example). For each iteration of the loop, the variable is set to the next property of the object. This makes it easy when you need to check or modify each of an object's properties.

▼ TRY IT YOURSELF

Working with Arrays and Loops

To apply your knowledge of loops, you will now create a script that works with arrays using loops. As you progress through this script, try to imagine how difficult it would be without JavaScript's looping features.

This simple script will prompt the user for a series of names. After all the names have been entered, it will display the list of names in a numbered list. To begin the script, initialize some variables:

```
names = new Array();
var i = 0;
```

The `names` array will store the names the user enters. You don't know how many names will be entered, so you don't need to specify a dimension for the array. The `i` variable will be used as a counter in the loops.

Next, use the `prompt` statement to prompt the user for a series of names. Use a loop to repeat the prompt for each name. You want the user to enter at least one name, so a `do` loop is ideal:

```
do {
    next = prompt("Enter the Next Name", "");
    if (next > " ") names[i] = next;
    i = i + 1;
} while (next > " ");
```

TIP

If you're interested in making your scripts as short as possible, remember that you could use the increment (`++`) operator to combine the `i = i + 1` statement with the preceding statement like so: `names[i++]=1.`

This loop prompts for a string called `next`. If a name was entered and isn't blank, it's stored as the next entry in the `names` array. The `i` counter is then incremented. The loop repeats until the user doesn't enter a name or clicks Cancel in the prompt dialog.

Next, your script can display the number of names that was entered:

```
document.write("<h2>" + (names.length) + " names entered.</h2>");
```

This statement displays the `length` property of the `names` array, surrounded by level 2 header tags for emphasis.

Next, the script should display all the names in the order in which they were entered. Because the names are in an array, the `for...in` loop is a good choice:

```
document.write("<ol>");
for (i in names) {
    document.write("<li>" + names[i] + "</li>");
}
document.write("</ol>");
```

TRY IT YOURSELF ▼

Working with Arrays and Loops

continued

Here you have a `for...in` loop that loops through the `names` array, assigning the counter `i` to each index in turn. The script then prints the name between opening and closing `<li>` tags as an item in an ordered list. Before and after the loop, the script prints beginning and ending `<ol>` tags.

You now have everything you need for a working script. Listing 18.4 shows the HTML file for this example, and Listing 18.5 shows the JavaScript file.

LISTING 18.4   A Script to Prompt for Names and Display Them (HTML)

```
<!DOCTYPE html>

<html lang="en">
  <head>
    <title>Loops Example</title>
  </head>
  <body>
    <h1>Loops Example</h1>
    <p>Enter a series of names and JavaScript will display them
    in a numbered list.</p>
    <script type="text/javascript" src="loops.js"></script>
  </body>
</html>
```

LISTING 18.5   A Script to Prompt for Names and Display Them (JavaScript)

```
// create the array
names = new Array();
var i = 0;

// loop and prompt for names
do {
    next = window.prompt("Enter the Next Name", "");
    if (next > " ") names[i] = next;
    i = i + 1;
} while (next > " ");

document.write("<h2>" + (names.length) + " names entered.</h2>");

// display all of the names
document.write("<ol>");
for (i in names) {
    document.write("<li>" + names[i] + "</li>");
}
document.write("</ol>");
```

▼ TRY IT YOURSELF

Working with Arrays and Loops

continued

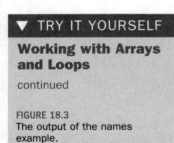

FIGURE 18.3
The output of the names example.

To try this example, save the JavaScript file as `loops.js` and then load the HTML document into a browser. You'll be prompted for one name at a time. Enter several names, and then click Cancel to indicate that you're finished. Figure 18.3 shows what the final results should look like in a browser.

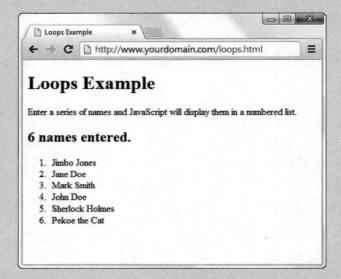

Summary

In this chapter, you've learned two ways to control the flow of your scripts. First, you learned how to use the `if` statement to evaluate conditional expressions and react to them. You also learned a shorthand form of conditional expression using the `?` operator, and the `switch` statement for working with multiple conditions.

You also learned about JavaScript's looping capabilities using `for`, `while`, and the `do...while` loops, and how to control loops further using the `break` and `continue` statements. Finally, you looked at the `for...in` loop for working with each property of an object.

Q&A

Q. What happens if I compare two items of different data types (for example, a number and a string) in a conditional expression?

A. The JavaScript interpreter does its best to make the values a common format and compare them. In this case, it would convert them both to strings before comparing. You can use the special equality operator `===` to compare two values and their types—using this operator, the expression will be true only if the expressions have the same value *and* the same data type.

Q. Why don't I get a friendly error message if I accidentally use = instead of ==?

A. In some cases, this does result in an error. However, the incorrect version often appears to be a correct statement. For example, in the statement `if (a=1)`, the variable `a` is assigned the value `1`. The `if` statement is considered true, and the value of `a` is lost.

Workshop

The workshop contains quiz questions and exercises to help you solidify your understanding of the material covered. Try to answer all questions before looking at the "Answers" section that follows.

Quiz

1. Which of the following operators means "is not equal to" in JavaScript?

    a. `!`

    b. `!=`

    c. `<>`

2. What does the `switch` statement do?

    a. Tests a variable or expression for a number of different values

    b. Turns a variable on or off

    c. Makes ordinary `if` statements longer and more confusing

3. Which type of JavaScript loop checks the condition at the *end* of the loop?

    a. `for`

    b. `while`

    c. `do...while`

4. Within a loop, what does the `break` statement do?

    a. Crashes the browser

    b. Starts the loop over

    c. Escapes the loop entirely

5. The statement `while (3==3)` is an example of which of the following?

    a. A typographical error

    b. An infinite loop

    c. An illegal JavaScript statement

Answers

1. b. The `!=` operator means *is not equal to*.

2. a. The `switch` statement can test the same variable or expression for a number of different values.

3. c. The `do...while` loop uses a condition at the end of the loop.

4. c. The `break` statement escapes the loop.

5. b. Because the condition `(3==3)` will always be true, this statement creates an infinite loop.

Exercises

▶ Modify Listing 18.4 to sort the names in alphabetical order before displaying them. You can use the `sort` method of the `Array` object, described in Chapter 16, "Using JavaScript Variables, Strings, and Arrays."

▶ Modify Listing 18.4 to prompt for exactly 10 names. What happens if you click the Cancel button instead of entering a name?

CHAPTER 19
Responding to Events

In your experience with JavaScript so far, most of the scripts you've written have executed in a calm, orderly fashion, quietly and methodically moving from the first statement to the last. You've seen a few event handlers in use in sample scripts used to focus your attention on other aspects of programming, and it is likely that you used your common sense to follow along with the actions—onclick really does mean "when a click happens." That alone speaks to the relative ease and simplicity of using JavaScript event handlers within your HTML.

In this chapter, you'll learn to use various event handlers supported by JavaScript. Rather than executing statements in a methodical order, the user can interact directly with different parts of your scripts when they invoke an event handler. You'll use event handlers in just about every script you write throughout the rest of this book, and in fact they're likely to feature prominently in most scripts you will write, period.

Understanding Event Handlers

As you learned in Chapter 14, "Getting Started with JavaScript Programming," JavaScript programs don't have to execute in order. You also learned they can detect *events* and react to them. Events are things that happen within the scope of the browser—the user clicks a button, the mouse pointer moves, or a web page finishes loading from the server (just to name a few). Various events enable your scripts to respond to the mouse, the keyboard, and other circumstances.

Events are the key methods JavaScript uses to make web documents interactive.

The script that you create and use to detect and respond to an event is generally referred to as an *event handler*. Event handlers are among the most powerful features of JavaScript. Luckily, they're also among the easiest features to learn and use—often, a useful event handler requires only a single statement.

Objects and Events

As you learned in Chapter 15, "Working with the Document Object Model (DOM)," JavaScript uses a set of objects to store information about the various parts of a web page—buttons, links, images, windows, and so on. An event can often happen in more than one place (for example, the user could click any one of the links on the page), so each event is associated with an object.

Each event has a name. For example, the `onmouseover` event occurs when the mouse pointer moves over an object on the page. When the pointer moves over a particular link, the `onmouseover` event is sent to that link's event handler, if it has one. In the next few sections you'll learn more about creating and using event handlers in your own code.

Creating an Event Handler

You don't need the `<script>` tag to invoke an event handler. Instead, you use the event name and code to invoke the event handler as an attribute of an individual HTML tag. For example, here is a link that invokes an event handler script when a mouseover occurs on a link:

```
<a href="http://www.google.com/"
   onmouseover="alert('You moved over the link.');">
   This is a link.</a>
```

Note that this snippet is all one `<a>` element, although it's split into multiple lines for readability here. In this example, the `onmouseover` attribute specifies a JavaScript statement to invoke—namely, an alert message is displayed when the user's mouse moves over the link.

You can invoke JavaScript statements like the preceding one in response to an event, but if you need to invoke more than one statement, it's a good idea to use a function instead. Just define the

NOTE

The previous example uses single quotation marks to surround the text. This is necessary in an event handler because double quotation marks are used to surround the event handler itself. You can also use single quotation marks to surround the event handler and double quotes within the script statements—just don't use the same type of quotation marks because that is a JavaScript syntax error.

function elsewhere in the document or in a referenced document, and then call the function as the event handler like this:

```
<a href="#bottom" onmouseover="doIt();">Move the mouse over this
   link.</a>
```

This example calls a function called `doIt()` when the user moves the mouse over the link. Using a function in this type of situation is convenient because you can use longer, more readable JavaScript routines as event handlers—not to mention you can reuse the function elsewhere without duplicating all of its code.

Defining Event Handlers with JavaScript

Rather than specifying an event handling script each time you want to invoke it, you can use JavaScript to assign a specific function as the default event handler for an event. This enables you to set event handlers conditionally, turn them on and off, and dynamically change the function that handles an event.

To define an event handler in this way, first define a function, and then assign the function as an event handler. Event handlers are stored as properties of the `document` object or another object that can receive an event. For example, these statements define a function called `mousealert`, and then assign it as the event handler for all instances of `onmousedown` in the current document:

```
function mousealert() {
    alert("You clicked the mouse!");
}
document.onmousedown = mousealert;
```

You can use this technique to set up an event handler for only a specific HTML element, but an additional step is required to achieve that goal: You must first find the object corresponding to the element. To do this, use the `document.getElementById` function.

First, define an element in the HTML document and specify an `id` attribute:

```
<a href="http://www.google.com/" id="link1">
```

TIP

For simple event handlers, you can use two statements if you separate them with a semicolon. However, in most cases it's just easier and more maintainable to use a function to perform these multiple statements.

TIP

Setting up event handlers this way enables you to use an external JavaScript file to define the function and set up the event, keeping the JavaScript code completely separate from the HTML file.

Next, in the JavaScript code, find the object and apply the event handler:

```
var link1_obj = document.getElementById("link1");
link1_obj.onclick = myCustomFunction;
```

You can do this for any object as long as you've defined it and therefore can reference it by a unique `id` attribute in the HTML file. Using this technique, you can easily assign the same function to handle events for multiple objects without adding clutter to your HTML code.

Supporting Multiple Event Handlers

What if you want more than one thing to happen when you click on an element? For example, suppose you want two functions called `update` and `display` to both execute when a button is clicked. It's very easy to run into syntax errors or logic errors such that two functions assigned to the same event won't work as expected. One solution for clean separation and execution is to define a single function that calls both functions:

```
function updateThenDisplay() {
    update();
    display();
}
```

This isn't always the ideal way to do things. For example, if you're using two third-party scripts and both of them want to add an `onload` event to the page, there should be a way to add both events. The W3C DOM standard defines a function, `addEventListener`, for this purpose. This function defines a *listener* for a particular event and object, and you can add as many listener functions as you need.

Unfortunately, `addEventListener` is not supported by older versions of Internet Explorer, so you have to use a different function, `attachEvent`, in that browser. In Chapter 21, "JavaScript Best Practices," you'll create a function that combines these two for a cross-browser event-adding script.

Using the event Object

When an event occurs, you might want or need to know more about the event in order for your script to perform different actions—for example, for a keyboard event, you might want to know which key was pressed, especially if your script performs different actions depending on whether the j key or the l key was pressed. The DOM includes an `event` object that provides this type of granular information.

To use the `event` object, you can pass it on to your event handler function. For example, this statement defines an `onkeypress` event that passes the `event` object to a function:

```
<body onkeypress="getKey(event);">
```

You can then define your function to accept the event as a parameter:

```
function getKey(e) {
    // more code
}
```

In Firefox, Safari, Opera, and Chrome, an `event` object is automatically passed to the event handler function, so this will work even if you use JavaScript rather than HTML to define an event handler. In Internet Explorer, the most recent event is stored in the `window.event` object. In the previous HTML snippet, this object is passed to the event handler function; so, depending on your browser, the wrong object (or no object) might be passed along in this scenario and your JavaScript code will need to do a little work to determine the correct object:

```
function getkey(e) {
    if (!e) e=window.event;
    // more code
}
```

In this case, the `if` statement checks whether the `e` variable is already defined. If it is not (because the user's browser is Internet Explorer), it gets the `window.event` object and stores it in `e`. This ensures that you have a valid `event` object in any browser.

Unfortunately, although both Internet Explorer and non–Internet Explorer browsers support `event` objects, these objects have different properties. One property that is the same in both browsers is `event.type`, which is the type of event. This is simply the name of the event, such as `mouseover` for an `onmouseover` event, and `keypress` for an `onkeypress` event. The following sections list some additional useful properties for each browser.

Internet Explorer event Properties

The following are some of the commonly used properties of the event object for Internet Explorer:

▶ event.button—The mouse button that was pressed. This value is 1 for the left button and usually 2 for the right button.

▶ event.clientX—The x coordinate (column, in pixels) where the event occurred.

▶ event.clientY—The y coordinate (row, in pixels) where the event occurred.

▶ event.altkey—A flag that indicates whether the Alt key was pressed during the event.

▶ event.ctrlkey—A flag that indicates whether the Ctrl key was pressed.

▶ event.shiftkey—A flag that indicates whether the Shift key was pressed.

▶ event.keyCode—The key code (in Unicode) for the key that was pressed.

▶ event.srcElement—The object where the element occurred.

Non–Internet Explorer event Properties

The following are some of the commonly used properties of the event object for modern browsers that are not Internet Explorer:

▶ event.modifiers—A flag that indicates which modifier keys (Shift, Ctrl, Alt, and so on) were held down during the event. This value is an integer that combines binary values representing the different keys.

▶ event.pageX—The x coordinate of the event within the web page.

▶ event.pageY—The y coordinate of the event within the web page.

▶ event.which—The key code for keyboard events (in Unicode), or the button that was pressed for mouse events. (It's best to use the cross-browser button property instead.)

▶ event.button—The mouse button that was pressed. This works just like Internet Explorer except that the left button's value is 0 and the right button's value is 2.

▶ event.target—The object where the element occurred.

> **NOTE**
>
> The event.pageX and event.pageY properties are based on the top-left corner of the element where the event occurred, not always the exact position of the mouse pointer.

Using Mouse Events

The DOM includes a number of event handlers for detecting mouse actions. Your script can detect the movement of the mouse pointer and when a button is clicked, released, or both. Some of these will be familiar to you already because you have seen them in action in previous chapters.

Over and Out

You've already seen the first and most common event handler, onmouseover, which is called when a user's mouse pointer moves over a link or another object. Note that onmouseout is the opposite—it is called when the user's mouse pointer moves out of the object's border. Unless something strange happens and the user's mouse never moves again while the viewer is viewing the particular document, you can count on onmouseout happening sometime after onmouseover.

onmouseout is particularly useful if your script has made a visual change within the document when the user's mouse pointer moved over the object—for example, displaying a message in the status line or changing an image. You can use an onmouseout event handler to undo the action when the pointer moves away.

TIP

One of the most common uses for the onmouseover and onmouseout event handlers is to create *rollovers*—images that change when the mouse moves over them. You'll learn how to create these later in the chapter.

Ups and Downs (and Clicks)

You can also use events to detect when the mouse button is clicked. The basic event handler for this is onclick. This event handler is called when the mouse button is clicked while positioned over the appropriate object.

For example, you can use the following event handler to display an alert when a link is clicked:

```
<a href="http://www.google.com/"
    onclick="alert('You are about to leave this site.');">
    Go Away</a>
```

In this case, the onclick event handler invokes the JavaScript alert before the linked page is loaded into the browser. This is useful for making links conditional or displaying a disclaimer before sending the user away to the linked page.

If your `onclick` event handler returns the `false` value, the link will not be followed. For example, the following is a link that displays a confirmation dialog. If you click Cancel, the link is not followed; if you click OK, the new page is loaded:

```
<a href="http://www.google.com/"
   onclick="return(window.confirm('Are you sure?'));">
   Go Away</a>
```

This example uses the `return` statement to enclose the event handler. This ensures that the `false` value that is returned when the user clicks Cancel is returned from the event handler, which prevents the link from being followed.

The `ondblclick` event handler is similar, but is used only if the user double-clicks on an object. Because links usually require only a single click, you could use this to make a link do two different things depending on the number of clicks. (Needless to say, this could be confusing to the user, but it *is* technically possible.) You can also detect double-clicks on images and other objects.

To give you even more control of what happens when the mouse button is pressed, two more events are included:

▶ `onmousedown` is used when the user presses the mouse button.

▶ `onmouseup` is used when the user releases the mouse button.

These two events are the two halves of a mouse click. If you want to detect an entire click, use `onclick`, but you can use `onmouseup` and `onmousedown` to detect just one or the other.

To detect which mouse button is pressed, you can use the `button` property of the `event` object. This property is assigned the value 0 or 1 for the left button, and 2 for the right button. This property is assigned for `onclick`, `ondblclick`, `onmouseup`, and `onmousedown` events.

As an example of these event handlers, you can create a script that displays information about mouse button events and determines which button is pressed. Listing 19.1 shows a script that handles some mouse events.

LISTING 19.1 The JavaScript File for the Mouse Click Example

```
function mousestatus(e) {
    if (!e) e = window.event;
    btn = e.button;
    whichone = (btn < 2) ? "Left" : "Right";
    message=e.type + " : " + whichone + "<br/>";
    document.getElementById('testarea').innerHTML += message;
}
obj=document.getElementById('testlink');

obj.onmousedown = mouseStatus;
obj.onmouseup = mouseStatus;
obj.onclick = mouseStatus;
obj.ondblclick = mouseStatus;
```

This script includes a function, mouseStatus, that detects mouse events.
This function uses the button property of the event object to determine
which button was pressed. It also uses the type property to display
the type of event, since the function will be used to handle multiple
event types.

After the function, the script finds the object for a link with the id
attribute testlink and assigns its onmousedown, onmouseup, onclick,
and ondblclick events to the mousestatus function.

Save this script as click.js. Next, you will need an HTML document to
work with the script; this is shown in Listing 19.2.

LISTING 19.2 The HTML File for the Mouse Click Example

```
<!DOCTYPE html>

<html lang="en">
  <head>
    <title>Mouse Click Text</title>
  </head>
  <body>
    <h1>Mouse Click Test</h1>
    <p>Click the mouse on the test link below. A message
    will indicate which button was clicked.</p>
    <h2><a href="#" id="testlink">Test Link</a></h2>
    <div id="testarea"></div>
    <script type="text/javascript" src="click.js"></script>
  </body>
</html>
```

This file defines a test link with the `id` property `testlink`, which is used in the script to assign event handlers. It also defines a `<div>` with an `id` of `testarea`, which is used by the script to display the message regarding the events. To test this document, save it in the same folder as the JavaScript file you created previously and load the HTML document into a browser. Some sample results are shown in Figure 19.1.

FIGURE 19.1
The mouse-click example in action.

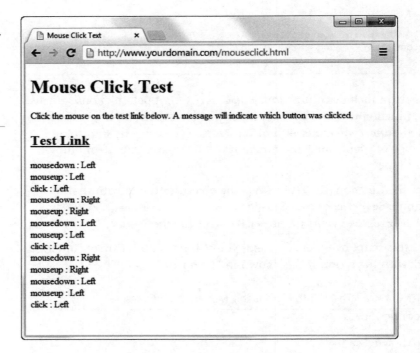

Using Keyboard Events

JavaScript can also detect keyboard actions. The main event handler for this purpose is `onkeypress`, which occurs when a key is pressed and released, or held down. As with mouse buttons, you can detect the down and up parts of the key press with the `onkeydown` and `onkeyup` event handlers.

Of course, you might find it useful to know which key the user pressed. You can find this out with the `event` object, which is sent to your event handler when the event occurs. In Internet Explorer, `event.keyCode` stores the ASCII character code for the key that was pressed. In non–Internet Explorer browsers, the `event.which` property stores the ASCII character code for the key that was pressed.

If you'd rather deal with actual characters than key codes, you can use the `fromCharCode` `String` method to convert them. This method converts a numeric ASCII code to its corresponding string character. For example, the following statement converts the `event.which` property to a character and stores it in the `key` variable:

```
var key = String.fromCharCode(event.which);
```

Because different browsers have different ways of returning the key code, displaying keys browser independently is a bit harder. However, you can create a script that displays keys for both Internet Explorer and non–Internet Explorer browsers. The following function displays each key as it is typed:

```
function displayKey(e) {
    // which key was pressed?
    if (e.keyCode) {
        var keycode=e.keyCode;
    } else {
        var keycode=e.which;
    }
    character=String.fromCharCode(keycode);

    // find the object for the destination paragraph
    var keys_paragraph = document.getElementById('keys');

    // add the character to the paragraph
    keys_paragraph.innerHTML += character;
}
```

The `displayKey` function receives the `event` object from the event handler and stores it in the variable `e`. It checks whether the `e.keyCode` property exists, and stores it in the `keycode` variable if present. Otherwise, it assumes that the browser is not Internet Explorer and assigns `keycode` to the `e.which` property.

NOTE

ASCII (American Standard Code for Information Interchange) is the standard numeric code used by most computers to represent characters. It assigns the numbers 0 to 128 to various characters—for example, the capital letters A through Z are ASCII values 65 to 90.

NOTE

The final lines in the `displayKey` function use the `getElementById` function and the `innerHTML` attribute to display the keys you type within a paragraph on the page—in this case, a paragraph with an id of `keys`.

The remaining lines of the function convert the key code to a character and add it to the paragraph in the document with the `id` attribute `keys`. Listing 19.3 shows a complete example using this function.

LISTING 19.3   Displaying Typed Characters

```
<!DOCTYPE html>

<html lang="en">
  <head>
    <title>Displaying Keypresses</title>
    <script type="text/javascript">
    function displayKey(e) {
        // which key was pressed?
        if (e.keyCode) {
           var keycode=e.keyCode;
        } else {
           var keycode=e.which;
        }
        character=String.fromCharCode(keycode);

        // find the object for the destination paragraph
        var keys_paragraph = document.getElementById('keys');

        // add the character to the paragraph
        keys_paragraph.innerHTML += character;
     }
   </script>
  </head>
  <body onkeypress="displayKey(event)">
    <h1>Displaying Typed Characters</h1>
    <p>This document includes a simple script that displays
    the keys you type as a new paragraph below. Type a few keys
    to try it. </p>
    <p id="keys"></p>
  </body>
</html>
```

When you load this example, type and then watch the characters you've typed appear in a paragraph of the document. Figure 19.2 shows the result of some typing, but you should really try it yourself to see the full effect!

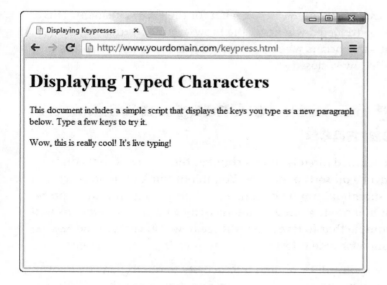

FIGURE 19.2
Displaying the output of the keys that were pressed.

Using the `onload` and `onunload` Events

Another event you might use often is `onload`. This event occurs when the current page (including all of its images) finishes loading from the server.

The `onload` event is related to the `window` object, and to define it you use an event handler in the `<body>` tag. For example, the following is a `<body>` element that uses a simple event handler to display an alert when the page finishes loading:

```
<body onload="alert('Loading complete.');">
```

Images can also have an `onload` event handler. When you define an `onload` event handler for an `<img />` element, it is triggered as soon as the specified image has completely loaded.

To set an `onload` event using JavaScript, you assign a function to the `onload` property of the `window` object:

```
window.onload = MyFunction;
```

> **CAUTION**
>
> Because the `onload` event occurs after the HTML document has finished loading and displaying, you should not use the `document.write` or `document.open` statements within an `onload` event handler, because it would overwrite the current document.

You can also specify an `onunload` event for the `<body>` element. This event will be triggered whenever the browser unloads the current document—this occurs when another page is loaded or when the browser window is closed.

Using `onclick` to Change a `<div>`'s Appearance

As you've learned already in this chapter, the `onclick` event can be used to invoke all sorts of actions. You might think of a mouse click as a way to submit a form by clicking on a button, but you can capture this event and use it to provide interactivity within your pages as well. In the example that follows, you will see how you can use the `onclick` event to show or hide information contained in a `<div>` element.

In this case, you will be adding interactivity to a web page by allowing the user to show previously hidden information when they click on a piece of text. I refer to it as a *piece of text* because, strictly speaking, the text is not a link. That is to say, to the user it will look like a link and act like a link, but it will not be marked up within an `<a>` tag.

Listing 19.4 provides the complete code for this example, which we'll walk through momentarily.

LISTING 19.4   Using `onclick` to Show or Hide Content

```
<!DOCTYPE html>

<html lang="en">
  <head>
    <title>Steptoe Butte</title>
    <style type="text/css">
    a {
       text-decoration: none;
       font-weight: bold;
    }
    img {
       margin-right: 12px;
       margin-bottom: 6px;
       border: 1px solid #000;
    }
    .mainimg {
       float: left;
    }
    #hide_e {
       display: none;
```

```
      }
      #elevation {
          display: none;
      }
      #hide_p {
          display: none;
      }
      #photos {
          display: none;
      }
      #show_e {
          display: block;
      }
      #show_p {
          display: block;
      }
      .fakelink {
          cursor: pointer;
          text-decoration: none;
          font-weight: bold;
          color: #E03A3E;
      }
      section {
          margin-bottom: 6px;
      }
  </style>
  </head>
  <body>
    <header>
        <h1>Steptoe Butte</h1>
    </header>

    <section>
        <p><img src="steptoebutte.jpg" alt="View from Steptoe Butte"
        class="mainimg" />Steptoe Butte is a quartzite island jutting out
        of the silty loess of the <a
        href="http://en.wikipedia.org/wiki/Palouse">Palouse </a> hills in
        Whitman County, Washington. The rock that forms the butte is over
        400 million years old, in contrast with the 15-7 million year old
        <a href="http://en.wikipedia.org/wiki/Columbia_River">Columbia
        River</a> basalts that underlie the rest of the Palouse (such
        "islands" of ancient rock have come to be called buttes, a butte
        being defined as a small hill with a flat top, whose width at
        top does not exceed its height).</p>
        <p>A hotel built by Cashup Davis stood atop Steptoe Butte from
        1888 to 1908, burning down several years after it closed. In 1946,
        Virgil McCroskey donated 120 acres (0.49 km2) of land to form
        Steptoe Butte State Park, which was later increased to over 150
        acres (0.61 km2). Steptoe Butte is currently recognized as a
        National Natural Landmark because of its unique geological value.
        It is named in honor of
        <a href="http://en.wikipedia.org/wiki/Colonel_Edward_
        Steptoe">Colonel Edward Steptoe</a>.</p>
```

```
      </section>

      <section>
        <div class="fakelink"
          id="show_e"
          onclick="this.style.display='none';
          document.getElementById('hide_e').style.display='block';
          document.getElementById('elevation').style.display='inline';
        ">&raquo; Show Elevation</div>
        <div class="fakelink"
          id="hide_e"
          onclick="this.style.display='none';
          document.getElementById('show_e').style.display='block';
          document.getElementById('elevation').style.display='none';
        ">&raquo; Hide Elevation</div>

        <div id="elevation">3,612 feet (1,101 m), approximately
        1,000 feet (300 m) above the surrounding countryside.</div>
      </section>

      <section>
        <div class="fakelink"
          id="show_p"
          onclick="this.style.display='none';
          document.getElementById('hide_p').style.display='block';
          document.getElementById('photos').style.display='inline';
        ">&raquo; Show Photos from the Top of Steptoe Butte</div>

        <div class="fakelink"
          id="hide_p"
          onclick="this.style.display='none';
          document.getElementById('show_p').style.display='block';
          document.getElementById('photos').style.display='none';
        ">&raquo; Hide Photos from the Top of Steptoe Butte</div>

        <div id="photos"><img src="steptoe_sm1.jpg" alt="View from
        Steptoe Butte" /><img  src="steptoe_sm2.jpg" alt="View from
        Steptoe Butte" /><img  src="steptoe_sm3.jpg" alt="View from
        Steptoe Butte" /></div>
      </section>

      <footer>
        <em>Text from
        <a href="http://en.wikipedia.org/wiki/Steptoe_Butte">
        Wikipedia</a>,photos by the author.</em>
      </footer>
    </body>
</html>
```

If you take a look at this code as rendered in your browser, you will see something like Figure 19.3.

FIGURE 19.3
The initial display of Listing 19.4. Note that the mouse pointer changes to a hand when hovering over the red text, despite the fact it is not an `<a>` link.

To begin, look at the 11 entries in the style sheet. The first entry simply styles links that are surrounded by the `<a></a>` tag pair; these links display as nonunderlined, bold, blue links. You can see these regular links in the two paragraphs of text in Figure 19.3 (and in the line at the bottom of the page). The next two entries make sure that the images used in the page have appropriate margins; the entry for `<img />` element sets some margins and a border, and the `.mainimg` class enables you to apply a style to the main image on the page, but not the set of three images at the bottom of the page.

The next four entries are for specific IDs, and those IDs are all set to be invisible (`display: none`) when the page initially loads. In contrast, the two IDs that follow are set to display as block elements when the page initially loads. Again, strictly speaking, these two IDs do not have to be defined as block elements because that is the default display. However, this style sheet includes these entries to illustrate the differences between the two sets of elements. If you count the number of `<div>` elements in Listing 19.4, you will find six in the code: four invisible and two that are visible upon page load.

The goal in this example is to change the display value of two IDs when another ID is clicked. But first you have to make sure users realize that a piece of text is clickable, and that typically happens when users see their mouse pointers change to reflect a present link. Although you can't see it in Figure 19.3, if you load the sample code on your machine and view it in your browser, the mouse pointer changes to a hand with a finger pointing at a particular link.

This functionality is achieved by defining a class for this particular text; the class is called `fakelink`, as you can see in this snippet of code:

```
<div class="fakelink"
     id="show_e"
     onclick="this.style.display='none';
     document.getElementById('hide_e').style.display='block';
     document.getElementById('elevation').style.display='inline';
">&raquo; Show Elevation</div>
```

The `fakelink` class ensures that the text is rendered as nonunderlined, bold, and red; `cursor: pointer` causes the mouse pointer to change in such a way that users think the text is a link of the type that would normally be enclosed in an `<a>` element. But the really interesting stuff happens when we associate an `onclick` attribute with a `<div>`. In the sample snippet just shown, the value of the `onclick` attribute is a series of commands that change the current value of CSS elements.

Let's look at them separately:

```
this.style.display='none';
document.getElementById('hide_e').style.display='block';
document.getElementById('elevation').style.display='inline';
```

In the first line of the snippet, the `this` keyword refers to the element itself. In other words, `this` refers to the `<div>` ID called `show_e`. The keyword `style` refers to the `style` object; the `style` object contains all the CSS styles that you assign to the element. In this case, we are most interested in the `display` style. Therefore, `this.style.display` means "the display style of the `show_e` ID," and we are setting the value of the `display` style to `none` when the text itself is clicked.

But three actions also occur within the `onclick` attribute. The other two actions begin with `document.getElementByID()` and include a specific ID name within the parentheses. We use `document.getElementByID()` instead of `this` because the second and third actions set CSS style properties for elements that are not the parent element. As you can see in the snippet, in the second and third actions, we are setting the display property values for the element IDs `hide_e` and `elevation`. When users click the currently visible `<div>` called `show_e`, the following happens:

▶ The `show_e` `<div>` becomes invisible.

▶ The `hide_e` `<div>` becomes visible and is displayed as a block.

▶ The `elevation` `<div>` becomes visible and is displayed inline.

Figure 19.4 shows the result of these actions.

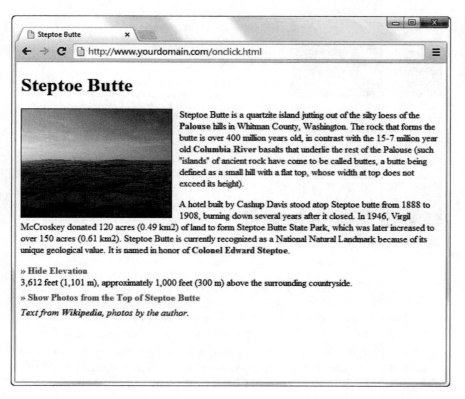

FIGURE 19.4
When Show Elevation is clicked, the visibility of it and other `<div>` elements changes based on the commands in the `onclick` attribute.

Another set of `<div>` elements exists in the code in Listing 19.4, the ones that control the visibility of the additional photos. These elements are not affected by the `onclick` actions in the elevation-related elements. That is, when you click either Show Elevation or Hide Elevation, the photos-related `<div>` elements do not change. You can show the elevation and not the photos (as shown in Figure 19.4), the photos and not the elevation, or both the elevation and the photos at the same time (see Figure 19.5).

FIGURE 19.5
The page after both Show Elevation and Show Photos from the Top of Steptoe Butte have been clicked.

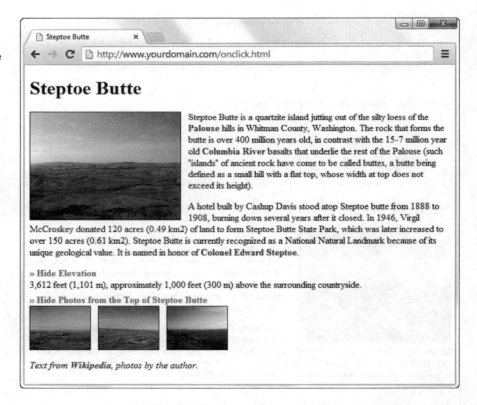

This brief example has shown you the very beginning of the layout and interaction possibilities that await you when you master CSS in conjunction with events. For example, you can code your pages so that your users can change elements of the style sheet or change to an entirely different style sheet, move blocks of text to other places in the layout, take quizzes or submit forms, and do much, much more.

Summary

In this chapter, you've learned to use events to detect mouse actions, keyboard actions, and other events, such as the loading of the page. You can use event handlers to perform a simple JavaScript statement when an event occurs, or to call a more complicated function.

JavaScript includes various other events. Many of these are related to forms, which you'll learn more about in Chapter 26, "Working with Web-Based Forms." In a longer example at the end of this chapter, you saw how to use onclick to show or hide text in a page with some design elements in it. Some new CSS was introduced: the use of the cursor property. Assigning a cursor property of pointer enabled you to indicate to users that particular text was acting as a link even though it was not enclosed in <a></a> tags as you are used to seeing.

Q&A

Q. Can you capture mouse or keyboard events on elements other than text, such as images?

A. Yes, these types of events can be applied to actions related to clicking on or rolling over images as well as text. However, other multimedia objects, such as embedded YouTube videos or Flash files, are not interacted with in the same way, because those objects are played via additional software for which other mouse or keyboard actions are applicable. For instance, if you click on a YouTube video that is embedded in your web page, you are interacting with the YouTube player and no longer your actual web page—that action cannot be captured in the same way.

Q. What happens if I define both onkeydown and onkeypress event handlers? Will they both be called when a key is pressed?

A. The onkeydown event handler is called first. If it returns true, the onkeypress event is called. Otherwise, no key press event is generated.

Q. When I use the onload event, my event handler sometimes executes before the page is done loading, or before some of the graphics. Is there a better way?

A. This is a bug in some older browsers. One solution is to add a slight delay to your script using the setTimeout method.

Workshop

The workshop contains quiz questions and exercises to help you solidify your understanding of the material covered. Try to answer all questions before looking at the "Answers" section that follows.

Quiz

Test your knowledge of JavaScript events by answering the following questions.

1. Which of the following is the correct event handler to detect a mouse click on a link?

    a. `onmouseup`

    b. `onlink`

    c. `onclick`

2. When does the `onload` event handler for the `<body>` element execute?

    a. When an image is finished loading

    b. When the entire page is finished loading

    c. When the user attempts to load another page

3. Which of the following `event` object properties indicates which key was pressed for an `onkeypress` event in Internet Explorer?

    a. `event.which`

    b. `event.keyCode`

    c. `event.onKeyPress`

Answers

1. **c.** The event handler for a mouse click is `onclick`.

2. **b.** The `<body>` element's `onload` handler executes when the page and all its images are finished loading.

3. **b.** In Internet Explorer, the `event.keyCode` property stores the character code for each key press.

Exercises

To gain more experience using event handlers in JavaScript, try the following exercises:

▶ Extend any (or all!) of the sample scripts in this section to check for specific values of key press actions before continuing on to execute the underlying JavaScript statements within their associated functions.

▶ Add commands to the `onclick` attributes in Listing 19.4 such that only one of the `<div>` elements (the elevation or photos) is visible at a time.

CHAPTER 20
Using Windows

Now that you've gotten your feet wet with basic JavaScript functionality, let's return to some specific aspects of the Document Object Model (DOM). In this short chapter, you'll learn more about some of the structural objects in the DOM—browser windows and dialog boxes—and how JavaScript can interact with them using the events you learned about in Chapter 19, "Responding to Events."

Controlling Windows with Objects

In Chapter 15, "Working with the Document Object Model (DOM)," you learned that you can use DOM objects to represent various parts of the browser window and the current HTML document. You also learned that the `history`, `document`, and `location` objects are all children of the `window` object.

In this chapter, you'll take a closer look at the `window` object itself. As you've probably guessed by now, this means you'll be dealing with browser windows.

The `window` object always refers to the current window (the one containing the script). The `self` keyword is also a synonym for the current window. As you'll learn in the next sections, you can have more than one window on the screen at the same time, and can refer to them with different names.

Properties of the `window` Object

Although there is normally a single `window` object available in a browser session, users might have more than one window object available in their browser session because they have multiple tabs open or a web page has opened a pop-up window. As you learned in Chapter 15, the `document`, `history`, and `location` objects are properties (or children) of the `window` object, and each open window object has these properties available for scripting purposes. In addition to these properties, each `window` object has the following useful properties:

▶ `window.closed`—Indicates whether the window has been closed. This makes sense only when you're working with multiple windows because the current window contains the script and cannot be closed without ending the script.

▶ `window.name`—The name specified for a window opened by a script.

▶ `window.opener`—In a new window opened by a script, this is a reference to the window containing the script that opened it.

▶ `window.outerHeight` and `window.outerWidth`—The height and width, respectively, of the outside of a browser window.

▶ `window.screen`—A child object that stores information about the screen the window is in—its resolution, color depth, and so on.

▶ `window.self`—A synonym for the current `window` object.

▶ `window.status`—The default message for the status line, and a temporary message to display on the status line. Some recent browsers disable status-line changes by default, so you might not be able to use these.

NOTE

The properties of the `window.screen` object include `height`, `width`, `availHeight`, and `availWidth` (the available height and width rather than total), and `colorDepth`, which indicates the color support of the monitor: 8 for 8-bit color, 32 for 32-bit color, and so on.

You can find a complete list of window properties (and methods) at https://developer.mozilla.org/en-US/docs/Web/API/Window.

Creating a New Window

One of the most convenient uses for the `window` object is to create a new window. You can do this to display a new document—for example, a pop-up advertisement or the instructions for a game—without clearing the current window. You can also create windows for specific purposes, such as navigation windows.

You can create a new browser window with the `window.open` method. A typical statement to open a new window looks like this:

```
myNewWindow=window.open("URL", "WindowName", "LIST_OF_FEATURES");
```

The following are the components of the `window.open` statement in the preceding example:

▶ The `myNewWindow` variable is used to store the new `window` object. You can access methods and properties of the new object by using this name.

▶ The first parameter of the `window.open` method is a URL, which will be loaded into the new window. If it's left blank, no web page will be loaded. In this case, you could use JavaScript to fill the window with content.

▶ The second parameter specifies a window name (here, `WindowName`). This is assigned to the `window` object's `name` property and is used to refer to the window.

▶ The third parameter is a list of optional features, separated by commas. You can customize the new window by choosing whether to include the toolbar, status line, and other features. This enables you to create various "floating" windows, which might look nothing like a typical browser window.

The features available in the third parameter of the `window.open()` method include `width` and `height`, to set the size of the window in pixels; `left` and `top`, to set the distance in pixels of the new window from the left side and top of the user's desktop, respectively; and several features that can be set to either `yes` (1) or `no` (0): `toolbar`, `location`, `status`, `menubar`, `personalbar`, `scrollbars`, and `resizable`, among a few others. You have to list only the features you want to use.

This example creates a small window with no toolbar or status bar:

```
newSmallWin = window.open("","small","width=100,height=120,
          toolbar=0,status=0");
```

Opening and Closing Windows

Of course, if you can open a window, you can use JavaScript to close windows as well. The `window.close` method closes a window. Browsers don't normally allow you to close the main browser window without the user's permission; this method's main purpose is for closing windows you have created. For example, this statement closes a window called `updateWindow`:

```
updateWindow.close();
```

As another example, Listing 20.1 shows an HTML document that enables you to open a small new window by pressing a button. You can then press another button to close the new window. The third button attempts to close the current window, and you'll see how well that works out later in this chapter.

LISTING 20.1 An HTML Document That Uses JavaScript to Enable You to Create and Close Windows

```
<!DOCTYPE html>

<html lang="en">
  <head>
    <title>Create a New Window</title>
  </head>
  <body>
    <h1>Create a New Window</h1>
    <p>Use the buttons below to open and close windows using
    JavaScript.</p>
    <button type="button"
            onclick="NewWin=window.open('','NewWin',
                     'toolbar=no,status=no,width=200,height=100');"
    >Open New Window</button>

    <button type="button"
            onclick="NewWin.close();"
    >Close New Window</button>

    <button type="button"
            onclick="window.self.close();"
    >Close Main Window</button>

  </body>
</html>
```

This example uses simple event handlers to do its work by providing a different handler for each of the buttons. Figure 20.1 shows the result of pressing the Open New Window button: It opens a small new window on top of the main browser window.

However, notice the error message shown in the JavaScript console in Figure 20.2. This error message appears after an attempt is made to close the main browser window from this script. As you can see, Chrome does not allow JavaScript to close the entire browser window, because JavaScript did not originally open the window.

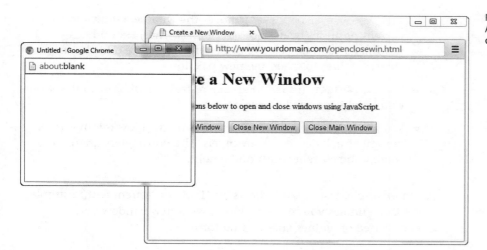

FIGURE 20.1
A new browser window
opened with JavaScript.

FIGURE 20.2
The console appropriately displays
an error when JavaScript tries to
close a window it did not open.

Moving and Resizing Windows

The DOM also enables you to move or resize windows that your scripts
have created. You can do this using the following methods for a `window`
object:

▶ `window.moveTo(x, y)` moves the window to a new position. The
parameters specify the x (column) and y (row) position.

▶ `window.moveBy(numX, numY)` moves the window relative to its current position, by `numX` or `numY` pixels. The `numX` and `numY` parameters can be positive or negative, and are added to the current values to reach the new position.

▶ `window.resizeTo(width, height)` resizes the window to the width and height specified as parameters.

▶ `window.resizeBy(numX, numY)` resizes the window relative to its current size, by `numX` or `numY` pixels. The parameters are used to modify the current width and height.

As an example, Listing 20.2 shows an HTML document with a simple script that enables you to resize and move a new window you've created based on values entered in a form.

LISTING 20.2   Moving and Resizing a New Window

```
<!DOCTYPE html>

<html lang="en">
  <head>
    <title>Moving and Resizing Windows</title>
    <script type="text/javascript">
    function doIt() {
    if ((document.changeform.w.value) &&
    (document.changeform.h.value)) {
       NewWin.resizeTo(document.changeform.w.value,
       document.changeform.h.value);
    }
    if ((document.form1.x.value) && (document.form1.y.value)) {
       NewWin.moveTo(document.changeform.x.value,
       document.changeform.y.value);
    }
    }
    </script>
  </head>
  <body onload="NewWin=window.open('','NewWin',
       'width=200,height=100');">

  <h1>Moving and Resizing Windows</h1>

  <form name="changeform">

  <p><strong>Resize to:</strong> <br/>
  <input size="5" type="text" name="w" /> pixels wide and
  <input size="5" type="text" name="h" /> pixels high </p>

  <p><strong>-- AND/OR --</strong></p>
  <p><strong>Move to:</strong> <br/>
```

```
    X-position: <input size="5" type="text" name="x" />
    Y-position: <input size="5" type="text" name="y" /> </p>
    <div><input type="button" value="Change Window"
        onclick="doIt();" /></div>
    </form>
    </body>
</html>
```

In this example, the `doIt` function is called as an event handler when
you click the Change Window button. This function checks whether
you have specified width and height values. If you have, it uses the
`self.resizeTo()` method to resize the current window. Similarly, if you
have specified x and y values, it uses `NewWin.moveTo()` to move the
window. If you have set both pairs of values, the script will both resize
and move your window. Load up this code in a web browser and give
it a try!

Using Timeouts

Sometimes the hardest thing to get a script to do is to do nothing at
all—for a specific amount of time. Fortunately, JavaScript includes
a built-in function to do this "nothing at all," which is also called
"sleeping." The `window.setTimeout` method enables you to specify a
time delay and a command that will execute after the delay passes.

You begin a timeout with a call to the `setTimeout()` method, which
has two parameters. The first is a JavaScript statement, or group of
statements, enclosed in quotation marks. The second parameter is the
time to wait in milliseconds (thousandths of seconds). For example, the
following statement displays an alert dialog box after 10 seconds:

```
timeoutID=window.setTimeout("alert('Time's up!')",10000);
```

A variable (`timeoutID` in this example) stores an identifier for the
timeout. This enables you to set multiple timeouts, each with its own
identifier. Before a timeout has elapsed, you can stop it with the
`clearTimeout()` method, specifying the identifier of the timeout to stop:

```
window.clearTimeout(timeoutID);
```

Normally, a timeout happens only once because the statement you
specify in the `setTimeout` statement is executed only once. But often
you'll want your statement to execute over and over. For example,

NOTE

Timeouts don't actually make
the browser stop what it's
doing. Although the statement
you specify in the `setTimeout`
method won't be executed until
the delay passes, the browser
will continue to do other things
while it waits (for example,
acting on other event handlers
and loading external content).

CAUTION

Like event handlers, timeouts
use a JavaScript statement
within quotation marks. Make
sure that you use a single quote
on each side of each string
within the statement, as shown
in the previous code snippet.

your script might be updating a clock or a countdown and might need to execute once per second.

You can make a timeout repeat by issuing the `setTimeout()` method call again in the function called by the timeout. Listing 20.3 shows an HTML document that demonstrates a repeating timeout.

LISTING 20.3   Using Timeouts to Update a Page Every Two Seconds

```
<!DOCTYPE html>

<html lang="en">
  <head>
    <title>Timeout Example</title>
    <script type="text/javascript">
    var counter = 0;

    // call Update function 2 seconds after first load
    timeoutID=window.setTimeout("Update();",2000);

    function Update() {
      counter++;
      var textField = document.getElementById("showText");
      textField.innerHTML = "The counter is now at " + counter;

      // set another timeout for the next count
      timeoutID=window.setTimeout("Update();",2000);
    }
    </script>
  </head>
  <body>
    <h1>Timeout Example</h1>
    <p>The counter will update every two seconds.</p>
    <p>Press RESTART or STOP to restart or stop the count.</p>
    <p id="showText"></p>
    <div>
     <button type="button"
             onclick="counter=0; Update();">RESTART</button>
     <button type="button"
             onclick="window.clearTimeout(ID);">STOP</button>
    </div>
  </body>
</html>
```

This script displays a message inside a specially named `<p>` element every two seconds, and includes an incrementing counter that displays as part of that message. The specific `<p>` tag has an `id` value of `showText` and the `Update()` function includes two lines that tell the script that the text should be placed between these two tags:

```
textField = document.getElementById("showText");
textField.innerHTML = "The counter is now at " + counter;
```

The first line creates a variable called `textField` that holds the value of the element given the `id` value of `showText`. The second line says that given that value, the text message about the counter and the counter number should be placed inside the starting and ending tags of the element with the `id` value of `showText`—that is the purpose of the `innerHTML` method, as you learned in previous chapters.

This script calls the `setTimeout()` method when the page loads, and again at each update. The `Update()` function performs the update, adding one to the counter and setting the next timeout. The RESET button sets the counter to zero and reasserts the `Update()` function, and the STOP button demonstrates the `clearTimeout()` method. Figure 20.3 shows the display of the timeout example after the counter has been running for a while.

FIGURE 20.3
The output of the timeout example, after it has been running for some time.

Displaying Dialog Boxes

The `window` object includes three methods that are useful for displaying messages and interacting with the user. You've already used these in some of your scripts. Here's a summary:

▶ window.alert(message) displays an alert dialog box. This dialog box simply gives the user a message.

▶ window.confirm(message) displays a confirmation dialog box. This displays a message and includes OK and Cancel buttons. This method returns true if OK is pressed and false if Cancel is pressed.

▶ window.prompt(message,default) displays a message and prompts the user for input. It returns the text entered by the user. If the user does not enter anything, the default value is used.

TIP

You can usually omit the explicit reference to the window object when referring to these methods because it is the default context of a script. For example, you can use alert("text") instead of window.alert("text").

When using the confirm and prompt methods, you should use a variable to receive the user's response. For example, this statement displays a prompt and stores the text the user enters in the text variable:

```
text = window.prompt("Enter some text","Default value");
```

As a further illustration of these types of dialog boxes, Listing 20.4 shows an HTML document that uses buttons and event handlers to enable you to test dialog boxes.

LISTING 20.4   An HTML Document That Uses JavaScript to Display Alerts, Confirmations, and Prompts

```
<!DOCTYPE html>

<html lang="en">
  <head>
    <title>Alerts, Confirmations, and Prompts</title>
  </head>
  <body>
    <h1>Alerts, Confirmations, and Prompts</h1>
    <p>Use the buttons below to test dialogs in JavaScript.</p>
      <button type="button"
              onclick="window.alert('This is a test alert.');">
              Display an Alert
      </button>

      <button type="button"
              onclick="window.confirm('Would you like to confirm?');">
              Display a Confirmation
      </button>

      <button type="button"
              onclick="window.prompt('Enter Text:',
              'This is the default.');">
              Display a Prompt
```

```
    </button>

  </body>
</html>
```

This document displays three buttons, and each button uses an event handler to display one of the three types of dialog boxes.

Figure 20.4 shows the script in Listing 20.4 in action. The prompt dialog box is currently displayed and shows the default value.

FIGURE 20.4
Showing a prompt dialog box as a result of clicking a button.

Summary

In this chapter, you've learned how to use the `window` object to work with browser windows, and used its properties and methods to set timeouts and display dialog boxes. Although this is not a long chapter, you did work through several examples in which you put all the pieces of the puzzle together from the previous several chapters: working with the Document Object Model to change content and window display, creating new functions, and invoking those new functions through events.

Q&A

Q. **When a script is running in a window created by another script, how can it refer to the original window?**

A. JavaScript includes the `window.opener` property, which lets you refer to the window that opened the current window.

Q. **What are some examples of using timeouts in JavaScript? I'm not sure why I would want code to go to sleep.**

A. Ideally, you want your code to execute all the time, but sometimes you need to wait for user input, or for long processes to finish, or even to ensure that users are not overloading your system by clicking on elements too often—you can include a timeout that effectively disables certain buttons for a certain amount of time, say to limit voting or "liking" something more than once every second.

Workshop

The workshop contains quiz questions and exercises to help you solidify your understanding of the material covered. Try to answer all questions before looking at the "Answers" section that follows.

Quiz

1. Which of the following methods displays a dialog box with OK and Cancel buttons, and waits for a response?

    a. `window.alert()`

    b. `window.confirm()`

    c. `window.prompt()`

2. What does the `window.setTimeout()` method do?

    a. Executes a JavaScript statement after a delay

    b. Locks up the browser for the specified amount of time

    c. Sets the amount of time before the browser exits automatically

3. True or False: JavaScript can take control of a browser window and resize it, even if the script did not open it.

    a. True

    b. False

Answers

1. **b.** The `window.confirm` method displays a dialog box with OK and Cancel buttons.

2. **a.** The `window.setTimeout()` method executes a JavaScript statement after a delay.

3. **b.** False. Only windows created by a script can be manipulated by the script.

Exercises

▶ Using timeouts and JavaScript to display date and time (which you learned earlier in this book), create a script to display a "live" clock with hours, minutes, and seconds shown.

▶ Modify Listing 20.4 to do something with the results of the `window.prompt()` dialog box—print the text, perform another action dependent on specific text, or do something that combines the two.

CHAPTER 21

JavaScript Best Practices

In this chapter, you'll learn some guidelines for creating scripts and pages that are easy to maintain, easy to use, and follow web standards. This is known as *unobtrusive scripting*: Scripts add features without getting in the way of the user, the developer maintaining the code, or the designer building the layout of the site. You'll also learn how to make sure your scripts will work in multiple browsers, and won't stop working when a new browser comes along. Additionally, and perhaps more important, these practices will help you become a better developer and a better member of the overall JavaScript developer community.

Scripting Best Practices

As you start to develop more complex scripts, it's important to know some scripting *best practices*. These are guidelines for using JavaScript that more experienced programmers have learned the hard way. Here are a few of the benefits of following these best practices:

- ▶ Your code will be readable and easy to maintain, whether you're turning the page over to someone else or just trying to remember what you did a year ago.

- ▶ You'll create code that follows standards and won't be crippled by a new version of a particular browser.

- ▶ You'll create pages that work even without JavaScript.

- ▶ It will be easy to adapt code you create for one site to another site or project.

- ▶ Your users will thank you for creating a site that is easy to use, and easy to fix when things go wrong.

WHAT YOU'LL LEARN IN THIS CHAPTER:

- ▶ Best practices for creating unobtrusive scripts
- ▶ Separating content, presentation, and behavior
- ▶ Following web standards to create cross-browser scripts
- ▶ Reading and displaying browser information
- ▶ Using feature sensing to avoid errors
- ▶ Supporting non-JavaScript browsers

Whether you're writing an entire AJAX web application or simply enhancing a page with a three-line script, it's useful to know some of the concepts that are regularly considered by those who write complex scripts for a living. The following sections introduce some of these best practices.

Don't Overuse JavaScript

It might seem counterintuitive to read, in a book about teaching you to become a competent developer using JavaScript, "don't overuse JavaScript," but it's true. Especially as HTML5 and CSS3 have matured, as has browser support for these advanced standards, there's much less of a need to use JavaScript for some of the enhanced interactions that we saw even just a few years ago. For example, some developers (myself included) spent years crafting useful JavaScript-based form validation scripts, all now rendered moot (or at least duplicative) with the inclusion of native HTML5 form field validation. So as you're thinking about what to build with JavaScript, keep the following in mind:

▶ Many of the visual effects that once needed to be coded in JavaScript can now be achieved perfectly well using CSS. When both approaches are possible (image rollovers and some types of menus come immediately to mind), CSS is usually preferable. It's well supported across browsers (despite a few variations) and isn't as commonly turned off by the user. In the rare case that CSS isn't supported, the page is rendered as standard HTML, usually leaving a page that's at least perfectly functional, even if it's not so pretty.

▶ Users are likely to spend most of their Internet time on sites other than yours. Experienced Internet users become accustomed to popular interface components such as menus, bread-crumb trails, and tabbed browsing. These elements are popular, in general, because they work well, can be made to look good, and don't require the user to read a manual first. Is familiarity with a site's operation likely to increase a user's productivity more than the potential benefits of your all-new JavaScript-heavy whizz-bang design?

▶ Users in many areas of the world are still using outdated, underpowered, hand-me-down computers and might also have slow and/or unreliable Internet access. The CPU cycles taken up by unnecessary JavaScript code might be precious to them.

► In some cases you might cost yourself a degree of search engine page rank because the search engines' spiders don't always correctly index content that's been generated by JavaScript or designs that require it for navigation.

Used carefully and with forethought, JavaScript can be a great tool, but sometimes you can have too much of a good thing.

Content, Presentation, and Behavior

When you create a web page, or especially an entire site or application, you're dealing with three key areas: *content*, *presentation*, and *behavior*—all of which you've learned about in the previous chapters.

► *Content* consists of the words that a visitor can read on your pages. You create the content as text, and mark it up with HTML to define different classes of content—headings, paragraphs, links, and so on.

► *Presentation* is the appearance and layout of the words on each page—text formatting, fonts, colors, and graphics. This is where the power of Cascading Style Sheets (CSS) comes into play.

► *Behavior* is what happens when you interact with a page—items that highlight when you move over them, forms you can submit, and so on. This is where JavaScript enters into the picture for enhanced front-end interactivity, along with server-side languages such as PHP, Ruby, and others.

It's a good idea to keep these three areas in mind, especially as you create larger sites. Ideally, you want to keep content, presentation, and behavior separated as much as possible. One good way to do this is to create an external CSS file for the presentation and an external JavaScript file for the behavior, and link them to the HTML document.

Keeping things separated like this makes it easier to maintain a large site—if you need to change the color of the headings, for example, you can make a quick edit to the CSS file without having to look through all the HTML markup to find the right place to edit. It also makes it easy for you to reuse the same CSS and JavaScript on multiple pages of a site. Last but not least, this will encourage you to use each language where its strengths lie, making your job easier.

Graceful Degradation

Among the earliest web browsers were some that didn't even support the inclusion of images in HTML. When the `<img />` element was introduced, a way was needed to allow those text-only browsers to present something helpful to the user whenever such an unsupported tag was encountered. In the case of the `<img />` tag, that facility was provided by the `alt` attribute. Web designers could assign a string of text to `alt`, and text-only browsers would display this text to the user instead of showing the image. At the whim of the page designer, the `alt` text might be simply a title for the image, a description of what the picture would have displayed, or a suggestion for an alternative source of the information that would have been carried in the graphic.

This was an early example of *graceful degradation*, the process by which a user whose browser lacks the required technical features to make full use of a web page's design—or has those features disabled—can still benefit as fully as possible from the site's content.

Let's take JavaScript itself as another example. Virtually every browser supports JavaScript, and only a small percentage of users turn it off. So do you really need to worry about that 2% of possible visitors who don't have JavaScript enabled? The answer is probably yes. One type of frequent visitor to your site will no doubt be the spider program from one of the search engines, busy indexing the pages of the Web. The spider will attempt to follow all the navigation links on your pages to build a full index of your site's content; if such navigation requires the services of JavaScript, you might find some parts of your site not being indexed. Your search ranking will probably suffer as a result.

But another important example lies in the realm of accessibility. No matter how capable a browser program is, there are some users who will access your site with other limitations, such as the inability to use a traditional mouse, or the necessity to use screen-reading software. These users are still part of your audience and presumably you want your site to be accessible to them as well, even without all of your JavaScript bells and whistles.

Progressive Enhancement

The counterpart of graceful degradation is *progressive enhancement*, in which the primary development principle is to keep the HTML documents as simple as possible so that they'll definitely work in even the most primitive browsers. After you've tested that and made sure that the basic functionality is there, you can dynamically add features that make the site easier to use or better looking for those with new browsers.

If you add these features unobtrusively, they have little chance of preventing the site from working in its primitive HTML form. Here are some guidelines for progressive enhancement:

▶ Enhance the presentation by adding rules to a separate CSS file. Try to avoid using HTML markup strictly for presentation, such as `<em>` for boldface or `<blockquote>` for an indented section.

▶ Enhance behavior by adding scripts to an external JavaScript file.

▶ Add events without using inline event handlers, as described in Chapter 19, "Responding to Events," and later in this chapter.

▶ Use feature sensing, described later in this chapter, to ensure that JavaScript code executes only on browsers that support the features it requires.

NOTE

The term *progressive enhancement* first appeared in a presentation and article on this topic by Steve Champeon. The original article, along with many more web design articles, is available on his company's website at http://hesketh.com/.

Adding Event Handlers

In Chapter 19, you learned that there is more than one way to set up event handlers. The simplest way is to add them directly to an HTML tag. For example, this `<body>` tag has an event handler that calls a function called `Startup`.

```
<body onload="Startup();">
```

This method still works, but it does mean putting JavaScript code in the HTML page, which means you haven't fully separated content and behavior. To keep things entirely separate, you can set up the event handler in the JavaScript file instead, using syntax like this:

```
window.onload=Startup;
```

Right now, this is usually the best way to set up events: It keeps JavaScript out of the HTML file, and it works in all modern browsers. However, it does have one problem: You can't attach more than one event to the same element of a page. For example, you can't have two different `onload` event handlers that both execute when the page loads.

When you're the only one writing scripts, this is no big deal—you can combine the two into one function. But when you're trying to use two or three third-party scripts on a page, and all of them want to add an `onload` event handler to the body, you have a problem.

The W3C Event Model

To solve this problem and standardize event handling, the W3C created an event model as part of the DOM level 2 standard. This uses a method, `addEventListener()`, to attach a handler to any event on any element. For example, the following uses the W3C model to set up the same `onload` event handler as the previous examples:

```
window.addEventListener('load', Startup, false);
```

The first parameter of `addEventListener()` is the event name without the `on` prefix—`load`, `click`, `mouseover`, and so on. The second parameter specifies the function to handle the event, and the third is an advanced flag that indicates how multiple events should be handled (`false` works for most purposes).

Any number of functions can be attached to an event in this way. Because one event handler doesn't replace another, you use a separate function, `removeEventListener()`, which uses the same parameters:

```
window.removeEventListener('load', Startup, false);
```

One problem with the W3C model is that Internet Explorer 8 doesn't support it—it has been introduced in IE9—and there are some industries that still use this browser and refuse to change (this is typical in large enterprise installations of desktop software such as hospitals, schools, and some government offices). Instead, Internet Explorer 8 supports a proprietary method, `attachEvent()`, that does much the same thing. Here's the `Startup` event handler defined Microsoft-style:

```
window.attachEvent('onload', Startup);
```

The `attachEvent()` method has two parameters. The first is the event, with the `on` prefix—`onload`, `onclick`, `onmouseover`, and so on. The second is the function that will handle the event. Internet Explorer also supports a `detachEvent()` method with the same parameters for removing an event handler.

Attaching Events the Cross-Browser Way

As you can see, attaching events in this new way is complex and will require different code for different browsers. In most cases, you're better off using the traditional method to attach events, and that method is used in most of this book's examples. However, if you really need to support multiple event handlers, you can use some `if` statements to use either the W3C method or Microsoft's method. For example, the following code adds the `ClickMe()` function as an event for the element with the `id` attribute `btn`:

```
obj = document.getElementById("btn");
if (obj.addEventListener) {
   obj.addEventListener('click',ClickMe,false);
} else if (obj.attachEvent) {
   obj.attachEvent('onclick',ClickMe);
} else {
   obj.onclick=ClickMe;
}
```

This checks for the `addEventListener()` method and uses it if it's found. Otherwise, it checks for the `attachEvent()` method and uses that. If neither is found, it uses the traditional method to attach the event handler. This technique is called *feature sensing* and is explained in detail later in this chapter.

Many universal functions are available to compensate for the lack of a consistent way to attach events. If you are using a third-party library, there's a good chance it includes an event function that can simplify this process for you.

Web Standards: Avoid Being Browser Specific

The Web was built on standards, such as the HTML standard developed by the W3C. Now there are a lot of standards involved with JavaScript—CSS, the W3C DOM, and the ECMAScript standard that defines JavaScript's syntax.

Microsoft, the Mozilla Project, Google, and other browser developers such as Opera Software continually improve their browsers' support for web standards, but there are always going to be some browser-specific, nonstandard features, and some parts of the newest standards won't be consistently supported between browsers.

Although it's perfectly fine to test your code in multiple browsers and do whatever it takes to get it working, it's a good idea to follow the standards rather than browser-specific techniques when you can. This ensures that your code will work on future browsers that improve their standards support, whereas browser-specific features might disappear in new versions.

TIP

The Yahoo! UI Library, like many other third-party libraries, includes an event-handling function that can attach events in any browser, attach the same event handler to many objects at once, and perform other nice functions. See http://yuilibrary.com/ for details, and see Chapter 22, "Using Third-Party JavaScript Libraries and Frameworks," for information about using various other available libraries.

NOTE

One reason to make sure you follow standards is that your pages can be better interpreted by search engines, which often helps your site get search traffic. Separating content, presentation, and behavior is also good for search engines because they can focus on the HTML content of your site without having to skip over JavaScript or CSS.

Handle Your Errors Well

No matter how good your development skills are or might become, your code will have errors. All code has errors at some point, and handling errors well is a sign of a careful developer. When your JavaScript program encounters an error of some sort, a warning or an error will be created inside the JavaScript interpreter and displayed in the JavaScript console of your web browser. Whether and how this is displayed to the user depends on the browser in use and the user's settings; the user might see some form of error message, or the failed program might simply remain silent but inactive.

Neither situation is good for the user; he or she is likely to have no idea what has gone wrong or what to do about it. As you try to write your code to handle a wide range of browsers and circumstances, it's possible to foresee some areas in which errors might be generated. Examples include the following:

▶ The uncertainty over whether a browser fully supports a certain object and whether that support is standards-compliant

▶ Whether an independent procedure has yet completed its execution, such as an external file being loaded

A useful way to try to intercept potential errors and deal with them cleanly is by using the `try` and `catch` statements. The `try` statement enables you to attempt to run a piece of code. If the code runs without errors, all is well; however, should an error occur, you can use the `catch` statement to intervene before an error message is sent to the user, and determine what the program should then do about the error. The syntax looks like this:

```
try {
    doSomething();
}
catch(err) {
    doSomethingElse();
}
```

Note the syntax:

```
catch(identifier)
```

Here, `identifier` is an object created when an error is caught. It contains information about the error; for instance, if you wanted to alert the user to the nature of a JavaScript runtime error, you could use a code construct like this to open a dialog containing details of the error:

```
catch(err) {
   alert(err.description);
}
```

Documenting Your Code

As you create more complex scripts, don't forget to include comments in your code to document what it does, especially when some of the code seems confusing or is difficult to get working. It's also a good idea to document all the data structures, variables, and function arguments used in a larger script.

Comments are a good way to organize code, and will help you work on the script in the future. If you're doing this for a living, you'll definitely need to use comments so that others can work on your code as easily as you can. Some examples include these:

▶ Using comments as a prologue to any object or function containing more than a few lines of simple code:

```
function calculateGroundAngle(x1, y1, z1, x2, y2, z2) {
/**
 * Calculates the angle in radians at which
 * a line between two points intersects the
 * ground plane.
 * @author Jane Doe you@yourdomain.com
 */
if(x1 > 0) {
    .... more statements
```

▶ Using inline comments wherever the code would otherwise be confusing or prone to misinterpretation:

```
// need to use our custom sort method for performance
reasons
var finalArray = rapidSort(allNodes, byAngle) {
    .... more statements
```

▶ Using a comment wherever the original author can pass on specialist knowledge that the reader is unlikely to know:

```
// workaround for image onload bug in browser X version Y
if(!loaded(image1)) {
    .... more statements
```

▶ Using comments as instructions for commonly used code modifications:

```
// You can change the following dimensions to your
preference:
var height = 400px;
```

Usability

While you're adding cool features to your site, don't forget about *usability*—making things as easy, logical, and convenient as possible for users of your site. Although there are many books and websites devoted to usability information, a bit of common sense goes a long way.

For example, suppose you use a drop-down list as the only way to navigate between pages of your site. This is a common interface element, and it works well, but do your users find it usable? Try comparing it to a simple set of links across the top of a page, and you might find that

▶ The list of links lets you see at a glance what the site contains; the drop-down list requires you to click to see the same list.

▶ Users expect links and can spot them quickly—a drop-down list is more likely to be part of a form than a navigation tool, and thus won't be the first thing they look for when they want to navigate your site.

▶ Navigating with a link takes a single click, whereas navigating with the drop-down list takes at least two clicks.

Remember to consider the user's point of view whenever you add any functionality, and especially potentially intrusive JavaScript functionality, to a site, and be sure you're making the site easier to use—or at least not harder to use. Also make sure that the site is easy to use even without JavaScript; although this might apply to only a small percentage of your users, that percentage is likely to include users of screen readers or other software packages necessary for people with visual impairments.

Accessibility

All developers must consider *accessibility*—making your site as accessible as possible for all users, including disabled users. For example, blind users might use a text-reading program to read your site, which will ignore images and most scripts. More than just good manners, accessibility is mandated by law in some countries.

The subject of accessibility is complex, but you can get most of the way there by following the philosophy of progressive enhancement: Keep the HTML as simple as possible, keep JavaScript and CSS separate, and make JavaScript an enhancement rather than a requirement for using your site.

NOTE

Ensuring that sites function without JavaScript is one of the first steps toward accessibility compliance. For more information on accessibility, see http://www.w3.org/WAI/.

Design Patterns

If you learn more about usability, you'll undoubtedly see *design patterns* mentioned. This is a computer science term meaning "an optimal solution to a common problem." In web development, design patterns are ways of designing and implementing part of a site that webmasters run into over and over.

For example, if you have a site that displays multiple pages of data, you'll have Next Page and Previous Page links, and perhaps numeric links for each page. This is a common design pattern—a problem many web designers have had to solve, and one with a generally agreed-on solution. Other common web design patterns include a login form, a search engine, or a list of navigation links for a site.

Of course, you can be completely original and make a search engine, a shopping cart, or a login form that looks nothing like any other, but unless you have a way of making them even easier to use, you're better off following the pattern and giving your users an experience that matches their expectations.

Although you can find some common design patterns just by browsing sites similar to yours and noticing how they solved particular problems, there are also sites that specialize in documenting these patterns, and they're a good place to start if you need ideas on how to make your site work.

TIP

The Yahoo! Developer Network documents various design patterns used on its network of sites, many of which are implemented using JavaScript. See https://developer.yahoo.com/ypatterns/.

Reuse Code Where You Can

Now that you have all of this JavaScript code sitting around, remember that, generally, the more you can modularize your code and make it reusable, the better. Take a look at this function:

```
function getElementArea() {
    var high = document.getElementById("id1").style.height;
    var wide = document.getElementById("id1").style.width;
    return high * wide;
}
```

The function attempts to return the area of screen covered by a particular HTML element. Unfortunately, it can work only with an element having an id with a value of id1, which is really not very helpful at all—it eliminates the possibility for you to use this code anywhere else, and if you want to do something similar, you're going to have to duplicate something like 98% of this function elsewhere.

Collecting your code into modules such as functions and objects that you can use and reuse throughout your code is a process known as *abstraction*. We can give the function a higher level of abstraction to make its use more general by passing as an argument the id of the element to which the operation should be applied:

```
function getElementArea(elementId) {
    var element = document.getElementById(elementId);
    var high = element.style.height;
    var wide = element.style.width;
    return parseInt(high) * parseInt(wide);
}
```

You could now call this function into action for any element that has an id, by passing the value of id as a parameter when the function is called:

```
var area1 = getElementArea("id1");
var area2 = getElementArea("id2");
```

Reading Browser Information

In Chapter 15, "Working with the Document Object Model (DOM)," you learned about the various objects (such as window and document) that represent portions of the browser window and the current web document. JavaScript also includes an object called navigator that you can use to read information about the user's browser. Knowing more about the browser can help your scripts determine whether or not to use certain elements of JavaScript—for example, if your script can tell that Internet Explorer 8 is in use, it might try to implement code written specifically for that browser rather than generic code that might fail.

The `navigator` object isn't part of the DOM, so you can refer to it directly. It includes several properties, each of which tells you something about the browser. These include the following:

▶ `navigator.appCodeName` is the browser's internal code name, such as `Mozilla`.

▶ `navigator.appName` is the browser's name, such as `Netscape` or `Microsoft Internet Explorer`.

▶ `navigator.appVersion` is the version of the browser being used—for example, `5.0 (Windows)`.

▶ `navigator.userAgent` is the user-agent header, a string that the browser sends to the web server when requesting a web page. It includes the entire version information—for example, `Mozilla/5.0 (Windows NT 6.1; WOW64; rv:29.0) Gecko/20100101 Firefox/29.0Safari/537.36`.

▶ `navigator.language` is the language (such as English or Spanish) of the browser. This is stored as a code, such as `en-US` for U.S. English. This property is supported by Chrome, Firefox, Opera, and Safari.

▶ `navigator.platform` is the computer platform of the current browser. This is a short string, such as `Linux i686`, `Win32`, and `MacPPC`. You can use this to enable any platform-specific features—for example, ActiveX components for Internet Explorer on Windows machines.

NOTE

As you might have guessed, the `navigator` object is named after Netscape Navigator, the browser that originally supported JavaScript. Fortunately, this object is also supported by Internet Explorer and most other recent browsers, despite its name.

Displaying Browser Information

As an example of how to read the `navigator` object's properties, Listing 21.1 shows a script that displays a list of the properties and their values for the current browser.

LISTING 21.1   A Script to Display Information About the Browser

```html
<!DOCTYPE html>

<html lang="en">
  <head>
  <title>Browser Information</title>
  </head>
  <body>
    <h1>Browser Information</h1>
    <p>The <strong>navigator</strong> object contains the
    following information about the browser you are using:</p>

    <script type="text/javascript">
    document.write("<ul>");
    document.write("<li><strong>Code Name:</strong> " +
      navigator.appCodeName);
    document.write("<li><strong>App Name:</strong> " +
      navigator.appName);
    document.write("<li><strong>App Version:</strong> " +
      navigator.appVersion);
    document.write("<li><strong>User Agent:</strong> " +
      navigator.userAgent);
    document.write("<li><strong>Language:</strong> " +
      navigator.language);
    document.write("<li><strong>Platform:</strong> " +
      navigator.platform);
    document.write("</ul>");
    </script>

  </body>
</html>
```

This script is wrapped inside a basic HTML document. JavaScript is used within the body of the document to display each of the properties of the `navigator` object using the `document.write()` statement.

To try this script, load it into the browser of your choice. If you have more than one browser or browser version handy, try it in each one. Firefox's display of the script is shown in Figure 21.1.

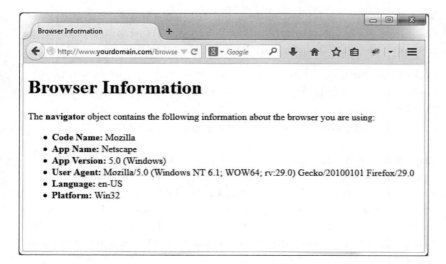

FIGURE 21.1
Firefox displays the browser information script.

Dealing with Dishonest Browsers

If you tried the browser information script in Listing 21.1 using certain versions of Internet Explorer, you probably got a surprise. Figure 21.2 shows how Internet Explorer 6.0 displays the script.

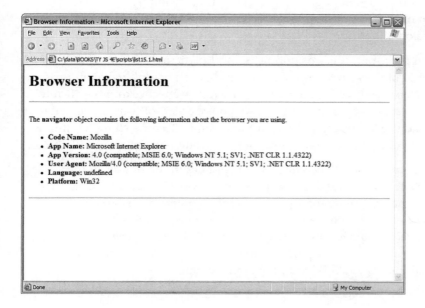

FIGURE 21.2
How Internet Explorer 6 displays the browser information script.

There are several unexpected things about this display. First, the `navigator.language` property is listed as undefined. This isn't much of a surprise because this property isn't supported by Internet Explorer.

More important, you'll notice that the word `Mozilla` appears in the Code Name and User Agent fields. The full user agent string reads as follows:

```
Mozilla/4.0 (compatible; MSIE 6.0; Windows 98)
```

Believe it or not, Microsoft did have a good reason for this. At the height of the browser wars, about the time Netscape 3.0 and IE 3.0 came out, it was becoming common to see "Netscape only" pages. Some webmasters who used features such as frames and JavaScript set their servers to turn away browsers without `Mozilla` in their user agent string. The problem with this was that most of these features were also supported by Internet Explorer.

Microsoft solved this problem in IE 4.0 by making IE's user agent read `Mozilla`, with the word `compatible` in parentheses. This allows IE users to view those pages, but still includes enough details to tell web servers which browser is in use.

You've probably already noticed the other problem with Internet Explorer 6.0's user agent string: the portion reading `Mozilla/4.0`. Not only is IE claiming to be Netscape, but it's also masquerading as version 4.0. Why?

As it turns out, this was another effort by Microsoft to stay one step ahead of the browser wars, although this one doesn't make quite as much sense. Because poorly written scripts were checking specifically for "Mozilla/4" for dynamic HTML pages, Microsoft was concerned that its 5.0 version would fail to run these pages. Because changing it now would only create more confusion, this tradition continued with IE 6.0.

Although these are two interesting episodes in the annals of the browser wars, what does all this mean to you? Well, you'll need to be careful when your scripts are trying to differentiate between IE and Netscape, and between different versions. You'll need to check for specific combinations instead of merely checking the `navigator.appVersion` value. Fortunately, there's a better way to handle this situation, as you'll learn in the next section.

Cross-Browser Scripting

If all those details about detecting different browser versions seem confusing, here's some good news: In most cases, you can write cross-browser scripts without referring to the `navigator` object at all. This is not only easier, but better, because browser-checking code is often confused by new browser versions and has to be updated each time a new browser is released.

Feature Sensing

Checking browser versions is sometimes called *browser sensing*. The better way of dealing with multiple browsers is called *feature sensing*. In feature sensing, rather than checking for a specific browser, you check for a specific feature. For example, suppose your script needs to use the `document.getElementById()` function. You can begin a script with an `if` statement that checks for the existence of this function:

```
if (document.getElementById) {
   // do stuff
}
```

If the `getElementById` function exists, the block of code between the brackets is executed. Another common way to use feature sensing is at the beginning of a function that will make use of a feature:

```
function changeText() {
   if (!document.getElementById) return;
   // the rest of the function executes if the feature is
      supported
}
```

You don't need to check for *every* feature before you use it—for example, there's not much point in verifying that the `window` object exists in most cases. You can also assume that the existence of one feature means others are supported: If `getElementById()` is supported, chances are the rest of the W3C DOM functions are supported.

Feature sensing is a very reliable method of keeping your JavaScript unobtrusive—if a browser supports the feature, it works, and if the browser doesn't, your script stays out of the way. It's also much easier than trying to keep track of hundreds of different browser versions and what they support.

NOTE

Feature sensing is also handy when you're working with third-party libraries, as discussed in Chapter 22. You can check for the existence of an object or a function belonging to the library to verify that the library file has been loaded before your script uses its features.

TIP

Peter-Paul Koch's QuirksMode, at http://www.quirksmode.org, is a good place to start when you're looking for specific information about browser bugs.

Dealing with Browser Quirks

So if feature sensing is better than browser sensing, why do you still need to know about the navigator object? There's one situation in which it still comes in handy, although if you're lucky you won't find yourself in that situation.

As you develop a complex script and test it in multiple browsers, you might run across a situation in which your perfectly standard code works as it should in one browser, and fails to work in another. Assuming you've eliminated the possibility of a problem with your script, you've probably run into a browser bug or a difference in features between browsers at the very least. Here are some tips for this situation:

▶ Double-check for a bug in your own code.

▶ If the problem is that a feature is missing in one browser, use feature sensing to check for that feature.

▶ When all else fails, use the navigator object to detect a particular browser and substitute some code that works in that browser. This should be your last resort.

Supporting Non-JavaScript-Enabled Browsers

Some visitors to your site will be using browsers that don't support JavaScript at all. These aren't just a few holdouts using ancient browsers—actually, there are more non-JavaScript browsers than you might think:

▶ Most modern browsers, such as Internet Explorer, Firefox, and Chrome, include an option to turn off JavaScript, and some users do so. More often, the browser might have been set up by the user's ISP or employer with JavaScript turned off by default, usually in a misguided attempt to increase security.

▶ Some corporate firewalls and personal antivirus software block JavaScript.

▶ Some ad-blocking software mistakenly prevents scripts from working even if they aren't related to advertising.

► More and more mobile phones are coming with web browsers these days, and most of these support little to no JavaScript.

► Some visually impaired users use special-purpose browsers or text-only browsers that might not support JavaScript.

As you can see, it would be foolish to assume that all your visitors will support JavaScript even though 98% of traffic is through JavaScript-enabled devices. Two techniques you can use to make sure these users can still use the site are discussed in the following sections.

NOTE

Search engines are another "browser" that will visit your site frequently, and they usually don't pay any attention to JavaScript. If you want search engines to fully index your site, it's critical that you avoid making JavaScript a requirement to navigate the site.

Using the `<noscript>` Tag

One way to be friendly to non-JavaScript browsers is to use the `<noscript>` tag. Supported in most modern browsers, this tag displays a message to non-JavaScript browsers. Browsers that support JavaScript ignore the text between the `<noscript>` tags, whereas others display it. Here is a simple example:

```
<noscript>
This page requires JavaScript. You can either switch to a browser
that supports JavaScript, turn your browser's script support on,
or switch to the <a href="nojs.html">Non-JavaScript</a> version
of this page.
</noscript>
```

Although this works, the trouble is that `<noscript>` is not consistently supported by all browsers that support JavaScript. An alternative that avoids `<noscript>` is to send users with JavaScript support to another page. This can be accomplished with a single JavaScript statement:

```
<script type="text/javascript">
window.location="JavaScript.html";
</script>
```

This script redirects the user to a different page. If the browser doesn't support JavaScript, of course, the script won't be executed, and the rest of the page can display a warning message to explain the situation.

Keeping JavaScript Optional

Although you can detect JavaScript browsers and display a message to the rest, the best choice is to simply make your scripts unobtrusive. Use JavaScript to enhance rather than as an essential feature, keep

NOTE

Google's Gmail application (http://mail.google.com), one of the most well-known uses of AJAX, requires JavaScript for its elegant interface. However, Google offers a Basic HTML View that can be used without JavaScript. This enables Google to support older browsers and mobile phones without compromising the user experience for those with modern browsers.

JavaScript in separate files, assign event handlers in the JavaScript file rather than in the HTML, and browsers that don't support JavaScript will simply ignore your script.

In those rare cases when you absolutely need JavaScript—for example, an AJAX application or a JavaScript game—you can warn users that JavaScript is required. However, it's a good idea to offer an alternative JavaScript-free way to use your site, especially if it's an e-commerce or business site that your business relies on. Don't turn away customers with lazy programming.

One place you should definitely *not* require JavaScript is in the navigation of your site. Although you can create drop-down menus and other fancy navigation tools using JavaScript, they prevent users' non-JavaScript browsers from viewing all of your site's pages. They also prevent search engines from viewing the entire site, compromising your chances of getting search traffic.

Avoiding Errors

If you've made sure that JavaScript is only an enhancement to your site, rather than a requirement, those with browsers that don't support JavaScript for whatever reason will still be able to navigate your site. One last thing to worry about: It's possible for JavaScript to cause an error, or confuse these browsers into displaying your page incorrectly.

This is a particular concern with browsers that partially support JavaScript, such as mobile phone browsers. They might interpret a `<script>` tag and start the script, but might not support the full JavaScript language or DOM. Here are some guidelines for avoiding errors:

TIP

The developer's toolbars for Firefox and Chrome include a convenient way to turn off JavaScript for testing.

► Use a separate JavaScript file for all scripts. This is the best way to guarantee that the browser will ignore your script completely if it does not have JavaScript support.

► Use feature sensing whenever your script tries to use the newer DOM features, such as `document.getElementById()`.

► Test your pages with your browser's JavaScript support turned off. Make sure nothing looks strange, and make sure you can still navigate the site.

As an example of unobtrusive scripting, you can create a script that adds functionality to a page with JavaScript without compromising its performance in older browsers. In this example, you will create a script that creates graphic checkboxes as an alternative to regular checkboxes.

Let's start with the final result: Figure 21.3 shows this example as it appears in Chrome. The first checkbox is an ordinary HTML one, and the second is a graphic checkbox managed by JavaScript.

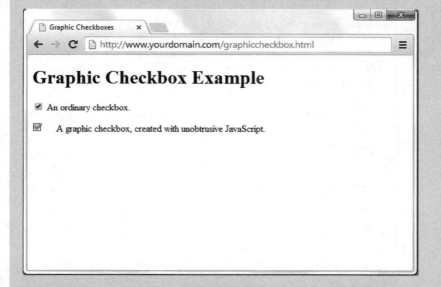

FIGURE 21.3
The graphic checkbox example in action, with the graphical checkbox checked.

The graphic checkbox is just a larger graphic that you can click on to display the checked or unchecked version of the graphic. Although this could just be a simple JavaScript simulation that acts like a checkbox, the implementation here is a bit more sophisticated. Take a look at the HTML for this example in Listing 21.2.

LISTING 21.2   The HTML File for the Graphic Checkbox Example

```
<!DOCTYPE html>

<html lang="en">
  <head>
    <title>Graphic Checkboxes</title>
  </head>
  <body>
    <h1>Graphic Checkbox Example</h1>

    <form name="form1">
```

▼ TRY IT YOURSELF

**Creating an
Unobtrusive Script**
continued

```
    <p><input type="checkbox" name="check1" id="check1"/>
    An ordinary checkbox.</p>
    <p><input type="checkbox" name="check2" id="check2"/>
    A graphic checkbox, created with unobtrusive JavaScript.</p>
    </form>

    <script type="text/javascript" src="checkbox.js"></script>
  </body>
</html>
```

If you look closely at the HTML, you'll see that the two checkboxes are
defined in exactly the same way, using a standard `<input />` element.
Rather than substitute for a checkbox, this script actually replaces the
regular checkbox with the graphic version. The script for this example is
shown in Listing 21.3.

LISTING 21.3   The JavaScript File for the Graphic Checkbox Example

```
function graphicBox(box) {
    // be unobtrusive
    if (!document.getElementById) return;

    // find the object and its parent
    obj = document.getElementById(box);
    parentobj = obj.parentNode;

    // hide the regular checkbox
    obj.style.visibility = "hidden";

    // create the image element and set its onclick event
    img = document.createElement("img");
    img.onclick = Toggle;
    img.src = "unchecked.gif";

    // save the checkbox id within the image ID
    img.id = "img" + box;

    // display the graphic checkbox
    parentobj.insertBefore(img,obj);
}

function Toggle(e) {
    if (!e) var e=window.event;

    // find the image ID
    img = (e.target) ? e.target : e.srcElement;

    // find the checkbox by removing "img" from the image ID
    checkid = img.id.substring(3);
```

```
    checkbox = document.getElementById(checkid);

    // "click" the checkbox
    checkbox.click();

    // display the right image for the clicked or unclicked state
    if (checkbox.checked) {
        file = "checked.gif";
    } else {
        file="unchecked.gif";
    }
    img.src=file;
}

//replace the second checkbox with a graphic
graphicBox("check2");
```

This script has three main components:

▶ The `graphicBox()` function converts a regular checkbox to a graphic one. It starts by hiding the existing checkbox by changing its `style.visibility` property, and then creates a new image node containing the `unchecked.gif` graphic and inserts it into the DOM next to the original checkbox. It gives the image an `id` attribute containing the text `img` plus the checkbox's `id` attribute to make it easier to find the checkbox later.

▶ The `Toggle()` function is specified by `graphicBox()` as the event handler for the new image's `onclick` event. This function removes `img` from the image's `id` attribute to find the `id` of the real checkbox. It executes the `click()` method on the checkbox, toggling its value. Finally, it changes the image to `unchecked.gif` or `checked.gif` depending on the state of the real checkbox.

▶ The last line of the script file runs the `graphicBox()` function to replace the second checkbox with the `id` attribute `check2`.

Using this technique has three important advantages. First, it's an unobtrusive script, in that the HTML has been kept simple and browsers that don't support JavaScript will simply display the ordinary checkbox. Second, because the real checkbox is still on the page but hidden, it will work correctly when the form is submitted to a server-side script. Last but not least, you can use it to create any number of graphic checkboxes simply by defining regular ones in the HTML file and adding a call to `graphicBox()` to transform each one.

To try this example, save the JavaScript file as `checkbox.js`, and be sure the HTML file is in the same folder. You'll also need two graphics the same size, `unchecked.gif` and `checked.gif`, in the same folder.

Summary

In this chapter, you've learned many guidelines for creating scripts that work in as many browsers as possible, and learned how to avoid errors and headaches when working with different browsers. Most important, you learned how you can use JavaScript while keeping your pages small, efficient, and valid by using web standards.

Q&A

Q. Is it possible to create 100% unobtrusive JavaScript that can enhance a page without causing any trouble for anyone?

A. Not quite. For example, the unobtrusive script in the "Try It Yourself" section of this chapter is close—it will work in the latest browsers, and the regular checkbox will display and work fine in even ancient browsers. However, it can still fail if someone with a modern browser has images turned off: The script will hide the checkbox because JavaScript is supported, but the image won't be there. This is a rare circumstance, but it's an example of how any feature you add can potentially cause a problem for some small percentage of your users.

Q. Can I detect the user's email address using the navigator object or another technique?

A. No, there is no reliable way to detect users' email addresses using JavaScript. (If there were, you would get hundreds of advertisements in your mailbox every day from companies that detected your address as you browsed their pages.)

Workshop

The workshop contains quiz questions and exercises to help you solidify your understanding of the material covered. Test your knowledge of unobtrusive scripting by answering the following questions. Try to answer all questions before looking at the "Answers" section that follows.

Quiz

1. Which of the following is the best place to put JavaScript code?

    a. Right in the HTML document

    b. In a separate JavaScript file

    c. In a CSS file

2. Which of the following is something you *can't* do with JavaScript?

   a. Send browsers that don't support a feature to a different page

   b. Send users of Internet Explorer to a different page

   c. Send users of non-JavaScript browsers to a different page

3. The modularization of code into reusable blocks for more general use is called:

   a. Abstraction

   b. Inheritance

   c. Unobtrusive JavaScript

Answers

1. b. The best place for JavaScript is in a separate JavaScript file.

2. c. You can't use JavaScript to send users of non-JavaScript browsers to a different page because the script won't be executed at all.

3. a. Abstraction.

Exercises

▶ Add several checkboxes to the HTML document in Listing 21.2, and add the corresponding function calls to the script in Listing 21.3 to replace all of them with graphic checkboxes.

▶ Modify the script in Listing 21.3 to convert all checkboxes with a `class` value of `graphic` into graphic checkboxes. You can use `getElementsByTagName()` and then check each item for the right `className` property.

CHAPTER 22
Using Third-Party JavaScript Libraries and Frameworks

Third-party JavaScript libraries, or code libraries written and maintained by another party for easy implementation in your own code, offer many advantages to always writing your own code. First and foremost, using these libraries enables you to avoid reinventing the wheel for common tasks. Additionally, these libraries enable you to implement cross-browser scripting and sophisticated user interface elements without first having to become an expert in JavaScript.

There are many third-party JavaScript libraries out there, and in this chapter you'll gain a brief introduction to a few popular ones (you'll look at one in depth over the next two chapters). Additionally, you'll learn a little about JavaScript frameworks, which—as the name suggests—provides you with some underlying structure for your development, as opposed to just building your own structure and using pieces (libraries) from elsewhere.

Using Third-Party JavaScript Libraries

When you use JavaScript's built-in and often-used `Math` and `Date` functions, JavaScript does most of the work—you don't have to figure out how to convert dates between formats or calculate a cosine; you just use the function JavaScript provides. Third-party libraries are those libraries not directly included with JavaScript, but they serve a similar purpose: enabling you to do complicated things with only a small amount of code, because that small amount of code refers to something bigger under the hood that someone else has already created.

WHAT YOU'LL LEARN IN THIS CHAPTER:

▶ Why you might use a third-party JavaScript library

▶ How to download and use one of the more popular third-party JavaScript libraries in your applications

▶ Understanding the benefits of JavaScript frameworks

Although in general most people are big fans of third-party libraries, you should be aware of some of the common objections:

▶ You won't ever really know how the code works because you're simply employing someone else's algorithms and functions.

▶ JavaScript libraries contain a lot of code you'll never use but the browser has to download anyway.

Blindly implementing code is never a good thing; you should endeavor to understand what is happening behind the scenes when you use any library. But that understanding could be limited to knowing that someone else wrote a complicated algorithm that you could not—and it's fine if that's all you know, as long as you implement it appropriately and understand possible weaknesses.

To the point about libraries containing a lot of extraneous code, that should be a consideration especially if you know that your target users have bandwidth limitations or the size of the library is disproportionate to the feature you're using from it. For example, if your code requires the browser to load a 1MB library just to use one function, look into ways to fork the library (if it is open source) and use just the sections you need, find other features of the library you can use to make it worth it, or just look for another library that does what you want but with less overhead.

However, regardless of the objections, there are numerous good reasons for using third-party JavaScript libraries, which in my opinion outweigh the negative objections. For example:

▶ Using a well-written library can really take away some of the headaches of writing cross-browser JavaScript. You won't have every browser always at your disposal, but the library writers—and their communities of users—will have tested using several versions of all major browsers.

▶ Why invent code that somebody else has already written? Popular JavaScript libraries tend to contain the sorts of abstractions that programmers often need to use—which means you'll likely need those functions too from time to time. The thousands of downloads and pages of online documentation and commentary generated by the most-used libraries pretty much guarantee that the code these libraries contain will be more thoroughly tested and debugged than the ordinary user's home-cooked code would be.

▶ Advanced functionality like drag and drop and JavaScript-based animation is, well, really advanced. Truly cross-browser solutions for this type of functionality have always been one of the trickiest effects to code for all browsers, and well-developed and -tested libraries to achieve these types of features are incredibly valuable in terms of the time and effort they will save you.

Using a third-party JavaScript library is usually as simple as copying one or more files to your server (or linking to an external but incredibly stable location) and including a `<script>` tag in your document to load the library, thus making its code available to your own scripts. Several popular JavaScript libraries are introduced in the following sections.

jQuery

Although the next two chapters focus exclusively on using jQuery, an introduction to this extremely popular library is in order in this chapter as well. The first implementation of jQuery was introduced in 2006 and has grown from an easy, cross-browser means of DOM manipulation to a stable, powerful library. This library contains not just DOM manipulation tools, but many additional features that make cross-browser JavaScript coding much more straightforward and productive. In fact, many JavaScript frameworks, which you'll learn about later in this chapter, rely on the jQuery library for their own functionality.

The current version (at the time of writing) is 2.1.1, and jQuery now also has an additional advanced user interface extensions library that can be used alongside the existing library to rapidly build and deploy rich user interfaces or to add various attractive effects to existing components. Again, we'll look at jQuery UI in greater detail in subsequent chapters.

jQuery has at its heart a sophisticated, cross-browser method for selection of page elements. The selectors used to obtain elements are based on a combination of simple CSS-like selector styles, so with the CSS techniques you learned in Part III of this book, you should have no problem getting up to speed with jQuery. Following are a few brief examples of jQuery code, to illustrate my point.

NOTE

jQuery's home page is at http://jquery.com/, where you can not only download the latest version, but also gain access to extensive documentation and sample code. The companion UI library can be found at http://jqueryui.com/.

TIP

If you don't want to download and store the jQuery library on your own local development machine or production server, you can use a remotely hosted version from a content delivery network, such as the one hosted by Google. Instead of referring to a locally hosted .js file in your HTML files, use the following code to link to a stable and minified version of the code:

```
<script
src="http://ajax.
googleapis.com/ajax/libs/
jquery/2.1.1/jquery.min.
js"
type="text/javascript">
</script>
```

In many cases, this provides better performance than hosting your own version, due to Google's servers being optimized for low-latency, massively parallel content delivery. Additionally, anyone visiting your page who has also visited another page that references this same file will have the file cached in their browser and will not need to download it again.

TIP

You can even extend jQuery yourself by writing further plug-ins, or use the thousands already submitted by other developers. Browse http://plugins.jquery.com/ to see lots of examples in searchable categories.

For example, if you want to get an element that has an ID of `someElement`, all you do is use this:

```
$("#someElement")
```

Or to return a collection of elements that have the `someClass` classname, you can simply use this:

```
$(".someClass")
```

We can very simply get or set values associated with our selected elements. Let's suppose, for example, that we want to hide all elements having the classname `hideMe`. We can do that, in a fully cross-browser manner, in just one line of code:

```
$(".hideMe").hide();
```

Manipulating HTML and CSS properties is just as straightforward. To append the phrase "powered by jQuery" to all paragraph elements, for example, we would simply write the following:

```
$("p").append(" powered by jQuery");
```

To then change the background color of those same elements, we can manipulate their CSS properties directly:

```
$("p").css("background-color","yellow");
```

Additionally, jQuery includes simple cross-browser methods for determining whether an element has a class, adding and removing classes, getting and setting the text or `innerHTML` of an element, navigating the DOM, getting and setting CSS properties, and easy cross-browser handling of events.

The associated UI library, which you'll learn about in a later chapter, adds a huge range of UI widgets (such as date pickers, sliders, dialogs, and progress bars), animation tools, drag-and-drop capabilities, and much more.

Prototype

Prototype, created by Sam Stephenson, is a JavaScript library that simplifies tasks such as working with DOM objects, dealing with data in forms, and remote scripting (AJAX). By including a single `prototype.js` file in your document, you have access to many improvements to basic JavaScript.

For example, in other sections of this book, you've used the `getElementById()` JavaScript method to obtain the DOM object for an element within a web page. Prototype includes an improved version of this: the `$()` function. Not only is the Prototype function easier to type, but it also is more sophisticated than the built-in function and supports multiple objects.

Adding Prototype to your pages requires only one file, `prototype.js`, and one `<script>` tag, such as the following (you can also get Prototype from a content delivery network and refer to it just as in the jQuery example in the preceding section):

```
<script type="text/javascript" src="prototype.js"></script>
```

NOTE

Prototype is free, open-source software. You can download it from its official website at http://www.prototypejs.org/. Prototype is also built into the Ruby on Rails framework for the server-side language Ruby—see http://www.rubyonrails.com/ for more information.

Script.aculo.us

By the end of this book, you'll learn to do some useful things with JavaScript, often using complex code. But you can also include impressive effects in your pages using a prebuilt library. This enables you to use impressive effects with only a few lines of code.

Script.aculo.us by Thomas Fuchs is one such library. It includes functions to simplify drag-and-drop tasks, such as rearranging lists of items. It also includes a number of combination effects, which enable you to use highlighting and animated transitions within your pages. For example, a new section of the page can be briefly highlighted in yellow to get the user's attention, or a portion of the page can fade out or slide off the screen.

After you've included the appropriate files, using effects is as easy as using any of JavaScript's built-in methods. For example, the following statements use Script.aculo.us to fade out an element of the page with the `id` value `test`:

```
obj = document.getElementById("test");
new Effect.Fade(obj);
```

Script.aculo.us is built on the Prototype framework described in the preceding section, and includes all the functions of Prototype; therefore, you could also simplify this further by using the `$` function:

```
new Effect.Fade($("test"));
```

NOTE

You will create a script that demonstrates several script.aculo.us effects in the next section.

Other Popular JavaScript Libraries

There are many more JavaScript libraries out there, and more are appearing all the time as JavaScript is taken more seriously as an application development language. Here are some more libraries you might want to explore:

▶ Dojo (www.dojotoolkit.org) is an open-source toolkit that adds power to JavaScript to simplify building applications and user interfaces. It adds features ranging from extra string and math functions to animation and AJAX.

▶ The Yahoo! UI Library (yuilibrary.com) was developed by Yahoo! and made available to everyone under an open-source license. It includes features for animation, DOM features, event management, and easy-to-use user interface elements such as calendars and sliders.

Adding JavaScript Effects Using a Third-Party Library

To see how simple it is to use an external library, let's create a sample script that includes the script.aculo.us library and uses event handlers to demonstrate several of the available effects.

For this example, we'll include script.aculo.us and Prototype in our HTML document by leveraging the Google content delivery network. To do this, simply use `<script>` tags to reference the code:

```
<script
    type="text/javascript"
    src="http://ajax.googleapis.com/ajax/libs/prototype/1.7.2.0/
    prototype.js">
</script>
<script
    type="text/javascript"
    src="http://ajax.googleapis.com/ajax/libs/scriptaculous/1.9.0/
    scriptaculous.js">
</script>
```

If you include these statements as the first things in the `<head>` section of your document, the library functions will be available to other scripts or event handlers anywhere in the page.

CAUTION

This example was created using version 1.9.0 of script. aculo.us, and version 1.7.2.0 of Prototype. The script should work with later versions, because developers tend to ensure backward-compatibility, but the underlying code might have changed since this was written. If you have trouble, you might need to use these specific versions.

After you have included the external code, you simply need to include a bit of JavaScript to trigger the effects. We will use a section of the page wrapped in a `<div>` tag with the `id` value `test` to demonstrate some of the effects that script.aculo.us makes possible. Each effect is triggered by a simple event handler on a button. For example, this code defines the Fade Out button:

```
<button onclick="new Effect.Fade($('test'))">Fade Out</button>
```

This code uses the `$` function built into Prototype to obtain the object for the element with the `id` value `test`, and then passes it to the `Effect.Fade` function built into script.aculo.us.

Once you have included the script.aculo.us library, you can combine effects with event handlers and some sample text to create a complete demonstration of script.aculo.us effects. The complete HTML document for this example is shown in Listing 22.1.

LISTING 22.1   The Complete Library Effects Example

```
<!DOCTYPE html>
<html lang="en">
  <head>
    <title>Testing script.aculo.us effects</title>
    <script type="text/javascript"    src="http://ajax.
    googleapis.com/ajax/libs/prototype/1.7.2.0/prototype.js">
    </script>
    <script type="text/javascript" src="http://ajax.googleapis.
    com/ajax/libs/scriptaculous/1.9.0/scriptaculous.js">
    </script>
  </head>
  <body>
    <h1>Testing script.aculo.us Effects</h1>
    <button onclick="new Effect.Fade($('testarea'))">Fade Out
      </button>
      <button onclick="new Effect.Appear($('testarea'))">Fade In
      </button>
      <button onclick="new Effect.SlideUp($('testarea'))">Slide
      Up</button>
      <button onclick="new Effect.SlideDown($('testarea'))">
      Slide Down</button>
      <button onclick="new Effect.Highlight($('testarea'))">
      Highlight</button>
      <button onclick="new Effect.Shake($('testarea'))">Shake
      </button>
    <hr/>
    <h2>Testing Effects</h2>
    <div
      id="testarea"
```

TIP

Of course, you could download script.aculo.us and Prototype to your local development machine or web server, and reference it accordingly. If you go down that path, try to keep all of your assets in separate directories, such as a `js` folder that contains all JavaScript libraries, and ensure that your `<script>` tag references the path accordingly.

TIP

This example demonstrates six effects: `Fade`, `Appear`, `SlideUp`, `SlideDown`, `Highlight`, and `Shake`. There are more than 16 effects in the library, plus methods for supporting Drag and Drop and other features. See http://script.aculo.us for details.

```
        style="background-color:#CCC; margin:20px; padding:10px;">
    This section of the document is within a &lt;div&gt; element
    with the <strong>id</strong> value of <strong>testarea</
    strong>. The event handlers on the buttons above send this
    object to the <a href="http://script.aculo.us/">script.aculo.
    us</a> library to perform effects. Click the buttons to see
    the effects in action.
    </div>
  </body>
</html>
```

This document starts with two `<script>` tags to include the third-party files that contain the JavaScript code that your own scripts will reference. The effects themselves are triggered by the event handlers defined for each of the six buttons. The `<div>` section at the end defines the `testarea` element that will be used to demonstrate the effects.

When you load this script in your web browser, the display should look as shown in Figure 22.1. After it has been loaded, you should be able to click on any of the six buttons at the top of the page to trigger the effects provided by the script.aculo.us JavaScript library.

FIGURE 22.1
The JavaScript-effects example ready for action.

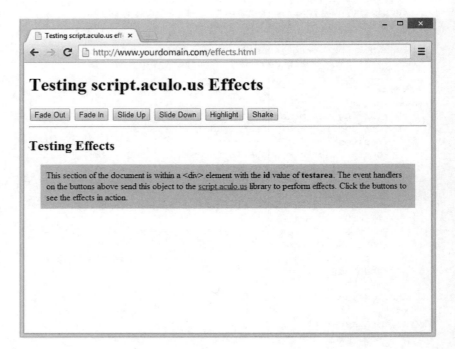

Using JavaScript Frameworks

There's a big difference between JavaScript libraries and JavaScript frameworks: simple libraries tend to be smaller and provide ready-made pieces of code that provide functionality meant to enhance your custom architecture, and frameworks are larger, are more complicated, and impose an architectural pattern upon your application such as the *model-view-controller* pattern. In a model-view-controller pattern, or MVC pattern, an application is conceived of as having three interconnected components:

▶ The **model**, which acts as the central component even though it's listed first in the name, holds application data, business rules, functions, and other logical elements.

▶ The **view** requests information from the model to show to the user.

▶ The **controller** sends information to the model for processing through user interactions.

You can think of it this way: In a web-based application, the user interacts with a controller that manipulates the underlying model, which updates the view, which the user then sees in the web browser.

In the traditional web-based application you will likely have experienced it this way: Both the model and the controller components sit on the back end, away from the browser, and are invoked through form elements or other interactions by the user that say, "Hey, back-end script, go do something with logic and data based on this input I'm giving you, and send the result back to the screen." The screen, in this case, would contain dynamically generated HTML (the view).

In a JavaScript-based MVC application, which most likely has been developed using one of the frameworks you'll learn about in a moment, all three components can sit on the client side—that is to say, a user can interact with data that is stored and manipulated entirely within the front end, never touching a back-end script or database. Or *most* of the three components sit on the front end, and use AJAX requests to invoke a script on the back end, which then sends results back into the view.

NOTE

AJAX (Asynchronous JavaScript and XML), also known as remote scripting, enables JavaScript to communicate with a program running on the web server. This enables JavaScript to do things that were traditionally not possible, such as dynamically loading information from a database or storing data on a server without refreshing a page.

AJAX requires some complex scripting, particularly because the methods you use to communicate with the server vary depending on the browser in use. Fortunately, many libraries have been created to fill the need for a simple way to use AJAX, and you'll try your hand at this later in this book.

By the end of the introductory lessons in HTML, CSS, and JavaScript found in this book, I wouldn't expect you or anyone else to be prepared to create a JavaScript framework of your very own—and please don't, because there are already 30 or more competing frameworks out there in the wild! But I would expect you to be able to start thinking about how a framework might be helpful in your work, and to be able to begin understanding one or more of the major frameworks in use today.

If you are building a predominantly read-only website and using a little JavaScript or jQuery for some display features, a framework would be considerable overkill. But if you begin to think about ways to extend that website to include user interactivity, you might think about laying a framework in to handle that work for you. Following are some major JavaScript frameworks in use today, all of which would be fine starting points for further exploration:

▶ **AngularJS** (angularjs.org)—A very powerful and flexible framework but it comes with a steep learning curve. However, it also comes with a very active user community that is ready to help new developers understand the framework.

▶ **Backbone.js** (backbonejs.org)—This framework has been around for quite some time (relatively speaking), and served as the inspiration for many other frameworks. It enables a new developer to get started quickly, but the downside of that, for some, is that your applications will contain a lot of unused templating code.

▶ **Ember** (emberjs.com)—Like Backbone.js, Ember enables a new developer to get started quickly. Although it appears "too magical" to some, Ember's strong adherence to common programming idioms can be a benefit to new developers.

▶ **Knockout** (knockoutjs.com)—Less popular than the frameworks previously listed, Knockout nonetheless provides a strong alternative as well as several nice tutorials for the new developer.

There are many more than these few JavaScript frameworks out there at the time of this writing, and I fully expect there will be more in years to come. To stay up to date or to get an overview of the core features of JavaScript frameworks and libraries, you can start by bookmarking and revisiting http://www.jsdb.io/.

Summary

In this chapter, you learned about some of the many third-party libraries available for JavaScript, which offer many advantages, including easy cross-browser scripting, selection and editing of HTML and CSS values, animation, and more sophisticated user-interface tools such as drag-and-drop. You used the script.aculo.us and Prototype libraries to put some basic JavaScript effects like this into action.

Additionally, you learned about the existence of popular JavaScript frameworks, and how these can be used to develop feature-rich web applications following standard software architecture patterns such as the model-view-controller pattern, or MVC.

Q&A

Q. Can I use more than one third-party library in the same script?

A. Yes, in theory: If the libraries are well written and designed not to interfere with each other, there should be no problem with combining them. In practice, this will depend on the libraries you need and how they were written, but many JavaScript libraries can be used together or will include a warning about incompatibilities.

Q. Can I build my own library to simplify scripting?

A. Yes, as you deal with more complicated scripts, you'll find yourself using the same functions over and over, and if they're functions you have created, then all the better to store them in a separate library file. This process is as simple as creating a `.js` file with your code, placing it on your server, and referencing it in a `<script>` tag as you would any other library.

Workshop

The workshop contains quiz questions and exercises to help you solidify your understanding of the material covered. Test your knowledge of JavaScript libraries by answering the following questions. Try to answer all questions before looking at the "Answers" section that follows.

Quiz

1. Which of the following objects *is not* a JavaScript library?

   a. script.aculo.us

   b. Yahoo! UI

   c. AJAX

2. How can you extend jQuery yourself?

   a. jQuery can't be extended.

   b. By writing server-side scripts.

   c. By writing a plug-in, or using a prewritten one.

3. What other JavaScript third-party library does script.aculo.us employ?

   a. Prototype

   b. Dojo

   c. jQuery

Answers

1. **c.** AJAX is a programming technique enabling your scripts to use resources hosted on your server. There are many libraries to help you employ AJAX functionality, but AJAX itself is not a library.

2. **c.** jQuery has a well-documented method for writing and using plug-ins.

3. **a.** Script.aculo.us uses the Prototype library.

Exercises

To further explore the JavaScript features you learned about in this chapter, you can perform the following exercises:

▶ Visit the script.aculo.us website at http://script.aculo.us/ to find the complete list of effects, and then modify Listing 22.1 to add buttons for one or more of these additional effects.

▶ Much like you practiced in this chapter using script.aculo.us, pick another third-party JavaScript library such as Dojo or Yahoo! UI and implement one or more of the library's custom features on your own.

CHAPTER 23

A Closer Look at jQuery

In the preceding chapter you learned a little bit about a few different JavaScript libraries and frameworks, such as how to include the functionality in your own site and (perhaps more important) why you might want to do so. One of the libraries discussed was jQuery, and this chapter is fully devoted to learning jQuery basics. By the end of the chapter, you will likely see why jQuery is so popular, and why developers continue to contribute plug-ins to this open-source project for the rest of the development community to use. With just a few keystrokes here and there, you'll see how useful this library can be for adding interactivity to your website or web-based application.

WHAT YOU'LL LEARN IN THIS CHAPTER:

▶ How to use jQuery's `$(document).ready` handler

▶ How to use jQuery to select page elements and manipulate HTML content

▶ How to chain commands together and handle events with jQuery

Preparing to Use jQuery

The current version of jQuery (at the time of writing) is 2.1.1, and the library itself—as well as extensive documentation—can be found at http://jquery.com/. As you learned in the preceding chapter, including any JavaScript library in your code is as simple as linking to it via a `<script>` element.

You have two options for storing the library: You can download and store it on your own server, or you can use a remotely hosted version from a content delivery network, such as the one hosted by Google or even the jQuery folks themselves.

If you download jQuery and keep it on your own server, I would suggest keeping it in a directory called `js` (for "javascript") or another directory specifically for assets (in fact, you could even call it `assets`)

NOTE

The "min" in the filename is for the *minified* version of the library, or a version that is fully functioning but has all the whitespace, line breaks, and other unnecessary characters removed from the source code. This minified version is thus smaller in size, which requires less time and bandwidth for the end user to download, while retaining all original functionality. Minified code is not easy for human eyes to read, but computers have no issues with it, because the unnecessary spacing doesn't matter to them.

TIP

Readiness means that the full DOM is ready for manipulation, but does not necessarily mean all assets (such as images and other multimedia) have been fully downloaded and are available.

so that it doesn't get lost among all the other files you maintain. Then, reference it like so:

```
<script src="/js/jquery-2.1.1.min.js" type="text/javascript">
</script>
```

I typically use the Google content delivery network, which means a `<script>` tag that looks like the following. Use whatever is more comfortable for you, as long as you know the difference.

```
<script
   src="http://ajax.googleapis.com/ajax/libs/jquery/2.1.1/jquery.
   min.js"
   type="text/javascript">
</script>
```

Becoming Familiar with the $(document).ready Handler

Previously in this book, you used the `window.onload` event handler—specifically, in Chapter 20, "Using Windows," you used this handler to open a new window when a page was loaded. jQuery has its own handler that serves the same purpose, but is perhaps more explicitly named; this handler ensures that nothing within the page can be manipulated until a state of readiness has been detected.

The syntax of the `$(document).ready` handler is simply this:

```
$(document).ready(function() {
   // jQuery code goes here
});
```

Pretty much all the jQuery code you write will be executed from within a statement like this. Like the JavaScript `onload` event handler you saw previously, the `$(document).ready` handler accomplishes two things:

▶ It ensures that the code does not run until the DOM is available; that is, it ensures that any elements your code might be trying to access already exist, so your code doesn't return any errors.

▶ It helps make your code unobtrusive by separating it from the semantic (HTML) and presentation (CSS) layers.

Listing 23.1 enables you to watch the state of readiness occur by loading a document and watching jQuery write a message to the console when the DOM is available and thus a state of readiness has been achieved.

LISTING 23.1   Ensuring a State of Readiness

```
<!DOCTYPE html>
<html lang="en">
<head>
   <title>Hello World!</title>
   <script
      src="http://ajax.googleapis.com/ajax/libs/jquery/2.1.1/
      jquery.min.js"
      type="text/javascript">
   </script>

   <script type="text/javascript">
       $( document ).ready(function() {
           console.log( "Yes, I am ready!");
       });
   </script>

</head>
<body>
   <h1 style="text-align: center">Hello World!<br/>Are you
   ready?</h1>
</body>
</html>
```

If you open your web browser, open Developer Tools, and switch to the console, you should see the "Yes, I am ready!" message printed to the console when you load this specific web page, as in Figure 23.1. This message is printed by jQuery when the document reaches a ready state.

After your document has reached a ready state—which should take milliseconds and is really imperceptible to human eyes unless you're looking for a console log statement—your page can continue on to be as interactive as you've planned.

FIGURE 23.1
jQuery has written a message to
the console, declaring readiness.

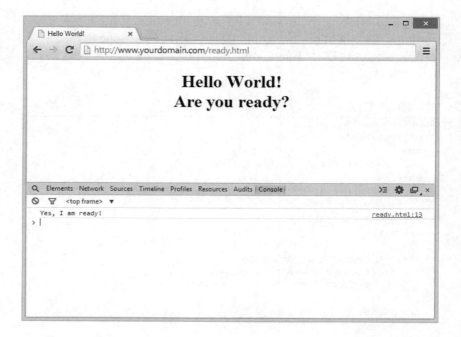

Selecting DOM and CSS Content

With your documents in a ready state, *you* should be ready to do more
with code. Before diving deeper into specific acts of manipulating
content with jQuery, let's take a look at some of the jQuery
statements that enable you to select HTML elements. The first step in
manipulating content is figuring out the content that you want to
manipulate, and the following statements help you out with that.

These jQuery statements each return an object containing an array of
the DOM elements specified by the expression that you see. Each of
these statements builds off the jQuery wrapper syntax: `$("")`.

```
$("span"); // all HTML span elements
$("#theElement"); // the HTML element having an ID of
                // "theElement"
$(".theClassname"); // HTML elements having a class of
                // "theClassname"
$("div#theElement"); // the <div> element with an ID of
                // "theElement"
$("ul li a.theClassname"); // anchors with class "theClassname"
                // that are within list items
$("p > span"); // spans that are direct children of paragraphs
$("input[type=password] "); // inputs that have the specified type
```

```
$("p:first"); // the first paragraph on the page
$("p:even"); // all even numbered paragraphs
```

These examples are all DOM and CSS selectors, but jQuery also has its own custom selectors, such as these:

```
$(":header"); // all header elements (h1 to h6)
$(":button"); // any button elements (inputs or buttons)
$(":radio"); // all radio buttons
$(":checkbox"); // all checkboxes
$(":checked"); // all selected checkboxes or radio buttons
```

If you notice, none of the preceding lines of jQuery has any actions associated with it. These selectors just get the required elements from the DOM. In the next few sections you'll learn how to work with the content you've selected.

Manipulating HTML Content

jQuery's `html()` and `text()` methods enable you to get and set the content of any elements you've selected (using the statements in the preceding section), and the `attr()` method helps you get and set the values of individual element attributes. Let's see some examples in the code snippets that follow.

The `html()` method gets the HTML of any element or collection of elements, and as such is very similar to JavaScript's `innerHTML` that you've seen in earlier chapters. In the snippet that follows, the variable `htmlContent` will contain all the HTML and text inside an element with the ID of `theElement`:

```
var htmlContent = $("#theElement").html();
```

Using a similar syntax, you can *set*, and not just retrieve, the HTML content of a specified element or collection of elements:

```
$("#theElement").html("<p>Here is some new content for within
    theElement ID.</p>");
```

However, if you want only the text content of an element or collection of elements, without the HTML that surrounds it, you can use the `text()` method:

```
var textContent = $("#theElement").text();
```

If the previous snippets were used in order in your script, the value of `textContent` would be `"Here is some new content for within theElement ID."`—note the lack of surrounding `<p>` and `</p>` tags.

You could again change the content—but now only the text content—of the specified elements, using the following snippet:

```
$("#theElement").text("Here is some new content for that element.");
```

In the snippets given previously, you can see how the use of jQuery selectors makes the process of selecting or referencing specific DOM elements pretty easy. In all of those snippets, you could swap out `$("#theElement")` with any of the selectors in the preceding section (and then some), as appropriate to your needs. Want to change the text of all anchor elements within a list to `"Click Me!"`? You can do that:

```
$("ul li a ").text("Click Me!");
```

You can also append content rather than replacing it outright:

```
$("#theElement").append("<p>Here is even more new content.</p>");
```

In this snippet, the element with the ID of `theElement` would now contain two paragraphs: the modified original from two snippets previous, and this new paragraph of content here.

Another useful trick is the capability to select specific attributes of particular elements. Using the `attr()` method, if you pass an argument containing the name of an attribute, jQuery will return the value of that attribute for the specified element.

For example, if you have an element such as

```
<a id="theElement" title="The Title Goes Here">The Title Goes Here</a>
```

then the following jQuery will return the value of the title attribute, or `"The Title Goes Here"`:

```
var title = $("a #theElement").attr("title");
```

You can also pass a second argument to the `attr()` method to set an attribute value:

```
$("a #theElement").attr("title", "This is the new title.");
```

Showing and Hiding Elements

Using plain old JavaScript, showing and hiding page elements usually means manipulating the value of the display or visibility properties of the element's style object. Although that works just fine, it can lead to pretty long lines of code:

```
document.getElementById("theElement").style.visibility =
'visible';
```

You can use jQuery's show() and hide() methods to carry out these tasks with less code. The jQuery methods also offer some useful additional functionality, as you will see in the following code snippets. First, here is a simple way to make an element or a set of elements visible by calling the show() method:

```
$("div #theElement").show(); // makes a <div> show if it has an
  ID of "theElement"
```

However, you can also add some additional parameters to spice up the transition. In the following example, the first parameter (fast) determines the speed of the transition. As an alternative to fast or slow, jQuery will happily accept a number of milliseconds for this argument, as the required duration of the transition. If no value is set, the transition will occur instantly, with no animation.

The second argument to the show() method can be a function that operates as a callback; that is, the specified function executes after the transition is complete:

```
$("div #theElement").show("fast", function() {
   // do something once the specified element is shown
});
```

The hide() method is, as expected, the exact reverse of show(), enabling you to make page elements invisible with the same optional arguments as you saw for hide():

```
$("div #theElement").hide("slow", function() {
   // do something once the specified element is hidden
});
```

Additionally, the toggle() method changes the current state of an element or a collection of elements; it makes visible any element in the collection that is currently hidden and hides any that are currently being shown. The same optional duration and callback function parameters are also available to the toggle() method:

TIP

The value "slow" corresponds to 600ms, and "fast" is equivalent to 200ms.

TIP

Remember that the `show()`, `hide()`, and `toggle()` methods can be applied to collections of elements, so the elements in that collection will appear or disappear all at once.

```
$("div #theElement").toggle(1000, function() {
    // do something once the specified element is shown or hidden
});
```

Animating Elements

In the preceding chapter, you saw one method for animating the appearance and disappearance of content using the script.aculo.us JavaScript library. As part of its rich feature set, jQuery also has methods for fading elements in and out, as well as optionally setting the transition duration and adding a callback function to the process.

To fade out to invisibility, use the `fadeout()` method:

```
$("#theElement").fadeOut("slow", function() {
    // do something after fadeout() has finished executing
});
```

Or to fade in, use the `fadeIn()` method:

```
$("#theElement").fadeIn(500, function() {
    // do something after fadeIn() has finished executing
});
```

You can also fade an element only partially, either in or out, using the `fadeTo()` method:

```
$("#theElement").fadeTo(3000, 0.5, function() {
    // do something after fadeTo() has finished executing
});
```

The second parameter in the `fadeIn()` method (here set to `0.5`) represents the target opacity. Its value works similarly to the way opacity values are set in CSS, in that whatever the value of opacity before the method is called, the element will be animated until it reaches the value specified in the argument.

In addition to fading elements in or out, you can also slide elements upward or downward without a change in opacity. The jQuery methods for sliding an element are direct corollaries to the fading methods you've just seen, and their arguments follow exactly the same rules.

For example, use the `slideDown()` method to slide an element down:

```
$("#theElement").slideDown(150, function() {
    // do something when slideDown() is finished executing
});
```

And to slide an element up, use the `slideUp()` method:

```
$("#theElement").slideUp("slow", function() {
    // do something when slideUp() is finished executing
});
```

To provide a visual change to the element in an animated way, you do so by using jQuery to specify the new CSS styles that you want to have applied to the element. jQuery will then impose the new styles but in a gradual manner (instead of applying them instantly as in plain CSS/ JavaScript), thus creating an animation effect.

You can use the `animate()` method on a wide range of numerical CSS properties. In this example the width and height of an element are animated to a size of 400×500 pixels; after the animation is complete, the callback function is used to fade the element to invisibility:

```
$("#theElement").animate(
    {
    width: "400px",
    height: "500px"
    }, 1500, function() {
        $(this).fadeOut("slow");
    }
);
```

> **NOTE**
>
> Most jQuery methods return a jQuery object that can then be used in your call to another method. You could combine two of the methods in the previous examples, through what is called *command chaining*, like this:
>
> ```
> $("#theElement").
> fadeOut().fadeIn();
> ```
>
> In this example, the selected element will fade out and then fade back in. The number of items you can chain is arbitrarily large, allowing for several commands to successively work on the same collection of elements:
>
> ```
> $("#theElement").
> text("Hello from jQuery").
> fadeOut().fadeIn();
> ```

Putting the Pieces Together to Create a jQuery Animation

Given what you've learned in this chapter so far, you can begin to put the pieces together into a more cohesive whole. Listing 23.2 shows a complete listing of the code used in a basic jQuery animation example; following the listing is an explanation of all the code used.

LISTING 23.2   A jQuery Animation Example

```
<!DOCTYPE html>
<html lang="en">
<head>
    <style>
        #animateMe {
            position: absolute;
            top: 100px;
            left: 100px;
            width: 100px;
            height: 400px;
```

```
            border: 2px solid black;
            background-color: red;
            padding: 20px;
        }
    </style>
    <title>Animation Example</title>
    <script
        src="http://ajax.googleapis.com/ajax/libs/jquery/2.1.1/
            jquery.min.js"
        type="text/javascript">
    </script>

    <script type="text/javascript">
        $( document ).ready(function() {
            $("#animateMe").text("Changing shape...").animate(
                {
                width: "400px",
                height: "200px"
                }, 5000, function() {
                    $(this).text("Fading away...").fadeOut(4000);
                }
            );
        });
    </script>
</head>
<body>
    <div id="animateMe"></div>
</body>
</html>
```

If you put the code from Listing 23.1 into a file and open it with your web browser, you will see something like what's shown in Figures 23.2 and 23.3—bear in mind that it's difficult to capture animation examples in screenshots!

Let's take a closer look at the code that produced these examples. First, in the <style> section of the script, an element with an ID of animateMe is defined as an absolutely positioned rectangle that is 100 pixels wide and 400 pixels high, with the upper-left corner of that rectangle positioned 100 pixels from the top and 100 pixels from the left edge of the browser. This rectangle has a red background and a 2-pixel solid black border, with an inside padding of 20 pixels on all sides.

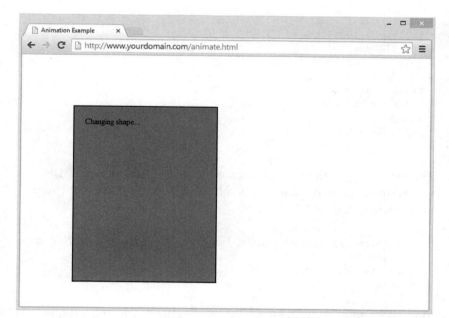

FIGURE 23.2
The animation example shows the element changing shape.

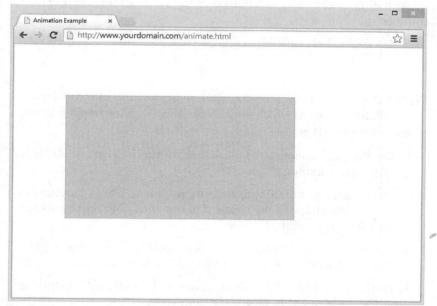

FIGURE 23.3
The animation example shows the element fading away after having changed shape.

```css
#animateMe {
  position: absolute;
  top: 100px;
  left: 100px;
  width: 100px;
  height: 400px;
  border: 2px solid black;
  background-color: red;
  padding: 20px;
}
```

The first `<script>` element contains a link to the Google Code CDN, which stores the particular version of the jQuery library we are using in this script, jQuery 2.1.1:

```html
<script
    src="http://ajax.googleapis.com/ajax/libs/jquery/2.1.1/jquery.
        min.js"
    type="text/javascript">
</script>
```

The magic happens in the next `<script>` element, which contains actual jQuery. First, ensure that the document is in a ready state by wrapping the primary commands in the `$( document ).ready()` handler:

```javascript
$( document ).ready(function() {
    // more code goes here
});
```

Within the `$( document ).ready()` handler is a chain of commands and callback functions which ensure that these actions happen to any element with an ID of `animateMe`:

1. Use the `text()` method to place text within the element labeled "Changing shape...."

2. Over a period of 5000 milliseconds, use the `animate()` method to change the shape of the element to one that is 400 pixels wide and 200 pixels high.

3. When the shape change is complete, use the `text()` method to place text within the element labeled "Fading away...."

4. Over a period of 4000 milliseconds, use the `fadeOut()` method to cause the element to disappear from view.

All the preceding steps are found in this chunk of the code:

```
$("#animateMe").text("Changing shape...").animate(
    {
    width: "400px",
    height: "200px"
    }, 5000, function() {
        $(this).text("Fading away...").fadeOut(4000);
    }
);
```

Finally, within the body of the HTML document, you see a `<div>` with an ID of `animateMe`. This `<div>`, which contains no text in the HTML, is the DOM element that all the jQuery code is manipulating:

```
<div id="animateMe"></div>
```

Although there's no text inside the `<div>` element originally, the jQuery `text()` method adds it in for display as the script executes. That's really all there is to it—you have some basic DOM elements that this powerful jQuery library can manipulate in many ways to produce an interactive experience for your users. Modifications to the display can happen automatically, as in the preceding example, or by capturing events that the user enacts, such as mouse clicks and key presses.

Handling Events with jQuery

All the examples in this chapter so far show jQuery that simply runs when the script is loaded in the browser. But as we've seen throughout this book and in your experience online in general, interactivity occurs when a user invokes actions through mouse clicks or key presses—click a button to start a process, hover over an image to see a larger version, and so on.

jQuery has its own syntax for handling events, which is as straightforward as the basic HTML and JavaScript you've seen in the previous chapters. For example, you can attach event handlers to elements or collections of elements—such as all `<a>` elements, an `<a>` element with given ID, all `<a>` elements with a given class name, and so on.

Capturing click events happens directly with the jQuery `.click()` event handler:

```
$("a").click(function() {
    // execute this code when any anchor element is clicked
});
```

You can also handle a click event, `.click()`, using a named function:

```
function hello() {
    alert("Hello from jQuery");
}
$("a").click(hello);
```

In both instances, the code within the curly braces or the named function (depending on which you have used) will be executed when any anchor is clicked. Note that the `.click()` event handler is not the only one available to you; other event handlers include the following:

- ▶ `.keydown()`—Handles a `keydown` JavaScript event
- ▶ `.keypress()`—Handles a `keypress` JavaScript event
- ▶ `.keyup()`—Handles a `keyup` JavaScript event
- ▶ `.dblclick()`—Handles a `dblclick` (double click) JavaScript event
- ▶ `.focusout()`—Handles a `focusout` JavaScript event
- ▶ `.mousedown()`—Handles a `mousedown` JavaScript event
- ▶ `.mouseenter()`—Handles a `mouseenter` JavaScript event
- ▶ `.mouseleave()`—Handles a `mouseleave` JavaScript event
- ▶ `.mousemove()`—Handles a `mousemove` JavaScript event
- ▶ `.mouseout()`—Handles a `mouseout` JavaScript event
- ▶ `.mouseover()`—Handles a `mouseover` JavaScript event
- ▶ `.mouseup()`—Handles a `mouseup` JavaScript event

For more information and documentation on other methods available in jQuery to handle JavaScript events, visit http://api.jquery.com/category/events/.

Summary

In this chapter, you took a closer look at the basics of using jQuery in your interactive sites, which begins by including the library and verifying the ready state of your document. From that point forward, you learned how to select page elements by referencing their element name, ID, class, or other position within the DOM, and how to manipulate the text within or the appearance of those elements.

Additionally, you learned about chaining jQuery commands together, and how to handle JavaScript events with jQuery so that users can initiate visual display or other changes through actions they take with their keyboard or mouse.

Q&A

Q. This chapter was short—isn't jQuery huge?

A. Remarkably, even though jQuery is very powerful, it is not in fact a huge codebase nor is it particularly unwieldy. Clocking in at 10,000 lines of code or so, and 275KB (when not minimized), it's definitely bigger than a web page, that's for sure! But it is true that packed into those 10,000 lines of code are many features we have not discussed here. We will talk a little more about the jQuery UI library in the next chapter, but even that is not sufficient to cover everything you might find in the technical documentation at http://api.jquery.com/ or in the more user-friendly documentation and tutorials site at http://learn.jquery.com/.

Q. Can I use jQuery in addition to other libraries and frameworks?

A. Yes, you can use jQuery with other libraries, and in fact many frameworks either include jQuery in their distribution or require that it be included as well. jQuery even provides a method for avoiding conflicts through the `noConflict()` method, which you can read about at http://learn.jquery.com/using-jquery-core/avoid-conflicts-other-libraries/.

Workshop

The workshop contains quiz questions and exercises to help you solidify your understanding of the material covered. Test your knowledge of JavaScript libraries by answering the following questions. Try to answer all questions before looking at the "Answers" section that follows.

Quiz

1. How could you select all page elements having a class of `sidebar`?

    a. `$(".sidebar")`

    b. `$("class: sidebar")`

    c. `$("#sidebar")`

2. The expression `$("p:first").show()` does what, exactly?

    a. Displays `<p>` elements before displaying any other elements

    b. Makes the first `<p>` element on the page visible

    c. Makes the first line of all `<p>` elements visible

3. When used with methods for fading, sliding, and animating elements, which of the following is not a valid value?

    a. `fast`

    b. `1000`

    c. `quick`

Answers

1. a. `$(".sidebar")`

2. b. Makes the first paragraph element on the page visible

3. c. `quick`

Exercises

To further explore the JavaScript features you learned about in this chapter, you can perform the following exercises:

▶ Modify the example in Listing 23.2 to react to mouse events, using jQuery.

▶ Go back to a few earlier chapters and find examples that use JavaScript events for interactivity. Rewrite those examples using basic jQuery as you've learned here.

CHAPTER 24

First Steps Toward Creating Rich Interactions with jQuery UI

In the preceding chapter, you took a closer look at the jQuery library, and saw how some of its built-in functions and methods can take the place of large chunks of JavaScript you'd otherwise have to write, test, and maintain on your own. The jQuery UI library is a similar beast—it is an additional library built on top of jQuery, which specifically provides a set of common UI interactions, effects, and widgets that make it significantly easier to provide your users with well-known interface elements without your having to reinvent the wheel.

In this chapter you'll have the opportunity to put the jQuery UI library into action, and learn how to apply effects to elements, implement generalized interactions such as dragging and dropping and sorting, and generally extend the functionality of your website even further.

Preparing to Use jQuery UI

The current version of jQuery UI (at the time of writing) is 1.10.4, and it requires jQuery version 1.6 or above. The library itself—as well as extensive documentation—can be found at http://jqueryui.com/. As you learned in the preceding chapter, including any JavaScript library in your code is as simple as linking to it via a `<script>` element.

You have two options for storing the library: You can download and store it on your own server, or you can use a remotely hosted version from a content delivery network, such as the one hosted by Google or even the jQuery folks themselves.

If you download jQuery UI (and jQuery) and keep it on your own server, I would suggest keeping it in a directory called `js` (for "JavaScript") or another directory specifically for assets (in fact, you

WHAT YOU'LL LEARN IN THIS CHAPTER:

▶ How and why to include the jQuery UI library

▶ How to use jQuery UI selectors

▶ How to dynamically position UI elements

▶ How to add effects when hiding, showing, or repositioning elements

▶ How to implement drag-and-drop functionality

TIP

If you decide to download jQuery UI, you can actually customize what is included. Go to the jQuery UI Download Builder at http://jqueryui.com/download/; select the parts of the code you know you're going to use, and leave out the code you know you don't need.

could even call it `assets`) so that it doesn't get lost among all the other files you maintain. Then, reference it like so:

```
<script src="/js/jquery-ui.min.js" type="text/javascript">
</script>
```

However, as I indicated in the preceding chapter when discussing the use of jQuery itself, I typically use the Google content delivery network. Use whatever is more comfortable for you; if you choose the CDN method, your links might look like this:

```
<script
   src="http://ajax.googleapis.com/ajax/libs/jquery/2.1.1/jquery.
   min.js"
   type="text/javascript">
</script>
<script
   src="http://ajax.googleapis.com/ajax/libs/jqueryui/1.10.4/
   jquery-ui.min.js"
   type="text/javascript">
</script>
```

Using Selectors in jQuery UI

Now that you have a plan (or at least a few options) for including the jQuery UI library in your script, let's start by working with three very specific selectors. One great feature of jQuery UI is the capability to extend the jQuery selectors that are already pretty extensive. These jQuery UI selectors make it easier to narrow down selections specific to UI elements.

First, the `:data()` selector enables you to filter elements based on keys added to those elements using the `.data()` jQuery method. In the code snippet that follows, you can see that a color value has been added to three elements: `<p>`, `<span>`, and `<div>`. The `:data()` selector is then used to set the colors on those elements; this selector can be useful when you want to change the appearance or behavior of an element based on the data associated with it.

```
// first provide the data for the colors of the elements
$("p").data("color", "red");
$("span").data("color", "blue");
$("div").data("color", "green");
```

```
// now set the colors on each of the elements
$(":data(color)").each(function(){
  $(this).css({color:$(this).data("color")});
});
```

Similarly, the :focusable selector enables you to limit elements to only those that can receive focus. For example, the following statement limits the changes to only those form elements that can receive focus. You can imagine using the :focusable selector to highlight a set of form fields that the user needs to complete.

```
$("form:focusable").each(function(){
  $(this).css({color:red});
});
```

Finally, the :tabbable selector is similar to the :focusable selector, in that it enables you to limit elements to only those that can be tabbed to. For example, the following statement limits the changes to only those form elements that can be tabbed to:

```
$("form:tabbable").each(function(){
  $(this).css({color:red});
});
```

This filter is very useful, especially when you're trying to exclude elements that are disabled.

Positioning UI Elements with jQuery UI

A great advantage that jQuery UI provides is the capability to position elements relative to other elements, and also handle collisions. This is done by extending the jQuery .position() method to allow for an options object that defines the relative positions between the jQuery element and other elements or event locations.

For example, to position an element #div1 to the right of #div2, you could use the following:

```
$("#div1").position({my:"left", at:"right", of:"#div2"});
```

Table 24.1 describes the options that jQuery UI provides to the .position() method.

TIP

You can use the :focusable selector for elements that have a negative tab index, but you cannot use the :tabbable selector for those elements.

TABLE 24.1   Option Settings Used When Elements Are Positioned with the jQuery UI `.position()` Method

Option	Description
my	Specifies the relative position of the current jQuery object used for alignment. Acceptable values are `right`, `left`, `top`, `bottom`, `center`. These values can also be combined, as in `left top`, `right bottom`, `left center`, `center center`. Finally, these positions can also be adjusted using numerical or percentage values. For example, the following places the item -10 pixels to the left and 20% of the height down: `left-10 top+20%`
at	Specifies the relative position in the target element to use for alignment. This option can be set to the same values as the `my` option.
of	Specifies a selector, a DOM element object, a jQuery object, or a JavaScript Event object. In the case of a jQuery object, the first element in the set is used. In the case of a JavaScript Event object, the `pageX` and `pageY` properties are used.
collision	Specifies how to handle instances in which the element overflows the window in some direction. When this option is specified and the object overflows the current window, it is moved based on the collision value. Accepted values are as shown here: ▶ `flip`—Flips the element to the opposite side of the specified target, and then runs the collision detection again. Whichever side allows more of the element to be visible is then used. ▶ `fit`—Repositions the element away from the edge of the window. ▶ `flipfit`—Tries to apply the flip logic by placing the element on whichever side allows more of the element to be visible. Then it tries the `fit` logic to ensure that as much of the element is visible as possible. ▶ `none`—Does not apply any collision detection.
using	Specifies a selector, a DOM element object, a jQuery object, or a JavaScript Event object. In the case of a jQuery object, the first element in the set is used. In the case of a JavaScript Event object, the `pageX` and `pageY` properties are used.
within	Enables you to specify the container object to use when determining whether there is a collision. This defaults to the JavaScript `window` object but can be set to a selector, a DOM element object, or a jQuery object.

In Listing 24.1, you can find the complete code used to position static image elements, as well as a dynamic one that moves with the mouse. You add some collision protections to keep the image from leaving a `<div>` element.

LISTING 24.1   Positioning Elements with jQuery UI

```
<!DOCTYPE html>
<html lang="en">
<head>
<title>Positioning with jQuery UI</title>

<script
   src="http://ajax.googleapis.com/ajax/libs/jquery/2.1.1/jquery.
   min.js"
   type="text/javascript">
</script>
<script
   src="http://ajax.googleapis.com/ajax/libs/jqueryui/1.10.4/
   jquery-ui.min.js"
   type="text/javascript">
</script>

<style type="text/css">
img {
  position: absolute;
  width: 150px;
  height: auto;
}
div {
  height: 500px;
  width: 450px;
  border: 3px solid #000;
}
</style>

<script type="text/javascript">
$(document).ready(function() {
   $("#img2").position({my:"left top", at:"right bottom",
   of:"#img1"});
   $("#img3").position({my:"left top", at:"right bottom",
   of:"#img2"});
   $("div").mousemove(function(e) {
       $("#img4").position(
         { my:"left top", at:"center", of:e, collision:"flip",
           within:"div" }
       );
   })
});
</script>
```

```
</head>
<body>
    <h1>Positioning with jQuery UI</h1>
    <div>
        <img id="img1" alt="Victoria" src="victoria.jpg" />
        <img id="img2" alt="British Columbia" src=
        "british_columbia.jpg" />
        <img id="img3" alt="Wyoming" src="wyoming.jpg" />
        <img id="img4" alt="Niagara Falls" src="niagarafalls.jpg"
        />
    </div>
</body>
</html>
```

As you step through the code, there shouldn't be anything unfamiliar to you until you get to the interesting lines within the jQuery `$(document).ready()` handler. The script begins with the standard inclusion of the jQuery and jQuery UI libraries, and then sets up some minimal styles for `<img />` and `<div>` elements. In this case, all images will be absolutely positioned, and are set at 150 pixels wide. Any `<div>`s will be 500 pixels high and 450 pixels wide, and will have a 3-pixel solid black border.

Skipping over the jQuery for a moment, the HTML itself is very simple: There is an `<h1>` heading followed by a single `<div>` that includes four images. Without the jQuery, you can imagine that these images would be displayed one right after the other, on a single line, until they ran out of space in the `<div>`, at which point one or more images would move to the next line. With the jQuery in place, however, this is not the case.

Instead, what you have is something like what's shown in Figure 24.1. I say "something like" because the placement of the fourth image is dependent on a mouse movement.

All the interesting bits of this code happen within the jQuery `$(document).ready()` handler—specifically, these two lines, which set up the placement of two of the four images:

```
$("#img2").position({my:"left top", at:"right bottom",
of:"#img1"});
$("#img3").position({my:"left top", at:"right bottom",
of:"#img2"});
```

Given that the first image is placed absolutely—its top-left corner in the top-left corner of its surrounding `<div>` element—this bit of jQuery and the extended jQuery UI `:position()` method instruct the browser to render the top left of the second image at the bottom right of the first image. Similarly, the top left of the third image is to be positioned at the bottom right of the second image. You can see this in the diagonal line of images in Figure 24.1.

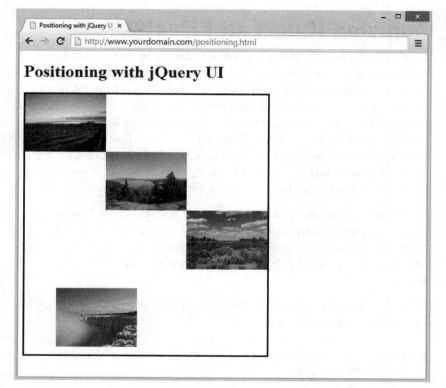

FIGURE 24.1
Showing images positioned with jQuery UI.

The final bit of code deserves a bit more explanation, because it controls the placement of the fourth image based on the user's mouse movement.

```
$("div").mousemove(function(e) {
    $("#img4").position(
    { my:"left top", at:"center", of:e, collision:"flip",
      within:"div" }
    );
})
```

This code essentially says that for any mouse movement within the selected `<div>` element, position the top-left corner of the fourth image wherever that mouse is within the <div>. If you try this yourself, you should see very clearly that the top-left corner of the image follows your mouse very closely. The value of collision is set to flip within the <div> element, meaning that even if your mouse goes outside the element, the image will stay within it.

Applying jQuery UI Effects

Now that you have a little experience applying jQuery UI methods to your code, let's take a close look at some of the interesting visual effects that the jQuery UI library can provide to you through the use of the .each() method. You'll also get a look at the easing functions that provide a variable aspect to how values are applied during the effect animation. To be clear, jQuery UI effects are just animations to CSS position, size, and visibility properties, but these changes are implemented in such a way as to create visual effects that give users a better, or at least more interesting, experience.

For example, suppose a user tries to log in with an invalid password. In addition to the form validation message, you can also use jQuery UI effects to make the login button shake, which might catch the user's attention better than just printing text to tell the user that the login failed.

Table 24.2 lists the jQuery UI effects along with the values that can be applied to manipulate them.

TABLE 24.2   Methods and Options for Effects When the jQuery UI .each() Method Is Used

Method	Option	Description
blind	direction	Provides the effect of "pulling the blinds" up by rolling the element up from the bottom. The value of direction can be set to up, down, left, right, vertical, or horizontal.
bounce	distance times	Provides a bouncing effect by repositioning the element up and down vertically. The value of distance is specified in pixels, and times is the number of times you want the element to bounce.

`clip`	`direction`	Slides the element down as the bottom is erased, simulating the bottom being clipped off. The value of `direction` can be set to `vertical` or `horizontal`.
`drop`	`direction`	Slides the element as it fades in or out. The value of `direction` can be set to `up`, `down`, `left`, or `right`.
`explode`	`pieces`	Slices the element into equal pieces that fade away in different directions. The value of `pieces` should be a perfect square (4, 9, 16, 25, etc.).
`fade`		Slowly fades the element in or out.
`fold`	`size` `horizFirst`	Folds the element in one direction, then in another. The value of `size` is equal to the number of pixels to fold down to, and `horizFirst` (`true` or `false`) specifies which direction to fold first.
`highlight`	`color`	Adds a color highlight to the image; `color` specifies the hex color (e.g., `#336699`).
`puff`	`percent`	Scales an element up at the same time it hides it, thus giving the effect of a puff of air. The value of `percent` is the percentage to scale the element to, such as `50` for a smaller image or `150` for a bigger image.
`pulsate`	`times`	Fades the element in and out quickly, simulating a pulsating effect. The value of `times` is the number of times to perform the fade action.

`scale`	`direction`
	`origin`
	`percent`
	`scale`
		Shrinks or enlarges the element to a vanishing point. The value of `direction` can be `both`, `vertical`, or `horizontal`. The value of `origin` is an array that specifies the vanishing point, such as `{"middle", "center"}`. The value of `percent` is the percentage to scale to, and `scale` specifies which part of the element to resize: `box`, `content`, or `both`.

NOTE

Before going off and adding effects all over the place, it's important to understand animation easing, so as to provide a better experience for users. The easing function sets a value path that the effect uses when animating the effect, and there are more than 30 easing functions in jQuery UI. Some of these functions appear in the code listings, but taking a moment to review the documentation and interactive examples at http://api.jqueryui.com/easings/ will likely be of great help to you.

shake	direction distance times	Animates rapid position changes vertically or horizontally. The value of `direction` can be `left`, `right`, `up`, or `down`. The value of `distance` is the number of pixels to shake, and `times` is the number of times to shake.
size	to origin scale	Animates the resizing of the element. The value of `to` specifies the new height and width, in the format `{height: value, width: value}`. The value of `origin` is the vanishing point, such as `{"middle", "right"}`, and `scale` specifies which part of the element to resize: `box`, `content`, or `both`.
slide	direction distance	Animates the element to simulate a sliding effect. The value of `direction` can be `left`, `right`, `up`, or `down`; `distance` indicates the distance to slide, up to the height or width of the element.

There are multiple ways to apply effects to jQuery objects. Effects can be added as a part of another transition, such as a class change or visibility change. You can also apply effects to an element using the `.effect()` method using the following syntax:

`.effect( effect [, options ] [, duration ] [, complete ] )`

In this syntax example, *effect* is the name of the effect (from Table 24.2) and *options* is an object containing the option values. The *duration* is specified in milliseconds, and you can add an optional *complete* handler function that will be executed when the effect has been applied.

The following example illustrates the full syntax of the `.effect()` method when a `size` effect is being applied to an `<img />` element:

```
("img").effect("size",
    {to:{height:100, width:100}, origin:["right","top"],
     scale:"box"},
    3000,
    function(){alert("effect complete");});
```

In Listing 24.2 you can see how to apply several effects to `<img />` elements—although you can apply effects to any element, these tend to be more visible for learning purposes when applied to images.

LISTING 24.2   Applying Effects to Images Using jQuery UI

```
<!DOCTYPE html>
<html lang="en">
<head>
<title>Applying Effects to Images Using jQuery UI</title>

<script
    src="http://ajax.googleapis.com/ajax/libs/jquery/2.1.1/jquery.
    min.js"
    type="text/javascript">
</script>
<script
    src="http://ajax.googleapis.com/ajax/libs/jqueryui/1.10.4/
    jquery-ui.min.js"
    type="text/javascript">
</script>

<style type="text/css">
div {
  height: 110px;
  padding: 6px;
  width: 150px;
  border: 2px solid #000;
  display: inline-block;
  position: fixed;
}
#frame1 {
    top: 80px;
    left: 20px;
}
#frame2 {
    top: 80px;
    left: 240px;
}
#frame3 {
    top: 80px;
    left: 460px;
}
```

```
#frame4 {
   top: 80px;
   left: 680px;
}
</style>

<script type="text/javascript">
$(document).ready(function() {
   $("#img1").click(function(e) {
      $(this).effect("shake", {direction:"down", distance:20,
       times:5}, 3000);
   });
   $("#img2").click(function(e) {
      $(this).effect("scale",
         {direction:"both", origin:["middle", "right"],
         percent:40, scale:"box", easing:"easeInBounce"}, 3000);
   });
   $("#img3").click(function(e) {
      $(this).effect("slide", {direction:"down", distance:200},
       3000,
         function() {
            $(this).effect("slide", {direction:"right",
             distance:200}, 3000);
      });
   });
   $("#img4").click(function(e) {
      $(this).effect("explode", {pieces:16}, 3000);
   });
});
</script>

</head>
<body>
   <h1>Applying Effects to Images Using jQuery UI</h1>
   <div id="frame1">
      <img id="img1" alt="Victoria" src="victoria.jpg" />
   </div>
   <div id="frame2">
      <img id="img2" alt="British Columbia" src="british_
      columbia.jpg" />
   </div>
   <div id="frame3">
      <img id="img3" alt="Wyoming" src="wyoming.jpg" />
   </div>
   <div id="frame4">
      <img id="img4" alt="Niagara Falls" src="niagarafalls.jpg"
      />
   </div>
</body>
</html>
```

When you step through the code just as you did with Listing 24.1, there shouldn't be anything unfamiliar to you until you get to the jQuery `$(document).ready()` handler. The script begins with the standard inclusion of the jQuery and jQuery UI libraries, and then sets up some minimal styles for `<div>` elements and some IDs. In this case, any `<div>` will be 110 pixels high and 150 pixels wide, and will have a 2-pixel solid black border, in addition to some padding. Some elements might have an ID, and four IDs are defined here to indicate fixed placement on the page. Skipping over the jQuery for a moment, the HTML itself is very simple: There is an `<h1>` heading followed by four `<div>`s that each include an image.

Back to the jQuery, which sets up specific `.click()` event handlers for each image. The first `.click()` handler, for the image with an ID of `img1`, applies the `shake` effect. Specifically, the image appears to shake five times, beginning by moving down 20 pixels at first, and the entire action takes 3000 milliseconds (or 3 seconds). The `.click()` handler for the second image applies the `scale` effect in both directions to the middle-right vanishing point, and scales the image down to 40%; note the use of `easeInBounce` easing to ensure a smoother animation flow. The `.click()` handler for the third image applies two effects: First, a `slide` effect moves the image down 200 pixels, and when that effect is complete, a `slide` effect moves the image to the right 200 pixels. Finally, the `.click()` handler for the fourth image applies the `explode` effect, which breaks the image into 16 pieces and fades the pieces away as they move apart.

Capturing effects is difficult in a screenshot, but in Figure 24.2 you can see the fourth image in the midst of its `explode` effect.

FIGURE 24.2
Applying jQuery UI effects to images.

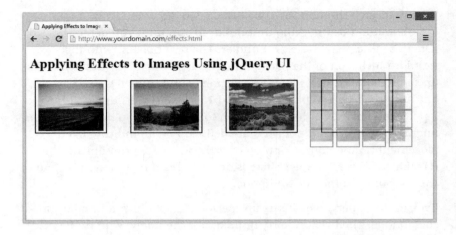

Adding Effects to Element Visibility Transitions

In addition to using jQuery UI effects with event handlers, you can also add effects when visibility changes. This effect can enable users to better visualize what is happening on their screen, and it provides them with a chance to follow the page flow better.

Visibility effects are applied in the same manner as the .effect() function you learned earlier in this chapter. You specify an effect from Table 25.2 and then set the desired options, including an easing function if you want to control the animation. Following are the element visibility transition methods that you can add effects to using jQuery UI:

- ▶ .hide(effect [, options] [, duration] [, complete])— Applies the effect with options while hiding the element.

- ▶ .show(effect [, options] [, duration] [, complete])— Applies the effect with options while showing the element.

- ▶ .toggle(effect [, options] [, duration] [, complete])— Either shows or hides the object based on its current visibility and applies the specified effect while doing so.

In Listing 24.3 you can see how to apply effects to visibility transitions. In this case, the example shows some rudimentary menus that appear to open (become visible) in interesting ways.

Listing 24.3   Applying Effects to Visibility Transitions Using jQuery UI

```
<!DOCTYPE html>
<html lang="en">
<head>
<title>Applying Effects to Visibility Transitions Using jQuery
UI</title>

<script
   src="http://ajax.googleapis.com/ajax/libs/jquery/2.1.1/jquery.
   min.js"
   type="text/javascript">
</script>
<script
   src="http://ajax.googleapis.com/ajax/libs/jqueryui/1.10.4/
   jquery-ui.min.js"
   type="text/javascript">
</script>

<style type="text/css">
span {
  display: inline-block;
  width: 130px;
  border: 2px solid #000;
  text-align: center;
  cursor: pointer;
}

div span {
  width: 120px;
  margin-left: 10px;
}

#showMenu {
  position: fixed;
  left: 130px;
  top: 80px;
}

#showMenu2 {
  position: fixed;
  left: 130px;
  top: 105px;
}
</style>

<script type="text/javascript">
$(document).ready(function() {
    $("#showMenu, #showMenu2, #toggleMenu").hide();

    $("#show").click(function(e) {
```

```
      $("#showMenu").show("fold", {size:22}, 2000);
    });

  $("#show2").click(function(e) {
      $("#showMenu2").show("scale", {origin:["top","left"]},
      2000);
    });

  $("#showMenu").click(function(e) {
      $("#showMenu").hide("fold", {size:22}, 2000);
    });

  $("#showMenu2").click(function(e) {
      $("#showMenu2").hide("explode", {pieces:9}, 2000);
    });

  $("#toggle, #toggleMenu").click(function(e) {
      $("#toggleMenu").toggle("blind",
          {direction:"up", easing:"easeOutBounce"}, 2000);
    });
});
</script>
</head>
<body>
  <h1>Applying Visibility Effects Using jQuery UI</h1>

  <span id="show">Show Fold</span><br/>
  <span id="show2">Show Scale</span><br/>
  <span id="toggle">Toggle Blind</span><br/>

  <div id="showMenu">
    <span>Fold 1</span><br/><span>Fold 2</span><br/>
    <span>Fold 3</span><br/><span>Fold 4</span><br/>
  </div>

  <div id="showMenu2">
    <span>Explode 1</span><br/><span>Explode 2</span><br/>
    <span>Explode 3</span><br/><span>Explode 4</span><br/>
  </div>

  <div id="toggleMenu">
    <span>Toggle 1</span><br/><span>Toggle 2</span><br/>
    <span>Toggle 3</span><br/><span>Toggle 4</span><br/>
  </div>

</body>
</html>
```

In this example, the CSS and the HTML set up some fake menu items—the CSS is all about placement, and the majority of the HTML simply creates four entries in each of the three menus. The interesting code is in the $(document).ready() handler, which opens by setting the visibility of three IDs (#showMenu, #showMenu2, and #toggleMenu) to hidden using the hide() method. This means that when the page is initially loaded, all three of the <div>s you see in the raw HTML will not be rendered on the page. The visibility of these <div>s changes when a click event is captured.

The first .click() handler, for the <div> with the ID of show, changes the visibility of the element with the showMenu ID and applies the fold effect. Similarly, the second .click() handler, for the <div> with the ID of show2, changes the visibility of the showMenu2 ID and applies the scale effect. The third .click() handler affects the showMenu ID again, applying the fold effect to a change in the visibility using the hide() method again. In other words, click on Show Fold once and the browser will fold the menu items into visibility, and if you click on any of those menu items that just appeared, the menu items will retreat into invisibility.

If you read through the remaining lines of the jQuery code, you'll quickly catch on that exactly the same process is happening with the remaining menu items, just with different effects used for the transitions. For example, if you click on any of the menu items labeled "Explode," they will retreat into invisibility by appearing to explode first, using the explode effect, and the final menu items will roll down and roll up as if they were window blinds.

Using jQuery UI Widgets for Advanced Interactions

As we move into more advanced work with jQuery UI, it's important to understand a little bit about widgets, because they are indeed fully featured pieces of jQuery that you can plug into your own code and immediately have access to rich interactions. All jQuery UI interactions are based on two main components that are already built into the core jQuery library—the jQuery.widget factory and the mouse widget.

The jQuery.widget factory provides the base functionality for all widgets, including creation, disabling, enabling, and option settings. The mouse widget provides the base mouse interactions with the widget that captures mouse events and allows the widgets to interact with them. The `jQuery.widget` factory defines an interface that is used by all jQuery UI widgets so that the options, methods, and events of the factory are available to all widgets.

Here's a quick list of methods and events available on all jQuery widgets:

▶ `create()`—Triggers an event each time the widget is created.

▶ `destroy()`—Removes the widget functionality completely.

▶ `disable()`–Keeps the widget functionality, but disables it.

▶ `enable()`—Enables the widget functionality.

▶ `option([optionName][, value])`—Returns an object with all option keys and values. If `optionName` is specified, it returns the specific option value; if `optionName` and `value` are specified, it sets an option value.

▶ `widget(name, [base,] prototype)`—Is used to create custom widgets. The `name` parameter is the string used to name and access the widget, the `base` parameter is the existing widget to inherit functionality from (if any), and `prototype` is an object defining the widget.

Even with just this little bit of information, you can move on and try your hand at the examples in the following sections. However, if you take a moment to understand the documentation at http://api.jqueryui.com/jQuery.widget/, you'll be all the more ahead of the game.

Understanding the Mouse Interaction Widget

The mouse interaction widget is automatically applied to all widgets. Typically, you will not need to interact with it much. However, it does expose a few options that are very useful at times. Those options are the following:

▶ `cancel`—Cancels interaction for specific elements. For example, to cancel mouse interactions for elements with a class of `label` in the element with an ID of `item1`, you would use this:

```
$( "#item1" ).mouse( "option", "cancel", ".label" );
```

▶ `delay`—Delays the time after the `mousedown` event occurs before the interaction takes place. For example, to add a 1-second delay for mouse interactions on elements with an ID of `item2`, you would use this:

```
$( "#item2" ).mouse( "option", "delay", 1000 );
```

▶ `distance`—Specifies the distance in pixels the mouse must travel after the `mousedown` event occurs before the interaction should start. For example, to set the distance to 10 pixels for mouse interactions with elements with an ID of `item3`, you would use this:

```
$( "#item3" ).mouse( "option", "distance", 10 );
```

Implementing Draggable Items

Now that you have reviewed the widget interface and the mouse interaction widget, you are ready to look at some of most common jQuery UI widgets: the `draggable()` and `droppable()` widgets. These widgets are designed to work in tandem to provide users with a richer and more interactive experience.

In brief, you can define one element to be draggable and then another to be droppable. When draggable elements are dropped on droppable widgets, you can apply JavaScript and jQuery code to provide whatever interaction for the user you would like.

The `draggable()` widget defines an element as draggable by holding down the mouse and moving it. This enables you to move the element to whatever position on the screen you would like. The `draggable()` widget handles scrolling elements and provides several options to control the visual effects on the screen that occur while the user is dragging an object.

Table 24.3 describes the more common `draggable()` options. The following line of code shows an example of attaching the `draggable()` widget to an element with the ID of `img1` while setting the `cursor` and `opacity` options:

```
$("#img1").draggable({cursor:"move", opacity:.5});
```

TABLE 24.3   Common `draggable()` Widget Options

Option	Description
axis	Can be set to `x` or `y`, or `false`. If set to `x`, drag is horizontal only; `y` drags vertically only, and `false` drags freely.
containment	Specifies a container to limit dragging within. Possible values are `parent`, `document`, or `window`.
cursor	Specifies the cursor to display while dragging.
helper	Defines what element is displayed when dragging. Values can be `original`, `clone`, or a function that returns a DOM object.
opacity	Sets the opacity while dragging.
revert	If Boolean, specifies whether the `original` object should return to its original position when dragging stops. If a string set to `valid`, revert occurs only if the object has been dropped successfully, and `invalid` reverts only if the object hasn't been dropped successfully.
stack	Is set to `false` or a selector. If a selector is specified, the item is brought to the top `z-index` of the element specified by the selector.
zIndex	Specifies the `z-index` value to use while dragging.

The `draggable()` widget also provides additional events so handlers can be attached to the element when dragging starts, is in progress, and stops:

▶ `drag(event, ui)`—Triggered while dragging; `event` is the event object and `ui` is an object with the following values: `helper` (object of the draggable item), `position` (object for the current CSS position), and `offset` (object for the current CSS offset).

▶ `dragstart(event, ui)`—Triggered when dragging starts.

▶ `dragstop(event, ui)`—Triggered when dragging stops.

For example, the following snippet of code shows the addition of a `dragstop` event to apply a `bounce` effect when the item is dropped:

```
$("#drag1").draggable({cursor:"move", opacity:.5});
$("#drag1").on("dragstop", function(){$(this).effect("bounce",
1000); });
```

In Listing 24.4 you can see some examples of draggable images using widgets; we'll step through the code in a moment.

LISTING 24.4   Applying Effects to Visibility Transitions Using jQuery UI

```html
<!DOCTYPE html>
<html lang="en">
<head>
<title>Draggable Images Using jQuery UI</title>

<script
   src="http://ajax.googleapis.com/ajax/libs/jquery/2.1.1/jquery.
   min.js"
   type="text/javascript">
</script>
<script
   src="http://ajax.googleapis.com/ajax/libs/jqueryui/1.10.4/
   jquery-ui.min.js"
   type="text/javascript">
</script>

<style type="text/css">
p {
  margin: 0px;
}
div {
  height: 115px;
  width: 150px;
  position: fixed;
}

#drag2 {
  top: 225px;
}

#drag3 {
  top: 375px;
}

img {
  width: 150px;
}
</style>

<script type="text/javascript">
$(document).ready(function() {
   $("#drag1").draggable({cursor:"move", opacity:.5});

   $("#drag1").on("dragstop", function() {
     $(this).effect("bounce", 1000);
   });
```

```
    $("#drag2").draggable({helper:"clone"});

    $("#drag2").on("dragstop", function(e, ui) {
      $("#drag2").animate(ui.offset);
    });

    $("#drag3").draggable();

    $("#drag3").on("drag", function(e) {
      $(this).children("p").html(e.pageX+", "+e.pageY);
    });

    $("#drag3").on("dragstop", function(e) {
      $(this).children("p").html("");
    });
});
</script>
</head>
<body>
    <h1>Draggable Images Using jQuery UI</h1>

    <div id="drag1">
      <img id="img1" alt="Victoria" src="victoria.jpg" />
    </div>

    <div id="drag2">
      <img id="img2" alt="British Columbia" src="british_columbia.
      jpg" />
    </div>

    <div id="drag3">
      <img id="img3" alt="Wyoming" src="wyoming.jpg" />
    </div>

</body>
</html>
```

The script begins with the standard inclusion of the jQuery and jQuery UI libraries, then sets up some minimal styles for `<p>`, `<img/>`, and `<div>` elements, as well as some IDs. In this case, any `<p>` element will have 0 margin; any `<div>` will be 115 pixels high, be 150 pixels wide, and have a fixed position; and any `<img/>` will have a width of 150 pixels. Some elements might have an ID, and two IDs are defined here to indicate fixed placement on the page. Skipping over the jQuery for a moment, the HTML itself is very simple: There is an `<h1>` heading followed by three `<div>`s that each include an image.

Back to the jQuery, which couldn't be simpler to implement now that we have widgets to use. In the first set of jQuery statements, the `draggable()` widget is added to the element with the ID of `drag1`, and sets the `opacity` to 50% while dragging occurs. A `dragstop` handler is added to ensure that when the user has let stopped dragging the item and has let go of the mouse button, the `bounce` effect is applied to the image.

Similarly, in the next set of statements, `draggable()` is implemented for the element with an ID of `drag2`. In this case, the helper option is set to clone so that the object stays in place while dragging; but next a `dragstop` event handler is added to animate changing the position from the original to the location of the helper clone. Notice that the offset is collected using the `ui` parameter.

Finally, the element with the ID of `drag3` has a `draggable()` widget, and this time the drag handler updates a previously unknown `<p>` element with the current mouse coordinates while dragging. The `dragstop` handler clears out the position text.

Capturing effects is difficult in a screenshot, but in Figure 24.3 you can see that these items are no longer in their original flush-left position on the page and instead have been dragged and dropped elsewhere.

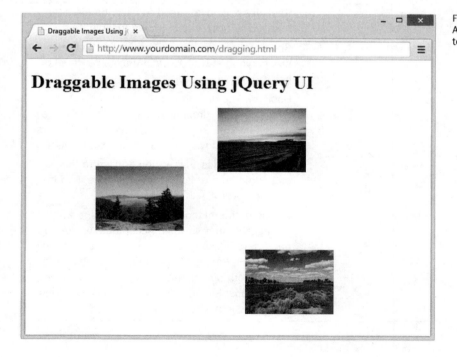

FIGURE 24.3
Applying jQuery UI dragging widgets to move images on the screen.

It's all well and good to create draggable elements, but if you want to produce droppable targets for your users, there are slight modifications to the code you've seen here already. But as you'll soon see, all of these widgets tend to follow a pattern, in that they have clearly defined options and a general syntax for use.

The `droppable()` widget defines an element as a valid drop container usable by draggable items. This enables you to provide interactions between elements using simple mouse controls. Similarly, the `droppable()` widget enables you to specify an `accept` function that can process the information about the event, such as mouse coordinates, as well as the draggable item involved.

Table 24.4 describes the more common droppable options. The following shows an example of attaching the `droppable()` widget to an element and specifying the `tolerance` level:

```
$("#div1"). droppable ({tolerance:"touch"});
```

TABLE 24.4 Common `droppable()` Widget Options

Option	Description
accept	Specifies a selector used to filter the elements that will be accepted by the droppable item.
activeClass	Specifies a class that will be applied to the droppable item while a valid draggable item is being dragged.
greedy	Boolean. The default is `false`, meaning that all valid parent droppable items will receive the draggable item as well. When `true`, only the first droppable item will receive the draggable item.
hoverClass	Specifies a class that will be applied to the droppable item while a valid draggable item is hovering over it.
tolerance	Specifies the method used to determine whether a draggable item is valid. Acceptable values are `fit` (draggable overlaps droppable entirely), `intersect` (draggable overlaps droppable at least 50% in both directions), `pointer` (mouse hovers over droppable), and `touch` (draggable overlaps droppable in any location).

The droppable widget also provides additional events so handlers can be attached to the element when dragging and dropping:

▶ `dropactive(event, ui)`—Triggered when a valid draggable item begins dragging; `event` is the event object and `ui` is an object with the following values: `draggable` (object of the draggable item), `helper` (object of the helper of the draggable item), `position` (object for the current CSS position), and `offset` (object for the current CSS offset).

▶ `drop(event, ui)`—Triggered when a draggable item is dropped on a droppable area.

▶ `dropout(event, ui)`—Triggered when a draggable item leaves a droppable area, based on `tolerance`.

▶ `dropover(event, ui)`—Triggered when a draggable item enters a droppable area, based on `tolerance`.

For example, the following snippet of code shows the addition of a `dropactivate` event to apply a `shake` effect when a droppable item is activated by a drag start:

```
$("#drop1").droppable({tolerance:"pointer"});
$("# drop1").on("dropactivate", function(){$(this).
effect("shake",
    1000); });
```

In Listing 24.5 you can see some examples of drag and drop used within a page. The first droppable element displays an image, and the second adds the image and `src` text to a list.

LISTING 24.5 Applying jQuery UI Drag-and-Drop Functionality

```
<!DOCTYPE html>
<html lang="en">
<head>
<title>Drag and Drop Using jQuery UI</title>

<script
    src="http://ajax.googleapis.com/ajax/libs/jquery/2.1.1/jquery.
    min.js"
    type="text/javascript">
</script>
<script
    src="http://ajax.googleapis.com/ajax/libs/jqueryui/1.10.4/
    jquery-ui.min.js"
    type="text/javascript">
</script>
```

```css
<style type="text/css">
div {
  display: inline-block;
  vertical-align: top;
}

img {
  width: 150px;
  margin: 0px;
}

#images {
  width: 150px;
  height: 115px;
}

#drop1, #drop2 {
  width: 300px;
  min-height: 110px;
  padding: 3px;
  border: 3px ridge white;
}

#drop1 img {
  width: 300px;
  height: auto;
}

#drop2 div {
  height: 115px;
  width: 290px;
  padding: 3px;
  border: 2px dotted black;
}

#drop2 div img {
  height: 115px;
  margin-right: 3px;
}

#drop2 div span {
  display: inline-block;
  vertical-align: top;
  font: 16px/70px sans-serif;
 }

.drop-hover {
  background-color:#BBDDFF;
}
</style>
```

```
<script type="text/javascript">
$(document).ready(function() {
  $("#drag1, #drag2, #drag3").draggable(
    {helper:"clone", cursor:"move", opacity:.7, zIndex:99});

  $("#drop1").droppable(
    {accept:"img", tolerance:"fit", hoverClass:"opaque"});

  $("#drop1").on("dropover", function(e,ui) {
    $(this).effect("pulsate");
  });

  $("#drop1").on("drop", function(e,ui) {
    $(this).html($("<img></img>").attr("src", ui.draggable.
    attr("src")));
    $(this).effect("bounce");
  });

  $("#drop2").droppable(
    {accept:"img", tolerance:"intersect",hoverClass:"drop-hover"}
  );

  $("#drop2").on("drop", function(e,ui) {
    var item = $("<div></div>");
    item.append($("<img></img>").attr("src", ui.draggable.
    attr("src")));
    item.append($("<span></span>").html(ui.draggable.
    attr("alt")));
    $(this).append(item);
  });
});

</script>
</head>
<body>
   <h1>Drag and Drop Using jQuery UI</h1>

   <div id="images">
     <img id="drag1" alt="Victoria" src="victoria.jpg" />
     <img id="drag2" alt="British Columbia" src="british_
     columbia.jpg" />
   </div>

   <div id="drop1"></div>
   <div id="drop2"></div>

</body>
</html>
```

The script begins with the standard inclusion of the jQuery and jQuery UI libraries, and then sets up some sizing, positioning, and font or color styles for the elements that will be involved in the dragging and the dropping. Skipping over the jQuery for a moment, the HTML itself is very simple: There is an `<h1>` heading followed by two `<div>`s that each include an image, and then two `<div>`s that are empty. Those empty `<div>`s are the droppable targets that will change in size and appearance when an item is dropped onto them.

In the first few lines of the jQuery, basic setup is taking place. In these lines the `draggable` widget is being added to the elements with the IDs of `drag1` and `drag2`. We use `clone` for the helper setting to keep the images in place, set the `cursor` and the `opacity`, and also set `zIndex` to a high number so that the images will show on top of other page elements, even while being dragged over.

Next, we add the droppable widget to the element with the ID of `drop1`—this is one of those empty `<div>`s noted previously. The value of `accept` is set to `img` so that only `<img />` elements will be accepted by the drop target. After that, a `dropover` event handler is added that applies a `pulsate` effect to the droppable box when the draggable item is hovering over it. Also, a `drop` event handler is added that will add an `<img />` element to the element with the ID of `drop1` with the same `src` attribute as the draggable element. A `bounce` effect is also added to show the user that the content changed.

Now moving on to the jQuery lines relevant to the second drop area, we implement `droppable()` on the element with an ID of `drop2`. Notice the user of `hoverClass`, which will cause the background to turn light blue when the box is hovered over by a droppable item. Also note the use of a `drop` handler function that adds a `<div>` element with the `<img />` and `src` text to the existing element with the ID of `drop2`. This serves to provide a bit of text, extracted from the dragged element, in the new area.

Figure 24.4 doesn't capture the interactivity, but it does show the original and dropped state of the two images in their new drop zones.

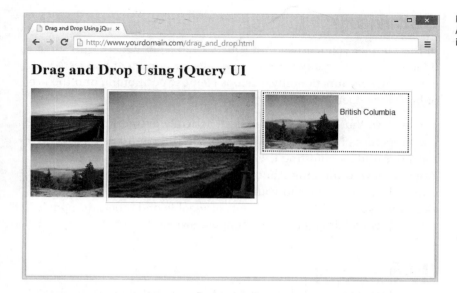

FIGURE 24.4
Applying jQuery UI drag and drop to images and elements.

Where to Go from Here

This chapter has given you a taste of the power of built-in jQuery UI widgets, and there are more where these have come from. If you visit and study the information at http://api.jqueryui.com/category/widgets/, you'll soon find that there are widgets for many of the common UI interactions that you encounter as a user, and all the better to provide those common interactions for your own site visitors. That is the point of the shared library, after all: No one needs to reinvent the wheel, and that includes users not needing to relearn interactions as they move from site to site.

If reading documentation isn't your thing, I recommend taking a look at *Sams Teach Yourself jQuery and JavaScript in 24 Hours*, which has several chapters wholly devoted to jQuery UI. Some of the examples in this chapter will seem familiar if you read that book, but there are many others that implement widgets we haven't covered here, such as autocomplete for forms, buttons, datepickers, dialog boxes, progress bars, sliders, spinners, tabs, and tooltips. There's plenty more to learn!

Summary

In this chapter you learned that jQuery UI extends jQuery with some additional functionality, such as new selectors, and it enhances existing jQuery functionality, such as element positioning and the use of built-in widgets.

You learned that jQuery UI effects are basically animations to the CSS properties of page elements, which you can control using easing functions and by adjusting the rate at which the changes occur. You saw how, using interaction widgets, you can easily provide some advanced features to your web pages such as drag-and-drop elements—you made some elements draggable and others droppable using jQuery UI draggable and droppable widgets.

Q&A

Q. Is there anything that can be done in jQuery UI that I can't do myself in jQuery and JavaScript?

A. No, but that's not the point. The real point is that jQuery and jQuery UI will save you a ton of time by not requiring you to reinvent an already stable wheel, and will enable you to present interactions to your users that they are likely to have experienced elsewhere.

Q. Is there a way to create custom easing functions?

A. Yes, you can create a custom easing function and attach it to `$.easing`. The function needs to accept the following parameters and return a new value based on those parameters:

▶ `tPercent`—Percentage of time passed in the animation from 0.0 to 1.0

▶ `tMS`—Milliseconds since the animation started

▶ `startValue`—Starting value of the property

▶ `endValue`—Ending value of the property

▶ `tTotal`—Duration of the animation

```
$.easing.myCustom = function(tPercent, tMS, startValue,
endValue, tTotal) {
    var newValue= <your code here>...
  return newValue;
}
```

Workshop

The workshop contains quiz questions and exercises to help you solidify your understanding of the material covered. Test your knowledge of JavaScript libraries by answering the following questions. Try to answer all questions before looking at the "Answers" section that follows.

Quiz

1. What jQuery UI selector would you use to isolate elements that happen to have a specific data value assigned to them?

2. How do you control the amount of time the effect will take?

3. When making an item draggable, what option should you use to keep the original in place while dragging?

4. What droppable event will be triggered when a draggable item is ready to be dropped in it?

Answers

1. `:data()`.

2. By setting the `duration` value of the effect.

3. Set `helper` to `clone` or another DOM object.

4. `dropover`.

Exercises

To further explore the JavaScript features you learned about in this chapter, you can perform the following exercises:

▶ Take the code in Listing 24.2 and apply all the other available jQuery UI effects to the images. Be sure to use the effect options where applicable, to experience the full range of functionality.

▶ Practice creating drop targets and the effects that are applied when an item has been dragged and dropped into the target area. Put together all the effects you've learned so far and see how they might be invoked in interesting ways based on that user interaction.

CHAPTER 25

AJAX: Remote Scripting

Remote scripting, also known as AJAX, is a browser feature that enables JavaScript to escape its client-side boundaries and work with files on a web server or with server-side programs. In this chapter, you'll learn how AJAX works and create two working examples of client-side to server-side interactivity using AJAX requests.

Introducing AJAX

Traditionally, one of the major limitations of JavaScript was that it couldn't communicate with a web server because it is a client-side technology—JavaScript runs within the browser. For example, although you can create a game purely in JavaScript, keeping a list of high scores stored on a server requires some form of submitting data to a server-side script, which JavaScript alone could not do (because it originally wasn't meant to do that).

Speaking purely about user interactions, one of the early limitations of web pages in general was that getting data from the user to the server, or from the server to the user, generally required a new page to be loaded and displayed. But in 2014, you would be hard-pressed to find some website in your daily browsing that *doesn't* allow you to interact with content without loading a new page every time you click or submit a button. For example, if you use web-based email such as Google or Yahoo! Mail, or if you use Facebook or Twitter, then you're interacting with some AJAX-based functionality.

AJAX (Asynchronous JavaScript and XML) was the answer to both of the problems indicated previously. AJAX refers to JavaScript's capability to use a built-in object, XMLHttpRequest, to communicate

NOTE

The term *AJAX* first appeared in an online article by Jesse James Garrett of Adaptive Path on February 18, 2005. It still appears here, which is well worth a read: http://www.adaptivepath.com/ideas/ajax-new-approach-web-applications.

with a web server without submitting a form or loading a page. This object is supported by Internet Explorer, Firefox, Chrome, and all other modern browsers.

Although the term *AJAX* was coined in 2005, the `XMLHttpRequest` object has been supported by browsers for years—it was developed by Microsoft and first appeared in Internet Explorer 5. In the past decade, it has become one of the cornerstones of advanced web application development. Another name for this technique is *remote scripting*.

In the next few sections we'll look at the individual components of AJAX in a little more detail.

The JavaScript Client (Front End)

Traditionally, JavaScript had one way of communicating with a server: through an HTML form submission. Remote scripting allows for much more versatile communication with the server. The *A* in *AJAX* stands for *asynchronous*, which means that the browser (and the user) isn't left hanging while waiting for the server to respond. Here's how a typical AJAX request works:

1. The script creates an `XMLHttpRequest` object and sends it to the web server. The script can continue after sending the request, and can perform other tasks.

2. The server responds by sending the contents of a file, or the output of a server-side program.

3. When the response arrives from the server, a JavaScript function is triggered to act on the data.

4. Because the goal is a more responsive user interface, the script usually displays the data from the server using the DOM, eliminating the need for a page refresh.

In practice, this happens very quickly—almost imperceptible to the user—but even with a slow server, it will still work. Also, because the requests are asynchronous, more than one request can be in progress at a time.

The Server-Side Script (Back End)

The part of an application that resides on the web server is commonly referred to as the *back end*. The simplest back-end script is a static file on the server—JavaScript can request the file with XMLHttpRequest, and then read and act on its contents. The back-end script is typically a server-side program running in a language such as PHP, Perl, or Ruby, but it could also be a static file full of data that is simply being returned to the user.

JavaScript can send data to a server-side program using GET or POST methods; these are the same two methods an HTML form uses. In a GET request, the data is encoded in the URL that loads the program. In a POST request, the data is sent separately and the packet can contain more data than a GET request. If it helps, think of the AJAX request as mimicking the action of an HTML-based form, only without the <form> and other related tags.

XML

The *X* in *AJAX* stands for *XML* (Extensible Markup Language), the universal markup language designed to store and transport data. A server-side file or program can send data in XML format, and JavaScript can act on the data using its methods for working with XML. These methods are similar to the DOM methods you've already used—for example, you can use the getElementsByTagName() method to find elements with a particular tag in the data.

Keep in mind that XML is just one way to send data, and not always the easiest. The server could just as easily send plain text, which the script could display, or HTML, which the script could insert into the page using the innerHTML property. In fact, over the past decade that AJAX has been in use, a shift has occurred such that it is more typical to see data transferred in JSON format than in XML format. However, "AJAJ" doesn't have the same ring to it.

Popular Examples of AJAX

Although typical HTML and JavaScript are used to build web pages and sites, AJAX techniques often result in *web applications*—web-based services that perform work for the user. Here are a few well-known examples of AJAX:

▶ Google's Gmail mail client (mail.google.com) uses AJAX to make a fast-responding email application. You can delete messages and perform other tasks without waiting for a new page to load.

NOTE

JSON (JavaScript Object Notation) takes the idea of encoding data in JavaScript and formalizes it. See http://www.json.org/ for details and code examples in many languages.

▶ Amazon.com uses AJAX for some functions. For example, if you click on one of the Yes/No voting buttons for a product comment, it sends your vote to the server and a message appears next to the button thanking you, all without loading a page.

▶ Facebook (www.facebook.com) uses AJAX all over the place, such as every time you "like" something.

These are just a few examples. Subtle bits of remote scripting are appearing all over the Web, and you might not even notice them—you'll just be annoyed a little bit less often at waiting for a page to load. Because remote scripting can be complicated, several frameworks and libraries have been developed to simplify AJAX programming. For starters, all the JavaScript libraries and frameworks described earlier in this book, such as JQuery, Prototype, AngularJS, and Backbone.js, include functions to simplify remote scripting.

Using XMLHttpRequest

You will now look at how to use XMLHttpRequest to communicate with a server. This might seem a bit complex, but the process is the same for any request. In fact, it's so similar that later in this chapter you will create a reusable code library to simplify this process.

Creating a Request

The first step to creating a request is to create an XMLHttpRequest object. To do this, you use the new keyword, just as when you create other JavaScript objects. The following statement creates a request object in modern browsers:

```
ajaxreq = new XMLHttpRequest();
```

This example works with Firefox, Chrome, Opera, and Internet Explorer 7 and above, but not with Internet Explorer below version 7. From this point forward, the sample code will only support IE7 and above, but if you want to support these old browsers, you have to use ActiveX syntax:

```
ajaxreq = new ActiveXObject("Microsoft.XMLHTTP");
```

The library section later in this chapter demonstrates how to use the correct method depending on the browser in use. In either case, the variable you use (`ajaxreq` in the example) stores the `XMLHttpRequest` object, and you'll use the methods of this object to open and send a request, as explained in the following sections.

Opening a URL

The `open()` method of the `XMLHttpRequest` object specifies the filename as well as the method in which data will be sent to the server: `GET` or `POST`. These are the same methods supported by web forms.

```
ajaxreq.open("GET","filename");
```

For the `GET` method, the data you send is included in the URL. For example, this command opens the `search.php` script stored on your server and sends the value `John` to the script as the `query` parameter:

```
ajaxreq.open("GET","search.php?query=John");
```

Sending the Request

You use the `send()` method of the `XMLHttpRequest` object to send the request to the server. If you are using the `POST` method, the data to send is the argument for `send()`. For a `GET` request, you can use the `null` value instead:

```
ajaxreq.send(null);
```

Awaiting a Response

After the request is sent, your script will continue without waiting for a result. Because the result could come at any time, you can detect it with an event handler. The `XMLHttpRequest` object has an `onreadystatechange` event handler for this purpose. You can create a function to deal with the response and set it as the handler for this event:

```
ajaxreq.onreadystatechange = MyFunc;
```

The request object has a property, `readyState`, that indicates its status, and this event is triggered whenever the `readyState` property changes. The values of `readyState` range from `0` for a new request to `4` for a complete request, so your event-handling function usually needs to watch for a value of `4`.

Although the request is complete, it might not have been successful. The `status` property is set to `200` if the request succeeded or an error code if it failed. The `statusText` property stores a text explanation of the error or `OK` for success.

Interpreting the Response Data

When the `readyState` property reaches `4` and the request is complete, the data returned from the server is available to your script in two properties: `responseText` is the response in raw text form, and `responseXML` is the response as an XML object. If the data was not in XML format, only the text property will be available.

JavaScript's DOM methods are meant to work on XML, so you can use them with the `responseXML` property. Later in this chapter, you'll use the `getElementsByTagName()` method to extract data from XML.

Creating a Simple AJAX Library

You should be aware by now that AJAX requests can be a bit complex, and to repeat that complex code in every page that calls it definitely makes for unwieldy pages that are no fun to maintain. To make things easier, you can create an AJAX library and simply reference it in your pages, as you do any external script. This library can then provide functions that handle making a request and receiving the result, which you can reuse any time you need AJAX functions.

The library in Listing 25.1 will be used in the two examples later in this chapter, and it shows the complete AJAX library, including a special case for very old browsers.

LISTING 25.1   The AJAX Library

```
// global variables to keep track of the request
// and the function to call when done
var ajaxreq=false, ajaxCallback;

// ajaxRequest: Sets up a request
function ajaxRequest(filename) {
   try {
    // modern browsers
    ajaxreq= new XMLHttpRequest();
   } catch (error) {
    try {
      // IE 5 or IE 6
```

```
        ajaxreq = new ActiveXObject("Microsoft.XMLHTTP");
      } catch (error) {
      return false;
      }
    }
    ajaxreq.open("GET", filename);
    ajaxreq.onreadystatechange = ajaxResponse;
    ajaxreq.send(null);
}

// ajaxResponse: Waits for response and calls a function
function ajaxResponse() {
   if (ajaxreq.readyState !=4) return;
   if (ajaxreq.status==200) {
      // if the request succeeded...
      if (ajaxCallback) ajaxCallback();
   } else alert("Request failed: " + ajaxreq.statusText);
   return true;
}
```

The following sections explain the library's code in a bit more detail.

The `ajaxRequest` **Function**

The `ajaxRequest` function handles all the steps necessary to create and send an `XMLHttpRequest`. First, it creates the `XMLHttpRequest` object. As noted before, this requires a different command for older browsers, and will cause an error if the wrong one executes, so `try` and `catch` are used to create the request. First the standard method is used, and if it causes an error, the ActiveX method is tried. If that also causes an error, the `ajaxreq` variable is set to `false` to indicate that AJAX is unsupported.

The `ajaxResponse` **Function**

The `ajaxResponse` function is used as the `onreadystatechange` event handler. This function first checks the `readyState` property for a value of 4. If it has a different value, the function returns without doing anything.

Next, it checks the `status` property for a value of 200, which indicates that the request was successful. If so, it runs the function stored in the `ajaxCallback` variable. If not, it displays the error message in an alert box.

Using the Library

To use this library, follow these steps:

1. Save the library file as `ajax.js` in the same folder as your HTML documents and scripts.

2. Include the script in the `<head>` of your document, using a `<script>` tag. It should be included before any other scripts that use its features.

3. In your script, create a function to be called when the request is complete, and set the `ajaxCallback` variable to the function.

4. Call the `ajaxRequest()` function. Its parameter is the filename of the server-side program or file. (This version of the library supports GET requests only, so you don't need to specify the method.)

5. Your function specified in `ajaxCallback` will be called when the request completes successfully, and the global variable `ajaxreq` will store the data in its `responseXML` and `responseText` properties.

The two remaining examples in this chapter make use of this library to create AJAX applications.

Creating an AJAX Quiz Using the Library

Now that you have a reusable AJAX library, you can use it to create simple JavaScript applications that take advantage of remote scripting. This first example displays quiz questions on a page and prompts you for the answers.

Rather than including the questions in the script, this example reads the quiz questions and answers from an XML file on the server as a demonstration of AJAX.

The HTML File

The HTML for this example is straightforward. It defines a simple form with an Answer field and a Submit button, along with some hooks for the script. The HTML for this example is shown in Listing 25.2.

CAUTION

Unlike most of the scripts in this book, this example requires a web server. It does not work on a local machine due to browsers' security restrictions on remote scripting.

LISTING 25.2   The HTML File for the Quiz Example

```html
<!DOCTYPE html>

<html lang="en">
  <head>
    <title>Ajax Quiz Test</title>
    <script type="text/javascript" src="ajax.js"></script>
  </head>
  <body>
    <h1>Ajax Quiz Example</h1>
    <button id="start_quiz">Start Quiz</button>

    <p><strong>Question:</strong><br/>
    <span id="question">[Press Button to Start Quiz]</span></p>

    <p><strong>Answer:</strong><br/>
    <input type="text" name="answer" id="answer" /></p>

    <button id="submit">Submit Answer</button>

    <script type="text/javascript" src="quiz.js"></script>
  </body>
</html>
```

This HTML file includes the following elements:

▶ The `<script>` tag in the `<head>` section includes the AJAX library you created in the preceding section from the `ajax.js` file.

▶ The `<script>` tag in the `<body>` section includes the `quiz.js` file, which will contain the quiz script.

▶ The `<span id="question">` tag sets up a place for the question to be inserted by the script.

▶ The text field with the `id` value `"answer"` is where the user will answer the question.

▶ The button with the `id` value `"submit"` will submit an answer.

▶ The button with the `id` value `"start_quiz"` will start the quiz.

You can test the HTML document at this time by placing the file on your web server and accessing it via the URL, but the buttons won't work until you add the XML and JavaScript files, as you'll learn about in the next two sections.

The XML File

The XML file for the quiz is shown in Listing 25.3. I've filled it with a few JavaScript questions, but it could easily be adapted for another purpose.

LISTING 25.3   The XML File Containing the Quiz Questions and Answers

```
<?xml version="1.0" ?>
<questions>
    <q>What DOM object contains URL information for the window?
    </q>
    <a>location</a>
    <q>Which method of the document object finds the
        object for an element?</q>
    <a>getElementById</a>
    <q>If you declare a variable outside a function,
        is it global or local?</q>
    <a>global</a>
    <q>What is the formal standard for the JavaScript language
        called?</q>
    <a>ECMAScript</a>
</questions>
```

The `<questions>` tag encloses the entire file, and each question and each answer is enclosed in `<q>` and `<a>` tags. Remember, this is XML, not HTML—these are not standard HTML tags, but tags that were created for this example. Because this file will be used only by your script, it does not need to follow a standard format.

To use this file, save it as `questions.xml` in the same folder as the HTML document. It will be loaded by the script you create in the next section.

Of course, with a quiz this small, you could have made things easier by storing the questions and answers in a JavaScript array. But imagine a much larger quiz, with thousands of questions, or a server-side program that pulls questions from a database, or even a hundred different files with different quizzes to choose from, and you can see the benefit of using a separate XML file.

The JavaScript File

Because you have a separate library to handle the complexities of making an AJAX request and receiving the response, the script for this example needs to deal only with the action for the quiz itself. Listing 25.4 shows the JavaScript file for this example.

LISTING 25.4 The JavaScript File for the Quiz Example

```
// global variable qn is the current question number
var qn=0;

// load the questions from the XML file
function getQuestions() {
   obj=document.getElementById("question");
   obj.firstChild.nodeValue="(please wait)";
   ajaxCallback = nextQuestion;
   ajaxRequest("questions.xml");
}

// display the next question
function nextQuestion() {
   questions = ajaxreq.responseXML.getElementsByTagName("q");
   obj=document.getElementById("question");
   if (qn < questions.length) {
      q = questions[qn].firstChild.nodeValue;
      obj.firstChild.nodeValue=q;
   } else {
      obj.firstChild.nodeValue="(no more questions)";
   }
}

// check the user's answer
function checkAnswer() {
   answers = ajaxreq.responseXML.getElementsByTagName("a");
   a = answers[qn].firstChild.nodeValue;
   answerfield = document.getElementById("answer");
   if (a == answerfield.value) {
      alert("Correct!");
   }
   else {
      alert("Incorrect. The correct answer is: " + a);
   }
   qn = qn + 1;
   answerfield.value="";
   nextQuestion();
}
// Set up the event handlers for the buttons
obj=document.getElementById("start_quiz");
obj.onclick=getQuestions;
ans=document.getElementById("submit");
ans.onclick=checkAnswer;
```

This script consists of the following:

▶ The first `var` statement defines a global variable, `qn`, which keeps track of which question is currently displayed. It is initially set to zero for the first question.

▶ The `getQuestions()` function is called when the user clicks the Start Quiz button. This function uses the AJAX library to request the contents of the `questions.xml` file. It sets the `ajaxCallback` variable to the `nextQuestion()` function.

▶ The `nextQuestion()` function is called when the AJAX request is complete. This function uses the `getElementsByTagName()` method on the `responseXML` property to find all the questions (`<q>` tags) and store them in the `questions` array.

▶ The `checkAnswer()` function is called when the user submits an answer. It uses `getElementsByTagName()` to store the answers (`<a>` tags) in the `answers` array, and then compares the answer for the current question with the user's answer and displays an alert indicating whether the user was right or wrong.

▶ The script commands after this function set up two event handlers. One attaches the `getQuestions()` function to the Start Quiz button to set up the quiz; the other attaches the `checkAnswer()` function to the Submit button.

Testing the Quiz

To try this example, you'll need all four files in the same folder: `ajax.js` (the AJAX library), `quiz.js` (the quiz functions), `questions.xml` (the questions), and the HTML document. All but the HTML document need to have the correct filenames so that they will work correctly. Also remember that because it uses AJAX, this example requires a web server.

Figure 25.1 shows the quiz in action. The second question has just been answered.

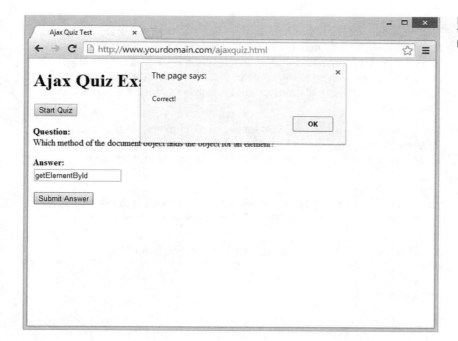

FIGURE 25.1
The quiz example loaded in a web browser.

Debugging AJAX-Based Applications

Dealing with remote scripting means working with several languages at once—JavaScript; server-side languages such as PHP, XML, or JSON; and of course HTML and CSS. Thus, when you find an error, it can be difficult to track down. Here are some tips for debugging AJAX-based applications:

▶ Be sure that all filenames are correct, and that all files for your application are in the same folder on the server.

▶ If you are using a server-side language, test the script without using the AJAX request: Load the script in the browser and make sure it works, and try passing variables to the script via the URL and checking the resulting output.

▶ Check the `statusText` property for the results of your request—an `alert` message or a message logged to the console is helpful here. It is often a clear message such as `"File not found"` that ends up explaining the problem.

▶ If you're using a third-party library, check its documentation—many libraries have built-in debugging features you can enable to examine what's going on.

▼ TRY IT YOURSELF

Making a Live Search Form

CAUTION

Once again, because it uses AJAX, this example requires a web server. You'll also need PHP to be installed, which it is by default by the vast majority of hosting services.

One of the most impressive demonstrations of AJAX is *live search*: Whereas a normal search form requires that you click a button and wait for a page to load to see the results, a live search displays results within the page immediately as you type in the search field. As you type letters or press the backspace key, the results are updated instantly to make it easy to find the result you need.

Using the AJAX library you created earlier, live search is not too hard to implement. This example uses a PHP program on the server to provide the search results, and it can be easily adapted to any search application.

The HTML Form

The HTML for this example simply defines a search field and leaves some room for the dynamic results. The HTML document is shown in Listing 25.5.

LISTING 25.5   The HTML File for the Live Search Example

```html
<!DOCTYPE html>

<html lang="en">
  <head>
    <title>AJAX Live Search Example</title>
    <script type="text/javascript" src="ajax.js"></script>
  </head>
  <body>
    <h1>AJAX Live Search Example</h1>
    <p><strong>Search for:</strong>
    <input type="text" size="40" id="searchlive" /></p>

    <div id="results">
      <ul id="list">
      <li>[Search results will display here.]</li>
      </ul>
    </div>
  <script type="text/javascript" src="search.js"></script>
  </body>
</html>
```

This HTML document includes the following:

▶ The `<script>` tag in the `<head>` section includes the AJAX library, `ajax.js`.

▶ The `<script>` tag in the `<body>` section includes the `search.js` script, which you'll create next.

▶ The `<input>` element with the `id` value `"searchlive"` is where you'll type your search query.

▶ The `<div>` element with the `id` value `"results"` acts as a container for the dynamically fetched results. A bulleted list is created with a `<ul>` tag; this will be replaced with a list of results when you start typing.

The PHP Back End

Next, you'll need a server-side program to produce the search results. This PHP program includes a list of names stored in an array. It will respond to a JavaScript query with the names that match what the user has typed so far. The names will be returned in XML format. For example, here is the output of the PHP program when searching for "smith":

```
<names>
<name>John Smith</name>
<name>Jane Smith</name>
</names>
```

Although the list of names is stored within the PHP program here for simplicity, in a real application it would more likely be stored in a database—and this script could easily be adapted to work with a database containing thousands of names. The PHP program is shown in Listing 25.6.

LISTING 25.6   The PHP Code for the Live Search Example

```php
<?php
  header("Content-type: text/xml");
  $names = array (
   "John Smith", "John Jones", "Jane Smith", "Jane Tillman",
   "Abraham Lincoln", "Sally Johnson", "Kilgore Trout",
   "Bob Atkinson", "Joe Cool", "Dorothy Barnes",
   "Elizabeth Carlson", "Frank Dixon", "Gertrude East",
   "Harvey Frank", "Inigo Montoya", "Jeff Austin",
   "Lynn Arlington", "Michael Washington", "Nancy West" );
if (!$query) {
   $query=$_GET['query'];
}
echo "<?xml version=\"1.0\" ?>\n";
echo "<names>\n";
while (list($k,$v)=each($names)) {
   if (stristr($v,$query)) {
      echo "<name>$v</name>\n";
   }
}
echo "</names>\n";
?>
```

TRY IT YOURSELF ▼

Making a Live Search Form
continued

▼ TRY IT YOURSELF

Making a Live Search Form
continued

This chapter is too small to teach you PHP, but here's a summary of how this program works:

▶ The `header` statement sends a header indicating that the output is in XML format. This is required for `XMLHttpRequest` to correctly use the `responseXML` property.

▶ The `$names` array stores the list of names. You can use a much longer list of names without changing the rest of the code.

▶ The program looks for a `GET` variable called `query` and uses a loop to output all the names that match the query.

▶ Because PHP can be embedded in an HTML file, the `<?php` and `?>` tags indicate that the code between them should be interpreted as PHP.

Save the PHP program as `search.php` in the same folder as the HTML file. You can test it by typing a query such as **search.php?query=John** in the browser's URL field. Use the View Source command to view the XML result.

The JavaScript Front End
Finally, the JavaScript for this example is shown in Listing 25.7.

LISTING 25.7   The JavaScript File for the Live Search Example

```
// global variable to manage the timeout
var t;

// Start a timeout with each keypress
function StartSearch() {
   if (t) window.clearTimeout(t);
   t = window.setTimeout("LiveSearch()",200);
}

// Perform the search
function LiveSearch() {
   // assemble the PHP filename
   query = document.getElementById("searchlive").value;
   filename = "search.php?query=" + query;

   // DisplayResults will handle the Ajax response
   ajaxCallback = DisplayResults;

   // Send the Ajax request
   ajaxRequest(filename);
}

// Display search results
function DisplayResults() {
   // remove old list
   ul = document.getElementById("list");
```

TRY IT YOURSELF ▼

Making a Live Search Form
continued

```
        div = document.getElementById("results");
        div.removeChild(ul);

        // make a new list
        ul = document.createElement("ul");
        ul.id="list";
        names = ajaxreq.responseXML.getElementsByTagName("name");
        for (i = 0; i < names.length; i++) {
           li = document.createElement("li");
           name = names[i].firstChild.nodeValue;
           text = document.createTextNode(name);
           li.appendChild(text);
           ul.appendChild(li);
        }
        if (names.length==0) {
           li = document.createElement("li");
           li.appendChild(document.createTextNode("No results"));
           ul.appendChild(li);
        }

        // display the new list
        div.appendChild(ul);
}
// set up event handler
obj=document.getElementById("searchlive");
obj.onkeydown = StartSearch;
```

This script includes the following components:

▶ A global variable, t, is defined. This stores a pointer to the timeout used later in the script.

▶ The StartSearch() function is called when the user presses a key. This function uses setTimeout() to call the LiveSearch() function after a 200-millisecond delay. The delay is necessary so that the key the user types has time to appear in the search field.

▶ The LiveSearch() function assembles a filename that combines search.php with the query in the search field, and launches an AJAX request using the library's ajaxRequest() function.

▶ The DisplayResults() function is called when the AJAX request is complete. It deletes the bulleted list from the <div id="results"> section and then assembles a new list using the W3C DOM and the AJAX results. If there were no results, it displays a "No results" message in the list.

▶ The final lines of the script set up the StartSearch() function as an event handler for the onkeydown event of the search field.

▼ TRY IT YOURSELF

Making a Live Search Form
continued

FIGURE 25.2
The live search example as displayed in the browser.

Making It All Work
To try this example, you'll need three files on a web server: `ajax.js` (the library), `search.js` (the search script), and the HTML file. Figure 25.2 shows this example in action.

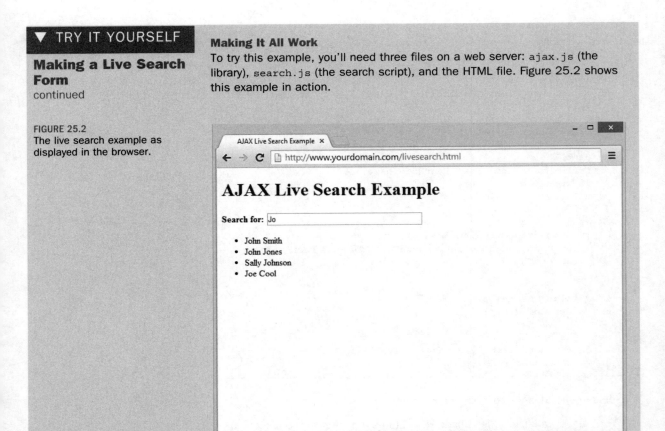

Using jQuery's Built-in Functions for AJAX

Having learned (and practiced) the "long" way to implementing AJAX requests in your website, you should know that jQuery has its own built-in functions for performing the same tasks. If you are already using jQuery, the following code snippets should make your programming life a lot easier.

There are numerous AJAX-related jQuery functions and methods, which you can read about in great detail at http://api.jquery.com/category/ajax/. For the purposes of a quick introduction, the following three jQuery shorthand methods enable you to do most of what you

NOTE

Of course, you can also include the jQuery library just to use its AJAX-related functionality, but if you do so, recognize you're requiring the user's browser to download a lot of code that you otherwise will not be using.

need in a basic AJAX implementation. To try these examples, you need to load the jQuery library via a `<script>` tag, as you learned in Chapter 23, "A Closer Look at jQuery."

The first of these shorthand methods is `load()`, which enables you to get a document from the server and display it as-is. This method is useful if you have a set of static HTML pages that you want to piece together to form a cohesive view. For example, in the code that follows, the jQuery `load()` method gets the content from the file on the server called `newContent.html`, and replaces the text of the element with an ID value of `newContentHere` with the content that is in the `newContent.html` document.

```
$(function() {
    $("#newContentHere").load("newContent.html");
});
```

If all of that seems a little too magical—if it hides the functionality from view and gives you less control than you would like—there are two other jQuery shorthand methods that provide more opportunities for AJAX scripting, both of which provide you with more control over what is going on. The `get()` and `post()` methods in jQuery enable you to specify a target script to either GET or POST, and enable you to send parameters and values along with your request.

In the example that follows, the `get()` jQuery method is used to send two parameters to the script called `serverScript.php`, via the GET HTTP method. These parameters are called `param1` and `param2`, with values of `value1` and `value2`, respectively. When the request has been made and has returned a result, an alert is displayed.

```
$.get("serverScript.php",
    {param1: "value1", param2: "value2"},
    function(data) {
        alert("Server responded: " + data);
    }
);
```

When the `post()` jQuery method is used, the syntax is essentially the same:

```
$.post("serverScript.php",
    {param1: "value1", param2: "value2"},
    function(data) {
        alert("Server responded: " + data);
    }
);
```

Summary

In this chapter, you've learned how AJAX, or remote scripting, enables JavaScript to communicate with a web server and retrieve results in a seemingly uninterrupted way for the user. You created a reusable AJAX library that can be used to create any number of AJAX applications, and you created a sample quiz using questions and answers stored in an XML file. Finally, you created a live search form using AJAX and PHP, and then learned you could perform all of these functions using jQuery's built-in AJAX functionality.

Q&A

Q. What happens if the server is slow, or never responds to the request?

A. When your server is slow, the callback function is called late or not at all. This can cause trouble with overlapping requests: For example, in the live search example, an erratic server might cause the responses for the first few characters typed to come in a few seconds apart, confusing the user. You can remedy this problem by checking the `readyState` property to make sure that a request is not already in progress before you start another one.

Q. In the live search example, why is the `onkeydown` event handler necessary? Wouldn't the `onchange` event be easier to use?

A. Although `onchange` tells you when a form field has changed, it is not triggered until the user moves on to a different field—it doesn't work for "live" search, so you have to watch for keypresses instead. The `onkeypress` handler would work; however, in some browsers it doesn't detect the Backspace key, and it's nice to have the search update when you backspace to shorten the query.

Workshop

The workshop contains quiz questions and exercises to help you solidify your understanding of the material covered. Test your knowledge of AJAX by answering the following questions. Try to answer all questions before looking at the "Answers" section that follows.

Quiz

1. Which of the following is the *A* in *AJAX*?

    a. Advanced

    b. Asynchronous

    c. Application

2. Which property of an `XMLHttpRequest` object indicates whether the request was successful?

    a. `status`

    b. `readyState`

    c. `success`

3. True or False: To support very old versions of Internet Explorer, you must create an ActiveX object rather than an `XMLHttpRequest` object when using AJAX.

Answers

1. **b.** AJAX stands for Asynchronous JavaScript and XML.

2. **a.** The `status` property indicates whether the request was successful; `readyState` indicates whether the request is complete but does not indicate success.

3. True. Internet Explorer 5 and 6 require ActiveX, whereas versions of Internet Explorer after version 7 support the `XMLHttpRequest` object natively.

Exercises

If you want to gain more experience with AJAX, try the following exercises:

▶ Build your own XML file of questions and answers on your favorite topic and try it with the quiz example.

▶ Use the AJAX library to add an AJAX feature to your site or create a simple example of your own.

▶ Rewrite the quiz example using one or more of jQuery's built-in AJAX functions.

CHAPTER 26

Working with Web-Based Forms

To this point, pretty much everything in this book has focused on getting information out to others. But you can also use your web pages to gather information from the people who read and interact with them.

Web forms enable you to receive feedback, orders, or other information from the users who visit your web pages. If you've ever used a search engine such as Google, Yahoo!, or Bing, you're familiar with HTML forms—those single-field entry forms with one button that, when pressed, gives you all the information you are looking for and then some. Product order forms are also an extremely popular use of forms; if you've ordered anything from Amazon.com or purchased something from an eBay seller, you've used forms. In this chapter, you'll learn how to create your own forms, but you'll learn only how to create the front end of those forms. Working with the server-side handling of forms requires knowledge of a programming language and is beyond the scope of this book.

How HTML Forms Work

An HTML form is part of a web page that includes areas where users can enter information to be sent back to you, to another email address that you specify, to a database that you manage, or to another system altogether, such as a third-party management system for your company's lead generation forms, such as Salesforce.com.

Before you learn the HTML elements that are used to make your own forms, you should at least conceptually understand how the information from those forms makes its way back to you. The

WHAT YOU'LL LEARN IN
THIS CHAPTER:

▶ How HTML forms work
▶ How to create the front end of an HTML form
▶ How to name pieces of form data
▶ How to include hidden data in forms
▶ How to choose the correct form input controls for the situation
▶ How to validate form data
▶ How to submit form data
▶ Using the form object with JavaScript

NOTE

PHP is the most popular server-side programming language; it's supported by any web hosting provider worth its salt. You can learn more about PHP at http://www.php.net/, or you can just dive right in to learning this programming language (plus database interactivity) from the ground up in *Sams Teach Yourself PHP, Apache, and MySQL All in One* (ISBN: 0672335433). Although several other books on PHP and related technologies are available, I am partial to this one because I wrote it. It is geared toward absolute beginners with PHP or any other programming language.

actual behind-the-scenes (the *server-side* or *back-end*) process requires knowledge of at least one programming language—or at least the ability to follow specific instructions when using someone else's server-side script to handle the form input. At that point in the process, you should either work with someone who has the technical knowledge or learn the basics on your own. Simple form processing is not difficult, and your web hosting provider likely has several back-end scripts that you can use with minimal customization.

Forms include a button for the user to submit the form; that button can be an image that you create yourself or a standard HTML form button that is created when a form `<input>` element is created and given a `type` value of `submit`. When someone clicks a form submission button, all the information typed in the form is sent to a URL that you specify in the `action` attribute of the `<form>` element. That URL should point to a specific script that will process your form, sending the form contents via email or performing another step in an interactive process (such as requesting results from a search engine or placing items in an online shopping cart).

When you start thinking about doing more with form content than simply emailing results to yourself, you need additional technical knowledge. For example, if you want to create an online store that accepts credit cards and processes transactions, there are some well-established practices for doing so, all geared toward ensuring the security of your customers' data. That is not an operation that you'll want to enter into lightly; you'll need more knowledge than this book provides.

Before you put a form online, you should look in the user guide for your web hosting provider to see what it offers in the way of form-processing scripts. You are likely to find a readily available Perl or PHP script that you can use with only minimal configuration.

Creating a Form

Every form must begin with an opening `<form>` tag, which can be located anywhere in the body of the HTML document. The `<form>` tag typically has three attributes, `name`, `method`, and `action`:

```
<form name="my_form" method="post" action="myprocessingscript.php">
```

The most common `method` is `post`, which sends the form entry results as a document. In some situations, you need to use `method="get"`, which submits the results as part of the URL query string instead. For example, `get` is sometimes used when queries are submitted to search engines from a web form. Because you're not yet an expert on forms, just use `post` unless your web hosting provider's documentation tells you to do otherwise.

The `action` attribute specifies the address for sending the form data. You have two options here:

▶ You can type the location of a form-processing program or script on a web server, and the form data will then be sent to that program. This is by far the most common scenario.

▶ You can type `mailto:` followed by your email address, and the form data will be sent directly to you whenever someone fills out the form. However, this approach is completely dependent on the user's computer being properly configured with an email client. People accessing your site from a public computer without an email client will be left out in the cold. Here's an example:

```
<form name="my_form" method="post" action="mailto:me@mysite.com">
```

The form created in Listing 26.1 and shown in Figure 26.1 includes just about every type of user input component you can currently use in HTML forms in modern browsers. Refer to this figure and listing as you read the following explanations of each type of input element.

NOTE

HTML5 has undergone many improvements and additions for creating forms and form elements, but as of this writing, not all of them can be used in ways you expect. The good news is that even if you use an input type in your form that an older browser doesn't technically support, it will still display a usable generic input field. Overall, this chapter discusses only the input types you can be confident using. To stay up to date on browser support for new form-related elements and attributes, check out "Can I Use..." at http://caniuse.com/#feat=forms, which aggregates information about browser support for HTML5 and CSS3.

LISTING 26.1 A Form with Various User-Input Components

```html
<!DOCTYPE html>

<html lang="en">
  <head>
    <title>Guest Book</title>

    <style type="text/css">

      fieldset {
         width: 75%;
         border: 2px solid #ff0000;
      }

      legend {
         font-weight: bold;
         font-size: 125%;
      }
```

```
        label.question  {
           width: 225px;
           float: left;
           text-align: left;
           font-weight: bold;
        }

        span.question  {
           font-weight: bold;
        }

        input, textarea, select {
           border: 1px solid #000;
           padding: 3px;
        }

        #buttons {
           margin-top: 12px;
        }

     </style>
  </head>
  <body>
    <h1>My Guest Book</h1>
    <form name="gbForm" method="post" action="URL_to_script">

    <fieldset>
       <legend>Personal Information</legend>

       <p><label class="question" for="the_name">
             What is your name?</label>
       <input type="text" id="the_name" name="the_name"
             placeholder="Enter your full name."
             size="50" required autofocus /></p>

       <p><label class="question" for="the_email">What is your e-mail
             address?</label>
       <input type="email" id="the_email" name="the_email"
             placeholder="Please use a real one!"
             size="50" required /></p>
    </fieldset>

    <fieldset>
       <legend>Survey Questions</legend>

       <p><span class="question">Please check all that apply:</span><br/>
       <input type="checkbox" id="like_it" name="some_statements[]"
             value="I really like your Web site." />
       <label for="like_it">I really like your Web site.</label><br/>
       <input type="checkbox" id="the_best" name="some_statements[]"
             value="It's one of the best sites I've ever seen" />
       <label for="the_best">It's one of the  best sites I've ever
```

```
            seen.</label><br/>
    <input type="checkbox" id="jealous" name="some_statements[]"
           value="I sure wish my site looked as good as yours." />
    <label for="jealous">I sure wish my site looked as good as
           yours.</label><br/>
    <input type="checkbox" id="no_taste" name="some_statements[]"
           value="I have no taste and I'm pretty dense, so your site
           didn't do much for me." />
    <label for="no_taste">I have no taste and I'm pretty dense, so
           Your site didn't do much for me.</label></p>

    <p><label for="choose_scale"><span class="question">Please rate my
           site on a scale of 1 (poor) to 10 (awesome):</span></label>
    <input type="number" id="choose_scale" name="choose_scale"
            min="0" max="10" step="1" value="5"/></p>

    <p><span class="question">Please choose the one thing you love
           Best about my web site:</span><br/>
    <input type="radio" id="the_picture" name="best_thing"
           value="me" />
    <label for="the_picture">That amazing picture of you</label><br/>
    <input type="radio" id="the_cats" name="best_thing"
           value="cats" />
    <label for="the_cats">All the cat photos, of course</label><br/>
    <input type="radio" id="the_story" name="best_thing"
           value="childhood story" />
    <label for="the_story">The inspiring recap of your suburban
           childhood</label><br/>
    <input type="radio" id="the_treasures" name="best_thing"
           value="Elvis treasures" />
    <label for="the_treasures">The detailed list of all your Elvis
           memorabilia</label></p>

     <p><label for="how_improve"><span class="question">How can I
           improve my web site?</span></label><br/>
     <select id="how_improve" name="how_improve" size="4" multiple>
           <option value="You can't. It couldn't be better.">You
           can't. It couldn't be better.</option>
           <option value="More about the cats.">More about the cats.
           </option>
           <option value="More about the family.">More about the
           family.</option>
           <option value="More about Elvis.">More about Elvis.
           </option>
     </select></p>
  </fieldset>

<fieldset>
   <legend>Free for All!</legend>
   <p><label for="message"><span class="question">Feel free to send
           more praise, gift offers, etc.:</span></label>
   <textarea id="message" name="message" rows="7" cols="55">
   </textarea></p>
```

```
        </fieldset>

        <div id="buttons">
          <input type="submit" value="Click Here to Submit" /> or
          <input type="reset" value="Erase and Start Over" />
        </div>

        </form>
      </body>
    </html>
```

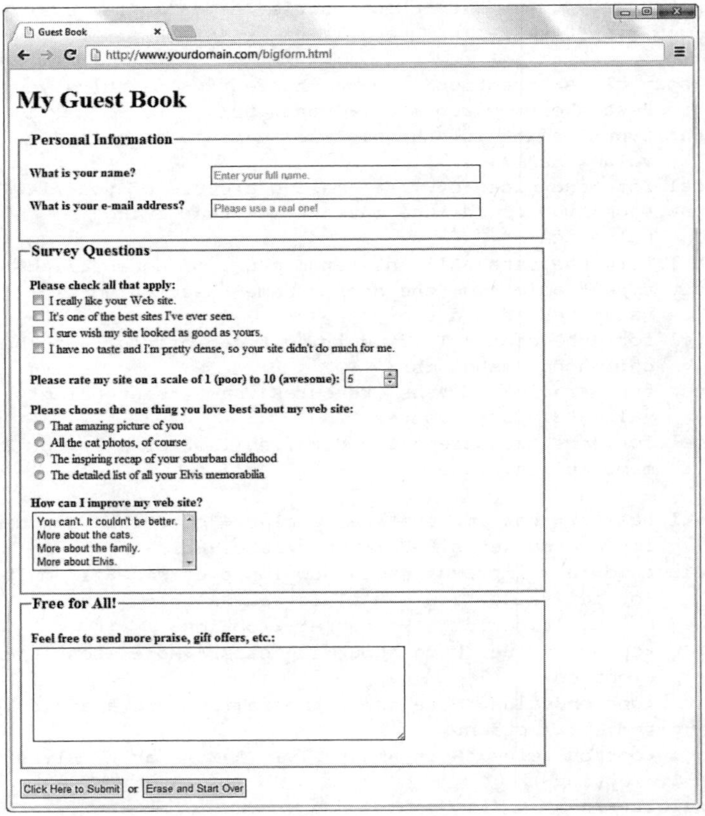

FIGURE 26.1
The code in Listing 26.1 uses
many common HTML form
elements.

The code in Listing 26.1 uses a `<form>` element that contains quite a
few `<input />` tags. Each `<input />` tag corresponds to a specific user
input component, such as a checkbox or radio button. The input,
select, and text area elements contain borders in the stylesheet, so it is

easy to see the outline of the elements in the form. Keep in mind that you can apply all sorts of CSS to those elements.

The next few sections dig into the `<input />` tag and other form-related tags in detail.

Accepting Text Input

To ask the user for a specific piece of information within a form, use the `<input />` tag. Although the tag does not explicitly need to appear between the `<form>` and `</form>` tags, it is good practice and makes your code easier to follow. You can place `<input />` elements anywhere on the page in relation to text, images, and other HTML tags. For example, to ask for someone's name, you could type the following text followed immediately by an `<input />` field:

```
<p><label class="question" for="the_name">What is your name?
</label>
<input type="text" id="the_name" name="the_name"
       placeholder="Enter your full name."
       size="50" required autofocus /></p>
```

The `type` attribute indicates what type of form element to display—a simple, one-line text entry box, in this case. (Each element type is discussed individually in this chapter.) In this example, note the use of the `placeholder`, `required`, and `autofocus` attributes. You'll learn about the `required` attribute later in this chapter; the `autofocus` attribute automatically focuses the user's cursor in this text field as soon as the browser renders the form. A form can have only one `autofocus` field. The `placeholder` attribute enables you to define some text that appears in the text box but disappears when you begin to type. Using this attribute, you can give the user a bit more guidance in completing your form.

The `size` attribute indicates approximately how many characters wide the text input box should be. If you are using a proportionally spaced font, the width of the input will vary depending on what the user enters. If the input is too long to fit in the box, most web browsers automatically scroll the text to the left.

The `maxlength` attribute determines the number of characters the user is allowed to type into the text box. If a user tries to type beyond the specified length, the extra characters won't appear. You can specify a length that is longer, shorter, or the same as the physical size of the

TIP

If you want the user to enter text without the text being displayed on the screen, you can use `<input type="password" />` instead of `<input type="text" />`. Asterisks (***) are then displayed in place of the text the user types. The `size`, `maxlength`, and `name` attributes work exactly the same for `type="password"` as they do for `type="text"`. Keep in mind that this technique of hiding a password provides only visual protection; no encryption or other protection is associated with the password being transmitted.

text box. The `size` and `maxlength` attributes are used only for those input fields meant for text values, such as `type="text"`, `type="email"`, `type="URL"`, and `type="tel"`, but not checkboxes and radio buttons since those have fixed sizes.

Naming Each Piece of Form Data

NOTE

Form-processing scripts are oversimplified here, for the sake of explanation within the scope of this book. The exact appearance (or name) of the variables made available to your processing script depends on the programming language of that script. But conceptually, it's valid to say that the name of the input element becomes the name of the variable, and the value of the input element becomes that variable's value on the back end.

No matter what type an input element is, you must give a name to the data it gathers. You can use any name you like for each input item, as long as each one on the form is different (except in the case of radio buttons and checkboxes, discussed later in this chapter). When the form is processed by a back-end script, each data item is identified by name. This name becomes a variable, which is filled with a value. The value is either what the user typed in the form or the value associated with the element the user selected.

For example, if a user enters `Jane Doe` in the text box defined previously, a variable is sent to the form-processing script; the variable is `user_name`, and the value of the variable is `Jane Doe`. Form-processing scripts work with these types of variable names and values.

To use this text field (or others) in JavaScript, remember that the text object uses the `name` attribute; you refer to the value of the field in the previous snippet like this:

```
document.formname.user_name.value
```

Labeling Each Piece of Form Data

Labeling your form data is not the same as using a `name` or `id` attribute to identify the form element for later use. Instead, the `<label>` `</label>` tag pair surrounds text that acts as a sort of caption for a form element. A form element `<label>` provides additional context for the element, which is especially important for screen reader software.

You can see two different examples in Listing 26.1. First, you can see the `<label>` surrounding the first question a user is asked (`What is your name?`). The use of the `for` attribute ties this label to the `<input />` element with the same `id` (in this case, `the_name`):

```
<p><label class="question" for="the_name">What is your name?
</label>
<input type="text" id="the_name" name="the_name"
       placeholder="Enter your full name."
       size="50" required autofocus /></p>
```

A screen reader would read to the user, "What is your name?" and then also say "text box" to alert the user to complete the text field with the appropriate information. In another example from Listing 26.1, you see the use of <label> to surround different options in a checkbox list (and also a list of radio buttons, later in the listing):

```
<p><span class="question">Please check all that apply:</span><br/>
<input type="checkbox" id="like_it" name="some_statements[]"
       value="I really like your Web site." />
<label for="like_it">I really like your Web site.</label><br/>
<input type="checkbox" id="the_best" name="some_statements[]"
       value="It's one of the best sites I've ever seen" />
<label for="the_best">It's one of the  best sites I've ever
       seen.</label><br/>
<input type="checkbox" id="jealous" name="some_statements[]"
       value="I sure wish my site looked as good as yours." />
<label for="jealous">I sure wish my site looked as good as
       yours.</label><br/>
<input type="checkbox" id="no_taste" name="some_statements[]"
       value="I have no taste and I'm pretty dense, so your site
       didn't do much for me." />
<label for="no_taste">I have no taste and I'm pretty dense, so your
       site didn't do much for me.</label></p>
```

In this situation, the screen reader would read the text surrounded by the <label> tag, followed by "checkbox," to alert the user to choose one of the given options. Labels should be used for all form elements and can be styled using CSS in the same manner as other container elements—the styling does not affect the screen reader, but it does help with layout aesthetics and readability.

Grouping Form Elements

In Listing 26.1, you can see the use of the <fieldset> and <legend> element three different times, to create three different groups of form fields. The <fieldset> element does just that—it surrounds groups of form elements to provide additional context for the user, whether they are accessing it directly in a web browser or with the aid of screen-reader software. The `<fieldset>` element just defines the grouping; the `<legend>` element contains the text that will display or be read aloud to describe this grouping, such as the following from Listing 26.1:

```
<fieldset>
    <legend>Personal Information</legend>
    <p><label class="question" for="the_name">What is your name?
    </label>
    <input type="text" id="the_name" name="the_name"
        placeholder="Enter your full name."
        size="50" required autofocus /></p>
...
</fieldset>
```

In this situation, when the screen reader reads the `<label>` associated with a form element, as you learned in the preceding section, it also appends the `<legend>` text. In the example above, it would be read as "Personal Information. What is your name? Text box." The `<fieldset>` and `<legend>` elements can be styled using CSS, so the visual cue of the grouped elements can easily be made visible in a web browser (as you saw previously in Figure 26.1).

Including Hidden Data in Forms

Want to send certain data items to the server script that processes a form, but don't want the user to see those data items? Use an `<input />` tag with a `type="hidden"` attribute. This attribute has no effect on the display; it just adds any name and value you specify to the form results when they are submitted.

If you are using a form-processing script provided by your web hosting provider, you might be directed to use this attribute to tell a script where to email the form results. For example, including the following code emails the results to me@mysite.com after the form is submitted:

```
<input type="hidden" name="mailto" value="me@mysite.com" />
```

You sometimes see scripts using hidden input elements to carry additional data that might be useful when you receive the results of the form submission; some examples of hidden form fields include an email address and a subject for the email. If you are using a script provided by your web hosting provider, consult the documentation provided with that script for additional details about potential required hidden fields.

Exploring Form Input Controls

Various input controls are available for retrieving information from the user. You've already seen one text-entry option; the next few sections introduce you to most of the remaining form-input options you can use to design forms.

Checkboxes

Besides the text field, one of the simplest input types is a *checkbox*, which appears as a small square. Users can click checkboxes to select or deselect one or more items in a group. For example, the checkboxes in Listing 26.1 display after text that reads "Please check all that apply," implying that the user could indeed check all that apply.

The HTML for the checkboxes in Listing 26.1 shows that the value of the name attribute is the same for all of them:

```
<p><span class="question">Please check all that apply:</span><br/>
<input type="checkbox" id="like_it" name="some_statements[]"
    value="I really like your Web site." />
<label for="like_it">I really like your Web site.</label><br/>
<input type="checkbox" id="the_best" name="some_statements[]"
    value="It's one of the best sites I've ever seen" />
<label for="the_best">It's one of the  best sites I've ever
    seen.</label><br/>
<input type="checkbox" id="jealous" name="some_statements[]"
    value="I sure wish my site looked as good as yours." />
<label for="jealous">I sure wish my site looked as good as
    yours.</label><br/>
<input type="checkbox" id="no_taste" name="some_statements[]"
    value="I have no taste and I'm pretty dense, so your site
    didn't do much for me." />
<label for="no_taste">I have no taste and I'm pretty dense, so your
    site didn't do much for me.</label></p>
```

The use of the brackets in the name attribute ([]) indicates to the back-end processing script that a series of values will be placed into this one variable instead of using just one value (well, it might be just one value if the user selects only one checkbox). If a user selects the first checkbox, the text string I really like your Web site. is placed in the website_response[] bucket. If the user selects the third checkbox, the text string I sure wish my site looked as good as yours. also is put into the website_response[] bucket. The processing script then works with that variable as an array of data rather just a single entry.

TIP

If you find that the label for an input element is displayed too close to the element, just add a space between the close of the `<input />` tag and the start of the label text, like this:

```
<input type="checkbox"
name="mini" />
<label>Mini Piano Stool
</label>
```

However, you might see groups of checkboxes that do use individual names for the variables in the group. For example, the following is another way of writing the checkbox group:

```
<p><span class="question">Please check all that apply:</span><br/>
<input type="checkbox" id="like_it" name="liked_site" value="yes"
       value="I really like your Web site." />
<label for="like_it">I really like your Web site.</label><br/>
<input type="checkbox" id="the_best" name="best_site" value="yes"
       value="It's one of the best sites I've ever seen" />
<label for="the_best">It's one of the  best sites I've ever
       seen.</label><br/>
<input type="checkbox" id="jealous" name="my_site_sucks" value="yes"
       value="I sure wish my site looked as good as yours." />
<label for="jealous">I sure wish my site looked as good as
       yours.</label><br/>
<input type="checkbox" id="no_taste" name="am_dense" value="yes"
       value="I have no taste and I'm pretty dense, so your site
       didn't do much for me." />
<label for="no_taste">I have no taste and I'm pretty dense, so your
       site didn't do much for me.</label></p>
```

In this second list of checkboxes, the variable name of the first checkbox is `"liked_site"` and the value (if checked) is `"yes"` when handled by a back-end processing script.

If you want a checkbox to be checked by default when the web browser renders the form, include the `checked` attribute. For example, the following code creates two checkboxes, and the first is checked by default:

```
<input type="checkbox" id="like_it" name="liked_site" value="yes"
       value="I really like your Web site." checked />
<label for="like_it">I really like your Web site.</label><br/>
<input type="checkbox" id="the_best" name="best_site" value="yes"
       value="It's one of the best sites I've ever seen" />
<label for="the_best">It's one of the  best sites I've ever
       seen.</label><br/>
```

The checkbox labeled `I really like your Web site.` is checked by default in this example. The user must click the checkbox to uncheck it and thus indicate that they have another opinion of your site. The checkbox marked `It's one of the best sites I've ever seen.` is unchecked to begin with, so the user must click it to turn it on. Checkboxes that are not selected do not appear in the form output.

If you want to handle values from the `checkbox` object in JavaScript, the object has the following four properties:

▶ `name` is the name of the checkbox, and also the object name.

▶ `value` is the "true" value for the checkbox—usually `on`. This value is used by server-side programs to indicate whether the checkbox was checked. In JavaScript, you should use the `checked` property instead.

▶ `defaultChecked` is the default status of the checkbox, assigned by the `checked` attribute in HTML.

▶ `checked` is the current value. This is a Boolean value: `true` for checked and `false` for unchecked.

To manipulate the checkbox or use its value, you use the `checked` property. For example, this statement turns on a checkbox called `same_address` in a form named `order`:

```
document.order.same.checked = true;
```

The checkbox has a single method: `click()`. This method simulates a click on the box. It also has a single event, `onClick`, that occurs whenever the checkbox is clicked. This happens whether the box was turned on or off, so you'll need to examine the `checked` property via JavaScript to see what action really happened.

Radio Buttons

Radio buttons, for which only one choice can be selected at a time, are almost as simple to implement as checkboxes. The simplest use of a radio button is for yes/no questions or for voting when only one candidate can be selected.

To create a radio button, use `type="radio"` and give each option its own `<input />` tag. Use the same `name` for all the radio buttons in a group, but don't use the `[]` that you used with the checkbox, because you don't have to accommodate multiple answers:

```
<input type="radio" id="vote_yes" name="vote" value="yes" checked />
<label for="vote_yes">Yes</label> <br />
<input type="radio" id="vote_no" name="vote" value="no" />
<label for="vote_no">No</label>
```

The `value` can be any name or code you choose. If you include the `checked` attribute, that button is selected by default. No more than one radio button with the same `name` can be checked.

NOTE

Radio buttons are named for their similarity to the buttons on old push-button radios. Those buttons used a mechanical arrangement so that when you pushed one button in, any other pressed button popped out.

When designing your form and choosing between checkboxes and radio buttons, ask yourself whether the question being asked or implied could be answered in only one way. If so, use a radio button.

As for scripting, radio buttons are similar to checkboxes, except that an entire group of them shares a single name and a single object. You can refer to the following properties of the `radio` object:

▶ `name` is the name common to the radio buttons.

▶ `length` is the number of radio buttons in the group.

To access the individual buttons in JavaScript, you treat the `radio` object as an array. The buttons are indexed, starting with `0`. Each individual button has the following properties:

▶ `value` is the value assigned to the button.

▶ `defaultChecked` indicates the value of the `checked` attribute and the default state of the button.

▶ `checked` is the current state.

For example, you can check the first radio button in the `radio1` group on the `form1` form with this statement:

```
document.form1.radio1[0].checked = true;
```

However, if you do this, be sure you set the other values to `false` as needed. This is not done automatically. You can use the `click()` method to do both of these actions in one step.

Like a checkbox, radio buttons have a `click()` method and an `onclick` event handler. Each radio button can have a separate statement for this event.

Selection Lists

Both *scrolling lists* and *pull-down pick lists* are created with the `<select>` tag. You use this tag together with the `<option>` tag, as the following example shows (taken from Listing 26.1):

```
<p><label for="how_improve"><span class="question">How can I
    improve my web site?</span></label><br/>
<select id="how_improve" name="how_improve" size="4" multiple>
    <option value="You can't. It couldn't be better.">You can't.
        It couldn't be better.</option>
```

```
<option value="More about the cats.">More about the
    cats.</option>
<option value="More about the family.">More about the
    family.</option>
<option value="More about Elvis.">More about Elvis.</option>
</select></p>
```

Unlike the `text` input type that you learned about briefly in a previous section, the `size` attribute here determines how many items show at once on the selection list. If `size="2"` were used in the preceding code, only the first two options would be visible and a scrollbar would appear next to the list so the user could scroll down to see the third and fourth options.

Including the `multiple` attribute enables users to select more than one option at a time; the `selected` attribute makes an option initially selected by default. When the form is submitted, the text specified in the `value` attribute for each option accompanies the selected option.

The object for selection lists is the `select` object. The object itself has the following properties:

▶ `name` is the name of the selection list.

▶ `length` is the number of options in the list.

▶ `options` is the array of options. Each selectable option has an entry in this array.

▶ `selectedIndex` returns the index value of the currently selected item. You can use this to check the value easily. In a multiple-selection list, this indicates the first selected item.

The `options` array has a single property of its own, `length`, which indicates the number of selections. In addition, each item in the `options` array has the following properties:

▶ `index` is the index into the array.

▶ `defaultSelected` indicates the state of the `selected` attribute.

▶ `selected` is the current state of the option. Setting this property to `true` selects the option. The user can select multiple options if the `multiple` attribute is included in the `<select>` tag.

▶ `name` is the value of the `name` attribute. This is used by the server.

▶ `text` is the text that is displayed in the option.

TIP

If you leave out the `size` attribute or specify `size="1"`, the list creates a simple drop-down pick list. Pick lists don't allow for multiple choices; they are logically equivalent to a group of radio buttons. The following example shows another way to choose `yes` or `no` for a question:

```
<select name="vote">
  <option
value="yes">Yes</option>
  <option value="no">
No</option>
</select>
```

NOTE

You can change selection lists dynamically—for example, choosing a product in one list could control which options are available in another list. You can also add and delete options from the list.

The `select` object has two methods—`blur()` and `focus()`—that perform the same purposes as the corresponding methods for `text` objects. The event handlers are `onBlur`, `onFocus`, and `onChange`, also similar to other objects.

Reading the value of a selected item is a two-step process. You first use the `selectedIndex` property, and then use the `value` property to find the value of the selected choice. Here's an example:

```
ind = document.mvform.choice.selectedIndex;
val = document.mvform.choice.options[ind].value;
```

This uses the `ind` variable to store the selected index, and then assigns the `val` variable to the value of the selected choice. Things are a bit more complicated with a multiple selection: You have to test each option's `selected` attribute separately.

No HTML tags other than `<option>` and `</option>` should appear between the `<select>` and `</select>` tags, with the exception of the `<optgroup>` tag (not shown in Listing 26.1). The use of `<optgroup>`, as in the following snippet, enables you to create groups of options (that's where the name `optgroup` comes from) with a label that shows up in the list but can't be selected as an "answer" to the form field. For example, the snippet

```
<select name="grades">
    <optgroup label="Good Grades">
        <option value="A">A</option>
        <option value="B">B</option>
    </optgroup>
    <optgroup label="Average Grades">
        <option value="C">C</option>
    </optgroup>
    <optgroup label="Bad Grades">
        <option value="D">D</option>
        <option value="F">F</option>
    </optgroup>
</select>
```

produces a drop-down list that looks like this:

```
Good Grades
    A
    B
Average Grades
    C
Bad Grades
    D
    F
```

In this situation, only A, B, C, D, and F are selectable, but the `<optgroup>` labels are visible.

Text Fields, Text Areas, and Other Input Types

The `<input type="text">` attribute mentioned earlier this chapter allows the user to enter only a single line of text. When you want to allow multiple lines of text in a single input item, use the `<textarea>` and `</textarea>` tags to create a text area instead of just a text field. Any text you include between these two tags is displayed as the default entry in that box. Here's the example from Listing 26.1:

```
<textarea id="message"  name="message" rows="7" cols="55">Your
     message here.</textarea>
```

As you probably guessed, the `rows` and `cols` attributes control the number of rows and columns of text that fit in the input box. The `cols` attribute is a little less exact than `rows` and approximates the number of characters that fit in a row of text. Text area boxes do have a scrollbar, however, so the user can enter more text than what fits in the display area.

The `text` and `textarea` objects also have a few JavaScript methods you can use:

- ► `focus()` sets the focus to the field. This positions the cursor in the field and makes it the current field.
- ► `blur()` is the opposite; it removes the focus from the field.
- ► `select()` selects the text in the field, just as a user can do with the mouse. All the text is selected; there is no way to select part of the text.

You can also use event handlers to detect when the value of a text field changes. The `text` and `textarea` objects support the following event handlers:

- ► The `onfocus` event happens when the text field gains focus.
- ► The `onblur` event happens when the text field loses focus.
- ► The `onchange` event happens when the user changes the text in the field and then moves out of it.

▶ The `onselect` event happens when the user selects some or all of the text in the field. Unfortunately, there's no way to tell exactly which part of the text was selected. (If the text is selected with the `select()` method described previously, this event is not triggered.)

If used, these event handlers should be included in the `<input>` tag declaration. For example, the following is a text field including an `onchange` event that displays an alert:

```
<input type="text" name="text1" onchange="window.
alert('Changed.');" />
```

Let's turn back to the basic `<input />` element for a minute, however, because HTML5 provides many more `type` options for input than simply "text," such as built-in date pickers. The downside is that not all browsers fully support many of those options (such as the built-in date picker). Here are a few of the different input types (some new, some not) that *are* fully supported but that we haven't discussed in any detail in this lesson:

▶ `type="email"`—This appears as a regular text field, but when form validation is used, the built-in validator checks that it is a well-formed email address. Some mobile devices display relevant keys (the @ sign, for example) by default instead of requiring additional user interactions.

▶ `type="file"`—This input type opens a dialog box to enable you to search for a file on your computer to upload.

▶ `type="number"`—Instead of creating a `<select>` list with `<option>` tags for each number, this type enables you to specify a `min` and `max` value, and the step-between numbers, to automatically generate a list on the browser side. You can see this in use in Listing 26.1.

▶ `type="range"`—Much like the `number` type just covered, this type enables you to specify a `min` and `max` value and the step-between numbers, but in this case, it appears as a horizontal slider.

▶ `type="search"`—This appears as a regular text field, but with additional controls sometimes used to allow the user to clear the search box using an x or a similar character.

▶ `type="url"`—This input type appears as a regular text field, but when form validation is used, the built-in validator checks that it is a well-formed URL. Some mobile devices display relevant keys (the `.com` virtual key, for instance) by default instead of requiring additional user interactions.

You can stay up to date with the status of these and other `<input>` types using the chart at https://developer.mozilla.org/en-US/docs/Web/HTML/Element/input.

Using HTML5 Form Validation

Many features in HTML5 have made web developers very happy people. One of the simplest yet most life-changing might be the inclusion of form validation. Before HTML5 form validation existed, we had to create convoluted JavaScript-based form validation, which caused headaches for everyone involved.

But no more! HTML5 validates forms by default, unless you use the `novalidate` attribute in the `<form>` element. Of course, if you do not use the `required` attribute in any form fields themselves, there's nothing to validate. As you learned in a previous section, not only are fields validated for content (any content at all) but they are validated according to the type that they are. For example, in Listing 26.1, we have a required field for an email address:

```
<p><label class="question" for="the_email">What is your e-mail
    address?</label>
<input type="email" id="the_email" name="the_email"
    placeholder="Please use a real one!"
    size="50" required /></p>
```

In Figures 26.2 and 26.3, you can see that the form automatically validates for the presence of content, but then also slaps you on the wrists when you try to enter a junk string in the field instead of an email address.

NOTE

Validation of email addresses begins and ends with the entry simply looking like an email address. This sort of pattern matching is really the only type of "validation" that you can do with email addresses, short of a time-consuming back-end processing script.

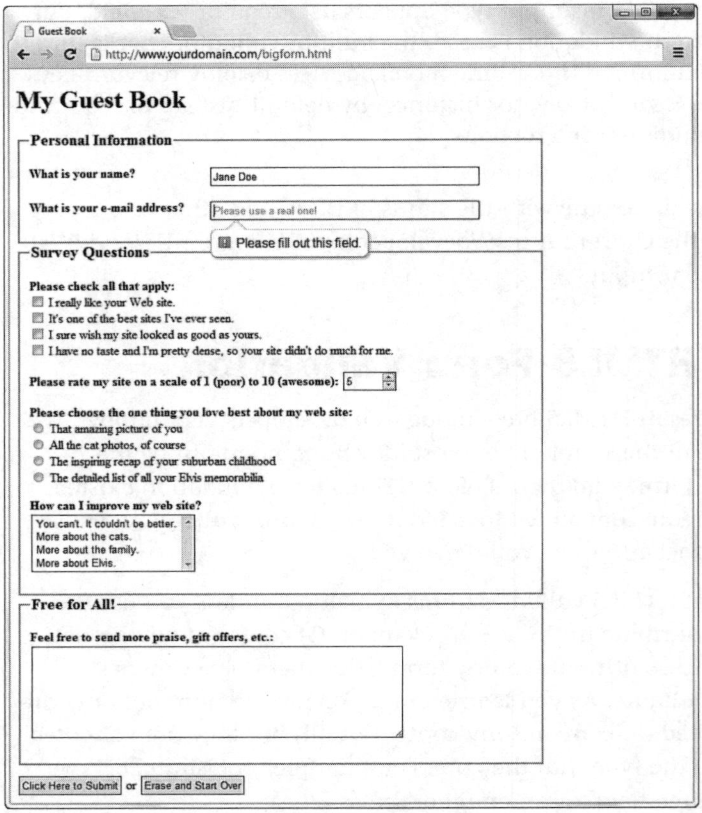

FIGURE 26.2
Attempting to submit a form with
no content in a required field
causes a validation error.

You can use the `pattern` attribute of the `<input />` field to specify your own pattern-matching requirements. The `pattern` attribute uses regular expressions, which is a large enough topic to warrant its own book. But consider a little example. If you want to ensure that your `<input />` element contains only numbers and letters (no special characters), you could use the following:

```
<input type="text" id="the_text" name="the_text"
    placeholder="Please enter only letters and numbers!"
    size="50" pattern="[a-z,A-Z,0-9]" required />
```

The pattern here says that if the field contains any letter between `a` and `z`, letter between `A` and `Z` (case matters), and number between `0` and `9`, it's valid. To learn more about regular expressions without buying an entire book, take a look at the online tutorial at http://regexone.com/.

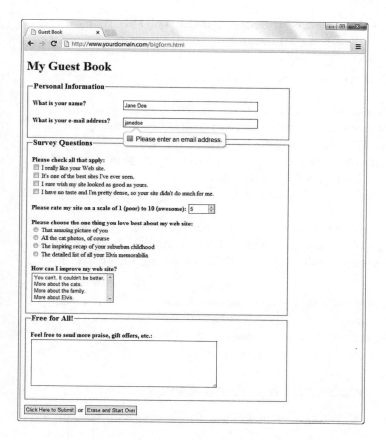

FIGURE 26.3
Attempting to submit a form with badly formed content in a field expecting an email address causes a validation error.

Submitting Form Data

Forms typically include a button that submits the form data to a script on the server or invokes a JavaScript action. You can put any label you like on the Submit button with the `value` attribute:

```
<input type="submit" value="Place My Order Now!" />
```

Unless you change the style using CSS, a gray button is sized to fit the label you put in the `value` attribute. When the user clicks it, all data items on the form are sent to the email address or script specified in the form's `action` attribute.

You can also include a Reset button that clears all entries on the form so that users can start over if they change their minds or make mistakes. Use the following:

```
<input type="reset" value="Clear This Form and Start Over" />
```

If the standard Submit and Reset buttons look a little bland to you, remember that you can style them using CSS. If that's not good enough, you'll be glad to know that there's an easy way to substitute your own graphics for these buttons. To use an image of your choice for a Submit button, use the following:

```
<input type="image" src="button.gif" alt="Order Now!" />
```

The `button.gif` image displays on the page, and the form also is submitted when a user clicks the `button.gif` image. You can include any attributes normally used with the `<img />` tag, such as `alt` and `style`.

The form element also includes a generic button type. When using `type="button"` in the `<input />` tag, you get a button that performs no action on its own but can have an action assigned to it using a JavaScript event handler (such as `onclick`).

Using JavaScript for Form Events

The `form` object has two methods: `submit()` and `reset()`. You can use these methods to submit the data or reset the form yourself, without requiring the user to press a button. One reason for this is to submit the form when the user clicks an image or performs another action that would not usually submit the form.

The `form` object has two event handlers, `onsubmit` and `onreset`. You can specify a group of JavaScript statements or a function call for these events within the `<form>` tag that defines the form.

If you specify a statement or a function for the `onsubmit` event, the statement is called before the data is submitted to the server-side script. You can prevent the submission from happening by returning a value of `false` from the `onsubmit` event handler. If the statement returns `true`, the data will be submitted. In the same fashion, you can prevent a Reset button from working with an `onreset` event handler.

Accessing Form Elements with JavaScript

The most important property of the `form` object is the `elements` array, which contains an object for each of the form elements. You can refer to an element by its own name or by its index in the array. For example, the following two expressions both refer to the first element in the form shown in Listing 26.1:

```
document.gbForm.elements[0]
document.gbForm.name
```

If you do refer to forms and elements as arrays, you can use the `length` property to determine the number of objects in the array: `document.forms.length` is the number of forms in a document, and `document.gbForm.elements.length` is the number of elements in the `gbForm` form.

You can also access form elements using the W3C DOM. In this case, you use an `id` attribute on the form element in the HTML document, and use the `document.getElementById()` method to find the object for the form. For example, this statement finds the object for the text field called `name` and stores it in the `name` variable:

```
name = document.getElementById("name");
```

This enables you to quickly access a form element without first finding the `form` object. You can assign an `id` to the `<form>` tag and find the corresponding object if you need to work with the form's properties and methods.

Displaying Data from a Form

As a simple example of interacting with forms purely on the client side, Listing 26.2 shows a form with name, address, and phone number fields, as well as a JavaScript function that displays the data from the form in a pop-up window.

LISTING 26.2 A Form That Displays Data in a Pop-up Window

```
<!DOCTYPE html>

<html lang="en">
  <head>
    <title>Form Display Example</title>
    <script type="text/javascript">
```

NOTE

Both forms and elements can be referred to by their own names or as indices in the `forms` and `elements` arrays. For clarity, the examples in this chapter use individual form and element names rather than array references. You'll also find it easier to use names in your own scripts.

```
    function display() {
      dispWin = window.open('','NewWin',
      'toolbar=no,status=no,width=300,height=200')

      message = "<ul><li>NAME:" +
      document.form1.name.value;
      message += "<li>ADDRESS:" +
      document.form1.address.value;
      message += "<li>PHONE:" +
      document.form1.phone.value;
      message += "</ul>";
      dispWin.document.write(message);
    }
    </script>
  </head>
  <body>
    <h1>Form Display Example</h1>
        <p>Enter the following information. When you press the Display
        button, the data you entered will be displayed in a pop-up.</p>
        <form name="form1" method="get" action="">
        <p>NAME: <input type="text" name="name" size="50" /></p>
        <p>ADDRESS: <input type="text" name="address" size="50" /></p>
        <p>PHONE: <input type="text" name="phone" size="50" /></p>
        <p><input type="button" value="Display"
                onclick="display();" /></p>
        </form>
  </body>
</html>
```

Here is a breakdown of how this simple HTML document and script
work:

- ▶ The `<script>` section in the document's header defines a function
  called `display()` that opens a new window and displays the
  information from the form.

- ▶ The `<form>` tag begins the form. Because this form is handled
  entirely by JavaScript, the form `action` and `method` have no value.

- ▶ The `<input />` tags define the form's three fields: `yourname`,
  `address`, and `phone`. The last `<input />` tag defines the Display
  button, which is set to run the `display()` function.

Figure 26.4 shows this form in action. The Display button has been
pressed, and the pop-up window shows the results. Although this is
not the most exciting example of client-side form interaction, it clearly
shows the basics that form a foundation for later work.

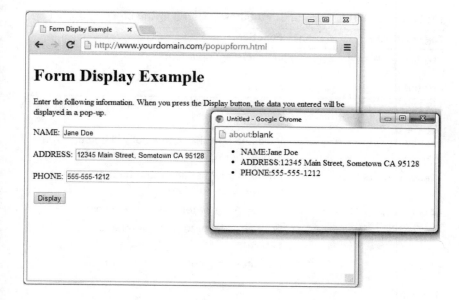

FIGURE 26.4
Displaying data from a
form in a pop-up window.

Summary

This chapter demonstrated how to create HTML forms, which enable your visitors to provide information to you when they are hooked up to a back-end processing script (which is outside the scope of this book).

You learned about all the major form elements, including a little about how form-processing scripts interpret the names and value attributes of those elements. When you are ready to try a back-end form-processing script, you'll be well versed in the front-end details, including how to access the form object in JavaScript.

We stopped short of doing anything in-depth with that information because server-side form handling requires an external script to process that form. However, there is plenty to do to set up a form that looks and acts just the way you want it to, including form validation, so you have a lot to practice before taking that next step into form interactivity.

Table 26.1 summarizes the HTML tags and attributes covered in this chapter.

TABLE 26.1   HTML Tags and Attributes Covered in Chapter 26

Tag/Attribute	Function
`<form>...</form>`	Indicates an input form.

Attributes	*Function*
`action="scripturl"`	Gives the address of the script to process this form input.
`method="post/get"`	Indicates how the form input will be sent to the server. Normally set to `post` rather than `get`.
`<label>...</label>`	Provides information for the form element to which it is associated.
`<fieldset>...</fieldset>`	Groups a set of related form elements.
`<legend>...</legend>`	Provides a label to a set of related form elements.
`<input />`	Indicates an input element for a form.

Attributes	*Function*
`type="controltype"`	Gives the type for this input widget. Some possible values are `checkbox`, `hidden`, `radio`, `reset`, `submit`, `text`, and `image`, among others.
`name="name"`	Gives the unique name of this item, as passed to the script.
`value="value"`	Gives the default value for a text or hidden item. For a checkbox or radio button, it's the value to be submitted with the form. For reset or submit buttons, it's the label for the button itself.
`src="imageurl"`	Shows the source file for an image.
`checked`	Is used for checkboxes and radio buttons. Indicates that this item is checked.
`autofocus`	Puts focus on the element when the form is loaded.
`required`	Indicates that the field should be validated for content, according to type (where appropriate).
`pattern="pattern"`	Indicates that the content of this field should be validated against this regular expression.
`size="width"`	Specifies the width, in characters, of a text input region.

`maxlength="maxlength"`	Specifies the maximum number of characters that can be entered into a text region.
`<textarea>...</textarea>`	Indicates a multiline text entry form element. Default text can be included.

Attributes	Function
`name="name"`	Specifies the name to be passed to the script.
`rows="numrows"`	Specifies the number of rows this text area displays.
`cols="numchars"`	Specifies the number of columns (characters) this text area displays.
`autofocus`	Puts focus on the element when the form is loaded.
`required`	Indicates that the field should be validated for content according to type (where appropriate).
`pattern="pattern"`	Indicates that the content of this field should be validated against this regular expression.
`<select>...</select>`	Creates a menu or scrolling list of possible items.

Attributes	Function
`name="name"`	Shows the name that is passed to the script.
`size="numelements"`	Indicates the number of elements to display. If `size` is indicated, the selection becomes a scrolling list. If no `size` is given, the selection is a drop-down pick list.
`multiple`	Allows multiple selections from the list.
`required`	Indicates that the field should be validated for a selection.
`<optgroup>...</optgroup>`	Indicates a grouping of `<option>` elements.

Attributes	Function
`label="label"`	Provides a label for the group.
`<option>...</option>`	Indicates a possible item within a `<select>` element.

Attributes	Function
`selected`	Selects the `<option>` by default in the list when this attribute is included.
`value="value"`	Specifies the value to submit if this `<option>` is selected when the form is submitted.

Q&A

Q. Is there any way to create a large number of text fields without dealing with different names for all of them?

A. Yes. If you use the same name for several elements in the form, their objects form an array. For example, if you defined 20 text fields with the name `member`, you could refer to them as `member[0]` through `member[19]`. This also works with other types of form elements.

Q. If HTML5 contains form validation, do I ever have to worry about validation again?

A. Yes, you do. Although HTML5 form validation is awesome, you should still validate the form information that is sent to you on the back end. Back-end processing is outside the scope of the book, but as a rule, you should never trust any user input—always check it before performing an action that uses it (especially when interacting with a database).

Workshop

The Workshop contains quiz questions and activities to help you solidify your understanding of the material covered. Try to answer all questions before looking at the "Answers" section that follows.

Quiz

1. What HTML code do you use to create a guestbook form that asks someone for his or her name and gender? Assume that you have a form-processing script set up at `/scripts/formscript` and that you need to include the following hidden input element to tell the script where to send the form results:

   ```
   <input type="hidden" name="mailto" value="you@yoursite.com" />
   ```

2. If you created an image named `submit.gif`, how would you use it as the Submit button for the form you created in Question 1?

3. Which of these attributes of a `<form>` tag determines where the data will be sent?

   a. `action`

   b. `method`

   c. `name`

Answers

1. You use HTML code similar to the following (with the appropriate DOCTYPE and other structural markup, of course):

```
<form name="form1" method="post" action="/scripts/formscript">
<input type="hidden" name="mailto" value="you@yoursite.com" />
<p><label for="name">Your Name:</label>
<input type="text" id="name" name="name" size="50" /></p>
<p>Your Gender:
<input type="radio" id="male" name="gender"
    value="male" /> <label for="male">male</label>
<input type="radio" id="female" name="gender"
    value="female" /> <label for="female">female</label>
<input type="radio" id="go_away" name="gender"
    value="mind your business" />
    <label for="go_away">mind your business</label></p>
<p><input type="submit" value="Submit Form" /></p>
</form>
```

2. Replace the code

```
<input type="submit" value="Submit Form" />
```

with this code:

```
<input type="image" src="submit.gif" />
```

3. a. The action attribute determines where the data is sent.

Exercises

▶ Create a form using all the different types of input elements and selection lists to make sure you understand how each of them works.

▶ Learn a little bit about regular expressions, and implement some custom validation using the pattern attribute.

▶ Investigate the form-handling options at your web hosting provider, and use a script that the web hosting provider made available to you to process the form you created in the first exercise.

CHAPTER 27
Organizing and Managing a Website

The bulk of this book has led you through the design and creation of static and dynamic web content, from text to graphics and multimedia, and with a little JavaScript interactivity thrown in for good measure. Along the way, I've noted some of the ways you can think about the life cycle of that content—but in this chapter, you'll learn how to look at your work as a whole.

This chapter shows you how to think about organizing and presenting multiple web pages so that visitors will be able to navigate among them without confusion. You'll also learn ways to make your website memorable enough to visit again and again. Web developers use the term *sticky* to describe pages that people don't want to leave. Hopefully this chapter will help you make your websites downright gooey!

Because websites can be (and usually should be) updated frequently, it's essential to create pages that can be easily maintained. This chapter shows you how to add comments and other documentation to your pages so that you—or anyone else on your staff—can understand and modify your pages. It also introduces you to version control so that you can innovate individually or as part of a team without overwriting work that you might want to have saved.

WHAT YOU'LL LEARN IN THIS CHAPTER:

▶ How to determine whether one page is enough to handle all your content

▶ How to organize a simple site

▶ How to organize a larger site

▶ How to write maintainable code

▶ How to get started with version control

By this point in the book, you should have enough HTML and CSS knowledge to produce most of your website. You probably have created a number of pages already, and perhaps even published them online.

As you proceed through this chapter, think about how your pages are organized now and how you can improve that organization. Have you used comments in your HTML or created a document for future website maintainers regarding your content organization? If not, now is a good time to start. Along the way, don't be surprised if you decide to do a redesign that involves changing almost all your pages—the results are likely to be well worth the effort!

When One Page Is Enough

Building and organizing an attractive and effective website doesn't always need to be a complex task. If you are creating a web presence for a single entity (such as a local event) that requires only a small amount of very specific information, you can effectively present that information on a single page with or without a lot of flashy graphics and interactivity. In fact, there are several positive features to a single-page web presence:

▶ All the information on the site downloads more quickly than on more extensive sites.

▶ The whole site can be printed on paper with a single print command, even if it is several paper pages long.

▶ Visitors can easily save the site on their hard drives for future reference, especially if it uses a minimum of graphics.

▶ Links between different parts of the same page usually respond more quickly than links to other pages.

Figure 27.1 shows the first part of a web page that serves its intended audience better as a single lengthy page than it would as a multipage site. The page begins, as most introductory pages should, with a succinct explanation of what the page is about and who would want to read it. A detailed table of contents enables visitors to skip directly to the section containing the material they find most interesting. If this "page" were printed, it would contain about six paper pages' worth of text about driving traffic to websites—something a visitor might think about printing and reading later, perhaps while also taking notes.

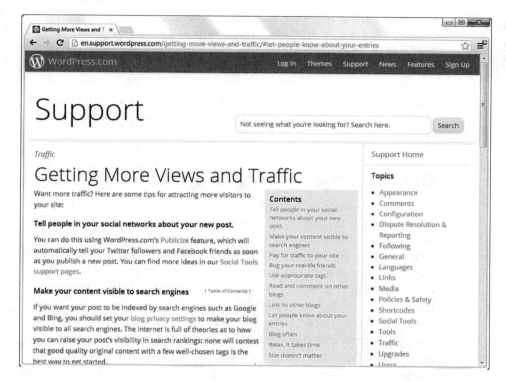

FIGURE 27.1
A good table of contents can make long pages easier to navigate.

When pages contain a table of contents to separate sections of information, it is also common for each short section to contain a link back up to the table of contents so that navigating around the page feels much the same as navigating around a multipage site. Because the contents of these types of longer pages are intended as a handy reference, visitors will definitely prefer the convenience of bookmarking or saving a single page over having to save 8 or 10 separate pages. The most common examples of single-page information websites are encompassed within Wikipedia, at www.wikipedia.org. If you consider each entry full of rich content to be its own "site," the single-page sites within Wikipedia—with their own tables of contents—represent millions of printed pages.

Having experienced many beautiful and effective graphical layouts online, you might be tempted to forget that a good, old-fashioned outline is often the clearest and most efficient way to organize long web pages full of text-based content within a site. This is especially true with the influx of single-page interfaces (also called single-page *applications*) that attempt to bring all the interactivity of desktop applications into a web browsing experience. These applications are often built using HTML and JavaScript frameworks and include significant visual design elements; in fact, these sites are often used to publish design portfolios rather than the type of text-based content you see here.

Organizing a Simple Site

With the exception of the aforementioned special cases of single-page applications and portfolio sites, single-page websites tend to serve as merely "coming soon" or placeholder purposes. If you spend any time at all on the Web, you'll quickly learn that most companies and individuals serve their readers better by dividing their site into short, quick-read pages surrounded by graphical navigation that enables them to gather almost all the information they could want within a few clicks. Furthermore, using multiple pages instead of a series of very long pages minimizes scrolling on the page, which can be especially bothersome for visitors who are using mobile devices to view the full site or who have relatively low-resolution monitors (less than 800×600).

The fundamental goal of a website is to make the individual or organization visible on the Internet, but also—and more important—to act as a portal to the information within the site itself. The main page of a site should give the user enough information to provide a clear picture of the organization, as well as traditional contact information and an email address to submit questions or feedback. It should also provide clear pathways into the highly structured information within other pages in the site. The main page shown in Figure 27.2 provides examples of all these good features: basic information, contact information, and paths to information for multiple audiences.

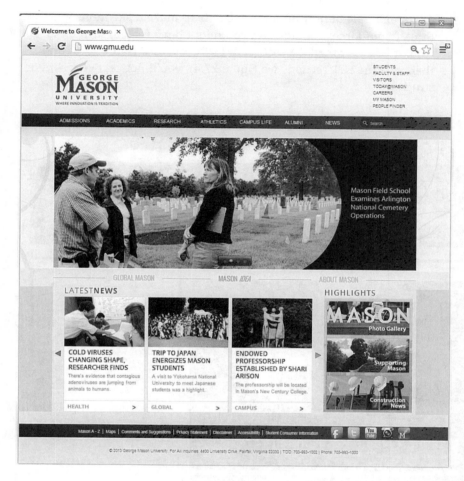

FIGURE 27.2
This university main page uses a basic design, minimal but useful graphics, and a clear structure to entice users to explore for more information.

One of the most common mistakes beginning website developers make is creating pages that look fundamentally different from other pages on the site. An equally serious mistake is using the same publicly available clip art that thousands of other web authors are also using. Remember that, on the Internet, one click can take you around the world. The only way to make your pages memorable and recognizable as a cohesive site is to make all your pages adhere to a unique, unmistakable visual theme. In other words, strive for uniqueness when compared to other websites, yet uniformity within the site itself.

TIP

Regardless of how large your site is, it's a good idea to carefully organize your resources. For example, placing the images for your web pages in a separate folder named `images` is one step toward organization. Similarly, if you have files that are available for download, place them in a folder called `downloads`. This makes it much easier to keep track of web page resources based on their particular types (HTML pages, PNG images, and so on). Additionally, if you organize your site into sections, such as Company, Products, and Press, put the individual pages into similarly named directories (`company`, `products`, `press`, and so on), for the same organizational reasons.

As an example of how uniformity can help make a site more cohesive, think about large, popular sites you might have visited, such as ESPN. com. If you visit the MLB section at ESPN.com (see Figure 27.3) and then visit the NFL section (see Figure 27.4), you'll notice a very similar structure.

FIGURE 27.3
The MLB section at ESPN.com.

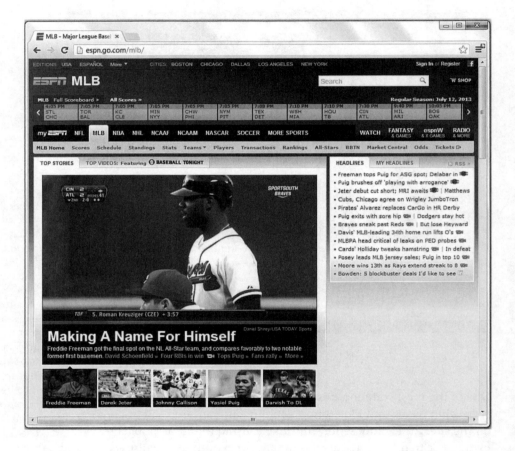

In both examples, you see navigation elements at the top of the page (including some subnavigation elements), a large area in the middle of the page for the featured item graphic, a rectangle on the right side containing links to top stories, and a set of secondary rectangles under the primary image leading readers to additional stories. The only difference between the MLB section and the NFL section is the color scheme: The MLB section is part of a predominantly blue color scheme, whereas the NFL section is predominantly green. However, in both sections, you know that if you want to read the popular news stories, you look to the right of the page. If you want to navigate to another section in the site or to the site's main page, you look to a navigational element at the top left of the page.

FIGURE 27.4
The NFL section at ESPN.com.

The presence of consistent design and organizational elements helps ensure that your users will be able to navigate throughout your content with confidence. From a maintenance perspective, the consistent structural template enables you to reuse pieces of the underlying code. This type of code reuse typically happens through dynamic server-side programming outside the scope of this book, but in general, it means that instead of copying and pasting the same HTML, CSS, and JavaScript over and over, that client-side code exists in only one place and is applied dynamically to the content. Therefore, instead of making changes to thousands of files to make a background change from blue to green, for example, you would need to make a change only once.

Organizing a Larger Site

For complex sites, sophisticated layout and graphics can help organize and improve the looks of your site when used consistently throughout all your pages. To see how you can make aesthetics and organization work hand in hand, let's look at examples of navigation (and, thus, underlying organization) for a few sites that present a large volume of information to several different audiences.

Figure 27.5 shows the main page of Amazon.com, specifically with the side navigation selected. Amazon is in the business of selling products, plain and simple. Therefore, it makes sense for Amazon to show product categories as the main navigational elements.

FIGURE 27.5
Amazon.com shows product categories as primary navigation elements.

Although Amazon is in the business of selling products, it still has to provide information regarding who it is, how to contact it, and other ancillary yet important information to enhance the business-to-consumer relationship. Links to this sort of information appear in the footer, or bottom portion, of the Amazon.com website—outside the viewing area of this screenshot. When creating your site template, you must determine the most important content areas and how to organize that content; also remember to provide users with basic information—especially if that information will enhance your image and make users feel as if you value what they have to say.

The next example is of a secondary page within the Peet's Coffee & Tea website (www.peets.com). All the pages in the Peet's website follow one of the common types of presenting navigation and subnavigation: a horizontal strip for main navigation, with secondary elements for that section placed in a vertical column on the left. As Figure 27.6 shows, the section the user is currently browsing (Community) is highlighted in the main navigation (through a subtle font color change), as is the specific page in the secondary navigation (using a background color change for the element). These types of visual indicators help users orient themselves within the site. Using a visual indicator is a useful tactic because your users might arrive at a page via a search engine or by a link from another website. After your users arrive, you want them to feel at home—or at least feel as if they know where they are in relation to your site.

As you can see by the different main navigation elements—Craft, Coffee, Tea, Stores, and Community—the Peet's website has to serve the needs of many different types of people who come to the website for many different reasons. As you organize your own site content, determine the information that is most important to you, as well as the information that is most important to your users, and create a navigation scheme that finds a happy medium between the two.

Figure 27.7 shows another example of a navigation style, this time with a twist on the standard top navigation/left-side navigation scheme. In this example, the left-side navigation (the secondary navigation, in this case) also appears in a drop-down menu under the main navigation (refer to Chapter 11, "Using CSS to Do More with Lists, Text, and Navigation," for information on how to do something like this). Hovering the mouse over any of the other main navigation elements shows similar menus. This scheme gives users an entire site map at their fingertips because they can reach any place in the site within one click of any other page.

FIGURE 27.6
This Peet's Coffee & Tea secondary page shows a main navigation element selected with secondary navigation on the left side of the page.

FIGURE 27.6
This Peet's Coffee & Tea secondary page shows a main navigation element selected with secondary navigation on the left side of the page.

Also notice that the Overview link in the side navigation window is styled a bit differently—with heavier purple text—than the other links in the window, indicating to visitors which page they are on. This visual detail, similar to what you saw on the Peet's site, is an unobtrusive way to give users a sense of where they are within the current navigational scheme.

You can choose among many types of navigation styles and ways of indicating to users where they are and where they might want to go next. Keep in mind the following fact: Studies have repeatedly shown that people become confused and annoyed when presented with more than seven choices at a time, and people feel most comfortable with five or fewer choices. Therefore, you should avoid presenting more than five links (either in a list or as graphical icons) next to one another, if at all possible—and definitely avoid presenting more than seven at once. Amazon.com gets a pass here because it is an Internet superstore, and users expect a lot of "departments" in which to shop when they get there. But when you need to present more than seven links in a navigation list, break them into multiple lists with a separate heading for each of the five to seven items.

FIGURE 27.7
The BAWSI.org website shows subnavigation attached to each main navigation element.

It will also help your readers navigate your site without confusion if you avoid putting any page more than two (or, at most, three) links away from the main page. You should also always send readers back to a main category page (or the home page) after they've read a subsidiary page. In other words, try to design somewhat of a flat link structure in which most pages are no more than one or two links deep. You don't want visitors to have to rely heavily, if at all, on their browser's Back button to navigate your site.

Writing Maintainable Code

If you've done any coding before reading this book, you already know how important it is to write code that can be maintained—that is, you or someone else should be able to look at your code later and not be utterly confused by it. The challenge is to make your code as immediately understandable as possible. A time will come when you'll look back on a page that you wrote, and you won't have a clue what you were thinking or why you wrote the code the way you did. Fortunately, there is a way to combat this problem of apparent memory loss.

Documenting Code with Comments

Whenever you develop an HTML page, CSS snippet, or JavaScript function, keep in mind that you or someone else will almost certainly need to make changes to it someday. Simple text web pages are usually easy to read and revise, but complex pages with graphics, tables, and other layout tricks can be quite difficult to decipher.

To see what I'm talking about, visit just about any page in a web browser and view its source code. Using Internet Explorer, right-click any page and select View Source. Using Chrome or Firefox, right-click any page and select View Page Source. You might see a jumbled bunch of code that is tough to decipher as pure HTML. This might be because content management software systems have generated the markup dynamically, or it might be because its human maintainer has not paid attention to structure, ease of reading, code commenting, and other methods for making the code readable by humans. For the sake of maintaining your own pages, I encourage you to impose a little more order on your HTML markup, style sheet entries, and JavaScript code. And remember: Proper indentation is your (and your future development partner's) friend.

As you have seen in several lessons throughout this book, you can enclose comments to yourself or your coauthors using the HTML beginning and ending comment syntax: `<!--` and `-->`. These comments will not appear on the web page when viewed with a browser but can be read by anyone who examines the HTML code in a text editor or via the web browser's View Source (or View Page Source)

NOTE

To include comments in a style sheet, begin comments with `/*` and end them with `*/` (your commented code should be between these characters).

The HTML `<!--` and `-->` comment syntax does not work properly in style sheets.

TIP

One handy use of comments is to hide parts of a web page that are currently under construction. Instead of making the text and graphics visible and explaining that they're under construction, you can hide them from view entirely with some carefully placed opening and closing comment indicators around the HTML that you do not want to appear. This is a great way to work on portions of a page gradually and show only the end result to the world when you're finished.

function. The following example provides a little refresher just to show you how a comment is coded:

```
<!-- This image needs to be updated daily. -->
<img src="headline.jpg" alt="Today's Headline" />
```

As this code reveals, the comment just before the `<img />` tag provides a clue to how the image is used. Anyone who reads this code knows immediately that this is an image that must be updated every day. Web browsers completely ignore the text in the comment.

TRY IT YOURSELF ▼

Commenting Your Code

It will be well worth your time now to go through all the web pages and style sheets you've created so far and add any comments that you or others might find helpful when revising them in the future. Here's what to do:

1. Insert a comment explaining any fancy formatting or layout technique before the tags that make it happen.

2. Use a comment just before an `<img />` tag to briefly describe any important graphic whose function isn't obvious from the `alt` message.

3. Consider using a comment (or several comments) to summarize how the cells of a `<table>` are supposed to align.

4. If you use hexadecimal color codes (such as `<div style="color: #8040B0">`), insert a comment indicating what the color actually is (bluish-purple).

5. Indent your comments to help them stand out and make both the comments and the HTML or CSS easier to read. Don't forget to use indentation in the HTML, CSS, or JavaScript itself to make it more readable, too, as discussed in the next section.

Indenting Code for Clarity

I have a confession. Throughout the book, I've been carefully indoctrinating you into an HTML code development style without really letting on. It's time to spill the beans. You've no doubt noticed a consistent pattern with respect to the indentation of all the HTML code in the book. More specifically, each child tag is indented to the right two spaces from its parent tag. Furthermore, content within a tag that spans more than one line is indented within the tag.

The best way to learn the value of indentation is to see some HTML code without it. You know how the song goes—"You don't know what you've got 'til it's gone." Anyway, here's a very simple table coded without any indentation:

```
<table><tr><td>Cell One</td><td>Cell Two</td></tr>
<tr><td>Cell Three</td><td>Cell Four</td></tr></table>
```

Not only is there no indentation, but there also is no delineation between rows and columns within the table. Now compare this code with the following code, which describes the same table:

```
<table>
  <tr>
    <td>Cell One</td>
    <td>Cell Two</td>
  </tr>
  <tr>
    <td>Cell Three</td>
    <td>Cell Four</td>
  </tr>
</table>
```

This heavily indented code makes it plainly obvious how the rows and columns are divided up via `<tr>` and `<td>` tags.

Consistent indentation might even be more important than comments when it comes to making your HTML code understandable and maintainable. And you don't have to buy into this specific indentation strategy. If you'd rather use three or four spaces instead of two, that's fine. And if you want to tighten things up a bit and not indent content within a tag, that also works. The main point to take from this section is that it's important to develop a coding style of your own (or your team's own) and then ruthlessly stick to it.

Thinking About Version Control

If you've ever used Google Docs, you have encountered a form of version control; when you're using Google Docs, Google automatically saves revisions of your work as you are typing. This is different from simply automatically saving your work (although it does that too) because you can revert to any revision along the way. You might have encountered this concept when using popular blog-authoring software such as Blogger or WordPress, or even when editing wikis—both of these types of applications also enable users to revise their work without overwriting, and thus deleting for all time, their previous work.

You might be wondering, "Well, what does that have to do with developing HTML, CSS, or JavaScript? You're just talking about documents." The answer is simple: Just as you might want to revert to a previous edition of an article or a letter, you might want to revert to a previous edition of your HTML, CSS, or JavaScript code. This could be because you followed a good idea to the end, but your markup just proved untenable and you don't want to start over entirely—you just want to back up to a certain point along your revision path. Or, let's say you developed a particularly involved bit of JavaScript and discovered that something in the middle of it just doesn't work with some browsers—you'll want to build on and extend the work you did, not throw it away completely, and knowing what you did in the past will help you in the future.

Version control involves more than just revision history. When you start using version control systems to maintain your code, you will hear terms like these:

- **Commit/check in and check out**—When you put an object into the code repository, you are committing that file; when you check out a file, you are grabbing it from the repository (where all the current and historical versions are stored) and working on it until you are ready to commit or check in the file again.

- **Branch**—The files you have under version control can branch or fork at any point, thus creating two or more development paths. Suppose you want to try some new display layouts or form interactivity, but you don't want an existing site to appear modified in any way. You might have started with one master set of files but then forked this set of files for the new site, continuing to develop them independently. If you continued developing the original set of files, that would be working with the *trunk*.

- **Change/diff**—This is just the term (you can say "change" or "diff") for a modification made under version control. You might also hear *diff* used as a verb, as in "I diffed the files," to refer to the action of comparing two versions of an object (there is an underlying UNIX command called `diff`).

- **Fork**—When you find an open-source GitHub repository that you want to use as the basis for your own work (or that you want to contribute to), you fork the repository to then create a copy of it that you can work on at your own pace. From the forked repository, you can push commits to your own version, fetch changes from the original repository, and issue pull requests to the owner of the original if you would like to contribute your changes to the original repository that you forked.

You will hear many more terms than just these few listed here, but if you can conceptualize the repository, the (local) working copy, and the process of checking in and checking out files, you are well on your way to implementing version control for your digital objects.

Using a Version Control System

Several version control systems are available for use, some free and open source, and some proprietary. Some popular systems are Subversion (subversion.apache.org), Mercurial (mercurial.selenic. com), and Git (www.git-scm.com). If you have a web hosting service that enables you to install any of these tools, you could create your own repository and use a GUI or command-line client to connect to it. However, for users who want to get started with a repository but don't necessarily want, need, or understand all the extra installation and maintenance overhead that goes with it, there are plenty of hosted version control systems that can even be used free for personal and open-source projects. These hosted solutions aren't just for individuals—all sorts of companies and organizations both big and small use hosted version control systems such as GitHub (www.github. com) or Bitbucket (www.bitbucket.org), just to name a few. For a few dollars, you can turn your free, public account into a private account, and keep your code to yourself.

For anyone wanting to get started with version control, I highly recommend GitHub for relative ease of use and free, cross-platform tools. The GitHub Help site is a great place to start: See http://help. github.com/. An added benefit of the already-free GitHub account is the capability to use Gist (gist.github.com) to share code snippets (or whole pages) with others (those snippets themselves are Git repositories and, thus, are versioned and forkable in their own right). GitHub repositories, including Gists, are also excellent ways to get started with version control of your work.

Using HTML and CSS Frameworks

If you use a content management system (CMS) such as WordPress (www.wordpress.org) or Drupal (www.drupal.org) to power your website, you will end up using a presentation template designed for one of those systems—but what about the people who do *not* want to use a CMS but *would* like a starting point for an advanced HTML and CSS presentation? Over the past few years, the web development world has seen the rise of HTML and CSS (or "front-end") frameworks, which can help solve this problem. Many of these frameworks are open source and available for download or forking from GitHub repositories. These frameworks often also include advanced JavaScript libraries, like the ones you learned about in Chapter 22, "Using Third-Party JavaScript Libraries and Frameworks."

I recommend three popular HTML and CSS frameworks:

▶ **Bootstrap**—Developed internally by engineers at Twitter, this framework is open-source software for anyone who wants to use it to get started with modern design elements. Learn more at http://getbootstrap.com/, which includes a simple "Get Started" section that explains what is included and how to use it.

▶ **Foundation**—Another open-source framework, Foundation emphasizes responsive design so that people with all kinds of devices, from desktops to phones, can enjoy and use your website. Learn more at http://foundation.zurb.com/, which includes an extensive "Getting Started" section that details the components of the display templates you can use.

▶ **HTML5 Boilerplate**—One of the leanest frameworks out there, this might be the most useful for beginners because it provides the basics of what you need without overwhelming you with the possibilities. Learn more at http://html5boilerplate.com/, and see the documentation maintained within the GitHub repository.

Although front-end frameworks can be incredibly useful for speeding up some of the foundational work of web development, you run the risk of falling into the "cookie cutter" trap, in which your site looks like all the others out there (at least, the ones using the same framework). However, with a little creativity, you can avoid that trap.

Summary

This chapter gave you examples and explanations to help you organize your web pages into a coherent site that is informative, attractive, and easy to navigate. Web users have become quite savvy and expect well-designed websites, and they will quickly abandon your site if they experience a poor design that is difficult to navigate.

This chapter also discussed the importance of making your code easy to maintain by adding comments and indentation. Comments are important not only as a reminder for you when you revisit code later, but also as instructions if someone else inherits your code. Indentation might seem like an aesthetic issue, but it can help you quickly analyze and understand the structure of a web page at a glance.

Because you likely will soon need code-management tools either for yourself or for yourself and other developers in your group, this lesson introduced you to a few concepts of version control. Version control enables you to innovate without losing your solid, production-quality work and also provides more opportunities for other developers to work within your code base.

Finally, you learned a little bit about HTML and CSS frameworks, of which there are many. These frameworks can help you speed up your web development project by giving you templates that already contain modern and validated markup.

Q&A

Q. Won't adding a lot of comments and spaces make my pages load more slowly when someone views them?

A. The size of a little extra text in your pages is negligible when compared to other, chunkier web page resources (such as large images and high-definition multimedia). You'd have to type hundreds of comment words to cause even one extra second of delay in loading a page. Also keep in mind that, with the broadband connections that many people use, text travels extremely fast. Multimedia components slow pages down, so although you need to optimize your images as best you can, you can use text comments freely. You can also learn more about the concept of "minifying" your HTML, CSS, and JavaScript at https://developers.google.com/speed/docs/best-practices/payload?hl=fr#MinifyHTML.

Q. Using version control seems like overkill for my tiny personal website. Do I have to use it?

A. Of course not—websites of any type, personal or otherwise, are not required to be under version control or other backup systems. However, most people have experienced some data loss or a website crash, so if you don't use version control, I highly recommend at least performing some sort of automated backup of your files to an external system. By "external system," I mean any external drive, whether a physical drive attached to your computer or a cloud-based backup service such as Dropbox (www.dropbox.com).

Workshop

The Workshop contains quiz questions and activities to help you solidify your understanding of the material covered. Try to answer all questions before looking at the "Answers" section that follows.

Quiz

1. What are three ways to ensure that all your pages form a single cohesive website?

2. What two types of information should you always include in your home page?

3. You want to say to future editors of a web page, "Don't change this image of me. It's my only chance at immortality." But you don't want users who view the page to see that message. How can you do this?

Answers

1. Use consistent background, colors, fonts, and styles. Repeat the same link words or graphics on the top of the page that the link leads to. Repeat the same small header, buttons, or other elements on every page of the site.

2. Use enough identifying information that users can immediately see the name of the site and understand what it is about. Also, whatever the most important message is that you want to convey to your intended audience, state it directly and concisely. Whether it's your mission statement or a trademarked marketing slogan, make sure that it is in plain view here.

3. Put the following comment immediately before the `<img />` tag:

```
<!-- Don't change this image of me.
    It's my only chance at immortality. -->
```

Exercises

▶ Open the HTML, CSS, and JavaScript files that make up your current website, and check them all for comments and code indentation. Are there areas in which the code needs to be explained to anyone who might look at it in the future? If so, add explanatory comments. Is it difficult for you to tell the hierarchy of your code—is it difficult to see headings and sections? If so, indent your code so that the structure matches the hierarchy and thus enables you to jump quickly to the section you need to edit.

▶ Create an account at GitHub, and create a repository for your personal website or other code-based project. From this point forward, keep your repository in sync with your work on your personal computer by committing your changes to the GitHub repository.

INDEX

Q–R

S

Safari web browser, 9
sans-serif font (text), 129
saving files
    files with HTML tags, 27
    .js files, 81
scaling images, 203-204
screen resolution, 207
Script.aculo.us JavaScript library, 533-536
<script> tags (JavaScript), 79-81, 84-85
scripting
    AJAX, 537, 589
        ajaxRequest function, 595
        ajaxResponse function, 595
        back end, 590, 603-604
        debugging applications, 601-606
        examples of, 591-592
        frameworks, 592
        front end, 590, 604-605
        JavaScript client, 590
        jQuery and AJAX-related functionality, 606-607
        libraries, 592-601
        live search forms, 602-606
        quiz building example, 596-601
        requests, 590-594, 603-605
        server-side scripts, 590, 603-605
        XML and, 591
        XMLHttpRequest, 592-594
    client-side scripting, 338, 349
    cross-browser scripting
        debugging browsers, 520
        event handlers and JavaScript, 508-509
        feature sensing, 509, 519
    effects (third-party libraries), 534-536
    error handling, 510-511

frameworks
    AngularJS, 538
    Backbone.js, 538
    Ember, 538
    Knockout, 538
    MVC pattern, 537
graceful degradation, 506
interpreted languages, 78
JavaScript
    accessibility, 513
    adding scripts to web pages, 86
    adding to web pages, 79-80
    advantages over HTML, 367
    AJAX, 83, 590, 598-600, 604-607
    arrays, 408-413
    best practices, 358, 362-363, 503-514
    break statements, 458
    breakpoints, 115-116
    capabilities of, 78, 82
    case statements, 453
    comments, 361-362, 511-512
    conditional expressions, 446-449
    conditional operators, 446-447
    continue statements, 459
    continuing loops, 459
    cross-browser scripting, 509, 519-520
    data types, 400-402
    Date objects, 84
    debugging via Developer Tools, 111-117
    design patterns, 513
    development of, 78
    do...while loops, 457
    documenting code, 511-512
    document.write statements, 80, 85
    Dojo library, 534
    DOM, 367-391, 489-499
    effects, 83
    else keyword, 448-452

    error handling, 89-91
    escaping loops, 458
    event handlers, 81-82, 357-360, 465-478, 507-509
    events, 81
    expressions, 399
    external scripts, 81
    flow control, 445-462
    for loops, 453-455
    for...in loops, 459-462
    form events, 632-633
    functions, 80, 354, 361, 419-424, 428, 435-438
    Gmail and, 522
    history of, 78
    if statements, 445-452
    infinite loops, 457-458
    jQuery library, 531-532, 541-554, 606-607
    jQuery UI library, 557-585
    .js files, 81
    JSON, 363-364, 591
    libraries (third-party), 529-536, 541
    logical operators, 447-448
    modifying scripts, 87-89
    navigating websites, 82
    non-JavaScript browsers, 520-525
    objects, 355-356, 361, 425-435, 438-440
    operators, 399-400
    order of script operation, 359-360
    output, 85
    overusing, 504-505
    parseFloat() function, 402
    parseInt() function, 402
    plus signs (+) in statements, 86
    progressive enhancement strategies, 363
    Prototype library, 532-533
    reading browser information, 515-518

LEARNING LABS

Fully Interactive Online Courses for Practical Skills

New!
Learn Online with Videos, Live Code Editing, and Quizzes

- **Read** the complete text of the book online in your web browser.

- **Watch** an expert instructor show you how to perform tasks in easy-to-follow videos.

- **Try** your hand at coding in an interactive code-editing sandbox.

- **Test** yourself with interactive quizzes.

Course Topics Include:

- **HTML5 and CSS3**

- **jQuery**

- **JavaScript**

- **Mobile Web Development**

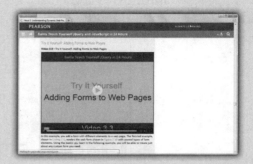

Watch Videos

Edit and Run Code

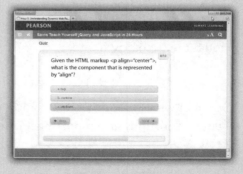

Quiz Yourself

Take a tour and try free samples at
informit.com/learninglabs